PRINCIPLES of
BUSINESS CREDIT

Eighth Edition

National Association of Credit Management

An NACM® Publication

Address inquiries to:
National Association of Credit Management
National Education Department
8840 Columbia 100 Parkway
Columbia, MD 21045

ISBN-10 1-888505-48-6
ISBN-13 978-1-888505-48-1

Printed in the United States of America

10 9 8 7 6 5 4 3 2 1

Principles of Business Credit

Editorial Acknowledgments

Chapters in the 8th Edition of the *Principles of Business Credit* have been infused with fresh content created and written by the graduates of NACM's Graduate School of Credit & Financial Management. Drawing from their team project papers, new content has been incorporated and provides a credit professional's perspective, suggestions and key points to consider on issues impacting credit policy, procedures and decision-making. NACM extends its sincere thanks to the following contributors by graduating class:

2013

Justin Blackford, CCE	Sue Herman, CCE	Eddie Olewnik, CCE	Michelle Sparks, CCE
Laura de Prato, CCE	Ralph Longo, CCE	Steven Porter, CCE	Christopher Southby, CCE
Doug Faust, CCE	Karen McGill, CCE	Matt Richard, CCE	

2014

Len Brown, CCE	Stephanie Dick, CCE	Doug Gregory, CCE	Jay Snyder, CCE
Jeff Butterfield, CCE	Mary Ellevold, CCE	Bob Lewis, CCE	Heather Swartzlander, CCE
Connie Caigoy, CCE	Don Giallanza, CCE	Kathryn Marsh, CCE	

2015

Jim Bailey, CCE	Rosanne Genise, CCE	Raj Mandlewala, CCE	Jennifer Thompson, CCE
Tami Behner, CCE	David Groom, CCE	Gerry Moran, CCE	Stacey Varuolo, CCE, CICP
Michelle Blanchard, CCE	Mike Hill, CCE	Sabrina Perez, CCE, CICP	
Estela Frias, CCE	Sandra Langdon, CCE	Brian Smith, CCE	

2016

Lisa Ball, CCE	Vivian Hoang, CCE	Alejandro Ojeda-Nonzioli, CCE	Eve Sahnow, CCE
Dawn Dickert, CCE	Kathie Knudson, CCE	Stacey Parker, CCE	Kenny Wine, CCE
Adam Easton, CCE	Tawnya Marsh, CCE	Jessica Pierre, CCE	John Zummo, CCE
Charles Edwards, CCE	Brendon Misik, CCE	Kevin Quinn, CCE	

The core content of this edition has benefited from the tireless efforts, writing and editing by the following individuals:

Walter (Buddy) Baker	Pamela Faulk-Turnbull, CCE	James McIntyre, CCE	Joanne Simone
Wanda Borges, Esq.	Jim Fullerton, Esq.	Ken Minton, CCE	Gwen Stroops, CCE, CICP
Michael Brittain, CAE	Michelle Herman	Dewanna Myers, CCE	Norman Taylor, CCE
Scott Cargill, Esq.	Wayne Hicks	Bruce Nathan, Esq.	Deborah Thorne, Esq.
Diana Crowe	Joanne Larson	Thomas Sauer, CCE	Clint Techmeyer, CCE
Stan DeGroot, CCE	Paula May, CCE	George Schnupp, CCE	Valerie Venable, CCE
Michael Dennis, CBF	Betty McDonald, CCE	Jim Sczudlo, CCE	Dawn Wallace-Cook, CCE
Marjorie Dyrnes, CCE	Paul McIntosh, CCE, CICP	Thomas Shimko, CCE	

NACM Staff Contributors

A special thanks to current and former NACM staff in their quest to *Make Principles Great Again:*

Robin An	Matthew Carr	Diana Mota	Ainslee Sadler
Jake Barron, CICP	Angela Culver	Kevin Naff	Robin Schauseil, CAE
Melanie Brohawn	Carol Fowle, CCE	Ben Noury, M.Ed	Brian Shappell, CBF, CICP

New Features

The 8th edition of *Business Credit Principles* has been thoroughly reviewed for its content and resources to ensure that it is the premier educational text for any credit professional. This edition either expanded or added the following elements to provide better structure and resources to facilitate learning the principles of business credit. The features include:

Enhancing the Structure

Expanded Content

The updated table of contents allows for easier navigation of the chapters. This includes easier access to specific content, concepts, figures and real world perspectives, which can be found throughout the chapters.

Themes within Credit

This edition is divided into themes, including *How Credit Works, The Legal Aspect, Extending Credit, Verifying Creditworthiness, Financing and Payment,* and *Bankruptcy,* to provide readers with a better understanding of the major topics that encompass being a credit professional.

New Chapter Elements

Essential Questions

The beginning of each chapter now includes questions that are essential to the overall understanding of the section. Designed to be answered with more than a simple "yes" or "no," these questions require the reader to have mastered the core ideas of the chapter in order to thoroughly and adequately respond to the questions. In many cases, there is more than one answer to each question; therefore, a reader who can answer a question thoroughly and defend his or her answer has truly mastered the core ideas within the chapter. This also provides instructors with topics to discuss before and after completing the chapter. Posing these questions at the beginning of a chapter allows for class discussion, the activation of knowledge and the identification of any misconceptions a reader may have so that they may be addressed and corrected by the end of the chapter.

Integrated Comprehension Checks

Each chapter features integrated comprehension checks, which are a tool for readers and instructors to check their progress throughout the chapter. The ability to correctly answer these questions provides readers with an opportunity to review the material as they read as well as to ensure that essential concepts are not being glossed over. It also provides the instructor with a great stopping point to check for student understanding.

Real World Perspectives

Real world perspectives provide the reader with a look into how concepts throughout the book are used daily by credit professionals. The stories from credit professionals provide an invaluable resource for handling complex situations that the credit department faces on a daily basis. Real world perspectives also give instructors a direct connection between the content and its real world application.

Chapter Summaries

This edition provides a streamlined summary of each chapter as a guide for reviewing concepts and highlighting key content presented in the chapter. Chapter summaries do not provide the same detail as the chapter, but allow the credit professional to view the necessary key concepts at a glance.

Principles of Business Credit

Contents in Brief

Comprehensive Table of Contents

Part VI: Bankruptcy

PART I

HOW CREDIT WORKS

Credit in the Business World

OVERVIEW

Credit is a privilege granted by a creditor to a customer to defer the payment of a debt, to incur debt and defer its payment, or to purchase goods or services and defer payment. This chapter provides an introduction to the topic of credit. It explores the history of credit, the primary reasons credit is offered and presents an overview of the credit process.

Additionally, the types of credit are defined and discussed. Lastly, the chapter provides an overview of the Federal Reserve System (Fed) and how it controls the U.S. economy.

? THINK ABOUT THIS

Q. How would business be conducted in a world without credit?

Q. A new tech startup and a company that is speculated to have poor financial management both place an order with your company, what factors would you take into account when extending credit?

Q. How does credit change based on the industry or the economic and business conditions?

DISCIPLINARY CORE IDEAS

After reading this chapter, the reader should understand:

- ✓ The historical development of credit.
- ✓ The primary reasons credit is offered.
- ✓ The important elements of credit.
- ✓ The credit process and where credit fits into a business cycle.
- ✓ The different types of credit.
- ✓ The Federal Reserve System and its impact on the economy.

CHAPTER OUTLINE

A Brief History of Credit

The idea of exchanging goods or services in return for a promise of future payment developed only after centuries of trade; money and credit were unknown in the earliest stages of human history. Nevertheless, as early as 1300 B.C., loans were made among the Babylonians and Assyrians on the security of mortgages and advance deposits. By 1000 B.C., the Babylonians had already devised a crude form of the bill of exchange so a creditor merchant could direct the debtor merchant in a distant place to pay a third party to whom the first merchant was indebted. Installment sales of real estate were being made by the Egyptians in the time of the Pharaohs.

Traders in the Mediterranean area, including Phoenicia, Greece, Rome and Carthage, also used credit. The vast boundaries of the Roman Empire encouraged widespread trading and a broader use of credit. In the disorganized period that marked the decline and fall of the Roman Empire, credit bills of exchange and promissory notes were widely used to reduce the dangers and difficulties of transferring money through unorganized trading areas.

During the Middle Ages, a period which spanned 1,000 years from about 500 to 1500 A.D., credit bills were essential to the trading activities of the prosperous Italian city-states. Lending and borrowing, as well as buying and selling on credit, became widespread practices; the debtor-creditor relationship was found in all classes of society from peasants to nobles. A common form of investment and credit, especially in Italy, was the "sea loan" whereby the capitalist advanced money to the merchant and thus shared the risk. If the voyage was a success, the creditor got the investment back plus a substantial bonus of 20 to 30 percent; if the ship was lost, the creditor stood to lose the entire sum.

Another form of credit was the "fair letter," which was developed at fairs held regularly in the centers of trading areas during the Middle Ages. The fair letter amounted to a promissory note to be paid before the end of the fair or at the time of the next fair. It enabled a merchant, who was short of cash, to secure goods on credit. This gave the merchant time either to sell the goods brought to the fair or to take home and sell the goods that had been purchased on credit.

Credit in Early America

The discovery of the New World provided new opportunities for the growth of capitalism and the expansion of credit. The first recorded use of open credit in early America took place with the establishment of the first permanent colony in New England. In September 1620, the Mayflower set sail from England for Virginia. Because of bad weather and navigational errors, the Pilgrims ended up off the coast of Cape Cod and eventually established the village of Plymouth in Massachusetts. Not only was the journey itself was a tremendous achievement, its financing was as well.

The Pilgrims had spent three years of arduous negotiations in England attempting to raise the funds necessary for the trip. A wealthy London merchant financed the trip and provided for "all credit advanced and to be advanced." In return, the Pilgrims contracted to work for seven years. At the end of that period, payment would be made to the creditors based on the size of the individual investment.

The original credit of £1800 could not be paid at the end of seven years, so an alternative arrangement was agreed upon: £200 to be paid annually for a term of nine years. This arrangement had to be renegotiated and finally, after 25 years, the last payment was made. This was the first example of credit in early America.

To finance the American Revolution, the Second Continental Congress made efforts to finance the Army of the United Colonies. The Congress had only three alternatives: borrow the money from sympathetic countries abroad, which was an impossible task since the Colonists' credit in the world stood at zero; impose taxes, which was unpopular and the very cause that had brought about the American Revolution; or issue bills of credit.

In June 1775, the Continental Congress authorized the printing of $2 million in various denominations ranging from one dollar to eight dollars. Trouble for the Continental currency began almost at once; each note had to be hand signed, which was not a simple task considering there were 49,000 of them. Counterfeiting of the currency was rampant. The principle behind the Continental currency was, in essence, a promise to pay the final bearer, at some point in the future, the face value in Spanish coins, the coins in widest circulation at that time.

In 1783, the Treaty of Paris was signed bringing an official end to the war and official recognition of the United States by England. Trading resumed and American importers and wholesalers extended generous terms to their customers. Generally, sales were made on terms of 12 months, but even where six- or nine-month terms were offered, it was not uncommon for an account to remain unpaid for a much longer period, sometimes up to 24 months or more.

With the restoration of pre-Revolutionary trade customs and habits, credit references assumed importance, although in most instances, proper information was still lacking. Some prospective purchasers took the precaution of using the names of prominent people they knew when placing orders on credit. While credit references sometimes accompanied orders, in most cases merchants took their chances. Terms of sale, as they developed during the 1800s, reflected the changes in the rapidly expanding economy. The 12-month period, which had prevailed, gradually became shorter. By the 1830s, the average term of sale was about six months.

Hard financial times hit the country in the mid-1830s. The population was rapidly growing and business was expanding. The sale of land on credit went virtually unchecked and the banking system was not centralized. By the summer of 1837, bank after bank closed its doors and thousands of businesses went into bankruptcy. The financial panic of 1837 saw the beginnings of the Mercantile Agency, established in 1841 by Lewis Tappan. It was this credit information agency that eventually became Dun & Bradstreet and helped transform credit and, with it, the course of American commerce.

 Comprehension Check
Explain the reasons credit has evolved.

The story of American credit was not solely influenced by Dun & Bradstreet. Another organization important for credit professionals worldwide was formed in 1896 in Toledo, Ohio. A group of credit executives, representing a hundred or so of their colleagues, organized a national association for credit professionals, the National Association of Credit Men. Their exchange of credit information was initially conducted on local and regional levels. The association expanded into the **National Association of Credit Management (NACM)**, which today with its network of Affiliated Associations, represents more than 14,000 credit professionals worldwide. NACM's purposes and objectives are:

Transition from Barter

It has been said that the growth of specialization is one of the distinguishing features of modern society. That may be so, but specialization surely began far back in the midst of time when one of our ancestors decided that he had just had too much! He couldn't do everything himself—hunt, fish, shape axe heads, fashion spears, and gather wood, salt and berries. Perhaps it was at that time that the revelation occurred. He was a good fisherman; his neighbor was not.

But that neighbor certainly knew how to turn out axe heads! He could give some of the surplus of fish to the neighbor in exchange for an axe head or two. Thus, the birth of barter.

A particularly fascinating type of barter, and one that implicitly established one as a creditor, was practiced by Native Americans: a form of exchange called potlatch. The social status of the giver rose in proportion to the magnificence of the gifts offered—and the accompanying influence that was gained by having others in your debt.

Simple barter, useful as it was, had some limitations: If your neighbor didn't want any of your fish, you had to find someone who did—and fast. Commodity money, which developed out of simple barter, overcame this difficulty. Commodity money was something that had assumed some accepted value. As a portable store of value, it could be exchanged for a wide variety of items. Cowrie shells, for example, were used in China 3,500 years ago and more recently in New Guinea, Africa, many Pacific Islands and in various parts of the Middle East. Cattle were, and still are, used as money in parts of the world. Salt was also a common medium of exchange (salt bars were still being used as money as recently as the 1920s). Early American colonists borrowed an idea from Native Americans—wampum (elaborate and beautiful strings of beads)—and declared it legal tender in Massachusetts in 1637. Other examples abound: fish hooks, feathers, amber, rice, human skulls, ivory, drums, nails, hoes and furs, to name but a few.

- To promote honest and fair dealings in credit transactions.
- To ensure good laws for sound credit.
- To foster and facilitate the exchange of credit information.
- To encourage efficient service in the collection of accounts.
- To promote and expedite sound credit administration in international trade.
- To encourage training for credit work through colleges, universities, self-study courses and other means.
- To foster and encourage research in the field of credit.
- To disseminate useful and instructive articles and ideas with respect to credit management techniques.
- To promote economy and efficiency in the handling of estates of insolvent, embarrassed or bankrupt debtors.
- To provide facilities for investigation and prevention of fraud.
- To perform other such functions as the advancement and protection of business credit may require.

Comprehension Check

Explain why organizations like **NACM** evolved.

Primary Reasons to Offer Credit

Business or **trade credit** has been part of the U.S. business scene for hundreds of years—and the use of credit in the purchase of goods or services is so common that it is taken for granted. Trade credit is, and continues to be, a very important source of funds for firms. It provides more financing to businesses than does commercial borrowing or corporate bond financing. Without business credit, the economic system would not exist.

The primary reason for a company to *offer credit terms to customers is to accommodate the sale of goods and services in order to create revenue.* The principal reasons companies offer credit are:

- **Increase Sales.** Extending credit to buyers often involves a trade-off between holding inventory or holding accounts receivable.
- **Competition.** Matching a competitor's credit terms may be a sales necessity.
- **Promotion.** A business may offer special credit terms as part of a promotional program for a product.
- **Credit Availability.** Some buyers may not have access to any other forms of credit. In tight credit times, seller trade terms or financing may be necessary.
- **Convenience.** Trade credit provides benefits not easily obtained from other payment arrangements. One of the biggest benefits is the simple convenience of paying for hundreds of purchases in a single transaction.
- **Demand.** Credit is extended in response to customer demand for a company's products or services. This implies that the sale may or may not take place without the extension of credit.
- **Price.** The granting of trade credit is an aspect of price. The time that the buyer gets before payment is due is one of the dimensions of the product, such as quality and service, which determines the attractiveness of the product. Like other aspects of price, the firm's terms of sale and credit-granting decisions affect its sales volume.

Comprehension Check

List and explain the reasons credit is offered.

Explain why a sale may not occur without credit.

Elements of Credit

Several essential points are always included in any definition of credit. First, there must be an exchange of values which sets up the transaction. Goods or services are obtained for a promise to pay, and payment is made when it comes due. This introduces the second factor: futurity and its companion, trust. The credit sale relationship between customer and supplier is based on trust and mutual need. The very derivation of the word "credit" from the original Latin **credere,** *to believe or trust, graphically describes the entire process of credit as a matter of mutual trust and confidence.* The buyer selects the supplier on the basis of its reputation as a source of a quality good at an acceptable price. The supplier accepts the order and extends the credit necessary to facilitate the sale if it believes the customer will honor the contract by paying the invoice according to the terms agreed. Thus, credit can be appropriately described as the transfer of economic value now, on faith, in return for an expected economic value in the future.

Where goods or services are exchanged immediately for cash, there is no futurity, no trust and no need for the seller to have confidence in the buyer. None of these is needed since economic payment is made at the time of purchase.

Credit sales represent an extension of the cash inflow timeline. When credit is granted, the seller does not require cash at the time of the sale, but rather permits payment to be made at a specific date in the future. When a payment is offered, the seller must decide whether or not to accept it. Many times company policy will guide the seller's action, while at other times a snap judgment may be necessary. Since the transaction involves futurity, trust and confidence, the credit concept is involved. The futurity of non-cash payments is short—just long enough for the payment to clear. Trust and confidence, however, are just as significant in this example as they are with longer terms. Once the seller has transferred goods to a buyer, legal steps are necessary to repossess these goods.

When unsecured credit terms are offered, the seller gives up goods or provides services in exchange for the promise of the buyer to pay at a specific future date. The seller is convinced that payment will be received when it is due—and that the buyer can be trusted. In a sale made on 30 or 60 day terms, for instance, the futurity aspect of credit is important; and as selling terms lengthen, the seller's analysis of the buyer's ability to pay on or by the due date becomes increasingly important.

There is no doubt that selling on credit is more costly than selling for cash. Those costs include the cost of the credit department, the investment of company funds in receivables, discounts for early payments, and the cost of converting receivables to cash and collecting bad debts. All of these factors comprise the cost of credit. No matter how great these costs, however, they are more than offset by distinct sales advantages. By offering credit terms, the seller can build a greater customer base, make more efficient use of production facilities, create greater goodwill, expand geographical markets, accept marginal risks, earn incremental profits and ultimately realize a greater return on investment.

> **Comprehension Check**
>
> What does the Latin term *credere* mean?
>
> •
>
> Explain why selling on credit is more expensive than cash, but ultimately beneficial.

There are several important elements of credit:

- **Risk of Nonpayment.** The purchaser may default in making any or all of the payments due to the seller.
- **Timing.** When credit is offered, the seller must wait for payment, even if that payment is received on time. This increases the risk of losing the use of funds that are tied up in financing the credit transaction or, if a payment is late, in carrying or financing the past-due customer.
- **Security.** As a means of gaining partial or full protection for the credit transaction, a seller may require the purchaser to pledge a form of collateral or provide a financial guarantee. This can be accomplished by pledging an asset, providing a personal, corporate or bank guarantee or entering into a security agreement.

- **Extra Costs.** The seller incurs expenses with granting credit, such as carrying receivables and the costs associated with the collection process.
- **Legal Aspects.** Federal and state laws have been enacted that affect both the credit grantor and debtor. Both businesses and consumers must be aware of applicable state and federal laws.
- **Economic Influences.** Changes in economic conditions, such as the rate of inflation and currency value fluctuations, can have strong effects on credit sales. For example, in inflationary times, a seller will not want to wait too long before getting paid and will likely impose stricter credit policies.

Companies are exposed to many changes: political and demographic changes, recessions, inflation and interest rate fluctuations. Companies within a particular industry confront additional risks relating to technological changes, shifting competition, rapid growth, regulation and the availability of raw materials and labor. Management competency, litigation and the company's strategic direction are additional sources of risk. All of these factors affect a company's operating performance, net income and cash flows, which affect the buyer's ability to pay. Credit in its broadest sense is based on the components of trust, risk, economic exchange and futurity.

Comprehension Check
List and explain the important elements of credit.

The Five Cs of Credit

Credit analysis is traditionally based on what is known as the **Five Cs of Credit:** (1) *Character,* (2) *Capacity,* (3) *Capital,* (4) *Collateral* and (5) *Conditions.* The Five Cs of Credit provide the credit manager or analyst with a framework for conducting a controlled investigation process and, therefore, deliver a credit evaluation that considers each component of credit risk associated with credit approval.

But are we *limited* to only the Five Cs listed? Consider the changes over the years in various industries not to mention the economy at large. *Competition* is also important since the credit analysis process can be influenced by terms or conditions the competition is offering in the marketplace. In addition, the credit professional must exercise *Common Sense;* if, on the surface, something doesn't seem right, then more questions should be asked, more information gathered and a harder look taken.

In each case the credit professional must measure the business credit account against every one of the Cs before issuing credit approval or a final recommendation. Sometimes the degree of credit investigation can depend on the customer's or potential customer's size or importance to the credit grantor and to the credit grantor company's established policy and procedures; thus, credit policy can require certain levels of credit investigation for different sizes or types of accounts. Therefore, it is possible for one C component to outweigh other C components.

Comprehension Check
What are the **Five Cs of Credit?**

Character

Character refers to the *willingness* of a debtor to pay its obligations and imputes a level of ethics, integrity, trustworthiness and quality of management that is provided or available to the business customer (proprietorship, corporation, etc.). Examining the business character of a customer requires that the credit professional learn about the previous business background of the people who own, manage or preside over that entity. Management that have been, or are currently in business on their own, or who have been officers of corporations, can be evaluated on the success or failure of the business in which they have been or are currently involved. A company with a long-standing record of operation without litigation or financial difficulty indicates a favorable business record. On the other hand, a company with a record of litigation or bankruptcy could suggest a possible risk. In both cases, a company reflects upon the people who managed it during times of success, setback or even failure. If a business applying for business credit involves ownership by a principal who has been involved in a business failure, the credit professional should determine the cause and then consider the reason in any subsequent credit decision. A previous business holding that was destroyed as a result of a force of nature could have a bearing on a decision to grant credit that is far different from a previous business holding that failed because of mismanagement or negligence.

When questions linger about a principal (or personal guarantor), it is reasonable to obtain a personal (consumer) credit report on the principal of the business that is applying for business credit. A "permissible purpose" and the written consent of the subject of the inquiry are required to obtain a consumer credit report.

Other *Character* considerations:

- Is this business able to redefine itself in a changing market?
- What is the impact of technological evolution on this business?
- How willing is the customer to share information?
- How diligently does the customer complete the credit application?

Capacity

Capacity deals with the inclination or propensity of a business to operate profitably and its ability to pay trade creditors, banks, employees and others as those debts become due. *Capacity* can be substantiated by a customer's ability to generate positive cash flow and by current and previous acts and deeds. The credit professional needs to know how the company handles large volume orders, exacting specifications or tight delivery schedules. Can the company grow and is it able to provide or obtain the needed capital and the necessary financing?

Capital

The value of a customer's business in excess of all liabilities and claims is referred to as its *equity* or *net worth,* and represents its financial strength in terms of **Capital.** *Capital* does not equate to cash; it is the amount of wealth available, in several forms, to be employed by a business in the production of more wealth—in the form of products/inventory purchased for resale, manufactured goods, or the purchase of permanent and fixed assets such as machinery or buildings. In evaluating *Capital,* the credit professional seeks to determine whether the customer possesses the *ability* to satisfy its obligations and lessen credit risk. This approach is different from the first "C," Character, which seeks to judge if the account is *willing* to pay. This factor highlights a company's financial condition and trend of operations. Each case is judged on its own merit, since many factors affect financial condition. Some industries need a large investment in fixed assets; others require only a minimum investment in machinery and fixtures. Similarly, some lines of business must have large amounts of ready cash and liquid assets to meet seasonal operating expenses, while others may rely on regular cash inflows to meet maturing debts.

Collateral

If the cash flow of a business customer is not adequate, the credit manager can request a second source of repayment called **Collateral:** property that may be pledged as security for the satisfaction of a debt. The type of property that can be pledged includes equipment, buildings, accounts receivable, stocks and bonds, inventory and other tangible assets that, once pledged, can be seized and sold by the creditor if the company defaults on the debt.

The credit manager must determine whether the business has additional resources in the form of equity in the assets pledged that can be liquidated for payment. Additionally, the credit professional must discover if the potential collateral is unencumbered or if it has been pledged to, and secured by, other creditors. If the asset pledged is not free and clear, then the creditor taking the security interest may be at the mercy of other creditors who took the same asset as security ahead of later entries. The position of the secured party is based on the legal principle of "first in time, first in right," which means that liquidation of security interests is based on what priority the security instruments were taken and filed.

Assets can be pledged voluntarily with the use of security agreements and filings. This type of pledge is best administered in advance of a credit sale. The security agreement should carefully identify items pledged as collateral.

Assets can also be obtained involuntarily using such legal instruments as liens or judgments then executed to liquidate property taken and used for repayment. Encumbering assets in this manner is usually after the fact of the credit sale, is not by agreement but rather by a function of state law, is not friendly and often involves additional time and expense.

Conditions

External events, occurrences, phenomena and factors that may interrupt or otherwise disturb the normal flow of business are **Conditions** the credit professional considers when examining a new or existing customer's credit. Some examples of *Conditions* are:

- National, regional or local economic environment.
- State and federal government regulations.
- Weather phenomena (hurricane, ice storm, drought, flood, etc.).
- Catastrophic events (fire, explosion, terrorist attack, etc.).

If providing credit to a customer who sells internationally, then other *Conditions* must be considered such as the stability of a foreign country's government and/or currency exchange rates.

The credit professional considers how sensitive the company's sales are to these *Conditions*. Will the company's sales fall dramatically or will they be relatively unaffected if faced with situations as described above? Companies with stable sales that are not tied closely to the overall economy (e.g., food and essential life products) are generally looked upon more favorably by creditor grantors. Similarly, the likelihood of a satisfactory credit experience is greater when the subject is in an industry that is in a period of growth.

It is important for the credit professional to know industry cycles and if a customer's industry is subject to periods of highs and lows. The credit professional will look more favorably on a business that demonstrates increasing sales, profits and net worth. Essentially, two words may summarize *Conditions: demand* for the product or service the customer offers, and *circumstances* that affect the business that are beyond management's control.

Comprehension Check

Why might one C be considered more important?

Canons of Business Credit Ethics

The cornerstone of the global business economy is the extension of commercial credit. As such, business credit executives, as the guardians of commercial receivables, play the vital and critical role of ensuring the flow of commercial goods and services that support world commerce.

In fulfilling their professional duties, business credit professionals pledge to conduct their duties within the constraints of law and to not maliciously injure the reputation of others. Further, business credit professionals pledge themselves to the highest professional standards and principles and to guarding and securing, in confidence, information obtained for the sole purpose of analyzing and extending commercial credit.

Credit professionals pledge to:

- Adhere to the highest standards of integrity, trust, fairness, personal and professional behavior in all business dealings.
- Negotiate verbal or written credit agreements, contracts, assignments, and/or transfers with honesty, fairness, and due diligence to and for the benefit of all parties.
- Render reasonable assistance, cooperating with impartiality and without bias or prejudice, to debtors, third parties, and other credit professionals.
- Exchange appropriate, historical and current factual information to support the process of independent credit decisioning.

Real World Perspectives

FIVE Cs OF CREDIT

When investigating a new customer or performing a review on a current customer who does not have financials to investigate, turn to a process that was employed nearly a half-century ago. The process is known as the 5 Cs of Credit: Character, Capital, Capacity, Conditions and Collateral.

A customer's character will define their willingness to pay for the product or service being provided. To develop an opinion on a customer's character, it is advantageous to review their management staff and see if they have been in the same form of business for a long period of time, or if this is their first time in the industry. If the business history is short, it is advisable to move with caution. Some of the steps a credit professional could take in this situation are to visit the customer, see how the business is set up and talk with the management to see what their growth plan or business plan is. Ask them if you can review their financials while you are there and discuss any flags that you may find. If the credit professional is unable to visit, a credit report could be pulled along with the references they provide to see what the payment history of the company is. Also check if the company has any judgments against them, if any of their accounts have been placed for collections, or if any liens have been established. When the credit professional performs the bank reference check, a review of the NSF checks that are reported and how long the bank account has been opened can also assist in defining character.

Unlike character, capital determines if the customer is able to pay their debts in a timely manner. Ideally, it is beneficial to have financial statements available for review. However, a credit professional is able to look at other factors if they are not available. A review of the customer's life cycle can define when the cash flow is at a high for the company and their expenses are at a high (i.e., a seasonal operation or companies that do not make payments at quarter end). A credit professional could use the third-party credit data that was pulled to see if there are any judgments or liens that might become due during the time frame when a payment would be expected. If the credit professional's industry has an Industry Trade Group, it would be beneficial to see how the company being reviewed is defined in the trade group ranking and see how they compare with companies that others in the industry sell to. If it is an existing customer and a review is being done, what the credit analyst has experienced with the customer could be taken into consideration when reviewing capital. If the credit analyst has developed a rapport with the accounts payable analyst, they may have additional insights as to how the company is performing based on previous conversations.

The capacity of a company shows the credit professional whether the customer has the proper legal structure to allow the corporation to continue making payments to the debtor. This can relate to the review of management that was performed in the character section by looking at the managers in charge of the three key business operations: marketing, financial and production. From the marketing standpoint, the credit professional could review the different business segments that the company is involved in as well as the company's marketing priority. From the financial standpoint, the manager that is in place can be researched to see what other companies they have been tied to. Look at the history of those companies and understand their general overall strategy. From the production standpoint, the credit professional could review the level of automation the company has to see if the it can keep up with changing demands of production. If the information on the managers is not available on the company's website, perhaps an Industry Trade Group would be able to provide the information, or use third-party credit ratings or certain websites such as Manta.com. Once the information about the managers is found, a great way to see their professional history and review the companies they worked for is to look on their LinkedIn profile.

When considering conditions, the general economic conditions that currently exist in the country where the company would be doing business are important. The credit professional would review the overall performance of the industry that they are operating in to help determine the amount of risk that is acceptable. A review of what the selling margin would be could possibly allow certain levels of risk to be overlooked, or if the customer also sells product to your company, a review of the payables due to them could help mitigate risk of open receivables.

Lastly, employing collateral would allow the credit professional to obtain a letter of credit as a payment option, a personal or a corporate guarantee from the company, any liens on equipment that might be able to be placed, and again, as in conditions, any payable that your company may owe them to offset any debtor obligation. If the credit professional is able to offset any liability with these options, the review of the customer could become easier.

Lisa Ball, CCE, Dawn Dickert, CCE, Kathie Knudson, CCE, Stacey Parker, CCE
Graduate School of Credit and Financial Management class of 2016

- Exercise due diligence as required to prevent unlawful or improper disclosure to third parties.
- Disclose any potential conflict in all business dealings.

Further, credit professionals acknowledge the importance of, and shall promote the benefits of, continued improvement of their knowledge, skills, and expertise in business credit. The pursuit of knowledge will support the strategic advancement of the commercial credit function as it leads businesses to profitability and growth.

The Credit Process

In simple terms, the credit process begins with a **buyer** *(a company or individual consumer)* deciding to purchase a product or service from a seller that either makes or provides a product or service. The buyer offers a means of trading value, or a medium of exchange, for the goods or service. Cash is most readily accepted by the seller, but the seller may also offer a form of deferred payment or credit.

The Credit Process
- Sales makes contact and order is taken.
- Credit department reviews customer for creditworthiness.
- Goods or service delivered on credit.
- Payment is made on time/within terms.

Credit is part of a company's **operating cycle.** *An* **operating cycle** *can be defined as the period of time between the acquisition of material, labor and overhead inputs for production and the collection of sales receipts.* During the operating cycle, a manufacturer is both a debtor and a creditor. Consider a typical operating cycle for a manufacturer: the operating cycle begins when the manufacturer purchases raw material from a supplier. The purchase of raw material is usually a business credit transaction. *The material is converted into goods during the* **production stage,** *and the* manufacturer must pay its supplier for the material. *The manufacturer then sells the finished goods to a customer, who ultimately pays for the goods that were purchased on credit during the* **collection stage.**

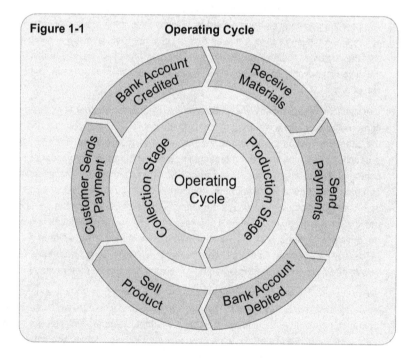

Figure 1-1   **Operating Cycle**

Bank Account Credited · Receive Materials · Production Stage · Send Payments · Bank Account Debited · Sell Product · Customer Sends Payment · Collection Stage · Operating Cycle

The purchaser becomes the debtor or user of credit, while the seller becomes the creditor or grantor of credit. *The purchaser's ability to obtain a product or service based on its promise to pay at a later date is called* **creditworthiness.**

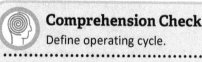

Comprehension Check

Define operating cycle.

Why will a manufacturer be both debtor and creditor at any given time?

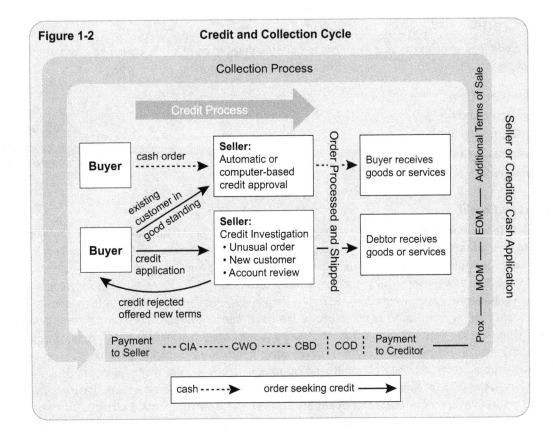

Figure 1-2   **Credit and Collection Cycle**

Types of Credit

Because of its different uses, credit can be broadly classified as either public credit or private credit. **Public credit,** *also known as government credit, is credit extended to or used by governments or governmental divisions, agencies or instrumentalities.* **Private credit** *is extended to or used by individuals or businesses to carry on the exchange of goods and services in the private sector.*

Public Credit

Public credit *includes the extension of, or borrowing by, any governmental unit.* All levels of government—federal, state and local—borrow money to meet public needs, including financing the cost of schools, highways, health and social welfare and military preparedness. Governments buy a wealth of products and services such as tanks, planes, food, office supplies, books, computer equipment, labor, electricity and so forth. Private sector businesses provide nearly all of these products and services. In all cases where financing needs exceed revenue, governments must draw upon their borrowing capacity. This is usually done by the issuance of state, municipal or federal bonds, or in the case of the federal government, through the issuance of shorter-term Treasury bills and notes. Currency itself can be regarded in a sense as a credit obligation of the federal government, though it is usually not classified as such. Analysis of public debt is usually made on the basis of a government's powers of future taxation.

On the other side of the equation is federal and state lending, which often has public policy objectives. Some of these loans include disaster loans, loans by the U.S. Small Business Administration, USDA business and industry loan programs and many others.

Comprehension Check
Define and give an example of **public credit.**

Private Credit

Private credit *is extended to or used by individuals or businesses to carry on the exchange of goods and services in the private sector.* Private credit can be divided into five broad categories:

1. **Investment credit.**
2. **Consumer credit.**
3. **Agricultural credit.**
4. **Business credit.**
5. **Bank credit.**

Comprehension Check

What are the major types of **private credit?**

Investment Credit

This refers to the placement of funds in productive assets to earn a profit. **Investment credit** *can be defined as the long-term borrowing of large amounts of money to finance productive assets.* It consists primarily of loans made to governments or businesses to raise capital to pay for expansion, modernization or public projects such as highways or schools. A borrower may be an institution, a corporation, the U.S. Treasury or a state, city, town or county; an investor is a lender who can buy bonds issued by U.S. companies, the U.S. Treasury or states, counties and cities. **Bonds** *are loans that investors make to corporations and governments* through which borrowers obtain the cash they need while lenders earn interest. **Corporate bonds,** *usually applied to longer-term debt instruments, with maturity of at least one year,* are higher risk than government bonds and thus higher yielding.

Companies often prefer to offer a bond rather than to issue stock to raise money because issuing additional stock may lessen the value of shares already owned by investors. Unlike stockholders who have equity in a company, bond holders are creditors. Corporate bonds are listed on the New York Stock Exchange. Since governments are not profit-making entities and cannot issue stock to raise money, bonds are the primary way for governments to raise money to fund capital improvements.

Bonds, or **fixed-income securities,** *are generally long-term (more than 10 years) securities that pay a specified sum (called the principal) either at a future date or periodically over the length of a loan, during which a fixed rate of interest may be paid on a regular basis.* Every bond has a fixed maturity date when the bond expires and the loan must be paid back in full. The interest a bond pays is also set when the bond is issued. The rate is competitive, which means the bond pays interest comparable to what investors can earn elsewhere. As a result, the rate on a new bond is usually similar to other current interest rates, including mortgage rates.

The word "bond" once referred to the piece of paper, which described the details of a loan transaction; the term is used more generally to describe a vast and varied market in debt securities.

Asset-backed bonds, created in the mid-1980s, *are secured or backed up by specific holdings of the issuing corporation such as equipment or real estate.*

Debentures *are the most common* **corporate bonds.** *They are backed only by the financial strength or standing of the organization issuing it, rather than by any specific assets.* A debenture buyer relies on the issuer's faith and credit as the only assurance of being paid the interest and principal.

Secured bonds *have specific titles attached to them, such as mortgage bonds, equipment and trust certificates and collateral trust bonds.* **Mortgage bonds** *are secured or collateralized with specific corporate assets such as real estate (land and buildings).* Mortgage bonds are backed by a pool of mortgage loans. **Equipment trust certificates (ETC)** *are bonds issued to pay for new equipment, secured by a lien on the purchased equipment.* ETCs are frequently issued by airlines, railroads and shipping companies to finance the purchase of railroad freight cars, airplanes and oil tankers. **Collateral trust bonds** *are similar to mortgage bonds except they are backed by securities of any company through the pledge of stocks and bonds.*

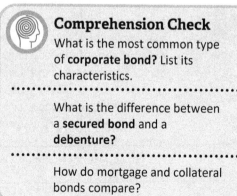

Comprehension Check

What is the most common type of **corporate bond?** List its characteristics.

What is the difference between a **secured bond** and a **debenture?**

How do mortgage and collateral bonds compare?

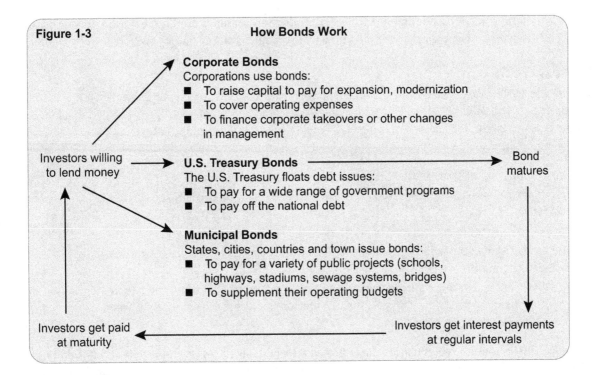

Figure 1-3   **How Bonds Work**

Corporate Bonds
Corporations use bonds:
- To raise capital to pay for expansion, modernization
- To cover operating expenses
- To finance corporate takeovers or other changes in management

Investors willing to lend money

U.S. Treasury Bonds
The U.S. Treasury floats debt issues:
- To pay for a wide range of government programs
- To pay off the national debt

Bond matures

Municipal Bonds
States, cities, countries and town issue bonds:
- To pay for a variety of public projects (schools, highways, stadiums, sewage systems, bridges)
- To supplement their operating budgets

Investors get paid at maturity

Investors get interest payments at regular intervals

Consumer Credit

Consumer credit *is defined as credit extended to a natural person primarily for personal, family or household purposes.* It excludes business and agricultural credit and loans exceeding $54,600 (subject to increase for inflation) that are not secured by real property or a dwelling. It must also be extended by a creditor. Common forms of consumer credit include credit cards, store cards, auto finance, personal loans (installment loans), consumer lines of credit, retail loans (retail installment loans) and mortgages.

Consumer credit can be classified as open-end, closed-end or incidental.

Open-end credit *is an agreement by a bank to lend a specific amount to a borrower and to allow that amount to be borrowed again once it has been repaid. Also called revolving credit or revolving line of credit.* In open-end credit, the creditor:

- Reasonably expects the customer to make repeated transactions.
- May impose a finance charge from time to time on the unpaid balance.
- Generally makes the amount of credit available again to the consumer as the outstanding balance is paid.

Closed-end credit *means credit which is to be repaid in full (along with any interest and finance charges) by a specified future date. Most real estate and auto loans are closed-end.*

Incidental credit *is extended by service providers, such as a hospital, doctor, lawyer or retailer and allows the client or customer to defer the payment of a bill.* There is no credit card involved. There is no finance charge and no agreement for payment in installments.

Agricultural Credit

Agricultural credit *encompasses any of several credit vehicles used to finance agricultural transactions, including loans, notes, bills of exchange and banker's acceptances.* These types of financing are adapted to the specific financial needs of agricultural operations, which are determined by planting, harvesting and marketing cycles. Short-term credit finances operating expenses,

Comprehension Check
Define **consumer credit**.
....

List and explain three ways consumer credit can be classified.

intermediate-term credit is used for farm machinery and long-term credit is used for real-estate financing. Agricultural credit often presents more risk to the creditor and is sometimes placed into its own unique category.

Business Credit

Business credit *refers to extensions of credit primarily for business or commercial purposes.* It is often referred to as business-to-business (B2B) credit. Outstanding trade credit represents nearly 20% of the annual U.S. GDP. Without business credit, the majority of companies would have a serious liquidity issue.

The important characteristics of business credit are:

- Selling terms are relatively short.
- Transactions are usually on open account or unsecured, but may be partially secured or secured in full.
- Cash discounts may be offered for payment before the net due date.
- The terms include transactions to manufacturers, wholesalers and retailers, but specifically exclude the consumer.
- The timeliness in reaching a decision whether or not to extend credit is often much more critical in the business setting. Delays in the manufacturing process can increase costs and reduce the quality of perishable goods.

The fact that business credit finances the intermediate and final stages of production and distribution distinguishes it from consumer credit. Business credit sales also yield a profit on goods sold rather than interest or investment income, which distinguishes it from bank and investment credit.

Unsecured, open account credit is the most widely used form of domestic business credit. In **open account credit,** *the creditor reasonably expects the customer to make repeated transactions and generally makes more credit available to the buyer as the outstanding balance is paid.* A typical business creditor who sells on open account terms is relying specifically on the full faith and credit of a purchaser. The seller establishes the terms of sale. Open account terms are also called *ordinary terms or standard terms.*

A **secured credit arrangement** *is one in which collateral is provided to the creditor.* By obtaining some form of security, the creditor can reduce repayment risk. Examples where secured credit may be useful are a start-up business or an undercapitalized business or an opportunity to sell an account that cannot justify a high credit exposure. Security is obtained not only when the buyer's financial condition is weak, but in order to guarantee payment if the buyer's financial condition changes. While it cannot strengthen a buyer's financial weakness, a secured credit arrangement does reduce the likelihood of loss. Secured credit is defined in Article 9 of the Uniform Commercial Code. It is important to note that drafts, trade acceptances and promissory notes are not forms of security. Each of these instruments is written evidence of debt. However, no security attaches to the instrument.

The ability to compete in the global marketplace is a necessity resulting in the globalization of credit. The procedure for an export credit decision includes more elements than for a domestic decision. In addition to the traditional Five Cs of Credit, other elements such as the risks associated with the economic stability of a country *(country risk)* must be evaluated. The strength and stability of foreign *currency* versus the exporter's currency play a major role in the success of an international credit transaction. Also, the buyer's *culture and customs* may influence the credit transaction. These factors— **country risk, currency issues** and **culture**—add three more dimensions to the Five Cs of Credit.

> **Comprehension Check**
>
> Explain what **open account credit** is.
> ....
> What is the difference between **unsecured** and **secured credit?**

Bank Credit

Bank credit *differs from business credit in a number of ways, but primarily in terms of the type of resource which changes hands in a transaction.* A bank furnishes money, while a business (supplier, wholesaler, manufacturer or other service provider) furnishes goods or services. After the transaction is completed, both the banker and the business supplier are creditors: the customer owes money to each entity.

The Federal Reserve and the U.S. Payment System

The **Federal Reserve Bank,** more commonly known as the Federal Reserve or simply the Fed, *is the United States' central bank, charged with ensuring the stability and flexibility of the nation's monetary and financial systems.*

The Federal Reserve is structured to be independent within the federal government. The Federal Reserve System is made up of the **Board of Governors,** the **Federal Open Market Committee** and 12 **regional banks.**

Structure

The Board of Governors

The Board of Governors, located in Washington, DC, is the "government agency" part of the **Federal Reserve System;** it is the Chairman of the Board of Governors who reports to Congress, and the Board of Governors that sets the regulations for the entire Federal Reserve System per its Congressional mandate.

There are seven members of the Board—themselves called governors—who are all appointed by the president of the United States and confirmed by the U.S. Senate. Each governor's term is limited to 14 years, and the terms of each governor are staggered so that one governor's term expires every other year. The Chairman and Vice Chairman of the Board—required to have been Board members themselves—each serve four-year terms.

Of the four monetary policy tools at the Fed's disposal **(open market operations, the discount rate, reserve requirements** and **contractual clearing balances),** the Board of Governors has sole control over reserve requirements and joint control over the discount rate (with the regional banks), but it does not control open market operations.

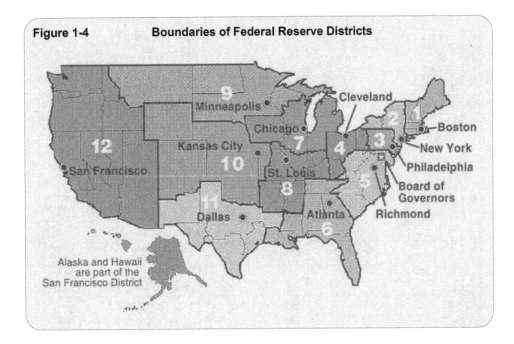

Figure 1-4 **Boundaries of Federal Reserve Districts**

Alaska and Hawaii are part of the San Francisco District

The Regional Banks

There are 12 regional banks within the Federal Reserve System. Each bank is run by a bank president and nine directors, chosen from outside the bank. Three of those directors represent member banks and the rest are from the public, designed to represent a diverse selection of the region's population.

The functions of the 12 regional banks include:

- Operating their portion of the nationwide payment system.
- Distributing currency throughout the region.
- Supervising regional member banks and bank holding companies.
- Serving as bankers for the U.S. treasury.
- Acting as a banker's bank—a depository institution for the regional banks (responsibilities include lending money to depository institutions through the discount window).

Each bank is assigned a number and a letter: look on any U.S. currency to see a number and a letter corresponding to the Federal Reserve Bank that distributed that piece of currency. To aid the regional banks in their supervisory and financial service responsibilities, many banks have branches throughout their districts. The following table lists the 12 regional Federal Reserve Banks and their branches.

Comprehension Check
Explain the structure of the **Federal Reserve.**

Figure 1-5 Federal Reserve Banks

Number	Letter	Bank	Branch
1	A	Boston	
2	B	New York	
3	C	Philadelphia	
4	D	Cleveland	Cincinnati, OH Pittsburgh, PA
5	E	Richmond	Baltimore, MD Charlotte, NC
6	F	Atlanta	Birmingham, AL Jacksonville, FL Miami, FL Nashville, TN New Orleans, LA
7	G	Chicago	Detroit, MI
8	H	St. Louis	Little Rock, AR Louisville, KY Memphis, TN
9	I	Minneapolis	Helena, MT
10	J	Kansas City	Denver, CO Oklahoma City, OK Omaha, NE
11	K	Dallas	El Paso, TX Houston, TX San Antonio, TX
12	L	San Francisco	Los Angeles, CA Portland, OR Salt Lake City, UT Seattle, WA

The Federal Open Market Committee

The third part of the Federal Reserve System is the **Open Market Committee,** *which is charged with buying and selling securities on the open market* in order to change the supply of money held in deposit at the Federal Reserve Banks.

The FOMC is made up of all seven governors from the Board of Governors, the president of the Federal Reserve Bank of New York and four presidents of other regional banks. The four positions for regional Bank presidents rotate each year.

The FOMC meets eight times a year to discuss current economic conditions in the United States. At that meeting, the FOMC sets a target **federal funds rate** which is the interest rate at which depository institutions (banks and credit unions) lend reserve balances to other depository institutions overnight, on an uncollateralized basis. It is a rate it perceives will affect the supply of and demand for money so as to stimulate the economy in the desired direction. After the federal funds target rate is set, securities are accordingly bought and sold on the open market by the Federal Reserve Bank of New York.

Federal Reserve Areas of Responsibility

Since the Fed was established by the Federal Reserve Act in 1913, its roles and responsibilities have evolved. The Fed has three primary areas of responsibility:

1. To guide **monetary policy** for economic stability.
2. To **regulate** and **supervise** banking institutions in the U.S.
3. To provide **financial services** to banking institutions, the U.S. government and foreign official institutions; as well as to play a major role in operating the nation's payment system.

Monetary Policy

The overall economic goals of the Federal Reserve are maximum employment, stable prices and moderate long-term interest rates. When reached, those goals indicate that the U.S. economy is strong and stable. The Federal Reserve uses four possible tools to control, to a certain extent, the amount of money in the economy.

The Discount Rate

The **discount rate** *is the interest rate Federal Reserve Banks charge their member banks for short-term loans.* These loans are conducted through the discount window at each of the regional Federal Reserve Banks. The discount window is often used by banks to satisfy not only their short-term funds needs, but also to fund longer-term loans (e.g., those needed to cover seasonal fluctuations in customer deposits and withdrawals).

Loans made through the discount window are transacted at the prevailing discount rate. If the Fed lowers the discount rate, for example, it becomes more lucrative than before for banks to borrow money from the Fed, so they do borrow, putting money into circulation in the economy. If, on the other hand, the Fed wants to decrease the amount of money in the economy, it can raise the discount rate, making it less lucrative for banks to borrow money from the Fed, so they borrow less, leaving more cash on deposit at the Fed and less in circulation in the economy.

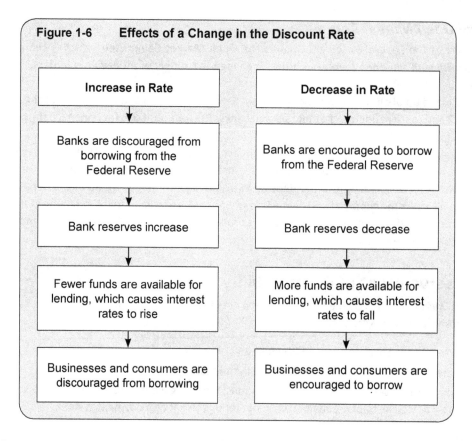

Figure 1-6   Effects of a Change in the Discount Rate

Increase in Rate	Decrease in Rate
Banks are discouraged from borrowing from the Federal Reserve	Banks are encouraged to borrow from the Federal Reserve
Bank reserves increase	Bank reserves decrease
Fewer funds are available for lending, which causes interest rates to rise	More funds are available for lending, which causes interest rates to fall
Businesses and consumers are discouraged from borrowing	Businesses and consumers are encouraged to borrow

Open Market Operations

Open market operations *is the purchase or sale of securities, primarily U.S. Treasury securities, in the open market to influence the level of balances that depository institutions hold at the Federal Reserve Banks and the rate at which banks lend each other money from their Federal Reserve Bank balances* (the **federal funds rate**). Open market operations are conducted at the Federal Reserve Bank of New York.

Even though banks are lending money from their Federal Reserve deposit accounts, the Fed cannot actually change the federal funds rate. Instead, the Federal Open Market Committee targets a federal funds rate that it believes would mean stability and strength for the economy on the whole. Then it engages in open market operations to try and get the actual federal funds rate close to the target rate.

Open market operations are based on the same principle as the discount rate: changing the supply of money. By selling government securities, for example, the Federal Reserve decreases the supply of money available to depository institutions (because it's effectively giving security notes in exchange for cash)—and that, in turn, increases the price of that money—the federal funds rate. Buying government securities, on the other hand, increases the supply of money available to depository institutions (it's effectively taking security notes in exchange for cash), which, in turn, decreases the price of that money—the federal funds rate.

The Reserve Requirement

The **reserve requirement** *is the portion of a member bank's deposits that it must hold in reserve in its own vaults or on deposit at its regional Reserve bank.*

By increasing the reserve requirement, it takes money out of the economy. By decreasing the requirement, it increases the money supply. In practice, the Fed rarely changes the reserve requirement more than once every few years.

Comprehension Check

Briefly explain the concept of **reserve requirement.**

What would the effect be if the Fed raised the reserve requirement? What if the requirement was lowered?

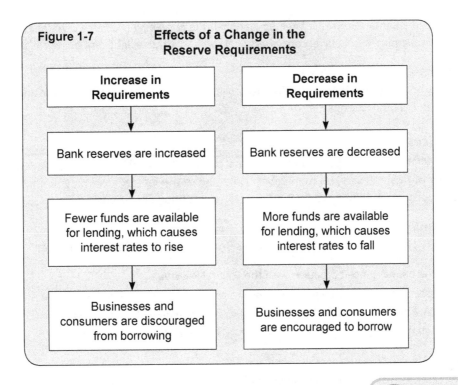

Figure 1-7   **Effects of a Change in the Reserve Requirements**

Increase in Requirements	Decrease in Requirements
↓	↓
Bank reserves are increased	Bank reserves are decreased
↓	↓
Fewer funds are available for lending, which causes interest rates to rise	More funds are available for lending, which causes interest rates to fall
↓	↓
Businesses and consumers are discouraged from borrowing	Businesses and consumers are encouraged to borrow

Contractual Clearing Balances

Contractual clearing balances *is an amount that a depository institution agrees to hold at its Federal Reserve Bank in addition to any required reserve balance.*

Comprehension Check

List the four major tools used by the Fed to expand or contract the money supply and to control interest rates.

Banking Supervision

One of the primary reasons that Congress created the Federal Reserve System in 1913 was to avoid banking crises like the one in 1907. One way the Fed does that is by backing up banks' deposits, if need be, through discount window loans. Another way the Fed works to ensure a stable banking system is through regulation and supervision.

The **Board of Governors** *is responsible for the regulation part, writing the rules that will keep the banking system stable and competitive.* The 12 regional banks, along with the Board, are responsible for supervision, enforcing those rules.

Safe, Sound and Competitive Banking Practices

Together, the regional Federal Reserve Banks supervise approximately 900 state member banks and 5,000 bank holding companies. Banks that are not supervised by the Federal Reserve, such as national banks and state banks that are not members of the Federal Reserve System, are supervised by the Office of the Comptroller of the Currency or the Federal Deposit Insurance Corporation, respectively.

The supervisory role of the Federal Reserve banks involves annual examinations of each bank's risk management and other performance measures. At each examination, the bank is given a performance rating from the Federal Reserve, which amounts to either a mark of approval or a warning to do better. Banks that do not get the mark of approval are monitored more closely throughout the year and can be mandated to make certain changes to come back within the bounds of the regulations.

Protection of Consumers in Financial Transactions

Congress has charged the Federal Reserve with making, interpreting, and enforcing laws that protect the rights of consumers, such as discrimination in lending and inaccurate disclosure of credit costs or interest rates.

Comprehension Check

Must all banks belong to the **Federal Reserve System**?

The Federal Reserve Banks also take a large educational role in helping consumers understand the rights they have in financial transactions, and helping consumers spot signs that those rights are being violated.

Stable financial markets

One of the roles of the Federal Reserve Banks is to provide stability to the financial system and contain systemic risk that may arise in financial markets.

Financial Services

In addition to guiding monetary policy and supervising and regulating member banks, the Federal Reserve also provides a number of **financial services** to member banks and to the federal government. These services include payment systems policies and solutions as well as currency distribution operations.

The Banker's Bank

The financial services that the Federal Reserve Banks provide their member banks include:

- Maintaining the banks' deposit accounts with the Federal Reserve.
- Providing payment services, including collecting and processing checks as well as bank-to-bank electronic fund transfers (EFTs) and automated clearing house (ACH) services.
- Distributing and receiving U.S. currency into and out of the banks' deposit accounts.

The Government's Bank

The financial services that the Federal Reserve Banks provide the federal government include:

- Acting as fiscal agents.
- Paying treasury checks.
- Processing electronic payments.
- Issuing, transferring and redeeming U.S. government securities.

Research and Information

The Federal Reserve System also conducts research on the U.S. and regional economies and distributes information about the economy to the public through published articles, speeches by board members, seminars and websites. This information is released to the public as part of the Fed's mandate to study the economy.

Two important outlets for this information are:

- Summary of Commentary on Current Economic Conditions by Federal Reserve District commonly known as **the Beige Book.** This report is published eight times per year. Each Federal Reserve Bank gathers *anecdotal information on current economic conditions in its District* through reports from Bank and Branch directors and interviews with key business contacts, economists, market experts and other sources. The Beige Book summarizes this information by District and sector. An overall summary of the twelve district reports is prepared by a designated Federal Reserve Bank on a rotating basis.
- **Fed Minutes** *are notes from discussions the Federal Open Market Committee has over economic policy.* They are released eight times a year, after each meeting. They often detail discussions between members over what policy to follow.

Comprehension Check

What two publications does the Fed release to the public as part of their mandate to study the economy?

Check Processing

The Federal Reserve Banks provide check collection services to depository institutions. When a depository institution receives deposits of checks drawn on other institutions, it may send the checks for collection to those institutions directly, deliver them to the institutions through a local clearinghouse exchange, or use the check-collection services of a correspondent institution or a Federal Reserve Bank. For checks collected through the Federal Reserve Banks, the accounts of the collecting institutions are credited for the value of the checks deposited for collection and the accounts of the paying banks are debited for the value of checks presented for payment. Most checks are collected and settled within one business day.

In the 1950s, the Federal Reserve developed and implemented the **magnetic ink character recognition (MICR) system** *for encoding pertinent data on checks so that the data could be read electronically. The characters are printed at the bottom of a check in what is called the* **MICR line.**

The first section, or the first nine digits, of the MICR line is called the **transit routing number,** which provides information about the financial institution on which the check is drawn. Additional sections of the MICR line identify the: **payor's account number, sequence number** and **encoded amount.** (*See* Figure 1-8)

> **Comprehension Check**
> What is the **MICR** system?
> ....
> What information does the MICR line contain?

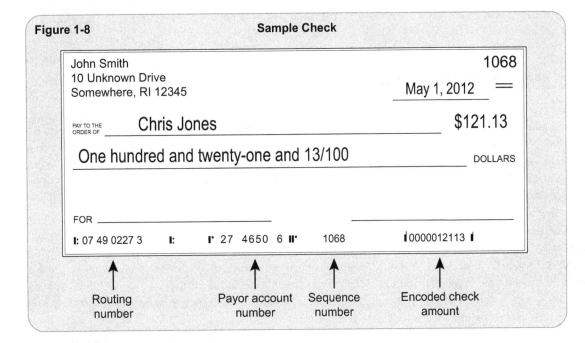

Figure 1-8 **Sample Check**

John Smith
10 Unknown Drive
Somewhere, RI 12345

1068

May 1, 2012

PAY TO THE ORDER OF Chris Jones $121.13

One hundred and twenty-one and 13/100   DOLLARS

FOR _____

I: 07 49 0227 3   I: I' 27 4650 6 II'   1068   I0000012113 I

↑ Routing number   ↑ Payor account number   ↑ Sequence number   ↑ Encoded check amount

In 1987, Congress enacted the **Expedited Funds Availability Act (EFAA)**, which limits the time that banks can hold funds from checks deposited into customer accounts before the funds are made available for withdrawal. The law, implemented in September 1988 through the Board of Governors' Regulation CC, Availability of Funds and Collection of Checks, also establishes rules designed to speed the return of unpaid checks.

The Federal Reserve has an availability schedule that details the time it takes to make funds available. *The delay between the time a check is deposited at the bank and the time the depositor's account is credited with collected funds by the bank is called* **availability float.**

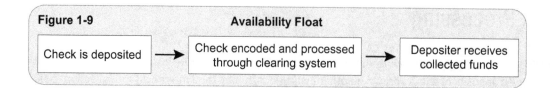

Figure 1-9   **Availability Float**

Check is deposited → Check encoded and processed through clearing system → Depositer receives collected funds

Availability float was affected by the Check Clearing for the 21st Century Act (Check 21), which became effective October 28, 2004. The purpose of **Check 21** *is to remove barriers to the electronic collection of checks allowing banks to "truncate checks."* **Check truncation** *is the process of taking the physical paper check out of circulation, capturing the check information electronically, and moving the electronic copy through the clearing system.* The paper check is destroyed or put into secured storage.

There are some practical effects of Check 21 that credit managers must take into account. When a customer claims payment was made, the credit manager must accept the substitute check as proper evidence of payment. According to the Act, courts, retailers and services providers are all required to accept the substitute check as proof of payment in the same manner as they would accept the original. From a credit manager's standpoint, the faster clearing process has two significant benefits:

1. Funds will end up in the creditor's accounts faster thus increasing their cash balances.
2. Checks drawn on an account with insufficient funds will be known sooner.

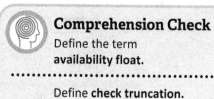

Comprehension Check

Define the term **availability float.**

Define **check truncation.**

Electronic Funds Transfer

Electronic funds transfer (EFT) *is the electronic transfer of money from one bank account to another,* either within a single financial institution or across multiple institutions, through computer-based systems and without the direct intervention of bank staff. There are several types of services for electronically transferring payments.

Automated Clearing House (ACH) *is an electronic network for financial transactions in the United States.* ACH processes large volumes of credit and debit transactions in batches. The Federal Reserve Banks (FedACH) and Electronic Payments Network (EPN) are the two national ACH operators.

Fedwire *is a real-time method of transferring cash value from one bank to another, using Federal Reserve account balances.*

SWIFT (Society for Worldwide Interbank Financial Telecommunication) *is a dedicated computer network to support funds transfer messages internationally between member banks worldwide.*

CHIPS (Clearing House Interbank Payments System) *is a worldwide bank-owned, private-sector U.S.-dollar funds-transfer system for cross-border and domestic payments.*

TARGET2 *is the real-time gross settlement (RTGS) system owned and operated by the Eurosystem. TARGET stands for Trans-European Automated Real-time Gross settlement Express Transfer system. TARGET2 is the second generation of TARGET.*

TIPANET (Transferts Interbancaires de Paiement Automatisés) *is an international payment system set up by the European cooperative banks.*

Comprehension Check

Define the term **electronic funds transfer.**

List the types of services for electronically transferring funds.

Federal Deposit Insurance Corporation

The Federal Deposit Insurance Corporation (**FDIC**) was created in 1913 as *an independent agency to preserve and promote public confidence in the U.S. financial system by insuring deposits in banks and thrift institutions for at least $250,000;* by identifying, monitoring and addressing risks to the deposit insurance funds; and by limiting the effect on the economy and the financial system when a bank or thrift institution fails. The FDIC insures approximately $9 trillion (as of 2016) of deposits in U.S. banks and thrifts—deposits in virtually every bank and thrift in the country.

The standard insurance amount is $250,000 per depositor, per insured bank, for each account ownership category. The FDIC insures deposits only. It does not insure securities, mutual funds or similar types of investments that banks and thrift institutions may offer.

The FDIC directly examines and supervises more than 4,500 banks and savings banks for operational safety and soundness, more than half of the institutions in the banking system. Banks can be chartered by the states or by the federal government. Banks chartered by states also have the choice of whether to join the Federal Reserve System. The FDIC is the primary federal regulator of banks that are chartered by the states that do not join the Federal Reserve System. In addition, the FDIC is the back-up supervisor for the remaining insured banks and thrift institutions.

The FDIC also examines banks for compliance with consumer protection laws, including the Fair Credit Billing Act, the Fair Credit Reporting Act, the Truth-In-Lending Act, and the Fair Debt Collection Practices Act, to name a few. Finally, the FDIC examines banks for compliance with the Community Reinvestment Act (CRA) which requires banks to help meet the credit needs of the communities they were chartered to serve.

The FDIC is managed by a five-person Board of Directors, all of whom are appointed by the president and confirmed by the Senate, with no more than three being from the same political party. It is headquartered in Washington, DC, but conducts much of its business in six regional offices, and in field offices around the country.

Comprehension Check
What does the **FDIC** *not* insure?

Online Business Banking

For credit professionals, the advent of **online business banking** has simplified money management. Enrolling in online business banking makes it easier to monitor accounts, financials, account history and statements; transfer funds between accounts and banks; pay bills and more.

With online business banking and remote deposit capture, it is not necessary to carry checks to the bank. They can be scanned in the office and deposited via a secure internet connection. Images of posted checks are available when necessary.

Online banking also allows for the assignment of different security levels for multiple users. In addition to secure deposits, all other transactions online are usually protected by a firewall and encryption technology to ensure the security of business information and financial data.

Other advantages include: automatic payments and debits, transaction alerts, cost savings and direct deposit, among others.

For businesses trading worldwide, there are international banks which provide access to bankers working in other countries. They can provide currency risk management and also help with foreign exchange, importing and exporting, wire transfers and inter-country payments.

Comprehension Check
What are some of the advantages of **online business banking**?

Key Terms and Concepts

Comprehension Check

1. The idea of exchanging goods or services on credit developed after centuries of trade. Explain some of the reasons why credit evolved.
2. Explain why organizations like **NACM** evolved.
3. List and explain the reasons credit terms are offered.
4. Explain why a sale may not occur, in the business setting, if credit is not offered.
5. What does the Latin term *credere* mean? How does it describe the credit process?
6. Explain why selling on credit is more costly than selling for cash, but ultimately beneficial. Give three reasons.
7. List and explain the important elements of credit.
8. List and explain the **Five Cs of Credit**. What are some additional Cs of Credit? Describe why one is considered more important than the others.
9. Define the term **operating cycle.**
10. Why will a manufacturer be both a debtor and a creditor at any given time?
11. Define and give an example of **public credit.**
12. Define and list the major types of **private credit.**
13. What is the most common type of **corporate bond**? List the characteristics of this type of bond.
14. What is the difference between a **secured bond** and a **debenture**?
15. How do mortgage and collateral bonds compare?
16. Define the term **consumer credit.**
17. List and explain three ways consumer credit can be classified.
18. Define and explain the important characteristics of **business credit.**
19. Explain what **open account credit** is.
20. What is the difference between **unsecured** and **secured credit**?
21. Explain the structure of the **Federal Reserve.**
22. Define the term **discount rate.**
23. Briefly explain the concept of **reserve requirement.**
24. What would the effect be if the Fed raised the reserve requirement? What if the requirement was lowered?
25. List the four major tools used by the Fed to expand or contract the money supply and to control interest rates. Explain the relationship between the tools and their influence on the money supply.
26. Must all banks belong to the **Federal Reserve System**?
27 What two publications does the Fed release to the public as part of their mandate to study the economy?
28. What is the **MICR** system?
29. What information does the MICR line contain?
30. Define the term **availability float.**
31. Define **check truncation.**
32. Define the term **electronic funds transfer.**
33. List the types of services for electronically transferring funds.
34. What does the **FDIC** *not* insure?
35. What are some of the advantages of **online business banking**?

Summary

- Credit has been documented to have been used as early as 1300 B.C. by the Babylonians and Assyrians. Credit also played a fundamental role in financing the United States during the American Revolution.
- Institutions like Dun & Bradstreet and NACM arose because of a clear need for information and resources, which include, but are not limited to the following:
  - Honest and fair dealings in credit transactions
  - Ensuring good laws for sound credit
  - Fostering and facilitating the exchange of information
  - Promoting and expediting information for international trade
  - Training credit professionals
- The seven reasons to offer credit are:
  - **To increases sales**
  - **Competition**
  - **Promotion**
  - **Credit availability**
  - **Convenience**
  - **Demand**
  - **Price**
- Credit involves trust and is ultimately more costly than dealing in cash, although the benefits can outweigh the costs.
- The **six elements of credit** are:
  - **Risk of nonpayment**
  - **Timing**
  - **Security**
  - **Extra costs**
  - **Legal aspects**
  - **Economic influences**
- The **Five Cs of Credit** are character, capacity, capital, collateral and conditions, but one might want to also consider competition and common sense as additional Cs.
- The two types of credit are public and private. Public involves the government, while private extends to businesses and individuals.
- The five types of **private credit** are:
  - **Investment credit**
  - **Consumer credit**
  - **Agricultural credit**
  - **Business credit**
  - **Bank credit**
- The **Federal Reserve** is composed of the Board of Governors, the Federal Open Market Committee and the 12 regional banks.
- The Federal Reserve has four main tools that control the money supply and the monetary policy of the U.S., which ultimately controls and manipulates various interest rates. They include: open market operations, the discount rate, reserve requirements and contractual clearing balances.

- Besides controlling monetary policy and interest rates, the Federal Reserve also ensures safe, sound and competitive banking practices, consumer protection, stable financial markets, financial services and published economic research.
- The **FDIC** insures approximately $9 trillion (as of 2016), which correlates to $250,000 per depositor, per insured bank.
- **Online business** banking has simplified money management making it easier to monitor accounts, financials, account history and statements, as well as facilitating the transfer of funds between accounts and bank assisting domestic and international business.

References and Resources . . . .

Board of Governors of the Federal Reserve System. *The Federal Reserve System: Purposes and Functions*, 2013.

"Credit Risk Review." NACM Graduate School of Credit and Financial Management project, 2016. Kathie Knudson, CCE; Lisa Ball, CCE; Stacy Parker, CCE; and Dawn Dickert, CCE.

Emery, Gary W. *Corporate Finance: Principles and Practices.* New York: Addison Wesley, 1998.

Gallinger, George W. and Jerry B. Poe. *Essentials of Finance: The Integrated Approach.* New Jersey: Prentice Hall, 1995.

Hill, Ned. C. and William L. Satoris. *Short-Term Financial Management: Text and Cases.* New Jersey: Prentice Hall, 1995.

2 Credit in the Company

OVERVIEW

Business is concerned with the sale of goods or services for a profit. This chapter discusses the role and structure of the credit department in a business setting from strategic and organizational points of view. It also covers the credit department's goals and the relationships between the various departments. The daily activities of the credit department including collections are described.

THINK ABOUT THIS

Q. How is the role of credit perceived by different departments in the company?

Q. How can the use of credit facilitate the overall direction and objectives of a company?

DISCIPLINARY CORE IDEAS

After reading this chapter, the reader should understand:

- ✓ Why credit is a function of business.
- ✓ The strategic role of credit.
- ✓ Where credit typically fits within the business organization.
- ✓ The role of credit in financial management.
- ✓ The role of credit in the operating cycle.
- ✓ The goals and core activities of a credit department.

CHAPTER OUTLINE

Credit as a Business Function

The word **business** *first appeared around the 14th century and originally meant "purposeful activity."* Today, the inclusive term "business" designates the activities of those engaged in the purchase or sale of commodities or in related financial transactions. In other words, a **business organization** *is a combination of functions, people and materials aimed at producing goods or services, and selling them to customers at a profit.* The sale of most commodities is accomplished through the extension of credit.

The credit department is an integral part of the business organization. It is the link between customers and many other business functions such as marketing, sales, production, shipping, customer service and accounts payable.

The role of the credit department continues to evolve. The credit department is involved from the time the order is solicited to the time the cash is collected. This **order-to-cash** responsibility reaches well beyond the financial evaluation of a customer's ability to pay and collecting that payment. The credit department represents a business decision that requires both financial and strategic decision-making to ensure that a proper balance of benefit is derived from sales against carrying the cost or potential loss.

Strategic decision-making is part of strategic planning, which is the key component that underlies credit policy and procedures. *The art of devising or using plans to achieve a goal is called* **strategy. Strategic planning** *entails the coordination of long-range plans with a particular focus on strategies, controls and desired results.*

External factors such as social, political, economic, legal, technological and competitive pressures impact a company's strategic plan. These external factors must be weighed in light of internal business factors such as production capacity, financial strength, human resources and sales. Both external and internal factors are assessed in terms of risk and reward. The role of strategic planning underlies the framework from which any policy, including credit policy, is formulated. Clearly defined goals affect the credit department's ability to shape the resulting credit policy.

> **Comprehension Check**
>
> Discuss what the term **business** means.
>
> What is meant by the term **order-to-cash?**
>
> Define the term **strategy.**
>
> What factors impact a company's strategic plan?

The Strategic Role of Credit

The credit department is involved with the customer cycle from placement of the order to the collection of payment. The cycle involves gathering and analyzing all information available which culminates in the best possible position to mitigate risk.

Consider the following broadly defined credit-related areas:

Amassing Information

The more information available about a customer or potential customer, the greater the quality of analysis. That same information also has strategic implications; it can strengthen a company's understanding of its customer base and lead to expanding that base. The credit department is, in effect, an information and business intelligence warehouse within any company. The information gathered by a credit department can be used by a purchasing department to screen vendors or by the sales department to help find new customers.

Credit Analysis

Credit analysis provides a business protection from financial risk and, depending on a company's strategic goals, becomes an important factor in the sales decision. By assessing the risk of whether a customer or potential customer has the ability, and/or willingness, to pay when the credit account becomes due, the credit grantor can avoid risk, improve profits, sell more to better-paying customers and forecast cash required to operate and invest.

Securitization

Securitization *includes but is not limited to letters of credit, Uniform Commercial Code (UCC) filings, liens and guarantees.* The credit department must ensure that all accounts are properly securitized to protect against defaults.

Collection

While the credit department is responsible for the enforcement of payment terms, credit terms are a part of a company's strategic business plan. Whether credit terms are restrictive or liberal will have a direct impact on that plan as well as on the credit process. Cash forecasting is a sequential event for the credit department.

Cash Application

Cash application is the function of matching and applying customer payments to accounts receivable, which represents transactions booked by the company for products or services sold to customers on unsecured, open account credit. This process is related to the timing of cash flow and the cost of carrying a receivable. The strategic implication of the cost of carrying receivables is related to a company's financial strength and its ability to gauge its need for cash flow or, in other words, properly forecast future cash requirements to meet payroll, expenses and other such demands for cash.

Deduction Resolution

The financial implication of the cost of carrying unresolved deductions or customer disputes affects a company's operating costs. Deduction resolution has very critical strategic implications because it is directly related to customer satisfaction, which in turn impacts sales.

> **Comprehension Check**
> Discuss a credit-related area that has both a financial and strategic implication.

Credit within the Business Organization

The credit department is responsible for the management of accounts receivable. From an accounting perspective, accounts receivable plays an important part in a business organization. Accounts receivable is a current asset and a component of **net working capital,** *which is the excess of current assets of a business over its current liabilities.*

Net working capital is calculated by subtracting current liabilities from current assets:

Net Working Capital = Current Assets – Current Liabilities

In larger companies, the finance department or the treasury department is responsible for the management of working capital. In smaller or family-owned businesses, the owners or top executives usually manage working capital.

As a result of this **balance sheet logic,** the vast majority of credit departments report to either the treasury or finance department. A 2015 NACM survey of its membership found that approximately half of participating credit executives said they meet with either a chief financial officer or treasurer once per month to discuss credit department performance, metrics, etc. Another 18% said they meet quarterly with upper management.

Some of the finance-related functions that the credit department manages include:

- Protecting and managing the investment in the accounts receivable portfolio.
- Cash forecasting.
- The timely conversion of receivables into cash.
- Financial analysis.
- Handling of collateral that secures a customer's account.
- Deposit of funds and the relationship with banks.
- Handling customer deductions.
- Evaluation of economic trends on sales, receivables and collections.

Comprehension Check

Using balance sheet logic, explain where the credit department falls within an organization.

List eight finance-related functions that the credit department manages.

The Role of Credit in Financial Management

Managers practice financial management when they:

- Obtain cash from investors.
- Use that cash to buy productive assets.
- Operate those assets to produce additional cash.
- Return cash to the business and/or investors.

Comprehension Check
What is the goal of cash management?

A key component of a company's financial activities is managing cash flow or cash management. *The goal of* **cash management** *is the efficient management and use of cash in a manner that is consistent with the strategic objectives of the business.* A major goal of cash management is to manage cash flows in order to increase the long-term value of the business while balancing the inflow and outflow of cash so that the business can meet its demands for cash by creditors, banks, investors, stakeholders and owners.

The management of cash flow can be divided into the following three broad areas:

Managing Cash Inflows

Cash inflows *are the funds collected from customers or obtained from financial sources.* Cash flows into the business from the sale of goods or services, from the return on interest-earning assets in the form of interest or from the return on equity securities in the form of dividends. Cash also flows into a business when it borrows money or obtains money from other sources outside of its normal operations.

Internal Cash Flow Management

This includes managing the company's cash reserves and investing cash or transferring cash among the operating units of a business or various bank accounts. Excess cash is usually invested so that it earns interest, becoming a productive asset.

Managing Cash Outflows

Cash outflows *are the funds disbursed from cash reserves to pay for purchases of inventories, to pay for operating expenses such as salaries, rent and insurance; to pay for the purchase of long-lived assets such as buildings or land; or for the repayment of debt principal or payment of dividends.*

The credit department plays a crucial role in managing the cash received from the sale of goods or services. The timely collection of cash is critical to maintain the proper balance of cash inflows and cash outflows.

Comprehension Check
List and describe the three broad areas of cash flow management.

Credit and the Operating Cycle

The **operating cycle** *comprises the activities a company performs to produce and sell its product or service.* A business must first purchase the resources it needs to make its product. It then sells that product and collects the funds from the sale. *Cash flows into and out of the business during the operating cycle. Cash flows out of the business during the production stage, when it purchases the resources needed. Cash flows into the business when it sells the product to a customer.* Rarely do these events occur at the same time; the challenge of business is to maintain sufficient levels of cash throughout the operating cycle to ensure smooth and ongoing operations.

The **collection stage** or **cycle** *begins after the sale of a product is made or services are rendered. With new or high-risk accounts, the collection cycle can begin as early as the credit department's receipt of an order or customer application as the credit department makes provisions for a strict collection plan strategy. In more routine sales, the collection cycle begins with the sale.*

The order is received and the customer placing the order is reviewed for creditworthiness to arrive at the credit decision. Sometimes, and depending on the credit policy, an order/customer passes all credit indicators and the order is approved. If the credit indicators point toward further credit investigation, the necessary steps are taken to make the sale while reducing the risk.

Upon approval, the order is recorded as a sale and an invoice is created. The events of recording the sale and creating an invoice are usually simultaneous. At this point the receivable is created. The invoice is, in effect, a memo or record of the sale and should include an itemization of products or services purchased.

The order is then shipped. The timing varies from company to company; sometimes the order is shipped as soon as the order is approved and the creation of the invoice follows. Sometimes, shipping and invoicing occur simultaneously. In other companies, the invoice is created after the order is shipped. The important point is that the work of the credit department continues after the order is shipped by monitoring the receivable.

In a perfect credit world, payments are received when due. The accounts receivable is reversed when the payment is received, and the cycle begins again. The reality is that not all invoices are paid as they come due. Among the reasons are errors, discount violations, incomplete or incorrect payments or deductions. The disputes must be settled with chargebacks or credit memos. In some cases, the order is canceled and a new invoice is issued. Invoice disputes are usually resolved by direct communication with the customer and other departments within the company key to the transaction. Financially distressed customers that do not pay invoices as they are due must be followed closely with an understanding yet aggressive collection effort. When a direct collection effort is not successful, a third party—a local NACM Affiliate, a collection agency or a collection attorney—can be used. In cases of insolvency, the business must be assessed to determine whether it can be financially rehabilitated or whether it should be liquidated. Depending on its policy and strategy, a company may or may not continue to offer credit to a financially distressed customer. Some businesses continue to sell to customers, even during a bankruptcy proceeding while other businesses terminate credit to customers based on the severity of the situation.

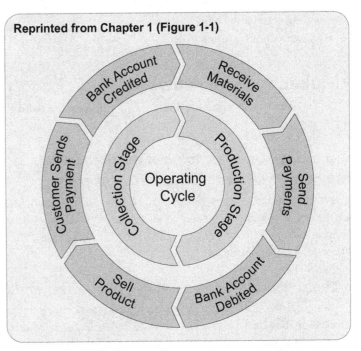

Reprinted from Chapter 1 (Figure 1-1)

Comprehension Check

Describe the **operating cycle**.

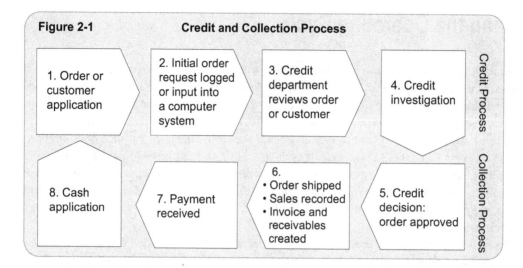

Figure 2-1   **Credit and Collection Process**

The Core Activities of the Credit Department

The credit function is a valuable asset to a company's business. Using creative methods to structure transactions so that sales can be approved, the credit department makes a significant contribution to sales and profit maximization by knowing when and how to accomplish the sale while minimizing risk.

The core activities of the credit department are:

- Customer and credit analysis.
- Developing credit policy.
- Managing the collection function.
- Setting credit availability thresholds.
- Management reporting.

> **Comprehension Check**
> List the core activities of the credit department.

Required Areas of Knowledge

To accomplish these goals and to perform these core activities, the following areas of knowledge or skill sets are required:

A Thorough Understanding of the Accounting, Financial Analysis and Finance Disciplines

All three of these disciplines come into play during the analysis of the customer. A mastery of both accounting and financial analysis is needed when interpreting information about a customer. Basic concepts in the area of finance, such as the time value of money, assist in determining the cost of offering credit terms from the perspective of both the buyer and seller.

A Comprehensive Understanding of Business and Credit Law

Many elements of the credit function require a thorough understanding of legal concepts. For example, a credit application may be used as a legal contract between the seller and the buyer. A cardinal rule of any credit investigation is: Know Your Customer (KYC). Is the customer a corporation, partnership or sole proprietor? Who are the owners? Antitrust laws, the Equal Credit Opportunity Act and the Fair Credit Reporting Act all affect what the credit department can and cannot do. Securing a credit transaction involves the Uniform Commercial Code.

Sound Business Communication Skills (Writing and Presentation)

The credit department must compose and send a variety of written communications to the customer as well as create meaningful reports for management. In management meetings, credit managers must be able to clearly explain credit issues in order to have input in general business policies and practices. Excellent verbal communication skills are critical when dealing with internal business functions and with customers.

General Management Skills Including Expert Negotiation Skills

As with most business functions, general management skills are a must. The ability to effectively manage, inspire and motivate credit department personnel is critical to the success of any credit department. As business changes, so do management techniques. There has been a shift to the team concept, which demands an understanding of how sales, credit and management/ownership work together to achieve the goals of the business. Additionally, expert negotiation skills are invaluable in the collection area. General management skills also include the ability to assign responsibility, delegate authority and maintain accountability for the results.

Customer Service Skills

The credit department interacts with the customer and also serves as the intermediary with a variety of other business units such as the sales department, the purchasing department, manufacturing or production and so on.

Analytical Skills

The ability to analyze both the customer's financial condition and general economic conditions and trends is key to a successful credit department.

Computer Skills

Most companies rely heavily on constantly evolving technology (e.g., computer automation software, Enterprise Resource Planning (ERP), cloud data storage, electronic credit applications, etc.) to enable the credit department to investigate the status of an order at any point in time. Often these specialized tools are critical to the credit function by helping managers analyze, plan and develop department objectives, policies and programs. More companies are using credit-scoring programs to evaluate credit and financial information on credit applications as these metrics can help reduce costs through automating some processes. This can include approving customers for open account credit automatically based upon applicants meeting specific criteria defined and determined by the credit, sales, management and ownership teams. Use of ERP systems, such as SAP and Oracle, as well as credit-focused bolt-on software options designed to close gaps left by "off-the-shelf" system options, continues to expand as companies increasingly find the efficiencies gained by implementing or upgrading a system justify the high cost and time commitment. Credit professionals are increasingly being asked to participate in ERP implementation in the early planning phases so potential problems can be addressed before the cost of fixing errors or closing gaps skyrockets. NACM members should consult the checklist, *Implementing ERP Systems,* posted in the NACM Knowledge & Learning Center.

Comprehension Check
Discuss some of the areas of knowledge or skill sets required for credit management.

The Credit Department's Goals

It is the responsibility of the credit department manager to plan and direct the activities of the credit function within the guidelines of company policy.

The goals and objectives of every credit department are:

• Increased sales and profits through skillful handling of the credit function.

- Improved quality of work performed due to greater accuracy, thoroughness and care exercised by every member of the staff.
- Decreased cost per unit of work performed resulting in improved planning, direction and supervision.
- Mitigating bad debt losses.
- Monitoring credit department costs.
- Measuring performance.

Comprehension Check
List six goals and objectives of every credit department.

The goal of the department is to achieve an optimum combination of profitable sales, turnover of accounts receivable investment, bad-debt expense and credit department operating expense.

The Credit/Sales Relationship

Continually fostering a symbiotic credit/sales relationship is one of the most important goals of the credit manager. A primary objective of the credit department is to support sales; with that support, sales can be made that otherwise would not have taken place. The credit/sales relationship should be evaluated on a regular basis to ensure that the expectations and goals of the organization are being met.

One of the major contributions of the credit department to the sales function is to work with customers and sales representatives and to find ways to approve orders. For example, a credit manager may be able to suggest a financing method not previously considered by the customer or may be helpful in locating sources of capital for a customer.

Also, what may be called a **marketing risk** should be distinguished from a credit risk. For example, to achieve adequate geographic distribution in marketing a name-brand product, it may be necessary to sell to a company that may not be creditworthy. **Marginal accounts** *or accounts with poor payment history, inadequate working capital or a deteriorating financial condition* are taken on for strategic reasons and should be identified as such when accounts receivable is analyzed. The credit department must communicate the risks to sales and management while guarding the confidentiality of the sources of information relating to the customer.

Comprehension Check
How can a less creditworthy company be used as a marketing strategy?

The Credit/Purchasing Relationship

Purchasing departments often check the financial condition of new supply sources through the credit department to ensure that the vendor or subcontractor will be able to deliver goods or services as agreed.

An interruption in the supply chain because a vendor could not get raw material or product on credit can cause a business to miss manufacturing or delivery deadlines and therefore affect sales and collection of accounts receivable—the company's cash flow. Worse yet, if the company is involved in a supply contract and cannot perform, then the company could be held in breach of contract. Knowing and understanding a company's suppliers and vendors is also a function of the credit department's responsibility to avoid risk except this potential risk is different from the typical credit function

Besides inquiring into the backgrounds of potential suppliers, the credit department can also analyze a supplier's financial condition. At times, the credit department is called upon to collect or adjust debit memos issued to cover claims for defective material or to settle other chargebacks. The credit department can assist in negotiating with suppliers. For example, it can arrange for other types of security, such as letters of credit, UCC-1 filings and liens. The credit department may also see to it that setoff rights are retained when its company both sells to and buys from another company. Under most state laws, a creditor has the right to offset mutual debts it owes against the debtor's liability to it.

The Credit/Manufacturing Relationship

When overproduction leads to excess inventory, it may be necessary to dispose of the goods through sales to accounts that may not ordinarily be viewed as creditworthy. Just as with marketing risk, the credit department should closely follow these production risk sales in order to minimize collection costs and bad debts.

Sometimes orders are put into production "subject to confirmation" by the credit department before shipment. An **approval subject to confirmation** *usually means that the customer is being asked to do something before goods are released, such as pay an overdue balance, reduce an outstanding balance to an acceptable level or submit an interim or annual financial statement.* This allows the goods to be manufactured for delivery on time to the buyer. While most of these conditional approvals result in the release of goods when they are ready, they do represent a production risk.

In periods of shortages, a customer may order goods well in excess of actual requirements in the hope that the amount allowed will be close to the quantity actually required. The credit department can be instrumental in spotting orders that are out of proportion to the relative size of the customer. A credit manager can usually recognize this practice and keep the sales and manufacturing departments from being misled into believing that growing sales have made additional production facilities necessary.

 Comprehension Check
Describe an approval subject to confirmation.

The Credit/Information Systems Relationship

As a company implements new technology, the first goal of the credit department is to get involved early in decision-making and planning in order to present valuable data about the credit process. Applying technology to the credit process requires a detailed examination of what information is necessary and what is not. *Breaking down key processes into primary activities, including actions, decision points and information/transportation flows,* is referred to as **process mapping** which is critical to implementing new technology. Technology can improve the flow of information, speed decision-making and standardize the credit process, which will continue to increase efficiencies and reduce costs.

Electronic Data Interchange (EDI) *is the movement of data electronically from one computer to another in a structured, processable format.* EDI has revolutionized the management of information and cash flow. The information needed in a typical business transaction may include items such as a request for a quote, a purchase order, a purchase order acknowledgment, shipping documents, an invoice, a payment advice and a freight bill. EDI converts these documents to electronic messages routed directly between the parties, either in a standard, widely-accepted format or in a proprietary, mutually agreed upon format.

 Comprehension Check
Define the term **electronic data interchange.**

Credit Department Relationships with Other Departments

Determining the status of a customer's account often requires close cooperation with the accounting department. The credit department frequently accounts for payments received and for collateral taken in settlement of customer accounts, credit adjustments and corrections of sales.

Federal and state laws, as well as the proper use of legal documents, play a critical role in business and require the credit department to interact extensively with the legal department or with counsel. The credit department also plays a key role in bankruptcy proceedings.

Comprehension Check

How does the credit department interact with other departments to meet the goals of the organization? Choose one and be specific.

In cases when a customer has difficulty with one of the company's products, it may be necessary for the credit department to consult with the engineering or manufacturing group about corrections or replacements to be made before payment of the account can be collected. Logistics may wish to determine the financial responsibility of carriers and may require assistance in the collection of claims for shortages or damages.

A close relationship must also exist with the human resources department. The credit manager should take an active role in creating job descriptions for credit personnel, recommend salary ranges and coordinate training programs.

Organizing the Credit Department

Each function performed must be planned for within the organizational structure of the credit department in order to ensure a smooth flow of credit. Two essential functions are **defining responsibility** and **staffing**.

The credit department's structure should be flexible, yet delineate responsibility for each function to be performed and for each customer account. Regardless of the size of a credit staff, a company must have continually educated, qualified individuals to address its workload. Key functions of the credit manager include forecasting staff requirements, working with human resources on accurate and current job descriptions as well as budgeting for growth and crucial training opportunities.

Day-to-Day Administration

The Credit Approval Process

Certain procedures must be followed before a credit decision can be made. The relationship with the customer must be established; essential information about the account must be obtained, analyzed and stored; and the data must be evaluated so that the processing of future orders may be facilitated.

Customer relationships are usually initially established through the sales department by direct sales calls, marketing and advertising programs. Customer orders come through the sales department, which furnishes the necessary credit information about the prospective customer.

Few companies make shipments on open account to a new customer without some sort of credit investigation. Trade experience, financial statements and bank references about the customer should be reviewed. Credit reports may also be used, as well as direct interviews or correspondence with the prospective customer and information gathered online.

The credit department is usually the only group, other than sales, to have substantial contact with the customer. This may happen when the credit investigation fails to provide sufficient data to warrant approval of the amount of credit requested. When additional information is required, correspondence should be sent or site visits arranged to meet the management team. Although the sales force is ordinarily not involved in the financial conversations with a customer, they should be kept informed of the discussions. Sales has the primary responsibility for dealing with customers, so communication is critical.

Special documentation may be necessary. The credit process may require involvement of legal counsel for both the seller and buyer. A security agreement along with filings under the Uniform Commercial Code should be made if collateral is required. Guarantees and/or subordination agreements should be at the ready in the event some form of indemnity is determined to be necessary to do business with a particular customer. A letter of credit and other special documentation may be called for in international dealings.

The credit file is the place for information on a customer's account, including its history and current status. It must be readily accessible but handled in a confidential manner. Many customers require that a confidentiality agreement be signed stating that all information will be held in confidence. Printed or digital credit files should be reviewed periodically to ensure customer information is manageable and not obsolete. Storage of this information—including on electronic, cloud-based platforms—must be done in a secure manner not just to keep customers happy, but to avoid potential legal problems and/or fines.

Financial statements should be analyzed with appropriate tools and techniques to aid the evaluation. Statements received directly from the customer should be promptly acknowledged.

All of this information, and more, helps the credit manager to make a decision regarding order approval while minimizing risks and easing potential responses in the event of a customer default. Establishing credit lines or limits can aid in processing further orders. The credit professional should communicate promptly with the customer regarding a credit decision and specify the parameters of the relationship. This will help minimize questions and future disputes.

Account Establishment

The ultimate responsibility for the status of a customer account rests with the credit department. It is essential, therefore, to set guidelines for account establishment. By having the customer complete a credit application, much of the needed information can be obtained.

The account must be precisely identified with its correct legal name and address. Additional identifiers may include an alpha-numeric identifier, a DUNS number, bank transit number or a Social Security or Employer Identification Number (EIN). It is important to obtain customer billing instructions and accounts payable contacts; credit terms should be clearly communicated and agreed upon.

Payment processors or receivers of electronic payments must have guidelines for handling errors, short payments or overpayments, and terms and discount violations. They should know how to communicate with customers and with the sales and credit departments to resolve problems.

Collectors should minimize customer slowness and resolve problems arising from such items as returns, shipping claims covering shortages and damage, pricing disputes or allowances for advertising and promotion.

Order Processing

Every order that falls within established credit parameters should be processed quickly for shipment to the customer. Orders over the limit, a new account or past due balances, etc. should be reviewed by the appropriate person along with the account status, the credit file or other pertinent information. Wherever possible, orders should be released for shipment quickly. If it is necessary to hold them until a credit deficiency is remedied, both the sales department and the customer should be notified.

Accounts Receivable Administration

The sum of all customer account balances must agree with the accounts receivable control account in the general ledger. This total reflects the company's investment in accounts receivable.

As a shipment is made, its invoice is posted to the customer account. Credits and payments are also posted, so at any time the sum of the open items represents the balance due from the customer. From a credit perspective, accounts receivable administration reflects the credit parameters established for customers, along with a historical summary of the transactions that have taken place. Thus, it may involve customer identifiers, credit limits, credit ratings, daily shipping amounts, aging of open items, terms and a payment summary. **Quantitative data** *for reports include number of invoices, checks, credits, discount or other terms violations, short payments and overpayments.* The ledger should also contain a summary of order activity along with the impact on the balance due of any orders that have been approved or held but not yet shipped. This will provide an accurate view of the account as it looks when those orders are shipped and billed.

Collections and Adjustments

The collection aspect consists of cash inflows from accounts receivable. Most customers pay invoices as they are due and need no special collection effort. They may send payments directly to the creditor, to a lockbox or to a third party.

Lockbox Operations

A **lockbox** *is a check collection system operated by a bank.* The bank receives and processes checks and then transfers the information to the company. The bank maintains post office boxes for receipt of payment at a central post office. Check and deposit information, along with other remittance data and any returned documents, are sent to the company after the deposit has been processed and the checks are entered into the clearing system.

Collecting Accounts Receivable

A collection effort is needed when payment is not received for invoices when they are due. It may only consist of a statement but can also include letters, phone calls, emails, visits and third-party collections. The resolution of disputes about how much is due is also a function of the collection effort. The customer may require an invoice copy or proof of delivery; clarification of prices, terms and discounts; information concerning damaged or undelivered merchandise; or explanation of some other adjustment claim. Usually sales and other departments are consulted to resolve these items.

Control and Follow-Up

The concept of control and follow-up is to identify and remedy reasons for nonpayment. For instance, credit policy and credit guidelines should define the actions for pursuing delinquent accounts and resolving disputes. Credit policy should also establish important benchmarks such as the industry average for payment trends.

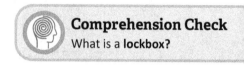

Comprehension Check
What are the day-to-day steps in credit processing?

Comprehension Check
What is a **lockbox**?

Key Terms and Concepts

Approval subject to confirmation, 2-9
Business, 2-2
Business organization, 2-2
Cash inflows, 2-4
Cash management, 2-4
Cash outflows, 2-4
Collection stage, 2-5
Defining responsibility, 2-10
Electronic Data Interchange (EDI), 2-9
Lockbox, 2-12

Marginal accounts, 2-8
Net working capital, 2-3
Operating cycle, 2-5
Process mapping, 2-9
Quantitative data, 2-11
Securitization, 2-3
Staffing, 2-10
Strategic planning, 2-2
Strategy, 2-2

Comprehension Check

1. Discuss what the term **business** means.
2. What is meant by the term **order-to-cash?**
3. Define the term **strategy.**
4. What factors impact a company's strategic plan?
5. Discuss a credit-related area that has both a financial and strategic implication.
6. Define the term **net working capital.**
7. Using **balance sheet logic**, explain where the credit department falls within an organization.
8. List eight finance-related functions that the credit department manages.
9. What is the goal of cash management?
10. List and describe the three broad areas of cash flow management.
11. Describe the **operating cycle.**
12. List the core activities of the credit department.
13. Discuss some of the areas of knowledge or skill sets required for credit management.
14. List six goals and objectives of every credit department.
15. How can a less creditworthy company be used as a marketing strategy?
16. Describe an **approval subject to confirmation**.
17. Define the term **electronic data interchange.**
18. How does the credit department interact with other departments to meet the goals of the organization? Choose one and be specific.
19. What are the day-to-day steps in credit processing?
20. What is a **lockbox?**

Summary......

- The term business dates back to the 14th century and encompasses all organizational functions that seek to create a product or service, which are then sold to a customer for a profit.
- The credit department is involved in the business process from **order-to-cash.**
- Credit plays a strategic role in a business' future goals and broadly involves **amassing information, credit analysis, securitization, collection, cash application and deduction resolution.**
- The credit department is responsible for a company's accounts receivable and is an integral part of a company's **working capital.**
- A credit department typically manages:
  - Protecting and managing the investment in the accounts receivable portfolio
  - Cash forecasting
  - The timely conversion of receivables into cash
  - Financial analysis
  - Handling of collateral that secures a customer's account
  - Deposit of funds and the relationship with banks
  - Handling customers' deductions
  - Evaluation of economic trends on sales, receivables, and collections
- The **collection cycle** commences directly after the sale of a product or service and it is important to understand that the work of the credit department continues even after the product is shipped.
- The core activities of a credit department are customer and credit analysis, developing credit policy, managing the collection function, setting credit availability thresholds and managing reporting.
- Goals of the credit department are, but are not limited to, the following:
  - Increased sales and profit
  - Decreased cost per unit of work
  - Mitigating bad debt losses
  - Monitoring credit department costs
  - Measuring performance
- The credit department maintains a relationship with other departments in a business including the sales, legal, purchasing and manufacturing departments.
- Day-to-day administration includes the credit approval process, account establishment, order processing, accounts receivable administration, as well as collections and adjustments.
- Credit policy is a critical component when extending credit, pursuing delinquent accounts and resolving disputes.

References and Resources

Emery, Gary W. *Corporate Finance: Principles and Practices.* New York: Addison Wesley, 1998.

Gallinger, George W. and Jerry B. Poe. *Essentials of Finance: The Integrated Approach.* New Jersey: Prentice Hall, 1995.

Hill, Ned C. and William L. Satoris. *Short-Term Financial Management: Text and Cases.* New Jersey: Prentice Hall, 1995.

"Leading the Journey from Isolation to Integration: The Future of Business Credit." *The Credit Financial and Management Review,* Vol. 3, No. 2, 2nd Quarter, 1997.

Reengineering the Credit Function. The Credit Research Foundation, 1995.

3 Organizing the Credit Department

OVERVIEW

The properly organized credit department plays a critical role in managing accounts receivable portfolio risk to protect profits, prevent potential losses and help the company sell more products or services.

This chapter discusses the role of the credit department from an organizational point of view. Proper structuring of the credit department—from a one-person operation to a multi-tiered, multifunctional entity—ensures that the role of credit contributes to the overall success of any company regardless of size.

THINK ABOUT THIS

Q. How do the operations of a business change the structure and function of the credit department and vice versa?

Q. What is a credit manager's role in setting credit policy, hiring and continuing the professional development of the credit department's staff?

DISCIPLINARY CORE IDEAS

After reading this chapter, the reader should understand:

- ✓ Organizational options for the credit department.
- ✓ Centralization vs. decentralization.
- ✓ Responsibilities of management.
- ✓ Effective credit policies and procedures.
- ✓ How to build a strong credit team.

CHAPTER OUTLINE

Organizing the Credit Department

The nature of a business and its size will determine the structure and staffing of the credit department. Unlike most other company operations, the credit department tends to remain fairly constant in size and scope of activities during periods of changing business conditions. This is due to increased support needed for full volume sales in good times and for increasing delinquencies when economic times are difficult. A credit department may face a greater number of collection problems in a depressed economy when inflation is rising and the money supply is tighter. During prosperous times, new account volumes create more upfront work for the credit department.

The organization of the department is particularly important; a measure of permanence and stability must be achieved that will ensure that the department functions under all conditions. Although the organization should not remain static, it is highly desirable to have experienced and capable employees available within the department. The credit manager should strive to achieve a balance of newly trained entry-level staff and experienced credit professionals. Alternatives exist to accommodate extra heavy workloads. Cross-training of personnel can lead to more flexibility. Accounting department personnel can be trained to perform routine tasks and called upon as necessary and temporary staff hired or tasks can be outsourced to companies specializing in credit-related functions such as cash application and dispute resolution.

Centralization vs. Decentralization

Although there may be variations among companies, the control and administration functions can usually be classified into two types of operations: *centralization* and *decentralization*. The question of whether to *centralize* or *decentralize* the credit function is faced by companies with geographically and culturally diverse operating units. It remains important as corporations continue to reengineer their business processes to leverage their technology. In a **centralized** structure, *the credit function is controlled and administered from a principal or central location.* In a **decentralized** structure, *the credit function may report to a principal location (headquarters) with credit personnel located at remote offices.*

Centralized—Credit Controlled and Administered at a Headquarters Office

A centralized department services credit operations that are based entirely at a company's main headquarters. It is the responsibility of the credit manager and staff to approve credit terms on most orders. Credit professionals may find themselves questioned by sales staff or even upper management if they decline an application to grant terms on an important or significant order. An increasing number of credit departments are using automated options that approve credit lines for perceived low-risk customers or low-amount credit requests as long as they meet certain pre-established criteria. This, in theory, allows credit managers and staff to focus on the most important customers and situations.

A centralized credit system may be modified in certain respects. In some companies, for example, most of the credit functions are carried on at headquarters, but collections offices are located in the field to work directly with customers, secure payments and make adjustments.

Figure 3-1 illustrates a credit department that is administered and controlled from a headquarters office. The senior ranking credit professional (e.g., director of credit, credit manager, etc.) is charged with ensuring department responsibilities are met and policies followed. That person is responsible for reporting to upper management staff, such as the treasurer or chief financial officer, as it is important for the credit function to maintain close and open communication with those responsible for the greater financial functions of a company.

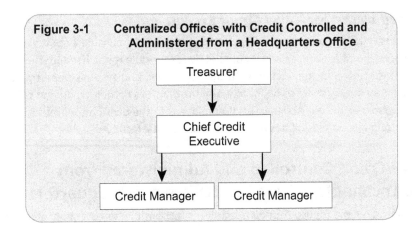

Figure 3-1   Centralized Offices with Credit Controlled and Administered from a Headquarters Office

Decentralized—Credit Controlled at Headquarters but Administered from Decentralized Location(s)

A mid-management level credit manager reports functionally to an executive-level credit manager at headquarters and also reports to the division head (the principle is the same for subsidiary or branch operations). *While authority in credit and collection is provided by the executive-level credit manager, in all other respects middle management establishes the procedures to which the credit professional must conform.* Figure 3-2 illustrates a decentralized operation under which the middle-level credit manager has a dual reporting role requiring close cooperation between the top-level credit executive and the division general manager.

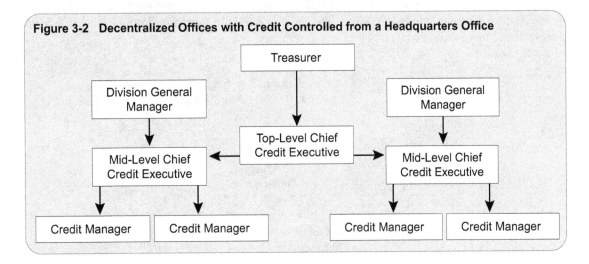

Figure 3-2   Decentralized Offices with Credit Controlled from a Headquarters Office

Authority of the Mid-Level Credit Manager

The mid-level credit manager is normally empowered by the division general manager to take care of personnel problems, operating expenses and all other nonfunctional matters within the scope of local policy.

The mid-level credit manager has authority to give final credit approval on all orders not exceeding a stipulated amount. Orders in larger amounts are referred to headquarters for processing and approval, usually with local recommendation. The mid-level credit manager may be authorized to give preliminary credit approval so the order can be processed.

Another method is to designate certain customers as "headquarters accounts" because of special circumstances. When this procedure is followed, the mid-level credit manager ordinarily has final approval authority for all other orders, and can recommend credit limits for accounts with sound financial resources whose orders normally exceed local authorization.

Authority Retained by the Top-Level Credit Executive

The top-level credit executive establishes credit policy for the divisions, considers approvals in cases that exceed the limits set for mid-level credit executives and is completely responsible for all headquarters accounts.

The top-level credit executive, in conjunction with the accounting and systems departments, also determines the procedures, techniques and practices to be followed by the divisions in their credit and collections operations.

Training of credit personnel and the assignment of employees to the divisions, with the agreement of the division manager, are also primary responsibilities of the top-level credit executive.

Decentralized—Credit Controlled and Administered from Decentralized Location(s) with a Staff Office at Headquarters

In this type of organization, the top-level credit executive is responsible for collecting information and preparing reports for management, providing advice and counsel to the field credit executives, and participating in major problem-risk analysis. Figure 3-3 illustrates a decentralized operation with a staff office maintained at headquarters. This arrangement requires the top-level credit executives to be responsible for order approvals and collections and to control their own unit credit departments.

The top-level credit executive usually establishes the overall credit policies. Divisions coordinate their activities based on industry best practices and select the best alternative action in the light of prevailing conditions. Compliance with the overall policies is especially important, so telephone calls, video conferences or field trips are key to monitoring the activities of credit personnel in the field. In cases where control is completely decentralized, the mid-level credit manager reports only to the division general manager and has complete authority in all credit and collection matters without reference to headquarters. The division is required to carry out the general credit policies of the company, but the operation within those policies is the responsibility of the division. Consequently, the division credit executive is responsible to the division general manager both for the performance of the function and for the operation of the division.

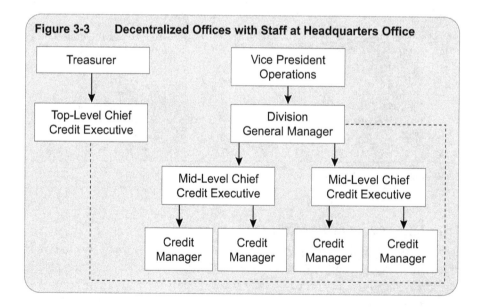

Figure 3-3   Decentralized Offices with Staff at Headquarters Office

Comprehension Check

Describe how the credit function would operate if credit is controlled at a headquarters office but administered from decentralized locations.

Benefits of Centralization

- **Economies of Scale.** When separate divisions serve common customers, a centralized credit office can mean a reduction in operating costs and a more efficient income stream, along with enhanced customer service.
- **Consistency and Control.** Adherence to standardization of policies, procedures and protocols is more manageable in a centralized environment. This has the advantage of providing consistent credit decisions across all business units which minimizes risk of satellite departments having undue influence. When information about a common customer is centralized, the credit function has more risk control over bad debt exposure and perhaps increased leverage in collection efforts. Closer proximity tends to encourage communication between staff members and management. Likewise, updates to policies, procedures and protocols can be disseminated more quickly.

> **Comprehension Check**
> List and discuss the benefits of a **centralized** credit operation.

Benefits of Decentralization

- **Internal and External Relationships.** Close proximity to customers can enhance a credit professional's relationship with marginal customers and lead to developing a better rapport with customers having a sizable dollar exposure. Being on site with other business functions promotes a better understanding of business goals and fosters the exchange of information about market and customer needs. It also enhances communication among departments and reduces the number of interdepartmental conflicts.
- **Involvement in Setting Strategic Priorities.** Credit can integrate its objectives with those of sales and marketing into divisional goals. Also, decisions made at a local level can be implemented immediately without going through additional levels of review.

> **Comprehension Check**
> List and discuss the benefits of a **decentralized** credit operation.

Management Responsibilities

Every department needs a clear philosophy of management that will not only permit full development of individual responsibility and strength, but at the same time give cohesive direction of effort, maintain teamwork and harmonize the goals of the individual and the enterprise.

The functions of management may be divided into five main areas:

1. Planning.
2. Organizing.
3. Staffing.
4. Leadership.
5. Control.

Planning

Planning establishes common objectives so everyone is aware of the values the department hopes to achieve. Planning helps to determine how to perform assigned duties, implement control measures as work progresses and formulate standards against which to check results.

Organizing

There are certain essentials in developing an improved organizational structure. Major functions should be combined into the overall department structure. Every function and every position should be described accurately, briefly and clearly. This process facilitates continuity of workflow, harmonious relationships, easy communication across all organizational levels and equitable appraisal and remedial action.

An ideal department structure requires careful planning. Major problems standing between the ideal structure and the present structure should be identified; viewpoints, objectives, vested interests, trends and personnel analyzed; and the use of present staff, resources and facilities reviewed. A decision may then be reached on what improvements can and should be made immediately, and a schedule of subsequent changes prepared.

Staffing

The top-level credit executive must establish and maintain basic controls governing the selection, compensation and development of department employees.

To succeed, there are three steps to consider:

1. Establish the results expected of each position and the criteria to be used to measure them.
2. Determine what the person in each position has to do in order to produce desired results.
3. Ascertain what knowledge, skills and personal qualifications are needed to perform the activities. Appropriate skills and abilities can be identified at points needed and instructions clearly specified.

Managers are responsible for the selection, performance, training and development of their employees. Outside trainers or training specialists may help, but the final responsibility rests with the department head. Effective training requires department objectives and standards and accepted criteria for performance measurement. Manuals and instructions for uniform interpretation of established practices are essential.

Leadership

Leadership, motivation and follow-through by the department head are important to identify opportunities for improvement and to point out areas where interim results or trends should receive immediate attention. Appraisals of employee performance, made regularly or for special reasons, are needed to identify gaps between actual performance and desired results, to ascertain specific training needs and to develop effective ways of meeting those needs.

The credit manager must guide and oversee subordinates, delegate authority and assign duties. Subordinates must understand policy and procedures and the reason for actions, be able to coordinate their actions in the department and communicate effectively.

Control

The department head should regularly review all operations to ensure conformity with established goals and objectives. Responsibility should be established for observance of credit policy compliance, reviewing procedures and standards of performance, and recommending changes.

Comprehension Check

What are some of management's responsibilities?

Business Organization

Business owners often begin to think seriously about credit management when they find they have insufficient cash flow to fuel their growth. In most companies, accounts receivable is the largest asset of the company.

Credit Policy and Procedures

A **credit policy** is a guiding principle used to establish direction for the credit function in an organization in order to achieve the objectives of minimizing risk and maximizing profitability, while maintaining a competitive advantage in the marketplace. A **credit procedure** is a series of steps to be followed for recurring credit situations to accomplish the goals outlined in the company's strategic planning framework and internal audit framework. Together, credit policy and credit procedures are used to empower the people responsible for the credit process, by providing the direction and consistency they need for successful execution.

Develop a Credit Application

The credit application should include enough information about the new customer to allow the credit manager to assess risk. It should be used in conjunction with commercial credit information and reports from agencies like NACM, D&B, Experian and Equifax that conduct external credit information research. NACM Affiliates host specialized industry credit groups to help credit grantors discover payment habits and trends of specific customers. Businesses can also learn about payment history from checking other trade references. NACM members can benefit from electronic credit checking tools made available to them.

The credit application should also serve as a legally binding document to be relied upon for enforcement of certain terms and conditions established by company policy and procedures or by owner or management discretion in the absence of any other controlling document.

Keep Credit Records

It is important to maintain accurate records for easy access while preserving confidentiality. Because most information is archived electronically, appropriate identification and back-up procedures are also necessary. Always consult with legal counsel to ensure that pertinent original documents are stored and maintained before destroying or archiving.

Produce Accurate Invoices

Businesses tend to lose a lot of time in the collection process due to billing discrepancies, such as pricing errors, billing the wrong customer, sending invoices to the wrong address, quantity of items shipped/delivered and missing information (purchase order information, etc.). Prompt payment is more likely when businesses send timely, clear and accurate invoices and statements to their customers.

Deal with Past Due and Delinquent Accounts

Credit departments should use a variety of methods to contact past due accounts such as collection letters, phone calls, personal visits and electronic correspondence. With regard to these attempts to encourage customer payment, the credit department should be cautious not to sever the relationship with the customer. Alternatively, letting a customer know that the company reports its accounts receivable trade data to NACM can encourage a customer to make timely payment. Properly structured credit departments must be considered as supporting all company sales efforts.

The credit department's constant challenge is how to maintain policies and procedures that are not so rigid that potential sales are inhibited or customers are lost to competition because of strict adherence to said credit policies. The credit department must have an arsenal of tools devised to help make the sale while ensuring payment or recovery of the account receivable asset.

Measure Effectiveness and Performance

The following metrics are commonly used to measure credit effectiveness and performance:

- Bad debt as a percentage of sales.
- Days sales outstanding in receivables—current.

- Days sales outstanding in receivables—past due.
- Percent collected by aging period.
- Aging of accounts receivable in dollars and as a percentage of total accounts receivable.
- Accounts opened as a percentage of applications received.
- Accounts over 90 days past due.
- Accounts on credit hold as a percentage of total open accounts.

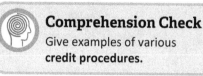

Comprehension Check

Give examples of various **credit procedures.**

Building the Credit Department Team

Understanding the specific duties and tasks to be performed is essential in hiring for and managing the credit department.

Job Description

A **job description** *is a statement of the duties, responsibilities and authorities of the position.* It helps define the amount and type of training required by qualified personnel for the various credit department tasks or functions. The description is also valuable when developing measures of performance. The components of the job description are the same whether for a staff of one or one hundred.

A **job specification** *is a statement of the qualifications that an individual should have to fill a particular job, usually including educational requirements, experience requirements and special characteristics and abilities.*

Components of a Job Description*

Job descriptions are an essential part of hiring and managing employees. These written summaries ensure applicants and employees understand their roles and what they need to do to be held accountable.

Job descriptions also:

- Help attract the right job candidates.
- Describe the areas of an employee's job or position.
- Serve as a basis for outlining performance expectations, job training, job evaluation and career advancement.
- Provide a reference point for compensation decisions and unfair hiring practices.

Overview

A job description should be practical, clear and accurate to effectively define the company's needs. Good job descriptions typically begin with a careful analysis of the important facts about a job such as:

- Individual tasks involved.
- The methods used to complete the tasks.
- The purpose and responsibilities of the job.
- The relationship of the job to other jobs.
- Qualifications needed for the job.

What to Avoid

Don't be inflexible with the job description. Jobs are subject to change for personal growth, organizational development or evolution of new technologies. A flexible job description encourages employees to grow within their position and contribute over time to the overall business.

What to Include

Job descriptions typically include:

- Job title.
- Job objective or overall purpose statement.
- Summary of the general nature and level of the job.
- Description of the broad function and scope of the position.
- List of duties or tasks performed critical to success.
- Key functional and relational responsibilities in order of significance.
- Description of the relationships and roles within the company, including supervisory positions, subordinating roles and other working relationships.

Additional items for job descriptions for recruiting situations:

- Job specifications, standards, and requirements.
- Job location where the work will be performed.
- Equipment to be used in the performance of the job.
- Collective bargaining agreements if the company's employees are members of a union.
- Salary range.

Proper Language in the Job Description

Keep each statement in the job description crisp and clear:

- Structure sentences in classic verb/object and explanatory phrases. Since the occupant of the job is the subject of the sentence, it may be eliminated. For example, a sentence pertaining to the description of a receptionist position could read: "Greets office visitors and personnel in a friendly and sincere manner."
- Always use the present tense of verbs.
- If necessary, use explanatory phrases telling why, how, where, or how often to add meaning and clarity (e.g., "Collects all employee time sheets on a bi-weekly basis for payroll purposes.").
- Omit any unnecessary articles such as "a," "an," "the," or other words for an easy-to-understand description.
- Use unbiased terminology. For example, use the he/she approach or construct sentences in such a way that gender pronouns are not required.
- Avoid using adverbs or adjectives that are subject to interpretation such as "frequently," "some," "complex," "occasional," and "several."

From the U.S. Small Business Administration.

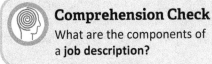

Comprehension Check
What are the components of a **job description**?

Selection of Personnel

Special Characteristics and Abilities

An individual may not possess the full qualifications listed below; however, the higher the position level, the more likely the credit professional will be able to:

- Determine appropriate methods of observing, organizing, analyzing and reporting data.
- Meet new situations and changing conditions with initiative, adaptability and ingenuity.
- Identify needs, unsatisfactory conditions and the causes of such conditions; handle unpleasant situations with tact, diplomacy and emotional stability.

- Analyze complex problems constructively and follow up difficult situations with resourcefulness.
- Make informed decisions and be willing to take considered risks for profitable company growth and development of sales potential.
- Direct the work of employees effectively, exercising considerate interest and fairness in dealing with people and communicating effectively and convincingly through speaking and writing.
- Handle customer and internal relations diplomatically and decisively when required.
- Acquire and maintain the required job knowledge, conduct affairs with integrity and persevere in eliciting confidential information.

> **Comprehension Check**
> What are the special characteristics and abilities to look for when selecting personnel?

Training

Training is an investment that creates an informed, knowledgeable and supportive employee. This translates indirectly into more profit for the organization. For the employee who takes advantage of the educational opportunities, training transcends the current job experience and always remains with the person.

Credit department personnel need formalized training, not only to train new employees but also to increase the skills and talents of experienced staff members. Any significant change in company organization may also require an expansion of the present training program. Whenever credit employees face greater responsibilities, some provision must be made for the continuing education of existing staff and for training new personnel.

Management personnel must continue to pursue training opportunities in order to carry out their responsibilities. Areas of credit and finance are increasingly important, and credit professionals must keep themselves qualified to perform these expanding roles and functions.

Preparation for Credit Training

Credit training is an opportunity for management to communicate effective credit function procedures from their company's point of view. Training encourages and reinforces the employee/trainee who may be eligible for future advancement within the department or company. Top management candidates are generally selected from among those employees or applicants with a thorough and applicable understanding of the importance of the function of credit in a company. Training should be both specific to the needs of the company/business/employer and general enough to address the fundamentals of business credit principles.

Considerations in a Sound Training Program

The primary objective of any training program is to provide employees with the opportunity to progress to whatever level of responsibility they can achieve. This requires programs for developing one's ability to think and to analyze and formulate workable solutions to problems. Knowledge is enriched, confidence inspired, and the traits and skills of leadership developed to ensure the widest possible use of the available human resources for the company's benefit.

A well-designed training program should:

- Develop a higher level of performance by being more proficient on the job. This includes the ability to handle customer relations and develop more harmonious working relations with other departments.
- Provide a broad concept of the company's place in the industry and the department's relation to the whole.
- Provide knowledge of general business functions enabling the employee to move into other job duties and responsibilities to which they may eventually aspire.

On-the-Job Training

Some credit skills and functions, such as the gathering of credit information, are best learned on the job through actual experience. When developing a training program, it is necessary that instructional materials be connected to the day-to-day operations of the credit department. Each program should be developed to meet the particular needs of the department where it will be used.

The extent of supervision depends on the position level, the employee's past academic background and experience, the speed of training and the individual's overall progress. Supervision should always be available to provide direction, answer questions, discuss problems and evaluate the individual. Any periodic progress reports should be discussed with the trainee, along with specific recommendations for improvement. Trainees on a new job must first learn the current methods of doing their work. When these techniques have been mastered, they should be encouraged to seek improved ways.

In-House Training

Dedication to quality *in-house training*, also known as **onboarding**, is especially important when dealing with credit professionals because of the wide range of functions members of this staff perform and the reality that most new credit professionals have not studied trade credit.

A well-conceived training program must reflect critical information regarding each employee's functions and responsibilities to the department as well as that of the greater business and the impact on company culture. Training programs should be designed with the goals of inspiring a common desire between departments to coordinate efforts, eliminating conflicting procedures and fostering a willingness to exchange ideas freely.

To accomplish these goals, training programs could include periodic meetings, even for current staff members, to discuss problems and necessary improvements within the credit department and the greater company. They can help employees learn how to apply recommended solutions.

A training program is often most effective when instruction is ongoing, so that staff can be knowledgeable regarding accepted and evolving best practices. It should also be highly interactive, because encouraging increased participation ("having a voice") in such processes will often foster a greater level of interest, involvement, buy-in and commitment, especially among non-management staff.

Observation Tours

Tours of other departments can help credit department employees understand more fully the working relationships between their department and other divisions.

Observation tours are a useful supplement to any training, since they give the observer an opportunity to see, in operation, certain processes they may have only read or heard about. This is particularly true in a company with a wide range of product lines and many different industrial classifications of customers.

Job Rotation Program or Cross-Training

It is sometimes desirable to include some provision for rotating trainees from one job to another within the department, and even from one department to another. Such experience generates a broader credit perspective. The specific plan of rotation depends upon the size, complexity and organizational setup of the department.

Popular on-the-job training methods include understudy assignments, also known as job shadowing, and job rotation. New employees often learn their jobs by shadowing a seasoned veteran or by **vertical rotation**. *The understudy serves under an executive as an observer or assistant to become familiar with the functions and area of responsibility.* Alternatively, **job rotation** or **horizontal rotation** *involves lateral transfers that enable employees to work at different jobs.*

The following benefits are likely to be attained with little expense or disruption of normal office routines:

- The department's overall flexibility is greatly increased. It is better able to meet emergencies caused by illness, vacation schedules and other work interruptions.

- Employees' enthusiasm for their work is increased. In addition, the discipline of having to think out and describe their jobs often leads credit personnel to develop better work habits and a better understanding of where their work fits in with that of others.
- Replacement of lower supervisory personnel is made easier since several persons in the department know several jobs.

Comprehension Check

What are the goals of a well-designed training program?

....

Name and describe some popular internal training methods.

Credit Library

Some companies have credit libraries containing books, articles, case histories, special reports and other pertinent reference materials. Employees are encouraged to become acquainted with and use them in their training. Online resources are also important elements for the credit department trainee.

Available to its members, the **National Association of Credit Management (NACM)** hosts an online Knowledge & Learning Center on its website at www.nacm.org. The Knowledge & Learning Center is a centralized resource of the vast amount of information NACM publishes providing members with the ability to comb through several different books and a decade of *Business Credit* magazines by keyword. Titles include:

- *The Manual of Credit and Commercial Laws*
- *Principles of Business Credit*
- *The Art and Science of Financial Risk Analysis*
- *The Construction Law Survival Manual*
- *Credit Beyond the Numbers*
- *Credit Management: Principles and Practices*
- *The Bankruptcy Abuse Prevention and Consumer Protection Act of 2005*

All of the forms found in the *Manual of Credit and Commercial Laws* are available and ready to use.

Searching through all of these books is similar to a Google search: type in a keyword and links to articles or places in the book where the keyword is listed appear.

The Knowledge & Learning Center also contains information authored by NACM's Graduate School of Credit & Financial Management (GSCFM) participants, who created a best practices guide to credit and collections, drawing upon their work experience. The sections pull together the work of groups of students from more than a dozen industries over several years. Participants will add content and new topics over time. The material draws together some of the best established minds in the industry along with the rising, future stars of credit. Topics include:

- Components of a Sound Credit Policy.
- Counseling a Distressed Customer.
- Developing an International Credit Score for Businesses.
- Going International.
- Implementing ERP Systems.
- Onboarding Credit Personnel.

Where relevant, NACM has added supplemental materials such as recorded audio teleconferences or webinars—enhancing and expanding this virtual guidebook. A credit professional, especially a new one, should consider the section on sound credit policy as a desktop checklist and reference of the most important things to remember.

Employee Enhancement

After the training phase is completed and the employee settles into a normal credit assignment, efforts should be made to involve the employee in assignments of a special or non-routine nature.

As a part of their internal training program, the credit department can hold periodic meetings on subjects relative to the department's structure. Outside speakers who specialize in credit and collection, bankruptcy, legal aspects and other activities pertaining to credit can also be invited to address the group. Participation in an NACM Industry Credit Group is also key to learning about an industry, current events, trends and changes in the business environment. In addition, the credit manager can conduct periodic group meetings with supervisory personnel to ensure a constructive team effort for all credit staff.

In order to help broaden credit understanding and as an additional aid for career planning, an accounting and financial analysis training program can also be established. Subjects may include such topics as taxes, financial analysis, auditing, banking, corporate accounting, foreign exchange, the law as it relates to contracts, torts and property or other industry specific areas that relate to the company's particular line of business.

Continuing Education

A continuing education program usually follows a conventional pattern with courses designed to cover a given area of instruction in an orderly manner. The purpose of such a program is to offer credit employees educational opportunities not provided by their company and to enable those outside the field to train for a credit position. There are continuing education programs for credit personnel at every level of experience. Continuing education is primarily based on courses offered by local colleges, professional organizations such as NACM and other groups.

NACM Affiliates conduct educational activities that can provide desirable supplementary training. Open forums, which emphasize participants' interaction, or conferences and seminars focusing on core credit topics or current trends are especially beneficial.

NACM-National Education Department

The NACM-National Education Department provides educational resources that promote life-long learning for those in the credit profession. Formerly known as the National Institute of Credit and founded in 1918, the National Education Department encourages NACM affiliates to offer a series of college-level courses designed to enhance a credit and financial professional's knowledge and understanding of business credit, financial and legal skills in a hands-on learning environment.

Through its Professional Certification Program established in 1974, NACM's Education Department establishes the standards and regulates the designation awards for the Certified Credit and Risk Analyst (**CCRA**), Credit Business Associate (**CBA**), Credit Business Fellow (**CBF**) and Certified Credit Executive (**CCE**).

The education-related needs of credit personnel are met through a variety of NACM resources. Live classroom programs are held at NACM's Credit Congress, as well as the NACM-National office. In 2009, NACM launched its Credit Learning Center (CLC), providing the opportunity to access credit education 24/7. Carefully selected, expert instructors present 50-minute learning modules on a wide array of topics. Through the CLC, students may work toward the completion of courses leading to an NACM designation or specialty certificate. Additionally, NACM hosts teleconferences and webinars focusing on current issues and topics in credit management.

The premier, internationally-recognized Association of Executives in Finance, Credit and International Business (FCIB), provides critical export credit and collections insight, practical advice and intelligence to companies of all sizes. Upon successful completion of FCIB's International Credit & Risk Management online course, participants are awarded the lifetime Certified International Credit Professional (**CICP**) designation. CICP designation holders interested in excelling beyond their CICP designation may apply for the prestigious International Certified Credit Executive (**ICCE**). ICCE candidates and holders are those interested in continuing to engage the global credit community.

Graduate School of Credit and Financial Management

Founded in 1941, the Graduate School of Credit and Financial Management (GSCFM) provides an executive-level program for qualified credit and financial professionals who wish to prepare for greater corporate responsibilities, perform their work more effectively, develop their leadership skills and increase their decision-making abilities. The program is held two weeks each summer for two consecutive years on a college campus. The intensive curriculum covers financial analysis, corporate strategy, economics, presentation techniques, legal environment of credit, leadership and advanced negotiations.

NACM's Credit Congress

Credit Congress, NACM's national, annual convention, offers working sessions, educational sessions and an Expo where attendees can view timely, state-of-the-art products and services offered by vendors to the credit management field.

Training Options for a One-Person, Centralized Credit Department

Among the resources for a centralized single-person credit department are:

- Training both on the job and in house.
- Training through NACM Affiliates, NACM-National and other continuing education conferences or seminars.
- Training through local colleges or self-study. The department manager can motivate individuals by offering to help them with comments and explanations.
- Online and on-demand credit training sessions, teleconferences and webinar sessions offered by NACM-National and its affiliates.

In smaller communities where outside educational facilities are limited, a number of small credit departments could pool their resources for training purposes. Group conferences, study groups and more formal courses can be arranged at a central location, either on company time or after working hours. Often NACM Affiliates can help with curriculum, material, instruction and meeting places.

Comprehension Check
Describe why continuing credit education is vital.

Key Terms and Concepts

Centralized structure, 3-2–3-3, 3-5

Credit policy, 3-7

Credit procedure, 3-7

Decentralized structure, 3-2, 3-3–3-5

Horizontal rotation, 3-11

Job description, 3-8–3-9

Job specification, 3-8

National Association of Credit Management
(NACM), 3-12–3-14

Onboarding, 3-11, 3-18–3-23

Vertical rotation, 3-11

Comprehension Check

1. Describe how the credit function would operate if credit is controlled at a headquarters office but administered from decentralized locations.
2. List and discuss the benefits of a **centralized** credit operation.
3. List and discuss the benefits of a **decentralized** credit operation.
4. What are some of management's responsibilities?
5. Give examples of various **credit procedures**.
6. What are the components of a **job description?**
7. What are the special characteristics and abilities to look for when selecting personnel?
8. What are the goals of a well-designed training program?
9. Name and describe some popular internal training methods.
10. Describe why continuing credit education is vital.

Summary

- The credit department tends to remain fairly consistent in size and scope during changing business conditions, whether the economic conditions are good or bad, due to an increased support role when sales volumes increase, as well as increased support needed when delinquencies increase.
- Large variations exist among companies, but a credit department is inevitably either **centralized** or **decentralized**.
- **Centralized** credit departments are entirely based in the company's main headquarters.
- **Decentralized** credit departments are not housed in the headquarters, but report to the headquarters from a remote office or offices.
- The role of the mid-level credit manager and the top-level credit executive play similar roles over decentralized and centralized organization structure. However, their authority and duties may differ depending on the credit policies enacted by the credit department.
- The benefits of a centralized credit department include:
  - **Economies of scale**
  - **Consistency and control**
- The benefits of a decentralized credit department include:
  - **Internal and external relationships**
  - **Involvement in setting strategic priorities**

- The functions of management can be divided into five main areas:
  - **Planning**
  - **Organizing**
  - **Staffing**
  - **Leadership**
  - **Control**
- **Credit policy** and procedure are the guiding principles that empower the credit department and credit managers toward successful management and execution of business credit.
- **Credit policy** and procedures include:
  - Development of a credit application
    - This can also serve as a legally binding document to enforce terms and conditions set by the business
  - Keeping credit records
  - Producing accurate invoices
  - Dealing with past due and delinquent accounts
  - Measuring effectiveness and performance
    - Valuable measures of effectiveness and performance include, but are not limited to the following:
      - Bad debt as a percentage of sales
      - Accounts over 90 days past due
      - Aging of accounts receivable in dollars and as percentage of total accounts receivable
- Clear and comprehensive jobs descriptions are essential to attracting the right candidates, describing the position, outlining performance expectations, qualifications, evaluation and job training, along with providing a reference point for compensation decisions.
- Training is an investment that is essential to any business and is essential to keep an informed, knowledgeable and up-to-date staff. Its primary responsibility is to allow employees to progress and reach whatever level of responsibility they can achieve within an organization.
- Training can be broken down into four general types each with their own individual benefits to an organization and employee:
  - **On-the-job training**
  - **In-house training**
  - **Observational tours**
  - **Job rotation program or cross-training**
- It is vital for credit professionals to continue their education because the business environment is always evolving. Without continuing education, a credit professional may put an organization at a higher risk of insolvency due to poor accounts receivable management, which inevitably affects an organization's cash flow.
- **NACM** provides outstanding continuing education programs on both a national and affiliate level. This includes a variety of live classroom courses, and online education through the Credit Learning Center (**CLC**), which can be accessed 24/7, as well as supplementary training that includes open forums, conferences, seminars and webinars.

- NACM's National Education Department manages a professional certification program, established in 1974, that sets the standards and regulations for professional certifications. The certifications include:
  - National Certifications
    - Credit Business Associate (**CBA**)
    - Certified Credit and Risk Analyst (**CCRA**)
    - Credit Business Fellow (**CBF**)
    - Certified Credit Executive (**CBE**)
  - International Certifications
    - Certified International Credit Professional (**CICP**)
    - International Certified Credit Executive (**ICCE**)
- The (**CICP**) can be earned after completing the internationally-recognized Associates of Executives in the Finance, Credit and International Business (**FCIB**) online course. The (**CICP**) is a lifetime award. Once the (**CICP**) is earned, those who aspire to continue their education and continue in the global credit community can apply for the (**ICCE**).
- Two additional options for continuing education are the Graduate School of Credit and Financial Management (**GSCFM**), as well as NACM's Credit Congress & Expo.

References and Resources

Business Credit. Columbia, MD: National Association of Credit Management. (This 9 issues/year publication is a continuous source of relevant articles and information. Archived articles from *Business Credit* magazine are available through the web-based NACM Resource Library, which is a benefit of NACM membership.)

Cole, Robert H. and Lon L. Mishler. *Consumer and Business Credit Management,* 11th ed. Boston: Irwin/McGraw Hill, 1998.

Dennis, Michael. *Credit and Collection Handbook.* Paramus, NJ: Prentice Hall, 2000.

Gahala, Dr. Charles L. *Credit Management Principles and Practices,* 4th ed. rev. Columbia, MD: National Association of Credit Management, 2013.

Hunter, James C. *The Servant: A Simple Story About the True Essence of Leadership.* Roseville, CA: Prima Publishing, 1998.

Ladew, Donald P. *How to Supervise People: Techniques for Getting Results Through Others.* Franklin Lakes, NJ: National Press Publications, 1998.

Price, Ron and Randy Lisk. *The Complete Leader: Everything You Need to Become a High-Performance Leader.* Eagle, ID: Aloha Publishing, 2014.

Small Business Administration. "Starting and Managing a Business." Web. 2015. http://www.sba.gov/content/writing-effective-job-descriptions.

"What is Onboarding?" NACM Graduate School for Credit and Financial Management project, 2015.

Supplementary Material

What is Onboarding?*

It is important to properly onboard, orient and train new employees as this process can pay huge dividends in the performance and overall success of the employee. **Onboarding** *is a strategic process of bringing a new employee into the company/organization and providing information, training, mentoring and coaching throughout the transition.* The process begins with the acceptance of an offer and continues throughout the first six to twelve months of employment.

The following checklist will guide the credit manager through the steps to effectively bring a new employee onboard at the company. Please note: not all items may be applicable to every department.

A manager may choose to assign some tasks to a First Friend/Mentor—a co-worker with a good performance standing and a positive point of view. However, the manager should maintain responsibility for the completion of these tasks. They should review the relevant items and plan time for the items on their schedule. They need to record the completion date for each item.

This checklist has been developed with a broad format approach for the Order to Cash/Credit Department. It may require additional checkpoints tailored to specific roles and responsibilities (Order to Cash Manager, Credit Manager, Collector, Grantor, Recovery Specialist, Billing Specialist, Accounting, Account Maintenance, Customer Service).

	PRE-ACCEPTANCE CHECKLIST	RESPONSIBILITY	Date Initiated	Date Completed
HR	Create job profile for credit roles	HR/Manager		
HR	Post job posting internally and/or externally with NACM Credit Career Center	HR		
HR	Compile and send resumes received to the hiring manager	HR/Manager		
HR	Consult with hiring manager to determine which candidates will be interviewed	HR/Manager		
HR	Organize interviews with candidates and hiring manager	HR/Manager		
HR	Conduct interviews with candidates	HR/Manager		
HR	Collaborate with hiring manager on best possible candidates	HR/Manager		
HR	Arrange and take part in subsequent interviews with chosen candidates	HR		
HR	Prepare offer letter once the appropriate candidate is chosen	HR		

	PRE-ACCEPTANCE CHECKLIST 2-3 weeks prior to arrival	RESPONSIBILITY	Date Initiated	Date Completed
S	Network/LAN access and user ID	Manager		
S	Add to corporate/department email distribution lists	Manager		
S	Request system/application access (e.g., mail, Intranet/portal, network directories)	Manager		
S	Order PC or laptop and any bolt-on systems for credit job function	Manager		
S	Order landline and/or cell phone	Manager		
S	Request/assign workstation	Manager		
S	Order VPN Key (remote access)	Manager		
S	Order secure ID tag	Manager		
S	Order parking permit	Manager		
S	Building alarm code and hours of operation	Manager		
T	Coordinate appropriate training plan with learning and development (L&D)/HR or training delegates	Manager		
T	Book training rooms	Manager/L&D		
T	Prepare training schedule handout for new hire on day of arrival	Manager/L&D		
T	Develop training plan specific to the role and new employees' skillset to ensure an overall understanding of the order to cash/credit processes. Reference material available through NACM, internal policies manager/L&D	Manager		
O	Update new hire 1 week prior to arrival on where to meet and any documentation required for HR and security	Manager		
O	If the budget permits, arrange breakfast or lunch with new employee on the first day	Manager		
O	Prepare and send announcement of new team member to division/company employees	Manager		

	FIRST DAY ARRIVAL CHECKLIST	RESPONSIBILITY	Date Initiated	Date Completed
O	Meet the new employee in the company lobby	Manager		
O	Welcome the new employee by introducing them to the team members/department (and/or direct reports/management team)	Manager		
O	Introduce the new employee to the First Friend/ Mentor	Manager		
O	Take new employee to HR to complete required paperwork	Manager/HR		
O	Take new employee to the security office to ensure photo ID/company badge is obtained. Register their vehicle with parking services and provide parking instructions	Manager/HR		
O	Have employee sign IT Security, Acceptable Use and Confidentiality Policy	Manager/HR		
O	Take new employee on company/building tour to get them familiar with the amenities (e.g., conference rooms, interoffice mail drop, copier, restrooms, cafeteria, fitness center, breakroom, etc.)	Manager		
O	Explain operation of office equipment: 1) Computer: user name and password, email account, signature, out of office messages and internet usage 2) Phone: voicemail and standard message 3) Other equipment: copier, fax, scanners, etc.	Manager		
O	Explain office security, safety and emergency operations plan	Manager		
O	Discuss appropriate dress code	Manager/HR		
O	Clarify office and IT "Do's & Don'ts"	Manager/HR		
O	Forward calendar meeting invites for upcoming/ ongoing meetings associated with credit job function	Manager		
O	Provide new employee universal calendar, holiday schedule, department/division/company phone list, important phone numbers (e.g., help desk)	Manager		
HR	Review and complete new employee paperwork, to include: benefits, pension plan, retirement savings plan	HR		
HR	Record employees personal contact information into payroll system	Payroll Services		
HR	Set up employee's payroll in accordance with employment offer	Payroll Services		
HR	Set up benefits, pension and retirement savings plan	Payroll Services		

			Date Initiated	Date Completed
HR	HR to provide new employee company handbook	HR		
HR	Ensure new employee completes paperwork for direct deposit	Payroll Services		
HR	Discuss time and attendance reporting policy. Discuss how to access the building after hours	Manager		
HR	Arrange for employee to attend first available HR/ new employee benefits orientation	Manager		
S	Organize workstation	Employee		
S	Activate voicemails	Employee		
S	Confirm all access to drives, networks, distribution lists	Manager		
S	Order purchase card	Employee		
S	Order business cards	Employee		
S	Notify switchboard or have employee update profile directory	Manager		
S	Ensure new employee is added to the department/ company distribution list	Manager		
T	Provide training schedule for First Month Checklist	Manager		

	FIRST MONTH CHECKLIST - weeks 1 to 4	RESPONSIBILITY	Date Initiated	Date Completed
O	Explain the company's mission/vision and goals	Manager		
O	Explain the department's mission/vision and goals and provide the department organizational chart	Manager		
O	Discuss how the new employee's role contributes to the overall success of department	Manager		
O	Familiarize new employee with company products, customers, brands, etc.	Manager/L&D		
O	Discuss and complete environmental health and safety required information (ergonomics)	Manager		
O	Follow up after new employee attends HR/new employee benefits orientation	Manager		
HR	Familiarize new employee with travel services, expense reporting, business credit card policy, etc.	Manager/HR		
T	Overview daily/weekly/monthly tasks	Manager		
T	Familiarize new employee with credit departments standard operating procedures (SOP) (guidelines, workflow instructions)	Manager		
T	Review and ensure an understanding of grants of authority level, approval presentation requirements and hierarchy of approvals	Manager		
T	Training with credit managers and understanding of credit policy/guidelines established by the company	Manager		

T	Review company's sales cycle and how the employees' role supports operations	Manager		
T	Review process of the customer cycle from approvals, billing and payment, collections, recovery, write-offs	Manager		
T	Arrange shadow sessions for new employee within order to cash/credit teams	Manager		
T	Understand different risk associated with the credit function	Manager		
T	Become familiar with legislation and regulations pertinent to business credit decision-making (e.g., SOX, PIPEDA, Red Flags)	Manager		
T	Ensure online access obtained to work with business credit reporting services	Manager		
T	Complete demos to gain an understanding of various business credit reporting services	Manager		
T	Review resources available to remain up to date on industry best practices. That includes participation in Credit Managers' Index survey, newsletters, credit chapters, credit monthly magazines, various NACM workshops/webinars, conferences	Manager		
T	Introduce new employee to sales teams they will be supporting	Manager		
T	Arrange time for new employee to relationship-build with teams	Manager		
T	Make sure new employee has an understanding of the business operations risk tolerance	Manager		
T	Send ongoing invites of regular sales strategy/ product launch meetings	Manager		
T	Give overview of credit department's Key Performance Indicators (KPIs)	Manager		
T	Provide new employee with useful company website links	Manager		
T	Explain department/division/company specific acronyms	Manager		
T	Check in that all access is obtained for programs, software, applications, websites (NACM), etc.	Manager		
T	Check in regularly for ongoing coaching sessions	Manager		

	ONGOING CHECKLIST - months 2-12	RESPONSIBILITY	Date Initiated	Date Completed
O	Introduce new employee to various company clubs, chapters, associations, etc.	Manager		
T	Establish and monitor standards of performance for credit personnel	Manager		
T	Review performance management development and professional development planning	Manager		
T	Review allowance for bad debt and write-off procedures	Manager/L&D		
T	Attend financial analysis class to understand ratio analysis and build technical competence	Manager/L&D		
T	Arrange meeting with customer relations representative of credit reporting services to meet with team and new employee	Manager		
T	Devote time to listen to new employee comments and concerns. Provide clarity to employee's questions	Manager		
T	Complete performance evaluation and forward to HR	Manager		
T	Request new employee for onboarding feedback for continuous improvement opportunities	Manager		
T	Continue ongoing job shadowing with business partners for relationship development	Manager		
T	Have employee participate in customer visits	Manager		
T	Continue ongoing coaching sessions	Manager/L&D		
T	Prepare professional development plan and include options such as courses/workshops through NACM and various certificate/designation options	Manager/ L&D/HR		

Legend
O: Orientation
HR: Human Resources
S: Systems
T: Training
L&D: Learning and Development

Resource
Reprinted from the NACM Graduate School for Credit and Financial Management project by Raj Mandlewala, CCE; Michelle Blanchard, CCE and Jennifer Thompson, CCE., class of 2015.

4 The Credit and Sales Partnership

OVERVIEW

The credit and sales relationship is symbiotic; one does not exist without the other in a successful organization. Both departments use much the same customer information to accomplish their objectives, albeit independent of the other, and each department can provide information that helps the other do its work more efficiently. This chapter looks at some ways credit and sales can work together to maximize efficiencies, make a positive impact on company profits and provide the best possible customer service.

THINK ABOUT THIS

Q. How can the actions of the credit and sales department enhance the credit-sales partnership?

DISCIPLINARY CORE IDEAS

After reading this chapter, the reader should understand:

- ☑ How credit can be a sales tool.
- ☑ Describe the Cs of the credit and sales partnership.
- ☑ Dealing with new or potential customers.
- ☑ Dealing with existing customers.
- ☑ How credit contributes to the sales department.

CHAPTER OUTLINE

The Basis for the Credit-Sales Partnership

Credit as a Sales Tool

Virtually every business transaction that concerns another business involves credit. Business credit is the single largest source of business financing by volume, even exceeding bank loans. Without business credit, the world economy would not exist.

Credit is an investment that a company makes in receivables; credit managers are responsible for managing this investment making them, in essence, the caretakers and managers of their company's investment. As an investment manager, the role of the credit manager is to maximize the benefit of the investment while minimizing the danger, looking for the greatest possible return at an acceptable risk. Simultaneously, credit management is the support system for the company's sales efforts; without sales, there would be no receivables—no investment—to manage.

It should come as no surprise that the extension of credit in our sales-based financial system is common; the few businesses that do not offer credit terms for purchases usually accept checks in lieu of cash, which is a form of short-term credit. The availability of credit is a powerful selling tool and is used to:

- Generate sales.
- Improve profit margins due to sound credit decisions, which increase sales volumes.
- Grow a potential market share.
- Provide good customer service.
- Strengthen customer loyalty.
- Meet customer demand.
- Remain competitive.

Figure 4-1   Credit and Sales

Credit and Sales: Are the Priorities Really That Different?

Credit and Collections

Meet financial objectives

Provide timely decisions

Maximize profitable revenue, managed risk

Provide a fair, consistent and predictable credit policy

Customer service

Keep stakeholders informed

Provide unique expertise to approve and retain customers

Proactive

An agent for process improvement

It Is Not a Tug of War

Sales

Meet sales objectives

Deal with fast-paced competitive environment

Profitable sales

Want a fair, consistent and predictable credit policy

Customer relationships

Be knowledgeable about account status

Able to identify "real" opportunities

Avoid shipment interruptions

Timely, accurate processes

The Cs of the Credit and Sales Partnership

The **Three Cs of Credit** best explain the sales and credit relationship. The first C is **Communication.** Here are a few ways that sales and credit can strengthen the lines of communication:

Sharing Information

Typically the customer relationship begins with the sales team and ends with the credit team. But the lines are much more blurred in the current business environment. The customer may make initial contact through the company's website or customer service department or even the credit department when the purchase will not be cash. Sales and credit may have different customer contacts, ranging from the CFO to the inventory manager, bringing different pieces of information that are all important when evaluating credit:

- **Purchasing.** Learning about competitors and what they did wrong, the price point for the product, order frequency and preferred lot size.
- **Inventory Manager.** Learning where to ship product.
- **The CFO.** Learning information about the company's financial results, both past and projected, the seasonality of the business, along with cash flow cycles, and the end customers.
- **Accounts payable.** Learning payment cycles and methods of payment.

The sales staff can be a valuable source of information for the credit department. They can observe and share details that may substantiate or negate other credit information, such as credit reports, credit references and financial statements. Observation of external building conditions, plant locations and general knowledge about a particular industry can add valuable information, which is particularly important with marginal prospects.

Using Technology

Technology can be leveraged to improve communications between sales and credit. Even if the sales and credit departments use different software they should have access to common network storage to view and retrieve data. Alerts may be set up regarding customer account status, especially if commissions are contingent on collections. Company Intranet sites can be used to publish credit policies for reference by the sales team.

Share Initial Credit Investigation Findings

Upon reviewing a customer's credit history, the credit professional should notify the sales team if a customer is deemed a high risk, so they can determine if this is a risk the company wants to assume, knowing payments may be slow and there is a higher probability of slow payments or bankruptcy.

Join the Sales Team

Sales meetings bring to light many of the obstacles they face just trying to move product out the door. Sales meetings tend to be positive and upbeat as opposed to credit meetings, which tend to focus on the problem accounts. Attending sales meetings also presents an opportunity to get "face time" with all the sales associates and managers at once.

Educate the Sales Team

The credit department may offer to provide training to sales team members to explain the credit application or the credit approval process so that they understand what is involved. Sales and a credit professional have very different vantage points.

The second C is **Collaboration.** When credit and sales share information about the customer, it is a win-win for the credit grantor. If open or extended terms are not suitable for a new account, the credit department may offer alternatives, such as guarantees, letters of credit, credit insurance or graduated terms. When credit and sales start to collaborate and find new ways to meet customer demands, both teams can be successful.

The credit professional can help leverage their time in front of customers by coming prepared with findings of a credit investigation with regards to risk assessment, customer credit history, personnel changes, financial results and refinancing activities, as well as their payment history with current suppliers. When a salesperson works in tandem with the credit department, they gain valuable information that will help them to maximize their chance of closing the sale.

Monthly credit/accounts receivable reviews that include members of both the sales and credit teams can be arranged to discuss:

- New accounts and potential sales volumes.
- Slow paying accounts.
- Material quality issues that have the potential to delay payments.
- Lost business.
- New target markets and accounts.
- Customers with favorable credit, where sales could be increased without increasing risk.
- Potential changes of payments terms, both extended or shortened.

Real World Perspectives

RWP 4-1

COMMUNICATION, COLLABORATION, COOPERATION

Almost 10 years ago, I was the chair of a small unsecured creditors' committee of manufacturers, and the experience reinforced my belief that sales and credit *can* work well together. It also produced a surprise or two and some humor as well.

I was working for a large northeastern vision care company, with the divisional line of business sunglasses and fashion eyewear. Part of my assignment was administering credit and collection management to a network of domestic wholesale distributors, eyeglass vendors and big box retailers. One of the small retail optical chains in the southern U.S. had run into hard times and surprised us somewhat with a Chapter 11 filing. Allegedly, bad weather had affected sales and their bank had called in the financing package. Because our products were featured brands, our company was the largest creditor outside of the banks, so I was tasked with setting up the unsecured creditors' committee and all the administrative duties that went with it.

The division of my employer that sold the product was in the process of being divested and sold to a new foreign parent—so all but absolutely essential travel related to the sale was highly restricted. The first 341 meeting of creditors was soon to take place in Texas, and I knew that it would be impossible to gain approval to go. Not a great way to start off as chair of the creditors' committee.

Our VP of finance and I discussed the travel ban, and who in our company located in Texas might be able to attend the 341 meeting in my place. Our regional sales manager in that area turned out to be a highly educated, solidly logical "go to" sort of guy, who would have the meeting date free and had the reputation of handling special assignments well for our senior management.

I called the U.S. Bankruptcy Court trustee in the case, explained our travel ban dilemma and that we had a substitute that should serve us well, with preparation from me, and that I would take over afterward. The trustee was a bit reserved about it, but said that as long as our representative didn't hold up the proceeding with improper questions or a lack of knowledge it should be okay.

So our regional sales manager and I spent several hours on the phone during the next two weeks holding a "commercial credit/ Chapter 11" primer session. The first week, I gathered together various materials (including excerpts from NACM's *Principals of Business Credit*) and overnighted the package to him, and we discussed the mechanics and concepts of the Chapter 11 bankruptcy process. The second week, I sent a similar FedEx that contained background documents on the specific customer that had filed for protection, and I familiarized the regional sales manager with the credit screening, payment turn stats, and sudden drop in regular payments that preceded the filing. Our sales manager absorbed all of this like water in a sponge, and I could tell he enjoyed the challenge. He told me he was "ready to go" and was anxious to experience this new task.

A few weeks later, I was in the middle of a hectic day—the kind that just rains down with one "I need it now" issue after another—and I received a call from the Texas bankruptcy trustee. I had been so busy that day I had even forgotten the 341

Customer Visits

A member of the credit team should make a point of traveling with the salespeople to visit both high risk customers as a "wellness check," as well as larger accounts that have a solid credit history. This can build mutual trust and create a learning experience for the credit team regarding the sales territory and customer base.

The third C is **Cooperation.** Without cooperation between sales and credit, each function could result in a silo environment, concerned only about its individual goals and objectives, which may create an adversarial atmosphere.

Credit and sales should work together to maximize the success of the company as a whole and minimize internal conflict. Conflict may arise when one perceives the other is impeding that success. The credit team might view a sale as too risky resulting in a possible loss for the company. The sales team may see credit as too conservative and obstructing a revenue-producing sale. Balancing these two extremes is essential to insure a healthy accounts receivable portfolio. This relationship can be strengthened by presenting options other than declining the sale:

- Joint Check Agreement.
- UCC Filing.
- Mechanic's Lien/Bond Claim.

RWP 4-1 continued...

meeting had just taken place. I asked her how my "shill" had done, and expected that because she had placed a special call an apology was in order. When I told her that, she laughed and said that was definitely not the case.

She said that our fellow did extremely well, and that she was calling to thank me for what was an entertaining and new experience for a 341 meeting. There were the usual questions for the debtor, and she said our guy had been right in there, slicing down the essence of the banks' secured financing, the alleged reasons for the decline in sales income and the usual dissection of the business crisis that caused the filing.

What had really made her laugh was what happened when the usual claim was made that "the sudden downturn in sales was due to conditions beyond the control of the debtor management." In this case, the product was sunglasses, and the principal was simply claiming that a stretch of bad, rainy weather in the region had caused his sales to tank. Our sales manager then stood up, gave a one-minute explanation that he had long ago started tracking the data points of sunglass sales versus umbrella sales as part of his career duties, and produced a chart for the time period in question showing the same as well as weather stats for the alleged poor weather period—entirely disproving what the debtor had said. Our guy then launched a series of questions from a sales standpoint and quickly exposed that the chain's decline in sales was due to a cutback in marketing efforts, a series of bad decisions on pushing product, and diverting available cash to non-value added projects instead. The trustee said everyone except the debtor and his attorney was smiling by the time our sales manager finished.

From that point, our sales manager went back to his duties, with heartfelt thanks from our finance area and from me. The subsequent unsecured creditors' committee meetings were held by telephone. Building on the details the sales manager had gathered in the 341 meeting and brought back, we exposed an imperfection in the debtor's security agreement with their bank. We hired an attorney to represent the committee, and eventually by chasing that point we managed to gain a carve-out concession from the bank that resulted in a partial distribution to the unsecured creditors. Without the original assistance and attentiveness of our sales manager at the 341 meeting, that concession might never have happened.

I had always believed that in a manufacturing environment sales and credit are part of a team that needs to work together, with the mutual goal of finding customers that can purchase as much product or service as possible that they can pay for, and then keeping and maintaining that relationship. But even with that mindset, our sales manager surprised me—and taught me that the diversity of our backgrounds and purposes, when combined, is a tremendous strength when trying to reach the mutual goal that brings success to our employer.

The sunglass business that I worked for moved their headquarters elsewhere, after radically changing the existing business. I stayed in the area working for other employers, but now when a customer or client files for Chapter 11 protection, I always stop and wonder where I can find that national sales manager, and smile...

Bob Steve

- Deposits.
- Credit Card/Electronic Check.
- Credit Insurance.
- 50% Down, 50% on Delivery.

Comprehension Check

What are the **Three Cs** in the credit-sales relationship?

Promoting the New or Potential Customer

A company's customer base is always changing. Customers go out of business, merge or are acquired. Some companies grow very large or change their product line. Still others may choose to purchase from competitors.

One way to offset account attrition, as well as a means for increasing sales, is to generate new customers. Credit professionals may place prospective customers into two categories: well-known established businesses with credit and financial history of varying degrees or newly-established, unknown businesses with little track record and few credit references. Because both types are new, they will require investigative work by the credit department.

Investigating Potential Customers

By requesting that the credit department conduct a credit investigation on a prospect before making an initial contact, the sales staff is assured it is spending its time and effort in pursuing legitimate prospects. This is particularly helpful to the prospective customer that has not yet submitted an application or is simply being solicited for business by the sales team. Preliminary investigation ensures that the customers' time is not wasted nor are they placed in the awkward position of being turned down for credit after having been solicited. However, not all companies prescreen prospects due to sales volumes or established company procedures. Some companies conduct these investigations on potential customers that may be out of their market area or in different industries. Still other firms may conduct information searches on only very large potential orders. Others may investigate only those companies that have a firm order pending.

The credit staff should receive complete and accurate prospect information from the sales department whenever a credit investigation is requested. Three pieces of information are helpful: the company's legal name, the complete company address and the names of the corporate owners, officers and registered agents. This preliminary investigation is the first line of defense against fraudulent activity. If the prospect does not meet established credit parameters, having information on the organization's owners, officers and agents will enable the credit department to investigate the possibility of extending credit with personal guarantees. As a result, what would otherwise have been a credit refusal can lead to an array of credit alternatives.

The sales department should include a realistic estimate of the prospect's current and future credit requirements as part of the request for credit. The more the credit department knows about a prospect's credit needs, the better it can determine if the company can meet them. Also, knowing the amount of credit that a prospect will need assists the credit department in determining the required depth of the credit investigation.

It may be more difficult for sales people to collect financial information, such as balance sheets, income statements, cash flow projections, lists of current guarantees, liens, pledges and leases. Most firms are cautious about releasing financial information in general and particularly wish to keep it out of the hands of their competitors. Both the credit and sales staff should be aware of these sensitive customer issues. Requests for such information should be treated with care and concern for the customer. The following suggestions may help the creditor obtain this information:

- Stressing the confidential nature of the information being requested. Credit information gathered should not be shared with any other department.
- Emphasizing that the information being requested is standard operating procedure and an acceptable industry practice.

- Asking for only necessary information and at the proper time. Potential customers shouldn't be asked for confidential credit information before they are convinced about the product or a sale is imminent.

It is important to protect the confidentiality of information entrusted to the credit staff. At times, unusual circumstances can require additional diligence in overseeing this information. For instance, independent agents are sales professionals who are self-employed or are employed by firms that exist completely apart from the seller's firm. In some industries, it is common to use independent sales agents, rather than company employees, to maintain all or part of the company's sales effort. For example, in the candy and snack industry, manufacturers often use "brokers" (a form of independent sales agent) for sales to grocery chains.

Because agents are not company employees, it should be carefully decided how much information will be given to them or obtained through them from potential customers. Company policy should address the collection and safekeeping of information.

Sales and credit should work together to estimate the profit margin that could be expected from a prospect's business. Generally, the greater the profit margin a company can make, the greater the risk it will assume. The seller is likely to give more latitude to a customer or potential customer that is a marginal credit risk when a high profit margin exists in a product line. Credit and sales should collaborate to convert the prospect into a customer while mitigating credit risk.

It should be noted that fraudulent buyers are often willing to enter into agreements or purchase merchandise regardless of price or terms, without negotiation, because they may ultimately have no intention of paying.

In addition to gathering information, the salesperson is well positioned to educate prospects and new customers about the seller's terms of sale and other conditions that must be agreed to for the convenience and privilege of receiving open account, unsecured credit. It is a best practice to define and explain terms early in the negotiating process, as this may prevent collection problems later. There are a number of steps the sales team can take with prospects to ensure that a good foundation is laid at the commencement of the credit relationship. It is equally important that the credit department assist in establishing communication with new accounts to ensure the customer understands the consistent message of the creditor company. Here are some suggestions for such communications:

- Once the sale has been confirmed, meeting with the potential customer and discussing or defining payment terms, what they mean and how they work. This may be an opportunity for credit staff to become involved.
- Making sure the prospect understands all aspects of the credit relationship with the company.
- Communicating the benefits of prompt payments.

Some prospective customers will not qualify for open, unsecured credit even though they may receive credit from competitors; this can be a source of frustration to the sales team. Remembering that the credit department is not declining the sale but just declining open terms, the credit/sales team may be able to negotiate cash in advance, letter of credit or similar terms to complete the sale. Sound communication and open dialog from the credit and sales departments will help the customer fully understand any decision that has been made.

The Established Customer

It is important for both the sales and credit teams to realize that the financial status of a customer will change over time; for this reason, established customers require periodic credit reviews. The failure to recognize changes in an existing customer's financial condition, buying patterns or payment habits with other suppliers could lead to credit risk and potential financial loss for the credit grantor. The same kinds of guidelines should be followed with established customers as with prospective customers relative to updating credit and financial information.

Figure 4-2
New Business/New Customer Information Form

New Business Account Tracking Number:

* Denotes Required Field

Sales Information Section

General Information Section:

Customer Name*

Sales Person*

Sales Director*

Sales VP*

Business Unit*

Award Letter Received*

Designate Production, Service, Both or Prototype*

Customer Part Numbers

Life of Program*

Tooling Required?*

Estimated Annual Sales Dollars*

Supplier Web Portal Information*

Customer Information Section:

Sold To Name*

Sold To Address*

Sold To City*	
Sold To State*	
Sold To Zip*	

Ship To Name*

Ship To Address*

Ship To City*	
Ship To State*	
Ship To Zip*	

Bill To Name*

Bill To Address*

Bill To City*	
Bill To State*	
Bill To Zip*	

Payer Name*

Payer Address*

Payer City*	
Payer State*	
Payer Zip*	

Buyer/Contact Name*

Buyer/Contact Email*	
Buyer/Contact Phone*	
Buyer/Contact Fax*	

Customer Accounting Mgr*

Customer Accounting Email*	
Customer Accounting Phone*	
Customer Accounting Fax*	

Customer A/P Contact*

Customer A/P Email*	
Customer A/P Phone*	
Customer A/P Fax*	

Figure 4-2   New Business/New Customer Information Form continued

Credit Management Section:

Completed Credit Application (signed by customer)*

Country Customer Bank is in*

Customer bank account number*

Customer bank routing number*

Opening Order Value/Order Frequency*

Payment Terms*

Sales Tax Exemption Form (signed for domestic)*

Tooling Payment Terms*

IT Information Section:

EDI Customer*

Note if yes to EDI, select items needed

☐ 850 - Purchase Order   ☐ 856 - Advanced Ship Notice   ☐ 824 - Application Advice
☐ 830 - Material Release   ☐ 997 - Functional Acknowledgement ☐ 820 - Remittance Advice
☐ 862 - JIT Schedule   ☐ 810 - Invoices   ☐ 866 - JIT Sequenced

Shipping Labels*   Production Labels*   Mixed Labels*   Master Labels*

Part Labels*   Is shipping audit required?*   Customer specs for EDI and Labels sent to IT

Customer IT Contact*	
Phone Number*	
Email*	
Customer Business Contact*	
Phone Number*	
Email*	

Committed date to customer*   IT Committed date   Delivered Date   Account at Customer*

Credit Management Section

Bank Statement*   Does this payer relate to alternative payer?*   House Bank*

Lockbox*   Previous Account Number*   Reconciliation Account*

Sort Key*   Tolerence Group*   ABCD Number*

Credit Representative*   MEMA Number*   Risk Category*

The Role of Sales with Established Customers

Companies should have a policy about the role of the sales department or individual salesperson if a payment problem arises. Some credit grantors want sales personnel involved in the collection process. Others follow a business philosophy that sales personnel are to limit involvement with the customer to selling only and do not encourage sales to inquire about an account payment. Still others empower the salesperson who originally sold the account to become involved. Regardless of company policy, the expectation is that sales will provide the credit department with any information that may affect credit risk.

When facing overdue invoices, sales may take one of the following roles:

- Having no collection responsibilities so they may focus on sales. In these companies, all collection efforts are handled by the credit and collection departments.
- Making the first attempt at collection. If that attempt is unsuccessful, the credit department assumes responsibility for collecting.
- Personally collecting past due balances. The rationale for this policy is that the sale is not complete until the bill is paid. Collecting cash is part of the sales cycle and, therefore, the salesperson's responsibility.

The salesperson's first action may be to contact the customer when there is a problem, such as a past due balance or a credit purchase that can't be processed. However, in some companies, the credit department will be the only point of contact regarding credit accounts. It is important that the process and best practice be established early in order to ensure consistent treatment of customers. When a customer's payment is late due to legitimate extenuating circumstances, the salesperson should facilitate good communication by advising the credit team as soon as possible. There are times when a late payment isn't really a collection problem, but rather the sign of a problem that occurred somewhere in the sales and delivery cycle. The sales staff may learn of these situations first. Among the reasons customers might not pay on time are:

- An allowance claim is pending.
- Shipment hasn't been received.
- Merchandise was received after the specified acceptable arrival date.
- Merchandise was misrouted.
- Customer received the wrong merchandise.
- Customer received only a partial shipment.
- Order was accidentally duplicated.
- Order was over-shipped.
- Some or all of the merchandise was damaged in transit or defectively manufactured.
- Merchandise was refused without being reviewed and then returned.
- Shipment was billed to the wrong company or department or the invoice contained the wrong prices, quantities, credit terms, etc.
- Missing documentation (missing purchase order).
- Service provided was incomplete or was unsatisfactory.
- Service provided was by an unauthorized purchaser.

When dealing with overdue balances, the sales and credit departments should work together to ensure that customers do not abuse the terms of sale: net payment dates, prompt-pay discounts, interest charges and special credit terms. This is another reason for strong communications between the departments. By closely monitoring payments, both departments can work together to resolve overdue payment situations quickly and without alienating the customer. The process can be a valuable

Comprehension Check

How can the sales department assist in the collection of past due accounts?

opportunity to educate the customer that slow payment and delinquency will not go unnoticed. It may also cause an otherwise slow-paying account to pay the creditor who is willing to follow through.

Credit's Role with Established Credit Customers

Another positive, pro-sales technique is to stress the service that the credit department can offer the customer. Often, the customer is unaware of the potential benefits found in the credit function. Some of the services the credit department can offer are listed in Figure 4-3.

Figure 4-3   Customer Assistance Credit Services

The credit professional has an opportunity to provide information and resources to customers based on their experience and expertise. Care should be taken when giving advice to troubled customers. Refer them to their company accountant or legal counsel. The following is a list of a few of these services:

Financial Analysis
The credit department may have financial information and industry comparison data that they can share with the customer to assist them in understanding their financial position relative to their own industry and marketplace.

Cash Flow Control
The credit department can analyze a customer's credit terms and help it identify ways to increase cash flow by using net due dates, discounts, saving interest or finance charges.

Credit References
The credit department can show a company how to develop a good credit reputation with suppliers and how to leverage that reputation in future business relationships.

Loan Referrals
The credit department may know of other companies or lending institutions that would be willing to extend credit or lend money to the buyer. As a courtesy these referrals can be made.

The Credit Department's Contribution to Sales

There are many opportunities for the credit professional to enhance the credit and sales relationship, such as:

- Having a neutral, open-minded investigation of all prospective and current customers.
- Monitoring established customers for changes in financial stability.
- Recommending when potential credit problems may be prevented or avoided with cautious credit terms and conditions.
- Working with sales to develop a collection approach that collects cash, reduces risk and enhances customer relations.
- Taking immediate action on overdue invoices by:
  - Promptly identifying these invoices.
  - Collecting all past due accounts quickly.
  - Using tact and diplomacy in dealing with overdue accounts.
- Assisting customers by providing educational services.
- Keeping information on accounts up to date by:
  - Providing consistent and clear communication to all concerned.
  - Keeping salespeople posted on the credit status of prospects and customers.
  - Informing customers about their accounts and changes in their credit terms.

- Maintaining good communication with company management, escalating issues when appropriate.
- Having a pro-sales attitude by:
  - Keeping open communications among sales staff and management.
  - Providing information and decisions as quickly as possible.
  - Being focused on increasing overall company sales, profits and cash flow while managing credit risk.
  - Being objective and fair.
  - Understanding the balance between increased sales and acceptable loss levels.
  - Identifying flexible credit approaches that promote sales volume increases.
  - Maintaining a credit program that is consistent with the industry, region and the customer's economic conditions.

Developing a strong and mutually supportive relationship between credit and sales is much easier if both departments focus on the core values and mission of the entire company. The common goal is to maximize company profits, strengthen cash flow and provide customer service.

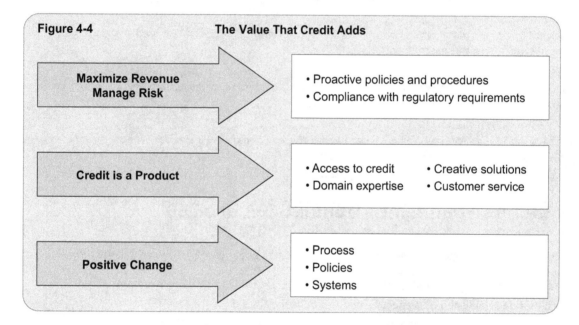

Figure 4-4   **The Value That Credit Adds**

| Maximize Revenue Manage Risk | • Proactive policies and procedures • Compliance with regulatory requirements |

| Credit is a Product | • Access to credit   • Creative solutions • Domain expertise   • Customer service |

| Positive Change | • Process • Policies • Systems |

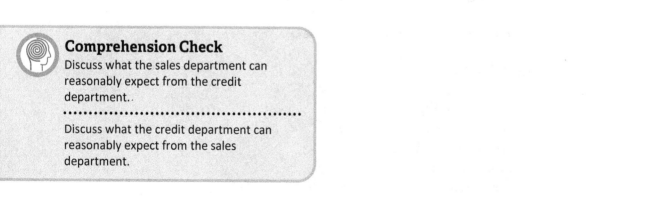

Comprehension Check

Discuss what the sales department can reasonably expect from the credit department.

· ·

Discuss what the credit department can reasonably expect from the sales department.

Key Terms and Concepts

Comprehension Check

1. What are the **Three Cs** in the credit-sales relationship?
2. How can the sales department assist in the collection of past due accounts?
3. Discuss what the sales department can reasonably expect from the credit department.
4. Discuss what the credit department can reasonably expect from the sales department.

Summary

- The credit and sales relationship should be a symbiotic one in order to foster a successful organization.
- Business credit is the single largest source of business financing by volume, even exceeding bank loans. When used correctly, the use of credit becomes a sales tool. Some of its features include:
  - Generating sales
  - Improving profit margins
  - Meeting customer demand
- The credit manager must maximize the benefit of investing while minimizing risk.
- The **Three Cs** of the credit and sales partnership include:
  - **Communication**
  - **Cooperation**
  - **Collaboration**
- By using the Three Cs as a standard of the credit and sales relationship, the overall information available to both the credit and sales department is increased, and ultimately should result in increased sales with decreased risk. The sales department will waste less time on higher risk clients, and the credit department will spend less time with collections.
- Conflict between the credit and sales department may arise when one perceives to be impeding the success of the other. However, the relationship between the departments can be strengthened by presenting alternative options instead of declining the sale. This may take a variety of forms such as using credit insurance or a mechanic's lien.
- With new or potential customers, the more information the sales department can obtain, the better the credit department can accommodate the terms for a sale, and the better the credit department can protect itself from fraudulent activity. The company's legal name, the complete company address and the name of the corporate owners, officers, and registered agents are good first steps in the process.

- It may be hard for the sales department to gain some of the information needed, stressing its confidential nature, acknowledging that the request is standard operating procedure and asking at the proper time may make it easier to obtain the necessary information.
- Companies should have a policy regarding the role of the sales department or individual salespersons if payment problems arise. In many cases, the salesperson may be the first person to learn of any payment problems and should communicate with the credit department in such a case.
- Late payments may not be a collection problem and may arise because of circumstances such as: shipment hasn't been received, merchandise was misrouted, or an order was accidentally duplicated.
- A credit department may also provide several **services to their customers** including:
  - **Financial analysis**
  - **Cash flow control**
  - **Credit references**
  - **Loan referrals**
- The credit department can make a large contribution to sales by monitoring established customer's financial stability, by recommending credit terms and conditions to reduce a potential credit problem, assisting the collection process, as well as many others.
- The relationship between the sales and credit department can be facilitated and supported if both departments focus on the core values and mission of the entire company. The common goal being, strengthen cash flow and provide customer service.

References and Resources

Business Credit. Columbia, MD: National Association of Credit Management. (This 9 issues/year publication is a continuous source of relevant articles and information. Archived articles from *Business Credit* magazine are available through the web-based NACM Resource Library, which is a benefit of NACM membership.)

Credit Professional's Handbook: The Technical Reference Manual for Credit and Customer Financial Management. The Credit Research Foundation, 1999.

"Credit Risk Review." NACM Graduate School of Credit and Financial Management project, 2016. Kathie Knudson, CCE; Lisa Ball, CCE; Stacy Parker, CCE; and Dawn Dickert, CCE.

Dennis, Michael. *Credit and Collection Handbook.* Paramus, NJ: Prentice Hall, 2000.

PART II

THE LEGAL ASPECT

5 The Legal Forms of Business

OVERVIEW

The legal form of a debtor's business may represent a key risk factor for creditors. Consequently, it is important that credit professionals understand the different forms of business, particularly as they affect the rights of creditors and debtors. State laws primarily govern the legal forms of business. For details of how the topics in this chapter relate to the states, consult the NACM *Manual of Credit and Commercial Laws.*

THINK ABOUT THIS

Q. Why should a seller understand a customer's legal standing? Does the buyer's form of business affect creditors' rights? Why or why not?

Q. What are the benefits of certain legal forms of business over others?

DISCIPLINARY CORE IDEAS

After reading this chapter, the reader should understand:

- ☑ The importance of the customer's legal form of organization in credit decisions.
- ☑ The major features of proprietorships.
- ☑ The different types of partnerships.
- ☑ The major features of corporate organizations.
- ☑ The major features of S corporations.
- ☑ The major features of limited companies, estates, common law trusts, joint ventures, cooperative societies and non-profits.
- ☑ Other features of organizations that are relevant to credit professionals.

CHAPTER OUTLINE

The Creditor's Interest in Legal Composition

The legal composition or form of business organization used by the debtor may have a direct effect on the creditor's ability to get paid in the event of business failure or death of a principal. The creditor needs to know who is legally liable and if the business will remain viable in adverse circumstances. This knowledge will be an important factor is the analysis of a firm.

Depending on the form of the business, the personal assets of the principals may or may not be available to support its debts. In smaller businesses controlled by an individual or a family, assets such as real estate used by the company can be easily manipulated so that they are outside the reach of the firm's creditors.

The four principal forms of business are proprietorship, partnership, corporation and limited liability company (LLC).

Comprehension Check

Why does a credit professional need to be concerned with what form of business a debtor is?

Proprietorships

General Considerations

A proprietorship *is a business owned and operated by one person.* This form of enterprise is the easiest to organize and requires a minimum of legal knowledge and financial resources. The business must engage in a legal activity and comply with local health, safety and zoning regulations. There may also be registration or qualification fees required by the state or local government, and an assumed name filing may be used.

Management

From the creditor's viewpoint, the greatest risk of a proprietorship is that the owner has total control over the business. The owner may direct all aspects of the business: marketing, production and financial management. If the owner gets sick or dies, the business may simply stop—and along with it the cash flow that was destined to pay creditors.

Another factor is that the owner may not possess all the skills required to successfully operate the company and, consequently, may hire one or more managers. The structure of a sole proprietorship makes it difficult to "take in a partner" if the business is successful. The mere act of "taking in a partner" changes the entity's legal status from a proprietorship to a partnership. The principals may then decide to incorporate, thereby changing the legal status to a corporation.

Continuity

The business of a proprietorship ceases when the owner dies or withdraws. In some cases it may be continued by the family or estate, provided that someone with suitable experience can be found to run the business. If the proprietor has a living trust will, the will may create an ongoing business.

In the event of a proprietor's death and liquidation of the business, creditors may not receive payment until the will is probated, creditor claims are filed and the estate is settled. This doesn't necessarily mean a loss of the money due, but payment may not be forthcoming for some time.

The creditor is also interested in the proprietor's health and the amount of life insurance carried. As the driving force in the business, the owner must be in good physical and mental condition. Often, the strain of running a business is great, particularly when it rests on the shoulders of one person. Banks have long made it a custom to require sufficient life insurance on the proprietor/borrower to pay off outstanding loans. That may be a good policy for a business creditor as well, depending upon how much money is at stake, with the proceeds of the insurance paid directly to the estate.

Capital

The proprietorship generally seeks credit based only on the assets of the business and those of the owner. If they are inadequate, the owner may be forced to moderate expansion plans or to allow outside interests to invest in the business. Therefore, the total amount of assets available to a proprietorship is usually limited.

The limited capital of the proprietorship may be a significant factor in a credit analysis. In some cases, it is a controlling influence, but in many others the capital invested is adequate for the scope of operations. The credit professional should be primarily interested in seeing that capitalization is sufficient for the current needs of the business and possible future growth and expansion.

The sole owner also receives the full benefit of a successful operation; the owner may retain as much of the business profits as they please, but the proprietor will pay taxes on those funds. This can be an advantage as it avoids the double taxation for the corporation and may provide extra capital for the business. In some cases, the credit decision will be influenced by what the owner does with the profits. Does the owner leave them in the business to strengthen its financial position, or does the owner use the profits and continue to rely on creditor financing for operating funds? From an accounting perspective, the money a proprietor takes out of the business for personal use is called the owner's "draw." Its counterpart in a corporation would be the salaries and dividends paid to the principals.

The draw in a sole proprietorship is meant to reflect the work done by the owner in the business—or the salary that would have to be paid if the owner hired someone to do the work. Other factors seem to have a greater bearing on the amount withdrawn, such as the owner's personal needs. If there is a costly illness in the family or if the owner has an expensive hobby, the business may be the only source of funds. The needs of the business must also be considered. There are many small companies that don't earn enough to compensate the owner for the time and energy put into the business. These factors can be a negative element in the credit decision.

Liability

The owner has personal, unlimited liability for the debts of the business, which makes the proprietor very vulnerable to creditors. With certain exceptions, personal assets may be claimed for the payment of business debts. This may not include, however, assets held jointly with the owner's spouse, unless they reside in a community property state (Arizona, California, Idaho, Louisiana, Nevada, New Mexico, Texas, Washington and Wisconsin with Alaska being an opt-in state that gives both parties the option to make their property community property).

The owner's personal liability for the debts of the business often can strengthen its credit position. The credit professional should be satisfied, however, that the personal liability means something in terms of assets. Frequently, the owner's personal wealth is tied up in the business, and the benefit to creditors of the personal liability is largely theoretical. Any personal wealth must be shared with all business creditors and personal creditors.

In cases where the company offers only marginal support for the credit requested, the credit professional should verify any outside assets the owner claims to have. If they are owned jointly with the spouse, the creditor will have difficulty in acting against them. A husband and wife can be a proprietorship in every state in the United States. Homestead laws passed in most states exempt certain real estate, depending on the state, from attachment or forced sale to meet general debts, including a proprietor's business debts. Refer to each state's current statutes for more information on the applicable laws.

> **Comprehension Check**
> What factors does a credit professional need to consider when dealing with a **proprietorship**?

Partnerships

General Considerations

A **partnership** is defined as *"an association of two or more persons to carry on as co-owners of a business in order to share the profits and losses."* While no particular form of contract is necessary to create a partnership, a partnership contract usually specified the partners' rights and duties and the extent of liability. A partnership may be formed by the method of doing business, such as sharing profits and losses, even though no formal contract exists.

The contract, if executed, formalizes the conditions of the business partnership and is the basis for solving any questions that may come up during the life of the partnership. The following points are usually covered:

- Type of business to be conducted.
- Amount of money or other valuable consideration to be invested by each partner.
- Division of profit and losses.
- Sharing of expenses.
- Powers and duties of each partner.
- Compensation to be paid to each in the form of salaries or draws.
- Duration of the partnership and how it is to be dissolved.
- Division of assets in case of dissolution.
- Provisions for withdrawal or admission of partners.
- How differences of opinion are to be settled.
- Provision for continuation in the event of one partner's death or incompetence.

The **Uniform Partnership Act (UPA),** enacted in certain states, *covers the rights and duties of partners.* Partners can change the provisions of the UPA as they create their own contract. In addition, the partners should know each other fairly well and be willing to cooperate in their common interest. Partnerships are of three types: general, limited and silent. The two more common types are described below.

Comprehension Check
Define the term **partnership.**

General Partnership

In a **general partnership,** *all partners are entitled to take an active part in the affairs of management, unless this is amended by the partnership agreement.* Despite their various roles, each partner is considered an agent for the firm; as such, each can commit the firm for business obligations and each has unlimited liability for the business. In comparison to a proprietorship, two or more partners will normally have more cumulative business experience, but there will be less flexibility in decision-making. With more than one principal in the business, there may be a greater pool of the production, marketing and financial management skills required to operate successfully.

Limited Partnership

The **limited partnership** differs from the general partnership in that it *is composed of one or more general partners and one or more limited partners.* The rights and obligations of the general partners are the same as those in a general partnership, except where they may be modified by the partnership agreement. The general partners control the management, have unlimited liability and actively participate in the day-to-day operation of the firm.

Comprehension Check
Describe the differences between a **general partnership** and **limited partnership.**

Limited partners, however, risk only the amount of their investment. In exchange for this limited liability, they remain passive and relinquish their voice in the management of the firm.

This type of partnership attracts people who are primarily interested in investment. They are not partners in the usual sense; rather, they depend upon return on investment much like those who invest their money in the stock market. The attraction is often a higher rate of return; it is also a convenient way of helping a relative or friend start a business as a backer without getting too involved.

Continuity

The partnership normally dissolves automatically upon the death or withdrawal of a general partner if there are only two partners, although it may continue long enough to enable the surviving partners to wind up the affairs of the business. This may be modified if the partners agree beforehand that the interest of the deceased partner will be purchased by the remaining partners and a new partnership will be formed simultaneously. Alternatively, the partnership agreement could provide that the interest of the deceased partner will pass to another partner. Failure to make such a provision may be detrimental to the firm's creditors. Moreover, the skills and experience lost upon the death of a partner may be difficult to replace. The death of a limited partner does not usually terminate the partnership. It may be necessary, however, for the remaining partners to purchase the interest held by the estate of the deceased partner.

The impact of ill health is not so great as it is in a proprietorship. One partner may become sick, yet the business may continue to operate in a satisfactory manner. Disagreements among the partners, though, may have a detrimental effect on the business. If they do not have the personal funds to buy each other's interest, they may be forced to remain together despite personal disagreements.

Capital

Compared to a proprietorship, the partnership may command more invested capital. Very often, partnerships are formed because one party can contribute business leadership and another party has the money to invest. Nevertheless, partnerships are usually confined to fairly small businesses given the ease of formation. Limited partnerships have the potential to attract large numbers of investors, because shares can be sold on a *pro rata* basis in much the same way as a corporation sells shares of ownership. Certain industries such as oil and gas producers and pipelines, leasing and real estate have huge limited partnerships run by a general partner that is itself a large corporation, formed primarily for certain tax advantages not available in most other business activities.

The general partners share profits equally, unless a written agreement has been reached by the partners. There are, however, no restrictions as to what provisions are included.

One of the attractions of a partnership is that it does not pay federal income taxes as a business entity; the partners pay individual income taxes on their proportionate shares of partnership income. Therefore, there is no double taxation on business profits, as there is when a corporation pays a tax on its profits and the shareholders pay a tax on their dividends. If the tax savings are retained in the business, the firm may be able to grow more rapidly than a corporation of comparable size.

Liability

All general partners are jointly and severally liable for the debts of the business. This means that every partner has unlimited liability for these debts. Under most state laws, creditors may sue any one partner, as well as the partnership, for the amount owed to them. Because creditors are always looking for the easiest way to collect their money, the most financially sound partners are the ones most likely to be sued. If made to pay, those partners, in turn, may be legally entitled to recover proportionate shares of this amount from the other partners.

Limited Liability Partnerships (LLPs)

General Considerations

The **limited liability partnership (LLP)** is very similar to a limited liability company (LLC). The difference is that an LLP *is designed for professionals who do business as partners in a partnership.* Its chief advantages include allowing the partnership to continue as a pass-through tax entity and limiting the personal liability of the partners. Texas was the first state to enact an LLP statute in 1991. Virtually all states have enacted LLP statutes.

An LLP must be formed and operated in compliance with its respective state statute. Created by the agreement of the partners, an LLP registers with the Secretary of State's office; its name must include either LLP or the words "Limited Liability Partnership." It is very important to keep informed about changes in the law regarding all LLCs and LLPs, since case law is evolving and requirements vary from state to state. In most states, LLP statutes are amendments to already existing partnership law. It is relatively easy to convert a traditional partnership into an LLP, because the firm's basic organizational structure remains the same. All of the statutory and common law rules governing partnerships still apply, except those modified by the LLP statute. Professional service firms, such as law firms, accounting practices and medical practices, find LLPs a useful structure for doing business. Family-run businesses, particularly family farms, are also attracted to the LLP structure.

Liability

In an LLP, partners are not held jointly and severally liable for the acts of other partners, as they would be in a regular partnership. Consider a large law practice that has been set up as a partnership. If one partner is sued successfully for malpractice and a large judgment is obtained, the rest of the partners are liable for the remaining debt once the limit of malpractice insurance has been reached. Conversely, in an LLP, partners avoid liability for the malpractice of other partners.

State laws differ as to the liability exemption if the LLP is "foreign" (formed in another state). There are questions concerning whose laws apply when statutes differ and an LLP formed in one state is doing business in another state. In Oregon, the LLP provisions cover all liabilities of the entity arising while the partnership was so registered, not just those relating to professional acts. Since liability parameters vary from state to state, it is wise to clarify the statutes in the state or states in which business is being done in terms of liability not associated with malpractice. Creditors often have varying amounts of protection. Most states apply the liability law of the state the LLP was formed in, regardless of the state they may be doing business in. The partner supervising the party committing the wrongful act or negligence is also liable. This is true for all forms of partnerships, including LLPs. When more than one partner is involved in the negligence, it is not clear how liability will be shared. Some state statutes provide proportionate liability—separate liability determinations for each partner involved in the negligence.

Dissolution

Limited liability partnerships can be dissolved by agreement of the partners, by death, incompetence, expulsion or withdrawal of a partner or by law (such as bankruptcy). Generally if an agreement is absent, a partnership must wind up its affairs and liquidate if an act of dissolution occurs. If an agreement to the contrary exists, the partnership may reform with a new composition.

Comprehension Check

Describe some basic characteristics of a **LLP**.

Corporations

General Considerations

The classic definition of a corporation was made by U.S. Supreme Court Chief Justice John Marshall (1755–1835). He termed it *"...an artificial being, invisible, intangible, and existing only in contemplation of the law."* A **corporation** may also be defined *as a voluntary association of persons, natural or legal (i.e., other corporations); organized under state or federal law and recognized by the law as being a person, fictitious in character, having a corporate name, and being entirely separate and distinct from the people who own it; having continuous life; and set up for some specified purpose or purposes.*

As a legal institution, the corporation has its roots in the medieval fiefdoms of England. One reason for its establishment was that it could get substantial things done—undertakings beyond the capacity of individuals or families. For example, one English corporation, the South Sea ("Bubble") Company, attracted and accepted money way beyond the firm's ability to earn a reasonable return with it. Its crash in 1720 so discredited the corporate institution that it was outlawed for nearly a hundred years afterward.

A corporation, being a creature of the state, has no "natural" rights and powers; it has only those granted by law. Therefore, the corporation must be organized in accordance with the laws of the state of its domicile. While it is afforded protection as a "person" by the U.S. Constitution, including its right to engage in interstate commerce, it cannot do business in another state without first getting permission from that state. *A corporation is known as a* **domestic corporation** *in the state in which it is incorporated; in other states it is considered a* **foreign corporation.** Its powers and purposes are fixed by charter and cannot be changed at will as in the case of an individual or partnership. Such a change as entering into a new type of business or increasing its capitalization—any variation from the rights, powers or purposes conferred by its charter—can only be effected by amending that charter in accordance with the laws of its state of incorporation. However, most corporate charters are drawn broadly enough so that the need for amendments rarely arises.

For purposes of credit analysis, the financial responsibility is that of the corporation. Nevertheless, the business backgrounds of the principals are an important deciding factor, for they are the conscience of the corporation.

 Comprehension Check
Define the word **corporation**.

Certificate of Incorporation

The **articles or certificate of incorporation** *(i.e., charter) include a description of the purposes and powers that the corporation expects to comply with and exercise respectively.* These are called the **express purposes** or **powers of the corporation.** In addition, there are certain **implied powers.** Examples of implied powers include *the right to buy and sell real estate when used as a plant or office location, the right to borrow, the right to have a bank account and the right to have a corporate seal as part of the corporate signature.*

The corporation is required to comply with the conditions of its charter. ***Ultra vires* acts**—*those acts outside the powers of the corporation*—are forbidden, and the officers and directors of the corporation may be held personally responsible for such acts. For example, in some states if corporate dividends are paid out of invested capital and not from earnings, the directors and officers may be required to replenish the capital from their personal assets.

Continuity

Nearly every corporation is granted a charter in perpetuity. The corporation survives the death of any principal. While new talents and new financing may be necessary, the surviving management generally has time to find them. The credit professional must keep an eye on the situation, but it is not like facing the problems that arise during a forced liquidation of a proprietorship or partnership.

Corporations, like the people who create them, are mortal; they are born, they have their season, and they pass from the scene. Responsibility for a corporation's overall performance is vested in the board of directors; stockholders elect members of the board at the corporation's annual meeting.

The board selects the officers who manage the corporation, sets their salaries, decides policy and has an oversight responsibility for the conduct of the business. This arrangement may create a sharp division between those who own the corporation and those who run it. The significance to creditors is threefold. First, the business is able to hire expert help in marketing, production and financial management; in short, it will be run by professionals. Second, there is less likelihood of the corporate wealth being siphoned off for the personal benefit of the owners. Third, even though shares of ownership may change hands, the creditor has an amount owing from the same debtor—the corporation. The relationship of the parties is not changed by the buying and selling of the common stock.

Capital

Because a corporation can issue stock, it usually has a larger potential source of capital for operations and expansion than other forms of organization. In addition, shares of stock in a corporation can be bought and sold by shareholders without any effect on its capital structure. This permits a continuity of operation and financial strength. That stability, so important to creditors of the corporation, can be jeopardized if one individual or family owns a majority of the shares. Such a situation is more akin to a proprietorship or partnership in that there is a potential for enriching the controlling shareholder at the expense of the company.

The corporation, being a legal entity, is required to pay taxes on its earnings in addition to those paid by its stockholders on corporate dividend payments.

Capital Stock

Stock certificates *issued by a company are evidence of corporate ownership in a proportion of the number of shares held to the total number of shares outstanding.* Some capital stock is issued with a **par value,** *a specific dollar amount that is shown on the face of the stock certificate.* This amount represents the minimum original investment in cash, property and services behind each share at the time of the original issue. As a company grows and matures, the par value becomes meaningless except from a historical perspective.

For that reason, in most cases, capital stock is authorized with no par value. A stated value is assigned when the stock is sold, which establishes the amount that is entered in a corporation's books as capital. Any funds received in excess of the par or stated value are shown on the books as capital surplus. The presence or lack of par value has no credit significance, nor has the classification of equity investments as capital stock or capital surplus. *The most significant number is the total equity.*

Common Stock

On the balance sheet, **common stock** *represents all or a portion of the money that was received when the company issued its shares.* The figure has virtually nothing to do with the market price of the shares. The market price of stocks is established by investors buying and selling shares from one another. Common stock represents the basic, and sometimes only, form of ownership in a corporation. By virtue of this ownership, common stockholders have certain rights:

- Voting and participating in the selection of directors.
- Sharing in the profits of the business by receiving dividends if and when they are declared by the directors.
- Sharing in the distribution of assets should a company be dissolved.

In addition, state laws, the corporation's charter or both can give stockholders **preemptive rights** *which allow the purchase of new stock in proportion to the stockholder's holdings at the time of a new issue,* preventing dilution of the stockholders' equity without consent. This ownership is in effect a semi-permanent investment, as common stockholders are not entitled to any distribution of earnings or assets until the respective prior claims of preferred stockholders, if any, have been satisfied. If there is no preferred or other special class of stock, common stock and capital stock are synonymous. Because common stockholders frequently have all the voting power, if it is concentrated in just a few hands, the credit professional should be interested in determining who actually controls the common stock. Closely held corporations have the potential to be drained of value by the payment of excessive salaries, rent, interest and dividends to those who control them. Creditors can often protect themselves by obtaining the personal guarantees of the principals. Occasionally, an organization may have established more than one class of common stock, maintaining voting rights in only one class, but permitting equal participation by both classes in dividends and giving each class equal rights in liquidation. There is a large variety of capital stock, much of it arising out of complex negotiations in mergers and acquisitions.

Preferred Stock

As implied by the name **"preferred,"** *the claims on assets of preferred shareholders generally have a higher priority than do the claims of common shareholders.* That is, in the event of a liquidation of the business, preferred stockholders are entitled to be paid before a distribution is made to common stockholders.

Preferred shares are also normally issued with a fixed cash dividend schedule, whereas common shares normally receive cash dividends on a discretionary basis based on business profits. A business' cash flow may be insufficient to permit payment of a preferred dividend. Whether the missed dividend is forfeited or "rolled into" later dividend cycles depends on whether the shares were issued as *cumulative* or *noncumulative.* With cumulative stock, the dividend continues to be a liability of the corporation and is paid when cash flow permits and generally must be paid before any distribution on common stock. With noncumulative, the dividend is forfeited.

Although the corporate charter may provide otherwise, preferred stockholders are usually denied the voting powers granted to common shareholders. This restriction may deny voting rights entirely, or it may provide the preferred shareholder with rights that are more limited than those given to common holders.

Preferred stock sometimes has the right of convertibility (usually into common stock) at the option of the holder, at a conversion ratio fixed at the time the stock was issued. This is of little consequence to credit professionals, for debt claims precede both types of stock.

The priority granted to preferred shareholders in dividend payments and liquidations is often more apparent than real. If a company is experiencing trouble and profits are not sufficient to pay common stock dividends, it is seldom able to pay preferred dividends either. Likewise in liquidation, any payment to stockholders is likely to be moot, for it is a rare dissolution that generates enough cash to pay administrative costs and all creditors, much less a payment to shareholders at any level.

Preferred stock may be redeemable after a certain period at the option of the corporation. One method is through **"sinking fund" preferred stock** *where the issuing company promises to buy back or redeem the preferred stock at some fixed time in the future; money can be deposited or set aside, so that over time preferred stock can be retired.* This provision creates a paradox for creditors. Outstanding preferred stock, because it is part of equity, provides a cushion for creditors. But if the issue has a buy-back or sinking fund provision, that cushion will be systematically reduced in the future.

It should be noted that many of the provisions of preferred stock (fixed dividends, redemption, limitations on voting rights) make it more similar to a *debt* instrument than an *equity* instrument.

Comprehension Check
What is **common stock** and what is **preferred stock?**

Liability

The stockholders have limited liability for the debts of the corporation. This liability is restricted to the amount each stockholder has invested. When the amount invested is equal to the par value of the stock, it is designated as fully paid and not assessable. Most states prohibit a corporation from issuing shares for less than par value (not fully paid for). Any amount owing for common stock is treated much like an account receivable. The stockholder is liable for the unpaid balance if the corporation becomes insolvent and the money is needed to pay creditors.

Despite the fact that stockholders may limit the amount of money they invest in a business, a creditor may ask the principals to guarantee the business obligations. The capital funds available for creditor protection may be larger than they would appear to be. Before a principal is asked for a guarantee, the creditor should ascertain whether there are tangible assets to support the personal guarantee. If not, there may still be some psychological value to the guarantee; a businessperson facing the decline of their company will likely have an incentive to first pay off those debts subject to guarantees. Should a bankruptcy be filed, such a pay-off may become a preference. Creditors can request a guarantee, and once a principal gives it to one creditor it may make little difference to them to do the same for any or all of the others.

The legal procedure for forming a corporation is more detailed and complicated than that required for a partnership or proprietorship. In addition, the corporation is subject to more control by state and federal governments, especially if it intends to offer its stock to the investing public. Much information about corporations, whose stock is publicly traded, must be filed with regulatory bodies. Such information is available to the public and can be readily obtained from data services companies and by contacting the local Secretary of State's division of corporations. Online material is available through sites such as the Securities and Exchange Commission's EDGAR portal (www.sec.gov/edgar.shtml). These online resources provide the credit professional with additional details about customer accounts.

Comprehension Check
To what extent do stockholders have liability for the debts of a corporation?

S Corporations

General Considerations

S Corporations were formerly known as Subchapter S Corporations. In 1958, some of the tax advantages enjoyed by proprietorships and partnerships were granted to small, newly formed corporations. This came about with the passage of the Technical Amendments Act, which modified the federal income tax laws to permit such corporations to be taxed as the individuals who owned or controlled them. The Tax Reform Act of 1976 gave shareholders of these pseudo corporations a variety of new benefits. The Internal Revenue Service has imposed strict limitations upon S Corporations as to when the election to become an S Corporation can be made, and when and how it can or must be eliminated.

Continuity

The lifespan of an S Corporation is the same as that for other corporations provided it meets certain requirements. It must have been organized in the United States and not be a member of an affiliated group of corporations responsible to a common parent. It must meet these additional requirements:

- Be a domestic corporation.
- Must have no more than 100 shareholders.
- Have only one class of stock.
- Have allowable shareholders (*may be* individuals, certain trusts and estates and *may not be* partnerships, corporations or non-resident alien shareholders). However, certain tax-exempt corporations, notably 501(c)(3) corporations, are permitted to be shareholders.

Every co-owner, tenant by the entirety, tenant in common and joint tenant is considered a shareholder when counting the total number. If husband and wife are treated as one stockholder because of the form of ownership, the death of either husband or wife or both will not change the number of stockholders, providing the stock continues to be held by their estates in the same proportion as before death.

The S Corporation must earn 75 percent or more of its gross income from its normal business function. If a company's passive earnings, such as rent, interest, royalties, dividends or capital gains, exceed 25 percent for three consecutive years, the S Corporation status will be terminated. In the meantime, if such earnings exceed 25 percent, then they are subject to the corporate income tax. When an S Corporation is created, every stockholder must agree to have the corporation taxed and the stockholders taxed as individuals. This consent is not needed when a new shareholder is added.

Comprehension Check
List the requirements of an **S Corporation.**

Capital

The net income of an S Corporation is divided into two general classes: that distributed to stockholders and that retained in the business. The distributed annual income from the corporation is taxed to the stockholders based on the amount each receives. Undistributed income is taxed to the stockholders based on the percentage of ownership. Undistributed income from prior years' earnings for which the owners have previously paid personal income tax can be distributed in later years to the stockholders without any tax liability. The credit professional can determine the amount of the available undistributed income by reviewing the capital section of the balance sheet. Where a corporation previously operated as a taxable corporation and had retained earnings not previously taxed to the stockholders, the balance sheet will distinguish between retained earnings and undistributed income.

Because S Corporations usually pay out profits each year, the net worth tends to remain the same, but cash funds may eventually be depleted. The stockholders often use these funds to pay their personal income taxes on distributed and undistributed earnings. In some cases, however, the stockholders will pay their personal income taxes and return any remaining cash to the business as a loan. With such a practice, stockholder loans will grow and **leverage,** *the relationship of debt to equity,* will deteriorate.

Liability

An **S Corporation** *is a corporation in all respects, except that the stockholders rather than the corporation pay the federal income taxes.* Likewise, any losses sustained by an S Corporation pass to the shareholders and can be used as deductions from other business income the stockholder may have on their personal tax returns. These losses are based on the percentage of stockholders' ownership and are limited to the total sum of the stockholders' investments in and loans made to the corporation.

From the creditor's point of view, shareholders of an S Corporation have the same immunity from business debts as any other shareholder. If their loans to the corporation become inordinately high, creditors should consider obtaining a **subordination agreement** or an *assignment* of the stockholders' loans receivable. Personal guarantees from the stockholders would also lend credit support.

Limited Liability Companies (LLCs)

General Considerations

Limited liability companies, or LLCs, came into existence in this country in 1977 in Wyoming. *The basic concept of the LLC is that an unincorporated business association, which desires to do business under the corporate structure, may do so by combining the benefits of a traditional C corporation and a partnership.* The C Corporation designation is only given to an "ordinary" corporation for tax purposes, as certain states may not authorize LLCs. The reluctance of states to enact LLC legislation and of businesses to enter into LLCs, even if available, stems from the question of whether or not the companies would retain the tax advantages of a partnership. Like an "ordinary" or C corporation, the members of LLCs (similar to stockholders) enjoy limited liability. At the same time, a properly structured LLC avoids the double taxation of C corporations and, therefore, enjoys the passthrough tax advantages of a partnership. LLCs are different from S Corporations in several ways:

- LLCs are not limited to a specific number of shareholders.
- They are not restrictive in the type of individuals who can hold an interest in the association or the amount of interest the association can hold in another corporation.

Throughout all of the discussion on LLCs, credit professionals should be constantly aware of the fact that LLCs are created for tax advantages only and do not differ in the overall corporate structure for those extending credit. They receive a distinct advantage when dealing with an LLC because it avoids the double taxation of corporate profits and that additional revenue could be used to satisfy the debts of creditors.

How an LLC is Formed

The advantage of the LLC is that it possesses both the limited liability of a corporation for the benefit of its members and the tax advantages of a partnership. If one were to lose the tax advantages of a properly structured LLC, there would be no use for an LLC as opposed to a traditional C corporation. In order to retain the tax status of a partnership, an LLC must conform to certain requirements established in federal law. Credit professionals should be familiar with these requirements, as the failure of a customer that is an LLC to comply with these standards could create a substantially adverse tax impact, which could seriously impair the entity's ability to pay its trade credit debts. It is for that reason that the requirements are listed here. In 26 CFR 301.7701-2(a)(1), the federal government outlined the six characteristics found in "pure corporations." They are:

1. Associates.
2. An objective to carry on business and to divide the gains there from.
3. Continuity of life "of the entity."
4. Centralized management.
5. Limited liability.
6. Free transferability of assets.

To be considered a partnership for federal taxation purposes, the Internal Revenue Service requires a business association, like an LLC, to possess more non-corporate than corporate characteristics. Since the government has acknowledged that the first two characteristics above are found in both partnerships and corporations, the remaining four characteristics are used to determine tax status. In other words, an LLC must not possess more than two of the remaining characteristics: continuity of life, centralized management, limited liability or the free transferability of assets.

Because one of the primary purposes of forming an LLC is to retain limited liability, one can usually assume this characteristic will be present in an LLC, although it is not necessary. This leaves the LLC with the ability to use only one of the remaining three characteristics. In order to gain the full benefit of an LLC, it must be carefully structured to avoid having two of these remaining three characteristics.

Comprehension Check

List the six characteristics of a *"pure corporation."*

Retention of Partnership Status

There are three specific ways one can avoid possessing the three characteristics that can tip the balance toward being more of a corporation and less of a partnership:

- **Continuity of Life.** If the LLC is structured so that other members of the association must agree to continue the LLC or it will be dissolved upon the withdrawal or removal of any member, it will be considered *not to possess continuity of life.*

- **Centralized Management.** It is known that more than 20 percent of equity must be represented in the management in order for an LLC *not to possess centralized management.* LLCs could be managed by its members or by other persons depending on the terms of its agreement.

- **Free Transferability of Assets.** If the LLC is structured so that a member may *not transfer any non-economic rights without the consent of all of the other members,* it will be considered *not to possess free transferability of assets.* This means that there must be a clear restriction on the transfer of membership interests, which can be a positive or a negative factor for the credit grantor.

A properly structured LLC will avoid at least two of the three characteristics. If it does, it will probably retain the past or retained tax benefits of a partnership, while permitting its members to enjoy the limited liability of a traditional corporation.

Considerations for Creditors

Initially, an unsecured creditor may think that dealing with an LLC is no different than dealing with an ordinary corporation. In most instances this is true, as absent a personal guarantee from one of the principals, the creditor can only look to the assets of the corporation to satisfy its obligations. In general, an LLC has the authority to conduct business, enter into contracts and transact any type of business in accordance with its bylaws just as if it were a C corporation. There are, however, some considerations that should be reviewed when dealing with an LLC:

- Usually, LLCs are startup operations and are not part of an established group of entities.
- While there are tax advantages for both profits and losses, the pass-through of losses to the members is a very distinct advantage.
- Many times, when it is assumed that the entity will be losing money in its early stages, the LLC structure (or an S Corporation) is chosen to maximize the tax benefits of the losses for those involved on an individual basis.

When dealing with an LLC, creditors should recognize that there may be an anticipation of losses by those who have formed the entity. Even though the entity itself will escape tax liability as it will be "imposed" upon the members, a creditor must assume that provisions for these taxes will be made by way of distributions to the members. Careful review of an LLC entity's annual financial statement should be undertaken to make sure that cash is not removed at such a rate which, while satisfying the tax obligations of the members, depletes the entity of cash needed in order to carry out its functions and pay its creditors in the ordinary course of business. If the principals of an LLC will not provide a creditor with personal guarantees, consideration should be given to securing a subordination agreement from the members that provides that the LLC may not distribute income to them unless and until the debts due to the creditor are current.

In many instances, this can have an even greater impact upon the individuals involved than would a personal guarantee. By monitoring the financial statements of the entity, the credit grantor can stay apprised of the situation, and make sure that the provisions are being honored. If a substantial amount of credit is being extended, it may be wise to receive an opinion from a legal or accounting professional for the LLC that it has been properly structured in order to receive the tax advantages. Were the LLC to anticipate the tax benefits but not receive them because of improper structuring, this could create a serious tax burden on the entity, which could interfere with the cash flow needed to pay debts in the ordinary course of business.

There is no reason or prohibition why a creditor cannot seek such an opinion from a legal or tax professional of a potential customer. Indeed, the reluctance to provide one could signal the possibility of a problem.

 Comprehension Check
How does an **LLC** differ from an **S Corporation?**

Estates

Proprietorships—Continuity

An estate normally operates a business for a short duration. It is the duty of the executor to take possession of decedent assets, pay administration expenses and creditor claims, and dispose of the balance of the estate in accordance with the decedent's will. If there is no will, the administrator will do the same in accordance with the laws of the state governing the distribution of the decedent's estate. In such a case, it is also possible for a creditor, or a group of creditors, to apply for and receive letters of administration. Creditors that become the representative of the estate must administer, not only for their own benefit, but also for the benefit of all interested parties. Creditors so proceeding are entitled to receive, in addition to the claim, the ordinary commissions and fees that the law allows.

Capital

If a significant amount of money is owed by an estate-run business, a creditor should verify that the assets are properly classified as business or personal and that they are not dispersed prematurely. The creditor should also be satisfied that the executor or administrator is qualified to manage the disposition of the estate. Unless the decedent's will provides otherwise, the executor must be bonded in the amount the court may direct; in the case of an administrator, a bond may be required.

Liability

Under the laws of most states, the representative, who may be either the executor or administrator, is required either to advertise for claims or to notify creditors to present their claims on or before a specified date. In some states, no such notice is required although creditors must file their claims within a time prescribed by law after the appointment of the representative.

Once a creditor determines that a customer has died, steps should be taken promptly to file a claim with the representative, without waiting for some official notice. Except for possible procedural difficulties and delay, the death of a debtor generally does not affect the validity of a debt. Where a debt has been reduced to judgment prior to death and has become a lien on real or personal property, the judgment lien generally continues as if death had not intervened.

Death usually does not shorten the applicable statute of limitations with respect to unsecured claims; in most cases, the time allowed to enforce collection is extended for a short period of time to enable creditors to assert their claims against the estate. It is suggested that notification should be sent return-receipt requested to ensure that claim is included. Mere written notice by the creditor to the representative of the estate generally suffices to stop the running of the statute of limitations without the necessity of instituting legal proceedings. Where written notice is given to the representative and the claim is acknowledged, the creditor does not need to do anything further, since the claim will generally be paid after the account has been audited or confirmed by the court.

If, after the passage of a **statutory period of time** *(from six months to one year in most states),* the representative has not paid the creditor nor filed an account for audit or confirmation by the court, a creditor may institute proceedings to compel the payment of the account.

If a creditor has given written notice of its claim and it is denied or disputed by the representative, the creditor must submit the claim directly to the court. Unless the creditor is prepared to prove the claim at the time of audit or institute legal proceedings against the representative, the claim will be barred.

Common Law Trusts

General Considerations

This form of organization, also referred to as a Massachusetts trust or business trust, has been used in England for centuries. It was first used extensively in Massachusetts and has since been recognized and used throughout the United States. It has been regarded more as a partnership than a **common law trust** in some states. Unlike the corporation, the powers of the common law trust are not generally derived from statutory law. Rather, they come from the trust agreement, subject to the rules that govern trusts generally. *It is formed by agreement between owners of property (or a business) and a trustee or group of trustees.*

The beneficiaries are issued trust certificates proportionate to their interests. The trustees hold legal title to all property of the business and manage its affairs. Some of their powers may at times be delegated to one of their number, though the trustees normally function as a unit. The certificate holders, or shareholders of beneficial interest as they are sometimes called, participate proportionately in the income from the trust. They also share proportionately in the proceeds when the trust is dissolved, much the same as the partners in a partnership.

Continuity

Depending upon the agreement creating it, a trust may continue for a specified duration or may continue into perpetuity. The death of a certificate holder does not cause a dissolution of the common law trust. The share passes through the estate of the deceased in much the same way as a share of corporate stock.

Capital

The capital of the common law trust is equal to the value of the property transferred to the trustees. Profits are generally distributed at the end of the fiscal period. For purposes of credit appraisal, the credit professional should obtain a balance sheet, income statement and statement of cash flows, as with any other type of business. Initially, the common law trust was not required to pay income taxes; instead, the beneficiaries paid personal income taxes on their proportionate earnings distributions. This advantage has been reduced over the years, and the common law trust has increasingly been taxed as a corporation.

Liability

Primarily, the credit professional will be interested in determining the liability of the beneficiaries for the debts of the business. In most cases where a trust has been organized, the certificate holders are protected from claims over and above the extent of their investments. The principal exception occurs when the beneficiary is shown to have a voice in the affairs of management. In those states where the common law trust is treated like a partnership, the certificate holders are not exempt from personal liability for debts. The creditor can then act as it normally would against a partnership.

Trustees are held accountable for the fiduciary affairs of the common law trust. They are accountable to the certificate holders for the property entrusted to them and for any loss due to misconduct or mismanagement. In acting with third parties, the trustees are personally liable for their commitments unless they have been absolved from this responsibility by agreement with the party with which they have made a contract.

In dealing with common law trusts, it is important for the creditor to know how that entity is viewed by the courts in the states where merchandise is to be shipped, as well as the state where the headquarters of the trust are located.

Joint Ventures

General Considerations

A joint venture, *also called a syndicate, is a combination of two or more persons including corporations formed to undertake a specific, and usually large, contract or project.* Often the transaction is too large in scope to be handled by any one of the venturers alone. For example, a large construction job, a public offering of securities or a large real estate transaction may be undertaken by a joint venture.

Participants often bring unique resources to the group, such as technical knowledge, capital, ability to negotiate for the business with the proper persons, competent personnel to handle the work and sources of materials that are needed to meet contract specifications. Occasionally, a firm will form a joint venture to develop a new product that is only partially within the range of their own expertise.

For credit analysis purposes, a **joint venture** is similar to a partnership. It is defined in case law as *an association of two or more persons (corporations) to carry out a single business enterprise for profit, for which purpose they combine their property, money, effects, skill, and knowledge.* In general, a creditor dealing with a joint venture can presume that the venturers can bind each other to contracts that are "reasonably necessary to carry on the business" they have undertaken. If the credit extended is for products or services that are not normally associated with the joint venture project, or if the amounts of credit involved are very large, the credit professional would do well to engage legal assistance in analyzing the liability of the parties.

 Comprehension Check
Define the term
joint venture.

Continuity

The continuity of the joint venture is fairly well-established by the length of time it will take to complete the transaction as specified in the contract. A contract drawn properly will bind the co-venturers to meet the obligations of the joint venture, either together or individually, if one or the other fails to perform. Naturally, when the project is completed the presumption is that co-venturers can no longer bind each other to an extension of credit.

Capital

The capital available to the joint venture includes all resources of the co-venturers, in a technical sense. It is usual for the venture to keep a separate set of books. In that way, the assets committed to the contract are segregated. Similarly, the creditor should set up a separate account for sales to the joint venture.

Liability

As mentioned above, co-venturers are usually held jointly and severally liable for the debts of the joint venture. However, there are some states where a different interpretation is given. In these states, the creditor may encounter difficulty in establishing that the co-venturers are individually liable for all debts of the joint venture. In such cases, the credit professional may ask the joint venture to state in writing who is liable for what.

Where the liability of the co-venturers is established, it is important to know the financial strength of the parties. A co-venturer that is not a good credit risk in other business transactions is not likely to be a better risk just because it entered into a joint venture. In such an instance, the credit position of the other co-venturers would weigh heavily in the overall analysis of the combination.

Other Forms of Organizations

Cooperative Societies

Cooperative societies *are organizations of mutual help and betterment, formed when individuals or corporate businesses combine their financial, capital and other resources to advance their particular trade or industry.* By this combination, they seek to obtain marketing and/or purchasing advantages. Savings are distributed to the membership periodically in the form of a patronage dividend, dependent upon each member's participation during the dividend period.

Methods by which cooperative societies obtain funds for their operation may vary from one state to another, or may be specified in the charter or bylaws of the society if not restricted by state law. Similarly, the liabilities of the society's officers, directors and membership may vary, as may the circumstances that affect its legal life. In general, cooperative societies are not heavily financed. Members may be small producers, such as dairy farmers, or even consumers who join a supermarket cooperative.

The extension of credit should be based on balance sheet numbers and member support as indicated by the profits earned.

Not-for-Profit or Nonprofit Organizations

The Internal Revenue Service recognizes the designation, not-for-profit, for certain organizations. **Not-for-profit organizations** *may be either corporations or associations.* They are often formed to carry out work or business as a service to the community rather than for profit.

Capital for the operation may come from governments, charitable endowments and social service agencies as well as fees for goods and services furnished to their constituents. Like for-profit businesses, they prepare financial statements that can guide creditors in their dealings with them.

Other Features of Organizations

General Considerations

In addition to knowing a customer's legal form of business, the credit professional is often asked to review the credit significance of organizational changes. Some of the more frequent situations are:

- Principals of one business are also principals of another, and there may be many transactions between them.
- Changes being made in legal composition, as when a proprietorship becomes a corporation.
- One company having its operations split into one or more divisions using separate names.
- Two or more businesses merging or consolidating, or one corporation acquiring another. In each instance, these actions could affect the customer's creditworthiness.

It may be advisable to determine the effect of these changes on the financial strength and credit position of the accounts. If no additional borrowing is required for these changes, the financial condition will not suffer. Should outside borrowing be necessary, however, another look at the credit position is in order.

In any case, the credit professional should determine if the change is brought about by favorable circumstances, such as a growth in business, or something unfavorable such as a decline in market strength and profitability.

Affiliated Interests

A person is said to have **affiliated interests** *when they are a principal in more than one company.* If each of these businesses is incorporated, they are all separate entities even though they may provide similar goods and services to their customers. A person may control a number of stores selling the same type of goods, yet each is a separate corporation. Legally, the assets of one store are not available for payment of the others' debts; the individual's personal assets are also insulated from the debts of each corporation.

The credit professional should examine the financial statements of each corporation involved. Getting one or more of the affiliated corporations to guarantee the debts of the weaker one may offset any weaknesses found. Affiliated interests are also important because they provide a more complete picture of the principal's character and capability. An unfavorable business record can often be uncovered by investigating the affiliates of a new concern.

Changes in Legal Composition

One of the more complex problems faced in credit analysis is a change in the legal composition of an account. A business often progresses from proprietorship to partnership to a corporation. As the business grows, changing the legal structure may provide advantages. The following three situations may appear similar on the surface but have differing ramifications to creditors. They demonstrate why further questioning is necessary when a corporation succeeds a partnership:

1. The corporation is formed. It then purchases the assets of the partnership and assumes its liabilities. In exchange for their proportionate holdings in the old partnership, the partners receive shares of stock in the new corporation.

2. The corporation is formed. The partnership is then liquidated and the partners receive a *pro rata* distribution of the proceeds of liquidation. They then invest their funds in the new corporation for shares of stock.

3. The corporation is formed. After the partnership is dissolved, the partners invest only a portion of the proceeds of liquidation in exchange for shares of stock in the new corporation.

From the viewpoint of credit analysis, three different situations are described above. In the first, there is no change in the net worth of the business. The change from the creditor's point of view is that a new corporate customer has come into being. However, the former partners have now insulated their personal assets from the claims of business creditors.

In the second situation, the new business is formed independently of the old partnership's liquidation. The partnership would pay all outstanding obligations before it could dissolve. Although there is now limited liability on the part of the principals, there has been no change in net worth or the financial strength of the business, provided the principals do indeed take the cash they will have in hand and invest it in the corporation as planned.

The third situation reflects a complete change in the form of organization, in the liability of the principals and in the financial strength of the business. By deciding to invest only a portion of the assets in the new corporation, the principals have held onto some of their interest in the old partnership.

It is not unusual for a business to be incorporated under the circumstances of the third illustration. The details are often left to the accountant and attorney. Consequently, the creditors may not be readily aware of the specific change nor of its effect on the financial condition of the concern. When a succession takes place, a typical incident that often confronts a credit professional is the following: In answer to a question on the ownership change, the principal may reply, "Yes, we have incorporated, but there is no other change in the business." This information can be misleading and may cause the credit professional to make an unjustified favorable appraisal of the account. It is always good practice to obtain the financial statements of the newly formed corporation. Any changes in equity, debt or the cash position should then be apparent.

Parent-Subsidiary Relationships

A corporation that owns more than 50 percent of the stock of another corporation is said to be the **parent of its subsidiary.** Therefore, subsidiaries may be partly owned or wholly owned. From a legal perspective, the parent and its subsidiary are generally considered as separate entities, with no intercompany liability for debts. It is therefore important to find out if the parent has guaranteed any debts of its subsidiary. Should that be the case, they represent a contingent liability claim on the parent's assets that may not be reflected on the parent's financial statement.

Under special circumstances, the courts have ruled that the parent and subsidiary are one organization. These cases have been decided on their individual merits, however, and do not fit in with the usual parent-subsidiary relationships. They have to be proved in court with the burden of proof on the creditor to show that, in effect, the subsidiary was an instrumentality of the parent and that the separate corporate indentures were ignored. This is normally very difficult to do. The safer approach is to regard the subsidiary as a separate entity and to rely upon analysis of its financial condition for appraisal of credit risk. Naturally, if the parent will guarantee the obligations of the subsidiary, the credit task is diminished (if the financial condition of the parent makes its guarantee meaningful).

Comprehension Check
Briefly discuss the relationship between a **parent corporation** and its **subsidiary.**

One of the most challenging situations for a credit professional is where a giant corporation sets up an operating subsidiary with virtually no equity and that subsidiary seeks credit. To ask the parent for a guarantee, which may involve getting approval from the giant company's board of directors, may appear insurmountable. In the majority of cases, the parent corporation will stand behind the debts of its subsidiary, but every now and then if serious money is at stake, a giant corporation may cut loose the subsidiary and wrap itself in the corporate veil.

Operating Divisions

When credit is extended to a division of a customer, the credit professional need not analyze the division as a separate entity. A **division** *is an internal arrangement of a corporation made for the convenience of its management.* It does not affect the legal status of the corporation. Therefore, there is no separation of credit liability.

Comprehension Check
What is an **operating division?**

Mergers and Consolidations

Mergers and consolidations *are statutory procedures regulated by state law.* They involve the complete integration of corporate entities and not just their assets and liabilities. In a merger of two corporations, the shares of stock in one company are exchanged by their holders for shares in the other, which will be the survivor corporation. The absorbed corporation files a certificate of succession and its files are assimilated by the survivor. The liabilities of the absorbed corporation are in effect taken over by the survivor corporation.

A consolidation is a somewhat different procedure. After a new corporation is formed, the shares of the corporations that are to be consolidated are exchanged for shares in the newly formed corporation.

Certificates of succession are filed by the corporations that will discontinue. Their files are absorbed by the brand new corporation and the liabilities of the old corporations are assumed by the new one.

The credit professional must determine what factors have been brought into the credit situation by the consolidation or merger of two or more companies. New capital resources may be available; new or different principals may be in control; and there is a new legal responsibility. In the consolidation, the creditor must look to the reorganized corporation for payment of debts existing before the change took place. The combination of facilities in the new organization may broaden the potential for expanded operations.

Purchase of Assets

This type of transaction between two corporations does not affect their positions as separate and unrelated concerns. Any assets may be purchased, although it will typically be inventory, fixed assets or intangibles such as methods, processes or patents. The purchase of assets is a private contract, and a variety of terms may be specified by the buyer and the seller. If assets are sold subject to liabilities, the purchaser assumes the secured debts on the assets bought. Such assumption, however, does not relieve the seller of its obligation to the creditor. Assets may also be sold net, in which case the seller pays any obligations from the proceeds of the sale. From the creditors' viewpoint, there is no change in the legal form of either corporation. The sale or purchase may affect their financial condition, but the two companies remain separate and unrelated.

Creditors of the selling companies have these further protections: If securities of the purchasing corporation are taken instead of cash, a creditor of the selling company can proceed against such securities if any judgment is unpaid. If the selling company goes bankrupt, its assets may be sold by the trustee with the approval of the court. If the assets purchased are subject to any outstanding obligations on them, the new owner is also responsible to the creditors of the original owner. Any purchaser of all or a substantial part of a firm's inventory assets is subject to Article 6 (Bulk Sales) of the Uniform Commercial Code to the extent still in effect in a particular state, and must notify creditors that the purchase is being made. This refers to the transfer of a major part of inventory outside the ordinary course of business. A transfer of a substantial part of equipment is also a bulk transfer if it is made in conjunction with a bulk transfer of inventory, but not otherwise.

Key Terms and Concepts

Comprehension Check

1. Why does a credit professional need to be concerned with what form of business a debtor is?
2. What factors does a credit professional need to consider when dealing with a **proprietorship?**
3. Define the term **partnership.**
4. Describe the differences between a **general partnership** and **limited partnership.**
5. Describe some basic characteristics of a **LLP.**
6. Define the term **corporation.**
7. What is **common stock** and what is **preferred stock?**
8. To what extent do stockholders have liability for the debts of a corporation?
9. List the requirements of an **S Corporation.**
10. List the six characteristics of a **"pure corporation."**
11. How does an **LLC** differ from an **S Corporation?**
12. Define the term **joint venture.**
13. Briefly discuss the relationship between a **parent corporation** and its **subsidiary.**
14. What is an **operating division?**

Summary ....

- The legal composition of a business may have a direct impact on a creditor's ability to get paid in the event of a business failure, change in legal composition or death. Depending on the legal status, a person's assets may or may not be available to pay back debts.
- A **proprietorship** is a business owned by an individual who assumes unlimited liability for the debts of the business. The proprietorship ceases when the owner dies or withdraws. In some cases it may be continued by the family or estate.
- There are three types of **partnerships:**
  - **General**
  - **Limited**
  - **Silent**
- In general, partnerships have command of more investment capital. General partners assume unlimited liability, while limited partners only assume the liability of the amount they invested. An attractive feature of partnerships is that it does not pay federal income taxes; rather, it partners pay taxes individually.
- In an **LLP,** the partners continue to have the benefit of a pass-through tax entity like in a general partnership. However, in an LLP, the partners are not held jointly accountable for other partner's actions. Parameters surrounding liability change by state, so it is important that credit managers consult their state laws in order to make an appropriate judgment of a debtor's accountability.
- A **corporation** under state law is considered as its own "person" or "entity," and having continuous life. A corporation has no natural rights; it only has rights that have been granted by law. Therefore, it can engage in interstate commerce, but cannot do business in another state unless given permission by said state. Corporations also have the ability to issue stock. Stockholders also benefit from the limited liability granted to corporations.
- The two types of stock issued by a corporation include: **common stock** and **preferred stock.** Although there are several differences, preferred stock normally has a higher priority to a company's claim than do those that hold common stock. However, common stock comes with other benefits such as voting rights within a corporation.
- **S Corporations** are a modified form of a corporation that allows the individual who owns or controls the corporation to only be taxed as an individual. This comes with certain restrictions that include:
  - Being a domestic corporation
  - No more than 100 stock holders
  - Only one class of stock offerings
  - Have allowable shareholders
  - It must earn 75% or more of its gross income from normal business function
- S corporations have the same immunity from business debts as any other shareholder.
- An **LLC** is a company that is created to model the traditional corporate structure while gaining the benefits of a partnership. LLCs are different from an S Corporation as follows:
  - LLCs are not limited to a specific number of shareholders
  - They are not restricted as to who can invest
- Apart from the six characteristics found in "**pure corporations,**" an LLC must be more non-corporate than corporate and normally do this by not possessing two of the following characteristics: continuity of life, centralized management or free transferability of assets.

- When dealing with **estates,** creditors can become a representative of the estate, and if there is a considerable amount of debt owed, they should ensure that the assets have been properly classified. Death does not shorten the statute of limitations on unsecured claims, but the time of enforcement may be lengthened.
- As a creditor, it is important when working with **joint ventures** to ask the joint venture to state in writing who is liable and for what part of the debt. It is also important to assess the individual financial strengths of each party.
- **Cooperative societies** should be given credit based on their balance sheet numbers and member support as indicated by the profits earned.
- **Non-profits** operate almost identically to for-profit businesses; therefore, their creditworthiness should be assessed based on their financial statements.
- Other features of organizations that may have a dramatic effect on the creditworthiness of a business are: when a person has affiliate interests, when there is a change in the legal composition of a company, when there is a parent-subsidiary relationship, or when mergers and consolidations occur.
- As a general rule, when extending credit to a division of a company, the analysis should not be done as if the division is a separate entity.

References and Resources

Business Credit. Columbia, MD: National Association of Credit Management. (This 9 issues/year publication is a continuous source of relevant articles and information. Archived articles from *Business Credit* magazine are available through the web-based NACM Resource Library, which is a benefit of NACM membership.)

Consumer and Business Credit Management. Boston: Irwin/McGraw Hill, 1998.

Manual of Credit and Commercial Laws. Columbia, MD: National Association of Credit Management, current edition.

Miller, Roger and Gaylord Jentz. *Business Law Today.* 5th ed. London: Thomson Learning, 2000.

6 The Legal Environment of Credit

OVERVIEW

There is a critical need to be aware of the specific government legislation that pertains to business credit. Government legislation not only creates and protects the rights of creditors but also imposes limitations on business activities. Credit department policies and procedures should be in place to ensure that all actions taken by the department and its employees are within the boundaries of the law.

THINK ABOUT THIS

Q. How has human behavior influenced the evolution of laws in the business environment?

Q. How has technology influenced the business and legal environment?

DISCIPLINARY CORE IDEAS

After reading this chapter, the reader should understand:

- ☑ The four cornerstone federal antitrust acts and why they were written into law.
- ☑ The Fair Credit Reporting Act and its applications in consumer and commercial credit.
- ☑ The applicable practices a creditor must follow under the ECOA and Regulation B.
- ☑ The purpose of the Consumer Financial Protection Bureau.
- ☑ The rules that a creditor must follow under the Fair Debt Collection Practices Act when collecting from a debtor.
- ☑ What information a creditor must disclose to a consumer applying for credit under the Truth in Lending Act and Regulation Z.
- ☑ What constitutes an e-signature and its relevant provisions.
- ☑ The procedures and requirements a holder of unclaimed property must follow.
- ☑ Why SOX was enacted and its requirements for corporate responsibility and accountability.
- ☑ The Red Flags Rules.

CHAPTER OUTLINE

Antitrust Regulation

Antitrust laws were initially enacted around the turn of the 20th century in response to the damaging effects that powerful monopolies, formed by corporate giants and others in the mid- to late-19th century, were having on small businesses. After the industrial revolution, monopoly power, along with many unfair trading practices such as price fixing and restraint of trade, was used to drive small businesses out of business. When monopolies were recognized as being out of control and damaging competition, federal antitrust laws started to appear in the United States to protect smaller businesses.

Four major federal acts have been passed over the course of the 20th century, each of which refined former laws by eliminating loopholes and establishing new provisions. These are the Sherman Act, the Clayton Act, the Robinson-Patman Act and the Federal Trade Commission Act. This chapter presents a summary of the four acts; the Acts are extremely complex and legal counsel should be sought when dealing with them. *The purpose of U.S. antitrust law is to encourage and protect competition.*

The latest edition of NACM's *Manual of Credit and Commercial Laws* is a source of additional information about these Acts.

Comprehension Check

What is the purpose of **U.S. antitrust law?**

The Sherman Act of 1890

The Sherman Act (15 USC §§1-7) was the first antitrust act passed in the United States. The Act was designed to prevent monopolies and unfair restraints of trade. *The Sherman Act prohibits contracts, combinations and conspiracies in restraint of trade in interstate commerce. It declares that every person who shall monopolize, or attempt to monopolize, or combine or conspire with any other person or persons, to monopolize any part of the trade or commerce among the several states, or with foreign nations, shall be deemed guilty of a felony, and, on conviction thereof, shall be punished by fine not exceeding $100,000,000 if a corporation, or, if any other person, $1,000,000, or by imprisonment not exceeding 10 years, or by both said punishments, in the discretion of the court.* In order for an offense to be considered a crime under the Sherman Act, a contract, combination or conspiracy between two or more persons or companies that has the effect of restraining or monopolizing trade or commerce within several states or with foreign nations must be made.

The purpose of the Sherman Act is to prohibit monopolies, contracts and combinations that would unduly interfere with the free exercise of their rights by those engaged, or who wish to engage, in trade and commerce; in short, its purpose is to preserve the right of freedom of trade. A seller of goods does not violate the Act by refusing to sell to others and may withhold goods from those who will not sell them at the prices suggested for their resale.

In determining if an action constitutes a conspiracy to commit an action that results in a restraint of trade, four elements must exist:

1. There must be knowledge of all the parities;
2. A common purpose;
3. An actual restraint of trade; and
4. Intent to restrain trade.

In short, the Sherman Act outlaws every contract, combination, or conspiracy in restraint of trade, and any monopolization, attempted monopolization, or conspiracy or combination to monopolize. Long ago, the Supreme Court decided that the Sherman Act does not prohibit *every* restraint of trade, only those that are *unreasonable*. For instance, in some sense, an agreement between two individuals to form a partnership restrains trade, but may not

Comprehension Check

What is the **Sherman Act** designed to prevent?

do so unreasonably and may be lawful under the antitrust laws. On the other hand, certain acts are considered so harmful to competition that they are almost always illegal. These include plain arrangements among competing individuals or businesses to fix prices, divide markets, or rig bids. These acts are *"per se"* violations of the Sherman Act; in other words, no defense or justification is allowed.

The Business Environment in the Early 1900s

In the early 1900s, entrepreneurs wanted to expand by buying other companies, which created new lending opportunities for New York bankers. The most powerful and wealthy of these entrepreneurs were called robber barons. The term robber baron described businessmen who allegedly used unscrupulous tactics in their business operations and on the stock market to amass huge personal fortunes.

In 1901, John Pierpont Morgan created U.S. Steel, the first billion-dollar corporation. U.S. Steel was a giant integrated steel trust. Capitalized with $1.4 billion at a time when the capitalization of all American manufacturing was $9 billion, U.S. Steel elevated both Wall Street and U.S. industry to a new plateau. When it came time for J.P. Morgan to sell U.S. Steel, approximately 300 underwriters disposed of the securities.

Many of the robber barons' massive businesses controlled a large majority of all activity in their respective industries, often arrived at through predatory pricing schemes that are now illegal. Some of the most notable were J.P. Morgan (banking), John D. Rockefeller (oil), and Andrew Carnegie (steel).

The Clayton Act of 1914

The Clayton Act finds its roots in the 1912 presidential election when the three parties at the time, the Republicans, Democrats and Progressives, promoted the position that the Supreme Court had been too lenient on large corporations and that antitrust laws needed to be strengthened. **The Clayton Act** (15 USC §§12-27 and 29 USC §§52-53) followed the Sherman Act and *was created to correct defects in the Sherman Act. It also supplemented the Sherman Act by giving certain administrative agencies the power to stop violations of the law in their development and before a threatened conspiracy ripened into actuality.* Congress passed the Clayton Act to promote competition through protection of viable, small, locally owned businesses.

Under the Clayton Act, it is unlawful to enter into:

1. Leases or sales on condition that lessee or purchaser shall not use or deal in the commodities of a competitor of the lessor or seller;
2. Exclusive dealing arrangements; and
3. Tying arrangements (an agreement by a party to sell one product but only on the condition that the buyer also purchases a different (or tied) product).

In addition, the Clayton Act restricts the acquisition of stock by one corporation from another where the effect of such acquisition may be substantially to lessen competition or to tend to create a monopoly. The Clayton Act prohibits any person serving as a director or officer in any two corporations under certain conditions where their service would result in an elimination of competition that would violate any of the antitrust laws. The Act was amended in 1955 to add two new subdivisions: The first gives the United States a right of action for actual damages sustained by reason of any violation of any antitrust law; the second amendment imposes a four-year statute of limitations on actions by private persons or by the United States to recover damages under the Act.

The Clayton Act is a major civil statute intended to protect competition and to keep prices from skyrocketing due to mergers, acquisitions, or other business practices. By giving the government the authority to challenge large-scale moves made by corporations, the Clayton Act provides a barrier against monopolistic practices. Section 7 of the Clayton Act prohibits mergers and acquisitions where the effect is to substantially reduce competition or to create a monopoly.

An illustration of the use of the Clayton Act is the action taken by the Department of Justice to block the acquisition of General Electric Company's appliance business by AB Electrolux and Electrolux North America Inc., whose brands include Frigidaire. The Justice Department argued that the $3.3 billion acquisition would combine two of the leading manufacturers of ranges, cooktops and wall ovens sold in the United States, eliminating competition that has benefited American consumers through lower prices and more options. The Department argued that purchasers in the United States spent over $4 billion on these major cooking appliances in 2014. The Justice Department took the position that Electrolux's proposed acquisition of General Electric's appliance business would leave millions of Americans vulnerable to price increases for ranges, cooktops and wall ovens, which are products that serve an important role in family life and represent large purchases for many households. The lawsuit also sought to prevent a duopoly in the sale of these major cooking appliances to builders and other commercial purchasers, who often pass on price increases to home buyers or renters. Ultimately, the acquisition was stopped and General Electric agreed to sell its appliance unit to Chinese manufacturer Haier Group.

The Federal Trade Commission Act of 1914

The Federal Trade Commission Act (15 USC §45) was the broadest of the important antitrust acts to be passed. *Its prohibitions include false advertising of foods, drugs, devices and cosmetics, and any other practice that is designed to deceive the public.* An example of an FTC Act claim, using Section 5, is a "Made in USA" claim in advertising and labeling.

Any practice that violates the Sherman Act, the Clayton Act or the Robinson-Patman Act—or even if it falls short of a violation but is related to the type of practice which they prohibit—may constitute an unfair method of competition in violation of the Federal Trade Commission Act. The ultimate aim of the Act is to protect the public from the actions likely to result from the destruction of competition or the restriction of competition to a substantial degree.

When the FTC was created in 1914 by this Act, its purpose was to prevent unfair methods of competition in commerce as part of the battle to bust the trusts. Over the course of time, Congress passed additional laws giving the agency greater authority to police anticompetitive practices. In 1938, Congress passed the Wheeler-Lea Amendment which included a broad prohibition against unfair and deceptive advertising practices. Since then, the Commission also has been directed to administer a wide variety of other consumer protection laws, including the Telemarketing Sales Rule, the Pay-Per-Call Rule and the Equal Credit Opportunity Act. In 1975, Congress gave the FTC the authority to adopt industry-wide trade regulation rules.

The Robinson-Patman Act of 1936

The Robinson-Patman Act (15 USC §13) was passed to supplement the Clayton Act. *The Robinson-Patman Act declares that it is unlawful for any person engaged in commerce or in the course of such commerce, either directly or indirectly, to discriminate in price between different purchasers of commodities of like grade and quality when either or any of the purchasers involved in such discrimination are engaged in interstate commerce, and where the commodities are sold for use, consumption or resale within the United States or any other place within its jurisdiction. This Act forbids price discrimination where the effect of such price discrimination is to substantially reduce competition or to create a monopoly in any line of commerce, or to injure, destroy or prevent competition with any person who either grants or knowingly receives the benefit of such discrimination or with customers of either of them.*

The Robinson-Patman Act is of particular importance to credit professionals. The term price discrimination includes the following types of business practices:

- **A different price charged to different purchasers.** A difference in price can only lawfully occur when the price difference results from differences in the cost of manufacture, sale or delivery resulting from the differing methods or quantities in which such goods are sold.

- **Differences in terms and conditions of sale.** For example, granting one purchaser free freight while charging freight costs to another is discriminatory.

- **Preferential credit terms.** Requiring one dealer to pay COD (cash upon delivery) while granting another dealer credit terms can support a price discrimination claim. Likewise, granting different credit terms to similar customers can be found to be discriminatory pricing. A creditor is entitled, however, to extend different terms to competing purchasers as long as the credit decision is made in a reasonable, nondiscriminatory manner so that the same standards of creditworthiness are applied to all customers who compete with each other.

- **Credit terms are an inseparable part of price according to a 1980 Supreme Court decision.** Anytime credit terms are fixed or adjusted, a price is being fixed. Allowing a customer to pay in 30 days, giving that customer the use of that money for that period of time, is of monetary value. There is a difference between COD and credit terms.

Comprehension Check

What does the **Robinson-Patman Act** specifically forbid?

Antitrust Regulations and Credit

Price-fixing

Perhaps the most serious of antitrust violations in which credit grantors can find themselves engaged is **price-fixing.** In the 1980 case of *Catalano Inc. v. Target Sales,* the United States Supreme Court held that *it is virtually self-evident that extending interest-free credit for a period of time is equivalent to giving a discount equal to the value of the use of the purchase price for that period of time.* The Supreme Court said that the terms of credit are an inseparable part of the price paid for a product. Since price-fixing is automatically illegal under federal antitrust law; the court said that credit-fixing must also be illegal. Therefore, credit terms must be characterized as an inseparable part of the price.

Price Discrimination

For any person to be found liable for **price discrimination,** there is no need for there to be an agreement, combination, association, or conspiracy. In order for a violation to occur, the person accused of price discrimination must have engaged in at least two transactions, crossing state lines and both of these sales must be for use, consumption or resale within the United States.

While the Robinson-Patman Act specifically states that it is unlawful for any person to discriminate in price between different purchasers of commodities of like grade and quality or to knowingly grant or receive a benefit from such discrimination, the case law that has resulted from the statute has broadened the definition of price discrimination and the kinds of transactions that will be included in that definition. The term, price discrimination, now includes the following types of business practices:

A different price charged to different purchasers

The Robinson-Patman Act clearly states that a difference in price can only occur when the price difference results from differentials in the "cost of manufacture, sale, or delivery resulting from the differing methods or quantities in which such" goods are sold. Price changes are allowable when they result from "changing conditions affecting the market for or the marketability of the goods concerned" [15 USC §13(a)].

Differences in terms and conditions of sale

Granting one purchaser free freight while charging freight costs to another purchaser is discriminatory. Charging one price for goods "delivered" to a customer and charging the same price for goods "delivered f.o.b. terminal" has been found to be discriminatory.

Preferential credit terms

Requiring one dealer to pay COD while granting another dealer credit terms can support a price discrimination claim. Likewise, granting different credit terms to similar customers can be found to be discriminatory pricing. Any person is entitled to extend different terms to competing purchasers as long as the credit decision is made in a nondiscriminatory manner so that the same standards of creditworthiness are applied to all customers who compete with each other. For example, history of late payments and financial difficulties are sufficient business justification for denial of credit.

Credit executives are not immune from antitrust responsibilities; it is not only the sales department that can be found culpable for antitrust activity. Through the years of case law, the courts have come to hold one doctrine to be true, time and time again: credit terms equal price.

Permissive Granting of Preferential Credit Terms

Meeting competition is the likeliest defense to a claim of unlawful price discrimination. While there are various criteria that must be met in order for this defense to be properly used, here are some primary ones:

Good Faith. A credit grantor (seller) must prove that it had good reason to believe that it is meeting an equal credit term (or price). The standard is that of a prudent business person responding simply and fairly to what is reasonably believable.

Verifying Competitive Offers. It is common knowledge and readily understood that written verification of a competitive offer by the buyer is not going to be forthcoming. Credit professionals should not contact competitors for this information, but there should be well-documented information on the steps that led to the decision to meet a lower offer or better credit terms. It is recommended that a record containing the following information be created and maintained:

- The date of the competitor's offer.
- The name of the competitor making the offer.
- The name of the customer.
- The terms and conditions of the offer.
- The source of the information.
- A statement as to why the source (e.g., Company X has been a customer for five years and has always been truthful. Therefore, there is no reason not to believe the customer at this time.)

Legitimate Business Reason. A price discrimination claim can also be defeated if the seller can prove there was a cost justification for giving a different price (credit term). The details required to establish this defense will be:

- Differences in the cost of manufacturing, sale or delivery.
- That difference resulted from market conditions (e.g. deterioration of products, seasonal goods, discontinued items).
- Establishing credit for a financially healthy customer while requiring a financially troubled company to pay COD or CIA (cash-in-advance) is legitimate because it is based on the company's credit risk.

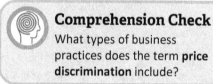

Comprehension Check
What types of business practices does the term **price discrimination** include?

Other Important Antitrust Legislation

Passed in 1974, **The Antitrust Procedures and Penalties Act** increased the penalties for offenses under the Sherman Act, changed consent decree procedures and revised the provisions for appellate review of antitrust cases. **The 1976 Antitrust Act** *grants the federal government new disclosure powers in antitrust litigation.* It also requires companies of a certain size to file pre-merger notices, and it permits a state attorney general to sue for damages on behalf of the state's residents. In addition to the above laws, almost all states have statutes prohibiting monopolies, contracts, conspiracies and combinations in restraint of trade.

Antitrust laws are complex and legal counsel should be consulted when dealing with them. Credit professionals should refer to the full text to ensure a thorough understanding of the Acts.

The Fair Credit Reporting Act

The Fair Credit Reporting Act (FCRA) is Title VI of the Consumer Credit Protection Act and became effective on April 25, 1971. *The purpose of the Act is to require consumer reporting agencies to adopt reasonable procedures that meet the needs of consumer credit, personnel (employment), insurance and other information that is fair and equitable to consumers.* The FCRA guarantees consumers the right to know what credit information credit bureaus and consumer reporting agencies maintain and to receive a specific reason why they, as consumers, were denied credit. The Act was intended to apply only to consumer credit transactions and not to commercial credit transactions.

Amendments to the FCRA were created by the Consumer Credit Reporting Reform Act of 1996, which took effect on October 1, 1997. The amendments to the Fair Credit Reporting Act deal with personal or consumer credit that is defined as "credit for personal, family or household purposes." The extension of business credit, provided that it does not cross over into consumer credit, is not affected by the amendments.

Since the law does not focus on the nature of the proposed or actual credit recipient (individual, partnership or corporation) but rather focuses on the use of credit (personal, family or household purposes), it does not affect credit extended to individuals who may be sole proprietors of businesses or partners in a partnership operating a business. It is important for the credit grantor to be certain that the credit extension is for business purposes. A one or two sentence certification to that effect on a credit application or other written document ensures that the credit grantor is protected. A credit extension is not for personal, family or household purposes if a credit grantor receives a sales tax or other type of tax exemption from the credit recipient.

If a creditor is seeking a credit bureau report containing consumer credit information, then the individual about whom the information is sought should sign a written consent. The law makes it clear that the use of a consumer credit report may not be initiated or requested without the written authorization of the individual involved unless there is a permissible business use specifically defined by the statute. These permissible purposes include the use of the information for the extension and/or review of business credit, employment purposes and the underwriting of insurance involving the consumer.

The law deals with the duties involved in connection with information provided to credit reporting agencies for consumer credit reports and furnished by consumer reporting agencies. As long as the information provided by a credit reporting agency or in connection with an industry group credit exchange is based upon credit for commercial purposes and not for personal, family or household purposes, the statute's regulations do not apply. Because the law only deals with consumer credit that is limited to personal, family or household purposes, there has been no change in the long-standing practice concerning the absence of a requirement to provide information or justification for a business credit decision. This is a complicated area that requires the advice of counsel should a particular issue arise.

Under Section 604(3)(F) of the Fair Credit Reporting Act, the requesting creditor may only request a consumer report if there is a legitimate business need for the information, meaning that the need is:

1. In connection with a business transaction that is initiated by the consumer; or
2. To review an account to determine whether the consumer continues to meet the terms of the account.

Generally, the consumer reporting agency will require the requesting creditor to certify the permissible purpose for which the report is being obtained and must certify that the report will not be used for any other purpose. Should this certification be inaccurate or incomplete, the credit grantor requesting the report can be held liable.

The term, consumer report, is defined in the law to mean any written, oral or other communication of any information by a consumer reporting agency detailing a consumer's creditworthiness, credit standing, credit capacity, character, general reputation, personal characteristics or mode of living that is used or expected to be used or collected in whole or in part for the purpose of serving as a factor in establishing the consumer's eligibility for:

• Credit or insurance to be used primarily for personal, family or household purposes.
• Employment purposes or any other purpose authorized under Section 604.

In general, a consumer reporting agency may not furnish a report unless the consumer has initiated the transaction or has authorized the agency to provide the report or the transaction consists of a firm offer of credit or insurance and other applicable provisions are met:

Comprehension Check
What is the purpose of the
Fair Credit Reporting Act?

- Extension of credit, or review or collection of an account of the consumer; or
- Intends to use the information for employment purposes.

The Equal Credit Opportunity Act and Regulation B

Purpose

The purpose of **The Equal Credit Opportunity Act and Regulation B (ECOA)** *is to promote the availability of credit to all creditworthy applicants without regard to race, color, religion, national origin, sex, marital status or age (provided the applicant has the capacity to contract).* It promotes the availability of credit without regard to the fact that all or part of the applicant's income derives from a public assistance program or to the fact that the applicant has, in good faith, exercised any right under the Consumer Credit Protection Act. The regulation also requires creditors to notify applicants of action taken on their applications and to retain records of credit applications.

The ECOA and Regulation B apply to all credit, commercial as well as personal, without regard to the nature or type of the credit or the creditor. It applies to credit extended to any individual, partnership or corporation for any purpose. It also applies to consumer leases. Each credit application, and all other means of obtaining information from a potential buyer, should also be evaluated to ensure compliance with ECOA requirements.

The wide breadth of the ECOA causes it to affect many businesses that routinely evaluate the creditworthiness of their customers. For this reason, it is important for all businesses involved in selling on credit to have procedures in place and employees trained in those procedures in order to ensure effective compliance with the law. Congress wrote the ECOA in broad language, and it is interpreted by Federal Regulation B in even more expansive terms.

All businesses that deal with any type of credit transaction need to be aware of the Act's provisions and be cognizant of simple steps they can take to avoid liability under the Act. Companies reviewing credit applications of their business customers are not immune from having charges made against them for ECOA violations. Many of these cases involve less visible ECOA provisions, such as its notification requirements. In a recent case brought in an Indiana federal court, the court found a bank liable under the Act for failure to provide a business applicant notice of an adverse action within 30 days.

 Comprehension Check
What is the purpose of the **Equal Credit Opportunity Act?**

The Basic Rules of ECOA and Regulation B

Businesses may not refuse to grant business credit or discourage a business credit applicant from asking for credit based on sex, marital status, religion, etc. The basic rules of ECOA and Regulation B state that a business credit grantor cannot:

- Discriminate against an applicant regarding any aspect of a credit transaction.
- Make any oral or written statement, in advertising or otherwise, to applicants or prospective applicants, that would discourage a reasonable person from making or pursuing an application.
- Inquire whether income stated in an application is derived from alimony, child support, or separate maintenance payments unless the creditor discloses to the applicant that such income need not be revealed if the applicant does not want the creditor to consider it in determining the applicant's creditworthiness.
- Inquire about the sex of an applicant.
- Inquire about birth control practices, intentions concerning the bearing or rearing of children, or capability to bear children.
- Inquire about the race, color, religion or national origin of an applicant.
- Request any information about a spouse of an applicant unless the spouse will be permitted to use the account; the spouse will be contractually liable on the account; the applicant

is relying on the spouse's income as a basis for repayment of the credit requested; the applicant resides in a community property state, or property on which the applicant is relying as a basis for repayment of the credit requested is located in such a state; or the applicant is relying on alimony, child support, or separate maintenance payments from a spouse as a basis for repayment of the credit requested.

- Inquire about the applicant's marital status unless the applicant resides in a community property state, or is relying on property located in such a state as a basis for repayment of the credit requested.

Personal Guarantees

The last two factors listed also come into play on personal guarantees. The ECOA does not permit a credit grantor to require a spouse to sign a personal guarantee if that spouse is not directly involved with the business credit applicant. Care must be taken to make sure that there are policies established for dealing with this, so that there is not an accidental noncompliance.

The law does permit a spouse to sign a personal guarantee, if certain detailed procedures are followed to first verify that the applicant does not have the financial statement or credit wherewithal to support a guarantee. Once the fact is independently established that the applicant does not meet certain creditworthiness criteria, the business credit grantor would have to deny the request or ask for additional financial information to support the request. Should the applicant volunteer the additional guarantee of a spouse, even though that spouse is not directly involved in the business, it is permissible for the spouse to also sign the guarantee. The key is that the business credit grantor may not require a spouse to sign the guarantee; it must be voluntary. This is a very complicated procedure, and competent legal counsel should be consulted in order to establish the appropriate policies and procedures for each company.

Credit applications are not required, but if used, must conform to the requirements of Regulation B.

Notification of ECOA Compliance, Action Taken and Statement of Specific Reasons

For the purposes of notification to consumers, the Federal Reserve Board created a distinction for trade credit to differentiate it from other types of business credit. The Board defines **trade credit** *as limited to a financing arrangement that involves a buyer and a seller such as a supplier who finances the sale of equipment, supplies or inventory; it does not apply to an extension of credit by a bank or other financial institution for the financing of such items.* The Board defines **factoring** *as a purchase of accounts receivable, and therefore factoring is not subject to the Act or the Regulations.* If there is a credit extension incident to the factoring arrangement, then the notification rules and the relevant provisions of the ECOA apply.

The Board created this distinction between trade and business credit in the area of noticing to curb discriminatory practices against women and small businesses seeking **working capital** (*the capital of a business that is used in its day-to-day trading operations, calculated as the current assets minus the current liabilities*) or **venture capital** (*capital invested in a project in which there is a substantial element of risk, typically a new or expanding business*). All business creditors must notify credit applicants that they comply with the Equal Credit Opportunity Act. The easiest way to comply with this requirement is to add the following language to a credit application:

Notice: The Federal Equal Opportunity Act prohibits creditors from discriminating against credit applicants on the basis of race, color, religion, national origin, sex, marital status, age (provided the applicant has the capacity to enter into a binding contract); because all or part of the applicant's income derives from any public assistance program; or because the applicant has, in good faith, exercised any right under the Consumer Credit Protection Act. The federal agency that administers compliance with the law concerning this credit is the Federal Trade Commission, Division of Credit Practices, 6th and Pennsylvania Avenue, NW, Washington, DC 20580.

Noticing Requirements Based on Gross Revenues of the Applicant

The Board establishes two types of business applicants.

1. Those with gross revenues of $1 million or less in their preceding fiscal year.

   A business credit (non-trade) grantor must notify applicant either orally or in writing within 30 days of receiving a completed application concerning the approval of, counter-offer to, or adverse action taken.

   If adverse action taken, within 30 days creditor must provide either statement of specific reasons for the action taken or disclosure of the applicant's right to a statement of the reasons for an adverse action. Notice of disclosure may be given at the time adverse action is taken or at the time the application is submitted provided that the disclosure is in a form the applicant may retain and contains the required ECOA notices.

Sample language of statement of specific reasons for action taken:

Thank you for applying to us for credit. We have given your request careful consideration and regret that we are unable to extend credit to you at this time for the following reasons:

Insert the appropriate reason, such as: value or type of collateral not sufficient, lack of established earnings record, slow or past due in trade or loan payments, etc.

Sample language of disclosure of applicant's right to request specific reasons for credit denial at time of application:

If your application for business credit is denied, you have the right to a written statement of the specific reasons for the denial. To obtain this statement, please contact [name, address and telephone number of the person or office from which the statement of reasons can be obtained] within 30 days from the date of this notification. We will send you a written statement of reasons for the denial within 30 days of receiving your request for the statement.

Insert the appropriate reason, such as: value or type of collateral not sufficient, lack of established earnings record, slow or past due in trade or loan payments, etc.

   For applications made solely by phone, a creditor may give an oral statement of the action taken and of the applicant's right to a statement of reasons for adverse action.

2. Those with gross revenues of more than $1 million in their preceding fiscal year. Small volume creditors are also given special noticing consideration.

   With respect to applications for trade credit, or for business credit, creditor must notify applicant either orally or in writing within a reasonable time of action taken. If applicant makes a written request for the reasons of the adverse action within 60 days, the creditor must give applicant a written statement of the specific reasons for the action and the ECOA notice.

Adverse Action

Four kinds of actions qualify as adverse:

1. A **refusal to grant credit** in substantially the amount or on substantially the terms requested in an application unless the creditor makes a counteroffer (to grant credit in a different amount or on other terms), and the applicant uses or expressly accepts the credit offered.
2. A **refusal to increase the amount of credit** available to an applicant who has made an application for an increase.
3. A **reduction of credit** availability on an existing account.
4. A **termination of an account** or an unfavorable change in the terms of an account that does not affect all or substantially all of a class of the creditor's accounts.

The following are *not* considered adverse actions:

1. A change in the terms of an account expressly agreed to by an applicant.
2. Any action or forbearance relating to an account taken in connection with inactivity, default, or delinquency as to that account.
3. A refusal or failure to authorize an account transaction at point of sale or loan except when the refusal is a termination or an unfavorable change in the terms of an account that does not affect all or substantially all of a class of the creditor's accounts or when the refusal is a denial of an application for an increase in the amount of credit available under the account.
4. A refusal to extend credit because applicable law prohibits the creditor from extending the credit requested.
5. A refusal to extend credit because the creditor does not offer the type of credit or credit plan requested.

> **Comprehension Check**
> The **ECOA** defines the term adverse action. List the four types of action that qualify as adverse under the ECOA.

Keeping Records

Business credit grantors must retain all information used in making a credit decision on an applicant for 12 months after the date on which the business credit grantor notifies the applicant of action taken on an application. However, for business applicants with gross revenues in excess of $1 million in its preceding fiscal year, creditors shall retain records for at least 60 days after notifying a business applicant. If, within that time period, the applicant requests in writing the reasons for adverse action or that the records be retained, the creditor must retain those records for 12 months.

Penalties

A creditor who violates a provision of the ECOA is liable for all actual damages sustained by the applicant either as an individual or as a member of a class. In addition to actual damages, punitive damages are also available. For creditors other than a government or governmental subdivisions or agency, punitive damages are capped at $10,000 for an individual creditor and $500,000 for a class action (or 1% of the net worth of the creditor).

Courts consider several factors when determining whether to award punitive damages and when determining the proper amount of punitive damages for violations of the ECOA. These factors include "the amount of any actual damages awarded, the frequency and persistence of failures of compliance by the creditor, the resources of the creditor, the number of persons adversely affected and the extent to which the creditor's failure of compliance was intentional." Additionally, it is important to note that attorneys' fees and costs are also available to plaintiffs in ECOA actions. In a recent Southern District of Indiana case, a plaintiff was awarded $10,000 in punitive damages and more than $55,000 in attorneys' fees and costs against a defendant creditor who failed to properly comply with the

Act's notice provisions. Therefore, it is important for companies to realize that once fees and costs are included, damages under the ECOA can be quite substantial.

Discrimination Measured by Effects Test

It is important to recognize that discrimination under the ECOA is measured by an "effects test" and is not simply based upon ill or malicious intent. Even if a creditor does not intentionally mean to discriminate, it can be held liable under the Act if the effects of its action result in discrimination toward one of the protected groups. To bring a suit under the ECOA, the plaintiff must:

1. Establish that it is a member of a protected class.
2. Demonstrate that it applied for and was denied credit.
3. Be denied credit.
4. Show that the creditor continued to approve credit applications for applicants with qualifications similar to those of the plaintiff.

Electronic Communication

Any disclosure required by Regulation B to be in writing may be provided by a creditor electronically in a clear and conspicuous manner and in a form the applicant may retain. A creditor must obtain an applicant's affirmative consent to obtain disclosures by electronic communications in accordance with the requirements of the E-Sign Act.

A creditor that uses electronic communication to provide disclosures shall:

- Send the disclosure to the applicant's electronic address; or
- Make the disclosure available at another location such as an Internet web site; and
- Alert the applicant of the availability of the disclosure by sending a notice to the applicant's electronic address (or to a postal address, at the creditor's option). The notice shall identify the account involved and the address of the Internet web site or other location where the disclosure is available; and
- Make the disclosure available for at least 90 days from the date the disclosure first becomes available or from the date of the notice alerting the applicant of the disclosure, whichever comes later.
- When a disclosure provided by electronic communication is returned to a creditor undelivered, the creditor shall take reasonable steps to attempt redelivery using information in its files.

Compliance

Compliance under the ECOA is not difficult, but it does require a review of current procedures to make sure effective procedures are in place. Establishing these now will protect a company in the event of a disgruntled customer down the road. There are five practices companies should adopt to make sure it limits liability under the Act.

1. Ensure that credit applications are worded neutrally, not asking for any prohibited information.
2. The criteria used to determine the creditworthiness of a potential customer must be easily measured and documented. Financial statements and financial references such as the customer's bank or other trade creditors from the buyer should be requested to assist in making a credit decision. Credit reports concerning the potential customer are another reliable source.
3. Establish and maintain a systematic method of complying with the Act's notification requirements. If a company determines that a customer is not creditworthy enough to

buy on credit, notify the potential buyer within the 30 days required under the Act. If the guarantee of an individual is requested, denials of the guarantor should be made timely. Incorporating a statement recording the date when the credit application was received and when notification was given is recommended.

4. Companies should develop a record retention policy that is in compliance with the Act.

5. Companies should educate employees about discrimination and require compliance with its notification and record retention policy.

Dodd-Frank Wall Street Reform and Consumer Protection Act

The Dodd-Frank Wall Street Reform and Consumer Protection Act of 2010 (Dodd-Frank Act) *established the* **Consumer Financial Protection Bureau (CFPB).** While the CFPB's primary mission is related to consumer lending, its oversight applies to commercial lenders and trade creditors in limited instances. For example, the Dodd-Frank Act transferred rulemaking authority under both the ECOA and the Home Mortgage Disclosure Act to the CFPB. This authority gives the CFPB responsibility for preparing fair lending reports to Congress and forcing compliance with law that requires lenders to report accurate data to credit reporting agencies.

There are many instances when a commercial trade credit grantor obtains and uses a consumer credit report in making its decision to extend credit. These instances may include extending credit to a sole proprietor, extending credit to a "mom and pop" business which is an artificial entity (such as a corporation or limited liability company) or accepting a personal guarantee in order to extend credit to a business.

Keep in mind that the ECOA notifications and disclosures to a credit applicant are only applicable when the trade credit grantor makes an adverse credit decision. If credit is granted, these notifications and disclosures are not required. With respect to these notifications and disclosures, the Dodd-Frank Act caused changes to the Fair Credit Reporting Act, which also was originally created to protect consumers. These Dodd-Frank Act changes to the FCRA impact the ECOA.

The ECOA requires disclosure of the principal reasons for denying or taking other adverse action on an application for an extension of credit. The FCRA requires a creditor to disclose when it has based its decision in whole or in part on information from a source other than the applicant or its own files. Disclosing that a credit report was obtained and used in the denial of the application, as the FCRA requires, does not satisfy the ECOA requirement to disclose specific reasons. For example, if the applicant's credit history reveals delinquent credit obligations and the application is denied for that reason, to satisfy the ECOA, the creditor must disclose that the application was denied because of the applicant's delinquent credit obligations. The FCRA also requires a creditor to disclose, as applicable, a credit score it used in taking adverse action along with related information, including the key factors that adversely affected the consumer's credit score. Disclosing the key factors that adversely affected the consumer's credit score does not satisfy the ECOA requirement to disclose specific reasons for denying or taking other adverse action on an application or extension of credit. To satisfy the FCRA requirement, the creditor must also disclose that a credit report was obtained and used in the denial of the application.

Comprehension Check
What is the purpose of the **Dodd-Frank Wall Street Reform Act?**

If a consumer credit report was used by the trade credit grantor in making its credit decision, the following language should be included in the notification to the applicant:

Sample language of notification to applicant when using a consumer credit report

Our credit decision was based in whole or in part on information obtained in a report from the consumer reporting agency listed below. You have a right under the Fair Credit Reporting Act to know the information contained in your credit file at the consumer reporting agency. The reporting agency played no part in our decision and is unable to supply specific reasons why we have denied credit to you. You also have a right to a free copy of your report from the reporting agency if you request it no later than 60 days after you receive this notice. In addition, if you find that any information contained in the report you receive is inaccurate or incomplete, you have the right to dispute the matter with the reporting agency.

Name: _____

Address: _____

[Toll-free] Telephone number: _____

If the trade credit grantor uses a credit score in making the credit decision, the following additional language must be added to its notification:

Sample language of notification to applicant when using a credit score

We also obtained your credit score from this consumer reporting agency and used it in making our credit decision. Your credit score is a number that reflects the information in your credit report. Your credit score can change, depending on how the information in your credit report changes.

Your credit score: _____

Date: _____

Scores range from a low of _____ to a high of _____

Key factors that adversely affected your credit score:

_____

_____

_____

_____

[Number of recent inquiries on credit report]

The Fair Debt Collection Practices Act

The Fair Debt Collection Practices Act, (15 USC §§1692-1692) was passed in 1977 and became effective on March 20, 1978. *Commonly known as FDCPA, the Act was created to make fair laws for the benefit of debtors when a creditor attempts to recover debts.* Ordinarily, the Act only applies to "consumer" debts or those incurred primarily for personal, family or household purposes, even if the debts have been reduced to judgment.

The FDCPA focuses on the collection activities of third-party collectors such as collection agencies and attorneys. Ordinarily, creditors are exempt from the FDCPA if they are collecting their own debts in their own name. A creditor loses this exemption if it uses any name other than its own so as to make it appear that a third party is attempting to collect its debts. Such conduct both violates the Act and renders the creditor liable to the same extent as a third-party debt collector.

Multiple cases have held that a creditor that purchases a debt after it is already in default will be treated as a debt collector under the Act and cannot maintain its creditor exemption. Therefore, companies that purchase portfolios of bad debts must ensure that their employees comply with the FDCPA.

The Federal Trade Commission has taken the position that the FDCPA may set standards for fair trade practices by creditors. The Commission has stated that under Section 5 of the FTC Act it could pursue creditors and collectors of commercial debts for the type of conduct that is prohibited by the FDCPA, even though such businesses are exempt from the FDCPA itself.

In addition to the FDCPA, many state laws restrict the actions of those who collect consumer debts. While there are many variations in the state statutes, both California and Pennsylvania have enacted statutes that apply the bulk of the FDCPA to creditors who are collecting their own debts in their own names. Texas, North Carolina and Florida have fair debt laws that impose substantial restrictions on creditors. Therefore, it is clear that a creditor that deals in retail debts would be wise to implement collection procedures that are consistent with the FDCPA.

Common FDCPA Prohibitions

The following is a partial list of the practices prohibited by the FDCPA:

- Misrepresenting the character or amount of a debt.
- Threatening to take action prohibited by law.
- Threatening to take action that is not intended to be taken.
- Using profane, obscene or abusive language.
- Making repeated calls for the purpose of harassment.
- Reporting a disputed debt to a credit bureau without disclosing that it is disputed.
- Reporting a "stale" debt to a credit bureau.
- Suing or threatening to file suit on a time-barred debt.
- Continuing to collect without first complying with a verification request.
- Communicating improperly with a third party.
- Communicating with a consumer who is known to be represented by an attorney.
- Communicating with a consumer at improper hours or at a time or place known to be inconvenient.
- Filing suit in an improper venue.
- Using any sort of false representations or deceptive means to collect a debt.

Businesses that violate the FDCPA can be sued for any actual damages resulting from the violation, together with statutory damages in the amount of $1,000 per suit and the attorney's fees incurred in prosecuting the suit. The Act also allows for class actions; in such an action suit, the defendant can be held liable for up to $500,000 or 1 percent of its net worth, whichever is less, plus the named plaintiff's individual claim and reasonable attorney's fees and costs incurred in pursuing the class action.

> **Comprehension Check**
> How does the **Fair Debt Collection Practices Act** affect the collection of a debt by a debt collector?

The Truth in Lending Act and Regulation Z

Congress passed **The Truth in Lending Act (TILA) Act** in 1968 with the intention of protecting and educating consumers in the field of purchasing credit. At the time, it was thought that the information given to consumers when purchasing credit was not thorough enough for them to establish whether or not they were receiving a good deal. President Johnson wanted consumers to be able to examine the use of credit in much the same way as they might purchase any other product. This Act and its companion Regulation Z, which comprises the Act's rules and regulations, attempt to give consumers the opportunity and right to shop for credit.

In an effort to protect and educate consumers, *sellers of credit are mandated by law to disclose certain information when offering credit.* Such information allows consumers to know exactly what interest rates, finance charges and fees will apply before accepting such credit. This information provides consumers with the opportunity to shop around and find which rates, terms and conditions are the best for them. While this Act only applies to consumer credit, it is important to remember that many exemptions apply to the Truth in Lending Act and Regulation Z. For example, if a credit purchase is not used primarily for personal consumer use such as business or agricultural, then it may be deemed exempt under this title.

TILA and Regulation Z exempt credit transactions involving extensions of credit primarily for: business; commercial or agricultural purposes; or to government or governmental agencies or instrumentalities; or to organizations. It also exempts:

- Transactions in securities or commodities accounts by broker-dealers registered with the Securities and Exchange Commission;
- Credit transactions, other than those in which a security interest is or will be acquired in real property or in personal property used or expected to be used as the principal dwelling of the consumer, in which the total amount financed exceeds $25,000; and
- Transactions under public utility tariffs, if the Board of Governors determines that a state regulatory body regulates the charges for the public utility services involved, the charges for delayed payment and any discount allowed for early payment.

Lastly, loans made, insured or guaranteed pursuant to a program authorized by Title IV of the Higher Education Act of 1965 are exempt under TILA and Regulation Z.

To protect consumers, the Act states that certain information must be disclosed to the applicant on the credit application: any finance charges that may or will be incurred (Regulation Z is very specific in explaining what charges may be considered finance charges and what charges are not) and the annual percentage rate (APR)—probably the most important disclosure mentioned in the Act. A consumer must know how much the APR is, whether it is paid yearly, quarterly or monthly, and so on. If an attempt is made by the issuer of credit to mask any information pertaining to charges to be incurred in the APR, they stand in clear violation of this Act. Other information that must be disclosed on the credit application is whether the consumer is applying for open-end or closed-end credit and what the differences between the two are.

Many rules must be followed under the title of the Truth in Lending Act and Regulation Z. Rules include the disclosure of particular information on applications for open-end consumer credit plans before a credit card is issued and periodic statements that must be sent to the consumer if an amount is owed at the end of a billing cycle. For closed-end credit disclosures, the disclosure must also be segregated from all other copy pertaining to the credit. If any part thereof is violated, a good chance exists that the **laws of usury,** *which pertain to the ceilings of interest rates,* have been violated as well. Different kinds of credit have different ceiling caps on allowable interest, which is a simple concept that becomes rather complicated very quickly. Although this doesn't directly deal with the Truth in Lending Act and Regulation Z, APR rates do make the two correlate on occasion. Therefore, it is pertinent that legal counsel be consulted when creating any documents that fall under the rules of TILA.

> **Comprehension Check**
> What is the purpose of the **Truth in Lending Act?**

The Fair Credit Billing Act

In 1975, the Truth in Lending Act was amended to create **The Fair Credit Billing Act.** The intention of this law is to take the hassle out of billing errors for consumers. *Creditors are required to correct errors promptly while at the same time preventing the errors from showing up on consumer credit reports.* Since this law was designed for consumer credit, discussion in this chapter is limited. For more information about the Fair Credit Billing Act, please refer to the Federal Reserve Board website and its Consumer Handbook to Credit Protection Laws at www.consumerfinance.gov/creditcards.

E-Sign Act

Electronic signatures and records as well as agreements entered into electronically, such as via email and facsimile, are generally valid and enforceable as long as the sender intended to affix their signature to the document. There are both federal and state statutes in place that provide for the validity of electronic signatures and the enforcement of contracts entered into by electronic communications.

In 2000, Congress passed **The Electronic Signatures in Global and National Commerce Act,** known colloquially as the **"E-Sign Act."** The goal of Congress in enacting the E-Sign Act was to facilitate the continued success of electronic commerce, by making electronic transactions and signatures have the same legal standing as conventional paper ones.

The E-Sign Act set the enforcement of electronic communications in motion and provided a template for laws governing electronic signatures and communications subsequently put in place throughout the country. In Section 7001(a), the E-Sign Act provides:

1. A signature, contract, or other record relating to such transaction may not be denied legal effect, validity, or enforceability solely because it is in electronic form; and
2. A contract relating to such transaction may not be denied legal effect, validity, or enforceability solely because an electronic signature or electronic record was used in its formation.

Comprehension Check
List two provisions of the **E-Sign Act.**

Electronic Signature Defined

In Section 7006(5), the **E-Sign Act** defines **electronic signature** *as an electronic sound, symbol, or process, attached to or logically associated with a contract or other record and executed or adopted by a person with the intent to sign the record.* The various statutes adopted by states around the country include similar definitions.

A basic principle of contract law known as the statute of frauds requires that certain types of contracts be in written form (as opposed to oral), including contracts for the sale of goods involving a minimum price. Various forms of communication, including letters, fax, telex and telegraph are regularly recognized by courts as fulfilling requirements in the Uniform Commercial Code (UCC) or other statutes that a contract be in writing. More recently, courts have added emails to that list and found that electronic signatures on emails and other documents are valid and enforceable as well, regardless of whether the signature is typed or written. Invoices, receipts, purchase orders, requisitions and agreements to purchase that are emailed, scanned, faxed or otherwise electronically transmitted can fulfill the requirement that a certain type of contract be in writing. Typically, courts have not required a written signature, finding that a typed signature is sufficient if the signatory acted with intent to sign.

The Validity of Electronic Communications

A string of emails or a confirmatory email setting forth the necessary contract terms may also constitute a valid and enforceable agreement entered into electronically. For example, the United States District Court for the Southern District of New York found in a case that emails between parties satisfied the signature and confirmation requirements of the statute of frauds because the company's president's typed signature appears at the signatory line of the attached letter and the letter is typed on company letterhead, the writing is sufficient against the sender. The court explained that the statute of frauds aims to guard against fraud and perjury by requiring some proof of contract, and the UCC's sale of goods provision is designed to require some objective guarantee, other than word of mouth, that there really has been some deal. An email suffices as much as a letter, a telegram or a fax to provide such objective indication of an existing agreement.

The validity of electronic communications is also relevant under a principle of contract law known as the merchant's exception, which permits enforceable contracts to emerge from the common commercial practice of entering into oral agreements for the sale of goods that are only later confirmed in writing. Finding that emails are commonly used by merchants and the public alike, the Southern District of New York found that emails can constitute the after-the-fact written confirmation under the merchant exception, and the email need only be sufficient against the sender. In most cases and depending on the applicable UCC or state contract law requirements, the email should include the subject of the contract, the specific terms of the agreement, and the price to be paid for the merchandise or products. In construing emails and electronic communications, courts have emphasized that, under the relevant state and federal statutes, the sender of the electronic communication must have intended to affix their signature.

Although emails between parties can constitute sufficient evidence of an agreement, the court found that an undated and unsigned letter sent attached to an email constituted an unbinding draft, rather than final letter, for a number a reasons. First, later letters were circulated on the issue indicating that the undated letter attached to the email was not the final word on the topic; second, the letter was written on letterhead for one entity over the name of a vice president for another entity, with no explanation of the named person's role in either entity; and third, the letter did not include a written signature but instead included a typed name, title and corporate affiliation in a format that would normally appear under a signature, not in place of one. With all of these reasons, the court found that there was "little or no evidence" that the alleged signatory to the letter intended to be bound.

Electronic Signatures in Commercial Transactions

Recognizing the growing use of electronic signatures in commercial transactions, a variety of applications and computer software programs now provide users with an easy platform to digitally insert signatures and electronically return signed documents, such as by email or facsimile. The best options of these types of platforms are those that warrant that they are fully compliant with the E-Sign Act and other similar statutes, such as DocuSign®. In addition, DocuSign® and a similar product, Adobe® EchoSign®, have created mobile applications for use on mobile applications to allow users to electronically sign and return documents at any moment, without any printing or scanning necessary.

Electronic Signatures and Credit

For the credit professional, an e-signature may eliminate a customer's need to download an application and mail the completed application with a handwritten signature. Some of the relevant provisions of the E-Sign Act are:

- Parties to the contract decide on the form of digital signature technology to validate the contract.
- Businesses may use e-signatures on checks.
- Businesses must require parties to the contract to make at least two clicks of a computer to complete a deal.
- The consumer decides whether to use an e-signature or handwritten signature.
- Cancellation and foreclosure notices must be sent on paper.
- E-signatures on adoptions, wills, and product safety recalls are not allowed.
- Records of e-contracts may be stored electronically.

In sum, electronic signatures are valid and enforceable so long as the signor intended to sign, and the party seeking to enforce the electronically signed agreement is able to reasonably demonstrate the signor's intent.

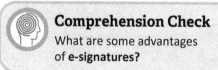

Comprehension Check

What are some advantages of **e-signatures**?

Unclaimed Property Law (Escheatment)

Post-September 11 and the States' Efforts to Find Untapped Revenue

States are incurring enormous financial costs for homeland security as a result of terrorist acts and are therefore looking for untapped revenue sources. The post-September 11 costs to state governments are estimated in the billions. For example, just New York property claims alone associated with the September 11 attacks reached into the billions. Local governments and cities report that municipal revenues have been affected by the September 11 attacks, and many are finding it difficult to meet budgets, in part, because of a decrease in tax collection and an increase in expenses to cover security. In this setting, states are looking for sources of revenue, and abandoned property, as the press reports, may be that untapped source for states. Escheatment revenue is an appealing revenue source from the states' view, as it does not require raising taxes. States are aggressive in their escheat efforts; several private firms are working on behalf of states on a contingency fee basis to locate abandoned property that should have been turned over to the state.

Escheatment Defined

Unclaimed property *is tangible or intangible property owed to a person or entity (the owner), yet held by another (the holder).* Generally speaking, under unclaimed property laws (historically referred to as laws of escheat or unclaimed money laws), a holder of unclaimed property that is not ultimately returned to its owner must report and remit that property to the proper state after a designated period of time, referred to as the dormancy period, which varies depending on the type of property involved. A holder that fails to perform these required duties can incur significant liability for the base unclaimed property amount and applicable interest and penalties.

Businesses and residents abandon over a billion dollars of tangible and intangible property annually. Every state has legislation that requires companies to escheat to the state after some period. California, for example, requires escheatment to the state after three years of abandonment. Escheatment includes all forms of property, both tangible and intangible.

For the credit professional, an account's credit balance may qualify as an abandonment of property. Escheatment laws provide that the state becomes the legal owner of abandoned property, based on the concept of state sovereignty. In looking at escheatment as a revenue source, states are considering those businesses that have failed to escheat.

> **Comprehension Check**
> Define **unclaimed property.**

Development of Escheatment Law

The history and background of unclaimed property goes back to 1066, the year William the Conqueror combined the best of Anglo-Saxon law with Norman law into English common law. In English common law there is the concept of **escheatment,** *which provided for the reversion of lands to the lord or to the crown upon the failure of capable heirs inheriting under the original grant.* The concept of escheat is referred to in the Magna Carta, written in 1215, and is considered to be the first step in a long historical process leading to the rule of constitutional law. Today, all laws are at the state level because the framers of the Constitution did not reserve the concept of escheat to the federal government. Under the reservation clause of the U.S. Constitution, all powers not granted to the federal government devolve to the states.

Uniform Disposition of Unclaimed Property Act

With the growing popularity of state unclaimed property statutes as a new source of state revenue in the 1950s, uniformity of such laws became a necessity, as controversies between states over conflicting claims to property developed. For example, if a corporation abandons credits it has based on a trade relationship with a vendor, several states might attempt to claim custody. The credits could be covered under the law of the state where the company was incorporated, or the state where the corporate headquarters was located. In addition, any state that was doing significant business with the corporation might claim the property.

In 1954, **The Uniform Disposition of Unclaimed Property Act (the Uniform Act)** *was introduced to unify the state statutory scheme of escheatment.* The Uniform Act was amended in 1966 and 1981. The Uniform Act attempts to prevent multiple state claims for property by designating the last known address of the owner as the basic test of jurisdiction. Under the Uniform Act, if two states claim the same property, the law of the state of the last-known address of the owner governs. If property is abandoned, the state must establish its right to the property by proving that the property is located within its territorial limits.

Generally, if the property is considered to have a situs, or the place to which, for purposes of legal jurisdiction or taxation, it is subject to escheat. The Uniform Act establishes a period for a presumption of abandonment for most types of property.

Every U.S. state, District of Columbia, Puerto Rico, the U.S. Virgin Islands and Quebec, British Columbia and Alberta in Canada have unclaimed property programs that actively and continuously find owners of lost and forgotten assets. Delaware receives a significant portion of escheated property, notwithstanding that its population is but 800,000. This is because a large percentage of corporations incorporate in Delaware. Under the escheat laws, a party forwards the abandoned property to the company's state of incorporation when the address of the owner can no longer be located.

Business-to-Business Exemption

While the concept of a business-to-business (B2B) exemption to unclaimed property reporting seems simple on its face, the intricacies of state-specific laws greatly complicate the matter. B2B exemptions can vary from a near complete exemption from reporting any property held in the ordinary course of business to a mere deferral of reporting until an ongoing business relationship ceases to exist. Some states take the position that businesses, unlike individuals, do not need the protections afforded by unclaimed property laws. States with B2B exemptions feel that businesses have the capability to ensure their property interests are secured and that taxpayer dollars should not be exhausted to protect these property interests. States with B2B exemptions choose not to interfere with business relationships and instead allow businesses to settle their contractual rights between each other.

Other states have more holder-friendly B2B exemptions, under which property held in the ordinary course of business is exempt from reporting, notwithstanding a lack of an ongoing business relationship with the owner. While holders are still required to attempt to return the property to the owners through due diligence procedures, any unreturnable property becomes the property of the holder.

Not all of these "ordinary-course-of-business" states provide the same breadth of exempt property under their B2B exemption. States such as Indiana, Iowa, Massachusetts, Michigan, North Carolina, and Wisconsin, only exempt credit balances from unclaimed property reporting, but still require the escheatment of uncashed checks and other types of property acquired in the ordinary course of business. Illinois, Kansas, Maryland, Ohio, and Virginia, on the other hand, have broad exemptions that cover most property held in the ordinary course of business and owned by another business, including credit balances and uncashed checks. These states are seen as the most business friendly with reference to their unclaimed property laws. Populous states are pushing for the location of the company's headquarters as the basis for jurisdiction for escheatment.

Risks of Not Escheating

Most states require businesses to review their records to determine whether any property has been unclaimed for the dormancy period and to make an annual report, especially post-September 11. State escheat statutes have harsh provisions for parties that fail to timely report or turn over unclaimed property. In addition to interest that runs from the period that the property should have been turned over, a state may assess fines, penalties and damages.

Escheatment Audit

A state generally enforces its escheatment law through an audit. Audits are generally handled by the state treasurer's office or controller. The scope of the audit can go back several years. The auditors typically request the following:

- Chart of accounts;
- General ledger/trial balance;
- Annual report;
- Journal entries;
- Bank reconciliations; and
- Accounting policies.

Steps to Protect Against Escheatment Claims

A credit executive should develop a game plan, and consider the following:

Step One: Determine the Situation
- Review past compliance. Has the company ever reported unclaimed property? If so, what, when and where?
- Has the company ever been subject to an escheatment audit? If so, what were the results?
- Are there any subsidiaries to be included? Has the company made any recent acquisitions that should be included?

Step Two: Determine Eligible Property
Does the vendor's company have some of the property types covered by most states? For the credit professional, these include:

- Vendor checks.
- Payroll checks.
- Customer credits.
- Refunds.

What states are represented among the names and addresses to be reported? If this is an initial filing, what about years that may not be on the books?

Step Three: Perform the Due Diligence
What due diligence is required by state? It is important to focus on:

- The minimum dollar amount,
- Timing, method, and
- Content notice.

What about operational due diligence? This might include developing a strategy to minimize unclaimed property liability and reviewing potentially reportable items. A due diligence letter should be prepared and include:

- Response deadline.
- Identification number and amount.
- Property type/reason.
- Instructions for claiming.

Step Four: Prepare Reports and Remittances

- Identify due dates for states.
- Prepare a cover sheet with signature.
- Use the proper media, paper, disk, etc.
- Use the proper report format.
- Include the remittance, which might be a check, wire transfer, etc.

Step Five: Filing Reports and Remittances

- File on time to avoid penalties and interest.
- If an extension is received, get it in writing. Only some states will grant them.

Step Six: Follow up and Reconcilement

- Reconcile general ledger to detail.
- Reconcile paid items to appropriate accounts/divisions.
- File any necessary holder reimbursement claims with the states.
- Establish a filing system for reports and work papers.

Credit professionals can also look to the following web site for guidance: National Association of Unclaimed Property Administrators: www.unclaimed.org.

Comprehension Check

If a holder determines it has unclaimed property, what due diligence is required?

Turning Over the Property

If the vendor's company decides to turn over the property to the state, most state statutes provide that the vendor should turn the property over to the state controller. Most legislation requires the vendor to make reasonable efforts to notify the owner of the property by mail that the owner's property will escheat to the state. The notice should be mailed not less than six months before the property is to be turned over to the state controller.

Depending upon the nature, all unclaimed property should either be delivered to the State Treasurer or Controller. When the unclaimed property is cash, delivery is made to the State Treasury; all other types of personal property go to the Controller. The party delivering the property is relieved and held harmless by the state from all claims regarding the property. No action or lawsuit may be maintained against the holder of the property.

Prior to delivery, the holder must furnish notice to the Controller. At a minimum, the notice must include the amount of cash, or nature or description of other personal property; the name and last known address of the person entitled to the property; and reference to a specific statutory provision under which the property is being transmitted.

Comprehension Check

Why is it important to properly report and remit unclaimed property?

POINTS TO CONSIDER

States require all unclaimed/abandoned amounts to be reported, regardless of dollar amount. It is these small amounts that have the greatest likelihood of going unclaimed. Unless a company can refute the presumption of abandonment by documenting that the credit resulted from internal arithmetic errors in invoicing, posting payments and issuing credits, the states can and will make a claim for these credit balances. These items will be used as a basis for creating a statistical sampling, which will likely be extrapolated back over several years.

Most of the states have a due diligence requirement for items over $50. In other words, letters should be sent for all amounts over $50. States (especially Delaware) expect to see a "positive confirmation" from the owner/customer stating that the credit is not due before the amount is considered not to be unclaimed. In the absence of a positive confirmation, the states can make a claim for these credit balances written off.

Some states require the letter to specify the amount outstanding, versus only the account number.

Sarbanes-Oxley Act of 2002

With so many cases of fraud-ridden bankruptcies brought into public view in the beginning of this century, Congress found it necessary to enact **The Sarbanes-Oxley Act of 2002 (SOX).** There is no doubt that the Enron and WorldCom bankruptcies had the most influence in the ultimate passage of this Act: *The SOX was created and enacted to protect investors by improving the accuracy and reliability of corporate disclosures made pursuant to the securities laws and for other purposes.* The sweeping reforms in the Sarbanes-Oxley Act address nearly every aspect and actor in our nation's capital markets.

SOX affects every reporting company, both domestic and foreign, as well as their officers and directors. The Act also affects those that play a role in ensuring the integrity of U.S. capital markets, such as accounting firms, research analysts and attorneys. The over-arching goals of the Act are far-reaching and include restoring investor confidence and assuring the integrity of United States. Within these goals, the principal objectives addressed in the Act can be grouped into the following themes:

- To strengthen and restore confidence in the accounting profession;
- To strengthen enforcement of the federal securities laws;
- To improve the "tone at the top" and executive responsibility;
- To improve disclosure and financial reporting; and
- To improve the performance of "gatekeepers."

The Act comprises 11 titles; what follows is a very broad discussion of this Act and how it pertains to credit. NACM's *Manual of Credit & Commercial Laws* contains a more in-depth presentation of the Act. The 11 titles are:

Title I: Public Company Accounting Oversight Board which provides for the establishment of a Public Company Accounting Oversight Board (the "Board"). As the watchdog for public companies, its intended result is informative, accurate and independent audit reports.

Title II: Auditor Independence prohibits any registered public accounting firm (and any person associated with that firm) to provide any non-audit related services.

Title III: Corporate Responsibility places the burden for proper audit procedures and financial reporting squarely on the shoulders of the principal executive officer or officers and the principal financial officer or officers or other persons performing the duties normally performed by such officers.

The Section 302 Certification can be broken down into three distinct parts:

1. Accuracy and fair presentation of the report's disclosure,
2. Establishment and maintenance of disclosure controls and procedures, and
3. Reporting of deficiencies in, and changes to, internal accounting controls.

A CEO and CFO must certify in any quarterly or annual report, including amendments to such reports that:

- They have reviewed the report;
- Based on their knowledge, the report does not contain any untrue statement of fact or omit a material fact to make the statements not misleading with respect to the period covered by the report; and
- Based on their knowledge, the financial statements, and other financial information included in the report (including, financial statements, footnotes to the financial statements, selected financial data, management's discussion and analysis of operations and financial condition and other financial information in the report), fairly present, in all material respects, the financial condition, results of operations and cash flows of the company as of, and for, the periods presented in the report.

Title IV: Enhanced Financial Disclosures requires financial reports to be prepared in accordance with generally accepted accounting principles (GAAP). This section addresses Management Assessment of Internal Controls.

Title V: Analyst Conflicts of Interest is an amendment to the Securities Exchange Act of 1934 requiring any stock or securities analyst, broker or dealer who has participated or is to participate in a public offering of securities disclose any conflict of interest that is known or should have been known at the time of any public appearance of its report.

Title VI: Commission Resources and Authority authorizes the Commission to carry out its duties and responsibilities.

Title VII: Studies and Reports directs the Comptroller General of the United States to identify factors that have led to the consolidation of public accounting firms since 1989 and the impact, present and future, of such consolidations on capital formation and securities markets.

Title VIII: Corporate and Criminal Fraud Accountability governs the criminal penalties for the destruction, alteration or falsification of records in federal investigations and bankruptcy. Section 806 of this Title is commonly known as the "whistle blower" section.

Title IX: White-Collar Crime Penalty Enhancements provides for penalties for attempts or conspiracy to commit fraud, mail fraud, wire fraud and violations of the Employment Retirement Income Security Act (ERISA) of 1974. Title IX can affect the credit department since the credit manager must certify the accuracy of the accounts receivable asset. This asset is reflected on the balance sheet and all financial reports certified by top management of the company. Failure to accurately certify this asset can result in penalties, fines and possibly imprisonment.

Title X: Corporate Tax Returns states that the corporate tax return should be signed by the chief executive officer of said corporation.

Title XI: Corporate Fraud Accountability establishes fines, penalties and imprisonment for destroying or altering records or impairs, or attempts to alter or impair, the integrity or availability of documents or records for use in official proceedings.

While SOX has received praise for increasing investor confidence in financial statements, SOX-related tasks have also resulted in internal control requirements that have filtered down to credit managers.

To ensure that financial statements are reliable, Section 404 of SOX mandates that rules for establishing responsibility be developed. Section 404 mandates that companies evaluate the effectiveness of their internal controls by having their certifying officers consider two basic questions:

1.   Do the employees of the company understand what they need to do to properly prepare external financial reports?
2.   What information do the company officers need to make sure their employees have complied?

Three steps can help address these two questions:

Step 1: Identify financial reporting risks and the controls that address them.

Step 2: Ensure that the controls work in practice.

Step 3: Report the conclusions on overall effectiveness and deficiencies.

Credit managers may be asked to sign off on documentation about accounts receivable and credit risk.

Auditors require that there should not be any misstatement of material facts. Credit managers should not let slip by anything that does not seem to be right about the way in which credit and receivables are being reported. SOX affords protections to someone willing to report wrongdoing. Record keeping is an important safeguard to support SOX enforcement. Important documentation to retain include credit applications, loan documents, analyses, financial data and copies of communications such as memoranda, letters and emails.

The SEC recommends that documents be retained for seven years. Its website (www.sec.gov/spotlight/sarbanes-oxley.htm) furnishes pertinent details concerning SOX.

Comprehension Check
Why did Congress enact the
Sarbanes-Oxley Act of 2002?

Red Flags

Identity theft and the protection of customer information has become an increasingly vital issue for businesses in recent years. The U.S. government has acted swiftly in the face of massive private information heists perpetrated by hackers that have put millions of customers' proprietary information at risk and have severely damaged the reputations of corporations.

In November 2007, a number of regulations that required financial institutions and creditors to develop and implement identity theft programs under the Fair and Accurate Credit Transactions Act (FACTA) were adopted by several federal agencies. In 2008, Sections 114 and 315 of FACT Act, referred to as the Red Flags Rule, went into effect.

Before presenting a discussion of the Red Flags Rule, it is important to note that the Federal Trade Commission (FTC) offered guidance on the extent to which the Red Flags Rule applies to business-to-business transactions involving trade creditors.

The process of determining whether or not a trade creditor has to comply with the Rule requires two steps: a trade creditor must determine whether or not it falls into the definition of being a creditor and second, if it is a creditor, it must then determine whether it has covered accounts that are subject to reasonably foreseeable risk of identity theft.

The Red Flag Program Clarification Act of 2010 limits the applicability of the Red Flags Rule to a creditor, as defined in the Equal Credit Opportunity Act (ECOA), that regularly and in the ordinary course of business:

1. Obtains or uses consumer reports in connection with a credit transaction;
2. Furnishes information to consumer reporting agencies in connection with a credit transaction; or
3. Advances funds to or on behalf of a person based on that person's obligation to repay the funds or repayable from specific property pledged by or on behalf of that person.

The term, advances funds, refers to money, rather than goods or services, narrowing this remaining category of creditor only to entities making loans. If a trade creditor does not meet the definition of creditor because, for example, it only deals with established corporate entities and does not rely on personal consumer credit reports or furnish information to consumer reporting agencies or make loans, then the Rule does not apply.

A trade creditor that does not fall into any one of these categories does not meet the definition of a creditor under the Red Flags Rule. Should a trade creditor regularly obtain and rely on an individual credit report in making credit decisions, whether the report is on the principal of a small business or a personal guarantor or a non-corporate entity like a mom-and-pop store or sole proprietorship, then the trade creditor is subject to the "Red Flags" Rule, meaning that, if it has covered accounts based on an analysis of its risk level, it must create its own written program for fighting identity theft.

Ultimately, if a company sells on a purely business-to-business basis, and does not fall into any of the defined categories of creditor, then it does not have to comply with the Red Flags Rule.

The Red Flags Regulations and Guidelines require most creditors and financial institutions to adopt a written program to detect, prevent and mitigate identity theft in connection with the new opening of a covered account or any existing covered account. Every creditor and financial institution covered by the rule must adopt a risk-based program that identifies red flags relevant to its own operation and, more importantly, how it will respond to them. The responsibility for rulemaking and enforcement was transferred to the U.S. Securities and Exchange Commission and the U.S. Commodity Futures Trading Commission.

Part I: Risk Assessment to Identify Relevant Red Flags

Red Flags *are any pattern, practice or specific activity that indicates the possible risk of identity theft; companies need to identify the Red Flags specific to it by identifying the types of accounts offered or maintained.* An important key to the Red Flags program is for every company to examine the methods by which it permits accounts to be opened along with its previous experience with identity theft.

Are documents, such as state- or government-issued forms of identification, presented during transactions? If so, what steps are taken to check for document alterations or forgeries? How is consistency in presented documents checked; does the person presenting match the documents? Is there a foreseeable risk of identity theft in connection with business accounts that may be opened or accessed remotely, through methods not requiring face-to-face contact such as the Internet or over the phone? How is a change of address monitored? For example, what if an increased line of credit is requested, or additional authorized account users are requested, immediately following a change of address notice? How is the identity of the purchaser verified on orders received via purchase order?

More and more, business is being done electronically, with companies offering access to accounts via the Internet or over the telephone. The Federal Bureau of Investigation's Cyber Division recently announced that crimes against U.S. businesses are increasing and that cyber criminals are becoming more brazen and effective at stealing financial information and perpetrating identity theft crimes.

The case of WESCO Distribution, discussed in the Fraud Chapter, highlights weaknesses in the trade credit industry. Criminals have posed as executives of various major corporations to pilfer hundreds of thousands of dollars of merchandise from unsuspecting companies by preying on salespeople eager to make or exceed sales targets. WESCO's Asset Protection Manager William Coe developed his own set of "red flags" that were distributed regularly to sales team members to prevent needless losses.

Coe understood that WESCO's identity was being used to defraud others and realized it was only a matter of time before criminals posing as another company would try and victimize WESCO. It wasn't long before WESCO staff caught fraudulent purchase orders being sent to them from individuals posing as major companies and customers of the distributor.

WESCO uses the following set of "red flags" when considering purchase orders or applications:

- The sender's email uses a generic service rather than a company name.
- Large quantities of the same item are ordered.
- The shipping address given differs from the company's address or is a new location for the customer.
- The language used in the emails is flawed, consistently misspelled and reads like it's from a foreign translation.
- Multiple credit cards are used for the purchase.
- The purchaser attempts to get net 30 terms.
- An alternative shipping method, faster than typical, is requested such as overnight air or rush pick-up.
- Multiple rush orders are received from the same company in a short period of time.

These factors are strikingly similar to several of the Red Flags identified by the FTC and provide a great starting point for all trade creditors in their efforts to prevent fraud. For example, in the case of fraudulent purchase orders sent to companies under the guise of WESCO, the purchase orders displayed a residential address not affiliated with the company and the phone numbers listed were incorrect or disconnected. Unfortunately, the salespeople and credit managers involved didn't further investigate the suspicious information. They rushed the shipments out the door and thousands upon thousands of dollars in merchandise were lost. WESCO ultimately had to send out alerts to all of the companies with which it does business about the theft of WESCO's identity and stated that if any company has the slightest bit of doubt about a purchase order received from WESCO, to please contact them.

Rush orders from new accounts may merit further checking. Many fraudulently placed rush orders are made citing holiday or seasonable demand. Generally speaking, sales teams have to work to solicit new business; when it happens the other way around and orders arrive too easily, it's a Red Flag that merits further investigation and verification.

Small initial orders from new customers, or from older customers under new management, may also be Red Flags. Most credit professionals would not consider approving a substantial order from a new customer without verifying its credit history and references; and yet, on small orders, overworked and understaffed credit departments may only conduct a cursory check on a new customer placing a small order. Conversely, large orders are often a Red Flag. It is a best practice in the commercial credit arena to check on why a large order is merited or needed.

Another Red Flag could be an answering service that offers to have a reference call back or, worse, a reference that provides an immediate, glowing report on an applicant—without ever having to look up records. An unusually large number of inquiries from other suppliers regarding a new account may be a Red Flag, signaling that the debtor is placing an extraordinary amount of orders.

If a company conducts counter sales, both corporate and personal checks may be a source for detecting Red Flags. As part of its check guarantee program, NACM Business Partner United Tranzactions (UTA) requires that company names be imprinted on corporate checks (no temporary checks) in addition to an address. While post office box numbers may appear on the check, a physical address must be requested and noted on all corporate checks. UTA also requires that a telephone number be recorded on the check, if it is not imprinted, in order for a check to be eligible for its check guarantee program. When inspecting personal checks, UTA requires the check writer's name to be imprinted on the check (no temporary checks), that a physical address be recorded on the face of the check in handwriting if only a post office box address is imprinted, and that a home telephone number be recorded. Identification is required and the signature must match the pre-printed name on the check.

Part II: Detecting Red Flags

Once the Red Flags that are relevant to a business are identified, policies and procedures must be established to detect them in day-to-day operations. For example, a Red Flag may be spotted when an order originating with the sender using a generic email account or when a new "ship to" address is verified. Red Flags can be indentified during a risk assessment when customers are authenticated, transactions are monitored or requests for address changes are verified. A description of what a company will do when a Red Flag is spotted should be included in a company's program. Some Red Flags may seem harmless on their own, but they can signal identity theft when paired with other events, such as a change of address coupled with the use of an address associated with fraudulent accounts.

Part III: Respond Appropriately to Any Red Flags Detected to Prevent and Mitigate Identity Theft

A written program policy provides for appropriate responses to the detected Red Flags to mitigate identity theft of a person or a company. Companies should consider factors that may heighten the risk of identity theft, such as a data security breach that resulted in unauthorized access to a customer's account records.

Once fraudulent activity is detected, credit department personnel must act quickly to protect customers and the company itself from loss and damage. Document the facts and findings supporting the conclusion that the transaction is fraudulent or authentic. As always, the proper protocol must be followed in presenting a written summary of the situation to management.

Part IV: Update the Written Program Periodically to Reflect Changes in Risks to Customers or to Business from Identity Theft

No matter how good a program looks on paper, the true test will lie in how well it works. It should include a description of how it will be administered covering topics such as how company management will maintain the program and keep it current on an ongoing basis. How a company will train staff to recognize the Red Flags and follow through with appropriate actions based on its program is described in this part. The program will also need to describe how a company will oversee service providers to ensure that their actions comply with these Red Flags Regulations and its Red Flags program. It is critically important to review and update a written Red Flags program to reflect changes in risks to customers or to the company from identity theft.

Should a company begin to experience higher incidences of fraud, it may be appropriate to change its methods of verifying the identity of customers. If new types of accounts are offered, the program will need to be updated accordingly. Any changes in a business such as a merger, acquisition, joint venture or changes in service provider arrangements need a program review.

Part V: Oversight of This Program

The FTC mandates that there be oversight of a company's Red Flags program by their board of directors, a committee of the board of directors or designated senior management. The oversight includes the assignment of the specific responsibility for the program's implementation, including the review of reports prepared by staff regarding compliance, and the approval of material changes to the program as necessary to address changing identity theft risks.

Companies will need to issue an annual report which discusses the effectiveness of its program and procedures, significant incidents involving identity theft and management's response and recommendations for changes to the program. Management is responsible for ensuring that any deficiencies raised within the annual report are addressed.

Penalties for Failure to Comply with the Red Flags Regulations

Many financial institutions covered by the Red Flags Regulations are subject to oversight by the appropriate federal banking regulators, which may impose penalties consistent with their regulatory authority.

Creditors who fall under these rules are regulated by the FTC. In the event of a known violation, which constitutes a pattern or practice of violations, the FTC may commence a civil action to recover a civil penalty in a federal district court. Penalties imposed by the FTC for violations of FACTA (Fair and Accurate Credit Transaction Act of 2003) may not exceed $3,500 per infraction.

In addition to regulatory enforcement actions, users of consumer reports who fail to comply with the address discrepancy regulations are subject to civil liability under §§ 616 and 617 of the Fair Credit Reporting Act.

 Comprehension Check
What is the **Red Rlags rule?**

Figure 6-1   Sample Policy for Red Flag Rules

Please note that the following sample policy suggests likely situations that may indicate possible identity theft fraud. Each company must conduct its own risk assessment and customize how it will respond as Red Flags are discovered.

[Insert Company Name] Identity Theft (Red Flags) Program

PROGRAM INTRODUCTION

This **RED FLAGS** program is designed to provide protocols and guidelines for the detection, prevention and mitigation of identity theft in connection with the opening of a covered account or any existing covered account. In preparing this program, [company name] has striven to identify patterns, practices and specific forms of activities, or Red Flags, that could indicate the possible existence of identity theft. This program better positions [company name] to stop identity theft at its inception. This program also serves as a testament to [company name]'s compliance with the FTC's Red Flags Regulations.

This program incorporates existing policies, procedures and other arrangements that control reasonably foreseeable risks to [company name]'s customers or reasonably foreseeable risks to the safety and soundness of [company name] from identity theft.

Throughout this policy, the term "covered account" means an account that [company name] offers or maintains—primarily for personal, family or household purposes—or that involves or is designed to permit multiple payments or transactions. A "covered account" is any other account that [company name] offers or maintains for which there is a foreseeable risk to customers or to the safety and soundness of [company name] from identity theft, including financial, operational, compliance, reputation or litigation risks.

The term "identity theft" means a fraud committed or attempted using the identifying information of another person without authority.

"Identifying information" means any name or number that may be used alone or in conjunction with any other information to identify a specific person, including any:

1. Name, Social Security number, date of birth, official state- or government-issued driver's license or identification number, alien registration number, government passport number, or employer or taxpayer identification number;
2. Unique biometric data, such as fingerprint, voiceprint, retina or iris image, or other unique physical representation;
3. Unique electronic identification number, address or routing code; or
4. Telecommunication identifying information or access device (as defined in 18 U.S.C. 1029(e)).

SECTION I: RISK ASSESSMENT/IDENTIFYING RELEVANT RED FLAGS

(Please note that these possible risk factors are merely suggestions; your company will need to identify its Red Flags based on its business, its customers, etc.)

[Insert company name] has considered the following factors in identifying relevant Red Flags for covered accounts:

Customize the possible risk factors listing:

1. The types of covered accounts your company offers or maintains
2. The methods your company provides to open its covered accounts (written application, verbal/over the phone, verbal/physical call by sales, online/Internet). Effective security management requires your company to deter, detect and defend against security breaches. That means taking reasonable steps to prevent attacks,

Figure 6-1   Sample Policy for Red Flag Rules continued

quickly diagnosing a security incident and having a plan in place for responding effectively.

3. The methods your company provides to access its covered accounts and

4. Your company's previous experiences with identity theft.

Customize the types of things that are Red Flags signaling the possibility of corporate identity theft:

1. The sender's email uses a generic service rather than a company name when placing an order

2. Large quantities of the same item are ordered; an unusual increase in the volume ordered by an existing customer

3. The shipping address given differs from the company's address or is a new location for the customer

4. Personal or common carrier pick-up of the goods ordered

5. An alternative shipping method, faster than typical mail, is requested such as Overnight Air

6. The language used in the emails is flawed, consistently misspelled and reads like it's from a foreign translation

7. Multiple credit cards are used for the purchase

8. The purchaser attempts to get net 30 terms

9. Multiple rush orders are received from the same company in a short period of time

10. The credit references are provided verbally and only telephone numbers for the references are provided (no physical address information)

11. The phone number of the credit reference can't be verified

12. The name of the business placing the order is confusingly similar to another well-known, successful business

13. Inability to reach the principals of the business

14. The order is placed by a business that had a recent change in ownership; the ownership change was not well-communicated or was downplayed

Customize notifications or warnings from a consumer reporting agency that constitute Red Flags:

1. A fraud or active duty alert is included with a consumer report.

2. A consumer reporting agency provides a notice of credit freeze in response to a request for a consumer report.

3. A consumer reporting agency provides a notice of address discrepancy.

4. A consumer report indicates a pattern of activity that is inconsistent with the history and usual pattern of activity of an applicant or customer such as:

   A. A recent and significant increase in the volume of inquiries

   B. An unusual number of recently established credit relationships

   C. A material change in the use of credit, especially with respect to recently established credit relationships

   D. An account that was closed for cause or identified for abuse of account privileges by a financial institution or creditor.

Figure 6-1   Sample Policy for Red Flag Rules continued

Customize suspicious documents presented to your company that are Red Flags:

1. Documents provided for identification appear to have been altered or forged.
2. The photograph or physical description on the identification is not consistent with the appearance of the applicant or customer presenting the information.
3. Other information on the identification is not consistent with readily accessible information that is on file with your company, such as a signature card or a recent check.
4. An application appears to have been altered or forged, or gives the appearance of having been destroyed or reassembled.

Customize suspicious personal identifying information:

1. Personal identifying information provided is inconsistent when compared against external information sources used by the financial institution or creditor. For example:
   A. The address does not match any address in the consumer report; or
   B. The social security number (SSN) has not been issued or is listed on the Social Security Administration's Death Master File.
2. Personal identifying information provided by the customer is not consistent with other personal identifying information provided by the customer. For example, there is a lack of correlation between the SSN range and date of birth.
3. Personal identifying information provided is associated with known fraudulent activity as indicated by internal or third-party sources used by the financial institution or creditor. For example:
   A. The address on an application is the same as the address provided on a fraudulent application;
   B. The phone number on an application is the same as the number provided on a fraudulent application.
4. Personal identifying information provided is of a type commonly associated with fraudulent activity as indicated by internal or third-party sources used by your company. For example:
   A. The address on an application is fictitious, a mail drop, or a prison; or
   B. The phone number is invalid, or is associated with a pager or answering service.
5. The SSN provided is the same as that submitted by other persons opening an account or other customers.
6. The address or telephone number provided is the same as or similar to the account number or telephone number submitted by an unusually large number of other persons opening accounts or other customers.
7. The person opening the covered account or the customer fails to provide all required personal identifying information on an application or in response to notification that the application is incomplete.
8. Personal identifying information provided is not consistent with personal identifying information that is on file with your company.

Figure 6-1   Sample Policy for Red Flag Rules continued

Customize the unusual use of, or suspicious activity related to, your company's covered accounts:

1. Shortly following the notice of a change of address for a covered account, the institution or creditor receives a request for a new, additional, or replacement card or a cell phone, for the addition of authorized users on the account.

2. A new revolving credit account is used in a manner commonly associated with known patterns of frauds. For example:

   A. The majority of available credit is used for cash advances or merchandise that is easily convertible to cash (electronics equipment or jewelry)

   B. The customer fails to make the first payment or makes an initial payment but no subsequent payments

3. A covered account is used in a manner that is not consistent with established patterns of activity on the account. There is, for example:

   A. Nonpayment where there is no history of late or missed payments;

   B. A material increase in the use of available credit;

   C. A material change in purchasing or spending patterns;

   D. A material change in electronic funds transfer patterns in connection with a deposit account;

   E. A material change in telephone call patterns in connection with a cellular phone account.

4. A covered account that has been inactive for a reasonably lengthy period of time is used, taking into consideration the type of account, the expected pattern of usage and other relevant factors.

5. The credit report reveals that all accounts are newly/recently opened and provides little or no historical credit information or payment trends.

6. Mail sent to the customer is returned repeatedly as undeliverable although transactions continue to be conducted in connection with the customer's covered account.

7. Your company is notified by the customer that he/she is not receiving paper account statements.

8. Your company is notified of unauthorized charges or transactions in connection with a customer's covered account.

9. Your company is notified by the customer, a victim of identity theft, a law enforcement authority, or any other person that it has opened a fraudulent account for a person engaged in identity theft.

Additional Options to Include in Your Company's Program

Your company's commitment to securing sensitive customer information:

1. Safeguarding sensitive data in your files and on your computers is just plain good business. After all, if that information falls into the wrong hands, it can lead to fraud or identity theft. A sound data security plan is built on five key principles:

   A. Know what personal information you have in your files and on your computers.

   B. State your company's policy on document retention.

   C. How is sensitive information protected while in the care of employees?

Figure 6-1   Sample Policy for Red Flag Rules continued

    D. How is sensitive information properly disposed of?

    E. Should there be a breach to sensitive data, state your company's response plan.

2. Does your company have a records retention manager to supervise the disposal of records containing customer information? If you hire an outside disposal company, conduct due diligence beforehand by checking references or requiring that the company be certified by a recognized industry group.

3. Discuss how information is disposed of; documents containing sensitive information should be burned, pulverized, or shredded so that the information cannot be read or reconstructed.

4. Discuss how computers, disks, CDs, magnetic tapes, hard drives, laptops, PDAs, cell phones, or any other electronic media or hardware containing customer information are destroyed, discarded or erased.

SECTION II: DETECTING THE RED FLAGS

For each instance identified in Section I, explain how your company will take action.

For example, since your company has identified that when an order is received by email and the sender used a generic service rather than a company-issued email account, credit department staff will verify the order by contacting the company through known contacts or will research contact information independently and research the order.

Since your company has identified that the shipping address supplied for an order differs from the company's address or is a new location for the customer, the credit department staff will verify the order by contacting the company through known contacts to verify the order.

SECTION III: RESPOND APPROPRIATELY TO ANY RED FLAGS DETECTED TO PREVENT AND MITIGATE IDENTITY THEFT

If fraudulent activity is detected, [insert company name] will act quickly to protect customers from loss and damage. Our employees will document the facts and findings in writing, supporting their conclusion that the transaction is fraudulent or authentic. The report will be presented to [insert who is to receive the report].

Customize the appropriate responses your company will make:

1. Monitoring a covered account for evidence of identity theft
2. Contacting the customer
3. Changing any passwords or security codes that permit access to a covered account
4. Reopen a covered account with a new account number
5. Not opening the account
6. Closing the account
7. Not attempting to collect on a covered account or not turning a covered account over to a third party collection agency
8. Notifying law enforcement
9. Determining that no response is warranted under the particular circumstances

Figure 6-1   Sample Policy for Red Flag Rules continued

SECTION IV: PERIODIC REVIEW OF THE WRITTEN POLICY TO REFLECT CHANGES IN RISKS TO CUSTOMERS OR TO BUSINESS FROM IDENTITY THEFT

[Insert company name] will update this policy [insert frequency (annually, semi-annually, quarterly)] to reflect changes in risks to customers or to [insert company name]'s safety and soundness from identity theft based on factors such as:

Customize the factors relevant to your company:

1. The experiences of your company with identity theft
2. Changes in methods of identity theft
3. Changes in methods to detect, prevent and mitigate identity theft
4. Changes in the types of accounts that your company offers or maintains
5. Changes in the business arrangements of your company, including mergers, acquisitions, alliances, joint ventures and service provider arrangements.

SECTION V: OVERSIGHT OF THIS PROGRAM

Oversight of this program will be the responsibility of [insert appropriate management official, committee, Board of Directors], which includes the responsibility and accountability for the program's implementation and the review of reports prepared by staff regarding compliance with this program.

An annual report discussing the effectiveness of the program and procedures, significant incidents involving identity theft and management's response and recommendations for changes to the program will be issued by [insert date].

Key Terms and Concepts

Comprehension Check

1. What is the purpose of **U.S. antitrust law?**
2. What is the **Sherman Act** designed to prevent?
3. What does the **Robinson-Patman Act** specifically forbid?
4. What types of business practices does the term **price discrimination** include?
5. What is the purpose of the **Fair Credit Reporting Act?**
6. What is the purpose of the **Equal Credit Opportunity Act?**
7. The ECOA defines the term **adverse action.** List the four types of action that qualify as adverse under the ECOA.
8. What is the purpose of the **Dodd-Frank Wall Street Reform Act?**
9. How does the **Fair Debt Collection Practices Act** affect the collection of a debt by a debt collector?
10. What is the purpose of the **Truth in Lending Act?**
11. List two provisions of the **E-Sign Act.**
12. What are some advantages of **e-signatures?**
13. Define **unclaimed property.**
14. If a holder determines it has unclaimed property, what due diligence is required?
15. Why is it important to properly report and remit unclaimed property?
16. Why did Congress enact the **Sarbanes-Oxley Act** of 2002?
17. What is the **Red Flags rule?**

Summary ....

- Understanding the legal environment surrounding business on national and state levels is critical to a credit professional's role. Legislation protects the rights of creditors as well as poses limitations to business activity. Penalties and criminal action that may be filed against individual credit professionals and the business if conduct is found to be outside the boundaries of the law.

- Antitrust regulation was enacted at the turn of the 20th century to mitigate the effect of powerful monopolies on small businesses. The four major federal acts combating monopolies include:
  - **The Sherman Act**
  - **The Clayton Act**
  - **The Robinson-Patman Act**
  - **The Federal Trade Commission Act**

- The **Sherman Act** was designed to prevent monopolies and unfair restraints of trade. Although it does not prohibit all restraints of trade, it does outlaw contracts, combinations, or conspiracy to restrain trade, and monopolization that is deemed unreasonable.

- The **Clayton Act** was created to correct the shortcomings of the Sherman Act. It gives administrative agencies the power to stop violations of the law before they develop into actuality. The law makes it unlawful to create exclusive dealing arrangements, as well as any deal containing arrangements that involved restricting the sale to or from a competitor. It also restricted companies from obtaining stock of other companies that would considerably lessen the competition in the market place.

- The **Federal Trade Commission Act** is the broadest act and prohibits any act that attempts or is designed to deceive the public.

- The **Robinson-Patman Act** is designed to target direct or indirect price discrimination. This is particularly important to credit professionals, and involves:
  - A different price charged to different purchasers of the same type
  - Differences in terms and conditions of sale
  - Preferential credit terms
  - Credit terms which are an inseparable part of price

- For a person to be found liable for price discrimination there is no need for an arrangement, combination, association or conspiracy. They only need to be engaged in at least two transactions crossing state lines, and for the consumption or resale within the United States.

- Meeting competition is the most common defense against claims of unlawful price discrimination.

- The **Fair Credit Reporting Act (FCRA)** requires consumer credit reporting agencies to adopt reasonable procedures to meet the needs of consumer credit, employment, insurance, and all other information that is fair and equitable to consumers. It concerns credit extended to consumers and not commercial credit transactions. The law states that a credit report may not be initiated or requested without the written consent of the individual and there is a permissible business use defined by statute.

- The **Equal Credit Opportunity Act and Regulation B (ECOA)** was created to promote the availability of credit regardless of one's race, color, religion, national origin, sex, marital status or age.

- With gross revenues of $1 million or less in the preceding fiscal year, the creditor must provide written or oral notice of **adverse action** within 30 days of receiving the application. Adverse actions are:
  - Refusal to grant credit
  - Refusal to increase credit on an existing account
  - Reduction of credit availability on an existing account
  - Termination of credit on an existing account
- A credit hold is not deemed adverse if the account has been slow to pay or is delinquent. If a creditor violates a provision of the **ECOA**, they are liable for actual damages sustained by the applicant. With all costs included, **ECOA** damages can be detrimental.
- Any disclosure can be provided electronically as long as it is clear and the creditor has obtained the applicant's affirmative consent to obtained electronic communication.
- The **Dodd-Frank Wall Street Reform and Consumer Protection Act** establishes a **Consumer Financial Protection Bureau (CFPB),** and has a primary mission to monitor consumer lending. It also requires the disclosure of the principal reasons for denying or taking adverse action against an application for an extension of credit.
- The **Fair Debt Collection Practices Act** was created to make fair laws for the benefit of debtors when creditors attempt to recover debts. The **FDCPA** focus is on the collection activities of third-party collectors. Prohibitions include, but are not limited to, the following:
  - Misrepresenting the character or the amount of a debt
  - Threatening to take action prohibited by law
  - Threatening to take action that is not intended to be taken
  - Making repeated calls for the purpose of harassment
- The **Truth in Lending Act (TILA)** was created with the intention of protecting and educating consumers in the field of purchasing credit. Sellers of credit are mandated by law to disclose certain information when offering credit. This includes information regarding the interest rates, finance charges and fees that will apply when accepting such credit terms.
- **E-Sign Act** was instituted to continue the facilitation of electronic commerce. It is vital to understand that e-signatures may not be denied legal effect, validity, or enforceability solely because they are in electronic form, and just because an electronic signature was used in the creation of a contract relating to a transaction. It is also important to understand that an email can constitute a valid and enforceable agreement.
- E-signatures make business on a domestic and international level faster and more efficient. They benefit both businesses and consumers from a legal standpoint, as well as reduce administrative work associated with printing, signing and rescanning a document in order to send it electronically.
- Due to the need for increased security after the events that took place on September 11th, states have looked for other sources of revenue, which has made escheatment an appealing source of revenue. **Escheatment** is the states right to unclaimed property. Laws differ by state, so it is important for credit professionals to know and understand the laws of escheatment in their particular state or fines, penalties and damages may be taken against a business.
- The **Sarbanes-Oxley Act (SOX)** was instituted to protect investors by improving the accuracy and reliability of corporate disclosures. The overarching goals of the act were to restore investor confidence and assure the integrity of business practices within the United States. The main objectives are to:
  - Strengthen and restore confidence in the accounting profession

- Strengthen the enforcement of the federal securities law
- Increase executive responsibility
- Improve disclosure and financial reporting

- The main components of the act include, but are not limited to, the creation of a **Public Company Accounting Oversight Board PCAOB),** the use of independent auditors, the requirement of executives to be responsible for the accuracy of all public documents, the use of **generally accepted accounting principles (GAAP)**, and the disclosure of any known conflict of interest.

- As of November 2007, the **Fair and Accurate Credit Transactions Act (FACTA)** requires financial institutions and credit managers to develop and implement identity theft programs. **Red Flags** are any potential risks that could arise in terms of identity theft.

- As a business, it is important to:
  - Do a risk assessment to identify relevant red flags
  - Detect red flags
  - Respond appropriately to red flags to mitigate risks of identity theft
  - Update the written program periodically to reflect changes in risks to consumers or to business from identity theft
  - Have oversight dedicated to a company's Red Flags program

References and Resources

Borges, Wanda. *Antitrust, Restraint of Trade, and Unfair Competition: Myth vs. Reality.* Columbia, MD: National Association of Credit Management, 1998.

Business Credit. Columbia, MD: National Association of Credit Management. (This 9 issues/year publication is a continuous source of relevant articles and information. Archived articles from *Business Credit* magazine are available through the web-based NACM Resource Library, which is a benefit of NACM membership.)

Business Credit and the Equal Credit Opportunity Act and Regulation B. Columbia, MD: National Association of Credit Management, 2001.

Government resources: The Federal Trade Commission at www.ftc.gov, the Federal Deposit Insurance Agency at www.fdic.gov and the Department of Justice at www.doj.gov.

Manual of Credit and Commercial Laws. Columbia, MD: National Association of Credit Management, current edition.

Miller, Roger and Gaylord Jentz. *Business Law Today.* 5th ed. London: Thomson Learning, 2000. *See* Unit 7.

Shenefield, John H. and Irwin M. Stelzer. *The Antitrust Laws: A Primer,* 4th ed. La Vergne, TN: AEI Press, 2001.

7 The Uniform Commercial Code

OVERVIEW

Laws governing sales began in England when merchants developed the law of merchants or a system of rules, customs and usages that regulated their transactions. Eventually, the law of merchants was combined with British common law. By 1882, the English Bills of Exchange Act was adopted by the British Parliament, followed by the Sale of Goods Act in 1893.

Using these two English laws as an example, two sets of laws were created by the National Conference of Commissioners on Uniform State Laws in the United States: the Uniform Negotiable Instruments Act (1896) and the Uniform Sales Act (1906). Other laws relating to commercial transactions were also created in the early 1900s such as the Uniform Warehouse Receipts Act (1906), the Uniform Stock Transfer Act (1909), the Uniform Bills of Lading Act (1909), the Uniform Conditional Sales Act (1918) and the Uniform Trust Receipts Act (1933). By the mid-1900s, it became clear that these various laws needed revision to keep current with business and to be integrated into one set of laws.

THINK ABOUT THIS

Q. Is the Uniform Commercial Code uniform? Why or why not?

Q. How would buyers and sellers conduct business without uniform laws across the 50 states?

Q. What are some expectations a buyer may have upon receiving a product or service?

Q. Under what conditions would a company want a tangible asset to secure an extension of credit?

DISCIPLINARY CORE IDEAS

After reading this chapter, the reader should understand:
- ✓ The history of the UCC.
- ✓ Article 2: Sales.
- ✓ Article 2A: Leases.
- ✓ Article 6: Bulk Sales.
- ✓ Article 9: Secured Transactions.

CHAPTER OUTLINE

A Brief Guide to the UCC

In 1942, the Uniform Commercial Code was designed as a joint project between the American Law Institute and the National Conference of Commissioners of Uniform State Laws. It took 10 years for the appointed editorial board and drafting committees to produce an official text, which underwent several revisions. Today, the Permanent Editorial Board (PEB) for the UCC is the body responsible for the uniformity of enactment and construction of the UCC and for evaluating and preparing proposals for amendment.

The UCC is **not** federal law; each state adopts the Code. Additionally, each state may adopt the code with numerous variations in the basic UCC, which requires considerable care in conforming to the local variations, so caution must be used and counsel should be sought. Pennsylvania was the first state to adopt the Uniform Commercial Code in 1954, and Louisiana is the only state that has not adopted the Code in its entirety. The Code applies to sales made in the District of Columbia and in the Virgin Islands, but it is not valid for sales made in Puerto Rico.

The basic premise on which the Uniform Commercial Code is based is that the personal property commercial transaction is a single subject of the law, involving the sale of and payment for goods. The concept of the UCC is to cover every phase of commercial transactions that can involve the sale and payment of goods.

The UCC is divided into nine articles and extends over the laws of sales, negotiable instruments, bank deposits and collections, letters of credit, bulk sales, documents of title, investment securities and secured transactions. The following lists each Article and the basic subjects covered:

Article 1	General Provisions	Purposes and policies, including definitions
Article 2	Sales	Contracts for Purchase/Sale of goods
Article 2A	Leases	Transfer of the right to possession and use of goods for a term in return for consideration
Article 3	Negotiable Instruments	Commercial paper, Promissory notes, Drafts, Checks, Certificates of Deposit, Money Orders,
Article 4	Bank Deposits and Collections	Deposit/Collection of checks
Article 4A	Funds Transfers	Electronic transfers of funds (CHIPS, Fedwire)
Article 5	Letters of Credit	Domestic and Foreign commercial letters of credit
Article 6	Bulk Sales	Special protection for creditors of seller in bulk inventory sales and transfers
Article 7	Documents of Title	Special rules for documents that evidence ownership or right to possession of goods, Bills of Lading, warehouse receipts
Article 8	Investment Securities	Stock Certificates
Article 9	Secured Transactions	Security interests, collateral, priority among secured creditors

Article 2: Sales (Effective 2002)

Comprehension Check
Article 2 applies to which kind of transactions?

Article 2 of the UCC applies to sale transactions in goods.

Goods

Goods are defined as *all things, other than money, stocks and bonds, that are movable.* Goods also include the unborn young of animals and growing crops. Goods that are not yet in existence or not yet under the control of people are called future goods. Examples of future goods are fish in the sea, minerals in the ground, goods not yet manufactured and commodities futures. Article 2 does not cover contracts to provide services or sell real property; these are covered by general contract common law and real property law.

Article 2 of the UCC is generally a part of the law of contracts; general contract common law applies to sales laws unless displaced by a particular provision of the UCC. And the **elements of contract common law**—*offer and acceptance, mutual assent, capacity to contract, legality of subject matter and consideration*—all apply. Article 2 states that a contract for the sale of goods for the price of $500 or more is not enforceable unless there is some writing sufficient to indicate that a contract for sale has been made between the parties.

Comprehension Check

Under Article 2, what rule applies to sales worth more than $500?

Merchant

The sales article of the UCC distinguishes between merchants and casual or inexperienced sellers. The UCC defines a **merchant** as *"a person that deals in goods of the kind or otherwise holds itself out by occupation as having knowledge or skill peculiar to the practices or goods involved in the transaction ..."* The UCC recognizes that more reliance can be placed on professional sellers like merchants—holding them, in effect, to a higher standard.

Comprehension Check

Why does Article 2 distinguish between a merchant and casual or inexperienced sellers?

Location of Title

A significant aspect of Article 2 is that it states the law without reference to the location of title. Historically, many controversies between buyers and sellers were answered by early common law decisions, and secondarily by the Uniform Sales Act, by determining the location of title to the goods. However, the drafters of Article 2 took the position that this "lump concept thinking," or merely determining the location of title to goods, created many uncertain and unfair results since it is frequently difficult to predict when title passes or is even established. Furthermore, passing of title may have no logical relationship to the rights in question. There is, however, a general title provision in Article 2.

Obligation of Good Faith

Within the UCC, every contract has an obligation of good faith or honesty in the transaction concerned in its performance. This is an important concept because if a contract contains an unfair or unconscionable clause, or if the contract as a whole is unconscionable, the courts have the right to refuse to enforce the unconscionable clause or contract.

Comprehension Check

Within UCC Article 2, every contract has an obligation of good faith or honesty in the transaction concerned. Why is this an important concept?

Tender Delivery

In general, the performance obligation of the seller is to tender delivery of goods, in a commercial unit, that conform to the contract with the buyer. A **commercial unit** is *any unit of goods that is treated by commercial usage as a single whole (as a machine or carload), a set of articles (as a suite of furniture) or a quantity (as a bale).* **Tender delivery** *means that the seller must make the goods available to the buyer. The basic obligation of the buyer is to accept the goods and to pay in accordance with the contract.* Additionally, the buyer has the right, before payment or acceptance, to inspect the goods, to reject the goods if they fail to conform to the contract or to accept the goods in spite of non-conformity. The seller has the right to correct or cure improper delivery. Acceptance of goods occurs when the buyer, having had a reasonable opportunity to inspect the goods, either accepts or rejects them.

The buyer must state the grounds for rejection where a defect in the tender could have been ascertained by reasonable inspection and could have been cured by the seller. The UCC introduces the concept of cover, which applies where the seller fails to perform; **cover** *gives the buyer an alternative right to purchase substitute goods and to recover from the seller the difference between the contract price and the purchase of the replacement goods as an absolute measure of damages, provided the buyer purchases in a reasonable manner.*

If the buyer refuses to accept goods that conform to the contract or repudiates the contract, the seller has a claim for damages against the buyer. The seller has two ways of determining the damages that the buyer is liable for because of the buyer's breach of contract: (1) the difference between the contract price and the market price at which the goods are currently selling, or (2) the profit the seller lost when the buyer did not go through with the contract.

If the buyer rejects a shipment, rightly or wrongly, the seller must first resell the goods at the best price obtainable and then sue for the difference between the proceeds and that which was due, plus any incidental damages. The only exception is where the merchandise is of a special nature and not readily salable at a reasonable price; in that case, the old rule still applies and the seller can sue for the full purchase price. If the buyer retains the shipment and then tries to return it much later, the seller is not obligated to accept the return and can sue for the full amount.

Comprehension Check

What does **tender delivery** mean?

....

What options does a buyer have if goods delivered by the seller do not conform to the contract?

....

If a buyer refuses to accept goods that conform to the contract, how can the seller determine the damages for which the buyer is liable because of the breach of contract?

There are many variations of this kind of problem and the UCC provides several rules to deal with them. Consequently, the seller can no longer hold rejected merchandise for a buyer and then sue for the purchase price; instead, they have to sell the goods first and then only sue for any loss. If the seller has no loss on the resale, then only the profit on the original sale can be recovered.

The UCC acknowledges that terms are frequently omitted from agreements or contracts by defining common trade practices. The UCC also recognizes that a contract for the sale of goods may be performed even though the price is not settled. An open-price term may occur when the parties intend to be bound by a contract but pricing will be set at a later date, if at all.

Title

The courts will initially consider one very specific question: did the parties contract as to when title passes? If the contract does not specify the passing of title, then the courts look to the UCC.

In its general title section, the UCC provides that title passes to the buyer when the seller has completely performed their duties concerning physical delivery of the goods. Therefore, if the contract only requires the seller to ship the goods, title passes to the buyer when the seller delivers the goods to the carrier. If the contract requires delivery of the goods by the seller, title passes to the buyer when the goods are delivered and tendered to the buyer. If delivery is made without moving the goods, the title passes at the time and place of contracting if the goods have been identified in the contract.

Comprehension Check

What does the general title section of the UCC state?

Risk of Loss

The UCC also has specific rules governing risk of loss, which is an issue separate and apart from title. Risk of loss depends on the terms of the agreement, the moment the loss occurs and whether one of the parties was in breach of contract when the risk of loss occurred. Risk of loss can be contractually addressed by using commonly accepted shipping terms.

The following are commonly used shipping terms that create shipment contracts, whereby the seller turns the goods over to a carrier for delivery to the buyer. In a shipment contract, both title and risk of loss pass to the buyer when the goods are given to the carrier; the seller has no responsibility for seeing that the goods reach their destination.

Commonly used shipping terms that create shipment contracts are:

- **FOB (Free on Board).** The place of shipment requires the seller to deliver the goods free of expense and at the seller's risk to the carrier.
- **FAS (Free Alongside).** At a named port requires the seller to deliver the goods, at their own risk, alongside the vessel or at a dock designated by the buyer.
- **CIF (Cost, Insurance and Freight).** The price of the goods includes the cost of shipping and insurance to a named destination. The seller bears this expense and the risk of loading the goods.
- **CFR (Cost and Freight).** The price of the goods includes the cost of shipping and freight to a named destination. The seller bears the risk of loading the goods.

If the contract requires the seller to guarantee delivery of the goods to a specific destination, the seller bears the risk and expense of delivery to that destination. Commonly used shipping terms that create destination contracts are:

- **FOB Destination or an FOB term with the place of destination of the goods** puts the expense and risk of delivering the goods to that destination on the seller.
- **Ex-Ship** places the expense and risk on the seller until the goods are unloaded from whatever ship is used.
- **No Arrival, No Sale** places the expense and risk during shipment on the seller. If the goods fail to arrive through no fault of the seller, the seller has no further liability to the buyer.

If no agreement has been made for either a shipment contract or a destination contract, then the risk passes to the buyer on receipt of the goods if the seller is a merchant. If the seller is not a merchant, the risk passes to the buyer when the seller tenders (offers) delivery of the goods.

Comprehension Check

List the conditions that relate to risk of loss.

What is a **shipment contract?**

What is a **destination contract?**

Reclamation and Stoppage of Delivery

Unless the seller has agreed to extend credit to the buyer, the buyer must pay for the goods at the time they are delivered. When the seller is ready to make delivery of the goods, they may withhold delivery until the payment is made, even in cases where they have agreed to extend credit to the buyer. If the seller discovers that the buyer is insolvent before making delivery, the seller has the right to withhold delivery until the buyer pays cash for the goods and for any goods previously delivered for which payment has not been made (the existing accounts receivable balance). If a seller discovers that a buyer is insolvent, the seller has the right to stop delivery of any goods in transit.

The seller has the right to require the insolvent buyer to return any goods obtained from the seller within the previous 10 days. Under the UCC, the seller must demand the return of merchandise from an insolvent buyer within 10 days of the receipt of the shipment. Insolvency under the UCC is defined to include the so-called equity rule (inability to pay debts as they mature) as well as the bankruptcy definition (liabilities exceeding assets).

Comprehension Check

What does **reclamation** mean under Article 2?

Figure 7-1   Reclamation: Stoppage of Delivery Notice

RECLAMATION: STOPPAGE OF DELIVERY NOTICE

_____, 20__

VIA EMAIL, FAX, FEDERAL EXPRESS, AND CERTIFIED MAIL, R.R.R.
[CARRIER/WAREHOUSE]
RE: STOPPAGE OF DELIVERY DEMAND: [NAME OF CUSTOMER]

Dear [INSERT]:

Demand is hereby made on you to stop delivery of all of the goods of the above customer in your possession, including, without limitation, all of the goods identified in the Schedule annexed hereto, pursuant to §§2-702, 2-703 and 2-705 of the Uniform Commercial Code.

Please contact the undersigned for instructions in connection with the return of the goods. We make this demand for stoppage of delivery without prejudice to all other rights and remedies available to us, at law or in equity.

Very truly yours,
[NAME OF CREDITOR]

By: _____

Title: _____

cc: [Name and Address of Debtor]

SCHEDULE TO STOPPAGE OF DELIVERY DEMAND

Invoice No.	Invoice Date	Invoice Amount	Bill of Lading No.

Real World Perspectives

RECLAMATION DEMAND CURES THE JOHN DOE BLUES

Many years ago, there was a regional retail chain customer in the Mid-Atlantic States, and for this story, let's call them, the John Doe Widget Company. They were always difficult to deal with: chronically late with payments, constantly needing several collection calls per invoice, and they always took deductions on anything and everything.

The company's name became a verb in our office lexicon, as in "We've been John Doe'd again!" This company set the standard now used by today's big-box stores that use accounts payable as a profit center with those same tactics. John Doe was the master of evasion and deductions!

Over several years, the John Doe Widget Company expanded by buying not one, but two, smaller chains that were in bankruptcy. With its expansion, they became even more difficult to deal with; payments got even slower, requests for deductions increased, constant calls were required for collections. More chasing. More frustration. Why were we surprised? We talked to supervisors, managers, the controller, the finance director, the chief financial officer—you name it, we talked to them to get paid.

After months of intense run-around, enough was enough. I was done playing their games and took a tough stance. The John Doe Widget Company account was flagged against any new business. That got their attention. Once the account was current, we shipped existing confirmed orders, but did not take any new ones. And the cycle would start again: slow payments, unreasonable requests for deductions, and again a flag was placed on their account. One day, they called, desperate to receive one of their confirmed orders. After getting a commitment from John Doe's finance director that they would overnight payment for their outstanding invoices in exchange for letting two more truckloads of products ship, I approved the new purchases.

As one can guess, the overnight did not arrive. One truck had already delivered; the other was in transit and I had no way to stop the delivery. No one was taking my calls—not even the finance director who made the promise the day before. "John Doe'd again!"

I was young, having just completed NACM's Credit Administration Program. With the information from the legal class fresh in my mind, I sent a reclamation letter overnight, demanding that my material be returned immediately. I immediately received a call from their legal counsel asking why I had sent the demand letter. In my youthful enthusiasm, I stated emphatically, "You're not meeting your debts as they come due, which is one definition of insolvency and apparently you don't have the money to pay me. If this is the case, then I would like to come and get my material." The attorney assured me that his client was indeed solvent and that this whole thing was unnecessary. I asked for immediate payment of everything, and he stated he would see what he could do.

After a few days and several unreturned calls to the attorney, I received a check for all open invoices with the attorney's letter restating that his client, the John Doe Widget Company, was indeed solvent. It was just a misunderstanding, he wrote, and enclosed were the appropriate payments.

Sixty days later, the John Doe Widget Company filed for bankruptcy, and 60 days after that came the notice from the bankruptcy trustee with a preferential payment demand for $40,000. I provided my reclamation documents and the attorney's letter assuring me of the debtor's solvency. Happily, I never heard from the trustee again. At least we got the last hurrah after years of being "John Doe'd."

Loretta April

Warranties

Article 2 addresses several warranty issues. A **warranty** *is a contractual promise by the seller regarding the quality, character or suitability of the goods sold.* An **express warranty** *is an oral or written statement, promise or other representation about the quality of a product.*

Examples of express warranties include:

- A statement of fact or promise made by the seller to the buyer that relates to the goods.
- A description of the goods which is made part of the basis of the agreement that the goods will conform to the description.
- A sample or model of the goods.

Whenever a seller of goods makes a statement of fact about the goods to a buyer as part of the transaction, an express warranty is created.

An **implied warranty** *is a warranty that is imposed by law rather than by statements, descriptions or samples given by the seller;* it relates to all sales transactions, whether they are business-to-consumer transactions or business-to-business transactions. Implied warranties are designed to promote high standards in business and to discourage harsh dealings. There are four basic types of implied warranties:

1. An implied warranty of merchantability.
2. An implied warranty of fitness for a particular purpose.
3. An implied warranty that is derived from a course of dealing or usage of trade.
4. An implied warranty of title (owner has title to the item).

Disclaimer of warranties is permitted as a matter of freedom of contract, but with the condition that the disclaimer must be conspicuous if placed in a written contract. To disclaim the implied warranty of merchantability the writing must mention the word "merchantability." **Merchantability** *is the concept that goods are reasonably fit for the general purpose for which they are sold.*

Comprehension Check
Define the term **warranty.**

What is an **express warranty?**

What is an **implied warranty?**

Article 2A: Leases (Effective 2002)

Leases *are defined as the transfer of the right to possession and use of goods for a term in return for consideration.* Leasing allows the lessee to use valuable assets without making an initial large capital investment and allows firms with limited capital budgets an alternative way to obtain resources. Additionally, leases are frequently tailored to meet the cash budget requirements of the lessee.

Included within the scope of Article 2A are transactions as diverse as the lease of a hand tool for a few hours and the leveraged lease of a complex line of industrial equipment. This Article generally preserves the concept of freedom of contract except that there are special rules for consumer leases. A **finance lease,** *a lease in which the lessor does not manufacture or produce the goods and only acquires the goods in connection with the lease,* is also governed by this Article.

A lease contract is enforceable if the total payments to be made, excluding payment for options to renew or buy, are less than $1,000 or if there is a written agreement. A lease contract can be made in any manner that shows agreement between the parties. If a court finds, as a matter of law, that a lease or clause is unconscionable at the time it was made, it can refuse to enforce the lease or clause. A lease imposes an obligation on each party that the other's expectation of receiving the performance will not be impaired.

A lease is also enforceable if the goods are to be specifically manufactured or maintained for the lessee and are not suitable for lease or sale to others in the ordinary course of business; or if a party admits that the lease was made; or if the goods have been received and accepted by the lessee.

Promises made by a lessor to a lessee create a warranty that the goods will conform to the promises made. Any description of the goods creates an express warranty that the goods will conform to the description; likewise, any sample or model used creates a warranty that the goods will conform to the sample or model. In a finance lease, there is an implied warranty of merchantability in a lease contract if the lessor is a merchant with respect to goods of that kind.

General Default

If either party is in default under the lease, the party seeking enforcement may obtain a judgment or otherwise peacefully enforce the lease by self-help or any available judicial or non-judicial procedure. If a lessor discovers the lessee to be insolvent, the lessor may refuse to deliver the goods; and if the lessee is in default, the lessor may peacefully take possession of the goods without judicial process. After default by the lessee under a lease contract, the lessor may recover from the lessee damages for goods accepted by the lessee and for conforming goods lost or damaged within a commercially reasonable time, accrued and unpaid rent, the value of the lease and incidental damages.

Comprehension Check
When is a lease contract enforceable?

Article 6: Bulk Sales (Effective 1989)

Bulk transfers have created special problems for business people. Merchants, owing debts, would sometimes sell out their entire inventory for less than what it was worth. This left creditors with no way of reaching and selling the goods to obtain the money owed to them. Article 6, Bulk Sales, protects creditors from this practice, known as bulk transfer. While many states have repealed their bulk sales statute, other states have either retained the existing Article 6 or revised Article 6. Consulting legal counsel in the state in which the transfer is taking place is recommended to determine which laws apply to that particular jurisdiction. For more details, refer to the NACM *Manual of Credit and Commercial Laws.*

A **bulk transfer** *is any transfer of a major part of the materials, supplies, merchandise or other inventory of an enterprise that is not made in the ordinary course of business;* under revised Article 6, the transferor must be going out of business as well.

The general concept of Article 6 is to protect the creditors of a merchant by voiding a bulk transfer of the merchandise not in the ordinary course of trade, unless the merchant (who is the transferee) gives written notice of the contemplated transfer to all known creditors before taking possession. The granting of a security interest for the performance of an obligation is not a bulk transfer under Article 6, but a legitimate financing transaction. Creditor protection under this Article is designed to prevent two types of fraud:

1. To stop the conveyance type of sale where both parties, the debtor and the buyer/transferee, may have conspired to defraud creditors by transferring goods at less than their true value so the debtor may then reestablish the business.

2. To prevent a debtor from selling the bulk of stock in trade, even for full value, to a buyer/transferee that may not be in collusion with the debtor, and then either dissipating the proceeds or disappearing with them, leaving creditors unpaid.

The UCC lists requirements that must be followed whenever a bulk transfer is made. If the requirements are not met, the transferee of the goods can lose all ownership rights to them. Further, creditors who suffer damages can demand the return of all goods bought, with no obligation to reimburse the buyer. Revised Article 6 gives creditors a united damage claim against the transferee. The requirements are:

1. The buyer/transferee must require the transferor/seller to furnish a list of any existing creditors with their addresses and amounts owing.

2. The parties must prepare a schedule of the property being transferred so that it can be identified.

3. The buyer/transferee must maintain or preserve the list and schedule for six months following the transfer and make it available for inspection.

4. The buyer/transferee must give notice of the transfer to all creditors from 10 to 45 days (depending on state law) before taking possession of the goods or paying for them, whichever happens first.

5. Revised Article 6 also requires the preparation of a schedule of distribution of proceeds to be given to all creditors by the seller, which enables the creditor and the transferee to know the disposition of the proceeds of the sale.

After following these requirements, the transferee may pay for and take possession of the inventory.

Creditors' Actions

A creditor receiving notice that a customer is selling under a bulk sale must immediately contact both the debtor and buyer to ascertain how much time will elapse before the sale; obtain a description of the property to be sold, its value, and the names of other creditors and the amounts due them; determine whether the debtor's debts are to be paid in full or in part from the proceeds; and find out where claims should be sent.

A creditor who did not receive any such notice but learns that a sale of the debtor's goods has been made, which may be subject to Article 6, should find out whether the debtor, the sale or both are subject to the UCC; whether a claim can be filed; or, if a claim cannot be filed, what rights creditors have against the buyer/transferee if either the debtor or buyer has failed to comply with the UCC. The creditor must move quickly in order not to be barred from relief under the law. Therefore, consult counsel once it's clear that a bulk transfer has occurred. Creditors who have not taken any action to interrupt the transfer lose their right to do so.

> **Comprehension Check**
>
> What is the general concept behind Article 6?
>
> ....
>
> Under UCC Article 6, five requirements must be followed whenever a **bulk transfer** is made. What are they?

Article 9: Secured Transactions (Effective 2013)

Overview

Whenever the payment of a debt is guaranteed or secured by personal property owned by the debtor or in which the debtor has a legal interest, the transaction becomes known as a **secured transaction.** The concept of the secured transaction is as basic to modern business practice as the concept of credit. Logically, sellers and lenders do not want to risk nonpayment, so they usually will not sell goods or lend funds unless the promise of payment is somehow guaranteed. Business could not exist without laws permitting and governing secured transactions.

The Terminology of Secured Transactions

A brief summary of the terms relating to secured transactions follows.

- **Collateral** is the *subject* of the *security interest* [UCC 9-102(a)(12)].
- A **debtor** is the "party" who *owes payment* or other performance of a secured obligation [UCC 9-102(a)(28)].
- A **financing statement**, referred to as the **UCC-1 form**, is the *document normally filed to give public notice to third parties of the secured party's security interest* [UCC 9-102(a)(39)].
- A **secured party** *is any creditor who has a security interest in the debtor's collateral*. This creditor can be a seller, a lender, a cosigner and even a buyer of accounts or chattel paper [UCC 9-102(a)(73)].
- A **security agreement** is an *agreement* that *creates* or provides for a *security interest* [UCC 9-102(a)(74)].
- A **security interest** is the *interest* in the collateral (personal property, accounts, etc.) that *secures payment or performance of an obligation* [UCC 1-201(35)].

These basic definitions form the concept of a secured transaction relationship between debtor and creditor.

Article 9 of the UCC contains the law of secured transactions for personal property and fixtures. It also contains the rules for obtaining a security interest in personal property and fixture collateral. A credit grantor must first satisfy all Article 9 requirements in order to obtain a valid and perfected security interest in all of the collateral securing payment of its claim against its customer or the performance of the customer's obligations. Then, a credit grantor must determine whether a secured creditor of its customer has satisfied all of the requirements for obtaining a perfected security interest that would confer upon it priority over junior secured and judgment lien creditors and a bankruptcy trustee.

Comprehension Check

Under UCC Article 9, what is a **secured transaction?**

What is a **security interest?**

Article 9 has been enacted and is currently in effect in all 50 states and the District of Columbia. Certain states, however, passed Article 9 with some changes to the official text. The following discussion is a review of the creation and enforcement of security interests in personal property; the general discussion, however, will not apply in all states. When creating a security interest, counsel should be sought in regard to a particular state's version of Article 9 to check for any variance from the official text.

Basic Coverage of the Uniform Commercial Code

While the UCC covers transactions that are intended by the parties to create security interests in personal property or fixtures to secure the future payment of debts or performance of obligations, certain types of personal property are specifically excluded. Unless one of the exceptions listed below applies, any transaction involving personal property is probably subject to the UCC. In any case not excepted, compliance with the UCC to create and perfect an enforceable security interest is required.

Excepted Transactions

If the transaction involves a security interest or lien on real estate, aircraft and certain vessels, wages or certain types of insurance claims that are not proceeds of UCC collateral or consumer tort claims, the UCC does not apply. Motor vehicles present a special problem since creation of a security interest may be subject to the UCC, but perfection is subject to other law.

- **Mechanic's Liens and Other Statutory Liens.** Statutory mechanic's, contractors' or similar liens are created by state law for persons furnishing labor or materials for the improvement of real property. The repair of vehicles or equipment or the feeding of livestock is also covered by statutory liens and not by UCC Article 9. The nature and extent of mechanic's liens and other statutory laws is the subject of state law and may vary widely from one state to another. Such liens often take precedence over security interests in the same property, including security interests under the UCC that attach before the work is done.
- **Aircraft, Ships and Motor Vehicles.** Certain types of aircraft, barges, oceangoing ships and other means of conveyance registered by the federal government under federal law are excluded from the operation of UCC Article 9 to a limited extent. Certain motor vehicles titled under state law are partially excluded. Security interests in aircraft and barges may be created under the UCC through the execution of a security agreement. The perfection of the security interest, however, is a question of federal law. Motor vehicles are subject to security interests created in a security agreement under the UCC, but generally perfected under the motor vehicle law of the state in which the vehicle is titled. Aircraft are covered by various federal and state laws, depending on whether they are aircraft being used for transport or whether they are aircraft sitting in a showroom of an aircraft dealer. In many states the notation of the security interest must be made on the vehicle's title issued by the state. Questions of the perfection of security interests in vehicles, ships and aircraft should be referred to counsel.
- **Wages.** The UCC expressly excludes the assignment of an individual's wages. This is rarely an issue in commercial sales of goods and the granting of commercial credit.
- **Insurance Contracts.** While UCC Article 9 generally traces a security interest in goods into any casualty insurance proceeds, as a general rule, Article 9 does not apply to the transfer or assignment of any interests in an insurance policy itself. Taking a security interest in

goods in most states automatically establishes a security interest in any proceeds if the goods are destroyed and covered by insurance. A security interest cannot be taken in most insurance policies. However, Article 9 applies to healthcare insurance receivables. They include claims under health insurance policies of the debtor's patients.

Comprehension Check

What transactions are excepted from Article 9?

Theory of UCC Sections on the Creation of Security Interests in Personal Property

Article 9 grants the parties a great deal of flexibility to tailor the creation of a security interest in many types of personal property to fit their particular transaction. The specific form of the security interest and its enforceability may be the subject of an agreement between the parties. In the absence of a specific contract setting out terms, the UCC provides specific remedies upon default.

A security interest may be limited to identified items of collateral or may be broad enough to cover all collateral of a particular kind or type, then owned or thereafter acquired by the debtor. One of the most flexible features of the UCC grants the parties *the right to create a security interest in property the debtor does not yet own or possess at the time that the security interest is created;* referred to as the **floating lien** of the UCC. A floating lien attaches to all of the debtor's property of a particular kind, properly described in the security agreement, even though the property of that kind is acquired long after the execution of the agreement. Property that is acquired thereafter is automatically covered and is likewise automatically released from the lien as items are sold by the debtor in the ordinary course of business.

The UCC further permits a secured creditor to trace a security interest to the proceeds received by the debtor upon the disposition of the collateral. Under certain circumstances, proceeds of the collateral to the debtor's bank account may be traced, or the collateral itself may be traced into the hands of the person buying the property from the debtor unless the buyer is a good faith purchaser.

Classification of Collateral

The first step in creating a secured transaction is to review the classifications of personal property under the UCC. No matter how designated in a particular industry, all collateral will fall within one of the classifications under the UCC. For the most part, be concerned with the types of property that will eventually become inventory or equipment in the hands of the purchaser (referred to here as the "debtor"). If the transaction is going to involve more than one type of collateral, greater care should be taken.

The categories of collateral covered under Article 9 include:

- Accounts and general intangibles.
- Deposit accounts.
- Goods, such as inventory and equipment.
- Instruments.
- Investment property, such as securities and brokerage accounts.
- Chattel paper (any writing evidencing a debt secured by personal property).

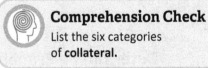

Comprehension Check

List the six categories of **collateral.**

Under Article 9, **accounts** *include the right to payment arising from the sale, lease, license and other disposition of all types of tangible and intangible property.* Accounts include:

- Fees and royalties payable under intellectual property licenses, such as patent, trademark and copyright licenses, the right to lottery winnings, the right to payment under an installment real estate sales contract and manufacturers rebates.
- Credit card receivables.

- Health care insurance receivables that are owed to healthcare providers. They are interests in claims under a policy of insurance evidencing a right to payment of money for providing healthcare goods and services.

Article 9 has a subcategory of general intangibles called **payment intangibles** *where the obligor's principal obligation is the payment of money.* Examples of payment intangibles include loan agreements or commercial debt instruments that may be sold. General intangibles also include software consisting of a computer program and any supporting information in connection with a transaction relating to the program. For example, a retailer's inventory of CDs containing computer programs for sale are general intangibles and not inventory. On the other hand, software consisting of a computer program embedded in goods and any supporting information provided in connection with a transaction relating to the program are goods with the program, and considered part of the goods.

Chattel paper *is any writing evidencing both a monetary obligation and a security interest in specific goods, including electronic as well as tangible chattel paper.* It also includes promissory notes as a subcategory of instruments.

A **commercial tort claim** *is a tort claim in favor of an organization or in favor of an individual that arises in the course of the individual's business or profession.* It does not include a personal injury or death claim.

A **deposit account** *is a bank account, such as a demand, time, savings, passbook or similar account, maintained with a bank.* A security interest can be granted in a deposit account as original collateral or the security interest can attach to the sums on deposit in the account as proceeds of other collateral.

A **letter of credit right** *is a right to payment or performance of a letter of credit.* This does not include the right to make a drawing under a letter of credit, which is reserved only to a letter of credit beneficiary.

Proceeds *include whatever is realized from the sale, exchange, collection or other disposition of collateral.* Proceeds also include rights arising from the lease or license of collateral, distributions on account of collateral and claims arising out of defects in or damage to collateral. Cash or stock dividends from pledged stock and claims against a third party for infringement of intellectual property collateral are, likewise, proceeds.

Under Article 9, a **security interest** automatically continues in identifiable proceeds of the original collateral. Cash proceeds and other non-goods proceeds are identifiable to the extent the secured party identifies the proceeds by a method of tracing, which is permitted under non-Article 9 law for commingled property of that type. Where the proceeds are goods that become commingled with other goods such that their identity is lost in the product or mass, identifiable proceeds include the entire product or mass.

Article 9 also includes **supporting obligations** that support payment or performance of other collateral, such as accounts. Where a creditor has a valid and perfected security interest in an account and payment of the account is secured by a letter of credit or guarantee, or other third-party support, the third party is automatically subject to the creditor's security interest.

The collateral categories are mutually exclusive and a particular item of collateral cannot fall into two classifications or categories at the same time in the hands of one debtor. Certain goods, depending upon whether they are being held for resale or for use by the debtor, may fall into a different class under limited circumstances. Proper classification is essential for determining the appropriate language to be used in a security agreement and financing statement as well as determining the proper method of perfecting the security interest through filing, control or possession.

Comprehension Check

List the items covered under Article 9's definition of **account**.

Determining Primary Use or Purpose

While the classification of certain types of collateral, such as accounts, does not change depending upon use, goods may be classified in several subcategories depending upon their primary use by the debtor. The difficulty faced by most secured parties is that a particular good may be held by different individuals for different purposes or uses and, therefore, fall into different classes. As the same item is passed from hand to hand through the chain of commerce, it may change classification. For example, a computer in the hands of a wholesaler or retailer is inventory, but may become consumer goods when sold to an individual for home use, or equipment if sold to a company for office use. Distinction in use is critical. A security agreement covering inventory would be ineffective if the debtor purchased the property for business use since the computer is no longer inventory. Likewise, a financing statement covering equipment would not be effective against the retailer holding the property as inventory for resale.

The classification of goods is usually obvious, except where a debtor uses machinery or other goods for more than one purpose. For example, a debtor operating a retail store selling equipment, but also using much of the equipment in a service business, will present special problems. The same item of goods that may be considered inventory if held for resale would be equipment if used by the debtor for repair of customers' purchases. If there is any question, a security agreement and financing statement should cover both classifications that the collateral may conceivably fall into. This may present special problems for manufacturers whose products would normally be purchased for resale. In such situations, the purchaser may also have financing covering both inventory and equipment used in the operation of the business. The primary lender may have already perfected a security interest in all inventory and equipment. The creation and perfection of a *purchase money security interest* in inventory and equipment require extra steps to prime or come ahead of existing security interests.

Comprehension Check

Why is determining primary use or purpose critical?

If there is any question concerning the classification of collateral in a particular debtor's hands, counsel should review the documentation, including a comprehensive summary of all financing statements and other documents of record.

Creation of Security Interests

The following requirements for the creation of a security interest must be satisfied in order to become a secured creditor:

- The creditor provided value to the debtor.
- The debtor has rights in the collateral and the power to transfer such rights to the secured party.
- There is a valid security agreement that describes the collateral in which the creditor is granted a security interest.

A **valid security agreement** *must contain a sufficient description of the collateral and be authenticated by the debtor.* A security agreement signed by the debtor is an authenticated record. It is no longer necessary for a debtor to actually sign a security agreement for it to be valid and enforceable. The term "authentication" refers to a manual signature or the use of any electronic means by which the debtor as an authenticating party could be identified and the authenticity of the record can be established. The parties no longer have to rely on paper as long as they can demonstrate in some retrievable form that the debtor intended to grant a security interest in particular assets. A **record** *is information that is inscribed on a tangible medium, such as on paper as a written security agreement, or which is stored in an electronic or other medium and is retrievable in perceptible form.*

A security agreement must describe the collateral by item or type. The collateral may be identified as accounts, instruments, chattel paper, documents, investment property, inventory, equipment and general intangibles. A generic collateral description of "all personal property" or "all assets" of the debtor is not sufficient. For most assets, the security agreement could describe the collateral as all present and future collateral or as a floating lien. This does not apply to commercial tort claims. When a security interest is granted in a commercial tort claim, the security agreement must contain a specific description of the claim. An adequate description would be "all claims arising out of the explosion at the debtor's chemical factory in Boston, Massachusetts, on July 1, 2015."

A security agreement could be a full-blown agreement; it could be contained in a purchase order or a confirmation, which provides the necessary security interest grant language, sufficiently describes the collateral and is authenticated by the debtor. While a written security agreement is not necessary where a security interest in the collateral could be perfected by possession or control, a secured party should insist upon one for such collateral as additional proof of its security interest.

Most security interests are created through an agreement that contains standardized provisions and with the blanks completed with the necessary information. Nonstandard security agreements may be used if they are carefully reviewed to meet the minimum requirements of UCC Article 9. The security agreement must contain the necessary minimum legal language to create a simple security agreement. (The *Manual of Credit and Commercial Laws* contains sample language for such, as well as instructions for completing an agreement.)

Article 9 continues the sole exception under the UCC to the requirement of a written security agreement where the creditor has possession or control of the collateral, provided that the possession or control is with the debtor's agreement. Questions may arise as to whether the debtor has provided permission, a best practice dictates that even in those situations when possession or control is taken, a written security agreement authenticated by the debtor should be obtained.

At a minimum, any security agreement should contain the following:

- **Identification of Parties.** A security agreement must contain a provision identifying both the debtor and the secured party. It must also contain the debtor's correct legal name and should include the mailing address.
- **Granting Clause.** The law requires the use of the magic words "expressly grants security interest" in all present and future collateral described in the security agreement to secure all present and future indebtedness of the debtor to the secured party.
- **Collateral Description.** The description of the collateral covered by the security interest is the essence of the security agreement. The form should either have a preprinted description of the collateral or provide a space for inserting a written description of the collateral. It should contain language stating that the security interest attaches to all similar types of collateral now owned or subsequently acquired by the debtor as well as to any proceeds generated by the disposition of the collateral and all supporting obligations relating to the collateral.
- **Debtor's Warranties, Covenants and Agreements.** While the UCC gives the parties great latitude in creating documentation to suit their particular transaction, it does not require that the debtor warrant that it owns or has the right to grant a security interest in the collateral or that the agreement contain any specific events of default. However, a typical form of security agreement contains provisions setting out assorted warranties (such as that the debtor owns or has the right to grant a security interest in the collateral) and gives a comprehensive list of events of default, an acceleration clause and anti-waiver clause. The contract language in the sample agreement is typical. Additional provisions, such as a provision for obtaining insurance for inventory collateral or governing accounts receivable generated by the sale of the collateral, are also common.

The basic elements of Article 9 are that a security interest is an interest in personal property granted by the debtor to secure repayment of a debt. Also, a security interest is consensual and requires that the debtor authenticate a security agreement, which describes the goods to be covered, known as the collateral. A security interest attaches when the security agreement is executed and the debtor acquires rights in the assets subject to the security interest. A security interest is perfected when the secured creditor either takes possession or control of the collateral or files a proper financing statement with the appropriate state authority. As a general rule, competing security interests have priority in the order they are perfected or, if all competing interests are unperfected, in the order in which they attached.

> ### Comprehension Check
>
> What requirements must be satisfied for the creation of a security interest?
> ....
>
> What is a **security agreement**?
> ....
>
> What does a security agreement establish?
> ....
>
> At a minimum, a security agreement should contain four essential elements. What are they?

Perfection

Perfection *is the process of taking the legal steps necessary to ensure that a secured party's interest in collateral will withstand attack by competing secured creditors, judgment lien creditors and a bankruptcy trustee.* A security interest is said to be perfected when all the steps have been taken to ensure its priority in the collateral described against all possible competing claimants. Generally, a security interest is perfected either through the taking of possession or control of the collateral or the filing of a financing statement under the UCC or both. In a limited number of cases, perfection is obtained through compliance with other state or federal law.

Perfection generally determines a creditor's priority to proceeds from the disposition of the collateral. Perfected security interests generally have priority from the date of perfection where the perfection was accomplished through filing, possession, control or some other means. Proper classification of the collateral into the appropriate category is essential since the proper means of perfection is based upon the classification of collateral.

Figure 7-2 will assist in determining the means of perfection applicable. Where two methods of perfection are listed, the method in bold is considered the preferred method. The subsequent explanation should assist in perfecting a security interest.

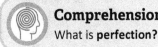

Comprehension Check
What is **perfection**?

Figure 7-2   Perfection Methods by Type of Collateral

Type of Collateral	Method of Perfection Under Article 9
Accounts	Filing (9-310(a))
Agricultural Liens	Filing (9-310(a))
Certified Securities	Possession or Filing (9-313(a))
Commercial Tort Claims	Filing (9-310(a))
Deposit Accounts	Control (9-312(b)), (9-314(a))
Electronic Chattel Paper	Filing (9-312(a)) Control (9-314(a))
General Intangibles	Filing (9-310(a))
Goods	Filing (9-310(a), 9-312(c)) Possession (9-313(a) and (b))
Healthcare Insurance Receivables	Filing (9-310(a)) Attachment (9-309(5))
Instruments	Filing (9-312(a)) Possession (9-313(a))
Investment property (other than certified securities)	Filing (9-312(a)) Control (9-314(a))
Letter-of-Credit Rights	Control (9-312(b)(2), 9-314(a))
Money	Possession (9-312(b)(3), 9-313(a))
Negotiable Documents	Filing (9-310(a), 9-312(a)) Possession (9-313(a))
Oil, Gas or Other Minerals Before Extraction	Filing (9-310(a))
Tangible Chattel Paper	Filing (9-312(a)) Possession (9-313(a))

Perfection by Possession

The secured party taking physical possession of the collateral may perfect security interests in most types of tangible collateral. The courts have generally held that if a secured party has exclusive control of, access to, or the use of the collateral, it has possession of it. Therefore, a negotiable instrument, such as a stock certificate in the company's safe, creates possession. Similarly, inventory or equipment stored in a warehouse in the company name is also in the company's possession. Article 9 also deals with the way to perfect a security interest where a third party has possession of the collateral. Notice of the security interest to the third party alone is not sufficient. The third party must acknowledge the security interest in an authenticated record that states that the third party is holding the collateral for the secured party's benefit.

Comprehension Check
Explain what is meant by the term **perfection by possession.**

Perfection by Control

Control *applies to situations where a secured party may not be in physical possession of the collateral but can still exercise a sufficient amount of power over the collateral to control it.* This frequently requires that a third party having possession of the investment property collateral, such as a bank, broker or other financial institution, enter into an agreement with the secured party where the third party agrees to comply with the secured party's instructions concerning the disposition of the collateral without the debtor's consent.

A secured party obtains control over a deposit account in a similar manner to obtaining control over investment property. Control over electronic chattel paper requires a unique "marking" of it. Control over a letter of credit right occurs when the secured party obtains the consent of the letter of credit issuer to the assignment of the proceeds of the letter of credit. However, there is automatic perfection of a security interest in a letter of credit right that is a supporting obligation of another category of collateral subject to a properly perfected security interest.

Comprehension Check
Explain what is meant by the term **perfection by control.**

Perfection by Filing

The most common method of perfecting a security interest under the UCC is through the filing of a **UCC financing statement.** A writing that meets all of the statutory requirements for a qualified financing statement must be filed with the proper authorities. The security interest must be continued to extend the validity of the perfection beyond the five-year period usually allowed. Article 9 contains the rules governing perfection by filing a UCC financing statement. These rules are designed to simplify procedures for UCC filings, reduce the cost of compliance by UCC filing and reduce the risk of inadvertent errors.

Comprehension Check
Explain what is meant by the term **perfection by filing.**

UCC Filing Rules

Article 9 substantially reduces the burden on a secured party by requiring the filing of a UCC financing statement for all types of collateral in the state where the debtor is located.

Where to File

A **registered organization**, such as a corporation, limited liability company and limited partnership, is located in the state where it is organized and registered. This term refers to *an entity organized solely under the law of a single state or the United States by the filing of a public organic record with the issuance of a public organic record by, or the enactment of legislation by the state or the United States.* The term includes a business trust that is formed or organized under the law of a single state if a statute of the state governing business trusts requires that the business trust's organic record be filed with the state. For example, a corporation is located in the state where it is incorporated. If a debtor is incorporated in Delaware and has its inventory in New Jersey and its chief executive office in New York, a UCC financing statement must only be filed in Delaware under Article 9.

Where the debtor is an unregistered organization, such as a general partnership, it is located in the state where it has its place of business; a UCC financing statement must be filed in that state. Where the debtor has a place of business in more than one state, it is deemed to be located in the state where it has its chief executive office, which is the state where a UCC must be filed.

Where the debtor is an individual, a UCC financing statement must be filed in the state of the debtor's principal residence. Where the debtor is a foreign entity that is located in a jurisdiction outside of the U.S. and the foreign jurisdiction does not provide for a public filing system that would enable a secured creditor to prevail over a subsequent lien creditor, the debtor is deemed to be located in the District of Columbia.

Article 9 simplifies the rules for filing a UCC financing statement in a particular state. Almost nationwide, the filing of a UCC financing statement is now done electronically with the Office of the Secretary of State. Louisiana remains an exception and requires filing at the local parish level, but such filing will constitute a statewide filing. An exception continues for fixtures where local filings continue to be required.

The filing of a UCC financing statement is deemed completed upon presentation of a proper UCC financing statement and the tender of the necessary filing fee or the acceptance of the UCC financing statement by the filing officer. Follow-up should be done for actual receipt and filing of the UCC financing statement. A secured party may wish to conduct a UCC search immediately after submitting the UCC filing to confirm that the UCC financing statement was properly filed and indexed.

Contents of UCC Financing Statement

A UCC financing statement must contain all of the following:

- **Name of Debtor.** A UCC financing statement must contain the debtor's correct legal name. The use of a trade name for a debtor that is a registered entity (such as a corporation) is not acceptable and may subject the secured creditor to the rights of a subsequent secured creditor. The question of whether an individual debtor's correct legal name must be used or whether a debtor may use a nickname has engendered substantial litigation and should discourage identifying individual debtors by their nickname.
- **Name of Secured Party or Its Representative**
- **Description of Collateral.** Under Article 9, a UCC financing statement can contain a generic "all asset" or "all personal property" description of collateral only if the description of collateral in the security agreement includes all categories of collateral or the security agreement otherwise authorizes it. However, the security agreement cannot contain such a generic "all assets" or "all property" description of collateral. Also, the extent of the perfected security interest is limited to the collateral described in the security agreement. For fixtures, the UCC must contain a real estate description and the name of the record owner of the real estate where the debtor does not have an interest in the real property, and should be filed in both the central location for personal property UCC filings and the real property records.

If a financing statement does not contain this information, it is ineffective and will not be accepted for filing. A financing statement should also contain the address of the debtor and secured party, the debtor's type and jurisdiction of organization and the debtor's organization identification number.

Article 9 does not require the debtor to sign a UCC financing statement. The debtor's authentication of a security agreement that describes the collateral referred to in the UCC financing statement authorizes the secured party to file a UCC financing statement. This facilitates the electronic filing of UCC financing statements and electronic UCC financing statement searches. As part of this rule, a secured party must obtain the debtor's authorization to pre-file a UCC financing statement where the debtor had not yet authenticated the security agreement.

Article 9 contains a uniform UCC financing statement. Virtually every state will now accept this uniform UCC form for filing (*see* Figure 7-3). In most states, Article 9 continues the rule that a UCC financing statement is effective for five years after the date of filing of the original UCC. The secured party must file a UCC continuation within six months prior to the fifth anniversary date of the original UCC filing. Unless a continuation is timely filed, the perfected security interest lapses the day after the fifth anniversary of the original filing. While a continuation does not have to be signed, a secured creditor should verify that its security agreement permits the continuation and does not contain a termination date which would disallow the filing of a continuation. Once filed, the continuation continues the perfection of the UCC financing statement for an additional five years, running from the end of the first five-year period and every succeeding five-year period, and not five years from the date of the filing of the continuation.

UCC filing amendments should be made: (1) when the name of the original debtor changes so that an existing UCC financing statement is "seriously misleading"; (2) to cover additional items or types of collateral and to correct

Figure 7-3   UCC Financing Statement

UCC FINANCING STATEMENT
FOLLOW INSTRUCTIONS

A. NAME & PHONE OF CONTACT AT FILER (optional)

B. E-MAIL CONTACT AT FILER (optional)

C. SEND ACKNOWLEDGMENT TO: (Name and Address)

Print   Reset

THE ABOVE SPACE IS FOR FILING OFFICE USE ONLY

1. DEBTOR'S NAME: Provide only one Debtor name (1a or 1b) (use exact, full name; do not omit, modify, or abbreviate any part of the Debtor's name); if any part of the Individual Debtor's name will not fit in line 1b, leave all of item 1 blank, check here ☐ and provide the Individual Debtor information in item 10 of the Financing Statement Addendum (Form UCC1Ad)

1a. ORGANIZATION'S NAME				
1b. INDIVIDUAL'S SURNAME	FIRST PERSONAL NAME		ADDITIONAL NAME(S)/INITIAL(S)	SUFFIX
1c. MAILING ADDRESS	CITY	STATE	POSTAL CODE	COUNTRY

2. DEBTOR'S NAME: Provide only one Debtor name (2a or 2b) (use exact, full name; do not omit, modify, or abbreviate any part of the Debtor's name); if any part of the Individual Debtor's name will not fit in line 2b, leave all of item 2 blank, check here ☐ and provide the Individual Debtor information in item 10 of the Financing Statement Addendum (Form UCC1Ad)

2a. ORGANIZATION'S NAME				
2b. INDIVIDUAL'S SURNAME	FIRST PERSONAL NAME		ADDITIONAL NAME(S)/INITIAL(S)	SUFFIX
2c. MAILING ADDRESS	CITY	STATE	POSTAL CODE	COUNTRY

3. SECURED PARTY'S NAME (or NAME of ASSIGNEE of ASSIGNOR SECURED PARTY): Provide only one Secured Party name (3a or 3b)

3a. ORGANIZATION'S NAME				
3b. INDIVIDUAL'S SURNAME	FIRST PERSONAL NAME		ADDITIONAL NAME(S)/INITIAL(S)	SUFFIX
3c. MAILING ADDRESS	CITY	STATE	POSTAL CODE	COUNTRY

4. COLLATERAL: This financing statement covers the following collateral:

5. Check only if applicable and check only one box: Collateral is ☐ held in a Trust (see UCC1Ad, item 17 and Instructions) ☐ being administered by a Decedent's Personal Representative

6a. Check only if applicable and check only one box:
☐ Public-Finance Transaction ☐ Manufactured-Home Transaction ☐ A Debtor is a Transmitting Utility

6b. Check only if applicable and check only one box:
☐ Agricultural Lien ☐ Non-UCC Filing

7. ALTERNATIVE DESIGNATION (if applicable): ☐ Lessee/Lessor ☐ Consignee/Consignor ☐ Seller/Buyer ☐ Bailee/Bailor ☐ Licensee/Licensor

8. OPTIONAL FILER REFERENCE DATA:

FILING OFFICE COPY — UCC FINANCING STATEMENT (Form UCC1) (Rev. 04/20/11)   International Association of Commercial Administrators (IACA)

Figure 7-4   UCC Financing Statement Amendment

UCC FINANCING STATEMENT AMENDMENT
FOLLOW INSTRUCTIONS

A. NAME & PHONE OF CONTACT AT FILER (optional)

B. E-MAIL CONTACT AT FILER (optional)

C. SEND ACKNOWLEDGMENT TO: (Name and Address)

[Print]   [Reset]

THE ABOVE SPACE IS FOR FILING OFFICE USE ONLY

1a. INITIAL FINANCING STATEMENT FILE NUMBER	1b. ☐ This FINANCING STATEMENT AMENDMENT is to be filed [for record] (or recorded) in the REAL ESTATE RECORDS Filer: attach Amendment Addendum (Form UCC3Ad) and provide Debtor's name in item 13

2. ☐ **TERMINATION**: Effectiveness of the Financing Statement identified above is terminated with respect to the security interest(s) of Secured Party authorizing this Termination Statement

3. ☐ **ASSIGNMENT** (full or partial): Provide name of Assignee in item 7a or 7b, and address of Assignee in item 7c and name of Assignor in item 9
For partial assignment, complete items 7 and 9 and also indicate affected collateral in item 8

4. ☐ **CONTINUATION**: Effectiveness of the Financing Statement identified above with respect to the security interest(s) of Secured Party authorizing this Continuation Statement is continued for the additional period provided by applicable law

5. ☐ **PARTY INFORMATION CHANGE**:

Check one of these two boxes: AND Check one of these three boxes to:

This Change affects ☐ Debtor or ☐ Secured Party of record   ☐ CHANGE name and/or address: Complete item 6a or 6b; and item 7a or 7b and item 7c   ☐ ADD name: Complete item 7a or 7b, and item 7c   ☐ DELETE name: Give record name to be deleted in item 6a or 6b

6. **CURRENT RECORD INFORMATION**:   Complete for Party Information Change - provide only one name (6a or 6b)

6a. ORGANIZATION'S NAME			
OR 6b. INDIVIDUAL'S SURNAME	FIRST PERSONAL NAME	ADDITIONAL NAME(S)/INITIAL(S)	SUFFIX

7. **CHANGED OR ADDED INFORMATION**:   Complete for Assignment or Party Information Change - provide only one name (7a or 7b) (use exact, full name; do not omit, modify, or abbreviate any part of the Debtor's name)

7a. ORGANIZATION'S NAME			
OR 7b. INDIVIDUAL'S SURNAME			
INDIVIDUAL'S FIRST PERSONAL NAME			
INDIVIDUAL'S ADDITIONAL NAME(S)/INITIAL(S)			SUFFIX

7c. MAILING ADDRESS	CITY	STATE	POSTAL CODE	COUNTRY

8. ☐ **COLLATERAL CHANGE**: Also check one of these four boxes: ☐ ADD collateral   ☐ DELETE collateral   ☐ RESTATE covered collateral   ☐ ASSIGN collateral

Indicate collateral:

9. **NAME OF SECURED PARTY OF RECORD AUTHORIZING THIS AMENDMENT**: Provide only one name (9a or 9b) (name of Assignor, if this is an Assignment)
If this is an Amendment authorized by a DEBTOR, check here ☐ and provide name of authorizing Debtor

9a. ORGANIZATION'S NAME			
OR 9b. INDIVIDUAL'S SURNAME	FIRST PERSONAL NAME	ADDITIONAL NAME(S)/INITIAL(S)	SUFFIX

10. OPTIONAL FILER REFERENCE DATA:

International Association of Commercial Administrators (IACA)

FILING OFFICE COPY — UCC FINANCING STATEMENT AMENDMENT (Form UCC3) (Rev. 04/20/11) errors in or to change the names and addresses of the debtor or secured party; and (3) for any amendment of an existing UCC financing statement. The UCC Amendment does not have to be signed, but it must be authorized by the debtor's authentication of the security agreement.

The Amendment refers to the original UCC filing by filing number, date and filing office and describes the change from the original UCC financing statement, such as a name change or change in collateral (*see* Figure 7-4).

Comprehension Check

List three elements that should be included in a UCC financing statement.

As a general rule, how long is a filing valid?

Mistakes in a UCC Financing Statement's Collateral Description Can Be Hazardous to a Perfected Security Interest!*

A trade creditor dealing with a financially distressed customer may seek a security interest in its customer's property to increase the likelihood of payment of the creditor's claim. One of the requirements for obtaining a valid security interest with priority over future security interests in the same collateral is for the creditor to properly identify its collateral in both (1) the security agreement executed by its customer, and, just as importantly, (2) the publicly filed UCC financing statement.

The holding of the United States Court of Appeals for the Sixth Circuit, in *1st Source Bank vs. Wilson Bank & Trust, et al.*, is a reminder of the unintended and harsh consequences of an inconsistency between the description of the collateral in the security agreement and the UCC financing statement. The Sixth Circuit held that a bank did not have a perfected security interest in certain trucking company debtors' accounts receivable because the bank had failed to include "accounts" or "accounts receivable" as part of the bank's collateral in its UCC financing statement, notwithstanding the inclusion of the term "accounts" as collateral in the parties' security agreement.

Requirements for Perfecting a Security Interest in Personal Property

A creditor seeking to obtain a security interest in personal property must satisfy the requirements included in Article 9 of the Uniform Commercial Code. First, a creditor must satisfy the requirements for the creation or attachment of a security interest in its collateral. A creditor obtains a security interest in personal property through a security agreement, signed by the debtor, which describes the collateral in which the creditor is granted a security interest. The security agreement must describe the collateral by class or type. For example, the collateral can be described as accounts, chattel paper, instruments, inventory, equipment, general intangibles and other categories of personal property.

Second, the creditor must perfect its security interest in the collateral. Perfection ensures that a creditor's security interest in the collateral will withstand attack by another secured creditor, a judgment lien creditor or a bankruptcy trustee. A creditor frequently perfects its security interest by filing a UCC financing statement in the appropriate filing office. A UCC financing statement must include the debtor's correct legal name, the name of the secured party and a description of the collateral. The description of the collateral in the security agreement must conform to the description of the collateral in the UCC financing statement.

The Facts of the Sixth Circuit Case

In 2004, 1st Source Bank (1st Source) sold or leased tractors and trailers to two trucking companies: K&K Trucking and J.E.A. Leasing (the Debtors). The parties' security agreements granted 1st Source a security interest in the Debtors' tractors and/or trailers, *accounts* and in the proceeds from the agreed upon collateral. On the other hand, the UCC financing statements, properly filed pursuant to Tennessee state law, contained a narrower description of 1st Source's collateral, identifying the collateral as tractors and/or trailers "together with all present and future attachments, accessories, replacement parts, repairs, additions and exchanges thereto and therefore, documents and certificates of title, ownership or origin, with respect to the equipment and *all proceeds thereof*, including rental and/or lease receipts." Significantly, 1st Source's financing statements, unlike the security agreements, did *not* include "accounts," "accounts receivable," or any other similar descriptive terms.

Wilson Bank & Trust, Pinnacle Bank, and TransCapital Leasing, Inc. (the Defendants) then lent money to the Debtors. The Debtors granted the Defendants a security interest in the Debtors' "accounts receivable now outstanding or hereafter arising." This security interest was reflected in a security agreement that the Debtors had executed.

In addition, the Defendants properly filed their UCC financing statements that, unlike 1st Source's UCC financing statements, specifically and correctly described the collateral as "all accounts receivable now outstanding or hereafter arising."

The Debtors defaulted on their loans in late 2009. 1st Source repossessed its collateral consisting of the Debtors' tractors and trailers. The Defendants collected the Debtors' accounts receivable in which they claimed a first priority security interest.

1st Source sued the Defendants alleging that 1st Source had a first priority security interest in the Debtors' accounts receivable because the language "and all proceeds hereof" included in 1st Source's financing statements, was sufficient to put third parties on notice of 1st Source's security interest in the Debtors' accounts receivable. The Defendants filed a motion for summary judgment seeking to dismiss 1st Source's complaint. The lower court granted summary judgment in favor of Defendants, holding that, under Tennessee law, 1st Source did not have a perfected security interest in the Debtors' accounts receivable because 1st Source's financing statements were insufficient to put the Defendants on notice that 1st Source's security interest extended to accounts receivable. In particular, the term "proceeds" as used in 1st Source's financing statements, could not be construed to include the Debtor's accounts's receivable.

The Sixth Circuit's Holding and Analysis

The Sixth Circuit upheld the lower court's decision. The court emphasized the importance of notice of a creditor's security interest in its collateral that its UCC financing statement is supposed to provide.

The priority of 1st Source's and the Defendants' security interests in the Debtors' accounts is governed by Chapter 9 of Tennessee's Commercial Code. Section 47-9-203 of the Tennessee UCC makes clear that 1st Source's security interest attached to the Debtors' "accounts" when the parties had entered into the security agreements. However, the issue was not whether 1st Source had a valid security interest in the Debtors' accounts, but, instead, whether 1st Source had a properly *perfected* security interest in the Debtors' accounts that had priority over the Defendants' later perfected security interest in the accounts. According to § 47-9-502(a)(3) of the Tennessee UCC, 1st Source was required to file a UCC financing statement that properly described the collateral (which 1st Source asserted included the Debtors' accounts) as a condition to properly perfecting its security interest in the Debtors' accounts.

The Sixth Circuit recognized that the filing of a UCC financing statement is required to notify third parties "that a person may have a security interest in the collateral indicated" in the financing statement. While minor mistakes in a UCC financing statement are excusable, a financing statement must be "sufficiently accurate such that third parties are put on notice." In addition, "only collateral that is adequately described in the financing statement will be perfected—*even where the security agreement confers a security interest in other collateral*" (emphasis added). In other words, if the collateral description contained in a publicly filed UCC financing statement is narrower than the collateral description contained in a security agreement, a subsequent secured creditor and/or bankruptcy trustee is only bound by the narrower (publicly ascertainable) collateral description included in a UCC financing statement.

The Sixth Circuit applied these principles observing that the "limiting language in 1st Source's financing statements identified the only items that were subject to the security interest," which did not include the Debtors' "accounts" or its "accounts receivable." The Defendants were not put on notice that 1st Source was claiming a security interest in the Debtors' accounts receivable, as the term was not referenced in the financing statements. Consequently, the Defendants' security interest in the Debtors' accounts receivable was superior to that of 1st Source by virtue of the Defendants' UCC financing statement identifying accounts as collateral.

The Sixth Circuit also rejected 1st Source's argument that the phrase "all proceeds thereof" included in the financing statements was sufficient to put third parties on notice that 1st Source had a properly perfected security interest in the Debtors' accounts receivable. Although the court recognized the very broad definition of "proceeds" included in the Tennessee UCC, 1st Source's interpretation of the term "proceeds" would render meaningless the term "accounts" (which is separately defined in § 47-9-102(a)(2) of the Tennessee UCC). The court was hesitant to expand the definition of the general term "proceeds" in a manner that would subsume the more specific term "accounts."

The Sixth Circuit also focused on how the Tennessee UCC's drafters sought to limit the definition of the term "proceeds" by explaining in the Tennessee UCC's commentary that the term "proceeds" does not include "income generated from the debtor's own use and possession of goods," where there was "no disposition of the goods by the security lease." Further, relying on the lower court's decision and other precedent, the Sixth Circuit held that in order for rights to "arise out of collateral," those rights "must have been obtained as a result of some loss or disposition of the party's interest in that collateral, not simply by its use" as "revenues earned through the use of collateral are not proceeds."

The Sixth Circuit's holding that "accounts receivable" cannot ever qualify as "proceeds" is disturbing and inappropriately broad. The court might have reached a different conclusion if the Debtors were selling or leasing tractors and trailers to third parties, instead of operating a trucking company. The tractors and trailers that the Debtors sold or leased would have been characterized as "inventory" under the Tennessee UCC instead of "equipment." Under these circumstances, the sale or lease of the tractors and trailers could be "dispositions" of collateral that would generate "proceeds." The first generation proceeds could take the form of "accounts" or "chattel paper." These first generation proceeds could then become cash proceeds when payment is received from a buyer or lessee of the tractors and trailers. In this scenario, 1st Source's financing statements should have automatically covered accounts as proceeds, regardless of whether the financing statements included the term "proceeds."

Conclusion

The litigation leading to the Sixth Circuit's decision could have easily been avoided if 1st Source had included a reference to "accounts" or "accounts receivable" in the description of collateral in the financing statements. All creditors seeking to perfect a security interest in assets taken as collateral for the payment of their claims should make it a practice to conform the description of their collateral in the security agreement and UCC financing statement. The alternative, which all creditors should strive to avoid, is costly ligation over the technical issue of what categories of collateral the terms used in a UCC financing statement actually cover and the risk that the creditor loses its perfected security interest in some or all of the collateral described in its security agreement.

Excerpted from "Mistakes in a UCC Financing Statement's Collateral Description Can Be Hazardous to a Perfected Security Interest!" by Bruce S. Nathan, Esq. and Eric S. Chafetz, Esq., Lowenstein Sandler PC.

Priority Rules

Article 9's long-standing rule is that *the first secured party to file a UCC financing statement or otherwise perfect its security interest has* **priority** *over competing secured parties.* However, there is an exception to this rule for certain categories of collateral: *A later perfection by possession or control of the collateral has priority over an earlier perfection by UCC filing.* For example, a security interest in an instrument that is perfected by possession has priority over a competing security interest that was previously perfected by a UCC filing. A security interest in tangible chattel paper that is perfected by possession also has priority over a competing security interest perfected by an earlier UCC filing, unless the latter security interest is legended on the chattel paper. In addition, a security interest in either electronic chattel paper or investment property that is perfected by control has priority over a competing security interest that is perfected by an earlier UCC filing (*see* Figure 7-2).

As a general rule, where two secured parties perfect by control, priority is determined by which secured party first obtains control. However, a *depository bank's security interest* or **right of setoff** with respect to a debtor's deposit account has priority over all other security interests in the account, whether such competing security interests are taken as original collateral or are proceeds of other collateral. A security interest in favor of the debtor's securities intermediary perfected by control of the debtor's brokerage account always has priority over a competing security interest in the account perfected by control.

A security interest in a letter of credit right that is perfected by control has priority over a secured party's interest in letter-of-credit rights that was automatically perfected as a supporting obligation.

A buyer of goods, such as inventory, in the ordinary course of business defeats a secured party that perfects by UCC filing. However, Article 9 provides that an ordinary course buyer of goods takes the goods subject to the rights of a secured party that has possession of the goods.

 Comprehension Check
How is **priority** established?

Purchase Money Security Interests

A **purchase money security interest** *is a security interest granted to a trade creditor in goods sold on credit terms to the debtor for the purchase price of the trade creditor's goods or a security interest granted to a third party lender in goods purchased by the debtor and paid for by loans or advances made by such lender.* Assets subject to a purchase money security interest are usually goods, such as inventory or equipment. A purchase money security interest can also be granted in software. There can be no purchase money security interest in intangible collateral.

A nexus, or connection, is required between the acquisition of the goods and the obligation to pay for them. A security interest does not qualify as a purchase money security interest if a debtor acquires property on unsecured credit terms and subsequently creates a security interest to secure the purchase price.

A purchase money security interest is granted superpriority status that has priority over existing perfected security interests. The secured party must take certain steps, depending on the type of collateral, to achieve this superpriority status. To obtain a purchase money security interest in collateral (other than livestock and inventory), such as a purchase money security interest in equipment, a secured party must have the debtor execute a security agreement containing the appropriate granting language in the collateral and file a UCC financing statement in the appropriate jurisdiction within 20 days after the debtor receives possession of the collateral. Where the purchase money collateral is inventory, the debtor must execute or authenticate a security agreement identifying the purchase money inventory collateral; file a UCC financing statement in the appropriate jurisdiction before the debtor gains possession of the inventory; and notify all secured creditors with UCC filings in the same type of inventory that the secured party intends to take a purchase money security interest in the inventory within five years of the debtor's possession of the inventory. However, a secured party with a possessory purchase money security interest in inventory that has not been delivered to the debtor does not have to give advance notice to existing secured parties to achieve superpriority status. Finally, a purchase money financier of livestock must notify earlier filed secured parties as in the case of inventory.

Under Article 9, the scope of a purchase money security interest in non-consumer transactions has a "dual status" rule. A purchase money secured creditor does not lose its superpriority purchase money status:

- Where the purchase money collateral also secures payment of other obligations.
- Where the obligation secured by the purchase money collateral is also secured by other collateral.
- Where the purchase money obligation is refinanced.

A creditor that satisfies all of the requirements for a purchase money security interest has priority over an earlier filed security interest in the same collateral as after-acquired property. A superpriority purchase money security interest in goods other than inventory extends to all identifiable proceeds of the goods to which the security interest is perfected. A purchase money security interest in inventory extends to identifiable cash proceeds received on or before delivery of the inventory and to chattel paper and instruments generated by the sale of the inventory if the secured party takes possession of, or places a legend on, the chattel paper or instruments. The superpriority status of a purchase money security interest in inventory does not extend to accounts arising from the sale of the inventory or to trade-ins. A purchase money security interest in inventory and equipment is subordinate to the security interest of a bank into which the cash proceeds of the collateral have been deposited.

Article 9 has created special priority rules for livestock financiers in proceeds of their purchase money collateral. A purchase money security interest in livestock extends to all proceeds, including accounts and all identifiable products in their unmanufactured states.

Finally, Article 9 changes the priority rules for multiple purchase money security interests. A supplier's purchase money security interest for the purchase price of the collateral has priority over a third-party lender's purchase money security interest for an enabling loan. Multiple purchase money security interests asserted by third-party lenders having made enabling loans rank in order of UCC filing.

 Comprehension Check
How is a **purchase money security interest** established?

PMSI (PURCHASE MONEY SECURITY INTEREST) HELPS LEAD THE WAY TO SATISFACTION

The Credit Situation: Historically, Donlamor, Inc. had been a high-volume retail customer of Pennsylvania House furniture (subsidiary of La-Z-Boy). In better times, the retailer had a high credit of $450,000. However, during difficult economic times, the retailer's financial condition deteriorated, causing a reduction of the credit limit to $150,000.

At the beginning of the year, Donlamor owed Pennsylvania House approximately $130,000. Due to cash flow constraints, the retailer's ability to pay the existing balance was questionable. The retailer had a backlog of consumer orders totaling $630,000 at wholesale cost. Consumer deposits on these orders were around $300,000. If the orders could not be filled, we determined that it would create tremendous consumer dissatisfaction with our brand name, even though our company would not be directly responsible for the unfilled orders.

Pennsylvania House inventory security included a purchase money security interest (PMSI) in the retailer's inventory and personal guarantees from the principals. Since any inventory released would be shipped immediately to consumers, the new inventory would not be available as collateral. The financial statements of the guarantors would not justify a significant increase in the credit limit.

The Problem: Whether to take a loss of the existing balance of $130,000 or to risk increasing the credit to as much as $650,000 so that the backlog orders could be filled.

The owner of Donlamor proposed granting Pennsylvania House a second mortgage in a warehouse (net equity of $230,000) and first lien in other floor samples (estimated wholesale value of $200,000). We could justify loaning 80 to 90 percent of the equity in the warehouse and 50 to 70 percent of the inventory value. On paper, this would have justified a credit increase of about $280,000 to $350,000.

To prevent the retailer from immediately exhausting the additional credit extension (and leaving half of the backlog orders unfilled), we required that 70 percent of each order released be paid immediately once the merchandise was loaded onto a truck and ready for shipment. The retailer's normal practice had been to collect the remaining balance from the consumer, once the furniture was ready for shipment. Our thought was that the consumer collections would partially or fully fund the 70 percent cash-in-advance requirement. The remaining 30 percent of each invoice would be added to a revolving promissory note secured by the warehouse and the other inventory. Ten monthly payments of around $35,000 would pay the revolving note in full (with interest at prime plus 1 percent). The benefits: (a) the existing balance could be paid over 10 months, (b) about $650,000 in new sales would be recognized by Pennsylvania House, (c) consumer dissatisfaction of cancelled orders would be avoided and (d) about $12,500 interest would be earned on the revolving note.

The Outcome: Pennsylvania House was aware of another retailer who expressed a desire to expand its business. After extensive negotiations, the Pennsylvania House "gallery" portion of the Donlamor business was sold and the selling price of $240,000 was pledged to Pennsylvania House, which also reduced exposure.

The entire transaction represented approximately $800,000 invoiced, including prior exposure and completed consumer shipments. The promissory note was essentially pre-paid as the customer remitted $365,000 within five weeks, and we transferred $160,000 of inventory to the new retailer. We also reduced the receivable by $240,000 based on a six-month interest bearing (prime plus 1 percent) signed by the new buyer and payable to Pennsylvania House.

We not only were able to protect our accounts receivable assets, but we also satisfied numerous deposit consumers. We subsequently shipped $300,000 to the new buyer for floor samples and back-up stock. The entire transaction resulted in more than $1.1 million of added sales for Pennsylvania House.

$800,000 — A/R
($400,000) — payments
($160,000) — inventory transfer
($240,000) — sale of Pennsylvania House gallery
$ 0.00 — net

Dave Carpenter

Consignments

Article 9 defines a **consignment** *as a transaction, regardless of its form, in which a person delivers goods to a merchant for the purpose of sale and the following:*

- The transaction does *not* create a security interest that secures an obligation.
- The goods are not consumer goods immediately before delivery.
- The merchant deals in goods of that kind under a name other than the name of the person making delivery; is not an auctioneer; and is not generally known by its creditors to be substantially engaged in selling the goods of others.
- With respect to each delivery, the aggregate value of the goods is $1,000 or more at the time of delivery;

This definition excludes consignments of consumer goods and consignments of small quantities of commercial goods (valued at less than $1,000). However, commercial consignments are not subject to Article 9 where the consignee is generally known by its creditors to be substantially engaged in selling the goods of others (which is difficult to prove).

A consignment is treated as a purchase money security interest in inventory. A consignor will have to follow the rules under Article 9 for the creation and perfection of security interests in inventory and the rules applicable to purchase money inventory security interests to obtain priority over existing floating inventory secured lenders.

There are three steps that a consignment vendor must take to properly protect its business transactions with its customer and protect its consigned goods.

1. **Enter into a properly written consignment agreement with the customer.** This consignment agreement should fulfill all the requirements of a business contract and must be signed by an appropriate person for each party involved.

2. **A consignment vendor must run a UCC search of its customer to determine what creditors have already filed UCC financing statements and perfected a lien against the customer's inventory.** The UCC search must be run where the customer is located. Location is specifically defined in the UCC. The definition of location differs depending on the customer. A corporation, limited liability partnership, limited partnership or other registered artificial entity is located in the state of its registration.

   Once the UCC search is run and the consignment vendor knows who has filed UCC financing statements before it, the consignment vendor must provide notification to each prior secured creditor that it is about to or has entered into a consignment agreement with the customer. While the UCC states that one only has to notify lien creditors that have liens in the same goods or types of goods as the trade vendor, it recommended to notify each and every prior secured creditor to eliminate future arguments over whether or not notice was required. Send the notification by certified mail or overnight courier so that the trade vendor has proof that the prior secured party received it.

3. **A UCC financing statement must be filed with the appropriate office (generally the Secretary of State) where the customer is located, as defined by the UCC.** If a consignment vendor is selling to an entity that has different corporate or other artificial entities, then a UCC financing statement must be filed with each appropriate office where each distinct corporate or artificial entity is located.

There is no protection for consigned goods until all three steps are achieved. Any one step missing leaves the consignment vendor at risk. A consignment vendor that delivers goods before each of these steps is finalized subjects its goods to the claims of a prior lien creditor's rights in inventory.

Comprehension Check
What is **consignment**?

CHAPTER 11 FILINGS CAUSE HAVOC FOR AN UNPERFECTED CONSIGNMENT CREDITOR

Sports Authority Holdings, Inc. and seven related corporations ("referred to herein as TSA") filed Chapter 11 proceedings on March 2, 2016. Approximately 170 consignment vendors sold inventory to TSA under various consignment or vendor agreements. Among the first-day motions filed by TSA was a motion to authorize TSA to continue to sell its consignment inventory in the ordinary course of business, provide replacement liens to consignment vendors in post-petition inventory and continue to pay consignment vendors in the ordinary course of business. TSA's motion stated how important consignment vendors are to its continued business operations because they allow TSA to "receive and resell a wide range of popular goods in [its] stores without having to commit working capital up front to cover the cost of selling such inventory." TSA stated further that it relies "on their ability to provide a wide selection of goods to meet customers' needs and drive customers' traffic."

Consignment vendors were excited to see this motion filed by TSA until the language within the motion was read carefully. Within that motion, TSA stated that it would only grant replacement liens to and/or pay the consignment vendors that have "[a] valid, enforceable, non-avoidable and perfected lien on consigned goods."

In one fell swoop, TSA promised protection to the consignment vendors and then took it away. As information has unfolded, it appears that about 90% of the TSA consignment vendors did not provide notification to prior secured creditors and did not file proper UCC Financing Statements.

TSA has now commenced a multitude of adversary proceedings (lawsuits) against consignment vendors seeking to have the Bankruptcy Court declare these consignment vendors to have unperfected security interests, permitting TSA to sell all inventory unfettered by these consignments and deem these consignment vendors to be nothing other than general unsecured creditors.

Clearly, that is a far cry from the protection these vendors intended to have when they entered into the original agreements with TSA.

A similar dispute took place in the Family Christian Bookstore Chapter 11 proceeding. That case was slightly different. Whereas in TSA, the Debtor has commenced the lawsuits to determine the consignment interests to be invalid, in the Family Christian Bookstore case, the consignment vendors banded together to prevent Family Christian from selling the consignment inventory. They claimed that the consignments were "true consignments outside the scope of Article 9" because the debtor is "generally known by its creditors to be substantially engaged in selling the goods of others." The consignment vendors claim that because of this exception, neither notification nor UCC filings were necessary to protect the consignment status of these vendors. The Family Christian litigation resulted in a settlement whereby the consignment vendors were paid a portion of the sale price of the consigned inventory so that they received somewhat better treatment than the general unsecured creditors.

This argument is now being discussed in the TSA case by myriad consignment vendors that have been sued. The outcome cannot be predicted at this time although one would hope that a settlement will be reached that will be favorable to consignment vendors.

The moral of this story is consignment vendors must take the necessary steps to protect one's consignment interest or risk diminished treatment. Even if a consignment vendor believes it can convince a court that its business with a customer is that of a "true consignment" a consignment vendor is best served by taking the steps described above to properly notice and perfect its consignment interest and not risk losing the protection and treatment it anticipated by entering into a consignment agreement in the first instance.

Wanda Borges, Esq.
Borges & Associates LLC

Merger/Successor Debtor

Article 9 addresses a number of issues generally referred to as double debtor. **Double debtor issues** *occur when collateral is either transferred to a successor debtor or the original debtor merges with a third party.*

A filed UCC financing statement remains effective with respect to collateral transferred to a third party, unless the secured party consents to the transfer free of its security interest or the transfer is an ordinary course of sale to a good faith or *bona fide* purchaser. The secured party does not have to file a new UCC under the name of the transferee unless the transferee is located (organized, such as incorporated) in a different state. Where the transferee is located in another state, the original UCC will become ineffective as against the transferred collateral unless a new UCC is filed within one year of the transfer.

Where a successor of the original debtor is subject to an existing security agreement because of a merger with an existing debtor, a reincorporation of an existing debtor, or after a transfer of collateral, and the successor is located (organized) in the same state as the original debtor, a UCC filed in the name of the original debtor will continue to be effective to perfect a security interest in assets acquired by the successor following the merger or transfer unless the UCC becomes seriously misleading. That would be the case where the name of the successor is not substantially the same as the name of the old debtor.

When the UCC filing becomes seriously misleading the secured party has four months to file a new UCC that names the successor as debtor. If the secured party does so, its security interest remains perfected in collateral acquired by the successor. Where the secured party fails to do so, its security interest will become unperfected in collateral that the successor acquires after the four-month period.

Where the successor or other new debtor is located (organized) in a different state than the original debtor, the UCC financing statement filed against the original debtor is no longer effective to perfect a security interest in collateral acquired by the successor or other new debtor immediately after the merger or other act that created the new debtor. The secured party must immediately file a new UCC in the name of the successor or other new debtor in the new state in order to continue the perfection of its security interest in collateral acquired by the debtor.

In a priority dispute between the secured party of the original debtor and the secured party of the successor or other new debtor, the original debtor's secured party will have priority in collateral transferred to the successor or other new debtor, even where the secured party of the successor or other new debtor was the first to file a UCC. However, the secured party of the successor or other new debtor will have priority in all new collateral acquired by that debtor.

Perfection of Security Interests in Certain Specialized Collateral

Security interests in certain assets are perfected through means other than a UCC filing. These assets include titled motor vehicles, aircraft, boats, trademarks and patents, and most copyrights. Consult with counsel concerning the requirements for perfecting a security interest in these types of assets.

Default and Enforcement

Although a debtor's possible default may be the last thing actually anticipated when credit is extended, sales and security documentation must be prepared as if default were certain. The whole point of having a security interest in the debtor's assets is the secured party's ability to dispose of those assets toward payment of the debt if default occurs. That assumes that the secured party correctly assesses the value of its collateral and the market available at the time of default. A creditor has two main concerns if the debtor defaults or fails to pay the debt as promised:

1. Satisfaction of the debt through the possession and (usually) sale of the collateral.
2. Priority over any other creditors or buyers who may have rights in the same collateral.

This section will generically outline the possible events of default, the alternative steps to take to realize on collateral after default and the steps necessary to preserve a right to a deficiency judgment against the debtor, guarantors and other secondary obligors if the collateral is insufficient to pay the debt. It focuses on commercial transactions, rather than consumer transactions where the rules may be different.

Definition of Default

While the UCC does not define default, it does provide the parties with latitude in defining the term in the security documentation. Unlike other provisions of the UCC, which generally define a term where the parties fail to do so, Article 9 makes no specific provision for a definition of default.

Even though the UCC does not require a definition of default in security documentation, it is generally advisable to do so. A secured party should define default in such a fashion as to cover most of the probable bases for the need to foreclose. A common definition of default in security documentation includes the following "events of default":

1. The debtor's failure to make any payment when due.
2. The debtor's failure to satisfactorily insure the collateral.
3. The debtor's refusal to allow an inspection of the collateral within a reasonable time after a request for inspection by the secured party.
4. The debtor's failure to pay taxes on the collateral when due.
5. The debtor's removal of the collateral permanently from the agreed location without the written approval of the secured party.
6. The debtor's failure to periodically provide financial statements and other financial information.
7. The debtor's sale of the collateral without the consent of the secured party.
8. The debtor's death or incapacity.
9. The debtor's cessation of business.
10. The debtor's filing of bankruptcy or a filing of an involuntary bankruptcy against the debtor.
11. The appointment of a receiver, conservator or trustee for the debtor's business and property or both.
12. The debtor's assignment of assets for the benefit of creditors.
13. The debtor's insolvency.
14. The debtor's failure to make payments of debts to other secured creditors or to its lender.
15. The secured party's determination that the prospect of repayment is impaired.
16. The debtor's breach of the terms or covenants contained in any related agreement between the debtor and the secured party or any other secured lender.
17. The destruction of, or substantial damage to, any of the collateral.
18. The encumbrance, seizure or attachment of any of the collateral by the IRS or any other governmental entity, or by any judgment creditor.

Comprehension Check
List at least five "events of default."

Assuming the debtor is in default, the secured party may pursue any of the following enforcement remedies.

Collection Rights

Under Article 9, following the debtor's default, the secured party may exercise collection rights with respect to intangible collateral, such as accounts and general intangibles, or to instruments or chattel paper. The secured party may notify an account debtor or other obligor to make payment directly to the secured party. The secured party could also compel the other obligor's performance of other obligations, such as enforcing warranties and obtaining injunctions regarding intellectual property rights. The secured party may also receive and apply funds in a deposit account over which it has control in reduction of its claim against the debtor.

Comprehension Check
What is a secured party entitled to under collection rights?

Nonjudicial Repossession of Collateral

Article 9 permits a lender to take possession of the collateral upon default without any court action if it may do so peacefully. Any nonjudicial attempt to repossess collateral that involves or threatens to result in the use of force by either the secured party or the debtor is probably improper and may result in the imposition of liability on the secured party. When in doubt, consult counsel on nonjudicial repossession rights.

The UCC specifically authorizes the secured party to place language in the security agreement requiring the debtor to assemble and deliver collateral to the secured party. In some cases it is impractical for a secured party to take possession of equipment or fixtures that are collateral.

Judicial Foreclosure of Article 9 Security Interests

A secured party may pursue judicial foreclosure in any court with jurisdiction over the parties. While federal jurisdiction may exist, generally foreclosures of Article 9 security interests take place in state court in the state where the collateral is located, unless the government is a party. It would be impractical to attempt to summarize the civil procedures of all states in which the UCC applies.

Generally, the foreclosure process will involve the retention of counsel and the filing of a complaint or petition with the appropriate court and the payment of a filing fee. The pleadings filed with the appropriate court will seek the foreclosure of security interests in the property, the sale of the property and the distribution of proceeds to the secured party. If there is any amount unsatisfied after sale of the collateral, judgment will be entered against the debtor for the deficiency. If there is a surplus, after application of the proceeds to the sale expenses and the outstanding debt (and the attorney's fees of the secured party to the extent provided for by agreement and not precluded by law) the surplus must be distributed back to any junior secured creditors and then the debtor. In some cases an Article 9 foreclosure action may be combined with a real estate foreclosure action where the collateral includes both personal and real property.

Disposition of Collateral after Default

Article 9 has clear rules governing a secured party's rights and obligations upon the disposition of collateral. A secured party may sell, lease, license or otherwise dispose of its collateral by public or private disposition and apply the proceeds in reduction of its secured claim. All subordinate interests in the collateral would be discharged by such disposition. Every aspect of the disposition must be commercially reasonable. A secured party's obligation to act in a commercially reasonable manner in disposing of its collateral cannot be waived by the debtor or guarantor or other secondary obligor.

As a general rule, a secured party must give advance notice of the disposition of collateral. That includes sending notice of the time and place of any public disposition, or reasonable authenticated notification of the time after which any private disposition of collateral will occur. However, no advance notice of disposition is required where the collateral is perishable; where there is a threat of a quick decline in its value; or where the collateral is of a type that is customarily sold on a recognized market.

The secured party must send notice of the disposition of collateral to the debtor and all guarantors and other secondary obligors. The debtor and guarantors and other secondary obligors may waive their advance right to notice of disposition in an authenticated agreement following default. The secured party must also give notice to all secured parties and lienholders with an interest in the collateral that is disclosed on a search of the proper filing office within certain time parameters.

Article 9 creates a number of safe harbors as it relates to the secured party's obligation to give advance notice of disposition of its collateral. In a commercial transaction, 10 days advance notice of the disposition is deemed to be commercially reasonable. Notice of disposition of the collateral would also be deemed proper if it follows the form of notice provided in the statute.

Under Article 9, a secured party's realization of a low price from its disposition of collateral does not by itself render a disposition commercially unreasonable. However, a low price may prompt a court to carefully scrutinize all aspects of the disposition. If a secured party or related party, or a guarantor or other secondary obligor, acquires the collateral at a price that is significantly below the price that would have been realized from a disposition to an unrelated party, the secured party's deficiency claim would be reduced to reflect the higher price that would have been paid by a hypothetical unrelated party.

Article 9 also allows a secured party to receive noncash proceeds, such as a note, from the disposition of its collateral. The secured party does not have to apply any noncash proceeds, prior to their conversion to cash, toward the payment of its claim unless a failure to do so would be commercially unreasonable. This enables the secured party to place a value on the noncash proceeds and apply an appropriate discount rate.

Article 9 affords a transferee of a disposition of collateral the benefit of any title, possession, quiet enjoyment and similar warranties (such as ordinary warranties arising from sales, or warranties of quality or fitness for a particular purpose) that would have accompanied the disposition of the asset by operation of non-Article 9 law had the disposition been under other circumstances. Article 9 also permits a secured party to disclaim or modify such warranties.

Finally, under Article 9, a secured party may purchase collateral through a public disposition, such as a public auction. A secured party may not purchase collateral by private disposition, unless the collateral is of a kind customarily sold on a recognized market or subject to standard price quotations.

Strict Foreclosure

Under Article 9, strict foreclosure is another remedy available to a secured party following the debtor's default and involves the secured party's acceptance of its collateral in full, or partial satisfaction of its secured claim. A strict foreclosure, like an ordinary foreclosure and disposition of collateral, discharges all subordinate interests in the collateral. This remedy is also available to a secured party in a commercial transaction even where the secured party does not have possession of its collateral.

As part of any full strict foreclosure, a secured party must send an authenticated notice to the debtor and all secured parties and other lienholders with a junior interest in the collateral where the secured party proposes to retain the collateral. If the secured party receives an objection from any of these parties within 20 days after sending the proposal, the secured party cannot retain the collateral. Otherwise, the secured party can retain its collateral in full satisfaction of its claim. The secured party's retention of its collateral over a long period without sending such notice does not give rise to a strict foreclosure.

Article 9 also permits a secured party to retain collateral in partial satisfaction of its secured claim, known as a partial strict foreclosure. The debtor must consent to a partial strict foreclosure in a record authenticated after default. The proposal must also be sent to all guarantors and other secondary obligors as well as to all junior secured parties and other lienholders with an interest in the collateral. If the secured party does not receive an objection within 20 days, the partial strict foreclosure can proceed; otherwise, it cannot.

The debtor and guarantors and other secondary obligors can waive this notice requirement or agree to a secured party's retention of its collateral in full or partial satisfaction of its secured claim following the debtor's default.

Application of Proceeds of Disposition

Under Article 9, a secured party can apply the proceeds of the disposition of its collateral first toward payment of the expenses of disposition, including attorney's fees, if provided for under the debtor's agreement with the secured party and not prohibited by law; then toward the payment of the secured party's claim; and then toward the payment of the claims of creditors with a junior lien in the collateral. Any remaining surplus proceeds would be paid to the debtor.

Accounting for Distribution of Proceeds

Under Article 9, the secured party must account to the debtor for the distribution of the proceeds of the disposition of collateral and pay any surplus to the debtor.

Remedies

Article 9 adopts a rebuttable **presumption rule** *where the secured party fails to comply with its provisions on the disposition of collateral.* Where the secured party fails to comply with Article 9, there is a presumption that *the value of its collateral equaled the amount of the secured claim, which eliminates its deficiency claim.* This presumption, however, is subject to rebuttal by the secured party.

Key Terms and Concepts

Comprehension Check

1. Article 2 applies to which kind of transactions?
2. Under Article 2, what rule applies to sales worth more than $500?
3. Why does Article 2 distinguish between a merchant and casual or inexperienced sellers?
4. Within UCC Article 2, every contract has an obligation of good faith or honesty in the transaction concerned. Why is this an important concept?
5. What does **tender delivery** mean?
6. What options does a buyer have if goods delivered by the seller do not conform to the contract?
7. If a buyer refuses to accept goods that conform to the contract, how can the seller determine the damages for which the buyer is liable because of the breach of contract?
8. What does the general title section of the UCC state?
9. List the conditions that relate to risk of loss.
10. What is a shipment contract?
11. What is a destination contract?
12. What does **reclamation** mean under Article 2?
13. Define the term **warranty**.
14. What is an **express warranty?**
15. What is an **implied warranty?**
16. When is a lease contract enforceable?
17. What is the general concept behind Article 6?
18. Under UCC Article 6, five requirements must be followed whenever a **bulk transfer** is made. What are they?
19. Under UCC Article 9, what is a **secured transaction?**
20. What is a **security interest?**
21. What transactions are excepted from Article 9?
22. List the six categories of **collateral.**
23. List the items covered under Article 9's definition of **account.**
24. Why is determining primary use or purpose critical?
25. What requirements must be satisfied for the creation of a security interest?
26. What is a **security agreement?**
27. What does a security agreement establish?
28. At a minimum, a security agreement should contain four essential elements. What are they?
29. What is **perfection?**
30. Explain what is meant by the term **perfection by possession.**
31. Explain what is meant by the term **perfection by control.**
32. Explain what is meant by the term **perfection by filing.**
33. List three elements that should be included in a UCC financing statement.
34. As a general rule, how long is a filing valid?
35. How is **priority** established?
36. How is a **purchase money security interest** established?
37. What is **consignment?**
38. List at least five "events of default."
39. What is a secured party entitled to under collection rights?

Summary

- The UCC is not federal law. Each state adopts the code, and each state may adopt variations to the basic code outlined in the UCC.
- The UCC was created in order to cover every phase of commercial transactions that can involve the sale and payment of goods. Specifically, Article 2 of the UCC applies to sales of transactions in goods.
- Goods are defined as all things, other than money, stocks and bonds, that are movable.
- The UCC distinguishes between merchants and casual or inexperienced sellers by defining merchants as "a person that deals in goods of the kind or otherwise holds itself out by occupation as having knowledge or skill peculiar to the practices or goods involved in the transaction," which in turn enables merchants to be held to a higher standard.
- It is also important to note, the courts have the right to refuse to enforce contracts that are deemed to contain unfair or unconscionable clauses.
- A buyer has the right to inspect goods before payment, reject the goods if they fail to conform to the contract or accept in spite of non-conformity. If the goods do not meet the contracted standard, the seller has the right to correct or cure improper delivery. The UCC institutes the concept of **cover**, by which the buyer has the right to purchase substitute goods and recover from the seller the difference between the contracted price and the purchase of replacement goods.
- If the buyer refuses an order that conforms to the contracted standard, the seller also has the right to claim damages against the buyer. The seller must first resell the goods at the best obtainable price and then sue for the difference.
- The UCC provides that the passage of title passes to the buyer when the seller has completely performed their duties concerning physical delivery of goods.
- Risk of loss can be contractually addressed by using commonly accepted shipping terms. The seller has no liability in shipping contracts when goods are given to the carrier. Commonly used shipping contracts:
  - **FOB (Free on Board)**
  - **FAS (Free Alongside)**
  - **CIF (Cost, Insurance and Freight)**
  - **CFR (Cost and Freight)**
- In destination contracts, the seller remains liable until the product is delivered to the specified destination. Common destination contracts include:
  - **FOB destination**
  - **EX-Ship**
  - **No Arrival, No Sale**
- If the seller discovers the buyer is insolvent before making the delivery, the seller has the right to withhold the delivery until the buyer pays cash for the goods and for any previously delivered items that have yet to be paid. This includes goods in transit. Sellers also have the right to demand the return of merchandise from an insolvent buyer within 10 days of the receipt of shipment.
- A warranty is a contractual promise by the seller regarding the quality, character, or suitability of the goods sold, and whenever a seller of goods makes a statement of fact about the goods to a buyer as a part of the transaction, an express warranty is created.

- The four basic types of **implied warranties** include:
  - **An implied warranty of merchantability**
  - **An implied warranty of fitness for a particular purpose**
  - **An implied warranty derived from a usage of trade**
  - **An implied warranty of title**
- Leasing allows the lessee to use valuable assets without making an initial large capital investment.
- If the lessee is discovered to be insolvent, the lessor may refuse the delivery of goods or fully take possession of the goods without judicial process.
- Bulk transfers create special problems for businesses. Therefore, Article 6 was created within the UCC to protect creditors from merchants who are debtors from selling their entire inventory for less than it is worth.
- The UCC lists requirements for the transfer of goods, which if not fulfilled, forfeits the rights to ownership of the goods. If this occurs, a creditor must move quickly to assess how much time will elapse before the sale, a description of the property being sold, the property's value, any other creditors and the amount due to them, and whether debts should be paid in full.
- Business could not exist without laws permitting secured transactions. Article 9 of the UCC contains the law of secured transactions in personal property and fixtures.
- The UCC does not apply to liens on real estate, aircraft and certain vessels, wages, or certain types of insurance claims. Motor vehicles may be subject to UCC, but perfection is subject to other law.
- A security interest must be classified under the following categories:
  - Accounts and general intangibles
  - Deposit accounts
  - Goods
  - Instruments
  - Investment property
  - Chattel paper
- It is vital that a creditor determines the primary use of the collateral, because when handled by different individuals the item may change classification.
- The following requirements are needed to create a **security interest**:
  - **Creditor provided value to the debtor**
  - **Debtor has rights to the collateral and the power to transfer rights to the secured party**
  - **There is a valid security agreement that describes the collateral in which the creditor is granted security interest**
- At a minimum, a **security agreement** should contain:
  - **Identification of parties**
  - **Granting clause**
  - **Collateral description**
  - **Debtor's warranties, covenant and agreements**
- Perfection is necessary to ensure the secured party's right to collateral given that other parties may have interest in the collateral. Generally, a security interest is perfected either through the taking of possession or control of the collateral or the filing of a financing statement under the UCC. Perfection can also occur if both steps are taken.

- A **UCC financing statement** should contain:
  - **Name of the debtor**
  - **Name of the secured party or its representative**
  - **Description of collateral**
- Priority rules can vary, but the longstanding rule is that the first secured party to file a UCC financing statement or otherwise perfect its security interest has priority over competing secured parties. The rules often vary depending on the category of collateral.
- For **purchase money security interests,** it is important to note that a security interest does not qualify as a purchase money security interest if the debtor acquires the property on unsecured credit terms, and subsequently creates a security interest to secure the purchase price. However, if done correctly, the secured party has superpriority status over existing perfected security interests.
- When a **merger or successor debtor** occurs, a creditor should research whether the UCC financial statement has become invalid and should be refiled. This commonly occurs if the debtor is located or changes states.
- The whole point of having a security interest in the debtor's assets is the secured party's ability to dispose of those assets toward payment of the debt if default occurs.
- If a debtor is in default, the secured party may pursue the following **enforcement remedies**:
  - **Collection rights**
  - **Nonjudicial repossession of collateral**
  - **Judicial foreclosure of Article 9 interests**
  - **Disposition of collateral after default**
  - **Strict foreclosure**
  - **Application of proceeds of disposition**

References and Resources

Borges, Wanda, Esq. "Consignment Agreements Under Fire: If Not Done Right, You Can Get Burned." *Business Credit.* Columbia, MD: National Association of Credit Management. May, 2016.

Business Credit. Columbia, MD: National Association of Credit Management. (This 9 issues/year publication is a continuous source of relevant articles and information. Archived articles from *Business Credit* magazine are available through the web-based NACM Resource Library, which is a benefit of NACM membership.)

Manual of Credit and Commercial Laws. Columbia, MD: National Association of Credit Management, current edition.

Manual on Trade Creditors' Rights of Reclamation & Stoppage of Delivery of Goods. American Bankruptcy Institute, 2002.

Miller, Roger LeRoy, and Gaylord A. Jentz. *Business Law Today,* Comprehensive 6th ed. South-Western/Thomson Learning, 2004.

Nathan, Bruce S., Esq. and Eric S. Chafetz, Esq. "Mistakes in a UCC Financing Statement's Collateral Description Can Be Hazardous to a Perfected Security Interest!" *Business Credit.* Columbia, MD: National Association of Credit Management. May, 2014.

Uniform Commercial Code and Related Procedures. Registré's, 2001.

www.law.cornell.edu/ucc/. The full text of the UCC can be found here.

PART III

EXTENDING CREDIT

8 Credit Policy and Procedures

OVERVIEW

A well-defined credit policy allows a business to achieve established goals and serves as a guide in determining how to handle a variety of situations. In the decision-making process, credit policy is interpreted and applied to actual situations with guidelines or procedures that are devised by credit professionals to standardize the requirements assigned to the department. Companies can publish procedure manuals as ready references for employees.

THINK ABOUT THIS

Q. Can a credit policy be flexible enough to accommodate a changing business and economic environment?

Q. As the company's goals change with the market, how does the credit department ensure that its policies can reflect those changes?

DISCIPLINARY CORE IDEAS

After reading this chapter, the reader should understand:

- ☑ The purpose of a credit policy.
- ☑ The advantages of an implied over a written credit policy.
- ☑ How a credit policy is developed.
- ☑ The components of a credit policy.
- ☑ How to create an effective credit department.
- ☑ Establishing terms of sale and credit limits.
- ☑ How to handle collections and bad debts.
- ☑ Types of credit procedures needed.

CHAPTER OUTLINE

Defining Credit Policy

A credit policy is designed to provide consistency across departmental functions. Because credit policy concerns the company as a whole, it is usually established by top management. The chief credit professional and associates along with the heads of other interested departments can also be consulted as policy is created and updated. The format of a credit policy is specific to the company preparing the policy; it must reflect the company's receivable management goals. Every credit professional should be provided with a written policy statement—one that is used as a training aid, is fully understood and accepted by sales as well as the credit staff.

An effective credit policy permits and encourages the fullest development of the opportunities in administering credit. It provides the latitude to plan departmental operations within the scope of the company policy, while creating effective procedures and techniques to implement that policy and establish adequate controls. It can assure that there is consistency in the company's dealings and interactions with its customers and it provides a means of recognizing the importance of the credit function to the company.

The first step is the formulation of credit policy which begins with the establishment of objectives. What does the company want to accomplish? If these objectives are to be attained, what should be the role of the credit department? The next step is a thorough analysis of the context within which the credit policy must operate, including the following factors:

- The established company policies.
- The objectives and policies of the other departments.
- The primary industry characteristics, such as current credit practices, the role of credit in competition, the company's position in the industry.
- The company's financial resources.

After these steps have been completed, the credit policy can be formulated. Within the given context, the credit policy sets a course of action that is expected to help the company meet its objectives.

> **Comprehension Check**
> What is a **policy**?

A Written Policy vs. an Implied Policy

There are two ways a policy can be disseminated: implied or written. An **implied credit policy** *exists, but it is not officially stated (or written).* It has little or no official expression of approval and can be difficult to perceive and, therefore, be left to interpretation. By definition, the understanding of unwritten policy depends on oral communication or on inference from the decisions made by senior credit personnel. A **stated credit policy** *is set forth in writing* and usually has the support and approval of senior management. As the policy is available to everyone in the same form, there are usually fewer misunderstandings. A stated policy indicates a basic honesty and integrity in intention. It generates confidence and stability and serves as a good training tool.

Consideration of a written policy by the professionals concerned also helps to reveal differences in their understanding of what the policy is and areas in which it is inadequate. A written policy is useful because it can be a source of stability and continuity in the operation, not only of the credit department but also of the company as a whole.

Individual credit professionals and other administrators tend to vary unconsciously in their credit thinking as they interpret and react to the conditions and problems with which they work. Unwritten policy is thus subject to gradual, unnoticed changes while a written policy lessens the possibility of this kind of variability; it requires that changes in policy be conscious and intentional. In this way, policy becomes a vehicle for reviewing the credit department's effectiveness.

Removing credit policy from dependence on the knowledge and experience of one or a few individuals tends to ensure consistency regardless of changes in department personnel. There is a greater probability of consistent decisions under a written policy, especially in large and complex credit organizations, where many people are dealing with the same types of problems and where they can be separated organizationally or geographically. If needed, customers may be shown a copy of the policy statement, so they can see that they are not being given unusual or discriminatory treatment.

Comprehension Check
What is the difference between an **implied** and a **stated** credit policy?

Importance of Credit Policy

A **credit policy** *is a guiding principle used to establish direction for the credit function in an organization, in order to achieve the objectives of minimizing risk and maximizing profitability, while maintaining a competitive advantage in the marketplace.* Credit is an investment that companies make through its receivables. The credit department manages this investment, maximizing the benefit of the investment while minimizing the cost of nonpayment and looking for the greatest possible return at an acceptable risk. The acceptable risk is defined through policy.

A **credit procedure** *is a series of steps to be followed on a consistent basis for recurring credit situations, to accomplish the goals outlined in the company's strategic planning framework and/or internal audit framework.* Together, credit policies and credit procedures are used to empower the people responsible for the credit process by providing the direction and consistency they need for successful execution.

All companies, whether they sell on credit or cash, should have a credit policy. The policy provides a framework for making effective credit decisions. When a company sells on credit, individual credit decisions follow a pattern consistent with the company's overall goals and objectives. Companies vary widely in how they express a stated policy. It is often formulated in very broad terms, such as "to maximize sales with minimum losses," and fails to differentiate one customer from another or to provide a useful basis for individual credit decisions. Cash only is a form of credit policy whereby the company adopted the policy that no credit will be extended.

Sound credit policy must be effectively communicated, both inside and outside the credit department. Whether policy is disseminated orally or in writing, there must be clear mutual understanding as to what it is and how it is to be applied. The company may also wish to make its credit policy known to organizations and individuals outside the company, such as its banks, credit insurers and customers. Depending on the situation, define the purpose such a publication is expected to serve, the nature and duration of the relationship and the competitive role of credit.

To be effective, policy must be directly and explicitly related to action. The top credit executive should take the steps necessary to translate broad, flexible policy statements into guides that can be used by credit personnel in the daily operation of the department. This usually begins with establishing short-term objectives and determining for the short run what the emphasis is to be within the range of decisions provided by policy. Probably the most significant single step when implementing credit policy is creating an atmosphere that encourages credit department staff to think in terms of policy and to be aware of the effect of their individual credit decisions on the company's commitment to the accounts receivable investment and to department and company operations.

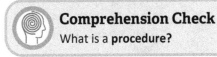
Comprehension Check
What is a **procedure?**

Developing a Credit Policy

A formal written credit policy should serve as a constant, practical guide for conducting all of the processes in a credit and collection function. A policy should be reviewed and updated periodically to align with organizational objectives and changing internal and external conditions.

There are four essential elements of credit policy:

1. **Establishing the credit standard.** This component describes the profile for an acceptable credit customer, including appropriate details and examples.

2. **Determining credit availability.** This component describes how the maximum amount of available credit is computed and managed, including decision criteria for reducing or increasing a customer's availability of credit.

3. **Setting credit terms.** This component stipulates the exact terms of sale for each class of customer.

4. **Defining collection policy.** This component provides criteria for regular collections and exception collection procedures for past due amounts.

The short-term application of **policy should be flexible,** consistent and fair, allowing for the credit professional's judgment. Some policy statements describe the degree of tolerance by using such phrases as "whenever possible" or "under usual conditions." Building in flexibility allows the policy to be used intelligently and in different approaches without the need for a formal change. Consistency ensures that the policy will be applied in a similar manner for like situations. Fairness ensures that all relevant facts and issues will be considered for each credit decision. Allowing for judgment encourages personal insight, develops better perspective and helps ensure a correct analysis of relevant matters.

The role of credit is influenced by a number of **general factors,** including the stability of demand for the industry's products and the rate of technological change. A company's current financial position can be decisive in the short-term application of policy. For example, severely limited working capital can require emphasis on prompt collections and rapid turnover of accounts receivable. New companies often have cash flow problems. As a start-up company matures and cash flow improves, policy can be changed. Changes in economic and political conditions and increased litigation in the collection of accounts can also prompt changes in policy.

The **type of customer** can have a limiting influence on the credit policies of all companies in an industry. Where the buyers' lines of business are characteristically short of capital, it is unrealistic for credit policy to be unduly restrictive. If an industry has many well-capitalized customers, the company that takes additional risk must expect additional return for this added risk. With enough good credit risks available to provide adequate profits, there must be an added incentive to make sales to fair or marginal risk customers. If the buyers are in control of the industry, the seller may have to offer longer terms.

The **geographic locations of customers** can have a direct bearing on policy with variations in credit terms offered. Widely separated markets require particular modifications in credit analysis and in collection efforts. A highly concentrated selling and buying area, on the other hand, involves a special type of price competition and service requirements.

Overall economic conditions can be significant in determining how policy is to be applied over shorter periods of time. When the business environment is stable and/or expanding, the ability of debtors to pay their invoices is somewhat improved; however, there is a danger that they may overbuy. If the business environment is contracting or slowing, debtors tend to delay payment of their invoices and credit requirements may tend to be stricter. Concurrently, companies are faced with the problem of meeting their bottom line in the face of decreasing sales and a customer base with more leverage.

Business conditions specifically affecting the areas or industries in which the company operates are also of major importance in policy application, such as those in a particular region, in the United States as a whole or in areas of foreign trade. Not all segments of the economy change at the same rate or in the same direction. The company can change emphasis, redefine responsibilities and adjust procedures in order to meet changing conditions. During prosperity and expansion, the credit department can help develop new markets or products. In a recession, the emphasis may be on greater care when selling to marginal accounts. The same credit policy is in effect during all phases of the cycle, but its application changes.

In many cases, the company's **competitive position** within its industry will influence how a company can apply its credit policy. While credit is not generally a competitive tool, a company can use the policy for competitive purposes. The credit professional must evaluate the company's long-range ability to compete and the competitive conditions within the industry. This would include analysis of the company's present position within the industry and its financial strength as well as an awareness of the strength of its sales organization and its position in product development. If a seller is not a major market leader, it may have to match the best terms, instead of being in firmer control over what terms it offers. For example, many companies whose position is undisputed or have substantial market share can demand strict credit policy whereas a start-up company may find it advantageous to be more lenient in its credit policy.

The **merchandising policy** of a company often influences credit policy. For example, a company may be required to place machinery in the hands of a limited number of franchised dealers on some basis to enable them to sell a maximum volume during a relatively short retail buying season. This may involve longer terms of sale in order to coordinate with manufacturing and shipment needs. Large extensions of credit can be required in relation to the financial responsibility of the dealers. Reliance is placed on the character and capacity of the dealer to a far greater extent than on capital. The essential factors are experience and proven ability in selling competitively, collecting effectively and operating profitably.

The **type of merchandise** affects the credit policy of the seller in a number of ways. The length of terms offered could be a function of the product's shelf life (those that can spoil will require shorter terms, so terms are usually net 7, 14 or 21 in the food industry), variations in demand (seasonal products can have differing terms depending on the time of year), and cost/price of the product (more expensive items such as jewelry can have longer terms while cheaper products can have shorter terms). Also, terms may be somewhat more liberal if the merchandise can be repossessed in the same condition as it was sold.

If goods have been stored in inventory for some time and an opportunity arises to dispose of them, credit policy should be sufficiently flexible to approve the transaction. An extreme example of this situation is the case of the shoe wholesaler that has stored some out-of-style shoes for a number of years and then receives an offer for the entire lot. Even if the customer wants extra terms or is not a good credit risk, it is doubtful that the shoe wholesaler will refuse the offer.

When merchandise can be obtained readily by the supplier, there is no need to restrict sales to customers unless warranted by financial or credit risks. When a particular item is scarce, however, credit policy can be influenced to the extent that stricter requirements are set for customers needing that item.

In the case of particular commodities, such as spirits and liquors, government regulations specify credit policies or procedures that must be followed by the seller. There, the overall policy must take the regulations into consideration.

Margins on the merchandise are important: when profit margins are slim, the credit department must be more vigilant with its oversight of its accounts. High-margin goods may enable credit professionals to approve sales to fair and marginal accounts more easily and more quickly as it may be more profitable to check orders and rely on overall profits to cover relatively bad-debt losses. Changes in profit margins can cause credit policy to change. For example, a new product line initially may have low profit margins. Accordingly, credit policy may be very tight. As profit margins increase, credit policy can probably loosen.

The price range of merchandise similarly influences credit policy. It is generally easier to establish a uniform liberal policy that applies to all customers when the unit price of merchandise is relatively low. Even on a wrong decision, the dollar amount of risk is not great. On a large ticket items, however, credit exposure is greater and a more detailed analysis is usually conducted before a customer order is approved.

Comprehension Check

List the four elements of a **credit policy.**

Foundational Components of a Credit Policy

There are several key questions which build the foundational components of the policy.

- What is the credit department's **mission**? This can also be called a vision or purpose. It states the overall objective for the credit function. The credit department's mission statement defines its goals, ethics, culture and norms for decision-making. The best mission statements define at least three dimensions: what the credit department does for its customers, what it does for its staff and what it does for its company.
- What are the **goals**? Goals can be specifically stated, such as a quantifiable measure, or more generally as an expressed desire to achieve improvement in a specific area.
- What are the roles and specific authorities of the credit management and staff? This defines the **boundaries of the credit function**, often in terms of interactions with other departments.

- What are the primary criteria for **evaluating customer credit**? This describes credit procedures in more detail, listing key aspects of the credit review and analysis processes.
- What are the company's **terms of sale**? Terms should be spelled out by major product line, with any qualifications or restrictions included.
- What are the **credit limits**? These should be set by the credit policy.
- What does **monitoring of accounts** consist of? The credit policy should set parameters for this function.
- What are the normal **collection procedures**? This describes the steps to be taken in customer collection activities.
- When is the account considered to be a **bad debt**? The credit policy describes the procedures for assessing an overdue account.
- What does **reporting to management** consist of? How often and to whom is a report made?

Comprehension Check

What questions build the foundational components of a credit policy?

Credit Department Mission Statement

The mission statement should express the long-range focus of the policy and define the purpose of the credit department. It will summarize how the credit function will contribute to sales growth and profitability though risk management and customer relationships.

📌 POINTS TO CONSIDER

- What is management's philosophy on risk tolerance?
- Should the credit function be liberal, moderate or conservative; can the company afford to take some risks?
- Will the company be flexible with payments beyond terms?
- How is the cash flow in the company?
- What is the financial strength of the company?
- What are the current and projected annual sales?
- What are the anticipated profit margins?
- What is the classification of products being sold (durable goods may have longer terms versus perishable goods with shorter terms)?
- What types of customers are in the customer base (large warehouse distributors versus small locally owned stores)?

- What is the geographic location of the customers and how will they be serviced (global distribution, national or local)?
- Are there any government regulations that may restrict terms or credit decisions?
- Are the policies and procedures Sarbanes-Oxley compliant?
- Should the credit function be centralized or de-centralized?
- What is the company's market position in the industry?
- Is the company striving to gain market share?
- How competitive is the industry the company operates in?
- What are the current economic trends?

Goals and Objectives of a Credit Department

The goals and objectives of the credit department should describe how the company expects to measure the effectiveness of its credit function. Goals should track with current market conditions, be consistent with the strategic direction of the organization and reviewed and updated annually. Goals and performance against goals should be communicated on a regular basis to the entire credit organization.

Five key credit department objectives:

1. Develop an optimal level of sales and cash flow, while limiting delinquencies and bad debt losses and working effectively with sales and other departments.
2. Minimize the carrying costs for accounts receivable.
3. Minimize risk and bad debt losses while maintaining a competitive advantage.
4. Monitor the costs incurred by the credit department such as operating costs and expenses within the credit department to benchmark standards.
5. The credit department must convert accounts receivable to cash as quickly as possible and communicate the condition, cost and trend of the company's investment in receivables to management.

To help the company achieve overall objectives, each department, including the credit department, should reach specific goals. Set forth in credit policy, these objectives define desired accomplishments for each department. The policy is established to meet the objectives of the company, which are determined before any other actions can be taken. Some factors to consider when developing goals could be:

- Terms of sale.
- Monitoring credit risk.
- Relationship to the sales department.
- Training and development of credit personnel.
- Amount of capital committed to accounts receivable.
- Measurement of the status of the accounts receivable investment.

Many companies monitor standard benchmark statistics, some of which are:

- Days sales outstanding.
- Days delinquent sales outstanding.
- Number of active accounts being managed by credit and collections.
- The average dollar size of these accounts.
- The average dollar size of invoices.
- The number of invoices being managed.
- The percentage of invoices over 30 days, over 60 days and over 90 days past due.
- Dollars collected by collector.
- Dollars collected per month per employee of the credit and collection function.
- Changes month over month in dollars collected per employee.
- The percentage past due for each collector.
- The number of deductions/debits outstanding.
- The dollar value of debits/deductions outstanding.
- The percentage of deductions over 30 days, over 60 days and over 90 days past due.
- Bad debt write-offs as a percentage of sales.

Boundaries: Organizational Roles, Responsibilities and Authority

While the organization of a credit department is not determined by credit policy, it plays an important part in putting policy into action through specific assignment of responsibility and delegation of authority. *Credit policy establishes the broad limits for decisions over a long period of time.* To make these limits a workable guide to decision-making, it is necessary to specify who has the authority to make different types of decisions and within what range personnel may exercise their judgment. For example, the authority to make exceptions to basic policy is usually limited to the chief credit professional. Authority for various levels of personnel is often stated in terms of the amount of credit involved. The definition of authority should make clear the channels through which an order must move until it is finally approved.

Defined organizational roles and responsibilities for each person involved in the credit function will help to achieve the most effective results possible. Clearly defined roles and responsibilities help streamline operations, prevent redundancy, provide clarity of tasks and improve productivity. An organizational chart will help clarify the role of each position in the company and show the nature over which authority exists and where decision-making should be made.

POINTS TO CONSIDER

- Has the company clearly communicated who has overall responsibility for the credit and accounts receivable functions?
- Who has the authority to approve credit applications?
- Who has the authority to change credit limits?
- What is the credit function's credit line approval hierarchy (how much each person is authorized to approve)?

- Do credit limits above a certain amount require approval from company's senior management?
- Who has authority to hold orders?
- Who has authority to shut off accounts?
- Does the sales department have authority to override the credit manager? What circumstances require the intervention of sales? Who has ultimate authority if sales and credit do not agree?

Credit Evaluation

Credit decisions should be based primarily on the credit applicant's willingness to pay, as evidenced by its payment history, and on its ability to pay, as evidenced by its financial situation. Other factors relating to the applicant, such as its legal form and the industry in which it operates, plus years in existence, should also be considered. After evaluating the information, however, the decision to offer or refuse credit to a customer is often at the credit manager's discretion.

When credit policy addresses a company's credit evaluation philosophy, the criteria to assess risk and determine credit limits is clearly established. The goal of defining and establishing how credit evaluations are conducted is to build consistency around the evaluation process.

The Five Cs of Credit are the basic components of credit analysis. Using the five Cs to evaluate a customer incorporates both qualitative and quantitative measures.

The Five Cs of Credit are:

1. **Character.** The history of the business and experience of its management are critical factors in assessing a company's ability to satisfy its financial obligations.

2. **Capacity.** Make sure to assess the capacity of the business to operate as an ongoing concern in every credit decision.

3. **Capital.** Analyze the financial strength of the organization in order to determine its ability to meet financial obligations in a timely fashion.

4. **Collateral.** Debtor support in terms of specific assets used as collateral can enhance a customer's creditworthiness. Resources such as liens on specific assets, letters of credit, pledges of stock or bonds and personal or corporate guarantees can each afford an opportunity to ultimately extend credit.

5. **Conditions.** General economic conditions in the world, the country, the community and the industry will exert a modifying influence on the financial analysis of an account.

The credit policy defines whether credit applications are required for all prospective customers.

The credit application begins the relationship-building process and is an initial source of information to begin a fact-finding, fact-verification mission about the applicant. In addition to using the credit application as an investigative tool, the credit application should create a contract between the seller and the customer.

It is very important for a seller to know its customer. To make sound credit decisions, organizations will typically leverage various information provided on a customer's credit application along with other external resources available. The credit policy defines which external resources are required as part of the credit investigation that culminates in the commercial credit-granting decision.

External resources include:

- Industry credit groups.
- Credit agency reports (NACM, D&B, Experian, Equifax).
- Financial statements.
- Trade references.
- Bank information and references.
- Public records.

Comprehension Check

What credit procedures are used in evaluating credit?

 POINTS TO CONSIDER

- Are credit applications obtained from all prospective customers?
- Do guidelines specify the types and sources of credit information to obtain on prospective customers?

- Are the company's methods for evaluating credit information and making credit decisions reasonable and consistently applied?
- Has the company considered dividing customers into categories based on sales volume and/or credit risk?

Terms of Sale

A credit policy should provide information about the terms of sale between the company and its customers. The policy should clearly detail who must approve requests for special terms. It is important for all parties to know when payment is expected for the product or service. If terms are varied due to certain customer classes, then the policy should include a discussion of the different types of terms that can be authorized.

- What sales terms are acceptable within the industry?
- Are terms clearly documented and communicated to the customer?
- Are requests for special terms documented and approved in advance by the credit manager or equivalent authority?
- Does the company consider antitrust laws, such as the Robinson-Patman Act, when it offers or grants special terms?
- Does the company have more than one product line that may require different terms?

- Does the customer understand at what point the terms begin (invoice date, date invoice is received by customer, or date product is accepted by customer)?
- If early payment discounts are offered, has management considered the cost of such discounts?
- Does the company assess late payment penalties against delinquent accounts? If so, does the company take into account the cost of calculating, billing and collecting the assessments?

Credit Limits

The credit policy should explain how the credit department establishes credit limits for all active customers. Credit limits should be based on each customer's credit rating, ability to pay and expected volume of purchases. Financial statements and trade information are sources of information typically used to assign credit limits. The credit policy should specify who is responsible for approving credit limits and if alternate approval is required for credit limits that exceed a certain amount.

The goal is to set credit limits that are flexible yet appropriate for the customer's risk level. Slower paying customers should be provided with more conservative credit limits while prompt paying (lower risk) customers should have more freedom with their credit limits. If credit limits are set correctly then slower paying customers will be more easily recognized more frequently for potential credit hold review and stronger payers will not.

Upon evaluating credit information, some companies use a strategy of segmenting customers into various credit limit parameters. One approach is to identify customers as low, moderate, or high risk. Segmentation helps to set credit limits and prioritize collections.

- Are credit limits assigned to customers to help control credit risk?
- Has the financial strength of the creditor been considered in establishing credit limit parameters?
- Are credit limits determined logically and consistently, then properly approved?
- Are sales and customers promptly notified of credit decisions and limits?
- Are customer's credit exceptions monitored daily, such as, exceeding credit limit and/or past due

situations, to proactively manage risk/customer exposure?
- Is written approval required by the credit manager if orders exceed the pre-approved credit limit or if the customer has past due invoices?
- Does the credit department review larger credit limits on a periodic basis?
- Are all credit limits subject to revision, based on changing levels of creditworthiness?

Monitoring Accounts

The credit policy should summarize the process of re-evaluating credit for existing customers along with the sources of information commonly used in the process. Establishing regular credit evaluation as part of the credit policy will allow the company to monitor any changes in the risk level of the receivable portfolio. The company can then adjust credit and collection policy accordingly. Specifically, if the portfolio is becoming a little more precarious than the company's tolerance for risk permits, the credit policy and collection plan should be tightened.

POINTS TO CONSIDER

- Do policies and procedures address how often to re-evaluate credit for existing customers?
- Are critical customers evaluated at least annually?
- Does management use other tools besides the A/R aging report to monitor credit?
- What other data sources are used for the purpose of account monitoring (sales associates, trade magazines, news wires, business and credit information companies)?
- Are credit re-evaluations for smaller customers performed at the first sign the customer is facing possible financial trouble?

- Do credit personnel check each customer's credit status (credit limits and past due invoices) before releasing orders?
- Who has the approval to release orders if a customer has exceeded its credit limit or if invoices are past due?
- Does the credit policy identify other approaches to reduce credit risks for marginal accounts, such as obtaining a security interest or guarantee?

Collections

The credit policy should identify what methods credit personnel will use to collect receivables, particularly past due accounts. The best collection process is one which is proactive and consistent, and which reflects the mission and goals of the credit department. The collection procedure should be prioritized according to both the customer's risk and exposure level.

This section should include:

- When to contact a customer.
- How to contact a customer.
- When to place an account on credit hold.
- How to resolve disputes, deductions, etc.
- When to turn over delinquent accounts to an outside collection agency or attorney.
- When to write an account off to bad debt.
- Authorizing settlements.

Real World Perspectives

TEXTING WORKS BEST

Connecting with clients who owe your business money can in some cases present a challenge. Particularly in a world with so many options for communication, from cell phones to email, finding the right medium to relay messages that an account is late, or very late, and must be paid is of the utmost importance. As we all know, the longer our business waits past the due date for payments, the less likely we'll see payment on that account.

When trying to reach high profile or troubled accounts, one method I began using more and more over the past four years is text messaging. In fact, these days I rarely leave a voicemail if I don't reach someone. That's because I don't think many people actually listen to voice messages nearly as much as they look at a text. A person may be in transit, busy or in a meeting. But even if someone is in a meeting, they can still respond to a text. And generally, my customers do. It doesn't work all of the time, but it usually works the first couple of times, at least until they realize who it is. Also, with clients who have an iPhone, I'm able to see if the person read the message. With voicemail or even email, it's common that people don't hear or respond in a timely way, if at all.

Texting technology has improved the collectability of accounts, and that's mainly a matter of the improved means of communication. The more communication you have, the more of a customer's story you have and the more likely you are to collect on your invoices. Now, just because you're in contact sooner with your customers doesn't mean they'll have the money to pay you, but it does mean you'll have the chance to understand their situation a little earlier in the process. Every customer has a finite amount of money, so if I can beat the other vendors to the table, then I've succeeded in reaching them that much sooner and will ultimately have fewer problems collecting down the road.

In terms of texting etiquette, we're still figuring that out as we go. The best method I find so far, though, is to first identify myself, then get to the point quickly by saying something like: "Hi, I'm with company X. Your account is past due. Give me a call to work out arrangements." If you don't identify yourself, it winds up slowing how the client responds to an unknown sender. Generally, I don't put dollar figures in the first text with a client, but if the conversation takes on a life of its own, then absolutely, I include dollar amounts. With one particular client that I've been texting back and forth with for a while, I'll send him a text with just a question mark. We're so familiar with each other, he'll understand that to mean "Where's my payment?" He'll eventually come around to paying me because he knows what I'm looking for. Another benefit to using text messages is that, unless the users have deleted the message string, they'll be able to quickly scan previous texts and grasp the gist of those collections conversations.

To date, most of our customers aren't paying through text messages. We do have Square (a credit card processing service) and are setting up Apple Pay (a mobile payment service), so we know we'll be able to receive payment this way, but it's not something we've taken on yet, though it's likely just a matter of time before we do.

Shane Norman, CCE, is the credit manager at Wheeler Machinery in Salt Lake City

Bad Debt

At some point, nonpaying customers have to be accounted for. This usually means deleting them from the company's books and from regular accounts receivable records by writing off the outstanding receivable as a bad debt. Some companies establish Allowance for Bad Debt Accounts, contra asset accounts, in order to recognize that write-offs are inevitable and to provide management with estimates of potential write-offs.

An account is written off when there is no probability that it will be collected and when it complies with Internal Revenue Service regulations regarding bad debt write-off. Some companies do not choose to set up allowance accounts; they keep the doubtful accounts on the A/R until such time as they qualify for partial or full write-off.

The policy should address:

- Conversion of an open account to a note.
- Customer counseling.
- Collection agencies.
- Use of outside attorneys and lawsuits.
- Customer bankruptcy, preference claims, bulk sales and assignments for the benefit of creditors.
- Authorization for accounts written off to bad debt.

 **POINTS TO CONSIDER**

- Does the company prepare a Reserve/Allowance for Bad Debt on a consistent basis?
- Is there a collection process in place to determine when an account balance should be considered uncollectable?

- Are bad debt write-off approval amounts assigned to departmental personnel, as set by the hierarchy of authorization levels?
- Do credit professionals participate on creditors' committees?

Other relevant items that may be mentioned in a credit policy include: comments on ethics, legality, quality, industry-specific programs, personnel, credit interchange and professional organizations, systems, deductions, returned checks, collection mechanisms, international trade and record retention.

POINTS TO CONSIDER

- Are deductions handled promptly to assure quality receivables?
- Do customer inquiries receive immediate attention?
- Does the company share receivables and trade information with credit bureaus or credit associations?

- Is business information shared in compliance with NACM's Canons of Business Credit Ethics?
- Does management periodically review and revise credit policies and procedures, as necessary, to reflect changing business conditions?

Deductions*

A significant challenge facing credit personnel in many industries is the issue of deductions. These deductions, also known as chargebacks, billbacks and many other names occur when a customer either short pays an invoice or takes a separate line item credit on their payment.

Deductions found their origin in the apparel industry with **penalties for non-compliance**, *either a set amount per incident or a percentage of the total invoice or order*, but soon migrated into all of consumer products manufacturing. With the advent of "Big Box" stores and mass merchandisers, getting paid through deductions became a normal course of business.

The challenge of deductions can range anywhere from ½ to 3% of annual sales, excluding **trade-related deductions**, *monies offered in exchange for promotion of a particular product*, and have been reported as high as 10% of a company's accounts receivable balance.

The reasons for deductions can vary greatly, but can typically be divided into three main categories:

1. **Planned deductions** are typically trade related and part of the budgets set up by sales departments for the promotion of their product. **Advertising**, *product promotion with specific dates, products and reduced pricing involved in the contract*; **billback allowance**, *special deals offered to incent customers to move a product where items are "billed back"' to the manufacturer*; **slotting fees**, *amounts charged by retailers to have products placed on their shelves*; and other similar claims typically comprise this category and represent a large percentage of incoming deductions. Because these deductions are expected and budgeted for, a credit professional should focus on quick resolution as there is very little opportunity for recovery of these claims unless the customer failed to abide by the **terms of the contract**, such as *deal dates and minimum buys*, couldn't provide **proof of performance** *(copy of ad or reduced pricing)* or other contractual issues. The sooner these deductions are credited to the correct **general ledger or promo account**, *a budget or "wallet" allocated by sales to customers on an annual basis*, the less impact they will have on aging.

2. **Preventable deductions** are taken for compliance-related claims. They include: EDI/ASN [**Electronic Data Interchange (EDI)**] *is the transfer of data from one computer system to another by standardized message formatting*. **Advance Shipment Notice (ASN)** *is a document that provides detailed information about a pending delivery)* issues, improper labeling, early or late shipments, pricing and any other violations of the **routing guide**, *(instructions and the rules of engagement for shipping products from suppliers to customers)*, provided by the customer. These items create a significant, negative impact to deduction balances, aging and the company's bottom line. The goal for these claims is to prevent them before they happen where possible. A proactive approach is necessary and will reduce the risk on the current balances as well as prevent future claims from being taken. These claims generally require cross-departmental cooperation from other areas such as shipping to resolve. Negotiations are common and can be used to not only reduce the amount being penalized, but also for a grace period to correct problems before future fines are assessed.

3. The last category is **painful deductions**. These can include items from the first two categories, but also cover shortage deductions (both full carton and concealed), post audits and **unearned cash discounts** *(a liability recognized over time)*. If a company offers terms, they list the percentage of the discount, normally 1-2%, and by when the customer must pay their invoice in order to earn the discount. For example, 2% 10, net 30 would mean a 2% discount is offered if the invoice is paid by the 10th day (normally, payment must be sent by the 10th date in order to receive the discount) If no discount is taken, the customer would have up to 30 days to pay. Other associated terms are **DOI** *(date of invoice)*, **ROI** *(receipt of invoice)* and **ROG** *(receipt of goods)*. These claims are

typically invalid, but take a significant amount of time and resources to resolve and recover. Consistent and regular follow-up on these items is critical to protect profit margins and to ensure the company does not become a target for abuse in the future.

A key to effective deduction management includes the following: identify, quantify, analyze and strategize.

The importance of properly **identifying** deductions can't be stressed enough. The credit professional can't manage a problem they don't understand. Knowing where the specific challenges lie helps to focus efforts and resources.

In addition to understanding the type of problem, being able to associate it with a dollar amount is crucial (**quantify**). Senior management will be more likely to provide assistance and support if they know how much the problem is costing the organization

The next key step is to **analyze** the deductions in more detail. Is the challenge in logistics, compliance or some other area? Once it is narrowed down, it is easier to identify the root cause of the problem. For example, if shortages are a challenge, the following questions can be asked:

- Is the challenge with concealed or full cases?
- Are the shortages coming from a particular distribution center or warehouse?
- Is it a particular **SKU** or **Stock Keeping Unit**, *a unique identification number assigned by the warehouse*, causing the shortages?

And so on ...

Once the analysis is completed, the credit department can begin to **strategize** a response and also identify what other departments or personnel need to be involved in the solution.

After research is complete, the next step is to quickly get the valid deductions cleared and off the aging report. If a claim is valid and there is no opportunity for recovery, it shouldn't remain on the trial balance sheet month after month.

Invalid deductions need to be addressed quickly and consistent follow-up given in order to bring them to resolution. Remember the goal is two-pronged: repayment and prevention

Not only should the invalid deduction be repaid, the situation should be prevented from happening again in the future.

Regardless of the approach, the more opportunities there are to be proactive when dealing with deductions, the more effective the management. Minimizing negative impact in this area of responsibility will be a key factor in long-term success.

Submitted by Diana Crowe, IAB Solutions LLC.

Reporting to Management

Reporting is delivered to senior management, executive management or the management team, which is generally a team of individuals at the highest level of organization management who have the day-to-day responsibilities of managing a company or corporation; holding specific executive powers conferred onto them with and by authority of the board of directors and/or the shareholders.

Companies have different approaches to management reporting for credit and collections and must determine what the right measures are, how often reports should be generated and reviewed, what action is to be taken and who is to take that action. A meaningful measure fills a need and meets a specific objective. Meaningful measures will support the organizations' mission and help reach organizational goals. A measure must be compared to some standard or it has no meaning. Goals can be set by identifying the current state, the past state and the direction of the performance being measured in accordance with past organization or industry values or trends. The right measure will express a value that complements and supports the objectives of the company, division, department or subgroup.

The statement that a sale is not complete until the cash is in the bank is both familiar and true. A business organization would soon run out of operating capital if it were not continuously replenished through collection of its receivables. Unless receivables are converted to cash on schedule, some of the company assets are unproductively tied up. Therefore, CFOs and management are concerned about credit and collections' impact on working capital and rely on accurate and informative reporting to understand the health of the business. Credit and collections reporting can be categorized in the following sections: cash flow forecasting and working capital management reporting and these can be separated into two disciplines—financial and operational.

Financial reporting is done to support the financial statements, i.e., detailing the support for the bad debt reserve. Operational reporting is to measure performance of activities or persons or groups that are responsible for actions.

POINTS TO CONSIDER

- Does the company prepare reports that monitor the performance of the accounts receivable function? Such as:
  - Accounts receivable aging analysis, including amounts and percentages of delinquent accounts in each aging category.
  - Accounts receivable turnover or days sales outstanding ratios.
  - Bad debt/recovery analysis.
- Are reports of such information prepared at least monthly, and the results compared to preceding periods and industry statistics?
- Are reports distributed to relevant parties as determined by guidelines or needs of the company (e.g., senior management, sales, controller, etc.)?

Review of Credit Policy

In order for a credit policy to maintain its relevance and continue to have a positive impact on cash flow and revenues, it must be reviewed at definite stated intervals and also in response to a changing economy, market conditions and the competitive environment.

One means of reviewing credit policy is by conducting a credit department audit. The audit should review all department activities in light of the overall policy. The result of the audit should be an objective evaluation of the department's effectiveness, as well as the identification of any areas that need improvement.

At the time of review, information must be gathered indicating the present position and progress of the department in relation to its objectives. Short-term goals provide convenient intermediate benchmarks toward long-term objectives. If performance is satisfactory, the existing policies should be reaffirmed or new objectives set. If credit performance is less than expected, there should be a critical examination of both the policy and the way it has been applied.

The steps for changing policy are much the same as those used for its initial development. Proposed changes should be discussed with the same people who participated in the formulation of the policy whenever possible. When the changes become definite, they should be carefully communicated to all the individuals and departments concerned.

Credit Policy Focal Points

When a company is developing a new credit policy or is reviewing an existing one, a number of factors should be considered. Some of these are internal in nature while others are external. Depending on the company, they vary in relative importance. Together they establish the context within which credit policy must operate. Here are the major focal points that could require a policy and/or procedure:

Focus on development of an optimal level of sales

1. New customers:
   a. Require credit application with each request.

    b. Communicate expected turnaround time for making a credit decision on new accounts.

    c. Define how the request for credit and the credit decision are communicated.

    d. Establish and maintain current credit department files, including contents of the files.

    e. Authorize and communicate credit limits.

2. Terms of sale:

    a. Terms established by industry; clear communication internally and to customers.

    b. Consistently applied and monitored discount chargeback follow-ups.

    c. Consistently applied and monitored late payment service charges.

    d. Requests for extended term arrangements; necessary approvals clearly specified.

    e. Blanket approvals (small orders below a specified amount are either cash or automatically approved).

    f. Consignment sales.

    g. Export sales and letters of credit

    h. Sales to a debtor in possession in Chapter 11 bankruptcies

3. Credit investigations:

    a. A sign-off policy for responsibility of the control of the account developed by the size of the account.

    b. Use of credit reporting agencies clarified by the requirements for types of reports to be utilized.

    c. Obtaining bank references detailing the type of information needed.

    d. Obtaining trade references with details of information needed.

    e. Financial statement requests from customers and analysis of statements with key focal points.

    f. Use of collateral (include sample documentation, specify authorized signatures and clarify the safeguarding of documents held in storage).

    g. Perfecting liens under Article 9 of the Uniform Commercial Code.

    h. Guarantees (personal and corporate).

    i. Warehouse receipts.

    j. Letters of credit (details by types of L/C).

    k. Subordination agreements.

    l. Lien searches.

    m. Pledge of stocks, bonds or certificates of deposit.

Minimize the carrying costs of receivables

1. Follow-up system for past-due accounts:

    a. Responsibility and time interval for initial follow-up.

    b. A systematic program for additional follow-up.

    c. Statements or collection letters.

    d. Holding orders.

    e. Deductions and open credits.

    f. Personal visits (written summary report required).

    g. Exchange of credit information related to customer payment experience.

    h. Unauthorized shipments.

2. Internal credit department reports (assign responsibility, clarify timing and include a distribution list for each report):
   a. Aging of receivables.
   b. Over credit limits report.
   c. Response on open items by category and age (deductions, credits, unearned discounts, service charges).
   d. High risk account report.
   e. Report for accounts with collection agencies or in litigation.
   f. Bad debt write-off report.
   g. Travel and expense reports.

Minimize bad debt losses

1. Conversion of an open account to a note.
2. Customer counseling.
3. Collection agencies.
4. Use of outside attorneys and lawsuits.
5. Customer bankruptcy, bulk sales and assignments for the benefit of creditors.
6. Credit professional participation on creditors' committees.
7. Authorization for accounts written off to bad debts.

Credit department organization and cost containment

1. A formal organizational chart that clarifies the positions of each member of the credit department (authority and responsibility should be clear).
2. Human resources within the credit department:
   a. Recruiting and hiring guidelines.
   b. Educational requirements by position.
   c. Experience requirements by position.
   d. Training and development guidelines.
3. Performance review criteria with a regular periodic performance review.
4. Membership in professional organizations.
5. Workshop and tuition reimbursement guidelines.
6. Promotion and termination guidelines.
7. Credit department budget guidelines:
   a. Responsibility for preparation and content.
   b. Specific items for which policies and procedures need to be developed, including salaries/incentives, space and equipment, supplies, training and education, travel and entertainment and collection and investigation expenses.

Checklist for a Well-Defined Credit Policy

A well-defined and complete credit policy includes:

1. Formal organization of department.
2. Job description, titles and review process.
3. Credit department budget guidelines.

4. Credit documentation required for credit file.

5. Methods of gathering credit information.

6. Time limits for credit decisions.

7. Establishment of terms of sale.

8. Established credit lines and procedure for establishing new lines.

9. Procedure for communicating the decision to the customer.

10. Procedure for communicating the decision to management.

11. Procedure for communicating the decision to the sales department.

12. Procedure for communicating the decision to operations.

13. Guidelines for dealing with and assisting marginal accounts.

14. A collection policy that reduces borrowing cost.

15. A collection policy that deals with slow-paying accounts.

16. A collection policy that minimizes bad debts.

17. A policy for unearned discounts/unauthorized deductions.

18. A policy for the handling of disputes.

19. A policy for the handling of returned and damaged merchandise.

20. Policies for using secured transaction for protection.

21. A policy for the use of a guarantee.

22. Guidelines for reporting to upper management.

Example of a Credit Policy

An example of a credit policy is shown in Figure 8-1. It is not presented as a complete or perfect policy statement, but it provides a concrete illustration of some of the concepts discussed. Like many policy statements, this one interweaves the department's objectives, such as "to help build a broad and durable customer relationship" and "with an aim toward promoting sales." These lead directly into policy statements: "The credit department shall endeavor to find a suitable credit basis on which to deal with every customer;" "Marginal credit risks are to be dealt with when they are needed to complete operating schedules, and as long as they constitute a source of added net profit to [company name]."

Specific practices are implied in the policy statement but are detailed in other documents. The procedures designed to find a credit basis for sales to every customer, for example, cover such matters as obtaining financial information, establishing terms of sale and setting credit lines.

Credit Procedures

Closely allied to assignment of responsibility is the development of detailed procedures for day-to-day operations. These translate the general policy instructions into clear-cut rules for specific situations, including such matters as order flow, maintenance of credit files and preparation of periodic reports.

One of the principles for delegating authority and establishing procedures is to include as many situations as possible in the routines administered by lower-level personnel. This allows credit professionals, who are more highly qualified by training and experience, to deal with more complicated situations.

The following questions could be included in Credit Procedures for Evaluating Credit:

1. Does the company consider the following data concerning the general business entity when evaluating credit applicants:
   - Confirmation of the legitimacy of entity via Secretary of State, credit agency report, etc.?
   - Form of entity (sole proprietorship, partnership, corporation, government agency)?
   - Industry in which the company operates and the applicant's position in the industry?
   - Years in existence?

2. Does the company evaluate the following factors concerning the credit applicant's supplier payment history:
   - Payment experience?
   - Consistent treatment of suppliers?
   - Length of relationship with suppliers?

    - Any suppliers restricting credit?

    - Any lawsuits, liens and/or judgments present?

3. Does the company evaluate the following factors concerning the credit applicant's banking relationship:

    - Loan payment experience?

    - Average deposit balances?

    - NSF History?

    - Availability and compliance on bank/credit lines?

    - Are loans/credit lines secured or unsecured? If secured, what is used as collateral?

4. Is the reliability of financial information on credit applicants considered, including the extent of outside CPA involvement, if any (i.e., audited/reviewed/compiled/etc.)?

5. Is the credit applicant's financial information evaluated and historically trended, using techniques such as:

    - Ratio analysis?

    - Cash flow analysis?

6. Are the results of the financial analysis clearly documented?

7. Are credit decisions and the support for those decisions documented for future reference?

8. Do certain accounts get automatic credit approval (based on dollar limits under a certain amount)?

9. What credit scoring techniques are used to evaluate credit worthiness?

10. Has the customer demonstrated the ability to pay bills in a prompt manner?

11. Is there a special process for riskier accounts?

12. How does the prospective customer compare to other companies in its peer group?

13. Are credit decisions made within a reasonable time frame, as outlined by the organization's guidelines?

The following could be included in Credit Procedures for Credit Approval and Administration:

- **Terms of Sale.** A complete list of the terms offered by the company and a brief explanation of how they are used.
- **Terms Codes.** Terms of sale can be coded to facilitate processing of information and the code should be shown on all sales orders and invoices. The procedure for administering the codes should be described, including the treatment of multiple codes and exceptions.
- **Credit Instructions.** Daily routines used to process all orders in accordance with prescribed credit lines and terms. Forms should be shown wherever used.
- **Credit Recommendations.** Organizations using referral limits that recommend credit for approval to a higher level should include the recommendation form.
- **Credit Files.** List of information that must be kept up to date, such as current credit agency reports, credit recommendations and financial statements.

The following could be included in Credit Procedures for Collections:

- **Normal Procedures.** Each account is a separate collection problem. Placing it into a category by size or type assists in determining the

> **Comprehension Check**
> What credit procedures are used for credit approval and administration?

intensity of collection effort required. Several means for collection follow-up are letter, email, phone, personal visit and joint credit and sales action. Copies of the series of form collection letters should be included.

- **Collection Schedule.** Collections should use a definite schedule that will provide for systematic review. Details should be described.
- **Lockbox System.** Descriptions, such as bank procedures and company guidelines for returned check processing, and other tasks, should be included.
- **Advance Payments.** Procedures for handling these items should be described.
- **Customer Deductions.** Copies of typical correspondence and departmental guidelines should be included.
- **Note Arrangements.** Copies of the notes used by the company should be included. In addition, important points in preparing notes should be included, such as correct maturity date, correct interest rate and correct signature.
- **Account Referral.** If normal collection procedures fail to net the necessary results, the account should be placed with an attorney or collection agency. Typical documentation should be included as exhibits.
- **Creditors' Extension Agreements.** As a major creditor, a company can initiate or join in a creditors' extension agreement to permit a debtor to set aside existing debt under an established plan. Standard documentation should be included.
- **Bankruptcy Proceedings.** Standard documentation and procedural guidelines should be included.
- **Allowance for Uncollectibles and Write-offs.** Guidelines for reporting and handling these items should be discussed.

Comprehension Check
What credit procedures are used for collections?

Key Terms and Concepts

Comprehension Check

1. What is a **policy?**
2. Why is the difference between an **implied** and a **stated** credit policy?
3. What is a **procedure?**
4. List the four elements of a **credit policy.**
5. What questions build the foundational components of a credit policy?
6. What credit procedures are used in **evaluating credit?**
7. What credit procedures are used for credit approval and administration?
8. What credit procedures are used for **collections?**

Summary

- A company's credit policy is typically designed and established by top-level management.
- The first step of a **credit policy** is to establish objectives.
- A credit policy can either be **implied** or **written**. A **written** or **stated policy** leaves fewer chances of error or misunderstanding across the organization or credit department. A written policy also ensures consistency throughout an organization as it pertains to managing its credit.
- Credit policy varies in complexity. For instance, cash only is a form of a credit policy that may be instituted by a business.
- Credit policy establishes the direction of the credit function within an organization, while credit procedures govern the steps used in the overarching principle. In order for a policy to be effective, it must be directly and explicitly related to action.
- The four essential elements of credit policy are:
  - **Establishing the credit standard**
  - **Determining credit availability**
  - **Setting credit terms**
  - **Defining collection policy**
- The short-term application of a policy should be flexible.
- **General factors** that influence the role of credit within an organization include:
  - **Type of customer**
  - **Geographic location of customers**
  - **Overall economic conditions**
  - **Business conditions**
  - **Competitive position**
  - **Merchandizing policy**
  - **Type of merchandise**
  - **Margins on the merchandise**
  - **The price range of merchandise**
- The mission of a credit department should establish the long-range focus of the policy and define the purpose of the credit department.
- The five key credit department **objectives** are:
  - **Optimize sales and cash flow**
  - **Minimize carrying costs for accounts receivable**
  - **Minimize risk and bad debt**
  - **Monitor the cost of the credit department**
  - **Convert accounts receivable to cash as quickly as possible**
- Several factors, such as terms of sale and credit risk, influence the goals of the credit department. Monitoring these factors using standard benchmarks, like days sales outstanding or average dollar amount of invoice, may be essential in reaching organizational goals.
- Within a credit policy, it is important to define organizational roles, responsibilities and authority surrounding credit decisions.
- When evaluating creditworthiness, it is always important to consider the Five Cs of Credit, while basing a decision primarily on the credit applicant's willingness to pay, taking into consideration their payment history and ability to pay, as shown by their financial situation.

- Credit policy should specify the following:
  - **Terms of sale**
  - **Credit limits**
  - **Monitoring accounts**
  - **Collections**
  - **Bad debt**
- It is critical to realize that a sale is not complete until payment is received.
- Credit and collections reporting can be categorized as: cash flow forecasting and working capital. Therefore, these can be separated into two disciplines: financial (reporting to support the financial statements) and operational (reporting to measure the performance of individuals or groups within an organization). Furthermore, a measure has no meaning unless compared to a standard.
- In order for a credit policy to remain effective, it must be reviewed and updated during specified intervals, in tandem with changing economic, market and competitive conditions. It should be reviewed based on its ability to meet the five key credit department objectives.
- Procedures must be set for both credit approval and administration and for collections. Procedures for credit approval may include: credit instructions, term codes and credit files. Procedures for collections may include: a collection schedule, advanced payments, note arrangement and bankruptcy proceedings.

References and Resources

Business Credit. Columbia, MD: National Association of Credit Management. (This 9 issues/year publication is a continuous source of relevant articles and information. Archived articles from *Business Credit* magazine are available through the web-based NACM Resource Library, which is a benefit of NACM membership.)

Cole, Robert H. and Lon L. Mishler. *Consumer and Business Credit Management,* 11th ed. Boston: Irwin/McGraw Hill, 1998.

Crowe, Diana. "Deductions." IAB Solutions LLC. Summit, PA, 2016.

Credit Executive Handbook. The Credit Research Foundation, 1986.

Dennis, Michael. *Credit and Collection Handbook.* Paramus, NJ: Prentice Hall, 2000.

Developing a Strategic Plan: A Guide to Promoting Your Credit Organization. The Credit Research Foundation, 1997. *How to Write a Credit Policy.* The Credit Research Foundation, 1996.

Manual of Credit and Commercial Laws. Columbia, MD: National Association of Credit Management, current edition.

NACM Graduate School of Credit and Financial Management projects, 2013. Laura de Prato, CCE; Chris Southby, CCE; Eddie Olewnik, CCE; Sue Herman, CCE; Steve Porter, CCE; and Gosia Sanders.

9 Credit Applications

OVERVIEW

A well-defined credit application provides the basis for gathering information and implementing the company's policies. The credit application is the primary document which allows the credit professional to "Know Your Customer (KYC)." It may also serve as a contract.

THINK ABOUT THIS

Q. Why does a company need a credit application?

Q. In a perfect world, what information should be included on a credit application?

Q. How does a credit application protect a buyer and seller?

DISCIPLINARY CORE IDEAS

After reading this chapter, the reader should understand:

- ☑ The purpose of a credit application.
- ☑ How to obtain banking information.
- ☑ How the credit application acts as a contract.
- ☑ What goes below the signature line.

CHAPTER OUTLINE

The Purpose of a Credit Application

Every credit professional appreciates the importance of a well-thought-out, informative and properly executed (signed) credit application. This document is crucial to the determination of the rights of the creditor (vendor/seller) in the event of a dispute with, or default of, a customer. Through the use of a well-drafted credit application, a credit professional may accomplish the dual goals of limiting credit risk, as well as addressing numerous contingencies that may arise in a credit relationship. A credit professional may also obtain a greater understanding of the nature of the customer's business simply by having more information with which to formulate questions about the customer's business dealings.

Gathering basic information about the customer, in compliance with current laws and regulations, is the core of the credit application process. In a perfect world, the credit manager should design (perhaps with the aid of counsel) a credit application that is concise and straightforward, yet contains all necessary information that will assist the credit analyst to make a credit decision, assist in the periodic review of the credit relationship, and provide support to counsel as needed, in the event of default. The credit application allows the credit professional to obtain information necessary to make decisions about a customer's ability and willingness to meet obligations within credit terms. This information can help increase sales of a company's products to new customers at the start of their business and to existing customers as the business grows. Credit applications can also make a significant difference in the collection of the account if a customer cannot or does not pay and must be compelled to do so through litigation.

Occasionally, obtaining information from some customers can be a sensitive issue. A customer may be disinclined to provide adequate information; unwilling to sign the credit application document; or become belligerent or uncooperative at the suggestion that the completed credit application is a prerequisite of the extension of credit. Credit grantors should keep in mind the nature of the exchange being requested: The customer wants products, merchandise or services without having to pay for them at the time of purchase. It is prudent for the credit professional to keep this fact in mind and point it out to the recalcitrant applicant. The credit application process is the credit professional's first, and sometimes only, opportunity to protect their company from risk of loss through credit sales and/or fraud. It should be routine to ask and insist that the customer/potential customer provide all of the information being requested on the credit application. The process of acquiring the requested information from the potential customer can also be indicative of future dealings with the customer, and should be considered in the credit review process.

The most advantageous time to ask for credit information is at the beginning of any buyer/seller relationship. Once the customer has been delivered products or services, the customer may no longer feel the need to be forthcoming with information or cooperate with the credit analyst. The opportunity to obtain information becomes inconsequential to the customer. Yet, the information that should have been obtained at the outset of the relationship is critical to the credit manager or analyst's credit review.

The key goal of a credit application is to assist the seller in learning as much as possible about the applicant before making a decision to extend credit. The credit application is often considered to be the cornerstone of the customer's file. It should provide basic information about the customer and be updated periodically to reflect changes in the company's policy and to obtain fresh information from the customer that better reflects the market and the various legal aspects affecting the credit function.

A properly constructed credit application can also serve as a document that can be relied upon for legal actions should litigation become necessary. One thing is certain about buyer/seller relationships: nothing is certain. Court dockets are filled with cases involving two parties litigating over that one little item that they were sure could never happen. In the absence of a written document like the credit application or a contract/agreement that spells out the way the two parties will conduct themselves, the judge, arbitrator or mediator is left to fill in the gaps using any factual evidence, parol evidence, the law of contracts and the UCC, which could have otherwise been spelled out in a credit application. It is unwise for the creditor grantor to leave the payment outcome to a third party without some written agreement.

A well-devised credit application is structured to assist the seller during the four stages of the buyer/seller relationship: (1) prior to extending credit, (2) during the credit relationship with the buyer, (3) during problems in a credit relationship and (4) during litigation.

It is very important for a seller to know its applicant. The credit application begins the relationship-building process and is an initial source of information to begin a fact-finding, fact-verification endeavor about the applicant.

In addition to using the credit application as an investigative tool, the credit application should create a contract between the seller and the buyer. The application should include all of the seller's desired terms and conditions of sale. A savvy customer will recognize the credit application as an agreement or contract to terms and negotiate the contract accordingly; the credit grantor should include every condition or term that addresses what has happened historically or could possibly occur in the industry or trade that would prevent the creditor from being paid on time or at all. It is far better to include in the credit application all terms and conditions to be negotiated rather than not including them at all. Not having a terms of sale clause included in the credit application may allow the customer's purchase order agreement to prevail in the event of a lawsuit, arbitration or mediation. In other words, in the absence of language favorable to the credit grantor, the credit grantor will lose to the customer on the basis that there was no [other] agreement to counter the customer's claim and subsequent documentation.

If a creditor wins a judgment in a legal proceeding, the credit application may also become a useful tool to help locate a judgment debtor's assets for collection purposes.

The Credit Application as a Source of Information

Basic Information

Date of application

By dating the application, it is easy determine the start date of the agreement. If financial information is supplied, the date will provide a frame of reference.

Applicant's complete legal name

Determining the correct legal name of an applicant ensures that the credit application truly functions as a contract and is legally binding. If it becomes necessary to go to court, bringing action against the correct person or entity is required. If the name of the entity is not correct, the case will be dismissed for lack of proper name.

In some industries, it is not unusual for a customer to use a commonly known name rather than the name under which the company is registered. In this event, it is important to thoroughly research the Secretary of State or other licensing records before filing suit.

Having the official, exact legal name is critical when searching for any lawsuits, tax liens, mechanic's liens or judgments as well as obtaining credit reports and assumed name filings. Such information could be considered a red flag or evidence that cash flow is not sufficient to pay certain taxes or other obligations. Public records of this sort indicate that demands could be made on cash intended to meet operating expenses or pay outstanding bills, possibly causing a collection problem for creditors. Based on these details, the credit grantor can also verify facts and information presented on the application.

Comprehension Check

Why is it important to have the correct legal name of a credit applicant?

Newly established DBAs (doing business as) should also be identified and added to the credit file.

Address information including mailing address, physical address, P.O. Box

Address information can be verified online. The sales department can help by verifying physical address information. Not only does an applicant's physical address pinpoint the location, it is likely that the applicant's assets will be located there as well. Be wary when an applicant lists a mail drop for the address, as most fraud occurs by this method.

Telephone number, fax number, email and website

Always verify telephone numbers, fax numbers, email addresses and the applicant's website. These simple steps can often uncover many irregularities or inconsistencies.

Federal Tax Identification Number (FEIN)

If a company is engaged in business, it should have a federal tax ID number in order to file a tax return. This number is important for issuing 1099s and other purposes. More importantly, it conveys a message of consistency and organization that the entity is in business and willing to take all necessary steps to operate within the structure of laws and regulations governing business. Absence of a valid federal tax ID number could be an indication of credit risk if the customer is affected by IRS intervention.

Accounts payable contact information

This information saves time should the creditor need to contact the accounts payable department.

Years in business

The longer a firm has been in business, the more stable it would appear to be—and more information should be available to the credit department. If the credit department cannot gather enough information about a company that has been in business for several years, then the credit manager must question the account.

Amount of credit requested

Determining the amount of credit requested by the customer will help the credit manager deal more efficiently with the application process.

Lease or own

Should a seller ever be in a position to seek assets to satisfy a judgment, knowledge about a debtor's ownership of real estate is very useful. For instance, if the premises (office, warehouse, retail space, etc.) are leased, then the landlord could be a source of information about payment trends. If the company were to default, disappear or file bankruptcy, then the landlord could obtain a lien on all property, inventory and other assets until the lease agreement is satisfied. This may pose a collection problem for the credit grantor.

Sales tax exemption

In some businesses, exemption from sales tax status is important information to have on hand before invoicing. The credit grantor should obtain sales exemption certificates.

Sample language for sales tax exemption

Sales Tax Permit #:

I certify that [name of applicant/debtor] located at [address, city, state of applicant] is engaged as a registered

☐ Retailer ☐ Manufacturer ☐ Lessor ☐ Other, and is registered with the state and cities listed on the attached use tax exemption certificate, within which seller/debtor would deliver purchases and that any such purchases are for wholesale, resale, ingredients or components of new products to be resold, leased or rented in the normal course of applicant's business. Applicant is in the business of retailing, manufacturing, leasing (renting) the following:

Description of Business:

I further certify that if any property so purchased tax free is used or consumed by the firm as to make it subject to a Sales or Use Tax, that applicant will pay the tax due directly to the taxing authority when state law so provides, or inform the seller/creditor for added tax billing. This exemption certificate shall be part of each order which applicant may hereafter give to seller, unless otherwise specified, and shall be valid until canceled by applicant in writing or revoked by the city or state.

Under penalties of perjury, I swear or affirm that the information on this form is true and correct as to every material matter.

Authorized Signature	Date	Title

U.S. Resale Tax exemption certificates

According to the Multistate Tax Commission, "Whenever a seller receives and accepts in good faith from a purchaser a resale or other exemption certificate or other written evidence of exemption authorized by the appropriate state or subdivision taxing authority, the seller shall be relieved of liability for a sales or use tax with respect to the transaction." Suppliers may obtain State Resale Tax Exemption Certificates from their reseller customers to avoid having to bill them for taxes. The customers must be resellers of the product and cannot be the end users.

The policy applies to customers who have "nexus" in a U.S. state. **Nexus,** defined as *"sufficient physical presence," is a legal term that refers to the requirement for companies doing business in a state to collect and pay tax on sales in that state.*

Regarding Resale Tax Certificates:

1. Usually, the credit department is responsible for obtaining copies of new customers' Resale Tax Certificates. The credit or tax department is then responsible for keeping them on file and requesting new ones before they expire (certain states only).

2. The states will audit companies to ensure they are obtaining and maintaining their customers' certificates. If the company cannot provide them to the auditors, they may be fined by the states. These fines can be very punitive.

4. The Multijurisdictional Uniform Sales & Use Tax Certificate can be used in lieu of obtaining forms from customers who do business in 38 of the states. *See* certificate below.

5. Not all states have a sales and use tax.

Sample language for uniform sales & use tax exemption/resale certificate — multijurisdiction

UNIFORM SALES & USE TAX EXEMPTION/RESALE CERTIFICATE — MULTIJURISDICTION

The following
states have indicated that this certificate is acceptable as a resale/exemption certificate for sales and use tax, subject to each state's laws. The issuer and the recipient have the responsibility to determine the proper use of this certificate under applicable laws in each state, as these may change from time to time.

Issued to Seller: _____

Address: _____

I certify that:

Name of Firm (Buyer): _____ is engaged as a registered:

Address: _____

_____ ☐ Wholesaler
_____ ☐ Retailer
_____ ☐ Manufacturer
_____ ☐ Seller
_____ ☐ Lessor
_____ ☐ Other (Specify) _____

and is registered with the below-listed states and cities within which your firm would deliver purchases to us and that any such purchases are for wholesale, resale, or ingredients or components of a new product or service to be resold, leased or rented in the normal course of business. We are in the business of wholesaling, retailing, manufacturing, leasing (renting) or selling the following:

Description of Business: _____

General description of tangible property or taxable services to be purchased from the Seller:

_____

Sample language continued

State	State Registration, Seller's Permit, or ID Number of Purchaser	State	State Registration, Seller's Permit, or ID Number of Purchaser
AL		MO	
AR		NE	
AZ		NV	
CA		NJ	
CO		NM	
CT		NC	
DC		ND	
FL		OH	
GA		OK	
HI		PA	
ID		RI	
IL		SC	
IA		SD	
KS		TN	
KY		TX	
ME		UT	
MD		VT	
MI		WA	
MN		WI	

I further certify that if any property or service so purchased tax free is used or consumed as to make it subject to a Sales or Use Tax we will pay the tax due directly to the proper taxing authority when state law so provides or inform the Seller for added tax billing. This certificate shall be a part of each order that we may hereafter give to you, unless otherwise specified, and shall be valid until canceled by us in writing or revoked by the city or state.

Under penalties of perjury, I swear or affirm that the information on this form is true and correct as to every material matter.

Authorized Signature: _____
(Owner, Partner, or Corporate Officer)

Title: _____

Date: _____

Check with each state's department of revenue for more information.

Type of business (wholesale, retail, distributor, manufacturer)

A general description of the business will help the seller understand the applicant's business. An applicant may have more than one type of business or it may be an indicator of fraudulent activity. If the nature of the business does not fit the need for the creditor's type of product, then the credit department has to ask, "Why are they buying our product and should we make an offer of open account, unsecured credit?"

NAICS Code

On the credit application, request the customer's **North American Industry Classification System (NAICS) code** *which identifies their product or service and industry.*

Below is an example of NAICS code 33461 (Manufacturing and Reproducing Magnetic and Optical Media):

- The first two digits of the code represent the firm's major industry
  31-**33**: Manufacturing
- The third digit tells the subsector
  33**4**: Computer and electronic product manufacturing
- The fourth digit identifies the industry group
  334**6**: Manufacturing and reproducing magnetic and optical media

- The fifth digit gives the industry
  3346**1**: Manufacturing and reproducing magnetic and optical media

The NAICS code 33461 tells us this about the customer: They manufacture optical and magnetic media and mass produce audio, video, software and other data on magnetic media.

NAICS codes enable the credit professional to:

Comprehension Check
What is an **NAICS code**?

- Know, at a glance, the primary industry in which the customer operates.
- Understand industry and competitive issues affecting the customer.
- Compare the customer to industry statistics and norms.

The Entity Itself—The Real Customer

Legal Status of Company: Corporation, LLC, Partnership, Sole Proprietorship

It is important to understand the legal structure of the applicant. If a creditor is selling to a sole proprietor, then the owner of the business is, literally, the business and is automatically liable for the entity's debts.

When dealing with a **general partnership**, *each individual partner can be held liable for all debt incurred as a result of the general partnership entity.* This is not an equal share formula. Any partner of the general partnership will be held liable for the entire debt of the general partnership—not an equal share. For example, if there are four partners involved in a general partnership entity, then any one of the partners may have to meet the obligation of the debt without consideration given to the other three partners. This simply means that the credit grantor can approach each partner until one of them satisfies the debt. The partners have an arrangement where they share equally in the investment and obligations. In a general partnership, the creditor need only trouble itself with collecting from any one of the various partners. The partner who finally pays may collect the appropriate sum of the paid obligation from each partner. It is not the creditor's duty or requirement to collect equal amounts from the remaining partners. Basically, the partner who has the money to pay, and does so, has a collection matter among the other partners.

A **corporation** *is an entity, usually a business, having authority under the law to act as a single person distinct from shareholders who run it and having rights to issue stock and exist indefinitely.* A corporation has an existence that is separate and apart from its shareholders. A corporation has the right to conduct business; to sue and be sued; and typically enjoys those rights and privileges provided under the laws of the state of its incorporation. As such, a great deal of information is commonly available relating to a specific customer who is incorporated through public record sources, Secretaries of State and possibly the Securities and Exchange Commission if the customer is an incorporated company that is publicly traded.

A **limited liability company (LLC)** *is an unincorporated association that, when properly structured, provides limited liability to its owners, referred to as members,* and provides tax advantages similar to S Corporations, formerly known as Subchapter S Corporations. Most states now recognize some form of a limited liability company.

With this type of entity, it can appear to the credit grantor that they are being asked to sell on open account credit to a general partnership. However, unlike the general partnership, the LLC entity behaves very similarly to a corporation with regard to sheltering assets and limiting liability for debts incurred by the entity.

The management philosophies of a corporation or LLC are often linked to its founders. As such, personal information about these individuals may play a key role in the credit-granting process. Later sections of this chapter address the ways in which personal information on owners, principals and members (of LLCs) can be properly and legally obtained when the credit grantor determines such details will be necessary in order to approve credit requested or increase credit limits to existing customers.

For the credit grantor, corporations and LLCs are the most common types of entities found. Selling to either one can present particular challenges to the creditor:

- Who has authority to enter into an agreement on behalf of the corporation or LLC?
- Who are its principals or members?

- What is the personal business background and history of the principals or members of the entity applying for credit?
- Who is ultimately liable for the corporation's or LLC's debt?

The credit grantor must first know the type of entity to which it is being asked to supply products or services in order to determine the risks and appropriate steps to take to protect itself from associated uncertainty or risk. Sometimes the creditor must consider using additional security instruments like a personal guarantee when selling to a corporation or LLC depending on the entity's creditworthiness.

A credit department can easily check the legal status of a company online with the Secretary of State's office to verify whether the company is in fact a corporation, its status (incorporated, dissolved, merged, fortified) and full legal name, the date of incorporation, the name of the resident agent and, in some states, the names and addresses of corporate officers and directors.

Other forms a business entity can take include a **limited partnership.** *A limited partnership consists of one or more general partners who are jointly and severally liable for the obligations of the partnership.* A limited partnership will also consist of one or more limited partners who are not responsible for the debts or liabilities of the partnership beyond the amount of the capital that each contributed to the entity. A general partner of a limited partnership may be a corporation. There is also what is known as a **master limited partnership,** *which is a type of limited partnership that is publicly traded over-the-counter or on a stock exchange;* a **joint venture,** *which is an association of two or more persons undertaking a single business enterprise for profit generally limited to one particular enterprise* (e.g., for the purpose of developing real property); a **municipal utility,** *which is a not-for-profit public entity owned and operated by the state or a political subdivision of the state* (for example, cities, public utility districts or a locally elected utility board); and a **cooperative,** *which is a private, independent entity owned and controlled by the members of the cooperative who use its services.*

Buyer's Obligation to Disclose Change of Name or Legal Status

A critical part of "Knowing Your Customer" (KYC) is for a seller to know the correct legal name and legal status of its customer. Specifically, a seller must ensure that it is contracting with the correct party. Otherwise, the seller might run into a later problem of being unable to collect its claim against a customer that is not identified correctly or has changed its legal status.

A seller can confirm its customer's correct legal name and legal status by performing a business name search with the Secretary of State's office of the applicable state. It is also imperative that a seller's terms and conditions account for a subsequent change in the customer's legal name or status. The terms should require that the customer notify the seller of a change in the customer's legal name and/or status and cooperate with the seller in modifying their contract as the seller deems appropriate. This would include the customer's agreement to enter into new agreements with the seller subsequent to any change in its legal name and/or legal status.

If a company changes its legal status, a new credit application should be signed. For example, if a sole proprietorship or general partnership incorporates or forms an LLC, the personal liability of the owner/proprietor or of the partners is extinguished. The credit application originally signed by the proprietor or partner is no longer valid for the new corporation or LLC. The same rule follows when mergers and acquisitions occur; a new credit application should be obtained replacing the previous agreement. In each case, these are new entities under the law. The credit agreement originally in place does not succeed.

Comprehension Check

Where can one check the legal status of a public corporation?

Principals, owners, officers and members

The credit department is charged with the responsibility of gathering the name of each person involved in the ownership of the entity whether it be for a sole proprietor, each partner of a general partnership, corporate officers or each member of a limited liability company. *Collecting social security numbers, home addresses and telephone numbers is a matter related to privacy issues; if credit grantors gather this type of information, then additional procedures are necessary as any personally identifying information must be kept strictly confidential. Likewise, the maintenance of personal and private information should be reviewed with counsel.*

It is important to know the ownership history to help the credit department gain confidence in the management of the business entity. Learning about the owners, officers, members (of an LLC) or principals is called antecedent information. This information tells the credit manager that the people who manage this company have experience or know the industry, which will help them succeed in the business venture. Antecedents help establish a record of successes or failures that the credit department can and should know in order to make credit decisions.

Laws and Regulations Covering Personal Information*

Various state and federal statutes and regulations require protection of defined categories of personal information. Some of them are likely to apply to corporations which possess any specified personal information about their customers. While the scope of coverage, the specificity of the requirements and the definitions vary among these laws, personal information is usually defined to include general or specific facts about an identifiable individual. The exceptions tend to be information that is presumed public and does not have to be protected such as a business address.

In general, a company must develop, implement and maintain a comprehensive information security program, including a risk assessment, containing detailed requirements for the information security program and detailed computer system security requirements.

The security requirements include:

- Encryption of all transmitted records and files containing personal information that will travel across public networks, and encryption of all data containing personal information to be transmitted wirelessly.
- Encryption of all personal information stored on laptops or other portable devices.
- Additional system security requirements are secure user authentication, secure access control, reasonable monitoring to detect unauthorized access, reasonably up-to-date firewall protection, reasonably up-to-date security software (including current patches and virus definitions), and education and training of employees.

Note that encryption is already required for federal agencies that have information about individuals on laptops and portable media. As encryption becomes a legal requirement in areas like these, it is likely to become the standard of what is reasonable.

The obligations don't stop, however, at protecting the confidentiality of information. Many states have laws that require notification concerning data breaches. While there are differences in their scope and requirements, they generally require entities that own, license or possess defined categories of personally identifiable information about individuals to notify affected individuals if there is a breach. Like the reasonable security laws, many of these laws apply to covered information about residents of the state. Some require notice to a state agency in addition to notice to consumers. Most of these laws have encryption safe harbors, which provide that notice is not required if the data is encrypted and the decryption key has not been compromised. Some states also now have laws that require secure disposal of paper and electronic records that contain defined personal information.

Comprehension Check
What security is needed to protect the confidentiality of customer information?

Reprinted with permission from David G. Ries, Esq., Clark Hill PLC, Pittsburgh, PA.

Related Business Ventures and Related Concerns

Ask about previous business ventures. What was the name of any previous business holding of the principal, and how was it concluded (sold/failed/bankruptcy/etc.)?

Additionally, ask if the principal is currently involved in any other business. After gathering these details, build a "family tree" of all the business holdings in which the principal is involved. This information will be insightful as to what degree of attention the principal may, or may not, pay to the actual business entity that is applying for credit. The information will also be helpful if one or another of the related concerns is not doing well financially or has been sued or has liens filed. If this is the case, then the question becomes: how much of the money that was available to pay outstanding invoices is now in demand for one, or more, creditors of the related concerns?

Bank and Trade Information

Bank References, Including Bank Name, Address, Account Numbers, Bank Loan Officer or Contact Name and Information

The seller may be able to contact the applicant's bank directly; therefore, it is helpful to obtain a contact name or a loan officer's name. Account numbers are important if post-judgment execution or garnishment action is ever required. Useful information about loans includes the type of loan, the original amount of any loan, the total amount due, loan payment trends and whether a personal guarantee was provided, or whether any collateral secures the loan.

The credit department looks for average balance information to determine if the amount of open account credit requested matches the available average bank balance normally carried in the customer's checking account: a customer requesting $50,000 of unsecured credit who carries an average bank balance in the "low four figures" ($1,000–$4,000) may require further scrutiny. The credit grantor also should determine whether or not any items have been returned unpaid (NSF) and, if the customer has a borrowing account, the payment history of active loans with the bank.

Many banks have policies concerning the release of customer information. Even though current laws do not prevent banks from providing information on the business/commercial bank customer, many banks have chosen to adhere to a standard "no information" policy. Banks are often limited to a larger degree because of banking regulations intended to protect bank information related to consumers. As a result, banks are inclined to view every credit inquiry as if it were a consumer inquiry and, therefore, decline a response to the request. Some banks will respond if they have written authorization from their customer to release information, but may charge a fee to the inquirer.

To help credit personnel obtain bank information on a customer, consider creating a separate signature line in the bank information section of the credit application for the customer/applicant to authorize the release of bank information on commercial or business accounts.

Sample language for bank authorization

I hereby authorize the bank named herein to release information requested for the purpose of obtaining and/or reviewing my company's credit from time-to-time.

Information about Banks and Other Creditor Security Interests

The offices of the Secretary of State may be able to provide useful information about an applicant. Using UCC-1 filings, credit grantors can review information about bank and other creditor security interests. UCC-1 filing reports are a matter of public record, are generally free and will tell the creditor if the applicant has borrowed money, purchased equipment or capital assets or entered into leases. Typical collateral seen in UCC-1 filings are accounts receivable, inventory and/or equipment encumbered by a present lien or security interest and blanket and hereafter acquired security. This means that everything the customer or applicant has is encumbered to a security holder. Names, addresses and telephone numbers of secured parties are included in each UCC-1 filing.

By reviewing such filings, the credit manager can tell by the filing date if lenders are willing to continue to loan money. The credit manager can also begin to determine whether the customer has financial flexibility or if the customer is too heavily encumbered to meet the potential credit grantor's requirements.

UCC-1 filings can also act as a secondary source of information. For example, if a customer defaults or, worse, closes its doors and cannot be located, a UCC-1 filing will identify the names, addresses and telephone numbers on each filing. With this information, the credit department will have possible leads in order to locate the customer—and possibly be able to secure return of goods or collect money.

Trade Reference Information

Most customers expect this question on a credit application and are ready with three, four or five references. While these direct references are valuable, they should not be the primary source of information on which the credit grantor bases a credit decision. The applicant will always provide the best references they can, therefore one would expect these references to be positive.

Beyond the applicant, a credit grantor may query fellow businesses for reference information. Care should be exercised, however, when credit information is shared among creditors. Any and all information exchanged should reflect only those transactions that have been completed and are in the past. There should be no discussion as to any future action a creditor may take—"We are going to file suit this week." There should also be no disparaging remarks about principals of the business or the business itself. Comments that reflect the historical nature of the relationship are appropriate as long as they are factual statements relating to payment habits and actions taken by the creditor providing the information. Such statements can describe: how long sold, date of last sale, high credit, total balance, amount current, past due 30, 60, 90+, and other historical comments (e.g., "They usually pay promptly"; "They take discounts"; "They are slow to 90 days but eventually pay"; "They were placed for collection"; "We had to sue"; etc.).

When seeking information, it is proper protocol to also provide information. A creditor should always be forthcoming when making an inquiry of a credit reference. For example, "This [customer/company] has applied for credit from our company and has given your company as a reference." All information exchanged is strictly confidential and should not be disclosed to any party outside of either company's credit department.

Free Flow of Information

Trade credit grantors enjoy the luxury of a free flow of information for the asking. They should be willing to share their current customer information when asked and to maintain confidentiality upon receiving such information from another business credit grantor.

The **NACM Canons of Business Credit Ethics** *establish standards relating to the proper exchange of credit information among creditors which contains historical and current factual information to support the process of independent credit decision-making.* No permission is required whatsoever to obtain a commercial/business credit report from any agency, including NACM Affiliates, Equifax, Experian, D&B and others about a business or potential business customer. The misconception in this area stems from consumer credit privacy laws that absolutely require permission to obtain personal information and from banks, which have internal policies that vary from bank to bank as to whether or not they will release commercial/business customer credit information.

The Antitrust Division of the Federal Trade Commission governs the gathering and dissemination of commercial/business information and is based on competition and restraint of trade while the Fair Credit Reporting Act and various consumer privacy protection laws govern the gathering and dissemination of personal consumer information.

Comprehension Check

What information should be required on a credit application?

The Credit Application as a Contract

The properly executed credit application is a binding contract when there is agreement to terms and conditions. Remember, the process of obtaining the signed application is a negotiation. As such, including all provisions in the credit application that protect or benefit the credit grantor is the objective. Negotiation generally means that neither party gets everything it wants. But if the questions aren't asked or if the conditions are not included in the credit application, they will certainly not be answered.

One way to think about this process is to consider everything that could possibly make the selling company successful in the event of default or other adversarial relationship with a customer. Then include language to address each issue on the credit application. While several will be addressed in this section of the chapter, every industry and each individual company should focus on those specific issues germane to their own business/industry. A customer or potential customer may negotiate some items, but some discussion will take place prior to the formation of a relationship that may avert an otherwise adversarial, and potentially costly, situation later. Negotiation of terms may be acceptable depending on the specific terms under discussion. The credit application should be a reflection of the challenges and situations a company has experienced over time. Therefore, include language to cover every situation experienced as a means to limit those occurrences from taking place again.

Agreement to Terms and Conditions of Sale and Credit Policy

The credit application is the only document necessary to form a contract for open account credit, absent a bid proposal or a subcontract agreement entered into by a supplier or subcontractor to which agreement to terms is a condition of the letting of the job or project. Aside from these instances, the credit application document sets forth the agreement between the two parties and describes, identifies and otherwise defines the terms and conditions upon which the parties will do business. Once signed, the credit application is legally binding, including all terms and conditions outlined within the agreement.

> **Sample language for terms and conditions**
>
> All invoices are due [per credit grantor terms]. All amounts for purchases from [name of credit grantor] are payable at [address]. COD restrictions may be placed on any past due account. I (We) agree to pay account promptly within terms stated.

Switching From Credit to Cash Terms

A seller selling on credit terms invoices its customer with payment due at some later date. The seller's terms and conditions should permit a switch to cash in advance terms when its customer fails to timely pay any invoice owing to the seller or the seller has a cause for concern about its customer's creditworthiness.

A provision for a change in payment terms can take a variety of forms. As is the case with most terms, a seller's ability to obtain favorable terms depends on its negotiating leverage. It might prefer the unfettered right to allow or terminate credit terms at its sole discretion. Alternatively, its terms might include the ability to switch to cash terms in the event a customer breaches its contract with the seller or the customer's financial condition has substantially deteriorated to warrant a termination of credit terms. This provision can also state that all amounts the customer owes the seller will be immediately due and payable when the seller changes payment terms.

> **Sample language for change in payment terms**
>
> The credit terms provided by seller are in its sole discretion and can be terminated at any time by seller; if at any time seller reasonably determines that buyer's financial condition does not justify the continuation of seller's performance, seller, at its sole discretion, may require full or partial payment in advance for the contracted goods from buyer; declare the total amount owed by buyer immediately due and payable; or, without any notice, suspend or terminate any performance without protest or penalty from applicant, including cancelling unfulfilled orders.

Terms and Conditions in Another Place

A seller will often have a set of terms and conditions on its website (or another location). Terms posted on the seller's website or in another place would be binding on a customer if the terms are incorporated by reference in a written signed agreement between the parties. Best practices require that a seller's credit application or other agreement signed by its customer includes the customer's agreement to be bound by the terms and conditions posted on the seller's website or other place. A link to the website where the applicable terms and conditions are located should also be included (and the link must actually work as a faulty link would likely result in the provision being deemed unenforceable). It is also good practice to require customers to periodically execute acknowledgments when the seller updates its terms and conditions to bind the customer to such updated provisions.

Buyer Modification of Terms

A customer's agreement to a seller's terms and conditions does not necessarily preclude the customer from subsequently submitting future purchase orders containing contradictory terms that could supersede the seller's more favorable terms. A seller can protect itself from this risk by including, as part of its terms, language that no modification or waiver of any terms by the customer will be enforceable without the seller's prior written approval and the seller's terms will govern to the extent of any discrepancy between its terms and those submitted by its customer in any sales quotation, purchase order or similar document.

Comprehension Check

Why do terms of sale have to be set forth in writing in a credit application?

Interest Charges

When considering a provision for service or finance charges, it is important to avoid violating state usury laws. Although most state usury statutes deal with consumer transactions, a customer may make a credit purchase using a business/trade credit account but then use the items purchased for their own personal use. Law governs this issue according to how the product or merchandise is used rather than how the product or merchandise is purchased.

Potential problems can arise when a customer does not pay for the merchandise or products within terms, and the credit grantor assesses interest, finance, late or similarly named delinquency charges. Even though a credit application may include language that says the customer understands that they are applying for business credit, the credit application contract terms will not prevail if any term violates the state usury law. If the products purchased on credit are used for "personal, family or household use," the transaction is of a consumer nature and consumer credit laws apply, including the amount of interest that may be assessed. State statutes vary, which further complicates matters.

> **Sample language for interest charges**
>
> All invoices are due [credit grantor terms of credit/sale]. A service charge of one and one-half percent (1½%) per month, or eighteen percent (18%) per annum, may be assessed on delinquent invoices but not to exceed at any time the highest legal rate of interest legally allowed.

This language may help to avoid a usury violation in states where the credit grantor may unknowingly make a consumer transaction to a customer for goods or services on open account and later attempt to collect any form of late payment charges on the transaction. This language may also help credit grantors prevail in the event of litigation involving collecting interest on non-usury commercial or business transactions. Courts will generally allow the interest rate agreed to in the signed credit application document as long as the goods or services were not used for personal, family or household use.

A seller should also include, as part of its terms, the reimbursement of attorneys' fees incurred in any lawsuit or through other actions to collect their past due claims or involving any disputes with their customer. The extent to which the seller will be reimbursed for its attorneys' fees can vary depending on the seller's negotiating leverage.

Certification of Use Provision

The objective is to attempt to avoid a defense by a customer that buys products or merchandise from a business credit grantor on open account ostensibly to use in a business manner but instead uses the products/merchandise for "personal, family or household purposes." Such usage shifts the transaction from business credit to consumer credit and, thereby, opens the door to consumer protection defenses.

> **Sample language for certification of use**
>
> I (We) certify that this request is for the extension of credit for business purposes only and is not intended for the extension of credit for personal, family or household purposes.

The nature of the transaction itself will dictate the outcome of this defense. How products or services were used is what a court will consider. Nonetheless, this language remains an important part of the credit application because it clearly states the intention of the parties entering the credit agreement or contract and puts the customer on notice that the creditor should be notified of a purchase that will be used for "personal, family or household purposes." Certification of use language may not be necessary for every industry or business unless a credit customer can potentially use products purchased for "personal, family or household use."

Venue Provision

The intent of including this provision on the credit application is to keep any litigation in the credit grantor's location; the venue provision affords the creditor that right. Without this provision, the credit grantor could be required to travel to the **venue** (*customer's location*) to bring suit or to defend a lawsuit. Including a venue provision in the credit application may cause the customer to reconsider payment on the delinquent account given that the customer would have to come to the creditor's location to defend against an action.

Comprehension Check
Why is it important to specify **venue** in the credit application?

Sample language for venue provision

It is understood that this agreement is entered into in the state of [ ], County of [ ], and is governed by the laws of the state of [ ].

OR

Applicant agrees that all issues and disputes relating to any credit arrangement extended hereunder shall be governed in accordance with a competent jurisdiction chosen at the discretion of [creditor] and that applicant expressly waives its venue rights without reference to conflicts of laws or legal principles.

Third-Party Collection Fees and Attorney's Fees

The general rule is that each party to a lawsuit must pay its own costs to collect and to defend a collection lawsuit. However, with a credit application provision that the customer agrees to pay, or to indemnify, the creditor whether or not a lawsuit is filed, the creditor then can recover fees paid to a collection agency.

In some states, attorney's fees may be automatically awarded to the prevailing party. However, absent language stipulating payment of third-party collection agency fees, courts generally do not award those fees.

Sample language for collection fees

In the event of default, and if this account is turned over to an agency and/or attorney for collection, the undersigned hereby agrees to pay all reasonable fees and/or costs of collection whether or not suit is filed.

Change of Ownership

The credit professional can avoid the shock of finding new owners in a previously approved customer's business by stipulating language in the credit application that addresses this issue.

Sample language for change of ownership

We [customer/credit applicant] understand that we must notify [credit grantor/supplier] in writing, and by certified mail, of any change in ownership, whether in the name of the entity or in the business structure of the entity under which credit is established, no later than 30 days after such change is effective.

Inclusion of this or similar language may personally bind the principal of a customer who sells the business or inventory to a new owner or who changes the status of the entity at some point after the establishment of business credit without providing notice. Such a modification (e.g., from proprietor or partnership to corporation or LLC) shifts the liability for purchases made after the change and affords protection from personal liability by virtue of the new status. Without knowledge of this event, the credit professional could unwittingly sell on open account terms to a customer when a personal guarantee may have been in order. It is imperative to then reevaluate the credit before continuing a relationship with the new owner or entity by way of a new credit application. It really is a new credit relationship and should be treated as such.

Certification of Credit Application Responses

Include language attesting to the fact that the information supplied is true and correct.

Sample language for certification of credit application responses

The applicant certifies under the penalty of perjury that the statements contained in the application are true and correct. Applicant understands that the seller intends to rely on all of the information presented in this application in determining its credit-worthiness.

Signature

An officer or principal of the company applying for credit does not necessarily have to sign the credit application agreement. If there is an authorized representative to sign such documents, then that signer can legally bind the company even if the signer is not an officer or executive of the company. Language to consider including in the credit application document that would appear above the signature line(s) should say substantially:

Sample language for authorization to sign

The person executing this agreement has authority to bind [the customer] and is authorized by [the customer] to enter into the terms and conditions set forth in this credit agreement.

Situations can arise in which a customer is reluctant to sign the credit application or feels it is a large enough business concern to evade the credit application signing process altogether. Insisting that the credit application be properly executed (signed) could stand in the way of making a sale by creating ill-will with the customer, the sales department and possibly management or ownership. A signed credit application document is a first defense in any dispute or potential litigation with a customer; therefore, it is essential that the credit application be signed by the customer or the customer's representative.

A signed credit application can also prevent a customer's after-the-fact effort to change terms later by their issuance of a purchase order or other document incorporating different terms of sale from those established in the credit application document. Absent a signed application, terms initiated in a later document may prevail causing the credit grantor to comply under unintended terms.

The credit professional is tasked with finding ways to say "yes" to customers regardless of information obtained or their disinclination to execute a credit application document. The credit professional must then determine how to manage the risk associated with the decision to sell on open account credit.

A signed credit application is pertinent only if there is no preceding signed document, such as a bid proposal, which incorporates terms if accepted by the issuer, or a subcontract or supply agreement in which agreement to terms is a condition of the letting of the job or project. The credit professional may or may not be involved in this process as these contracts and bid proposals are frequently authorized without input from the credit department. The credit professional can be of assistance, however, by making management aware of objectionable terms included in such contract documents and by knowing where to find resources to help their company avoid perilous terms in contracts.

If a contract term is dubious or uncertain in nature, the rule is simple: "When in Doubt—Line it Out." *See* the Crest Ridge case study for more details.

The following options are suggested as alternative methods that may be considered whenever a customer is averse to signing the credit application:

Comprehension Check

Whose signature is needed on the credit application?

Credit Card Authorization Agreement

This form can be offered to the customer in lieu of the credit application. Such an agreement simply means that the credit professional will charge purchases made by the customer at the time the order is placed.

Electronic Funds Transfer Authorization (EFT)

Using this method, the customer agrees to allow the credit professional to simply transfer funds from its bank account at the time the order is placed.

Management Indemnification Form

A form signed by management, or the individual who overrides the signed application requirement, protecting the credit professional if the customer appeals to a higher authority than the credit professional, in order to obtain credit without a signed credit application.

Shipment Terms

Understanding when the ownership of goods sold changes hands is a very important subject that credit department personnel at all levels should understand clearly. The transfer of goods from seller to buyer presents an element of risk. The goods can be lost, damaged or destroyed while in the care of a transportation carrier. Therefore, the issue of who is responsible for the risk of loss must be defined.

The Uniform Commercial Code has specific rules governing risk of loss, which is an issue separate and apart from title (ownership). Risk of loss depends upon the terms of the agreement, the moment the loss occurs, and whether one of the parties was in breach of contract when the risk of loss occurred. Risk of loss can be contractually addressed by using *commonly accepted shipping terms* **(Incoterms®)**. In addition to the shipping terms, the following is commonly used to create shipment contracts, whereby the seller turns the goods over to a carrier for delivery to the buyer. In a **shipment contract,** *both title and risk of loss pass to the buyer when the goods are given to the carrier.* The seller has no responsibility for seeing that the goods reach their destination.

No Arrival, No Sale *places the expense and risk during shipment on the seller.* If the goods fail to arrive through no fault of the seller, the seller has no further liability to the buyer.

If no agreement has been made for either a shipment contract or a destination contract, then the risk passes to the buyer on receipt of the goods if the seller is a merchant. If the seller is not a merchant, the risk passes to the buyer when the seller tenders (offers) delivery of the goods. The UCC Article 2 definition of **merchant** is "*a person who deals in goods of the kind or otherwise by his occupation holds himself out as having knowledge or skill peculiar to the practices or goods involved in the transaction or to whom such knowledge or skill may be attributed by his employment of an agent or broker or other intermediary who by his occupation holds himself out as having such knowledge or skill.*" **Seller** is "*a person who sells or contracts to sell goods.*" So a merchant deals in goods and a seller sells goods.

Comprehension Check

In a **shipment contract,** when do title and risk of loss pass to the buyer?

Figure 9-1

Credit Card Authorization Form

The following form was originally developed by NACM MidAmerica of Oklahoma City, OK. All rights reserved.

[VENDOR] COMMERCIAL CREDIT CARD PAYMENT PROGRAM

[APPLICANT] agrees to the following terms and conditions regarding payment by credit card.

AGREEMENT TO PAY

[APPLICANT] agrees to honor all credit card charges for product purchased from [VENDOR]. Should the credit card be declined, [APPLICANT] may demand payment, prior to any further shipments.

PAYMENT OF OBLIGATIONS

[APPLICANT] agrees to pay to [VENDOR] at such place designated by it, obligations evidencing credit extended by [VENDOR] in accordance with the applicable payment, finance and service charge schedule in effect from time to time.

CHARGEBACKS

[APPLICANT] agrees that any disputed charge, request for chargeback or adjustment, will first be reported to [VENDOR]. [VENDOR] will have 10 business days to resolve the dispute with [APPLICANT].

[APPLICANT] has 30 days to dispute, or request a chargeback, any credit card charge. [APPLICANT'S] failure to dispute the charge, or request a chargeback, 30 days after payment constitutes a waiver of any right to chargeback the payment.

AUTHORIZATION FOR PAYMENT

[APPLICANT] hereby authorizes [VENDOR] to charge its credit card for any and all purchases. The following representatives of the [APPLICANT] are authorized to use the [APPLICANT'S] credit card.

Credit Card Number: _____

Expiration Date: _____

Address of Account Holder: _____

Phone Number of Account Holder: _____

Email Address of Account Holder: _____

Individual/Personal Card _____ Corporate/Company Card _____

Cardholder authorizes payment of/up to: _____

A legible enlarged photocopy of the front and back of the credit card must accompany this authorization request.

All payments on credit cards will be charged upon receipt.

_____	_____
Representative	Title
_____	_____
Representative	Title
_____	_____
Representative	Title

[APPLICANT] *agrees to inform* [VENDOR] *within 10 days of any changes to those authorized to use its credit card.*

WARRANTIES AND REPRESENTATIONS

[APPLICANT] warrants and represents that the signature on the claim slip will be genuine and authorized by cardholder and not forged or unauthorized.

Figure 9-1   Credit Card Authorization Form continued

TRANSACTIONS COSTS

[APPLICANT] is not entitled to a cash discount for payments by credit card.

TRANSFERABILITY

This agreement is not transferable by [APPLICANT] without [VENDOR'S] consent. Any attempt by [APPLICANT] to assign the Agreement in violation of this paragraph shall be void.

FAILURE OF CUSTOMER TO FULFILL OBLIGATIONS

Should [APPLICANT] fail to fulfill any of the obligations under this agreement, [VENDOR] may declare the entire balance due and immediately payable, and may proceed to enforce the full payment of such balance, including finance and service charges. In event of suit to collect such payment balance, [VENDOR] shall pay all reasonable attorney fees and actual court costs.

GOVERNING LAW

All transactions involving the credit extended under this agreement shall be governed by the laws of the State of [   ], which are expressly adopted to control all transactions under this agreement.

WAIVER OF STATUE OF LIMITATIONS

[APPLICANT] expressly waives the defense of the statute of limitations for the period permitted by law.

AGREEMENT OF CUSTOMER

[APPLICANT] expressly agrees to the provisions contained in this agreement and manifests this agreement by his/her signature.

RECEIPT OF COPY OF AGREEMENT

[APPLICANT] acknowledges receipt of a copy of this agreement.

Date: _____,   By: _____

       [APPLICANT]

Date: _____,   By: _____

       [VENDOR]

INDIVIDUAL PERSONAL GUARANTEE

Date _____, 20xx

I, (name) _____, residing at address _____, for and in consideration of your extending credit at my request to (company) _____ (hereinafter referred to as the "Company"), of which I am (title) _____, hereby personally guarantee to you the payment at _____ in the state of _____ of any obligation of the Company and I hereby agree to bind myself to pay you on demand any sum which may become due to you by the Company whenever the Company shall fail to pay the same. It is understood that this guarantee shall be a continuing and irrevocable guarantee and indemnity for such indebtedness of the Company. I do hereby waive notice of default, non-payment and notice thereof and consent to any modification or renewal of the credit agreement hereby guaranteed.

Signature _____

Social Security No. _____

Witness _____

Address _____

Real World Perspectives

The following case study describes what can happen when a creditor moves forward without a signature on his/her credit application.

CREST RIDGE CONSTRUCTION GROUP, INC. VS. NEWCOURT INC.

The impact of terms contained on a credit application was recently illustrated in litigation between Crest Ridge Construction Group, Inc. ("Crest Ridge") and Newcourt Inc. ("Newcourt"). Crest Ridge, a construction company, won a subcontract to build certain sections of the Liberty Science Center in Jersey City, New Jersey. One portion of the subcontract required Crest Ridge to supply architectural wall paneling for the Center. The principals of Crest Ridge began discussions with Newcourt, a low-cost foam paneling supplier. Shortly after the discussions began, Newcourt issued a price quotation to Crest Ridge which stated that it was "subject to credit department approval." Newcourt also furnished Crest Ridge with a credit application. The terms and conditions in the credit application and price quotation did not state any specific required credit terms.

Crest Ridge returned the credit application to Newcourt a few weeks later. The completed credit application form stated that Crest Ridge had been established in 1985 and listed one banking and four trade references. Newcourt checked out the banking reference and attempted to verify the trade references. The bank reported that Crest Ridge did have an account and had an average balance of $5,000. Newcourt was not able to verify the trade references. Because it was concerned about the creditworthiness of Crest Ridge, Newcourt began to investigate other methods of guaranteeing Crest Ridge's payment.

Meanwhile, Newcourt and Crest Ridge continued to discuss the project. Crest Ridge issued a purchase order to Newcourt quoting a price and referencing Newcourt's original price quotation. Newcourt supplied samples of its wall paneling material, job specifications and calculations, three revisions of shop drawings and final drawings showing where each panel would be placed at the Center. Three months later, Newcourt wrote to Crest Ridge suspending all further work on the wall paneling project and demanding payment in full within two weeks. The letter did not mention any credit problems but instead stated that full payment was required because of the "encumbering and confusing progress and lack of receiving pertinent data necessary to satisfy the requirements on the above-referenced project." Crest Ridge attempted to contact Newcourt several times but there was no response. Crest Ridge finally went to another supplier and covered with higher-priced paneling. Newcourt never shipped any paneling to Crest Ridge.

Crest Ridge sued Newcourt for breach of contract. Newcourt argued that there never was a contract because Crest Ridge did not obtain the approval of Newcourt's credit department. The court held that although Newcourt "required" that the price quotation

was subject to credit department approval, it did not act in a manner consistent with that language. It went ahead and exchanged price quotes, showed its product and acted in many ways consistent with the existence of a contract. Thus, the court ordered Newcourt to pay damages equal to the difference in amount Crest Ridge was required to pay the higher-priced supplier.

Lessons to Be Learned from Newcourt

Newcourt appears to have had a credit application procedure which left something to be desired. It required references and other information that gave it reason to be concerned about whether it would receive payment from Crest Ridge. It also supplied certain terms and conditions on its credit application that Crest Ridge executed. Newcourt did not act consistent with its terms. Although Newcourt's credit department had apparently not given its approval, Newcourt's behavior gave every indication that a deal had been made. It provided material samples, three revisions of shop drawings, fastening details, stipulations as to the color of each panel and final drawings showing where each panel would be placed. Crest Ridge believed that it had a contract with Newcourt. The court examining these facts also believed that Newcourt acted as if a contract had been made. The court found that Newcourt's demand that it be paid in full prior to any manufacturing or shipment was unjustified under the terms and conditions set forth in the credit application. The court noted that Newcourt did not supply any credit terms to Crest Ridge.

Courts are predisposed to finding that a contract exists. The court considering the Crest Ridge/Newcourt dispute was no different. The court was willing to determine that based upon the terms and conditions contained in the credit application or through the actions of the parties that Crest Ridge and Newcourt had a contract between them. In this instance, the court found that the credit application terms were for the most part disregarded by Newcourt as evidenced by its actions. Had Newcourt really wanted to rely upon its terms and specifically the requirement that its credit department must approve the transaction, then Newcourt would have had to refrain from moving ahead with performance and discussions until such time as the credit department approved the relationship or perhaps sent a letter stating that it could not proceed without the approval of its credit department. It did not. In fact, Newcourt acted as if a contract did exist up until it stated that payment must be made in advance. Newcourt had set up its credit application in many ways that should have protected it, yet Newcourt acted inconsistently in such a way that the court found that its actions dictated the terms of its contract and it was found to have breached the contract.

This material originally appeared in a past issue of Business Credit *magazine and was written by Deborah Thorne, Esq., while a partner in the law firm of Barnes & Thornburg LLP.*

Supplemental Information

Other provisions may be included on the credit application that may be beneficial to specific industries and businesses or in certain circumstances. A credit professional may include these terms on the credit application as supplemental language to other terms and conditions or as replacement language for items discussed that do not apply to certain industries or businesses.

Waiver/Duty to Inspect

Use of this provision requires a customer to inspect and notify creditor of any dispute within a specific period of time or surrender the right to do so later. This language strengthens the case for prompt collection of delinquent accounts and avoids the practice of some customers who would withhold payment of any portion of an invoice where there may be a dispute on a smaller portion of the invoice.

> **Sample language for waiver/duty to inspect**
>
> Applicant agrees to examine immediately upon receipt, each of [creditor's] invoices and/or statements, and to advise [creditor] of any disputed transactions or billings/statements within 10 days of receipt, together with a written statement specifying the reasons for such dispute. Failure to notify [creditor] of any dispute with respect to defective goods or billing shall constitute a waiver of all such disputes.

Escheatment/Inactivity

Every state has legislation that requires individuals and companies to **escheat,** *which is defined as the "reversion of property to the state in consequence of a want of any individual competent to inherit." (Black's Law Dictionary,* Abridged Tenth Edition, 2014).

Escheatment includes all forms of property, both tangible and intangible, including a customer's credit balance. Escheatment laws provide that the state becomes the legal owner of abandoned property based on the concept of state sovereignty. To write down a seller's escheatment exposure, a credit professional may consider imposing a reasonable inactivity fee to the credit balance.

> **Sample language for escheatment/inactivity**
>
> [Creditor] imposes an inactivity fee of $_____ per month against any credit balance presumed abandoned by applicant. An account is presumed abandoned if there is no activity for one year.
>
> **OR**
>
> [Creditor] reserves the right to assess a monthly service charge on account paid outside credit terms to the maximum amount permitted per jurisdiction.

Setoff Rights

Setoff rights are a significant state law remedy that can help a trade creditor reduce its exposure on a claim against a financially distressed customer. Setoff enables a creditor to net out the amount it owes its customer from the amount the customer owes the creditor. For example, a seller might be owed $100 for goods sold to a customer on credit, but the seller might separately owe $100 to the customer in connection with an entirely separate business transaction. Setoff allows the seller to net out and set off the amounts owed which results in full payment of its claim.

Creditors that sell to and buy from their customers can include a setoff provision as part of their terms. A typical setoff provision will permit the seller to offset any indebtedness owing to the customer against the seller's claim against the customer.

Therefore, in the example, in the event the customer is unable to pay the $100 it owes to the seller, the seller can cancel its $100 debt to the customer, resulting in a 100% recovery on its claim. In the context of the customer's bankruptcy, a seller's setoff right is like a secured claim where the seller could reduce its claim against its customer on a dollar-for-dollar basis by concomitantly reducing its indebtedness to the customer. This contrasts with the seller being relegated to general unsecured creditor status with a far lower likelihood of recovery of its claim in the absence of any setoff right.

Creditors that do business with affiliated entities might attempt to broaden their setoff rights to allow them to net their claim against one affiliate to reduce their obligation to another affiliate. This is called a "triangular setoff." Taking the example, in this situation a seller is owed $100 for goods sold on credit to its customer, but the seller separately owes $100 to the customer's affiliate. The seller can include a term that permits it to offset its indebtedness to its customer or its affiliates against the seller's claim against the customer, with the applicable affiliates doing business with the seller agreeing to be bound by this particular provision.

Alternatively the seller, its customer, and the customer's affiliates can enter into a separate setoff agreement. Trade creditors should note, however, that while triangular setoff provisions are enforceable under state law in a non-bankruptcy context, bankruptcy courts have refused to enforce this provision in a bankruptcy setting. Therefore, even in a case where a seller, its customer and the customer's affiliate unambiguously agree to grant the seller triangular setoff rights against the affiliate, the seller will likely lose its triangular setoff rights upon the filing of bankruptcy by the customer and its affiliated entities. The seller could minimize the risk of loss of its triangular setoff rights by obtaining the affiliate's guarantee of the customer's obligations to the seller.

Waiver of the Right to a Jury Trial

It is important to seek the agreement of the customer to waive its right to a jury trial. Virtually every state will permit the waiver of a jury trial by a business debtor, provided that it is created in a commercial setting.

Prejudgment Remedy Waiver

Sample language for prejudgment remedy waiver

Applicants do hereby expressly and irrevocably waive any notice and/or hearing, which may be required for prejudgment remedies under the statute of the state of [state].

Alternative Dispute Resolution (ADR)

Consider language in the credit application that provides for binding arbitration or mediation should a dispute arise. Mediation or arbitration usually can be set in a matter of days with an arbitrator or mediator experienced in collection or business disputes. Conversely, a hearing or trial by jury could take months or years to be heard by a judge. Arbitration is binding and eliminates litigation or trial by jury whereas mediation is not binding and does not circumvent litigation if either party is not satisfied with the mediator's decision. The decision to add an arbitration or mediation provision in a credit agreement is one that should be made after careful deliberation with management and counsel, to ensure that all appropriate factors are considered.

Use this tool judiciously as binding arbitration also eliminates litigation as an alternative.

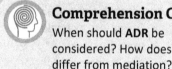

Comprehension Check

When should **ADR** be considered? How does it differ from mediation?

Sample language for alternative dispute resolution

Applicant agrees that applicant will submit all disputes to final and binding arbitration (or mediation) in [State,] in accordance with the American Arbitration Association or the National Association of Arbitrators (if arbitration is selected). Applicant agrees to be bound by the arbitrator's (or mediator's) decision.

Security Instrument/Agreement

Although perfection of the security agreement is required to properly demonstrate the right to collateral, the credit application can contain language that creates the security interest and will then be considered a security agreement.

Sample language for security instrument/agreement

Applicant hereby grants to the [creditor] a security interest in [ ] and any and all purchases made by Applicant from creditor (the "Collateral"), and hereby authorizes the [creditor] to execute and file on behalf of the applicant any such UCC financing and continuation statements as the [creditor] deems necessary to perfect its and/or its Assignee's security interest in the Collateral.

Financial Information

For customers that are small companies, financial statements can be difficult to obtain since they may not have audited annual financial statements. If this class of customer represents the largest part of the customer base, include an easy-to-complete balance sheet and income statement form as part of the application. If the customer base is made up of larger companies, financial statements should be available. In either case, it is crucial for the creditor to obtain financial information, signed by an authorized officer, and to attach such financial information by reference into the credit application.

A section should be included in the credit application stating that the applicant agrees to provide updated financial information upon request. Financial statements can detect changes in legal status.

> ### Sample language to obtain financial statement
>
> Attached to (or included within) this credit application is the most recent financial statement of the applicant/undersigned. The undersigned agrees to provide to creditor updated financial information on request, and to timely provide an annual financial statement to creditor as a condition of the continuation of this credit.

If the applicant is a corporation, a balance sheet can be copied from an 1120 tax return. Not all applicants can provide an audited financial statement, but it is recommended that the seller obtain financial information to evaluate creditworthiness.

The application can include a question about whether the applicant has ever filed for bankruptcy and/or has been involved in an involuntary bankruptcy proceeding, an assignment for the benefit of creditors or a composition agreement, which are all insolvency proceedings.

Buyer's Obligation to Provide Financials

A seller's terms should also require that their customers periodically deliver financial statements to the seller. There are several reasons why this can be informative. First, a seller's knowledge of its customer's financial condition by reviewing the customer's financial statements would be helpful in any decision concerning future business. A seller's review of its customer's financial statements would also assist the seller in deciding whether to tighten credit terms or switch from credit to cash terms.

Limitations on Liability

A seller's terms should also impose a cap on its liability to its customer. These provisions should limit a seller's and their affiliates' cumulative liability to the total amounts their customer had paid to the seller.

> ### Sample language for limitations on liability
>
> The aggregate cumulative liability of seller and its affiliates under common control with it, directors, officers, employees, representatives and agents for all claims arising hereunder, notwithstanding the form in which any such action is brought, whether in contract, tort (including negligence), or otherwise, shall be limited in the aggregate to the total amounts paid by applicant to seller under any invoice or order confirmation.

Any such provision should also confirm that a seller would not be liable for consequential, incidental, indirect, special, exemplary or punitive damages, third-party claims, loss of revenues, loss of profits or loss of savings.

A seller should also include a provision that requires its customer to inspect the goods purchased from the seller and raise complaints within a short period of time. For example, requiring a customer to assert all complaints in writing within seven days of delivery of the seller's goods and providing for a customer's waiver of claims that were not timely and properly asserted will increase the likelihood of full payment of a seller's claim against the customer.

> ### Sample language for customer inspection of goods
>
> Applicant is under an obligation to inspect contracted goods immediately upon receipt for correctness, completeness and conformity. Incorrect, incomplete or nonconforming contracted goods must be reported to seller in writing within seven (7) days from the date of delivery of the contracted goods. Otherwise, buyer shall be deemed to have accepted the contracted goods. Upon written notice from buyer, seller will correct incorrect and/or incomplete orders at its own expense. For nonconforming contracted goods, seller, at its sole discretion, will (i) repair the product or part thereof; (ii) furnish a replacement product or affected part thereof; (iii) issue a refund in an amount equal to the original selling price for the item; or (iv) deny the claim according to those terms.

A seller should also include language that shortens the statute of limitations for a customer to commence a lawsuit against the seller for breach of contract and other claims. Article 2 of the Uniform Commercial Code (which governs transactions for the sale of goods) stipulates that the statute of limitations is four years for any lawsuit asserting breach of contract or breach of warranty claims. However, the contracting parties can shorten the statute of limitations to as low as one year. Therefore, a seller's terms should state that a customer must commence an action alleging a breach of warranty or any other breach of contract claim within one year after the cause of action arises.

Limitations on Warranties

Article 2 of the Uniform Commercial Code also provides that certain implied warranties will be read into sales contracts, unless the contract waives such warranties. Article 2 creates an implied warranty of merchantability that requires goods sold to be merchantable (i.e., fit for the ordinary purposes for which such goods are used). Article 2 also contains an implied warranty of fitness of purpose where the customer is relying on the seller's expertise in making sure the goods are suitable for the customer's intended purpose. There might be other implied warranties arising through course of dealing or usage of trade.

A seller's terms and conditions should include a disclaimer of all implied warranties. Only those warranties that the seller and the customer agreed to include as part of the disclaimer should be binding on the seller. Some states allow general disclaimers of all implied warranties, while other states require listing each specific warranty that is being disclaimed.

As a best practice, a seller's terms should include a disclaimer of all implied warranties of any kind, including, without limitation, warranties as to performance, merchantability, or fitness for a particular purpose, and warranties arising by statute or otherwise, or from a course of dealing or usage of trade.

> **Sample language for disclaimer of implied warranties**
>
> Except as provided in seller's products warranty, warranty of title or infringement, seller does not make or give any representations, guarantees, warranties or conditions of any kind, express or implied, including, without limitation, warranties as to performance, merchantability, or fitness for a particular purpose, and warranties arising by statute or otherwise, or from a course of dealing or usage of trade.

Stating that all goods are sold "as is" can also serve to alert the customer that the goods are being sold without any implied warranties of any kind. Lastly, a seller should make sure provisions limiting warranties are in bold font and/or capital letters since the Uniform Commercial Code requires that any provision excluding warranties be conspicuous.

Liquidated Damages

Liquidated damages *are damages that the parties agree will compensate an injured party upon a specified breach*. Liquidated damages typically include a customer's damages arising from a seller's late delivery of goods or provision of services. Liquidated damages clauses are often expressed as a percentage of the overall value of the sale or service in question.

Absent including a liquidated damages clause as part of a seller's terms, courts will be left to determine actual damages, which is often difficult, and can vary depending on the circumstances. As such, best practice is for a seller to include a liquidated damages clause in its contracts in order to attain cost certainty in the event of a dispute. While liquidated damages may turn out to be greater than actual damages in certain circumstances, the seller would at least gain comfort from having a clearer understanding of its overall risk profile.

Indemnification

A seller's terms should also include a seller's indemnification in favor of its customer and vice versa. Indemnification provisions can take several different forms. The seller's objective should be to have as narrow an indemnity in favor of the customer as possible. Customers often seek to include broad indemnification provisions where the seller indemnifies its customer for all customer claims regardless of which party is at fault. Despite the fact that these broad indemnification provisions are unenforceable in certain states, sellers should try to narrow their scope at the outset. A reasonable indemnity from the seller's perspective imposes liability on the seller to indemnify its customer for actions that are solely the seller's fault.

A seller should also seek its customer's indemnity for certain claims that might be brought against the seller in connection with a transaction. For instance, a seller might wish to seek protection from product liability claims. The seller's terms can require the customer's indemnification of the seller for product liability claims brought against the seller where the customer's intervening act had caused the product defect. This provision would be beneficial where the customer receives the product from the seller and the customer's subsequent improper installation causes a malfunction and exposes the seller to potential liability. The customer should bear the cost where it was clearly at fault.

Force Majeure

A seller's terms should also state that the seller is not responsible for its failure to perform under an agreement with a customer if such failure is the result of a force majeure event. **Force majeure** *events can include "acts of God," such as floods, earthquakes and hurricanes, as well as other events, such as war, terrorist activities, labor disputes and electrical failures*. The seller's objective should be to define a force majeure event as broadly as possible so as to assign as much risk as possible to the customer.

Below the Signature Line

Consent to Obtain Consumer Credit Report—FCRA Authorization

After completing the investigation of the potential business customer, or review of the existing business customer, the credit professional may believe that the customer represents a questionable credit risk. The credit professional must then determine whether to sell or to continue to sell on open account credit basis to this customer and/or at current credit limits. The credit professional may decide that a review of the personal credit history of the principal of the business entity is warranted in order to make an appropriate credit decision.

In this case, the credit professional will want to obtain a consumer credit report. In order to legally obtain this report, the **Fair Credit Reporting Act (FCRA)** requires a two-pronged test. First, there must be a "permissible purpose" to obtain the report. Second, "written authorization" from the individual whose report will be reviewed must be obtained. A provision in the credit application seeking general authority for the credit professional to obtain a consumer credit report on a proprietor, partner, officer/principal of a corporation or member of an LLC will not be sufficient to obtain such a report.

With regard to the first test element, "permissible purpose," the credit grantor automatically has the existing applicant's permission because there is either a request to enter into a business credit relationship with the credit grantor or there is already an established business credit relationship.

Sample language for the second test FCRA element

The undersigned individual who is principal, proprietor or partner of the entity applying for business credit, and therefore desirous of a business relationship with [creditor], recognizing that his or her individual credit history may be a factor in the evaluation of the credit history of the applicant, hereby consents to the use of the consumer credit report of the undersigned by [creditor] as may be necessary in the credit evaluation process and for periodic review for the purpose of maintaining the credit relationship.

The FCRA goes on to say that this authorization must be "conspicuous" in that the applicant must be clear that permission is being given to obtain their personal credit report. In order to meet the "conspicuous" test, the FCRA suggests that the language be printed in bold, all caps or otherwise stand out from other terms and conditions in the credit application. This language may also be treated as an addendum to the credit application and offered to the customer as a separate document for the principal's signature.

Personal or Corporate Guarantee

A personal guarantee can be a valuable tool for the credit department when information available on the business entity itself is unavailable or unsatisfactory. A **personal guarantee** *is obtained from a principal of an entity such as a president or other officer or shareholder; a member or multiple members of an LLC; or from any third-party source unrelated to the business but who can be offered as a signatory.* A **corporate guarantee** *is used when a corporation agrees to be held responsible for completing the duties and obligations of a debtor to a lender, in the event that the debtor fails to fulfill the terms of the debtor-lender contract.*

The objective for the credit department when obtaining a personal guarantee is to ensure "pass-through" to the personal assets of the individual signing the guarantee in order to offset the risk the credit grantor may be taking by providing open account, unsecured credit. Individuals who sign a personal guarantee acknowledge, via their signature, that they understand that should the business entity for which they are offering their guarantee default in any manner then the credit grantor may look to them for satisfaction of any and all debt incurred by the entity.

Personal guarantees are unnecessary for an entity structured as a proprietorship or general partnership because the proprietor, owner or partners of a general partnership are automatically personally responsible for debts incurred by the business entity owned or controlled by them.

The difference between a personal guarantee and a corporate guarantee is that an individual person or persons are attesting to their faith and trust in the company or business entity to meet their obligations to the creditor named. They will "stand-in-the-shoes" of the customer in the event of default. The result is the same for a corporate guarantor except that the guarantor is actually another company that will be approached for payment in the event of default of the business entity to which the creditor is being asked to extend open account, unsecured credit.

In the personal guarantee the consent language is *not* required to appear separate and apart from the guarantee form itself because the guarantor and the person consenting to the request to obtain consumer information should be one and the same. This is unlike the credit application process wherein an authorized representative can enter into the credit application terms and conditions. The authorized signer on the credit application, however, may not be the person whose consumer credit report will be required. The signer of the credit application cannot provide consent for the acquisition of another party's credit report. Therefore, a separate signature area for consent is necessary, including those instances in which the authorized signer of the credit application and credit report subject are one and the same.

Credit professionals must understand that, under certain circumstances, it is possible to have three separate signatories in the process of obtaining a credit application: the signatory of the credit application, the signatory of the consent to obtain a consumer credit report and the signatory of the personal guarantor.

In the process of obtaining consent to obtain consumer credit information, the credit professional will generally require the social security number of the individual whose consumer report is be obtained. In gathering personal information of this nature, the credit professional should be reminded that the **Gramm-Leach-Bliley Act** and certain other privacy regulations must be considered when gathering and keeping this personal information. A review of company policy with appropriate legal counsel is warranted and recommended.

Guarantee language can be included on the credit application form itself or it can be an addendum. If the guarantee appears on the credit application form, then it is advisable for the guarantee language to appear below the signature line where the customer would agree to the credit application's terms and conditions. There are numerous reasons for doing so; the main one has a great deal to do with FCRA requirements to obtain personal information on the guarantor. *Any personal or corporate guarantee is only as good as the person (or company) signing it. If they are not creditworthy, then the guarantee could be of little value when enforced. It is not necessary to comply with FCRA regulations regarding a corporate guarantee, as a creditor is not required to have a "permissible purpose," or to obtain permission, written or otherwise, to obtain credit information on a business entity regardless of their structure.*

Key terms of a personal or corporate guarantee are:

- It should be termed a "payment guarantee" as opposed to a "performance guarantee." This means that the guarantor agrees to pay the creditor and not perform on a contract.
- It should be "absolute and unconditional," meaning there is no mistake and that the creditor is not required to fulfill some condition in advance of demanding payment under the guarantee.
- It should be a "continuing" guarantee. That is, the guarantee continues in force as long as debt exists.
- It should be "irrevocable," which means the guarantor cannot avoid, or otherwise destroy, the efficacy of the guarantee without written notice to the credit grantor and acceptance by the creditor of the revocation.

Additional terms to consider when drafting a personal or corporate guarantee:

- Guarantors agree to seller's specified interest rates.
- Guarantors agree to pay all costs of collection (attorney's fees and court costs).
- Guarantors agree to the specified governing laws.
- Guarantors agree to be joint and severally liable with the debtor to the seller.
- Guarantor's consent to jurisdiction (optional).
- Guarantor's waiver of a jury trial (optional).
- Guarantor's waiver of counter claims.
- Guarantor's signature.
- Guarantee should be witnessed and notarized.

Sample language to consider in the Personal Guarantee

- In consideration of credit extended by Seller to Buyer, I assume personal and individual responsibility, etc.
- The guaranty is open, continuous and not limited in time.
- This guaranty shall remain force until Seller receives notice from me that this guaranty is terminated.
- I knowingly and voluntarily waive any right to trial by jury.

It is advisable to seek legal counsel to ensure that any guarantee entered into with a customer is in compliance with current policies and is written in such a way as to achieve the payment protection desired.

Corporate guarantees should always include a corporate resolution from the company or entity guarantor. This step ensures that no claim will come forth that the corporation did not authorize entering this obligation without knowledge and consent on behalf of the principals, shareholders and board of directors of the corporate entity.

The ECOA does not permit a credit grantor to require a spouse to sign a personal guarantee if that spouse is not directly involved with the business credit applicant.

If a guarantee of another corporation, an affiliated corporation, a parent or a subsidiary is obtained, obtain a corporate resolution authorizing the obligation. A parent corporation can guarantee the debt of its subsidiary. The official corporate seal should be placed on the documents.

 Comprehension Check
What are the essential elements of a **personal guarantee**?

Sample language for personal guarantee

PERSONAL GUARANTEE

For valuable consideration, the receipt of which is acknowledged, including but not limited to the extension of credit by [Company Name] to _____ the undersigned, individually, jointly and severally, unconditionally guarantees to [Company Name] the full and prompt payment by _____ _____, of all obligations which Guarantor presently or hereafter may have to [Company Name] and payment when due of all sums presently or hereafter owing by Guarantor to [Company Name]. Guarantor agrees to indemnify [Company Name] against any losses [Company Name] may sustain and expenses [Company Name] may incur as a result of any failure of Guarantor to perform including reasonable attorney's fees and all costs and other expenses incurred in collecting or compromising any indebtedness of debtor guaranteed hereunder or in enforcing this guarantee against guarantor. This shall be a continuing guarantee. Diligence, Demand, Protest or notice of any kind is waived. It shall remain in full force until guarantor delivers to [Company Name] written notice revoking it as to indebtedness incurred subsequent to such delivery. Such delivery shall not affect any of guarantors obligations hereunder with respect to indebtedness heretofore incurred.

The undersigned personal guarantor, recognizing that his or her individual credit history may be a necessary factor in the evaluation of this personal guarantee, hereby consents to and authorizes the use of a consumer credit report on the undersigned, by the above named business credit grantor, from time to time as may be needed, in the credit evaluation process.

Sign Name _____ Print Name _____ Date _____

Sign Name _____ Print Name _____ Date _____

Witness _____ Date _____

Equal Credit Opportunity Act (ECOA) Notice

The **ECOA** *prohibits a business credit grantor from discriminating with respect to the extension or renewal of credit based on race, color, religion, national origin, sex, marital status or age.* It is important that a credit application does not contain questions which could be interpreted as discriminatory. The following language is required and can be placed in the footer of the credit application:

Sample language for required ECOA notice

The Federal Equal Credit Opportunity Act prohibits creditors from discriminating against credit applicants on the basis of race, color, religion, national origin, sex, marital status, age (provided the applicant has the capacity to enter into a binding contract); because all or part of the applicant's income devices from any public assistance program; or because the applicant has in good faith exercised any right under the Consumer Credit Protection Act. The federal agency that administers compliance with this law concerning this creditor is the Federal Trade Commission, Division of Credit Practices, 6th Street and Pennsylvania Avenue, NW, Washington, DC 20580.

Comprehension Check

What is contained in the **ECOA** regulations?

Figure 9-2   Terms and Conditions Sample Form

1. The undersigned Applicant agrees to the use of its signature on this application as authorization to release credit information from Applicant's bank and from all other sources of credit information regarding the Applicant.

2. Should credit availability be granted by COMPANY to Applicant, all decisions with respect to the extension or continuation of this credit shall be at the sole discretion of COMPANY.

3. When requested, the undersigned Applicant agrees to provide annual financial information to properly substantiate the continuation of credit extension as required by COMPANY.

4. Applicants from whom COMPANY will require security in exchange for the extension of credit will cooperate as necessary to enable COMPANY to perfect an appropriate security interest including, but not limited to, a security interest in the goods sold by COMPANY to the Applicant.

5. The undersigned Applicant hereby agrees that all amounts due for goods and services purchased from COMPANY are payable at the remittance address shown on the invoice and according to the terms specified by COMPANY as stated on each invoice. The undersigned Applicant hereby agrees to remit the total amounts due as reflected on COMPANY'S invoices. If the Applicant believes an adjustment to any invoice is warranted, the Applicant shall request in writing that appropriate credit be issued and shall cooperate with COMPANY in verification of the propriety of such credit.

6. No term or condition contained in any purchase order, offer, writing or other communication to COMPANY shall be valid and binding upon COMPANY unless agreed to in writing by an authorized representative of COMPANY or is identical to the written terms and conditions of sale of COMPANY.

7. The undersigned Applicant agrees to apply cash discount to credit memos, as long as cash discount is part of the Applicant's payment terms. Promotional credits are not subject to cash discount.

8. In the event that COMPANY takes possession of Applicant's existing stock ("Lift Out Inventory") through a stock lift, Applicant warrants good title to the Lift Out Inventory. Applicant agrees to identify, prepare and supply COMPANY with any releases or terminations of security interests, financing statements and liens affecting the Lift Out Inventory accepted by COMPANY. Applicant warrants that the removal and disposal of Lift Out Inventory by COMPANY will not (a) violate any loan agreements, security agreements, credit sales agreements, other agreements, bulk sales laws, tax consents or clearance requirements or court or administrative orders, contractual agreements or other legal obligations to which Applicant is a party or subject; or (b) give rise to claims against COMPANY of any kind by anyone claiming by or through Applicant an interest in or contractual rights regarding the Lift Out Inventory. Applicant also assigns to COMPANY all warranty rights, chooses in action and general intangible rights pertaining to the Lift Out Inventory.

9. The undersigned Applicant acknowledges that in the event of default, including payment default, (defined as payment received beyond terms as designated on invoices), COMPANY reserves the right to take any or all of the following actions:

(a) Impose a moratorium on order shipment.

(b) Reduce the credit limit.

(c) Conduct a credit investigation of the business entity which will require updated trade and bank reference information.

(d) Require financial statements to clarify the customer's financial status.

(e) Require some type of security such as a UCC-1/Purchase Money Security Agreement, Cross-Corporate Guarantee, Personal Guarantee or Letter of Credit.

(f) Require immediate payment of the account balance in full.

(g) Revoke open account terms.

Figure 9-2   Terms and Conditions Sample Form continued

10. The undersigned Applicant agrees to notify the COMPANY credit department of any changes of ownership and further agrees to remain liable for all purchases made prior to such change unless COMPANY otherwise agrees in writing.

11. The undersigned Applicant agrees to pay a fee of $50 for any check returned for non-sufficient funds.

12. The parties shall endeavor to resolve within 90 days any dispute arising out of or relating to this Agreement by mediation under the CPR Mediation Procedure then currently in effect. Unless the parties agree otherwise, the mediator will be selected from the CPR Panels of Distinguished Neutrals. Any controversy or claim arising out of or relating to this Agreement, including the breach, termination or validity thereof, which remains unresolved by mediation shall be submitted to binding arbitration in accordance with the CPR Rules for Non Administered Arbitration then currently in effect, by three independent and impartial arbitrators, of whom each party shall designate one; provided, however, that if one party fails to participate in the mediation as agreed herein, the other party can commence arbitration prior to the expiration of the time periods set forth above. The arbitration shall be governed by the Federal Arbitration Act, 9 U.S.C. §§ 1-16, and judgment upon the award rendered by the arbitrators may be entered by any court having jurisdiction thereof. The place of arbitration shall be CITY, STATE and the governing law shall be the laws of STATE without regard to STATE'S rules on conflict of laws. A party may file a complaint at any time before arbitrators have been selected to seek a preliminary injunction or other provisional judicial relief, if in its sole judgment such action is necessary. Despite such action the parties will continue to participate in the procedures specified in this Agreement.

13. The undersigned Applicant agrees to pay, in the event the account becomes delinquent and is turned over to a collection agency, all attendant collection costs and attorney's fees as allowed by law in the state of STATE.

14. The Applicant understands that if a return is accepted to cover delinquent debt, COMPANY reserves the right to charge a 10% handling fee on the credit memo. Freight costs on the return are the responsibility of the debtor.

15. The Applicant hereby certifies the accuracy and truth of the information provided in this application, and in the information provided in addition to this application, and acknowledges that such information is given for the purpose of inducing COMPANY to extend credit to Applicant and to assist in the investigation of the Applicant and the subsequent decision on the extension of credit to the Applicant. By signing this application, the signatory represents and affirms that he/she is a duly authorized representative of the Applicant with full power and authority to agree to the terms and conditions set forth in this application and to bind the Applicant hereto.

16. I affirm that the information contained in this application is complete and accurate. COMPANY is relying on this information as affirmed. All information contained herein is material and any omission and/or misstatement could result in immediate termination of credit extended by COMPANY.

Signed and dated_____

The investigation and eventual credit availability decision by COMPANY will be executed in compliance with the Federal Equal Opportunity Act as administered by the Federal Trade Commission which prohibits discrimination on the basis of race, color, religion, national origin, sex, marital status or age.

Reprinted from the NACM Graduate School of Credit and Financial Management project, 2016.

Key Terms and Concepts

Alternative dispute resolution (ADR), 9-22

Canons of Business Credit Ethics, 9-11

Cooperatives, 9-8

Corporate guarantees, 9-26—9-27

Corporations, 9-7

Electronic funds transfer (EFT) , 9-16

Equal Credit Opportunity Act (ECOA), 9-28

Escheat, 9-20

Fair Credit Reporting Act (FCRA), 9-25

Federal Tax Identification Number (FEIN), 9-4

Force majeure, 9-25

General partnerships, 9-7

Gramm-Leach-Bliley Act, 9-26

Incoterms®, 9-16

Indemnification, 9-24—9-25

Joint ventures, 9-8

Liability, limitations, 9-23

Limited liability companies (LLC), 9-7

Limited partnerships, 9-8

Liquidated damages, 9-24

Master limited partnerships, 9-8

Merchants, 9-16

Municipal utilities, 9-8

NAICS Code, 9-6—9-7

Nexus, 9-5

No Arrival, No Sale, 9-16

Personal guarantees, 9-26—9-27

Sellers, 9-16

Shipment contracts, 9-16

Triangular setoffs, 9-21

Venue, 9-14

Warranties, limitations, 9-24

Comprehension Check

1. What information should be required on a credit application?
2. Why is it important to have the correct legal name of a credit applicant?
3. What is an **NAICS code**?
4. Where can one check the legal status of a public corporation?
5. What security is needed to protect the confidentiality of customer information?
6. Why do terms of sale have to be set forth in writing in a credit application?
7. Why is it important to specify **venue** in the credit application?
8. Whose signature is needed on the credit application?
9. In a **shipment contract**, when do title and risk of loss pass to the buyer?
10. When should **ADR** be considered? How does it differ from mediation?
11. What are the essential elements of a **personal guarantee?**
12. What is contained in the **ECOA** regulations?

Summary ....

- The credit application is crucial to the determination of the rights of the creditor in the event of a dispute with, or default of, a customer. With a well-drafted credit application, a credit professional may accomplish dual goals of limiting credit risk, addressing contingencies that may arise in a credit relationship.

- The credit application is the credit professional's first, and sometimes only, opportunity to protect their company from risk of loss through credit sales and/or fraud. This is most advantageous to obtain at the beginning of the buyer/seller relationship.

- The credit application is structured to assist the seller in four stages of the buyer/seller relationship:
  - **Prior to extending credit**
  - **During the credit relationship with the buyer**
  - **During problems in a credit relationship**
  - **During litigation**

- The credit application is usually the primary source of information on a business looking for credit. Basic information for any credit application includes:
  - **Date of application**
  - **Applicants legal name**
  - **Address information including mailing address, physical address, P.O Box**
  - **Telephone number, fax number, email and website**
  - **Federal Tax Identification Number (FEIN)**
  - **Accounts payable contact information**
  - **Years in business**
  - **Sales tax exemption**
  - **Lease or ownership of real estate**
  - **Type of business**
  - **NAICS code**

- Understanding the legal structure is also an essential component of any credit application because it allows a credit manager to understand who is liable for any debts accrued by the organization.

- A creditor can easily check the legal status of a company online with the Secretary of State's office. If a company changes it legal status, a new credit application should be signed.

- It is critical for any credit professional to understand the law and regulations surrounding personal information. Many states also require notification to individuals concerning data breaches.

- Obtaining bank references may be necessary when extending credit. However, even though current laws do not restrict banks from providing creditors information regarding business customers, many banks have chosen to adhere to a standard "no information" policy.

- Trade credit grantors enjoy the luxury of a free flow of information, and should be willing to share their current customer information, while maintaining confidentiality if obtaining customer information from another business credit grantor. The **Canons of Business Credit Ethics** establish standards relating to the proper exchange of credit information among creditors which contains historical and current factual information to support the process of independent credit decision-making.

- It is important to remember that the process leading up to a signed credit application is a negotiation.
- It is also important to avoid violating state usury laws. Law governs how the product is used rather than how it is purchased. Therefore, the amount of interest specified can only be collected if it is in the signed agreement and has been used for business/commercial purposes, aside from "personal, family, or household purposes." A Certification of Use Provision can be added to a credit agreement to avoid a defense by a customer who uses their business credit to buy products they intend to use for personal use. This is only necessary if the products have potential for "personal, family, or household use."
- A **venue** provision is essential part of a credit application to ensure credit grantors will not be required to travel to bring or defend a lawsuit.
- In order to be awarded attorney fees, it is suggested that this be stipulated in the credit agreement to ensure that it is not overlooked in court proceedings.
- During a change in business ownership, a reevaluation of credit before continuing business with the organization is imperative. A new credit application should be the beginning of this new relationship.
- An authorized representative can legally bind the company even if the signer is not an officer or executive of the company.
- Alternative methods of authorizations if customers are averse to signing a credit application include:
  - Credit Card Authorization Agreement
  - Electronic Funds Transfer Authorization (EFT)
  - Management Indemnification Form
- Due to the fact that transfer of goods from seller to buyer can present substantial risk, it is important to establish who is liable in these circumstances. Based on Uniform Commercial Code, risk of loss depends upon the terms of the agreement. This can be addressed by using the commonly accepted shipping terms (Incoterms®).
- Other supplemental information that may be included in the credit application includes:
  - **Waiver/duty to inspect**
  - **Escheatment/inactivity**
  - **Right of offset**
  - **Waiver of the right to a jury trial**
  - **Prejudgment remedy waiver**
  - **Alternative Dispute Resolution (ADR)**
  - **Security instrument/agreement**
- Big or small, financial information for a company should be provided. If the company is small, a variation of financial information should be provided, like an easy-to-complete balance sheet or income statement. For larger companies, financial statements should be provided.
- It is important to follow **ECOA** laws when obtaining a personal guarantee, but keys to a personal or corporate guarantee are:
  - **Payment guarantee**
  - **It should be "absolute and unconditional"**
  - **It should be "continuous"**
  - **It should be "irrevocable"**
- The ECOA also prohibits discrimination based on race, color, religion, national origin, sex, marital status or age.

References and Resources······································

Business Credit. Columbia, MD: National Association of Credit Management. (This 9 issues/year publication is a continuous source of relevant articles and information. Archived articles from *Business Credit* magazine are available through the web-based NACM Resource Library, which is a benefit of NACM membership.)

Cole, Robert H. and Lon L. Mishler. *Consumer and Business Credit Management,* 11th ed. Boston: Irwin/McGraw Hill, 1998.

"Credit Risk Review." NACM Graduate School of Credit and Financial Management project, 2016.

Dennis, Michael. *Credit and Collection Handbook.* Paramus, NJ: Prentice Hall, 2000.

Manual of Credit and Commercial Laws. Columbia, MD: National Association of Credit Management, current edition.

Nathan, Bruce S., Esq., Lowell A. Citron, Esq. and Chad S.Pearlman, Esq. "Mind Your T's and C's." New York: Lowenstein Sandler PC, 2016.

Ries, Esq., David G. Clark Hill PLC, Pittsburgh, PA.

Terms and Conditions of Sale

OVERVIEW

Arrangements that specify the contractual conditions of transactions between sellers and buyers for the sale of goods or services are known as **terms and conditions of sale.** In other words, these arrangements are the rules that govern the sales transaction. They include **payment terms,** which specify whether or not open credit is to be part of the sales transaction, the length of time for which credit is to be granted and other features such as discounts. Although this chapter will focus on payment terms, *terms and conditions of sale* also include other nonpayment conditions, such as warranties, return privileges and insurance coverage. From a legal standpoint, the words terms and conditions are interchangeable and will be treated accordingly in this chapter.

The impact of terms on an organization's operations is significant. The granting of time for the customer to make payment represents a commitment of operating funds by the seller. Also, in most instances, the granting of open credit will permit the customer to receive product and/or services before payment is rendered. This situation increases the seller's risk of loss in the event of customer insolvency or irreconcilable disputes. Both of these elements, the seller's ability to finance its receivables and exposure to losses from bad debts or disputes, must be factored into the seller's credit policies with respect to terms decisions.

? THINK ABOUT THIS

Q. How can terms of sale benefit the buyer or seller? Are there occasions in which the terms benefit the seller more than the buyer and vice versa?

Q. What aspects of a product can change the terms of sale?

Q. How can terms of sale and interest rates impact a company's profitability?

DISCIPLINARY CORE IDEAS

After reading this chapter, the reader should understand:

- ☑ The role played by terms in day-to-day business transactions.
- ☑ The major factors that influence terms.
- ☑ The key elements of terms.
- ☑ The types of terms and how they differ.
- ☑ The impact of payment timing and discounts on profitability.

CHAPTER OUTLINE

Important Considerations

Application of a Seller's Credit Policies to Its Terms

There are many different payment terms, ranging from prepayment by **ACH** *(Automated Clearing House)* or wire transfer to the allowance of considerable time to pay for goods or services received by a buyer. From a practical standpoint, there is a direct relationship between the terms of sale and the seller's perception of the buyer's ability to pay. Sellers are allowed to require cash in advance from a prospective customer or to take adverse actions to restrict terms offered to existing accounts, based on internally-developed credit standards. At one extreme, if the seller has little or no confidence in the buyer's paying ability, the immediate payment of cash by certified check, ACH or wire transfer may be required. On the other hand, if the seller believes that the customer is a good credit risk, goods or services can be delivered on an unsecured basis and *a period of time will be allowed for the buyer to render payment* **(open credit terms)**. Careful thought and understanding of all of the elements of terms of sale is critical to selecting the appropriate terms for a customer.

Generally, terms decisions will be based on the seller's credit policies. With regard to customers to whom open credit is declined and/or adverse actions are taken, conformity to the regulations of the Equal Credit Opportunity Act is essential.

Contractual Considerations with Respect to Terms

It is important to understand that not all sales transactions are governed by signed contracts, especially where there is frequent routine business activity between a buyer and a seller. In such situations, buyers, sellers and sometimes intermediaries exchange conflicting documents. The rules that govern these conflicts are discussed in The "Battle of the Forms" (*see* page 10-21).

Antitrust Implications

A seller's terms will be heavily influenced by the competitive situations that have developed in the industry in which the seller operates. However, each seller must set **standard terms** *(the basic terms offered uniformly to all accounts)* independently from other sellers and without collusion or conspiracy with other sellers, to avoid violation of antitrust laws. Also, in instances where a seller offers different terms to different customers, caution must be used to ensure antitrust laws are not violated. Terms are considered an aspect of price, and many of the actions that constitute violations of antitrust laws with respect to price (e.g., the Robinson-Patman Act) also constitute violations with respect to terms.

> **Comprehension Check**
> How does the Robinson-Patman Act apply to terms of sale?

Influencing Factors

General Considerations

Once terms of sale are established, they can be quite difficult to change. Because terms have both marketing and financial aspects, it is important that decisions related to establishing or changing them be made jointly by the company's sales and financial management teams. Terms may vary widely according to products and marketing situations within the same industry. These variations are in the broadest sense a reflection of **competition** and **market and product characteristics.**

Competition

Credit is extended in response to either direct or indirect customer demand for the firm's products or services. Where competition exists, as it does in most situations, the implication is that sales may not occur without the extension of credit. The decision to extend credit and the decision about the terms offered can be viewed as similar to a decision regarding the price of the product or service. Price is the result of a great number of market forces, some controllable, some not. Although the company's products or services may be similar to those offered by competitors, sufficient diversity of product or service may be created by the company through customer relations, pre- and post-sale services, pricing policies or payment terms.

Any reference to decisions to lengthen terms includes decisions to extend credit to customers who would be required to pay in advance under more conservative circumstances. Decisions to shorten terms would also include a more conservative stance as to extending credit.

A company that contemplates offering payment terms that differ significantly from its standard terms for a product line, or from the most common industry terms, must weigh competitive aspects and the subsequent influence on profits. Unless the product holds a large share of the market or is priced much lower than competing items, terms that are shorter than standard can divert business to competitors that offer less stringent arrangements. While unusually long payment terms may help build sales, they produce higher risks, greater capital investment and cost of carrying accounts receivable, higher collection expenses, heavier losses from bad debts and reduced profit margins.

Any competitive advantage may only be temporary because it can lead competitors to offer other inducements to the same customers. Shorter terms reduce the seller's burden of financing the transaction, but buyers seek longer terms or larger cash discounts. Payment arrangements balance these opposing interests. Payment terms are an element much like prices in the overall competitive scene. Uniformity of terms within an industry minimizes their competitive aspects but, even under these circumstances, a change in competitive conditions is likely to produce changes in terms. For instance, in a buyer's market there is a tendency to offer longer terms as an inducement to buy. When demand for products or services exceed their availability, terms can be expected to shorten.

Market and Product Characteristics

Market and product characteristics range widely in impact and complexity, from production time to physical characteristics of raw materials. There is a direct relationship between the time it takes buyers to convert goods or acquired services into cash and the time they need to repay the debt created by the purchase of these inputs. The customer would prefer that payment terms cover their **operating cycle,** which is *the period of time between the acquisition of material, labor and overhead inputs for production and the collection of sales receipts.*

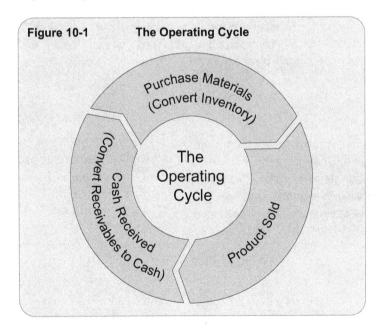

Figure 10-1   The Operating Cycle

In practice, a portion of the customer's operating cycle is usually funded by its own capital, especially if there is further production involved or if the goods are not ready for resale when purchased. During the inventory-conversion period, raw materials are purchased; machinery and labor transform it into a product before it is sold. The collection period is the time required to convert receivables to cash. If selling terms are shorter than the customer's operating cycle, the supplier is said to have a favorable spread. If longer, then the buyer is said to have the advantage. In the latter case, for instance, suppliers could be furnishing a disproportionate share of funding for a customer that buys on long terms and sells on short terms.

Basic materials are sold to manufacturers on shorter terms than intermediate or finished goods, primarily because of the short period of time raw materials retain their original form in the hands of the manufacturer. Terms of sale rarely exceed the customer's normal manufacturing cycle and storage time. Chemical products, such as agricultural oils and minerals, are normally sold on longer terms than their raw components. In the textile industry, unfinished cotton goods frequently call for shorter terms than finished fabrics.

Many institutional lenders treat *work in process* (**WIP**) inventory differently than raw materials or finished goods. That is, a lender may make a secured loan to a buyer based on raw and finished goods values, but not WIP. This is because WIP has little or no intrinsic value while in that state. This can create problems for buyers as they seek to finance their operating cycles.

Perishable items, such as meats, fresh vegetables and dairy products, have a short shelf life, rapid turnover rate and short selling terms. It is fairly common to find 7, 14 or 21-day terms in the food industry and certain products allow heavy security rights to be granted to the seller under the **Perishable Agricultural Commodities Act (PACA).** Less perishable foods, such as canned goods and manufactured or processed foods products, have a longer turnover period, since they can be stocked in larger quantities by the retailer. They are sold on longer terms.

Merchandise having a seasonal demand often carries longer terms during the off season than during the active period. For instance, accounts receivable generated from the sale of toys builds up during the year in anticipation of the holiday season. The supplier finances a great portion of the buyer's needs, but maintains steadier production levels during the year and reduces storage problems that could be created by large pre-season stocks.

Goods protected by trademarks or those in very high demand enjoy widespread consumer acceptance and frequently turn over more rapidly than unknown brands. This may translate into shorter terms for the more popular products. Inexpensive items tend to be sold on shorter terms than more costly products. For example, terms for drug items are shorter than terms for floor coverings and many furniture items. Diamonds and expensive jewelry, which generally have a longer operating cycle than any of the above products, are purchased by retailers on terms that range from four to six months. Automobiles and other products may be sold under floor plan arrangements requiring extensive financing by the seller.

A seller's internal situation with regard to order bookings may also influence credit policy with respect to payment terms. For example, a manufacturer operating at full capacity may temporarily seek to shorten terms or reduce the credit risk exposure in its receivables portfolio. The latter may be accomplished by withdrawing credit from existing high-risk accounts or tightening standards for new account prospects.

Class of Customer

Companies often offer different terms to different types or classes of customers. Customers can be classified in many ways, such as by size of order or by type of buyer. Retailers may receive one set of terms, wholesalers another and institutional buyers still another. For example, a paint manufacturer may grant longer terms to retailers than to industrial accounts purchasing for use rather than resale.

Profitability

Products with higher profit margins may allow longer terms than products with lower margins. Selling terms should take this factor into consideration. In practice, competition may nullify short terms on low margin items by forcing a seller to lengthen terms for lines where depressed prices yield little or no profit. An example of this scenario would be commodity products, such as aluminum, petroleum or grain.

Comprehension Check

What factors influence credit terms? Provide an explanation for each factor.

Categories of Terms of Payment

Terms of sale can be separated into three different categories: **cash, open** and **special.** Regardless of the kind of terms used by a seller, they should be clearly communicated in writing and agreed to by the buyer.

Cash and Prepayment Terms

Cash terms, also referred to as **prepayment or closed terms,** *call for payment before the transaction or at the time of the transaction.* Cash terms do not ordinarily offer any discount or anticipation rights. Offering only these terms indicates that the seller does not wish to extend credit to the buyer. However, cash terms are sometimes simply the standard terms offered to all customers for a given product such as certain raw materials. The following terms are the most restrictive terms from a buyer's standpoint since the seller assumes little or no risk:

- **Cash in Advance (CIA)** terms require the buyer to make payment via one of the cash methods (e.g., electronic transfers, company check, certified check, cashier's check, etc.) before an order will be shipped. CIA terms are most often used for very weak credit or when unsatisfactory, limited or no credit information is available.
- **Cash before Delivery (CBD)** terms are synonymous with CIA: no delivery is allowed until the buyer has made payment. Otherwise, the seller could bear the same risks as Cash on Delivery.
- **Cash with Order (CWO)** terms are offered when the seller requires payment before manufacturing of a product can take place.
- **Cash on Delivery (COD)** terms require payment to the transportation company for the full invoice amount at the time of the delivery. There is the risk that the buyer will not accept the shipment or cannot pay for the shipment at time of delivery, which means that the seller will have to bear the costs of freight to and from the buyer's location, preparation and packaging costs and possible deterioration of the product. Also, in the case of seasonal products, such non-acceptance may cause the seller to lose the opportunity to resell the goods to others. Another risk is that the delivery agent may fail to pick up payment. These risks may encourage the seller to consider CIA terms. COD terms are used extensively where credit has not been established, where deliveries are frequent, where products are perishable and where the merchandise is standard. It should also be noted that acceptance of a company check is the normal method of COD payment (even though it may create a non-sufficient funds (NSF) risk for the seller) as buyers seldom have time beforehand to go to the bank to arrange a wire, certified or cashier's check.

> **Comprehension Check**
>
> What are the categories of credit terms?
>
> ....
>
> What are **prepayment terms**?
>
> ....
>
> List four types of prepayment terms.

Short Terms

Short terms are of limited duration and are usually offered as a matter of industry practice (for example, highly perishable goods); in situations where credit limits are very tight; or where the seller wishes to provide some token amount of credit support. Despite the shortness of terms, the customer may at least gain the advantage of quickly examining the product before payment is rendered.

- **Bill-to-Bill terms** are also called "drop ship," "drop delivery" or "load-to-load" terms and require payment for the previous shipment when a new delivery is made. These terms are often found in lines involving weekly deliveries. Perishable foods sold to retail stores and gasoline sold to retail service stations are representative of this type of credit term.
- **Receipt of Invoice terms** require the customer to render payment immediately upon receipt of seller invoice or on some predefined short dating. Typically payment must be received before the next order is to be shipped, therefore making it similar to Bill-to-Bill in its intent.

With credit card and purchasing debit card transactions, the seller receives payment quickly but the structure of the sale differs from other types of short terms.

- **Credit Card Payment** indicates that the seller obtains the promise of payment from a financial institution on behalf of the buyer rather than extending credit. That financial institution extends credit to the buyer and renders payment to the seller. The duration of payment timing is determined by the contractual agreement with the institution involved. The institution must issue, to the buyer, advance approval of the transaction. The payment received by the seller will involve a discount from the sales price taken by the financial institution as a fee for its handling of the transaction. Sellers should be aware that most credit card transactions permit the buyer to deduct for disputes at a later date; therefore, the risk of loss through dispute is not eliminated. Credit cards are used widely in consumer transactions and are widely accepted for purchasing by governmental units and in business-to-business (B2B) transactions.
- **Purchasing Debit Card (P-cards)** are used extensively in industries characterized by high volume, spontaneous purchasing. These purchases often occur in market locations distant from the home offices of buyers and sellers. This type of purchase is funded directly by the buyer's bank account; the transfer of funds occurs from the buyer's bank account to the seller's bank account. Like credit cards, most transactions require the pre-approval of the funding institution. In industries where these terms are used, the buyer's accounts payable departments have essentially been eliminated. As with credit card payments, later deductions for disputes may be an issue for the seller. Consider use of a credit or purchasing debit card authorization agreement when determining whether to accept such forms of payment.

There are several kinds of **cash.** Cash can mean *a buyer's company check, a certified check or a cashier's check.* A **cashier's check** *is drawn by a bank on its own funds.* In assessing risk, the seller looks to the bank's financial stability. Therefore, the risk to the creditor is the credit risk of the bank itself when a cashier's check is accepted. Courts have held that payment cannot be stopped on a cashier's check because the bank, by issuing it, guarantees the check in advance. Where a **certified check** is involved, *a bank guarantees that funds are on deposit when the check is certified.* At the request of either the depositor or the holder, the bank acknowledges and guarantees that sufficient funds will be withheld from the drawer's account to pay the amount stated on the check. There is some risk of bank offset in several states, so the guarantee of a certified check is not perfect creating some risk for the credit grantor. More banks are encouraging the use of cashier's checks for these purposes and discouraging the use of certified checks.

Other cash payment methods include *wire transfer and electronic funds transfers (EFT).* In a **wire transfer,** *the buyer arranges to move funds from its bank account to the seller's bank account electronically.* The most common method to do this is via the Federal Reserve's Fedwire Funds Service system, to which all banks have access. Funds move in a real-time mode via Fedwire, and all Fedwire transfers are final and irrevocable. Banks handling the transfer can provide a Fedwire identification number to verify that the transfer has been completed. **Electronic funds transfers (EFTs)** are made via the *Automated Clearing House (ACH).* In an ACH transaction, customers can initiate the transfer by instructing their banks to use the ACH, or they can allow their supplier to automatically debit their bank account by using an ACH debit transfer. ACH transfers are not real-time, but require up to two business days to be completed. They are also not final and can be returned, much like a check that does not have enough funds on deposit to cover the clearing. ACH transfers are substantially cheaper than Fedwire transfers. Many financial institutions offer software that can be used to alert the seller immediately as to the receipt of wires, which facilitates release of orders. Third-party service providers that are recognized by the Federal Reserve System offer commercial and retail credit grantors the opportunity to initiate EFT payments via the Internet or proprietary software. Customers can make one-time payments for cash/COD/CIA sales, for past due collection purposes of open account receivables and for recurring payments of accounts.

Electronic payments are the typical form for international, cross-border payments, as foreign checks are not governed by U.S. banking rules and can be returned NSF long after deposit. Sellers may be able to recognize a cost savings with buyers that pay electronically, making such buyers qualify as a separate class of customer entitled to its own set of credit terms. In some industries, buyers may grant the sellers permission to electronically draft their accounts at time of shipment, usually in exchange for favorable discounts. In addition, Check 21 regulations have created expedited clearing of electronically-initiated payments.

Another important consideration for cash terms involves the exact timing of the funds transfer and its impact on possible preferential payments should the buyer file bankruptcy subsequent to the sale. If the seller's intent is to receive cash before shipment or cash on delivery, and somehow the funds are actually received by the seller at a later time, the **contemporaneous exchange defense** to a preference may be invalid. This can happen if the seller ships on CIA terms on *promise* of payment or delivers on CBD terms on promise of payment, and the wire or check is received *after* shipment or delivery respectively.

A problem also exists when buyers render a NSF or stop payment check that they replace with "good funds" at a later date. Under current bankruptcy law, where a check is involved, the **date of receipt of payment** is considered to be *the date a check for good funds was received by the seller.* Therefore, contemporaneous exchange defenses can be negated because shipment occurred before receipt of payment. These instances of forced credit create a serious credit risk problem for open account credit grantors.

Open Account Terms

Open account terms include at least three elements: the **net credit period** and, if terms include a discount option, the **cash discount** and the **cash discount period.** Therefore, **Credit Terms = Net Credit Period + Cash Discount Elements.**

The **net credit period** *is the length of time allowed for payment of the* **face amount** *(non-discounted amount) of the invoice.* **Cash discount elements,** if any, include *(a) the amount of the discount, usually expressed as a percentage of the invoice face amount excluding freight and other third-party charges and (b) the length of time allowed for the buyer to pay on a discounted basis.* In other words, credit terms provide the buyer with information that indicates the due date for payment on a discounted basis, the amount of the discount and the due date for payment after the discount period passes (i.e., 1% 10, net 30 days).

The most common open terms category is known as **terms based on invoice date.** That is, *the net credit period is a certain number of days from the date the invoice was billed or it can be computed from the date the goods are received by the customer.* An example of such a term is "net 30": payment must be made in full within 30 days of the date of the invoice.

In some industries, **single payment terms** are observed. That is, *purchases made over a period of time*, usually a month, are assigned a single due date, usually in the following month. While these arrangements can simplify bookkeeping for both seller and buyer, they can create at least two problems for sellers. First, disputes can sometimes arise wherein the buyer claims goods and/or invoices were received too late to be paid in the current cycle, thereby delaying payment until the next cycle. Such disputes can delay the seller's cash receipts by 30 days or more, whereas under terms based on invoice date, the delay would merely be a few days. Second, to maximize the total time for payment, buyers often request that all shipments be concentrated at the early end of the cycle. These requests can create numerous difficulties for the seller, such as inventory management and labor and transportation scheduling. Examples of single payment terms are as follows:

- **End-of-Month (EOM) Terms.** Shipments made during a given month are billed as of the last day of that month and assigned a single due date in the following month (usually the tenth of the following month). This term is expressed as "Net 10 EOM." A single statement, rather than individual invoices, is rendered to the buyer (although the statement does reflect actual shipment dates and amounts for matching purposes). Where a discount is offered, the cash discount period and net credit period are identical. That is, any payments made after the single due date are delinquent and must be made at face value with no discount applied.

  In some industries, the cut-off date for EOM billings is changed from the last day of the shipping month to (for example) the 25th day (i.e., from March 30 to March 25). This permits the buyer several extra days to receive and process the invoice and merchandise prior to the due date. However, this usually does not alleviate the shipment concentration issue.

- **Middle of the Month (MOM) Terms.** Shipments made from the 1st through the 15th of a given month are invoiced as of the 15th of that month; shipments made from the 16th through the end of a given month are invoiced as of the end of that month. The credit and discount period is normally 10 days after each of these invoice dates. Note that whereas EOM terms approximate 25 or 30 days on average, MOM terms approximate 17 days and are therefore shorter.

- **Proximo Terms.** Proximo, abbreviated "prox," is Latin for "next" or "next following." Net 10th Prox terms are similar to Net 10 EOM terms except that, under prox terms, individual invoices are usually billed at time of shipment rather than on a monthly basis. Also, prox terms may offer a net period that is different from the discount period. For example, while terms of "2% 10th Prox" are identical to "2% 10 EOM," terms of "2% 10th prox net 30th" permit the undiscounted payment to be delayed until the 30th day of the month following shipment.

  In the automotive industry, a special form of prox terms is sometimes used: the combination of Net 10th prox and Net 25th prox. In other words, invoices dated from the first through the 15th of a given month are due on the 10th of the following month, and those dated from the 16th through the end of the month are due on the 25th of the following month.

Discount Terms

A cash discount is calculated from the invoice amount if the customer pays within a specified period of time called the **discount period.** The discount is usually expressed as a percentage but can also be stated as a dollar amount. Terms of **1% 10 net 30,** for example, allow the buyer to deduct 1% from the face amount if the invoice is paid within 10 days. If the buyer does not take the discount, the full amount of the invoice is due within 30 days. The discount rate is 1% and the discount period is 10 days.

The offered discount normally will not apply to common carrier freight charges added to the invoice or any other third-party add-on charges, such as insurance, for which the seller may not reap a corresponding benefit.

The following are examples of payment timing for various discount terms:

- **8% 10 EOM.** An 8% discount is earned if payment is made by the 10th of the month following shipment. If paid later, discount is forfeited and the invoice is also past due.
- **8% 10th Prox.** Similar to 8% 10 EOM.
- **2% 10 MOM.** Shipments made from the first through the 15th of a given month are due on the 25th of the month; those made from the 16th through the end of the month are due on the 10th of the following month, with the credit period being the same as the discount period.
- **2% 10th Prox, net 30th.** A 2% discount is earned if payment is made by the 10th of the month following shipment. The full, undiscounted amount is due by the 30th of the month following shipment.

Policies vary in the credit community as to the date used for receipt of payment. Clarification of the seller's discount policy, on contract documents or policy releases, is a necessity and should be spelled out on the credit application agreement or contract in the terms and conditions section.

Anticipation *is a form of early payment allowance wherein a discount is allowed based on the number of days an invoice is paid early, using a pre-established annual rate converted to a daily rate.* Such discounts are usually based on the prime rate or the prime rate adjusted by a certain number of basis points (i.e., prime less 100 basis points = prime less 1%). The discount amount is the annual rate divided by 365 days multiplied by the number of days paid early. Anticipation is usually offered by sellers who are trying to maximize cash flow due to (a) an attractive opportunity for their own investments, (b) a need for improved liquidity to meet their own debt obligations or (c) a need to expand to meet demand for their products. One disadvantage is that the seller may face problems communicating a change in rate to the buyer when the prime rate changes, or other disputes can develop as to the exact offered rate. However, as compared to other discounts, anticipation offers the advantage of better flexibility in changing the offered rates.

Trade discounts *are allowances offered to purchasers because of industry custom or the volume of purchases.* They should not be confused with cash discounts, since trade discounts bear no relationship to time of payment and may be deducted regardless of when the bill is paid. Trade discounts may consist of (a) a standard percentage offered to all customers in a given trade class or (b) a standard set of volume discounts offered to all such customers. For example, manufacturers may offer trade discounts to wholesalers or retailers; wholesalers may offer trade discounts to retailers, etc. Seek legal counsel when considering a discount program to ensure compliance with antitrust laws, as a discount term is an element of pricing and must be offered to all like customers.

Chain discounts, or successive discounts from the original price, *represent a manner in which a trade discount and a payment discount can be combined in a single set of terms.* In such instances, the sequence of the discounts can change the outcome if the buyer takes the trade discount but fails to earn the payment discount. In other words, for a buyer forfeiting payment discount, offering a 10% trade discount and a 5% payment discount produces a higher total discount to the buyer than does 5% trade and 10% payment.

Dynamic discounting allows buyers more flexibility to choose how and when to pay their suppliers in exchange for a lower price or discount for the goods and services purchased. The "dynamic" component refers to *the option to provide discounts based on the dates of payment to suppliers.* In most cases, the earlier the payment is made, the greater the discount. Dynamic discounting enables buyers and their suppliers to initiate early-pay discounts on an invoice-by-invoice basis. Dynamic discounting requires both parties to view invoices through a web-based platform and select approved invoices for early payment. The main benefit of dynamic discounting is that the buyer can use their own balance sheet or excess cash to generate additional purchasing discounts. The seller benefits by reducing working capital and getting paid earlier.

Comprehension Check

What are the types of discount terms?

Enforcement

If cash discounts are to serve their purpose, the seller is discouraged from allowing unearned discounts because of their influence on cash flows and profits. However, enforcement of discount terms varies widely; implementation of any grace period and collection of a chargeback should be guided by company policy developed for consistent treatment for all customers.

Unearned Discounts

From time to time, customers send in *a check for the amount due less the discount even though the discount period or terms have expired.* This is commonly referred to as **unearned discounts.** In these cases, a decision whether to accept payment as a completed transaction must be determined before depositing the payment.

Inconsistent treatment of unearned discounts and enforcement of terms will create the potential for antitrust claims under the Robinson-Patman Act. The principle behind a claim of violation of this type involves preferential pricing, which is a form of discrimination and can lead to a competitive advantage for the customer who receives an unearned discount.

For example, customer A pays its open account credit invoice within stated terms and takes a discount. Customer B (a "like-customer" to customer A) does not pay its open account credit invoice within stated terms but takes the discount nonetheless. The creditor allows the discount taken by customer B by not enforcing policy to disallow the unearned discount.

In this example, customer B receives a price advantage by the fact that the creditor allowed a discount that was not earned or, in other words, was taken by the customer outside the stated terms. A price advantage was given to customer B that was not provided to customer A. Based on the time value of money, customer B basically paid less than customer A because customer B was allowed to hold onto its money for a longer period of time. Therefore, customer B gained a competitive advantage over customer A when the creditor allowed customer B to take a discount that was not earned. The creditor in this example has likely violated the Robinson-Patman Act based on the concept of price advantage.

If the creditor chooses not to accept the payment as a completed transaction, then the options include the following:

- Notify the customer by phone immediately and follow up in writing
- Invoice the customer for the unearned discount amount
- Return the check and demand full payment

If a discount is allowed by a creditor outside the discount terms, then the creditor must note in the customer's file the reason why the unearned discount was allowed in order to avoid future claims of violation made by a customer or class of customer that any antitrust violation occurred.

In cases where a creditor receives payments directed to a lockbox, the check is already accepted by the time the bank advises the creditor of the payment. Therefore, notification and the generation of an invoice for the unearned discount are the only available options.

Factors Influencing Offering of Discount Terms

The necessity and value of cash discounts is controversial; cash discounts offer substantial financial advantages to buyers. Assuming that a majority of customers pay within the discount period, the seller can expect a quicker turnover of funds, with reduced net working capital requirements, reduced credit and collection expenses and reduced delinquencies and credit losses. However, these advantages are sometimes disputed, with the argument being that prompt payment may at least partly be a matter of habit or fulfillment of agreement upon terms. This presumes that collections would be as prompt on terms of net 10 days as on 1% 10 net 30 days. This assumption may be valid if the seller's customers are all strong financially and if competitors also sell on terms of net 10 days.

Competitive conditions often dictate that sellers conform to the standard industry terms. If such terms include a discount structure, any given seller may likewise feel compelled to offer an equal discount.

If cash discounts shorten the average collection period, they could be a very real advantage to suppliers who have exhausted most of their possible sources of financing or have a strong need for faster turnover of their accounts receivable. Suppliers who suffer widespread or recurring abuse of discount terms may not benefit and may choose to terminate discount programs.

The credit manager should play an important role in determining discount terms. By using a time value of money approach to capture relevant cash inflows and cash outflows associated with selling the firm's products or services, the credit manager can show whether or not offering discounts can enhance the firm's value. For slow-paying customers to whom a firm has offered a cash discount, the credit manager can use the **cost to the buyer** technique to help convince the buyer that a bank loan can be less expensive than trade credit. In this way, the credit manager helps the buyer add value to the buyer's firm. The result may be a more loyal and timely paying customer.

The following are among the most compelling reasons to offer discounts:

- To meet competitive conditions in the market.
- To reduce total credit exposure, and to reduce delinquencies and credit losses by shortening the payment cycle.
- To reduce credit and collection expense.
- To reduce borrowing costs of the seller's firm.
- To improve the ability to put collected funds to use more quickly in the seller's firm. The **opportunity cost** *represents the return that the seller can obtain by investing funds elsewhere at comparable risk or by investing funds in corporate growth through acquisitions or other means.* Opportunity cost should be compared to the costs of offering discounts as calculated below.

Analyzing the Cost of Offering Cash Discounts from the Seller's Perspective

The credit manager, together with the seller's management team, must not overlook the issue of whether a cash discount will add economic value to the firm. Decisions to offer early payment discounts or to change the amount of the discount often require detailed analysis of their economic impact. In the following sections, various concepts used to determine the cost considerations necessary to make these decisions are examined.

Analysis of the Time Value of Funds

Net Present Value

The seller's price should take into account three factors: the required profit, *the risk of possible nonpayment* (**risk premium**) and the cost of carrying the receivable until maturity. While the first two factors are usually included in a seller's overall pricing strategy, the latter is often overlooked. The cost of carrying receivables requires using present value formulas to translate future dollars to current dollars.

As time passes, receivables lose value for two reasons: the cost of the lost use of the money and the possible increasing likelihood of the failure of the debtor. The cost of lost use includes several concepts. In times of inflation, customers who are granted time to pay bills will be paying with "deflated dollars," and the supplier will have to replace sold inventory at a higher price. In addition, presuming the supplier must borrow money to service its own debts while awaiting payment, interest costs become a cost of carrying receivables. Even if borrowing does not become a necessity for suppliers, they lose the opportunity of investing the proceeds of their sales in interest-bearing instruments, corporate growth, etc. If the costs of carrying receivables are ignored, the oversight could force the seller to absorb a cost not considered when setting prices.

To analyze the costs of carrying a receivable, the concept of **net present value** can be used. *The value of any receivable to be paid in the future must be discounted backwards in time to determine its present value.* The discount rate percentage to be used in the analysis of expected profits is based on factors which are numerous and subjective, and could yield a multiplicity of answers. Therefore, most sellers use their own annual **cost of capital** (represented below as the value k) as the discount rate.

The following formula is used to calculate the net present value of a receivable due at a future date, assuming monthly compounding:

$$PV = FV/(1 + k)^n$$

PV is the resultant net present value to be derived, FV is the given future value, k is the monthly compound equivalent of the annual cost of capital, and n is the time period in months.

For example, assume that the supplier has an annual cost of capital of .1288 (.01015 compounded monthly for 12 months), and expects to collect $100 at the end of the 12-month period. The present value of that $100 would be:

$$\$1.00/(100 + .01015)^{12} = \$88.59$$

The following is a simpler formula that can be used to approximate present value:

$$PV = FV - FV(k \times n)$$

Using this formula, if the firm's annual cost of capital (k) is .1288, the monthly cost of capital is .01073 (.1288/12), and if the receivable expected to be collected is $100 due in 12 months, the approximated present value is:

$$PV = \$100 - \$100(.01073 \times 12) = \$87.12$$

Using the same formula, the present value of a $100 invoice due in 30 days is:

$$PV = \$100 - \$100(.01073 \times 1) = \$98.93$$

And the present value of $100 due in 60 days is:

$$PV = \$100 - \$100(.01073 \times 2) = \$97.85$$

A seller wishing to recover the profit erosion caused by the time value of the funds in the 30-day example could add $1.07 to the price and in the 60-day example could add $2.15 to the price.

Using the simple formula, assuming a $100 net scale, with monthly cost of capital of .01073, Figure 10-2 displays the present value of future receipts based on collections made in 30-day increments.

Figure 10-2 Present Value of Future Receipts
Based on an Annual Cost of Capital of 12.88%

Receipts	Days	Cost of Captal	Present Value
$100	0	0	$100.00
100	30	.0107	98.93
100	60	.0215	97.85
100	90	.0322	96.78
100	120	.0429	95.71
100	150	.0537	94.64
100	180	.0644	93.56
100	210	.0751	92.49
100	240	.0859	91.42
100	270	.0966	90.34
100	300	.1073	89.27
100	330	.1181	88.20
100	360	.1288	87.12

Future Value

To recover the profit erosion caused by the time value of funds, a seller would determine the present price at the required profit, then project the resulting value forward to the maturity date by applying the cost of capital factor. The formula used to determine this required **future value** is:

$$FV = V(1 + k)^n$$

Assuming that the seller wishes to establish a price equal to $100 plus the cost of carrying the receivable for 30 days, the calculation is:

$$FV = \$100(1 + .01015)^1 = \$101.02$$

As with present values, a simpler model may be used by which the future value may be approximated, i.e.:

$$FV = PV + PV(k \times n) \text{ where } k = \text{annual cost of capital divided by } 12$$

Using this formula, the selling price for the 30-day example above becomes:

$$FV = \$100 + \$100(.01073 \times 1) = \$101.07$$

Where relatively short time periods are involved, the simple model provides a workable alternative. For longer periods, which stretch into years, significant variances develop in the results of the two formulas and the compound model should be used.

Effect of Discount Terms on Profit

The concept of time value of funds is useful for understanding how cash discount terms offered by the firm affect its receivables, cost of capital and profit. For instance, if regular selling terms are 2% 10 net 30 and k is .1288, then the firm's profit on any particular receivable will vary according to when the buyer pays the invoice.

This may be shown by a series of comparable sales situations. In all instances that follow, selling price is $100, terms are 2% 10 Net 30, and the costs of goods or services sold (except k) are $86.

Immediate Payment

When a customer pays cash and takes the discount, the invoice price is reduced by the discount amount. The other figures require no time value adjustment, since they are in the present. Costs of $86 are subtracted from the $98 received and the profit is $12. In this instance, there is no capital cost of carrying the receivable.

Sales (Receivable)	$100.00
Cash Discount	(2.00)
	98.00
Cost at Present Value	(86.00)
Profit at Present Value	$ 12.00

Payment on the 10th Day

When payment is received on the 10th day, or the last day of the discount period, the firm sustains two types of profit reduction: the customer is entitled to deduct the discount, and the seller's firm has incurred the capital cost of carrying the receivable for 10 days. Therefore, while receipts are $98, the cash or present value of the receipt is $97.65 because it has cost 35 cents to carry the $100 for the 10 days. With the deduction of $86 in costs, the profit becomes $11.65.

Sales (Receivable)	$100.00
Cash Discount	(2.00)
	98.00
Cost of Carrying Receivable (simple formula)	.35 ($100 × 10 days (.1288/365))
Cash or Present Value	97.65
Cost at Present Value	(86.00)
Profit at Present Value	$ 11.65

Payment on the 11th Day

If the customer pays on the 11th day but does not take the discount (admittedly, an unlikely situation, since once discount is lost the buyer would probably carry the item to full maturity), the seller firm gains the cash discount at the expense of one more day's capital cost of carrying the receivable. This sets the cash or present value of the receivable at $99.61 and the profit at $13.61.

Sales (Receivable)	$100.00
Cash Discount	0.00
	100.00
Cost of Carrying Receivable	.39 ($100 × 11 days (.1288/365))
Cash or Present Value	99.61
Cost at Present Value	86.00
Profit at Present Value	$ 13.61

Payment on the 30th Day

When payment is received on the maturity date of the receivable, the seller has carried the receivable for one month and incurred the corresponding cost of capital of $1.06. However, the payment is for the full amount of the invoice, or $100, and the profit is $12.94.

Sales (Receivable)	$100.00
Cash Discount	0.00
	100.00
Cost of Carrying Receivable	1.06 ($100 × 30 days (.1288/365))
Cash or Present Value	98.94
Cost at Present Value	86.00
Profit at Present Value	$ 12.94

Payment on the 60th Day

For the last illustration, it is assumed that payment is received on the 60th day, or 30 days past due, and no interest for the late payment is charged. No discount cost is applicable, but it has been necessary to carry the receivable for 60 days making the cost of capital $2.12. This reduces the cash value of profit to $11.88.

Sales (Receivable)	$100.00
Cash Discount	0.00
	100.00
Cost of Carrying Receivable	2.12 ($100 × 60 days (.1288/365))
Cash or Present Value	97.88
Cost at Present Value	86.00
Profit at Present Value	$ 11.88

This illustrates the undiscounted payment on the 11th day after invoice date as yielding the greatest profit to the seller. The next most profitable is payment on the maturity date (30 days). Immediate payment is the third most profitable. The analysis also shows that the firm makes higher profits on the payment received 30 days slow than it does on the discounted payment received on the last day of the discount period. The examples described above are illustrated in Figure 10-3.

Figure 10-3 PV of Sales at Different Payment Dates When Discount is Offered

Payment Date	0	10	11	30	60
Sale	$100.00	$100.00	$100.00	$100.00	$100.00
Cash Discount	2.00	2.00	0.00	0.00	0.00
	98.00	98.00	100.00	100.00	100.00
Cost of Carrying	0	.35	.39	1.06	2.12
Cash or Present Value	98.00	97.65	99.61	98.94	97.88
Cost at Present Value	86.00	86.00	86.00	86.00	86.00
Profit at Present Value	$ 12.00	$ 11.65	$ 13.61	$ 12.94	$ 11.88

It is a simple exercise to repeat these calculations for different terms of sale and different costs of capital. By doing so, the firm can determine the cost/profitability tradeoffs when it is studying its discount terms or the possible use of late payment charges. Once implemented, discount terms must be monitored and tested in relation to the creditor's cost of money (borrowed funds).

Analyzing Profits from Discounted Sales

Profits resulting from discount terms will also vary in relation to the increase or decrease in sales that result in any change of discount terms. A firm planning to change the percentage of discount or eliminate the discount should calculate the estimated effect of the terms change on total sales and resulting profits.

Assume that total monthly sales are $250,000 in a firm whose annual k is .1288. If terms of sale are 2% 10, Net 30 and the supplier is being paid in 10 days, the profit less discount and carrying costs would be:

Sales	$250,000
Cash Discount	-$ 5,000
	$245,000
Cost to Carry	-$ 882 = $250,000 × 10 days × (.1288/365)
Profit at Present Value	$244,118

Assume that the firm changes terms to Net 30 days. If elimination of the early payment discount results in a 10% loss of total sales, and if customers who paid promptly at 10 days begin to pay on an average of 40 days (10 days beyond the terms of sale since there is less incentive to pay on time) the profit, less carrying costs (no reduction for discounts allowed) would be:

Sales	$225,000
Cost to Carry	-$ 3,178 = $225,000 × 40 days × (.1288/365)
Profit at Present Value	$221,822

Under this scenario, the elimination of the discount produced unfavorable results.

This exercise can be repeated for different terms of sale, changes in sales volume, and different costs of capital. In this way, the firm will be able to understand the cost and profitability tradeoffs of anticipated changes. It should also be noted that if increases or decreases in sales volume also result in changes in the costs of goods sold, these cost changes will also result in changes to the firm's profits.

Analyzing the Cost to the Buyer of Not Taking Cash Discounts

The seller's credit team can use the **cost to the buyer formula** to help convince the buyer that a bank loan may be cheaper than trade credit when discount terms are available. The formula to be used for this purpose is as follows:

Formula for Approximate Costs of Foregoing the Discount (annualized)

$$\frac{\text{Discount Percent}}{100 - \text{Discount}} \times \frac{365}{\substack{\text{Number of Days Until Paid} \\ \text{Less Discount Period}}} = \substack{\text{Approximate} \\ \text{\% of Costs}}$$

A customer who previously paid in 30 days, forgoing discount, would receive the following annual benefit by paying in 10 days:

$$\frac{1}{100 - 1} \times \frac{365}{30 - 10} = .01 \times 18.25 = 18\%$$

If customers can borrow funds at a rate lower than 18%, they will generate internal profits by discounting. Customers who pay beyond terms—and who would have to spread the discount benefits across a longer timeline—may see little incentive to discount. Assume that the customer in the example above has been paying 30 days slow.

$$\frac{1}{100 - 1} \times \frac{365}{30 - 10} = .01 \times 7.3 = 7\%$$

In the second example, the equivalent annual benefit is significantly lower and may not provide sufficient incentive for the customer to borrow funds to take advantage of the cash discount. Unless the creditor charges late payment penalties, holds shipments or services or uses other means to shorten the payment cycle, the slow customer will continue to benefit from paying late.

The equivalent annual interest rates applicable to various discount terms are shown in Figure 10-4. The first column lists the various cash discount percentages, ranging from ½% to 5%. Various terms are shown in the remaining six column headings. Below each is the cash discount equivalent annualized rate for that set of terms. For example, under terms of ½% 15, net 30 days the equivalent annualized rate is 12%; with 1% 15, net 30 the rate is annualized at 24%; and so on. The same procedure is used in the other columns.

Figure 10-4 Annual Interest Rates Applicable to Discount Terms

Cash Discount Percent (X%)	X% 15 Net 30 Days	X% 10 Net 30 Days	X% 30 Net 60 Days	X% 15 Net 60 Days	X% 10 Net 60 Days	X% 30 Net 90 Days
½	12%	9%	6%	4%	3.6%	3%
1	24	18	12	8	7.2	6
1½	36	27	18	12	10.8	9
2	48	36	24	16	14.4	12
2½	60	45	30	20	18.0	15
3	72	54	36	24	21.6	18
3½	84	63	42	28	25.2	21
4	96	72	48	32	28.8	24
4½	108	81	54	36	32.4	27
5	120	90	60	40	36.0	30

Late Charges

When goods or services are purchased on credit, the supplier finances the purchase during the time provided by the credit terms. This financing is regarded as a necessary cost of business and is included in determining the selling price. However, unless the bill is promptly collected at maturity, the cost for carrying the account thereafter is an additional cost of business. **Late charges** *assessed upon receipt of late payments represent a way in which the seller can recover these costs*. Late charges should be clearly distinguished from **interest payments,** which are *charges made by financial institutions for loans*. The credit application agreement should identify these charges and how they will be assessed.

Reasons for imposing and enforcing late charges include the recognition that late payments may cause one or more of the following situations:

- Use of the supplier's capital without consent.
- Allows delinquent customers an unfair net price advantage.
- Increases the supplier's collection expenses and, usually, bad debt expenses.

Reasons for not imposing late charges include:

- Fear of losing customer goodwill.
- Belief that competitors do not impose or enforce similar charge.
- Difficulty in collection of late charges.
- Heavy administrative costs for businesses that generate significant numbers of invoices at relatively low invoice amounts.
- Costs of carrying overdue accounts are considered to be comparatively small.

Like unearned discounts, late charge policies must be applied uniformly to all customers or to like groups of customers, or they may be interpreted as a form of price discrimination under the antitrust laws. The premise is exactly the same interpretation as unearned discounts. It is recommended that credit grantors seek the advice of legal counsel before instituting a late charge program to make sure it is applied properly under the law. The issue is not the validity of using late charges but, rather, proper implementation and enforcement of the policy once it is instituted. In some states, late charges may constitute a violation of the usury laws if: a credit sale is made for products or services primarily for personal, household or family use; and the interest rate charged is in excess of the maximum permitted by state law.

Special (Other) Terms

The following are examples of special terms primarily used in specific situations or in certain industries. Some of these terms are simply variations of open credit terms.

Receipt of Goods

Receipt of Goods (ROG) terms *permit the buyer to compute the cash discount period or net credit period from the date the merchandise is received rather than from the invoice date.* A distant buyer experiencing lengthy transit time receives a compensating benefit and is not pressed to remit before examining the shipment, as can happen when the terms begin on the invoice date. In some industries, the net credit period is calculated from the invoice date while the discount date is based on receipt of goods. ROG terms are common in the importing of raw sugar and other occasions where long transit times exist. With these terms, enforcement places a burden on the seller to determine when the merchandise arrived at the buyer's facility. In some industries, regularity and predictability of transit times permit the use of a standardized matrix which calculates delivery dates.

Comprehension Check
What are receipt-of-goods terms?

Bill and Hold

Bill and Hold (B&H) terms are used in some industries, such as textiles, *to permit sellers to invoice buyers under normal payment terms on the agreed-upon completion date, whether or not shipment has actually occurred.* This provides protections to the seller, which minimizes inventory risk, especially where fashion or customized products are concerned. The customer is required to render payment on the normal due date regardless of the actual shipping schedule of merchandise. In several states, the UCC provides further protection to sellers in certain industries by providing for a seller's lien on any B&H inventory still in the seller's possession. In the event of nonpayment by the buyer, the seller may liquidate this inventory to others and use the proceeds to reduce the buyer's debt. Regulations of the Securities and Exchange Commission contain many provisions that apply to B&H transactions, and these should be carefully observed before rendering a B&H invoice.

Consignment

Consignment terms offer an alternative to an open account sale. *Consignment is not a true sale until the buyer, called the* **consignee***, actually sells the goods to a third party or moves them from consigned inventory into the buyer's own inventory. Until the goods are thus sold or moved, title remains with the supplier, usually the manufacturer, who is called the* **consignor.**

The consignee's reward for handling the sale is either (a) a commission or (b) the goods can be sold at regular markup with the profit being retained by the consignee.

The execution of a consignment agreement between the parties helps avoid misunderstandings about the terms. While it is often true that consignees are permitted to return unsold goods to the seller, such issues, and the timeframe permitted for returns, are spelled out in a consignment agreement.

Consignment terms are often used for other than credit reasons, such as the following:

- Penetrating new market segments.
- Introducing new or more costly product lines.
- Displaying inventory for sale prior to an expected seasonal demand.
- Attempting to sell goods that are out of season or style or for which there is no current market.

There is an obligation for the consignee to account for the proceeds when the goods are sold or to return the goods according to the terms of the agreement if they are not sold. The seller may also require the consignee to maintain adequate insurance on all consigned goods with the seller as beneficiary.

In addition to defining returns and insurance issues, consignors should also take care to ensure that consignment agreements allow them to receive regular inventory reports. Consignors should also consider perfecting a security interest under the UCC. Compliance with the perfection requirements of the UCC protects ownership of inventory in the event of a dispute over goods.

Consignment terms are often used where inventory is expensive and/or slow moving, such as the fine jewelry trade.

Comprehension Check
What is a consignment term?

Floor-Plan Financing

Floor-plan financing *involves an inventory financing company, called the floor-plan creditor, that has contractual arrangements with both the seller and the buyer.* In some cases, the seller can serve as the financing company. The supplier ships the product to the buyer but sends the invoice to the financing company. The financing company pays the supplier, and the buyer pays the financing company over a longer period of time, with interest. A floor-plan agreement, which states all terms (e.g., repayment terms, repurchase agreements and recourse), must be developed and signed by all parties involved. Floor-plan financing is used when individual goods or items are very expensive. For example, motor vehicle and boat dealers and retailers and distributors of furniture and household appliances commonly use floor-plan financing.

Comprehension Check
What is **floor-plan-financing**?

UCC security agreements are often used with this form of financing. The manufacturer, as the secured party, can protect its interest by filing a **blanket financing statement** and/or a **purchase money security interest** covering the goods and proceeds without having to execute new agreements as more items are sold.

Contra Account

Some companies find themselves in the position of having reciprocal seller/buyer relationships with their customers. In such situations, the parties maintain contra accounts so only the net amount due to one party or the other needs to be paid regularly. A **contra account** *offsets the balance in another, related account with which it is paired. If the related account is an asset account, then a contra asset account is used to offset it with a credit balance. If the related account is a liability account, then a contra liability account is used to offset it with a debit balance.* In certain industries, such as energy, netting arrangements of this sort facilitate payments without the need to move large amounts of offsetting funds. The technique of contra account settlement can be perfectly natural between two strong companies, but it can also be useful in cases where a strong supplier wants to protect itself against a customer that is financially weak. A contractual agreement acceptable to both seller and buyer will clarify the contra account arrangements. It is important for a creditor to know if a customer has made such arrangements with other suppliers, since the supplier with the contra account arrangement has a potentially stronger claim to the customer's assets.

Extra Dating

Extra dating terms *can be used to extend the net period and/or the discount period.* For example, terms of 2% 10, 60 extra extend both the discount period and the net credit period to 70 days from the date of the invoice. Since these extra

Comprehension Check
What are **extra dating arrangements**?

terms have identical discount and net credit periods, there is no inducement for the buyer to pay prior to maturity. To overcome this, extra terms can sometimes be expressed as follows: 3% 10, 2% 10 60 extra. This indicates that 3% can be deducted if payment is made within 10 days, but only 2% is deductible if payment is made by the end of 70 days.

Seasonal Dating

Seasonal dating terms *are used when there is a high seasonal demand for a product and sellers wish to encourage off-season purchases. Seasonal terms postpone payments to coincide with the buyers' heavy selling seasons. These terms are common in the toy (December dating) and agricultural (crop terms) industries, among others.* The customer benefits from having the goods on hand without an immediate investment of funds for the purchase of inventory (although warehousing expenses are still a factor). The seller benefits by having more consistent sales and production throughout the year and production cycles with lower storage requirements. The seller usually bills at date of shipment to the buyer—but with a single due date based on a predetermined date during the peak selling season. Incentives may be offered to the buyer in the form of anticipation for early payment. Seasonal dating creates the problem of a buildup of accounts receivable for the seller and can create substantial additional credit risk.

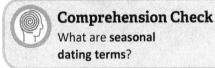

Comprehension Check
What are **seasonal dating terms**?

Security Interest

Creditors may enhance their position by taking a secured position in assets such as inventory, bank accounts and real estate. Secured interests can be useful when a sale is made to a new business, a high-risk account, if the terms of payment are long, if a large dollar amount is involved or if material is going to be at the customer's location for an extended period of time.

Advances

When work is done to the customer's specification, it is customary to ask for a partial payment with the order to provide the seller with some working funds for the job and to offer some protection in case the customer cancels the order. Where advances are not the customary practice, they can nevertheless be requested for partial protection when a customer is not in a strong financial condition, when there is the possibility of refused shipments on COD or sight draft, and similar situations.

Progress Payments

Partial payments are sometimes made on a contract as it progresses, especially when manufacturing or construction time is long and the creditor cannot afford to finance production. These are examples of progress payment terms used in the machinery industry:

- In the engineering industry: 15% upon receipt of drawings, 20% upon receipt of curves; 15% upon receipt of motors or partial shipment, 40% upon receipt of the complete shipment; 10% retention not to exceed 180 days upon inspection of material.
- For machinery: 30% in advance, 30% upon initiation of production, 30% upon delivery and 10% upon acceptance.

Other Terms and Conditions of Sale

These are usually found on the reverse side of purchase orders and acknowledgments. Some of the more common items include:

- **Warranties.** Seller's obligations to the buyer for the products or services.
- **Delivery.** Conditions that constitute valid delivery of the product.
- **Termination of Contract.** Conditions that provide the parties with the right to terminate the obligations of the order.
- **Title/FOB point.** At what point does title pass from the seller to the buyer?
- **Force Majeure.** Acts of God" that may release the parties from complying with the terms of the order.
- **Indemnification.** The seller's assumption of the buyer's liability for specified occurrences under the order.
- **Liability.** Obligations of the seller and buyer.
- **Conditions Precedent to Buyer's Obligation.** Conditions that must happen or be performed by the parties before any obligation or liability attaches to the parties.
- **Arbitration Clauses.** Language that binds parties to the use of arbitration in lieu of a judge and/or jury in resolving a dispute.
- **Conditions of Default.** These define what acts or failures to act constitute defaults of the agreements spelled out in the order.
- **Applicable Law.** Defines which state or international laws will regulate the transaction.

Export Terms

Pro Forma Invoice

Widely used in the export trade, a **pro forma invoice** *is an abbreviated invoice sent in advance of a shipment*, usually to enable the buyer to obtain an import permit, an exchange permit or both. The invoice closely approximates the weights and values of the shipment, but it is not binding on the seller until the order is confirmed. This device enables the buyer to receive goods without unusual delays and the exporter to receive payment without lengthy exchange restriction delays. It can be used domestically when sent in advance of shipment and treated as a memo item. It does not become the seller's account receivable until the shipment is made at which time an actual invoice is sent to the customer.

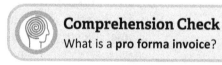

Comprehension Check
What is a **pro forma invoice**?

Barter Arrangements

Barter arrangements as a form of payment *allows a buyer to pay with merchandise instead of currency, often using a third-party clearinghouse as an intermediary*. The intermediary facilitates the transaction and collects a fee for its services. The intermediary can also function as a broker, working with buyers and sellers that wish to take part in barter arrangements. Barter is often used when a country does not have a fully convertible currency or is in an early stage of development and the country risk is significant.

Incoterms®

Because of additional risks often encountered with export and import business throughout the world, standard terms related to freight, insurance, clearance of goods through customs, and other such costs have been standardized by the International Chamber of Commerce. These terms, known as **Incoterms®,** short for *International Commercial Terms,* are *a set of internationally recognized trading terms, defined by the International Chamber of Commerce (ICC), and are used for the purchase and shipping of goods in the international marketplace.*

The "Battle of the Forms"*

Let's think again about the way modern commerce works. Material suppliers send offers and contractors send back purchase orders. Both offers and purchase orders often have detailed "fine print." The fine print terms on the offer often conflict with the fine print terms on the purchase order.

This is the Battle of the Forms, and it determines what provisions exist in the contract between a buyer and a seller. The first thing to remember is that these parties have a contract on the terms on which there is agreement—It doesn't matter that some terms are missing or in complete conflict, according to the Uniform Commercial Code (UCC).

Firm Offers and Price Quotes

The terms of the offer will be an enforceable contract, if the offer is accepted. It can be important in establishing the terms of the contract whether the buyer or seller made the initial offer. Once an initial offer is made, the recipient must object to terms in the offer or those terms will be part of the contract. Additional or different terms in a response do not become a part of the contract if there is an objection or if those additional or different terms "materially alter" the agreement.

Accordingly, it is easier to establish terms in an initial offer than via a response. All buyers and sellers would prefer to "fire the first shot" in the Battle of the Forms by making the first firm offer. It is sometimes difficult to tell whether a correspondence is a firm offer or simply conversation. An offer must be sufficiently detailed regarding the product, quantity and price so that an acceptance would result in an enforceable contract.

Some prejudice seems to exist in the courts regarding seller quotes as firm offers. Price quotes are not typically considered offers, but rather a "mere invitation to enter into negotiations." Submission of a purchase order by a buyer is generally viewed as an offer. Sellers should be particularly careful to include all important terms in proposals or quotes and clarify that the documents are an "offer" that can be accepted by acknowledgment or calling for delivery.

A seller should either sign the offer or ensure there is no signature line for the seller. An offer should not state that all orders are subject to review and acceptance at seller's place of business, as this would mean that there was no offer ready for acceptance. A seller can overcome prejudice offers by making sure an offer is clearly expressed and ready for acceptance.

Responses and Confirmations

When the second party (buyer or seller) sends the return document (which is definitely accepting or confirming an agreement), the parties will have a contract even though the confirmation contains provisions adding to or differing from the original offer.

Under common law prior to the UCC, the "mirror image" rule required that the buyer's acceptance be the same as the seller's offer. If the acceptance is not a mirror image of the offer, it rejects the initial offer and operates as a counteroffer. This is still the rule for most contract negotiations unless the contract involves the sale of goods. In that event, the UCC controls.

The UCC rejects the mirror image rule and converts a common law counteroffer into an acceptance even if it states additional or different terms." It states:

A definite and seasonal expression of acceptance or a written confirmation which is sent within a reasonable time operates as an acceptance even though it states terms additional to or different from those offered or agreed upon, unless acceptance is expressly made conditional on assent to the additional or different terms.

This means that if there is a timely response to an offer that indicates an acceptance, the parties have a contract even if the response has additional or different terms than the offer. In a response, there is a difference between "additional" terms (that add some new term to the offer) and "different" terms (that conflict with a term in the offer).

The UCC considers "additional terms" to be "proposals for addition to the contract." If the transaction is between merchants, these additional terms will become a part of the contract unless the additional provisions: (1) "materially alter" the agreement, (2) the other party objects to the new terms or (3) the original offer was expressly limited to the terms of the offer. The UCC states that:

The additional terms are to be construed as proposals for additions to the contract. Between merchants, such terms become part of the contract unless:

- the offer expressly limits acceptance to the terms of the offer;
- they materially alter it; or
- notification of objection to them has already been given or is given within a reasonable time after notice of them is received.

Courts have disagreed on the fate of "different" terms that conflict with terms in the offer. Some courts follow the same rule as for additional terms and the different terms become a part of the contract if there is no objection. The majority view, however, is the "knockout" rule." The conflicting terms in the offer and acceptance eliminate each other from the contract. **UCC gap fillers** are terms used to fill in the gaps. The contract would be the terms agreed by the parties, which would be the terms in the offer and acceptance that do not conflict, plus the contract terms added by the UCC.

It is important to join the "Battle of the Forms" within the meaning of the UCC. It is not enough to respond with a confirmation that is silent about the terms in an offer. The recipient must expressly reject or object to any objectionable terms of sale or propose different terms. Sending purchase orders that only acknowledge the material and pricing, but were otherwise silent, constitutes an acceptance of a supplier's proposal and cannot be a "counteroffer" proposing a sale with no terms. Telephoning a supplier and verbally requesting shipment of materials, as often happens, also constitutes an acceptance of a supplier's proposal and would not be a counteroffer. Even terms limiting the seller's liability may be included in an initial offer and will become a part of the contract unless the buyer expressly objects.

A response or confirmation can be made conditional on an agreement to the additional or different terms. A buyer could respond to an offer by stating, "I will agree to this only if you agree to remove your limitations of liability and extend your payment terms to 90 days." This would not be an acceptance. This is a counteroffer and even though courts differ on the exact wording required to make one, there is no contract unless the additional or different terms are accepted.

If additional or different terms are added in a response or confirmation (and the response or confirmation is not made conditional on an agreement to the additional or different terms), it becomes relevant whether the additional or different terms were "material." Lawyers can spend a long time and a lot of a company's money arguing about whether the additional provisions "materially altered" the contract. This exception is possible protection if a return purchase order has a very important and costly provision in the fine print. It is normally better and easier, however, to limit acceptance of an offer and object to any new terms added later.

Terms that would not be material alterations in a response or confirmation would include provisions for reasonable interest on unpaid invoices, limiting remedies for delays outside the seller's control, or a clause fixing a reasonable time for complaints. Courts have held that addition of an attorney's fee provision is a material alteration. An indemnification clause or a "no damage for delay" clause would materially alter the terms of an agreement. If the offer had included warranties, then a confirmation containing a disclaimer of warranties and limitation of remedies would "materially alter" the agreement. On the other hand, if the offer had excluded warranties, then a confirmation adding warranties would "materially alter" the agreement. This difference exemplifies the importance of making the first firm offer.

Establishing Limitations

It is important to be first to make a firm offer. Changing terms later is more difficult. It is also easier to limit acceptance of an offer than to make a response acceptance conditional. A signed agreement from the other party may be necessary, or is at least advisable, to change the terms of an offer. Sellers should clearly express any offers as a definite offer to buy or sell, with enough detail regarding the goods and the price to be an enforceable contract and including strong terms of sale.

There is an opportunity in an initial offer to establish limitations on the warranties and liability, establish venue for any dispute or establish the right to attorney's fees on default. These terms will be established, unless the other party affirmatively objects. Adding or changing any of these terms in a response, however, would be a "material alteration" that would not be effective and there is no need to affirmatively object.

It is also always preferable to get a signed agreement, rather than depending on a "Battle of the Forms" to establish terms. A signed agreement will eliminate much uncertainty and make it much harder for the other party to add or modify terms.

Perhaps the best advice is to expressly limit acceptance of all proposals, offers, purchase orders or confirmations. Offers sent out should state that "This proposal is subject to the terms and conditions on the reverse and any acceptance of this proposal shall be limited to the terms described in this proposal." This would make it more difficult for the return "acceptance" to change the terms of the agreement.

Even if the initial offer limited acceptance to the terms of the offer, the other party could send a response or confirmation that expressly rejects the terms of the offer and states that any contract must be on the terms of the response. Although some court rules differ, this is typically considered a "counteroffer," and no contract exists unless there is agreement to the changes. If shipping or accepting product at this point, however, seller is taking a risk that the initial offer will not apply and that the response terms do apply. This is another instance where it is important to read any mail and send written objections if a confirmation is received that does not accurately describe an agreement. A final signed agreement is also advisable to eliminate doubt regarding terms.

It is important to have strong and clear forms available for offers, proposals, purchase orders and confirmations. The provisions a seller has in the fine print of a firm offer will be a part of the contract unless they are expressly rejected. A fairly low-cost, one-time investment to establish these can considerably reduce a company's risks and costs for years to come.

A sample supplier proposal could state:

Acceptance is limited to terms of this Proposal. Seller objects to any different or additional terms contained in any purchase order, offer or confirmation sent or to be sent by Buyer, which are expressly rejected. The price offered will be held firm only if acknowledgment is received by Seller or Buyer calls for delivery within 30 days of this Proposal, either of which shall be an acceptance of all terms herein. This Proposal is conditional on Buyer's agreement to all terms and Seller is otherwise unwilling to proceed with this transaction. This is the final expression of this agreement and here will be no waiver or modification of any of these terms unless in writing signed by both parties. If Seller does expressly make any further agreement regarding these goods, all terms of this Proposal shall be incorporated into and shall become a part thereof.

If sending a return document or "confirmation," a company has an opportunity to change or neutralize some of what it perceives to be harsh terms of the original offer it received. To effectively change terms, a response acceptance or confirmation must be expressly conditional on assent to those different terms. It is not enough to say that "acceptance is limited to the different terms and conditions." A response acceptance or confirmation must clearly express an unwillingness to proceed with the transaction unless there is assurance of assent to the different terms. It is advisable to both parties to get an actually signed contract at this point if it is important to know the terms of the final agreement.

A buyer purchase order should state something similar the following:

Acceptance is limited to terms of this Purchase Order. Buyer objects to any different or additional terms expressed or implied in any quote, proposal, offer or confirmation sent or to be sent by Seller, which are hereby expressly rejected and superseded by this Purchase Order. This Purchase Order is expressly conditional on Seller's assent to all terms herein and Buyer is unwilling to proceed in this transaction without that assent. The first to occur of Seller's acceptance of this order or shipment of goods shall constitute Seller's agreement to all of the terms and conditions in this Purchase Order. This is the final expression of this agreement and there will be no waiver or modification of any of these terms unless in writing signed by both parties.

Credit Agreements or Master Supply Agreements

A buyer or seller may have a "Master Agreement" that applies to all sales for years, followed by quotes or purchase orders for each individual sale. For most material suppliers, this takes the form of a "Credit Agreement," which should affirmatively state that it will apply to all future sales to this customer.

A Master Agreement or Credit Agreement can be modified in a subsequent agreement for any particular sale, including agreements established through a battle of forms. Terms could be extended for one project, for example. Staff reviewing offers and responses need to notice that they modify Master Agreement terms and consider whether the company is willing to do that.

It may be tempting to state in a Master Agreement or Credit Agreement that it cannot be modified in a subsequent agreement. However, that is probably ineffective. Any agreement can be modified by unanimous consent, even the part of the agreement that says it cannot be modified. It also would seem that any business would want the flexibility to modify existing agreements in some instances.

Modification of Contracts

Provisions can be added or subtracted from a contract after that original contract exists. These additions or subtractions are "modifications to the contract."

Modifications may occur in long-term contracts with successive, repeated deliveries. For example, a concrete ready mix plant may take set deliveries of cement or stone each week for months or years. The price may be set for long periods of time or it may fluctuate with the market. Such price changes would be modifications to the supply contract. Modifications can also occur in short-term or single-delivery contracts.

Modifications to contracts for the sale of goods need no consideration to be binding. This means seller could modify a contract, even inadvertently, without receiving anything in exchange. It can be important to read any mail and object to any suggestions or assertions that would change the contract detrimentally.

End of the Battle of the Forms

So, when does the Battle of the Forms end? It does seem clear that an actually signed and complete agreement would be final. Subsequent letters and emails cannot change the terms of the agreement, unless they qualify as modifications to the agreement.

In the absence of a signed and complete agreement, it is not clear that the Battle of the Forms ever ends.

Submitted by James D. Fullerton, Esq. of Fullerton & Knowles, PC.

Key Terms and Concepts......

Comprehension Check

1. How does the Robinson-Patman Act apply to terms of sale?
2. What factors influence credit terms? Provide an explanation for each factor.
3. What are the categories of credit terms?
4. What are **prepayment terms**?
5. List four types of prepayment terms.
6. What are the types of **discount terms**?
7. What are **receipt-of-goods** terms?
8. What is a **consignment** term?
9. What is **floor-plan-financing**?
10. What are **extra dating arrangements**?
11. What are **seasonal dating terms**?
12. What is a **pro forma invoice**?

Summary

- There is a direct relationship between the terms of the sale and the seller's perception of the buyer's ability to pay. In an extreme example, if a seller has no faith that a buyer will pay, the immediate payment in cash, or in other forms, may be required
- It is important to note that not all sales are governed by signed contracts, especially when there is frequent activity between the buyer and the seller.
- When changing terms, or when changing **standard terms** for a particular buyer, the seller must ensure that they are not in violation of antitrust laws, particularly price discrimination laws set by the Robinson-Patman Act. Legal counsel in these circumstances is suggested.
- Two major influencing factors for terms of sale are **competition**, and **market and product characteristics**.
- When there is competition in the market, a sale may not take place without the extension of credit. Price is an extension of various factors including competition, and it is necessary to view the terms of a sale as a component of price.
- Customers prefer terms that cover their **operating cycle**. Having terms that are shorter or longer than a buyers operating cycle may indicate more favorable terms for either the buyer or the seller.
- Terms differ widely by industry. Common terms for perishable items are 7, 14, or 21-day terms, while chemical products that have a longer storage time generally have longer terms of sale.
- Class of customer or profitability of a product may also lend itself to different terms.
- The three categories of terms of payment are as follows
  - Cash and prepayment terms
    - **Cash in advance (CIA)**
    - **Cash before delivery (CBD)**
    - **Cash with order (CWO)**
    - **Cash on delivery (COD)**
  - Short term
    - **Bill-to-bill**

- Receipt of invoice terms
- Credit card payment
- Purchasing Debit Card (P-cards)
- Cashier's check or certified check
- Wire transfer
- Electronic funds transfers (EFTs)
  - Open account terms
    - End-of-month (EOM) terms
    - Middle of the month (MOM) terms
    - Proximo Terms
- **Open account terms** include at least three elements: **net credit period, cash discount** and the **cash discount period**.
- Electronic payments are the typical form for international, cross-border payments.
- It is a necessity to spell out any discount policy on the credit application or in the contract in the terms and conditions section.
- Types of discounts include:
  - Anticipation
  - Trade discounts
  - Chain discounts
  - Dynamic discounting
- Enforcement of discounts varies widely. However, it is essential to create a company policy that is used consistently on all customers, because unearned discounts can create potential antitrust claims under the Robinson-Patman Act.
- The credit manager should play an important role in determining discount terms. Some of the most compelling reasons to offer discounts include:
  - Competitive conditions
  - Reduction of credit exposure, delinquencies, credit losses
  - Reduction of credit and collection expense
  - Reduction of borrowing costs
  - Improvement of cash flow and investment opportunity
- Decisions to offer early payment discounts or to change the amount of the discount often require a detailed analysis of their economic impact. This includes an analysis of how the net present value affects the profitability of terms.
- The seller's credit team can also use the **cost to the buyer formula** to convince a buyer that taking a bank loan may be a cheaper option for the buyer. This allows a buyer to generate internal profits, but also improve the speed of payment for the seller.
- If a bill is not collected at maturity, it may be necessary to institute **late charges**, because late payments incur costs that have not been accounted for by the seller.
- Special terms may be beneficial for certain industries or special circumstances that a buyer and seller may find themselves in. **Special terms** include:
  - **Receipt of Goods**
  - **Bill and Hold**
  - **Consignment**
  - **Floor-Plan Financing**
  - **Contra Account**
  - **Extra Dating**

- **Seasonal Dating**
- **Advances**
- **Progress Payments**

• There are also special terms for international trade known as **export terms**. Some export terms are as follows:

- **Pro Forma Invoice**
- **Barter Arrangements**
- **Incoterms®**

References and Resources

Business Credit. Columbia, MD: National Association of Credit Management. (This 9 issues/year publication is a continuous source of relevant articles and information. Archived articles from *Business Credit* magazine are available through the web-based NACM Resource Library, which is a benefit of NACM membership.)

Cole, Robert H. and Lon L. Mishler. *Consumer and Business Credit Management,* 1st ed. Boston: Irwin/McGraw Hill, 1998.

Dennis, Michael. *Credit and Collection Handbook.* Paramus, NJ: Prentice Hall, 2000.

Fullerton, James D., Esq. "Battle of the Forms." Clifton, Virginia: Fullerton & Knowles PC, 2016.

Manual of Credit and Commercial Laws. Columbia, MD: National Association of Credit Management, current edition.

11 Credit Investigations

OVERVIEW

One of the core functions of the credit department is credit investigations. The greater the effort made to gather information at the beginning of the buyer/seller relationship, the easier it may be to collect accounts later. This chapter discusses all phases of gathering credit information—from the legal right to do so to the reasons such investigations are important to setting up the process. Sound credit decisions can only be made on the basis of adequate information about a customer's business, its financial condition, the character of the principals and other business matters.

THINK ABOUT THIS

Q. What ethical considerations should be taken into account when investigating a customer's credit worthiness?

Q. When does a customer visit become beneficial to a credit professional?

Q. What value does an industry credit group bring to a credit investigation?

DISCIPLINARY CORE IDEAS

After reading this chapter, the reader should understand:

- ☑ How to conform to the legal requirements and ethical principles of credit investigation.
- ☑ The sources of direct credit investigations.
- ☑ The sources of indirect credit investigations.
- ☑ The importance of conducting credit investigations on existing accounts.
- ☑ The sources of international credit investigations.

CHAPTER OUTLINE

Legal and Ethical Aspects of Credit Investigations

The credit department, owners, officers, sales management and other key management personnel must have a secure knowledge of their legal right and privilege to gather and disseminate credit information about mutual business customers to which open account credit is provided by the company. They must also know, and understand, the ethical implications of this process.

Exchange of Credit Information—The Legal Perspective

The exchange of credit experience information on a particular customer is legal only if the information exchanged is restricted to factual, historical data. Since 1925, various U.S. courts have recognized in numerous decisions the legitimate business interest in the exchange of factual credit information among businesses with legitimate interests. One important case supporting the right to gather business and trade credit information is the 1925 U.S. Supreme Court case that held:

> "... The gathering and dissemination of information which will enable sellers to prevent a perpetration of fraud upon them, which information they are free to act upon or not as they choose, cannot be held to be an unlawful restraint upon commerce, even though, in the ordinary course of business, most sellers would act upon the information ..." *(Cement Manufacturers Protective Association vs. United States,* 268 US 588, 603–604)

In a 1976 case, the U.S. Court of Appeals for New York commented on the exchange of credit information as follows:

> "... Unlike exchanges regarding prices which usually serve no purpose other than to suppress competition, and hence fall within the ban of the Sherman Act ... the dissemination of information concerning the creditworthiness of customers aids sellers in gaining information necessary to protect themselves against fraudulent or insolvent customers. ... Given the legitimate function of such data, it is not a violation of the Sherman Act to exchange such information, provided that any action taken in reliance upon it is the result of each firm's independent judgment, and not of agreement." *(Michelman vs. Clark Schwebel Fibre Glass Corp.,* 534 F2d 1036)

These cases are the foundation for conducting all business and trade credit investigations and exchanging business credit information on specific customers among competitors. These cases, however, do not permit the exchange of credit information or allow for gathering of credit data on consumers who obtain credit for "personal, family or household use." While commercial (business and/or trade) credit is specifically set up to avoid "personal, family or household use," there may be cases where under the law special consideration is needed. Every business-to-business credit grantor should recognize the respect the law itself discerns for business credit grantors and should adhere to those legal and regulatory parameters as well as to the ethical standards observed in the realm of business credit.

Antitrust, anti-defamation and confidentiality are the core principles for exchanging business credit information in industry credit group meetings *or any setting*—whether among two or 200, in a formal meeting or office, or in a parking lot or restaurant. These principles must also be adhered to in conversations among business credit grantors by phone, fax or electronically.

Comprehension Check

What are the three core principles that should be followed when exchanging business credit information in industry credit group meetings or other settings?

Antitrust in Credit Investigation

Figure 11-1   Antitrust

The object of this discussion [in an industry credit group meeting] is the collection and exchange of credit experience information relevant to the credit of accounts based upon actual experience or present knowledge as it relates to past and completed transactions only. It does not imply in any manner that the creditors [party to such exchange] recommend that any credit relationship be conducted or modified in any way.

There should be no agreement or understanding, express or implied, to fix or determine to whom sales should be made or credit extended, establish joint or uniform prices, terms or conditions under which sales are made or credit extended; and creditors may not boycott or blacklist any customers or suppliers. Creditors may not plan with another, or report, any future actions or policies.

Creditors may not give advice or otherwise attempt to influence the independent judgment of other creditors in the extension of credit.

Figure 11-1 focuses on the antitrust concerns a credit grantor must consider when inquiring or disseminating information about a customer's credit history, payment pattern, etc. In the context of information exchanged among commercial/business credit grantors, the primary objective is to avoid violating various antitrust laws. The intent of these antitrust regulations is to avoid any behavior that could lead to conspiracy, restraint of trade, price setting or fixing, or boycotting certain customers or suppliers. At the same time, the regulations also attempt to allow for the free-flow of credit information in a very specific manner so that creditors and competitors can avoid fraud, including the non-payment of an outstanding debt. U.S. antitrust laws are designed to give creditors the right to ask and find out how a customer or potential customer meets its obligations. The credit grantors who exchange such information must do so in a manner consistent with these laws.

The credit grantor must limit comments to the history of the customer's account. How long has the subject of the inquiry been a customer? What has been the highest amount of credit given/allowed? What were the credit terms offered to the customer? Does the customer owe money now? How much of what the customer owes is current? How long is the account past due 30 days, 60 days, 90 days or longer? How did/does the customer usually pay the account? What has been the experience with this customer regarding credit dealings and transactions?

No credit grantor may suggest that credit be either extended or denied or offered in such a way as to create, or appear to create, any form of agreement to sell or not sell a customer in any way other than by each creditor's independent decision. To do so could be considered a conspiracy in restraint of trade, which is a potential violation of the Sherman Act. Comments such as "I wouldn't sell (customer) on credit if I were you," "If we (all) sell (customer) on COD terms," or "Maybe we should" could indicate a threat of antitrust violation.

A credit grantor cannot enter into discussions of any nature with regard to prices. For the credit department, this relates to the terms and conditions of sale or credit. Under the Robinson-Patman Act, sales term, common vernacular that is often used interchangeably with credit terms, is an element of price. In some instances, a credit grantor will not release information regarding terms of sale when asked in order to avoid any concern about the question of price as it relates to the Act. Robinson-Patman does permit the inclusion of this information as it relates to the credit information trade line; however, if a company sets its own policy to prohibit sharing this information, then a customer's payment history in relation to sales/credit terms will likely not be available.

Credit grantors may not agree to do business with certain customers according to certain terms or conditions (i.e., conspiracy in restraint of trade). Nor may they report something that has not yet occurred or been acted upon such as: "We will never sell this customer on open account terms again"; "This customer is permanent COD"; "We are going to file suit"; "We are filing liens today." These comments are stated in such a way as to indicate that the actions themselves have not yet occurred. This means that the customer still has time to redeem itself and prevent these intended actions from taking place. When comments like these are shared, the recipient of the information tends to factor them into its credit decision. If the provider of the future action comment does not act on the comment because the customer subsequently pays or makes arrangements to pay, or management determines not to take action, then the customer may have been harmed and an antitrust violation will have occurred.

Each credit grantor must use the information obtained as a basis to make independent, unilateral credit decisions in accordance with their own company credit policy and/or judgment without influence, suggestion or coercion to make a credit decision in any manner.

Conspiracy, Restraint of Trade, Joint Actions

While the courts have held the exchange of factual credit information to be legal and proper, any agreement, express or implied, between competitors on any action concerning a common customer or class of customers is clearly illegal. Such an illegal agreement or conspiracy could be an agreement not to do business with a certain customer or class of customers or it could be an agreement on terms to be offered to a customer or class of customers. While exchange of factual information about the credit experience with customers is perfectly proper, care should be taken that no agreements are made for any common action, nor should there be any effort made to influence the credit decision of another company. Any joint action can have the effect of eliminating the element of competition from the marketplace; to do so is unlawful.

> **Comprehension Check**
>
> What types of behavior constitute **antitrust** when exchanging business credit information?

Defamation in Credit Investigation

Figure 11-2 Anti-Defamation

Libelous statements among creditors must be carefully avoided; they may subject all creditors to major damage suits by persons who consider themselves to have been defamed.

Creditors must also avoid giving opinions or making statements which imply that any individuals are dishonest, fraudulent or immoral since no specific damages need to be proven in court to recover for these kinds of statements.

Statements which might be considered *libelous* or *hearsay* should not be used unless it can be proved from clear evidence that the statement is true.

People operate businesses. As such, it is common to discuss a business credit transaction with the owners, partners or principals of the business credit customer. This is the issue referred to in Figure 11-2. Even though the customer is the business entity itself, the principal of the entity is looked to for management decisions such as payment of invoices. It is impractical to consider the business without considering the management of the business. Whoever makes management decisions, that *person's* track record, previous business experience and knowledge have an impact on current and future business credit decisions.

Credit grantors who are party to any such objectionable or disparaging remark or writing about the character or personal conduct of an owner or principal of a common customer can be sued by that customer. Defending the remark or writing is solely the legal burden of the parties involved in making the writing or remark. The only legal defense to the claim is "fact" or "truth." The injurious claim made by a customer is called defamation.

Libel and Slander

Defamation *is a false statement made to others that injures the name or reputation of a third party.* The two types of defamation are libel and slander. **Libel** *is defamation in some permanent form, such as printed media or writing in any form, including electronically-generated emails, computer files, folders or documentation.* **Slander** *is defamation in a temporary form, such as speech.*

The law has always been very protective of the reputation of businesses and business individuals. Legislatures and the courts have recognized that a person or business firm may suffer real damages by being lowered in the esteem of any substantial and respectable group, especially when that group may represent suppliers.

Examples of Libel and Slander

While it is proper to pass on information that is of public record to another supplier, such as the filing of liens, legal actions or criminal convictions, such information should not be reported with any malicious intent. For instance, continuous reference to a person's or company's unfavorable past history could hinder that person or company with such a record from being reestablished in society. This is especially pertinent where many years of good conduct have ensued or where nothing either good or bad is definitely known about the intervening years.

It is not defamatory to say that a customer is past due, has broken payment commitments, has bounced a check, is cautious with money or has led an eventful life. These statements lack the element of personal disgrace necessary for defamation in the eyes of the law. However, saying that a business "refuses to pay its bills" or that a firm is "insolvent" (unless it is an established fact) obviously damages that entity in the business community and may result in a charge of defamation.

Matter of Libelous Per Se

Generally, *matter libelous per se is any communication that falsely suggests a criminal act or immorality, or which tends to deprive a person in business of public confidence and esteem.* Examples would be to accuse someone of fraud or of being dishonest. The charge need not be made in a direct, positive and open manner. If the words used, taken in their ordinarily accepted sense, convey a degrading imputation—no matter how indirectly—they are libelous. A written communication that states a particular debtor has not paid debts that are owed and past due is not libelous, if true. If written communication imputes insolvency, bankruptcy or lack of credit on the basis of this fact, it becomes libelous.

The following are examples of libelous per se:

1. To charge by letter that a person knowingly made false representation with intent to deceive, or lacks veracity.
2. To publish a false statement imputing insolvency to a merchant or trader.
3. To charge falsely that a person has failed in business or has made an assignment for the benefit of creditors.
4. To falsely claim that the person committed a crime of moral turpitude (conduct that is considered contrary to community standards of justice, honesty or good morals).
5. To charge in writing that a business individual is embarrassed, inferring insolvency or lack of creditworthiness.

The best way to explain this aspect of anti-defamation is to say: if it hasn't happened yet, then it should not be reported. If a statement is made that a customer has filed bankruptcy, the creditor making the comment should have the case number, date of the filing or other information evidencing the fact of the bankruptcy. Therefore, there should be no speculation or further discussion about a customer filing bankruptcy unless newspaper articles, the public record or other written documents are published for all to know. Comments based on speculation from salespeople, management, other creditors, the trade or others do not constitute evidence that can be cited as support of the fact that the action has been taken or that the comments are based on public knowledge.

The element of **publication,** *communication of the libel to some third person,* is essential to an action in libel. Communication to the defamed person alone is not actionable because no third person has learned of the defamatory matter; consequently, there is no possible injury to the defamed party's reputation.

Defenses to Charges of Libel

Truth is a complete defense to an action in libel and must be so pleaded. Where several statements are published, however, of which only some are true, the defamer does not escape liability. Some defamatory statements are not actionable as libel because they are **privileged communications:** *statements made by one person in pursuance of a duty to another person having a corresponding duty or interest.* Such privilege is conditional, however, in that a community of interest must exist and must be exercised in good faith; malicious intent or a wanton and reckless disregard of the defamed person's rights will destroy the privilege. A person bringing suit must prove the existence of malice in order to sustain the action.

The courts have considered the following as privileged communications:

1. Statements made by a former employer whose name has been given as a reference to a prospective employer of an employee.
2. Communications between creditors of the same debtor in reference to their respective claims.
3. Communications by banks, such as a statement as to the financial standing of a person offered as a surety.

Comprehension Check
Explain the terms **libel**, **slander** and **matter libelous per se,** providing an example of each as it pertains to credit management.

Exchange of Credit Information—The Ethical Perspective

There are two cardinal principles in the exchange of credit information: *confidentiality* and *accuracy* of inquiries and replies. Confidentiality includes the identity of inquirers and sources, which cannot be disclosed without their permission. Adherence to these and other principles embodied in this age-tested code is essential as offenders jeopardize their privilege to participate further in the exchange of credit information.

Confidential Nature of Credit Information

Confidentiality relies upon the fidelity, or trustworthiness, of the party with whom information is being exchanged. All parties involved trust that the information has been requested for a legitimate purpose and will not be used indiscriminately.

When conducting a credit investigation, the identity of the inquirer should not be divulged without its authorization. Similarly, the identity of the source of the information should not be made known without its authorization.

Figure 11-3   Confidentiality

All information obtained by credit grantors must be considered strictly confidential and not to be divulged or discussed with any person outside of the creditors own credit department under any circumstances.

The facts presented must be accurate because the reference is one of the most pertinent sources of credit information. When discussing data, favorable or unfavorable, the responding party must give a reply that is restricted to or based on fact. If a discrepancy is discovered within a reasonable time after an inquiry has been answered, and is considered to be significant in relation to the purpose of the inquiry, it is prudent and ethical that the discrepancy be disclosed to the inquirer. It is expected that, as a matter of professional courtesy, no liability will be attached to, or result from, the good faith exchange of information.

The law protects the free interchange of credit information among business credit grantors. Without these laws, the flow of information could not survive. However, it is important that information either provided or being provided can be trusted. In this respect, confidentiality can be viewed in two ways. Each creditor party to any credit information exchange must have confidence that the information exchanged is accurate and without personal or emotional overtones. There is also the expectation that the party receiving the credit information will conduct itself in such a way as to protect the provider and/or the recipient of the information from any undue harm, injury, embarrassment or other unnecessary complication as a result of either providing information requested or obtaining information from a willing provider.

The credit grantor must trust that information:

- Being provided by a responding credit grantor's request is accurate and factual.
- Provided by the credit grantor to the inquiring party will be used solely by that individual to make a credit decision.

- Received will not be used for any purpose other than to make a credit decision and that it will not be repeated to any other party including the business customer on which the inquiry is made.

Ethical principles are violated when one creditor either purposefully or inadvertently violates the confidence of another credit grantor who provided credit information about a customer. In rare cases, competitors have been known to use accurate but adverse credit information to undermine a customer/seller relationship in order to gain a competitive edge. A creditor who intentionally provides false information may violate certain laws.

Can the party receiving the information be trusted to know how to handle it after the fact in order to avoid a "breach of confidence" from occurring? Consider the following scenario:

> You provide factual credit information about a customer to another credit grantor to whom the customer gave your name (company) as a credit reference. You provide factual, accurate credit information about the customer: the customer has a specific history of late payment with your company. Later, the customer contacts you and takes issue with the negative or derogatory reference about their company's credit experience with your company.

In the scenario above, a *breach of confidence* has most likely occurred. In other words, the credit details you provided in confidence were repeated to the customer, or yet another party, by a credit grantor.

This breach may set up a lengthy customer service and satisfaction process between your company and the customer that can involve the sales and management teams and even go so far as to involving legal counsel for one or both parties and possibly beyond, depending on the extent of the complaint.

This is only one of several types of ethical issues that can occur if a credit grantor is not familiar with the inquiring party and does not know if the party will treat the information confidentially.

When a breach of confidence occurs, there is likely no legal recourse available; the credit management profession more or less polices itself by limiting credit information to other credit grantors whom they know and can trust. In the event that a breach occurs, the credit grantor who has been affected may put restrictive conditions in place, such as withholding credit information from the party who has failed to treat the confidential information properly. In other words, credit information "dries up."

The process of exchanging information among creditors in confidence is strictly voluntary. It is important to know and recognize the ethical principles involved in such exchanges—whether between two parties exchanging credit information—or among several credit grantors who participate in specialized industry credit groups. Open email credit information exchanges are not recommended.

Summing Up Ethical Considerations

The purpose of a credit investigation should be to obtain information to make a specific decision about granting credit to a company. The goal of the investigation is to obtain factual and accurate information that will lead to an appropriate credit decision.

Personal Behavior. The credit professional has an obligation to their employer and to the credit community in general to behave professionally and to guard against violating, even unintentionally, any laws against restraint of trade.

Honesty. The credit professional should always present their company's experience honestly to any party requesting credit information. Misrepresenting oneself or one's company can have serious legal and ethical consequences.

Objectivity. Information requested must be factual. It is important to phrase questions and requests objectively in order to foster clear communications and avoid relying on someone else's opinion.

Topics to Avoid. Credit professionals should avoid discussing the following topics with anyone outside the credit department of their own company: future prices, future terms or future discounts. Furthermore, credit professionals should avoid any conversations touching on discriminatory trade practices or anything that might be construed as restraint of trade or in violation of antitrust legislation. For example, it is inappropriate to agree with other companies not to sell supplies to another business. That is forming an illegal boycott and is in violation of one or more of the federal antitrust laws.

Company Policy

Information gathered during the investigation must be kept confidential within the organization itself. A policy should be established as to who is permitted to access credit files. This policy must be appropriate to the size of the organization, the extent and nature of information contained in the files, and the use to be made of the information. An untrained person could seriously jeopardize the relationship between the customer and the company, and even subject the company to a lawsuit, by unwarranted or unguarded revelations of information that the customer might consider detrimental to its reputation or character. Therefore, it is important that all persons dealing with credit inquiries be properly trained in the legality and ethics of communicating credit information both inside and outside the company. Correct and accurate information, readily available at all times, is critical when reporting to management and the sales department, or when disclosing information to another credit grantor upon request, to a credit reporting agency or to an industry credit group.

Direct Credit Investigations

Direct investigation *occurs when the creditor collects credit information either through direct contact with the customer or through direct contact with noncommercial sources of information such as competitors, banks and other trade references that may have relevant details to share.* Sources of direct investigation include customer-supplied trade references, bank references and financial statements; information obtained from a Secretary of State's office; information found in public records; details collected through personal or telephone interviews with principals; and material found in search engines such as Google, Yahoo and others, as well as the customer's, or potential customer's, website.

Direct investigations were once the norm, but given the incredible amount of information online today, their frequency and value has diminished. However, they are still useful when information is not readily available or if the investigating company does not use commercial information services. Direct investigations can also be used to verify information obtained on a credit report or other online source, especially when a current or potential customer is high risk, a new business or has a high exposure.

Direct investigations can be labor intensive and should be conducted with a certain knowledge and understanding of the process. For instance, specific questions other than those relating to facts and completed transaction experience are inadvisable. Also, making an inquiry to a competitor without disclosing that the subject is a prospect is unethical, and when this information is properly disclosed, the reply is at the discretion of the account holder (respondent).

 Comprehension Check
Define **direct credit investigation.**

Customer Visits

The benefits of customer visits by credit department representatives include:

- Developing and enhancing the customer relationship.
- Strengthening the relationship with the sales department.
- Observing customer facilities (the inventory, condition of the equipment, the plant, the location and attractiveness of retail operations, etc.).
- Discussing financial information in more depth.
- Reviewing financial information that might otherwise be unavailable.
- Observing how other suppliers' products are being used.

- Developing connections between various internal company functions and the customer's counterparts (i.e., logistics departments, advertising departments, etc.).
- Resolving disputes.
- Sharing best practices.
- Discussing account status and collection of payments.

Comprehension Check

Explain the benefits of visiting a customer.

Building Customer Relations

Customer visits provide many valuable opportunities to build customer relationships. Visits may include representatives from credit, sales and other members of company management. Joint customer visits may have an additional benefit of enhancing internal communications among sales, credit and other departments instrumental to the maintenance of the account. A customer visit delivers a strong and unified message to the customer that its business is important to the creditor and that the protocol for doing business with the credit grantor has certain expectations. A good customer visit should be educational with regard to the expectations of both the creditor and the customer.

It is important for company representatives to review key discussion points prior to the visit so that management, credit, sales, production, distribution and other departments clearly understand the goals and objectives of the customer meeting. Based on these pre-visit discussions, a clear vision of the outcome of the visit will be ensured.

Comprehension Check

What questions can a credit manager ask a customer during a visit?

Figure 11-4 suggests possible questions to ask a customer during a visit. Not all questions will apply to every customer or every visit. It is important that the credit professional analyze the customer's situation and prepare to ask pertinent questions.

Figure 11-4   Questions to Ask Customers

1. What is their corporate structure?: Is it a corporation, partnership, LLC, LLP or proprietorship?

2. Do they have affiliated companies? If so, what is their relationship to the company being investigated (vertical: supplier or end-user; horizontal: differentiated by product type or geography, etc.)?

3. What is their product cycle, from ordering to shipment of raw materials to finished product to receipt of cash? What is the impact of seasonality on their business?

4. What are their inventory policies? Are there markdown procedures in place, or other plans to relieve slow-moving stock? What is the size of order backlogs?

5. Who are the principal customers of the company being investigated? How would their creditworthiness be described?

6. What terms of sale do they offer to their customers? What is the payment performance of their customers?

7. What is their market share? What is their product niche? Who is their competition, their advantages or disadvantages (price/quality/delivery), and their relative market shares?

8. Are there plans for expansion, new product developments or curtailments of unsuccessful lines? How will any expansion be financed? How will overhead be eliminated or absorbed if unsuccessful lines are curtailed? Are the facilities owned or leased? If leased, what are the expense implications if facilities are closed? Are the plans realistic?

9. Who are their major suppliers? What terms do they offer? Do any of them hold letters of credit, guarantees or security instruments such as liens?

10. What are projections for sales and income? What factors would influence possible variances?

11. What are their borrowing arrangements (availability, advance rates, factoring arrangements, security held, mandatory cleanup periods)?
    - What is the impact of seasonality?
    - Is refinancing under consideration?
    - Are personal assets or assets of affiliated companies pledged?

Observe the Facilities

A great deal can be learned from viewing the customer's operations first-hand. An observant credit professional can note irregularities and inconsistencies with information that has been previously provided by the customer. For example, a recent financial statement may indicate a large volume of inventory on hand. If the inventory seems low during a facilities tour, the credit professional can point out the discrepancy and allow the customer to offer an explanation. Customer visits break down barriers to understanding the customer. Plan to visit the most important sites first, but not necessarily the ones the customer seems most inclined to have you visit. Credit professionals can observe an operation and the subject company's performance relative to similar businesses that have been visited.

- What is the condition of inventory?
- What is the appearance of the equipment?
- Is retail traffic light or heavy?
- Are stores well located?
- Are the office facilities too extravagant or in need of modernization?
- Are a competitor's products in use and in what quantities?

When visiting a customer's facilities:

- Observe the impact of competition in terms of product use, amount on hand, etc. Try to ensure that you are not misled by what you observe. If there is a large backlog, what factors are involved (heavy buying in advance of season, poor acceptance of the suppliers' product, spot buying due to advantageous pricing, purchase of supplier's product due to credit problem, etc.)?

Real World Perspectives

RWP 11-1

RECLAMATION FROM DOLLARS TO TEARS

Clarence, the store owner, forcefully and purposefully handed me the keys to the store and said to me, "It's yours!" I was in shock by the turn of events, never expecting a customer to simply hand me the keys to their business! Although not prepared for this drama, I told Clarence that I was there to find a mutually agreeable solution to address the pharmacy's delinquency issues. Clarence began to listen to me closely, while cautiously still displaying some fear and trepidation.

Reflecting back to my interactions with Clarence before our first face-to-face meeting, maybe his behavior should not have surprised me. Clarence, the owner of a small drug store in St. Louis, would never commit to a payment plan and with great reluctance he agreed to our meeting. The meeting time also was unusual—7:00pm, after the store had closed. Clarence's slow opening of the store's entrance door confirmed a lack of trust and a feeling of dread to meeting with the "Credit Manager" from Chicago! The behavior may have been a tip off, the store keys being handed to me by Clarence, however, seemed to be a little over the top. All I knew was that I was going to have my work cut out for me.

The pharmacy was built in 1894, and Clarence certainly had a long history with the pharmacy. He told me about working in this drug store in high school and purchasing the drug store shortly after graduating from pharmacy school, fulfilling his boyhood dream. Clarence went on to tell me about the quadruple bypass surgery that he had in the prior year and the resulting health complications which led to his current financial difficulties. Being unable to work for six months, Clarence had to hire a pharmacist and manager for the store, increasing his expenses significantly. Furthermore, the newly hired personnel mismanaged the drug store.

My face-to-face meeting with Clarence would not be my last, although it helped build a foundation of trust on both personal and business levels between Clarence and me. I appreciated Clarence's sincere and honest overview of his financial difficulties, and I could tell that Clarence was truly a man of good character. I asked Clarence to put together the store's financial information and told him I would visit the next time I was in St. Louis. Clarence agreed to my request.

- Observe what other suppliers are present in the on-hand inventory. This may provide reference information that can be used for follow-up after the visit.
- Observe the efficiency of customer logistics. Is the facility located advantageously to customer locations and supply routes?
- Observe the traffic flow of employees' work areas, receiving and shipping facilities.
- Observe manufacturing efficiency and productivity. Look for signs of excess capacity.
- Are they busy? Depending on the industry, be aware of the kind of activity that should be taking place.
- Does employee morale seem high or low? If possible, ask employees to describe their functions in the organization.
- What is the condition of equipment and other fixed assets?
- Are there plans to relocate any facilities?
- Include the salesperson in the visit to help explain the facility and add their interpretation. Ask the salesperson to compare this operation to competitors' facilities.

Comprehension Check

What key factors should be observed during a customer visit?

Discuss and Review Financial Information

Many privately-held companies will only permit onsite examination of financial information. In such instances, if there were no visit, financial information would be unavailable to the credit department. It is important in these cases to capture as much information as possible during a customer visit. If the customer will permit it, take notes.

Even when copies have previously been given to the credit manager, a face-to-face discussion with customers about their financial statements provides a clearer understanding of the numbers. There are two reasons for this.

RWP 11-1 continued...

Two weeks later, I was again on a plane to St. Louis to see my friend Clarence. When I arrived we went back to the prescription dispensing counter as we had done at our first meeting to review the financial statements (if that was what you would call them). Essentially, it was a list of assets written on a green legal pad. It even included a bicycle from the 1950s used to deliver prescription orders! We went through the inventory items and discussed inventory management opportunities to improve his cash flow along with the store's operating performance and profitability. At the end of our meeting, we arrived at a mutually agreeable payment plan. Clarence told me that the payment plan would also require the approval of his attorney.

As I returned to Chicago, I thought that I was in a continuous loop leading to no resolution. I had already made a substantial investment with my time. I expected that the attorney, who was a friend of the family, would put up additional roadblocks due to the fact that I was requesting to become the only secured creditor for all of the business assets.

I did go through a challenging tug-of-war with Clarence's attorney and was now ready to finalize our agreement. Once again, I was on a plane to St. Louis to see Clarence. When I arrived, Clarence happily greeted me and we walked to the prescription dispensing counter. I went through each document and explained its purpose and significance. Clarence appreciated my attentiveness to these details and then I advised him where he needed to sign and date the documents in order to fully execute our agreement. Clarence slowly and carefully raised the documents to view at eye level and then he began to cry, telling me, "Shane, I thought there was no way out." I put my arm around his shoulder and told him that everything was going to be all right.

The next day Clarence's attorney called me by phone to thank me for helping her client and that it was a pleasure to work with me. A week followed and Clarence called me to tell me how he appreciated everything I had done for him. The whole experience was now indelibly stamped into my mind.

By helping business owners, I have learned that you not only can make a difference in their lives, but also make a difference in the lives of their families, the employees and their families, and the communities they serve. Look for the "Clarences" in your business and make a difference in their lives!

Shane Stevenson, CCE

First, the assets may now be visible to the credit professional. Second, there is usually more unrestricted time allotted for the review than for a telephone conversation. This permits more time for clear, concise questions and the ability to observe how the customer responds to certain questions.

A visit is a good time for the credit manager to learn in detail about the components of the customer's cash flow, especially if balance sheet analysis indicates weakness (heavy debt to worth ratios or lower than desired working capital). The credit manager can determine and observe if inventory or accounts receivable are turning within a normal range for the industry and/or the current economy. Suggestions may be offered that could help the customer take corrective measures and improve certain functions. For example, could the customer turn receivables and/or automate inventory management?

The credit professional can learn about opportunities the customer has explored, while observing the customer's responses to suggestions and inquiries that may reveal management philosophy and implementation skills.

A credit professional should be alert to the attitude the customer takes during the visit itself. Answers to complex questions that are inconsistent or inaccurate could be indicative of a cavalier approach to what should be a serious discussion about the importance of a future relationship with this customer. Here, the credit professional can observe the customer's body language in response to certain inquiries or listen for conflicting answers from different employees to the same question. The credit professional should use the opportunity to observe the company and management for signs of fraud or misrepresentation.

Industry knowledge and advance preparation are crucial to a successful customer visit. A strategy for the visit itself is also important. The customer should not be surprised by the nature of questions being asked during the visit. If financial information is to be discussed, then the customer should be asked to prepare this information in advance of the meeting. There should be no surprises for the creditor representatives during the visit. If certain sensitive questions are to be asked of the customer, then all participants joining the discussion should be aware and in agreement about the questions to be asked. Because interaction between the sales and credit departments and the customer can be sensitive, it is important for all participants to be fully aware of the information to be discussed.

Sometimes customers are reluctant to discuss financial information in the presence of the sales representative. This issue should be addressed before the visit through individual conversations with those involved. Usually, it is best to arrange for a time when the credit professional and management can meet privately to discuss financial information.

Resolve Disputes, Develop Interaction

The credit department is in a unique position to help avoid situations that could lead to disputes, claims and other problems that can negatively affect prompt payment within terms. The credit department has more opportunities to monitor interactions between the customer and other departments, including sales, distribution, production and management. For example, if a dispute exists from a drop-shipment made directly to the end-user (the customer's customer), or there is a quality issue, breakage, pricing or product application misunderstanding. A customer visit provides an opportunity for the parties to reach a resolution or settlement.

Freight and Logistics

Differences in interpreting or accepting routing guides are often reduced to a paper war between the logistics departments of two companies. The credit department, by virtue of its role in resolving customer deductions, is able to coordinate joint visits to address these problems. Quite often, an understanding can be reached eliminating the problem entirely, offering the subject company competitive advantages.

Pricing and Terms

Visiting a customer is an opportunity to clarify terms and conditions that may be conflicting or ambiguous. Once conflicts are identified, it is important to follow up with the customer service department so that future purchase orders from the customer can be monitored based on the information gathered during the visit.

Advertising

Interpretation can differ widely between supplier and customer on cooperative advertising programs. These are often not properly understood at time of sale and become apparent only when deductions surface. Credit's role in arranging onsite meetings of the advertising functions of both companies can become instrumental in resolution of the dispute.

"Team" Approaches to Visits

Many companies follow a "team" concept. That is, members of several different departments may form teams to visit customers to address broad supplier/customer strategies. Wherever possible within the framework of company policy, a credit professional should work toward becoming part of these teams. This allows the credit department to be seen as a vital resource to overall customer relations.

Customer Education and Best Practices

The credit professional may be in a position, due to their knowledge and experience, to provide suggestions to the customer. This is particularly true with a small or start-up business that may not have the resources available or the information needed to resolve a problem. The credit professional can share successes and best practices that have worked well internally, can suggest publications and referrals to various trade organizations and help mentor the business to growth. This willingness to be of assistance strengthens a customer/supplier relationship and builds loyalty from the customer's perspective.

Account Status and Collecting Money

Part of the customer visit may include a discussion of the customer's account status and collection of payment for past due accounts. Preparation is very important, the credit professional will want to have all pertinent facts with them and be knowledgeable prior to the discussion. The discussion may be deemed a sensitive one, so that a sales or manufacturing representative may be excused during this portion of the meeting. The credit professional has the opportunity to set the tone for the discussion and close the meeting amicably. Even when collection of payment is the primary purpose of the visit, the credit professional should take advantage of the onsite trip and include other discussion points when appropriate.

Preparation

There is no substitute for preparation. The credit professional should prepare for each customer visit with a written agenda, list of questions, time frames and participants. This list may be reviewed with company management prior to the visit to ensure their information needs are met. Including management in the preparation of visit objectives also provides the credit professional with an opportunity to stress the value of credit department attendance at these meetings.

The following preparation checklist will help ensure a successful visit:

- Define the objectives of the meeting.
- Determine who will attend the meeting and arrange a brief pre-meeting conference to agree on objectives and visit details.
- Schedule the meeting with all parties so that ample time is allotted for all necessary discussions.
- Review all relevant receivables and financial information such as detailed account status, financial statements and credit file material, noting any additional information needed.
- Obtain as much information as possible from other departments. What is the sales department's opinion of the account? Are distribution and other policies being properly observed by the customer? What is the unshipped order position? Review customer purchase orders for terms, prices or other issues. Are invoices being billed to the correct address?
- Contact other credit managers who may have visited the account recently and be certain credit investigation information is up to date.
- Prepare a follow-up list of things to be accomplished or learned.

After the Visit

Once the customer visit is completed, it is important to make immediate notes about the meeting's discussions, decisions and outcomes, etc. These reports may be referred to as: trip reports, call reports, meeting minutes or customer memos. The documentation of these meetings should be kept in the customer file and may first be circulated among the internal meeting participants or reviewed with company management. Observations made about the facilities, financial information discussed and questions specific to the customer's business should be clearly noted in the documentation.

Several items were most likely discussed and possibly assigned to various meeting participants, e.g., the credit professional was to check on an invoice problem, the company president was to provide a copy of their most recent financial statements, the sales representative was to inquire about a backorder that had been promised last week, etc. Most companies use an automated tickler system to track task due dates; other firms use a shared calendar. However tracked, it is critical that a follow-up practice be in place and that someone is responsible for managing completion of the tasks. The credit professional is well-positioned to serve as a central point of communication.

Figure 11-5 Sample Customer Visit Memo

Customer Name: _____

Location of Meeting: _____

Date/Time/Duration: _____

Key Discussion Points: _____

_____

_____

Assignments: _____

_____

_____

Responsible Participant: _____

Task: _____

_____

_____

Due Date: _____ Date Completed: _____

Responsible Participant: _____

Task: _____

_____

_____

Due Date: _____ Date Completed: _____

Submitted By: _____ Date: _____

Comprehension Check

What are some important steps in the follow-up process?

Trade References

A **trade reference** *is the payment experience information provided by a supplier on its customer*. Information from other trade creditors (trade references) describes how the customer actually pays its vendors, regardless of other strictly financial facts that might indicate the company's ability to pay or not pay. The payment record should be examined for specifics, including payment trends, and should be reconciled with the condition indicated by the customer's financial statements if warranted and available. Though slow trade payments are often a sign of trouble, they may also characterize a business that is having growing pains but is substantially healthy; the slowness may also be seasonal or due to expansion. Trade references are comprised of base variables, which represent the creditworthiness of the suppliers' customers, such as the following:

- Reporting date.
- Manner of payment, whether customer payment is prompt or slow, and by how many days.
- Rolling 12-month high credit (highest amount of credit used).
- Current total amount owing.
- Current total past due.
- Selling terms or days beyond terms.
- Date of last sale.
- Length of time the supplier has sold the account.
- Whether supplier referred account to a collection agency or if a history of NSF checks.
- Other facts about the customer's purchase and payment records.

Bank Information

Though many banks are cautious about releasing information about customers, they are valuable sources of credit information. Creditors can make direct inquiries of the customer's bank, or may ask their own banks to inquire of the customer's bank. In either case, the information is helpful in establishing a complete picture of the customer's record and financial ability.

The caution existing in the banking environment creates a common problem when seeking bank credit information. Banks are regulated by a set of "lender liability" rules and laws that do not affect trade creditors, causing banks to create policies regarding the release of credit information.

A proper inquiry should contain:

1. **Subject.** The subject of the inquiry should be identified as completely as possible including full name of the entity, address and name(s) of principals.
2. **Purpose.** The reason for the inquiry should be given in sufficient detail to allow the recipient to make an appropriate response.
3. **Experience.** If the inquirer has had experience with the subject, a summary of that experience should be provided. Doing this creates an exchange of information between the parties. Each gains important credit information on the mutual customer.

Comprehension Check

When contacting a bank about a potential account, what information should the inquiry contain?

How to Properly Request Information from Banks and Suppliers

Each inquiry should specifically indicate its purpose. One of the most important elements of an inquiry is its purpose. The creditor receiving the inquiry has a right to know why the information is needed. If no purpose is given, there is no obligation to respond. Knowing and understanding the purpose of an inquiry places the recipient in a better position to respond with the type and amount of information needed to satisfy the inquirer. When the purpose of the inquiry is solicitation, acquisition, merger, competition or legal action, replying is at the discretion of the respondent.

When contacting a creditor, the inquirer should state the initial steps taken, as well as the information on hand, in order to avoid duplication of effort.

Clearly identify the inquirer's organization. The legitimate use of credit information is to assist an inquirer who expects to extend credit or to otherwise rely on the subject of the inquiry in business dealings. The inquiry may not be answered without the creditor first determining its legitimacy and establishing the organization making the request. For example, when the creditor receives a telephone inquiry, information may not be disclosed on the first call unless the creditor has already identified the organization. Most creditors will request contact information (especially the main telephone line of the business) and then return the call to establish the identity prior to releasing information. Many creditors will not provide references over the phone and will suggest s written request be sent to them or simply provide access to the commercial credit repository that they share their information with electronically.

Clearly communicate the amount involved. Providing the amount of credit requested is standard procedure and helps provide the creditor with information about their existing customer. When initial trade credit is involved and no amount is established, the inquiring party should provide the normal size of its transactions. A range of figures such as $500-$1,000 or $50,000-$100,000, etc., is acceptable. If for some reason there is no amount involved, the inquirer should state this in a manner that would logically satisfy the respondent to the overall purpose of the inquiry.

To ensure accuracy and consistency in interpretation, figure ranges, as provided by the Risk Management Association (RMA), should be used:

Figure 11-6 RMA's General Figure Ranges

Low 4 figures	$1,000 to 1,999
Moderate 4 figures	$2,000 to 3,999
Medium 4 figures	$4,000 to 6,999
High 4 figures	$7,000 to 9,999

The ranges are adjustable to accommodate all amounts in the following manner:

Nominal	under $100
3 figures	from $101 to $999
4 figures	from $1,000 to $9,999
5 figures	from $10,000 to $99,999
6 figures	from $100,000 to $999,999, and so on

Comprehension Check

If a bank reports that an account balance is in the medium four-figure range, what is the numeric balance range for this account?

••

Provide the numeric figure ranges for the following dollar ranges: (a) Nominal, (b) 5 figures.

Statement of Principles for the Exchange of Credit Information

In 1955, recognizing the need to foster and maintain a high level of ethical standards in the exchange of business credit information between banks and business credit grantors, the NACM and RMA (www.rmahq.org) formed a joint committee that developed a *Statement of Principles for the Exchange of Credit Information between Banks and Business Credit Grantors*. The *Statement of Principles* was revised in 1978 to reflect current usage. Figure 11-7 lists the seven principles with explanatory comments.

Other Sources of Direct Investigation

The following sources are by no means exhaustive of the information available for credit investigations.

County and State Government Offices

Perhaps the office contacted most frequently is that of the Secretary of State, which possesses information about a company's incorporation status: the date, the officers, the type of corporation/LLC, any changes to the articles of incorporation or operating agreement of the LLC and whether assumed names must be registered with the state. Depending on the customer, it may be prudent to obtain a copy of the articles of incorporation or operating agreement of the LLC. [Secretary of State, Headquarters, National Association of Secretaries of State (NASS), Hall of States, 444 N. Capitol Street, NW, Suite 401, Washington, DC 20001 (phone 202-624-3525, fax 202-624-3527 or web http://nass.org/)]. Other items to check at the state level are professional licenses and permits, driver's licenses and UCC filings.

The county courthouse is another resource as its records can provide details about lawsuits filed or judgments rendered against a customer or potential customer. Tax and/or mechanic's liens filed by or against a customer may also be researched. This information can serve as a red flag that there may be contingent demands by taxing authorities or other creditors that could lead to the seizure of assets or otherwise usurp a creditor's claim. Assets that the creditor assumed would be available could be reallocated as a result of these legal filings.

Bankruptcy Court Information

To research a bankruptcy filing or possible filing, the credit professional needs to know the name of the owner, the name of the company and in what county of the state the company was doing business. Information about bankruptcy cases can be found online through the United States Judiciary's Public Access to Court Electronic Records (PACER) system. This resource can be found at http://pacer.psc.uscourts.gov. Creditors can also contact the office of the U.S. Bankruptcy Court Clerk with jurisdiction for the particular county of the businesses' residence. This information is also available online and is listed in the *Manual of Credit and Commercial Laws.*

Internet

The Internet is a resource for direct investigation that brings general information to the credit professional almost immediately. Because of the legal implications, payment, banking and other pertinent credit data are not available to the general public on free Internet websites. Likewise, because of the confidential nature of critical data, email is not generally recommended as a medium of exchange since emails may or may not be private and confidential at all times. If email is to be used as a method for exchanging credit information, the credit professional should take every precaution to maintain standard levels of confidentiality. This may mean using encryption or other security measures to secure messages and transmissions. Security also encompasses controlling access to the computer where email messages are stored.

For general information, Google, Yahoo, Wikipedia, Ask.com and similar search engines can reveal information about a company or the principals of a company. The amount of general information available online can be drawn from resources such as publications, periodicals and news services. Internet access makes research easy, and the various search engines can help narrow the search for very specific information.

Online tools such as Google alerts on key customers can help creditors stay abreast of any newsworthy events, and online mapping tools can shed significant insight into whether the customer's address is truly at their business location or simply a ship to or mail/post office box storefront. When among other credit professionals, it can be helpful to identify particular sites that have yielded useful and pertinent information. Take the time to review the company's online presence.

Customer Website

A considerable amount of information can be gleaned about a customer from their website, or lack of one. At best, it is likely to provide useful details including the number of employees, a full accounting of owners or officers, its geographical reach, related concerns (family tree of companies), history of the company, how long in business, management plans for expansion, product lines (which may lead to additional credit references) and other data that can be verified against the information offered in the credit application or customer information questionnaire. At worst, the lack of a website or a non-functioning site, may be a red flag.

Like references listed on a credit application, a company's website is subjective and presents the company in the best perspective possible. Investigation is necessary to confirm and verify information obtained from this source.

The following actions may be helpful:

1. Investigate site to see if there are any upcoming projects or jobs that would require the company's products.
2. See if the customer has an investor relations section, including financial statements.
3. Learn other current news or information that would be pertinent to establishing credit.
4. Add any information to the credit file and discuss with sales if needed, i.e., in case the requested credit limit needs to be adjusted.
5. Check date of the company's domain name or website to validate when they initiated their online presence. Use online programs or IT department to obtain this information.
6. Check social media sites to validate the information received about the company and the officers and to learn how the company markets itself.
7. Google the company's and/or officers' names for additional information.
8. Social media sites can validate information already received, or can spark new questions for the customer or sales before opening an account.
9. A customer's website can help the credit analyst determine if any other investigations are necessary.

> **Comprehension Check**
> In addition to trade references and banks, what sources are available when conducting a direct investigation?

Indirect Credit Investigations

An **indirect investigation** usually refers to *acquiring information from* **third-party sources** *that are in the business of preparing information on businesses/companies as opposed to individuals (principals of businesses/companies). These third-party sources are referred to as commercial credit agencies, bureaus or "repositories."* A credit report purchased from a commercial credit reporting agency is an example of information obtained by indirect credit investigation. In early American credit history, these third-party resources were referred to as "mercantile agencies" or agencies that gathered payment information on merchants. Credit reporting agencies have existed in America since 1841.

Third-party sources exist because gathering credit information directly can be time consuming and costly in terms of labor. Credit reporting agencies have on file, or can gather quickly, large quantities of data at a cost that is lower than the labor, time and overhead (such as telephone, postage, supplies, storage and related operating expenses) otherwise needed.

Industry Credit Groups

Sometimes, the credit grantor needs or desires more detailed and/or industry-specific credit information. Industry credit, or trade, groups can often fill in possible gaps. In their capacity as a form of credit reporting, such groups usually operate as a service feature or division of an agency that gathers and disseminates commercial credit information for banks and suppliers.

An **industry credit group** *is composed of credit managers from a number of different companies who share factual credit information about mutual customers and prospects.* The first credit group was established in 1875 by stationery and office equipment merchants. The concept mushroomed, and, today, NACM Affiliates sponsor and operate more than 1,200 industry credit groups throughout the United States. Still others are sponsored by private agencies.

An industry group pools information related to customer payment habits, financial histories, business changes (e.g., ownership, address, merger or acquisition), and problems such as NSF checks, judgments, liens and accounts placed for collection. Group members supply accounts receivable and other information to NACM Affiliates or servicing organization database. The service provider compiles the data, generates formal credit reports and makes them available to industry group members. In the early days, all of this was done manually. Over the years, automation on all sides has helped to reduce the time involved—and has improved the currency, freshness and completeness of the information in most groups. Today, many groups (and/or their hosts) require electronic full A/R file reporting to participate. Membership in a credit group can often lead to opportunities to gather more complete customer credit histories. Groups also keep members up to date on new legal rulings, developments in technology and continuing credit educational opportunities. NACM Affiliate staff facilitates group meetings to ensure compliance with the antitrust laws and regulations.

Industry groups can be local, regional, national or international. Local industry groups usually encompass a city or metro area, several counties or an entire state and meet the most frequently, often on a monthly basis. An industry credit group can be regarded as both a direct and indirect investigation resource of information.

Industry credit groups allow credit managers and analysts who sell to a common customer base to engage in discussions designed to examine the current payment patterns and practices of specific customers. They permit credit managers and analysts to separate "fact from fiction" by comparing the customer's reasons for slow or non-payment to what other industry group members are experiencing.

Commercial (Business) Credit Reporting Agencies

When it comes to determining customer creditworthiness, commercial credit grantors rely heavily on credit bureau reports as key sources of information. While there are many choices available, and the task to determine the best sources to use may seem daunting, it is easy and inexpensive to obtain good quality information to support a business transaction. Researching, comparing and choosing which sources to use is a key component of the credit professional's role.

Credit reports seek to help the user assess several, if not all, of the five Cs of credit by providing insight into corporate structure, type of business, industry, ability to pay, willingness to pay, existence and performance of secured and unsecured debt, existence and status of liens, judgments or even bankruptcy. Most credit bureaus or reporting agencies provide reports on all types of business structures.

Reporting agencies typically provide basic business and trade credit reports that may reveal payment history, business background, public records, collection activity, banking relationships, UCC filings and credit scores.

In addition, some credit reporting agencies will include more specialized reporting features such as:

- 'Flash' or 'alerts' representing pertinent events.
- Financial and operating statements.
- Accounts payable contact information.
- Antecedent information on principals of the business entity.
- History of the entity ownership.
- Description of the business' operations.
- Related concerns or family tree information.

There are *general, specialized* and *aggregating* credit reporting agencies. **General credit reporting agencies** *gather credit information on any business regardless of industry or upon receipt of an inquiry from a subscriber or member, delivering the information to the inquirer and then storing that information on file for future delivery and updating of the subject file.* **Specialized credit reporting agencies** *are more restrictive in the scope of the industries on which credit information is gathered and of the type of information reported.* They usually serve a particular industry for which they gather very specific credit information. The jewelry and furniture industries are two such examples that use specialized credit reporting. Manufacturers inquire about wholesalers, and wholesalers inquire about retail stores or shops in order to determine exactly how the particular customer pays other wholesalers or manufacturers within the industry. Other reporting agencies that offer more focused industry information include agencies or services that provide credit reports for the apparel, textile, aerospace, automotive, chemicals, golf and giftware industries; seafood; and toy and drug wholesalers. While all agencies gather information from creditors, members and subscribers about how a subject of an inquiry pays vendors and suppliers, they also may source other information unrelated to payment history that is of value. **Aggregating credit reporting agencies** *are typically resellers of the general or specialized agencies and use either individual data elements or entire credit reports from these agencies, and may also include news feeds and external econometric or publicly available data, to create a consolidated report.* Aggregated reports are an excellent way to compare sources of information and to reduce the likelihood of a "no record."

Commercial credit reports can be also defined as compiled or developed, or a combination of both. **Compiled reports** *are pulled together from automated sources of data and are matched, merged, de-duplicated and updated without any or much human intervention.* **Developed reports** *are usually freshly investigated, potentially using compiled reports as a source, but often including interviews with the subject itself and direct verification of references.* Both are valuable, with developed reports usually priced much higher due to the intensive work required.

While certain suppliers and vendors may report to, or participate in specialized repositories, their participation does not preclude them from reporting to general credit reporting agencies as well. Many companies report to several types of credit reporting agencies for many reasons.

There are four major general credit reporting agencies that offer business credit reporting services to subscribers, users and members: D&B, Experian, Equifax and NACM. All are national in their scope of coverage, report on multiple industries and offer unique features that distinguish them from the other agencies.

While some creditors use one source exclusively, given the diverse and substantial amount of information available, along with pricing flexibility, it is suggested that comparisons on a diverse range of clients be done on a periodic basis to determine the best sources.

As each creditor's customer mix, risk tolerance, budget, staffing, profit margins, industry, size and quantity of new orders are different, what may work well for a peer in the same industry may not be the best fit for a specific company. Many credit reporting agencies are usually willing to provide a reasonable number of sample reports free of charge for this purpose.

Comprehension Check

What sources are available when conducting an indirect investigation?

....

What are the types of commercial credit reporting agencies?

Figure 11-8   Sample NACM National Trade Credit Report

MAXIMIZE THE IMPACT OF REPORTING TO NACM

You can create goodwill with your customers while setting the stage for improved payment performance from those slower to pay. Consider sending this letter to all of your customers (or to just your slower pay or delinquent customers) to advise them that your company reports its customers' payment histories to the National Association of Credit Management (NACM). Your good-paying customers will appreciate your support, your customers with legitimate disputes may contact you to resolve them, while others will simply send in payment. Those that don't take any action may warrant additional review.

INITIAL NOTICE LETTER

Dear Valued Customer,

In today's business environment, we understand the vital role that good credit plays in every company's ability to access capital. We know that many companies today, of all sizes, have to rely on lines of credit to buy inventory, supplies or even to meet payroll. As a commercial trade supplier, we want to do everything we can to support your businesses—whether large or small—in building a complete and robust credit history. This will ensure that valued customers like you will continue to have access to the commercial credit you've earned and deserve.

To support our goal of meeting best-in-class commercial credit practices, we are active members of the National Association of Credit Management (NACM). NACM's mission is to promote honesty and integrity in commercial credit transactions. Without business credit, our global economic system would not exist. Business credit is, in reality, the capital required to conduct business.

Next month, we will report all open and paid account balances to NACM. This information will become a part of your business' credit history and may be accessed by your existing and future creditors—those within our industry and others, such as banks, leasing companies, service providers, transportation companies, advertising or construction firms, etc.

Reporting your payment history will help your company to not only build, but to also maintain a strong credit history in a database that is instantly accessible to NACM members worldwide. NACM is not only our go-to source for information, it is also a trusted source to businesses across our industry.

We hope that you'll review the enclosed open invoice(s) and act upon them within the next few days. We'd like the information we report to NACM to be factual and as up-to-date as possible.

Thank you for your support and for your continued business!

FINAL NOTICE LETTER

Dear Valued Customer,

We've made repeated attempts to collect the past-due balance on your account. Since your account has not been brought current, we are prepared to take further action. In 30 days, your account will be turned over to a collection agency, at which point you may be liable for added collection fees and court costs. On that same date, the past-due status of your account will also be reported to the National Association of Credit Management (NACM). As you know, this information will become a part of your business credit history and may be accessed by your existing and future creditors as they review the creditworthiness of your company.

To avoid such actions, please review the enclosed invoice(s) and remit payment immediately for before collection actions are initiated.

Figure 11-8   Sample NACM National Trade Credit Report continued

The accuracy of this report is not guaranteed. Its contents have been gathered in good faith from members but no representation scan be made as to the accuracy of the information gathered and contained in the report. This bureau disclaims liability for the negligence of any person or entity resulting in an inaccuracy in the report. This report is prepared and distributed for use in the extension only of commercial and business credit.

Figure 11-8 Sample NACM National Trade Credit Report continued

TRADELINES

MBR	IND CODE	REPT	OPEN	LAST	DBT	HIGH CREDIT	BALANCE	FUTURES	CURRENT	1-30	31-60	61-90	91+	TERMS / COMMENTS
TAMPA														
253	RFSP	0315		1111	51	$15,840	$1,110	$0	$0	$444	$222	$222	$222	
10001	AGRI	0115	0107	0714	2	47,728	6,550	0	5,600	950	0	0	0	P30NET 30
ATLANTA														
	HWRS	0315		0614	9	193,112	193,112	0	89,254	101,743	815	(22)	1,322	
	PLWH	0315		0514	0	3,960	630	0	1,285	0	0	(655)	0	N10
BIRMINGHAM														
	LEIS	0315		0614	0	190,696	284	0	972	2,048	(81)	(2,655)	0	NET 90
	HTWH	0215		1113	48	2.18M	353,720	0	190,420	0	0	0	163,300	
BOSTON \ HARTFORD \ PROVIDENCE														
	FTWR	0315	1001	0514	14	301,882	209,505	0	64,112	126,125	17,883	0	1,385	
	COSV	1114		0913	0	778	538	0	538	0	0	0	0	NET30
CHICAGO														
	HWRS	0315	0507	0614	5	17,320	16,932	0	10,760	6,172	0	0	0	NET 30
	HMCR	0315		0614	19	46,769	46,769	0	38,113	0	0	114	8,542	
DALLAS														
	COSV	0315		0614	0	29,091	29,091	0	29,091	0	0	0	0	US
	CHWH	0315		0612	103	25,745	1,752	0	0	0	0	0	1,752	
HOUSTON \ NEW ORLEANS														
	TRAN	0315	1103	0514	14	515,630	148,289	0	85,820	27,855	30,534	4,080	0	
	CNST	0215		1113	8	1,409	1,409	0	663	746	0	0	0	NET 30
INDIANA \ MICHIGAN \ OHIO														
	HWRS	0315	0312	0614	6	11,105	7,368	0	4,402	2,966	0	0	0	N45
KNOXVILLE														
	NEWS	0315	0196	0514	0	284,200	284,200	0	281,480	2,720	0	0	0	NET 30
	APRL	0315	0108	0514	17	691,281	217,292	0	7,777	193,433	30,527	(2,452)	(11,993)	NET 30
LOS ANGELES \ NORTH CALIFORNIA \ LAS VEGAS \ RENO														
	BRCS	0315		0614	6	2,169	2,169	0	1,349	820	0	0	0	1%10N
LOUISVILLE \ MEMPHIS														
	APRL	0315	0111	0514	5	144,927	144,927	0	99,213	45,714	0	0	0	Varies
	HTWH	0315		1012	0	0	(105)	0	0	0	0	274	(379)	
MINNEAPOLIS														
	CERM	0215		0512	15	40,666	5,924	0	0	5,924	0	0	0	
	APRL	0315	0509	0514	0	29,282	18,142	0	19,334	0	0	0	(1,192)	VARIED
NASHVILLE														
	CNEQ	0215	0911	0314	41	7,436	7,436	0	3,686	1,028	0	0	2,722	NET 10
OKLAHOMA CITY														
	FLWH	0315	0194	0514	0	118	118	0	118	0	0	0	0	NET 30
ORLANDO \ CAROLINAS \ VIRGINIA														
	ELDS	0215		0414	0	713	713	0	713	0	0	0	0	
		0315		0311	65	4,201	3,444	0	0	1,294	0	675	1,475	Due Upo
PITTSBURGH														
	PETR	0215		0414	0	566	566	0	566	0	0	0	0	0
PORTLAND														
	APRL	0115	0199	0713	8	45,379	45,379	0	38,117	(93)	6,697	420	238	NET 30
	APRL	0315	0198	0614	17	243,220	243,220	0	185,775	16,653	4,763	3,203	32,826	NET 30
SALT LAKE CITY														
	ADVT	0315		0614	0	171,480	171,480	0	171,480	0	0	0	0	
	APRL	0315		0614	0	271,238	184,360	0	183,452	0	0	293	615	VARIED
SAN DIEGO \ COLORADO \ NEW MEXICO														
	WLSP	0315	0110	0514	0	39	39	0	39	0	0	0	0	NET 30
	ELDS	0315		0514	5	1.44M	607,200	0	544,800	0	51,600	10,800	0	NET 30
SEATTLE \ ALASKA \ HAWAII														
	ELCT	0315		0514	6	1,821	811	0	745	0	0	66	0	ROI
	FLMF	0215		0214	0	363	383	0	383	0	0	0	0	CCP
SPOKANE														
	HDWE	0315		0614	0	139	139	0	327	0	0	0	(188)	
	NEWS	0315	0600	0514	0	61,533	61,533	0	62,681	(1,148)	0	0	0	NET 30
ST.LOUIS														
	FTWR	0315		0514	50	565,861	565,861	0	12,786	74,102	293,019	182,451	3,503	VARIED
UPSTATE NEW YORK														
	NEWS	0315	0111	0614	12	32,293	11,943	0	10,086	0	0	1,857	0	DISCNT
(39) TRADELINE TOTAL			AVG		14	$3.59M		$0	$2.15M	$609,496	$435,979	$198,671	$204,150	
			WT		18			0%	60%	17%	12%	6%	6%	

Figure 11-8 Sample NACM National Trade Credit Report continued

F — COLLECTION CLAIMS

MBR	IND CODE	ENTRY DATE	STATUS	CLAIM AMOUNT	CURRENT BALANCE
DALLAS					
	CNEQ	03/02/2012	Open	$418.41	$595.44
PORTLAND					
	FURN	07/26/2013	Open	$400.00	$302.00
COLLECTIONS: 2					

G — ALERTS

MBR	IND CODE	DATE	CODE	AMOUNT	MISC COMMENTS
ATLANTA					
	MISC	08/26/2013	NON SUFFICIENT FUNDS	$1,266.74	
DALLAS					
	MISC	02/02/2014	MISCELLANEOUS, PAST DUE	$221.57	
ALERTS: 2					

H — FINANCIAL INSTITUTIONS

MBR	IND CODE	REPT DATE	OPEN DATE	INST	TYPE	ORIG	CUR	COMMENT
410	BANK	02/17/2014	01/01/2012	BANK	CHECKING	M5	L5	
FINANCIAL INSTITUTIONS: 1								

I — PUBLIC RECORDS

DATE	TYPE	COUNTY	BOOK/INSTR #	PAGE	LIENOR	AMOUNT	OWNER
TAMPA							
04/13/2015	JDG	BREVARD COUNTY			DEMO CORPORATION	$15,230.00	
11/07/2014	STL	PINELLAS COUNTY		3424	DEMO CORPORATION	$5,600.00	JON P
		Property: SOUTH TAMPA			Satisfied Date: 03/01/2014 Satisfied Book: 9999 Satisfied Page: 3424		
PUBLIC RECORDS: 2							

J — BANKRUPTCIES

DATE	ATTORNEY NAME	STATUS	CHAPTER	CASE NUMBER	ASSETS
TAMPA					
11/05/2012	JON SMITH	CONFIRMED	7	12-56789	
BANKRUPTCIES: 1					

K — UCC FILINGS

REFERENCE #	FILED	EXPIRES	SECURITY/ADDRESS
TAMPA			
7800098012	01/06/2013	01/06/2019	JOHN DOE TRACKER COMPANY 123 ORANGE AVE TAMPA, FL 33622
	Comments: FARM EQUIPMENT		
UCC FILINGS: 1			

L — CORPORATE INFORMATION

TAMPA (02/07/2014)

CORPORATE NAME/ADDRESS				REGISTERED AGENT/ADDRESS	
DEMO CORPORATION 123 MAIN STREET ANYWHERE, FL 32309					

DOC#/FILING NUMBER	FEI/EIN	TYPE	STATUS	INC. DATE (STATE)	LAST FILED
FL123-06890	54-4874946	Domestic For Profit	Active	08/26/1985	01/02/2014

YRS IN BUSINESS	# OF EMPLOYEES
	150

COMMENTS

Comment section of Corporate Data.

OFFICER NAME	OFFICER TYPE	OFFICER ADDRESS
TAMPA		
STAN SMITH	PRESIDENT	123 MAIN ST ANYWHERE, FL 32309
WILLIAM SAMPLE	OWNER, PRINCIPAL, RABBI, TREASURER	111 ELM STREET OLDSMAR FL 33711
DALLAS		

M — NOTES

DATE	CREATED BY	NOTE	FOLLOWUP
11/11/2014	Jonp	Public records searched and nothing new found.	02/18/2015
NOTES: 1			

N — INQUIRIES

MBR	IND CODE	DATE
253	MACH	04/13/2015
253	MACH	04/10/2015
253	MACH	04/09/2015
INQUIRIES: 6		

O — REQUESTOR INFO

Accessed: 04/28/2015 11:22:55 AM
253 (sjh)
XYZ Member Company
5521 W Cypress St
Suite 200
Tampa FL 33607
(813) 269-1022

Figure 11-8   Sample NACM National Trade Credit Report continued

(A) In the **HEADING** section, you'll find the contact information for the NACM Affiliate furnishing the report. The name and address of the business subject appears on the left; on the right, the "InFile" date and time signals when the file on the subject was initially created.

The "Other Names" section shows any AKA, DBA, FKA (Also Known As, Doing Business As and Formerly Known As); related business subjects are included in the "Related Subjects" section and can be consolidated into one online virtual report at no additional charge.

(B) **PREDICTIVE SCORE:** Based on the unique tradelines gathered by NACM Affiliates, the scoring model predicts late payments and severe delinquency looking forward 6 months. The predictive variables include current aging status, historical aging (including trends and variance in payment trends) and other business characteristics. From the data on hundreds of thousands of businesses, common characteristics are examined on the business subject and, depending on how closely or remotely that subject matches the characteristics, the score is assigned a range, from high risk to low risk. In cases where not enough data exists, no score is assigned. If the business subject is already delinquent to the degree that the score is trying to predict, no score is assigned in the Low to High range because there is no need to predict something that has already occurred. Each report contains a complete credit score explanation.

(C) **CHARTS:** Past due percentages are used for the past due trend analysis, which compares the prior year to the current; DBT figures are used to graph the DBT trending for the past year.

(D) **MONTHLY & QUARTERLY Trending:** Total number of tradelines reported by month and quarter (report date is the month/year/quarter the tradeline was reported).

(E) **TRADELINES** supplied by the members of the Affiliate furnishing the report are always displayed first. NACM member numbers are displayed only for the members of the Affiliate furnishing the report honoring the longstanding "local" credit report tradition. Subsequent trade data is displayed by participating NACM Affiliates; member numbers do not appear, but industry codes do. YOUR member is NOT displayed or shared if the report is purchased by a member of ANOTHER participating NACM Affiliate. Protecting the identity of your company is a top priority for NACM.

DBT (days beyond terms) is automatically calculated by the database using a system-wide algorithm.

HIGH CREDIT is the highest balance owed in the past 6 months, on a rolling basis.

Any COMMENTS or remarks provided by the member/source are displayed.

TRADELINE TOTAL displays the total of ALL tradelines and AVERAGE DBT.

WT: DBT x balance for each tradeline then summed and divided by the total balance.

(F) **COLLECTION CLAIMS** include claim status, amount and current balance. Balances are updated when payments are made. Member numbers and industry codes are displayed for members of the NACM Affiliate furnishing the report and are always shown first. Subsequent claim data is displayed by contributing NACM Affiliates and is identified by industry codes (no member numbers).

(G) **ALERTS** are reported by NACM members and reflect pertinent changes in account activity. Some examples are NSF checks, past due status, accounts placed with attorneys, ownership changes, etc. Subsequent alert data is displayed by participating NACM Affiliates and is identified by industry codes (no member numbers).

(H) **FINANCIAL INSTITUTIONS** data, reported by banks, savings and loans, credit unions, etc., may include account types (such as checking, savings, construction loans, credit lines, etc.). The data may also include original and current amounts and comments.

(I) **PUBLIC RECORDS** are furnished by many different sources and may include, but are not limited to, judgments, state or federal tax liens, release of liens, mechanic's liens, etc. They also include country information, book, page numbers, lienors, amounts, etc. (Third Party Data may be available for purchase.)

(J) **BANKRUPTCIES** data may include, but is not limited to, attorney name, chapter, case number, date filed and possible assets. (Third Party Data may be available for purchase.)

(K) **UCC FILINGS** (Uniform Commercial Code) data may include, but is not limited to, reference numbers, dates filed, expiration dates and secured party information. (Third Party Data may be available for purchase.)

(L) **CORPORATE INFORMATION** may include, but is not limited to, any officer/director names on file with the Secretary of State. (Third Party Data may be available for purchase.)

OFFICER data may include, but is not limited to, any officer names on file with the Secretary of State. (Third Party Data may be available for purchase.)

(M) **NOTES** are key items of relevance pertaining to the business subject added by a Participating Affiliate report provider.

(N) **INQUIRIES** display other companies recently inquiring about the subject. Identity is NOT disclosed.

(O) **REQUESTOR INFO** displays information about the requestor: date and time accessed, member number, operator's initials and contact information. This information is only visible on the Requestor's/Purchaser's report.

Figure 11-8   Sample NACM National Trade Credit Report continued

NACM National Trade Credit Report

Why Should My Company Report Its Credit Information?

✓ Increase leverage with customers
✓ Reduce fraud
✓ Reward prompt payers
✓ Enhance your customers' creditworthiness profiles
✓ Protect your company
✓ Save time in preparing for NACM industry credit group meetings
✓ Save staff time responding to credit reference requests*
✓ Meet "best in class" corporate standards
✓ Support the NACM credit community

Credit is a privilege granted by a creditor to a customer. The decision to extend trade credit is based in part on current, factual information, which includes payment habit history.

Increase Your Leverage

You can create goodwill with your customers while setting the stage for improved payment performance by those that may be slower to pay. Your good-paying customers will appreciate your support, your customers with legitimate disputes may contact you to resolve them, while others will simply send in payment. Those that don't take any action may warrant additional review. Better customer payment habits improve your own DSO.

Reduce Fraud

Billions of dollars worth of goods and services are transacted daily through the business credit process. In many instances, fraudulent activity can be detected by carefully reviewing the information on a credit report. The more data reported, the more focused the picture becomes.

Enhance Your Customers' Creditworthiness Profiles

Reported accounts receivable information becomes a part of your customers' credit histories, reviewed by existing and future creditors—those within your industry and others such as banks, leasing companies, service providers, transportation companies, advertising or construction firms, etc. Reporting your customers' payment histories will help them not only build, but also maintain a strong credit history in a database that is instantly accessible to NACM members worldwide.

Protect Your Company

Without business credit, the world's economic system would not exist. Business credit is, in reality, the capital required to conduct business. Reporting your company's payment data will strengthen your customers' financial position by keeping their credit history robust, accurate and current.

Save Time

By electronically contributing your full A/R data file, you'll substantially reduce the amount of time it takes to prepare for an NACM industry credit group meeting. You'll also save time and resources by not responding to file revision or Poll My Group requests.*Depending upon availability, you may be able to direct non-member inquires to an online portal to electronically check credit references, saving even more time.

Meet "Best in Class" Corporate Standards

A lack of information interferes with the free and complete ability of a business to make a sound, accurate and equitable credit decision and is an impediment to the commerce of this country. If every business around the world reported data, commerce would grow. Great companies are growth leaders.

Support the NACM Credit Community

NACM is the go-to source for information; more than 15,000 businesses nationwide rely on NACM for credit information. By contributing your data, you're supporting the entire NACM commercial credit community!

Share credit where credit is due!

✓ It's easy, free and legal!
✓ NACM can accept your data in most formats:
  · D&B, Equifax and Experian
  · Spreadsheets (saved as .csv)
✓ Data can be transmitted via email, FTP or through an NACM Preferred Software Partner. Where available, members may upload a file directly from their participating Affiliate (once successfully logged in).

Sharpen the Focus

Trade payment information paints a powerful picture. Help maintain the crisp, sharp focus by contributing your company's data today. NACM's data is used exclusively in the credit decision process by its members—it's never used for marketing purposes.

For more information on business credit reporting and other great services, contact your local NACM Affiliate or visit us at:

www.tradecreditreport.com
www.nacm.org

NACM's mission is to promote honesty and integrity in commercial credit transactions. Join the cause.

International Credit Investigation

Credit information is available on international customers and their countries, but financial statements are more difficult to obtain. Furthermore, they are difficult to evaluate because accounting practices and tax regulations differ widely from country to country. The time required to gather information is greater than in domestic cases, so many export credit professionals build a comprehensive file of information on prospective global customers so they may make quick decisions when necessary. Credit information sources range from the customer to the comprehensive economic and business data compiled by U.S. governmental agencies, the international departments of banks, private trade promotion organizations and publishers and organizations that foster commerce globally.

Customer-Supplied Information

The best starting point for international credit information is the customer. At best, the buyer may volunteer data, including financial reports, a detailed biography of the principals and a history of the business going back over several generations. At worst, the buyer will provide no information at all, feeling that such a request reflects upon the integrity of the principals. Due to differences in accounting methods, international financial statements generally cannot be analyzed in the same way as domestic statements.

Bank Information

An excellent source of credit information is the exporter's bank. An inquiry directed through this source stands a better chance of obtaining useful information than one directed to the foreign customer's bank. Bank information generally includes a history of the foreign firm, antecedents of the principals and some financial data. A fairly complete picture of a firm's credit standing may often be obtained; however, depending on the seller's risk, bank reports should be supplemented by information from other sources.

Banks usually have extensive credit information on many international firms. Credit information on a buyer may already be in the bank's record or may be obtainable from other domestic sources. In other cases, it may be necessary for the bank to obtain the information from its international correspondents.

Banks vary widely in their cooperation with requests for information; similar to information received from the customer, the credit information secured directly from the bank varies in value. It may include business history, business background of the principals and financial data, or it may consist merely of a comment that the buyer is a respected member of the community.

Exporter's Foreign Sales Representative

The exporter's sales representative abroad can also be a valuable source of information. In all probability, the sales agent has had the opportunity to study the customer's business practices first-hand. The agent is known in the customer's trade circle and has access to credit information from local banks and commercial sources. The representative can therefore offer a fair picture of a customer's financial condition, as well as confidential data that would be difficult to obtain from any other source.

International Credit Reporting Agencies

A number of agencies provide business information reports on companies located outside the United States. Some of these also provide domestic credit reports, while others focus primarily on non-U.S. companies. FCIB, D&B, Experian and Equifax are some of the groups that report on non-U.S. companies. Reports on international companies are similar in content and format to domestic reports. They may be purchased individually or contracted for in advance.

FCIB

The **Finance, Credit and International Business Association (FCIB)**, is a wholly-owned subsidiary of NACM, which serves professionals involved in worldwide export financing, credit, treasury and international subsidiary management. FCIB's purpose is to raise the level of expertise and professionalism of members and to provide enhanced job enrichment through relevant discussion and exchanges of experiences. Among the services are:

- **International Credit Reports.** FCIB offers access to top independent credit reporting resources at attractive prices. The reports can be customized to answer specific questions and contain credit recommendations within the report as well as currency trend analysis.
- **Country Reports.** These reports summarize current experiences of international finance and credit professionals, capturing timely, in-depth information on the credit risks of export sales. FCIB's country reports assist international credit professionals to forecast foreign exchange availability, transfer risks and prospective currency changes.

Organization for Economic Cooperation and Development (OECD)

The **OECD** *is a Paris-based intergovernmental organization, established under a 1960 convention, whose purpose is to provide its 34 member countries with a forum in which governments can compare their experiences, discuss problems they share and seek solutions that can be applied within their own national contexts.* The fundamental task of the OECD is to enable its members to consult and cooperate with each other in order to achieve the highest sustainable economic growth in their countries and to improve the economic and social wellbeing of their populations.

Original OECD members were the countries of Europe and North America. Next to join were Japan, Australia, New Zealand and Finland, followed by Mexico, the Czech Republic, Hungary, Poland, Korea and the Slovak Republic. In 2010, Chile, Slovenia, Israel and Estonia became the latest members. The OECD is currently engaged in "enhanced" membership discussions with Brazil, China, India, Indonesia and South Africa; several other countries are in various stages of membership discussions. Visit the OECD website at www.oecd.org for additional information.

Comprehension Check
What sources are available when conducting an international investigation?

Investigating Existing Accounts

When to Investigate an Existing Account

Periodic Updating

It is recommended that credit applications be updated whenever there is a change in the credit grantor's policies or credit terms, or at certain timeframes (e.g., annually, every three years, every five years). In the process of verifying information, the credit professional should take the opportunity to review the contents of the file and archive or destroy all outdated or irrelevant materials. This will prevent duplication and oversight and make it easier to find items when they are needed.

Special Event Updating

Reviews for updates should occur for any of the following events:

- An account that usually purchases small amounts, suddenly placing large orders.
- A prompt payer suddenly beginning to pay slowly.
- A lot of inquiries suddenly coming in about an account.
- A change in ownership or legal business structure of an account.

It is not necessary, legally or ethically, to obtain a customer's authorization to order a commercial/business credit report. No personal or private information about the individual owners or principals of the business entity exists on a commercial credit report that would create a violation of privacy.

Comprehension Check

When should existing accounts be reviewed?

RWP 11-2   **Real World Perspectives**

SURVEY QUESTION:
HOW OFTEN SHOULD YOU UPDATE AND REVIEW CUSTOMER FINANCIAL STATEMENTS?

- **Credit consultant:** The frequency of reviews should be aligned with the perceived risk associated with extending open account credit terms to a particular individual customer.

- **A producer of long steel:** Quarterly or yearly. A higher risk account should be reviewed quarterly until the analyst is comfortable enough to change the schedule to once a year. Regular review on active customers will help minimize loss exposure.

- **Credit consultant:** The risk involved must be judged for what the company considers (dollar size-wise) is a large dollar amount to risk. For some firms a $5K open credit limit is a lot of exposure, where for others a $10 million dollar exposure is small. Quarterly or yearly depends upon the dollar risk size, the level of importance that the customer holds for the company and any "disturbing news" about that particular customer.

- **A designer and manufacturer of analog, mixed-signal and DSP integrated circuits:** They review high balance customers yearly, high risk customers semi-annually, distributors yearly and any customer requesting higher limits—they ask for an interim review at that point.

- **A fluid power distribution company:** The timing is determined by their industry and the dollar risk size they are comfortable with. Review times and limits are as follows: >$500K every three months, >$250K every six months, >$50K every 12 months. They suggest that each company decide as a team what it considers a big risk or a small risk and adjust from there.

- **A manufacturer of backup power generation products for residential, light commercial and industrial markets:** They obtain financials quarterly or annually depending upon the risk, which could either mean a large balance and/or financial stress. For a few highest risk accounts, they obtain statements monthly. The financials are not audited, reviewed or compiled, but allow them to see any unusual or large changes monthly and watch for trends.

- **A leasing company:** It depends on many things. For example, where they have approved LOCs in place, they do reviews annually, but it depends on the exposure and utilization. Large public companies are done every quarter upon release of their interims and for large private companies, they request interims depending on what the financial position was at the time of the LOC approval being put into place for 12 months. It also depends on the industry, so with the downturn in the oil sector, a lot more scrutiny and review of large, particularly non-core business transactions, would be looked at on a case-by-case basis and recent financial statements would be reviewed again.

- **A manufacturer of valves:** Most of the company's customers are private companies or partnerships, so they don't get access to their financials. In that case, they check the news regularly for any mention of them and of course, any change in payment habits leads to a look. Also remember, that in some countries, it is important to stay on top of what the government is doing. In Argentina, for example, it's quite possible for a business to be very healthy, but the government limits how much they can pay each month since the payment is leaving the country.

Strengthening Customer Relations

Written Communications

Credit correspondence should not be limited to collection letters, but should also include all facets that will build a solid customer relationship.

Periodic Requests for Financial Statements

Business finances can change greatly from one period to the next, so financial statements covering the year, or even a shorter period, are very important. A request can point out that the frequency is routine for all customers and that current statements are used to continue or expand the customer's credit line.

Revision of Credit Availability

If the creditor makes it a practice to notify customers of their credit limits, the revision of a limit offers an opportunity to express the seller's position to the customer. With a marginal account, particularly, notification may be important. To be most effective, it should emphasize that the increased credit line is a direct result of the customer's payment performance and financial growth. More difficult is the letter to a customer notifying of a downward revision, also known as an adverse action. It is best to state the facts about an adverse action in a logical, friendly manner, with sufficient explanation. If possible, the communication should close on a hopeful note that the circumstances causing the downward revision will soon be remedied and again evaluated for reconsideration.

There are four kinds of adverse actions as defined by the **Equal Credit Opportunity Act (ECOA):**

1. Refusal to grant credit.
2. Refusal to increase credit on an existing account.
3. Reduction of credit availability on an existing account.
4. Termination of credit on an existing account.

When an adverse action is made, "... the creditor must notify the applicant *either orally or in writing* within a reasonable time of the adverse action taken."

Sales Reps

Through frequent calls on customers, salespeople may receive early news of changes in sales trends, collections or movement of inventory. When changes are promptly reported, the credit department can be alerted to investigate further.

Comprehension Check

How can customer relations be strengthened?

Sources of Information

The sources of information for updating a credit file are the same ones used for opening a new account. In addition, it may be useful to search online to check a customer's website to determine what the customer is saying about their business. Using search engines, the credit department can immediately access articles or news items about a customer. The reporting of a creditor's entire A/R and the corresponding daily or weekly monitoring of those customers can provide excellent indicators of potential problems before they impact the creditor's own receivables. Many credit sources also provide monitoring services, and some may provide daily or weekly listings of warnings free of charge. If they are integrated into the daily process of the credit department, these warnings or triggers can stave off losses and more than pay for the costs of the credit service many times over.

Key Terms and Concepts

Comprehension Check

1. What are the three core principles that should be followed when exchanging business credit information in industry credit group meetings or other settings?
2. What types of behavior constitute **antitrust** when exchanging business credit information?
3. Explain the terms **libel, slander** and **matter libelous per se**, providing an example of each as it pertains to credit management.
4. Define **direct credit investigation**?
5. Explain the benefits of visiting a customer.
6. What questions can a credit manager ask a customer during a visit?
7. What key factors should be observed during a customer visit?
8. What are some important steps in the follow-up process?
9. When contacting a bank about a potential account, what information should the inquiry contain?
10. If a bank reports that an account balance is in the medium four-figure range, what is the numeric balance range for this account?
11. Provide the numeric figure ranges for the following dollar ranges:
    a. Nominal
    b. 5 figures
12. In addition to trade references and banks, what sources are available when conducting a direct investigation?
13. What sources are available when conducting an indirect investigation?
14. What are the types of commercial credit reporting agencies?
15. What sources are available when conducting an international investigation?
16. When should existing accounts be reviewed?
17. How can customer relations be strengthened?

Summary ....

- The exchange of credit information is legal as long as the information transferred is restricted to factual, historical data. In particular, the information given cannot represent any action that has yet to occur.

- The core principles for exchanging business credit information in any setting are: **antitrust, anti-defamation** and **confidentiality.**

- This is particularly important as it pertains to antitrust regulations. The intent of antitrust regulation being to avoid any behavior that could lead to conspiracy, restraint of trade, price setting or fixing, or boycotting certain customers or suppliers.

- A creditor must be careful to avoid any kind of defamation. **Defamation** being any occurrence of **libel** or **slander.** This includes matter **libelous per se.** A simple way to understand it is to say: if it hasn't happened yet, then it should not be reported.

- Truth is a complete defense to an action in libel. Some defamatory statements are not considered actionable because they are considered privileged communications, unless the purpose of the actions can be proved to be of malicious intent.

- The relationship between credit professionals needs to be one of trust. A credit professional must feel confident that the information they are providing will remain confidential. That being said, the person seeking the information must take extra care to keep the information confidential. Any breach of confidence may cause the exchange of credit information too simply "dry up."

- The credit granter must trust that:
  - Information provided is accurate and factual
  - The information will be used solely by that individual to make a credit decision
  - The information will not be repeated to any other party

- Ethical considerations should be made for the following:
  - Personal behavior
  - Honesty
  - Objectivity
  - Topics to avoid

- Direct credit investigation used to be the norm, and its use has since diminished as the availability of online information has increased. Direct credit investigations include:
  - **Customer visits**
  - **Trade references**
  - **County and state government offices**
  - **Bankruptcy court information**
  - **The Internet**
  - **Customer website**

- Customer visits may be essential to ensure the creditworthiness of a customer. The following are a few benefits of visiting the customer:
  - Enhancing the customer relationship
  - Strengthening the relationships between departments
  - Discussion of financial information in more depth or that is otherwise unavailable
  - Observing the facilities

- It is essential to be prepared when going on a customer visit. The credit professional should be prepared for each visit with a written agenda, list of questions, time frames and participants.
- Banks may have their own rules about providing customer information, and may be cautious when releasing the information about their customers. When requesting information from banks and suppliers, creditors should do the following:
  - Indicate the purpose of the inquiry
  - Clearly identify the inquirers organization
  - Clearly communicate the amount involved
- Indirect investigation includes:
  - **Industry credit groups**
  - **Commercial credit reporting agencies**
    - **General credit reporting agencies**
    - **Specialized credit reporting agencies**
    - **Aggregating credit reporting agencies**
- The four major credit reporting agencies are: NACM, D&B, Experian and Equifax. Third-party sources, such as the ones mentioned, have on file, or can gather information directly, that could be too time consuming or costly for most businesses.
- International credit information is available, but more difficult to obtain. The information can be obtained from customers, banks, the exporter's foreign sales representative or international credit reporting agencies. An excellent example of an international reporting agency would be the Finance, Credit and International Business Association (FCIB), which is a subsidiary of NACM.
- Investigating existing accounts should occur periodically due to special events, such as a sudden increase in purchase volume or a prompt payer suddenly beginning to pay slowly.
- Investigating existing accounts can strengthen customer relations and improve sources of information, ultimately reducing the risk to the creditor.

References and Resources

Business Credit. Columbia, MD: National Association of Credit Management. (This 9 issues/year publication is a continuous source of relevant articles and information. Archived articles from *Business Credit* magazine are available through the web-based NACM Resource Library, which is a benefit of NACM membership.)

Cole, Robert H. and Lon L. Mishler. *Consumer and Business Credit Management,* 11th ed. Boston: Irwin/McGraw Hill, 1998.

Credit Executive Handbook. The Credit Research Foundation, 1986.

Credit Professional's Handbook: The Technical Reference Manual for Credit and Customer Financial Management. Cavendish Publishing, 1999.

"Credit Risk Review." NACM Graduate School of Credit and Financial Management project, 2016. Kathie Knudson, CCE; Lisa Ball, CCE; Stacy Parker, CCE; and Dawn Dickert, CCE.

Institute of Management and Administration. "Customer Visits: A Real Step Toward Improving the Quality of Receivables." *Managing Credit, Receivables and Collections*. October, 1998.

Institute of Management and Administration. "How to Make the Most of Those Important Customer Visits." *Managing Credit, Receivables and Collections*. October, 1998.

Manual of Credit and Commercial Laws. Columbia, MD: National Association of Credit Management, current edition.

PART IV

VERIFYING CREDITWORTHINESS

12 Business Credit Fraud

OVERVIEW

Predatory individuals perpetrate crimes of theft against companies by manipulating credit terms through misleading statements or actions which can cause significant financial losses. The real-life cases discussed in this chapter have been distilled into a variety of situations, circumstances and occurrences that, when identified, most often result in financial losses involving credit. These fraud warning signs are intended to serve as primary clues that a fraud against a company may be in progress.

The objective of this chapter is to provide a description of those known circumstances that most frequently reveal the trail of fraud and help credit professionals identify the steps necessary to protect their firms from financial loss through credit risk.

? THINK ABOUT THIS

Q. What are the key the warning signs of business fraud?

Q. What can be done by a credit professional to identify possible fraudulent activity?

DISCIPLINARY CORE IDEAS

After reading this chapter, the reader should understand:

- ✓ Hallmarks of bust-out and same name scams.
- ✓ Why unsolicited orders are suspect.
- ✓ Why a large number of reference requests should be checked out.
- ✓ How the credit professional can be used as a reference in a fraud.
- ✓ Why unverifiable references, increased orders and unusual product mixes are suspect.
- ✓ How to spot misrepresentations.
- ✓ How to spot the warning signs of hidden ownership, the principal being unavailable, NSF and counterfeit checks.
- ✓ How to spot financial irregularities.
- ✓ What assets may be removed from a business.
- ✓ How to spot identity theft.

CHAPTER OUTLINE

Bust-Out and Same Name Scams

Whenever the business economy faces a difficult time, thieves will find ways to use the problem to their advantage. There continues to be more variations on old scams and greater sophistication in newer scams. This being the case, companies that remain vigilant will be the ones least likely to be affected by business identity theft.

The definition of **fraud** describes the nature of bust-out scams and same name scams: *an intentional perversion of the truth for the purpose of inducing another to rely on it to part with some valuable thing. It is false representation of a matter of fact, whether by words or conduct, by false or misleading statements or by concealment of that which should have been disclosed, which deceives and is intended to deceive another so that a person shall act upon it to their legal injury.*

Bust-Out Scam

Spectacular corporate frauds led to the bankruptcies of companies like Enron and WorldCom and the bust-out scam continues to wreak havoc on businesses without the resources to shut it down.

Bust-out fraud, also known as **sleeper fraud,** *is primarily a first-party fraud scheme. The fraudster makes on-time payments to maintain a good account standing with the intent of bouncing a final payment and abandoning the account.* During the process, the fraudster builds up a history of good behavior with timely payments and low utilization. Over time, the fraudster obtains additional lines of credit and requests higher credit limits. Eventually, the fraudster uses all available credit and stops making payments. Overpayments with bad checks are often made in the final stage of the bust-out, temporarily inflating the credit limit and causing losses greater than the account credit limit.

In a classic bust-out, a company is contacted by someone with an offer to buy large quantities of merchandise on cash on delivery terms. The supplier delivers the goods in exchange for a check drawn on a business account. When the check is returned for insufficient funds, the customer makes apologies for the mistake and sends another check. Often, by this time, another truckload of goods is on its way, but subsequent checks have no more cash behind them than the first. The accounts are real but unfunded. By the time the supplier realizes they've probably been taken, the stolen goods have been sold and the company has skipped out or disappeared.

Same Name Scam

Since the beginning of credit ratings, fraudsters have taken advantage of systems designed to rate business's creditworthiness. To illustrate how the same name scam works, consider that there is a reputable business with an excellent credit rating in Detroit named Detroit Distributing. The enterprising fraudster knows that credit professionals don't always order credit reports for businesses with excellent credit ratings or particularly when the dollar amounts are relatively small.

The fraudster sets up an office or warehouse under a similar, if not identical, name to Detroit Distributing. In this case, the new business is called Detroit Distribution and is located in Detroit. The variation on the name is a very subtle difference, and will probably not be noticed by the majority of suppliers who receive orders. Most credit departments have a credit scoring system that allows orders under a given level to be shipped, depending upon the credit rating.

The fraudster proceeds to place a number of small- to modest-sized orders using the name Detroit Distribution. Unwary suppliers, finding the excellent rating of Detroit Distributing, ship without a thought. By the time the invoices come due a month later, the phony operation is long gone.

Upon further observation, most credit professionals will point out that there is a flaw to this scheme. Suppose the supplier already sells to the real Detroit Distributing and sends the invoice to the real company. Immediately upon receipt of the invoice, the real company's purchasing or payables department will likely call the supplier and point out that they never ordered the product in question. And, should the supplier review the ship-to address, they may find that the shipping address is not connected with the real Detroit Distributing. The best way to trip up a potential same name scam is for the credit professional to pay attention to detail; it simply won't work if addresses are verified.

Unsolicited Orders

One sign that something may be amiss is an unsolicited order. Generally speaking, no matter how good a product, the sales force needs to work hard to come up with business. When an order arrives from an unsolicited customer, it is often a warning sign of fraud.

A company may receive unsolicited orders in any number of ways, but they generally arrive online, via phone or at a trade show. The definition of an unsolicited order can be tricky. Many companies receive the vast majority of their business via unsolicited orders. For example, catalog businesses receive calls soliciting their goods routinely. Sometimes, as a result of a presence at a trade show, orders increase from unknown sources. As a credit professional, the questions to ask are: (1) how common is an unsolicited order and (2) is there a rational explanation for the order? Does it make sense?

Another clue is the relationship between sales and the customer placing the order. If the customer seems to be trying just a little too hard to give what is normally looked for; it is time for the credit professional to back off and be more careful. The key statement to remember is the often quoted, "If it seems too good to be true, then it probably is."

Unverifiable References

One of the foundations of the credit investigation process is the credit reference. The theory behind reference checking is that past performance can be an indicator of future performance. Often, with modest-sized accounts, a credit professional has little other than references on which to base a credit decision. Businesses applying for credit may know this and are unlikely to submit unfavorable references. Worse still, in the case of fraudulent operators, a potential creditor can simply invent their own references. In fact, 50 percent of all business credit frauds have fake references.

As with other fraud warning signs, it is important to recognize that most references are completely legitimate. However, there are certain questions that can be asked about the references being checked:

- Are the entities providing the references unknown?
- Do some or all of the references sound vaguely similar to known businesses?
- Do the references have an ostentatious sounding name?
- Are most of the references in the same general geographic area as the prospective customer?

If the answer to any of the questions is yes, further investigation is merited. The first and easiest step to take is to simply check the reference's locale. This small step may uncover many frauds. If the reference is found and the facts don't add up, a second step to help verify the legitimacy of references is to pull a credit report. Is the reference listed at all? If it is listed, is it in a line of business that makes sense? If not, and they are offering a glowing reference, it is a warning sign.

Another tip-off that a credit professional might be dealing with a questionable reference is the use of a mail drop or answering service. While a business that sells some product or service might operate from a mail drop, most businesses generally need a physical location.

The credit professional should be able to reach a reference. If they find that they are leaving messages at answering services, when a return call is received, the credit professional should say that they are momentarily tied up and state the need to call back. If the reference gives their answering service number again, the credit professional should ask for the number at the current location, as they will be calling in just a minute. Fraud operators hate to give their number, as they don't want their location known.

Often, fraud operators will stall indefinitely with a myriad of excuses as to why they will not be in their office and ask the credit professional to leave their number with the answering service. The excuses generally will sound plausible, so good, common sense judgment is required. As with all situations, there are a number of legitimate reasons why a business person might want to give an answering service number. However, when this pattern of activity is seen and the references in question are overly glowing, the reports should be treated with more than a small amount of skepticism.

A post-mortem of credit frauds shows that many achieved success by relying on references that called back with glowing reports. A credit professional should still look for obvious discrepancies in the reference's story. If they have done their homework, and found that a reference does exist, does its story make sense in light of other information that they might have about the potential new customer? For example, is the reference reporting sales for longer than the new account appears to have been in business? Or is the figure given for high credit too high, in light of the size of the reference? If so, then the information received from the reference should be discounted and, perhaps, more questions asked.

Comprehension Check
List four basic questions that can be asked about a credit reference to protect from business credit fraud.

One of the best indicators is a credit professional's instinct. When something feels wrong, a little extra investigation will usually dispel any qualms.

Large Number of Reference Requests

Typically, clever bust-out artists establish a good credit history on a relatively smaller scale with several companies. They plan to use those companies as references when they begin placing larger orders. Often there is very little a credit professional can do to detect that this is a problem until the inquiries begin flooding in.

What constitutes a large number of inquiries? Most credit departments routinely receive credit reference requests; what is normal for one might not be normal for another. When something deviates from what is perceived as routine, it should be considered a red flag and more investigation is needed.

Often, there may be an explanation for the product or service ordered. Perhaps the inquiries relate to a major customer that is expanding. The best action for a credit professional to take is to simply call the customer and ask why they are giving their company as a reference so often. A legitimate company will be quite open and have a plausible explanation.

Bust-out artists are thoroughly prepared for questions about their ordering. Numerous companies that have established credit over a period of time used the excuse of expansion to justify huge increases in ordering from suppliers. A two-store chain is suddenly opening six more; or a wholesaler is suddenly going national. Stories may be similar, but if the company is not really known, it often pays to dig deeper.

Comprehension Check
Explain how an unusually large number of credit reference requests may indicate a possible business credit fraud.

If the customer claims to be opening new stores, has a sales representative visited the locations? What do the locations look like? Are they well stocked? Do they even have locations? Many companies claiming they were expanding were able to give only a vague explanation. It's the credit professional's job to pin down the buyer and ask for specifics. Why can't they give exact locations for their stores, if their new stores are the reason for increased orders?

Being the Credit Reference in a Possible Fraud

High inquiry rates also raise the question of what credit professionals should do when their company is used as a reference. Suppose many calls have been received and the credit experience has been quite good. What if the customer is fairly long term and has had substantially high credit and prompt payments? If the credit department is being flooded with inquiries, it may be a signal that fraud is in the making and liability may become a problem.

When companies begin to receive numerous inquiries about a particular customer, and then conclude that something is wrong, it is tempting to stop offering references altogether. Not responding to reference inquiries reduces the valuable flow of information at a time when it is needed most. The credit professional should keep to the facts and leave interpretation to others; there is no reason not to offer credit references in a suspected fraud.

Increased Orders and Unusual Product Mixes

Increased Orders

The primary goal in any business endeavor is to get customers to increase their orders. But this can also be a warning sign of potential fraud

In most credit fraud situations, the fraudster ultimately wants to order as much as possible. The window of opportunity for the heavy ordering is often just a few months. There comes a time in almost every credit fraud when ordering increases drastically because of greed. If they're going to take the business down, they can't resist doing it on a big scale. The results are orders that are out of proportion to the size of the business.

Like all fraud indicators, a credit analyst can only make use of this indicator in the context of other factors. Without knowing something about the business's history, its previous order history or its ability to move products, the credit analyst can't really make a judgment about whether a significant rise in orders is a warning sign. Here are some things to be aware of:

- If the order is from a retail store, what is the square footage?
- How many locations does the business have?
- Has a sales representative visited any of the stores or the headquarters? What did they find?
- If the customer is a wholesaler, is the reason for the increase known? Under normal circumstances, a wholesaler knows their sales team. If this is a mystery, try to find out who needs the product.
- Does the business have the usual signs of permanence?
- Are the backgrounds of the principals known?

When in doubt, a credit professional should ask their own sales team for help; a good sales representative can be one of the best fraud-fighting allies. If significant increases in ordering are being experienced, coupled with any of the other fraud warning signs, the odds are something is wrong.

When questioned after the fact, many fraud operators have told law enforcement agencies that an increase in ordering should be viewed by credit professionals as a red flag. Normal businesses do not routinely increase each order, but for bust-outs, this is par for the course. When a bust-out is gearing up, the orders generally increase each time.

Like all fraud warning signs, this may be merely a circumstantial red flag—something that should cause a careful look at the customer in question. Investigation should continue prior to authorizing increased credit.

Unusual Product Mixes

A classic indicator that a fraud may be in progress is the receipt of an order for an unusual product mix. This indicator usually comes in two forms. First, it can be a customer placing an order for a product that it wouldn't normally require (for example, a single restaurant ordering 12 copiers). Second, it can be a routine customer who places an order for a mix of product that does not seem to make sense (for example, six of every item).

Credit professionals should examine the first situation, regardless of the product or service sold, and develop a sense for the type of customer from whom orders are normally received. When an order is received that seemingly deviates from the norm, it generally stimulates that sixth sense. When this situation occurs, the game plan should always be the same; the normal credit investigation routine should be thrown out and the credit professional should become a detective. They should not stop until the reason for the odd order is understood. As with all fraud warning signs, it is important to keep in mind that many situations which look suspicious on the surface are easily explainable after further investigation. A conversation with the customer may alleviate fears of questionable activity or confirm original suspicions.

Another way in which this indicator can manifest itself is when the customer seems routine, but the order seems unusual. Generally, most credit professionals don't take the time to look at what is being ordered; the dollar value is what drives an investigation. The composition of the order is often a clue that the order is not valid. At trade shows, bust-out artists often place orders for each and every item in a company's catalog. Conversely, they might place an order for only one product, when normally an order would be a variety of items.

Through experience, this sense of which orders are unusual can be developed. Bust-outs have been detected by alert credit professionals who noticed that an order came in at a higher price than normal (retail, instead of wholesale, for example); an indicator that price is not a big concern. Be alert to the composition of orders. When in doubt, the investigation should continue until the reason for the order is understood.

Comprehension Check
Why can a sudden increase in orders or an unusual product mix be an indicator of a business credit fraud?

Misrepresentations

The question of whether something is a fraud ultimately rests on whether there is intent, and a misrepresentation of some sort generally proves intent. Therefore, anytime a misrepresentation is spotted, a warning flag should go up.

Anything can be misrepresented, including financial information, business or educational background, or reasons for a late payment. A credit professional may stumble onto a misrepresentation accidentally. Everything else about the potential account might look positive, causing the credit professional to ignore the one minor piece that points to something being amiss. Any misrepresentation, however small, is ignored at the peril of the creditor. While there may be occasional reasons to use an assumed name, it is a warning sign that more investigation is in order.

As with most fraud-spotting techniques, diligence and knowledge of the industry are the two elements needed to spot misrepresentations. The latter is critical because it sets off a red flag when something doesn't fit the norm for an industry. But even when there is no obvious sign of something wrong, diligence is really the key. When it comes to the **Five Cs of Credit,** the C for character is the most important of all. Evidence of a misrepresentation is critical in an analysis of a person's character.

Undisclosed Changes in Ownership

Changes in ownership occur every day, and the vast majority are completely legitimate. However, there are many individuals who specialize in buying businesses with the sole intention of driving them into insolvency, keeping the assets for themselves and leaving creditors unpaid. This form of business credit fraud causes greater losses than all other forms put together.

There are several key warning signs that signal questionable ownership changes. One warning sign is a new owner with a track record of bankrupting businesses. Unfortunately, most are not so obvious. A second warning sign is an ownership change with little or no notice given to creditors. In most instances, suppliers (trade creditors) and others associated with the business are notified of an ownership change. But credit fraud operators often like to capitalize on the good name of the business, and downplay the new ownership.

Another indication that something might be wrong is a new owner with little or no background information available. Often, fraud operators, also called take-down artists, take over businesses through fronts. The real owner, or take-down operator, has such a bad track record that their name cannot appear on a business without raising suspicions. The object is to find a clean front man. In this case, there may be a new owner of a business whose prior business experience seems insufficient to have provided either the capital or the experience to purchase and operate the business in question.

Another warning sign is when a company is owned by a series of corporations, and a trace up the corporate ladder only seems to reach more parent companies—no actual people. After all, people run a business and a business is only as good as the people running it. If it's impossible to identify who is in charge, it may be an indication that something is being hidden purposefully when transparency in business conduct is so important.

The credit professional should work upstream in an attempt to determine the owners of the ultimate top parent. If it's been specifically advised that the names of the owners are not going to be released, this is clearly a warning sign.

Unverifiable Backgrounds of Principals

Perhaps the most important criteria in the evaluation of the creditworthiness of a business is the background of the principals. If someone has a long and verifiable track record, a credit analyst can feel comfortable that a successful past will likely be a prologue to a good future.

When studying a business for the extension of credit, it is a best practice to pay particular attention to the antecedents of the principals. Experience and criminology studies have shown that white-collar criminals will continue their schemes until caught. After the first bust-out, fraud operators have several choices: (1) they can tell credit agencies and creditors the truth, in which case, credit likely will be withheld; (2) they can make up a background; or (3) they can simply defer it.

The first scenario isn't likely, but it does occur. Some debtors are upfront about their past problems and attempt to convince creditors that they have turned over a new leaf. While this works occasionally, the second or third options are more likely scenarios.

Bust-out operators will sometimes supply credit agencies with personal background information which, for whatever reason, cannot be verified. They do this by saying they worked for firms which are now bankrupt or which never existed. Access to online information and credit reports has gone a long way toward closing the information gap.

Dealing with an Unverifiable Background

When in possession of a large order, the credit professional should ask questions until comfortable with the principal's background. The key is to ask for specific addresses of previous employers. Once this information has been obtained, it is easier to verify the background. Another method is to ask for the principal's supervisor at a particular company. If the person is reluctant to supply this information, it should be a clear red flag for the prospective creditor.

Hidden Ownership

As already stated, the most important C of the **Five Cs of Credit** is character: knowing all about the owners of customer companies is critical to good credit analysis. While there may be some legitimate reasons why someone would want to conceal their ownership of a business (such as being a publicity shy celebrity), in most instances, it should be a warning sign to the credit analyst. There are two questions: how can a business operate with a hidden owner and, assuming they are hidden, what then?

The first situation is more common than one might think. Because the second question is tougher, hidden ownership most often occurs after an ownership change, meaning that control changes should be monitored very carefully. Whether there are new owners or not, here are a few warning signs:

1. **Reluctance of the listed principals, or managers, to make decisions without consulting someone else** is a clue that it could be a front. Generally speaking, when dealing with an owner of a business, they are able to answer routine questions. However, if someone is merely a front for a hidden owner, they will be unable to answer questions without first checking with the real owner.

2. **A control change where the owners are not immediately disclosed.** Most ownership changes are not kept secret; if they occur with little or no fanfare, the individuals who are

represented as principals need to be checked to see if they have backgrounds commensurate with their new positions.

3. **A confusing chain of command at a company.** Ask company representatives at suspect businesses for the names and titles of the principals at the company. If they respond that someone is simply the boss when they are not the highest-ranking principal, it is possible that something is amiss.

4. **A confusing corporate structure.** While it is possible that a corporation takes over a long-time customer, it is important to find out who owns the corporation. Sometimes, individuals with checkered backgrounds hide behind a series of corporations. This tactic also makes it harder for the eventual lawsuits to reach them. In cases where there is a series of corporations going up the ladder, each with unknown principals, a credit analysis should not continue until the actual people with titles and responsibilities are reached. This sometimes happens legitimately, of course, but it is also a method used by con artists to remain hidden from the scrutiny of creditors and regulators.

5. **Signers on checking accounts.** An old adage in white-collar crime investigations is "follow the money." If a situation is questionable, and the real owners may not be known, the credit professional should try to determine who the signers on checking accounts are. When it is found that the signers are different than the purported owners, it clearly raises the question as to why someone other than the owner has control of the funds.

Sources of Information

While it is possible to find out about hidden ownership on one's own, it is often very difficult, and simply happens by accident on many occasions.

Key areas that provide help:

1. **The sales force.** Some of the best leads may come from credit professionals who paid attention to what their sales departments tells them. Keeping open lines of communication with sales is one of the best ways to gather useful information about the customer base.

2. **Industry credit groups.** Industry credit groups are an invaluable source of information about ownership changes and irregularities.

Principal Unavailable

The unavailability of a principal over a period of time may signal that an operation is winding down. There are also many instances where fraudulent debtors are unavailable at the time of ordering. Frequently, this occurs with operations that place orders for delivery to mail receiving agencies or mini-storage warehouses. Because "the customer is always right," it is possible to overlook warning signals and to fill orders even from blatantly questionable operations. If customers are difficult to reach to discuss an order, the odds of reaching them after a shipment or to collect a past due only decreases. Some of the classic excuses by fraudulent debtors include:

- He's in the field, collecting from our customers. It's hard to fault someone who's out trying to shore up cash flow; most credit professionals can relate to this excuse.

- She's overseas, on a buying trip. While this may be what creditors' hear, there is often no basis in reality for such statements.

- He's had a heart attack. White-collar criminals are known to have multiple heart attacks when creditors are trying to reach them to discuss delinquency issues.

- A principal may be unavailable because the person listed on paper as the principal may, in fact, be a front for another. In such a case, it will be unlikely the listed principal will deal with the creditor on matters of substance.

Any of these scenarios should raise a red flag for the credit professional. Most importantly, the unavailable principal is a clue that can help define the nature of the transaction.

Comprehension Check

Describe why a change in ownership, unverifiable background of principals, hidden ownership and unavailable principals need further investigation and may be warning signs of fraud.

NSF Checks Received

Like virtually all potential signs of fraud, NSF (non-sufficient funds) checks should only be taken in the overall context of the business. The NSF check is simply one more indication that something may be amiss. The key in determining fraud is state of mind and intent. Most of the time, an NSF check simply reflects poor management or a miscalculation and may not reflect a fraud. However, when dealing with a fraud, a bounced check is probably intentional. Some factors to consider are:

1. **Patterns of activity.** While not generally admissible in court, patterns can serve as strong circumstantial evidence that something is amiss. NSF checks can be an indication that something more than poor management is involved.
2. **Fraud audits conducted after the fact often uncover other NSF checks going into a fraudster's checking account.** The checks are often submitted from related parties just prior to the issuance of a flurry of NSF checks. The perpetrator can then claim that money was in the account, and show deposit slips to prove intentions were good.
3. **An increase in ordering at the time an NSF check is submitted.** An NSF check that precedes a large order could serve as a tipoff that a fraud may be in the making.

An NSF check is not necessarily an indication of a fraud. But looked at in connection with other information, it can be one more clue of a potential fraud, rather than a routine business transaction.

Counterfeit Checks Received

Check fraud is a challenge given the advent of inexpensive desktop publishing systems, laser printers and color copiers, an individual con man can manufacture checks quite easily.

The following tips may help spot forgeries and save costly errors in trusting too much in appearances. Part of the trick in catching check forgeries is to focus special attention on those accounts that appear suspect. The warning signs to look for when a bad check is suspected:

- Check numbers do not change.
- Checks drawn on new accounts.
- Checks with no account or routing number.
- Inverted watermark on paper.
- Misspelled words.
- Poor printing quality.
- Checks presented near the end of the business day by customers who seem unwilling to wait until the next business day for their order.
- Checks received from customers whose accounts are themselves suspect.
- Normal checks presented to honor a previously submitted bad check.

- Irregular signatures, such as those with an interruption or gap where the pen has lifted off the paper completely.
- First four digits of routing code are not valid.
- District in routing code does not match District in transit number.
- Bank identification number in routing code does not match bank identification number in transit code.
- Check identification in optical scan numbers at bottom of check does not match check number on face of the check.

Comprehension Check
List some warning signs of a bad check.

Financial Statement Irregularities

One of the best ways to uncover potential frauds is through the careful analysis of a business's financial statements. It is not necessary to be a CPA; all that is needed is a working knowledge of the basics along with an eye for detail.

Financial statement analysis gets to the core of the **Five Cs of Credit**. Statements are used to determine whether the capital and collateral of a business are sufficient to extend credit. Unless the character of the maker of the financial statements is totally sound, the analysis will be based on faulty information. There have been countless decisions wrongly made because they were based on phony information.

Context is critical in helping a credit professional determine that a financial statement has been fabricated or doctored. Statements should always be examined in the context of all other information known about a business. A financial statement is designed to paint a picture of a business both at a given point in time (through the balance sheet), and of its progress over time (the income statement/statement of activities). Both statements should make sense in light of other information that exists about the business. In the context of other information, each piece should fit together; misrepresentations often do not fit. This is where knowledge of a particular industry and the economy will help identify a financial statement that may not be fully reflective of a business's true picture.

Often, credit professionals and investment professionals are taken completely by surprise by the bankruptcy of a company that appeared, based on years of audited statements, to be making money. W. T. Grant's notable bankruptcy in the early '70s is a great example of a surprise bankruptcy, which, in retrospect, offered clues in its financial statements that it was destined for failure. Unfortunately, those taken by surprise suffered their greatest losses as a result.

W.T. Grant, one of the largest retailers in the country, had shown good income numbers over the years leading up to its sudden bankruptcy. While it did pay slowly, creditors felt comfortable that the risks were reasonable, given the fact that W.T. Grant was an old-line, profitable account. The missed clue in the financial statement was severely negative cash flow.

It is important to keep in mind that generally accepted accounting principles (GAAP) allow businesses wide latitude in accounting policies. Those with very aggressive policies may often overstate the soundness of their financial status. W.T. Grant's negative cash flows gave significant advance warning, but its income statement did not. It made money only based on highly aggressive policies, which were within GAAP until it declared bankruptcy.

Assets Removed

Assets removed are the essence of any business credit fraud. While bust-outs are often thought of in terms of the removal of inventory, a business is made up of far more assets than inventory, and any asset of a business is subject to looting. Generally, the removal of assets is not noticed until it is too late, but in some instances, a credit or finance professional can spot this early, before the damage is too severe.

In an effort to show intent, one question to ask is, does the removal of assets occur to such a degree that keeping the business afloat is impossible? In many instances, the rapid speed and huge quantity of assets removed make it obvious to any creditor that a business was being pillaged solely for the purposes of enriching its owner, and there was no intent to keep it a going enterprise, and pay creditors.

What may seem obvious to professionals may not be obvious in a court of law. It is difficult to determine mal-intent when studying the removal of assets. Even if too much of a business's assets are removed, showing intent can be challenging. Legitimate businesses fail every day, and the owners continue to draw salaries right up to the end.

One way to show intent, in the case of removal of assets, is a misrepresentation. One example is the case of Coats Distributors, a business purchased by convicted bust-out operator, Jon Miller. Miller claimed to be infusing money into the business. He actually transferred hundreds of thousand dollars into Coats. However, investigators found that it was only a partial return of an even greater amount that he had already removed from Coats' operating accounts. On a net basis, Miller had removed more than $400,000 almost immediately after gaining control of the business while, at the same time, purporting to be infusing cash into the business. This appears obvious, but at the time, credit, financial and law enforcement investigators didn't have the benefit of seeing the whole picture. They only had the word of Jon Miller to believe.

Any Asset Can Be Removed

Asset removal is not only limited to inventory or operating cash. Corporate pirates will take anything of value. Look at any balance sheet; there are all kinds of items of value. One of the biggest is, of course, accounts receivable; they simply can be collected and pocketed, or they can be sold or factored to a third party. Many fraudsters, when factoring their accounts receivable, supplement the real receivables with phony receivables.

Even harder assets, such as equipment or real estate, can be converted to the owner's use, through sales or sale-leaseback arrangements.

Despite the difficulty of proving intent, credit and finance professionals should always keep a lookout for a business removing assets at a fast pace. It can be more than mismanagement. The removal of assets can be at once the most obvious or the subtlest of all the fraud warning signs.

> **Comprehension Check**
> Why is it important to keep an eye on a customer's assets and make sure they are not improperly removed?

Identity Theft and Social Engineering

Business identity fraudsters do not need to steal much of the information needed to impersonate a business; more often than not it is publicly available at no cost or legally purchased. In most states, businesses are required by law to post documents that contain many of their key identifiers such as sales tax number, business license number, etc. Unlike the protections provided for consumer credit reports, if a business has a credit report, virtually anyone can order a copy because business credit reports are intended to foster and promote commerce. Unfortunately, business credit reports contain a wealth of information that can also be misused by crafty business identity thieves.

Business EINs

In some respects, an **EIN**, a *business' federal employer identification number*, is a business form of a Social Security number because of the ways it is commonly used to uniquely identify the business. An EIN is not provided the same protections as an SSN. Many business identity theft schemes occur, and many fraudulent accounts can be opened, with only a business's name, address and EIN. State business registration information is public record showing details about the business's legal structure, ownership, officers, directors, registered agent and registered address. In some cases, copies of documents that contain the owners' or officers' signatures are legally available to anyone who is ambitious enough to look. Of course, there is the Internet black market where the stolen confidential information of millions of consumers and businesses is routinely purchased, sold and traded every day. Fueled by wide-scale data breaches caused by hacking, theft, loss, or human error, there are countless consumer and business credit card numbers, account numbers and other sensitive information available for the taking.

> **Comprehension Check**
> Explain how **EINs** make identity theft easier.

Corporate Identity Theft

Identity theft and social engineering are among payment scams that are neither new nor particularly complicated. Fraud perpetrators target companies in what they believe are routine, business-to-business transactions. Bad actors pretend to be a company, with just enough information through social engineering to get funds wired to their account.

Criminals impersonating legitimate business owners or businesses have gotten ever more sophisticated as public attention to their chosen, illegal profession has increased. With the Internet making company information readily accessible, many potential fraudsters can easily copy company logos, letterheads or other paperwork from a company's website to make their communications with targeted businesses seem less suspicious. Still, these applications often contain a number of red flags in their details and operational history. Credit professionals can save their company from losses with thorough investigation.

The key to detecting a fraudster using a legitimate company to place orders is to take a hard look at the actual applications and orders, which often have errors on them, (e.g., misspellings, etc.). Credit professionals should take the time to compare the information provided on an application with the information included in a company's report to reveal the potential buyer's identity. Take advantage of the resources available such as an NACM National Trade Credit Report to verify the information provided and check the inquiry rate on the NACM report. Contact and shipping information should also sound alarms for credit professionals aiming to ensure that their potential sale is legitimate. Fraudsters often ship to residences and mailbox locations which may be detected by conducting a reverse look up on the shipping address. Examine the email address carefully; a lot of fraud is coming from legitimate company@yahoo, Hotmail, Gmail and other free, untraceable email addresses. Beware of email addresses and phone numbers that are slightly different than those of the verified legitimate company.

Many companies and credit professionals may think that the longer a company has been in business, the less of a risk it is to sell to them. But an application or report that shows a company has been incorporated for several years doesn't guarantee that the buyer is legitimate. Sometimes the fraudsters will establish a company, or incorporate four or five companies, and let them become dormant. These shell companies will often be inactive as they rack up the number of years incorporated and then suddenly see a flurry of activity. While this doesn't automatically indicate the presence of fraud, a potential customer who has been dormant for a long time and suddenly begins seeking credit should be investigated further.

Fraud on the Rise

Many domestic companies were affected by payment fraud in recent years. Federal Trade Commission research shows that, of 30 types of fraud complaints, the top three are identity theft, debt collection schemes and imposter scams, which together accounted for more than one-third of all reported incidents. Businesses with otherwise sterling reputations are finding themselves fielding complaints, some of which end up with the Better Business Bureau or Attorneys General offices in various states. Once the business customer clicks on an email link, often to accounts through Gmail or Outlook rather than a company's ".com" or ".org" domain, or takes a phone call and provides information without checking the source, the process of fraud is off and running. Despite all the warnings about scams over the years, such schemes continue to be alarmingly successful.

Whether it's a bust out, where either a criminal or a shell company set up by the criminal will buy goods without ever intending to pay for them; or corporate identity theft, where a criminal pretends to be from another legitimate business and submits an application for credit; another online scam or another form of cybercrime, thieves will exploit the weakness of an industry, an owner, or a company to get what they're after. Moreover, by seeking certain amounts according to certain business conditions and characteristics, these thieves can also keep themselves from getting caught. Depending on the size of the company, a fraudster or identity thief might seek $5,000, $10,000, $25,000 or even up to $100,000 worth of credit, or a commensurate amount of goods. If a company usually writes off a certain percentage of bad debt, and is expecting to write more off during the recession, a criminal can often put in the application, get it approved quickly and then never even face a cursory investigation by the company itself.

All of these instances add up. Business identity theft currently costs companies $50 billion a year in the U.S., and this isn't just a problem for large firms. Certain industries face greater threats due to the resalable nature of their products, like electronics, computers, technology and even food, but identity thieves find small businesses just as profitable as large ones. No matter the business situation, identity theft is a sizeable and costly problem that requires diligence on the part of company credit staff to make sure the person or company asking for money or goods is who they say they are.

Bust-Out King Reveals Secrets to a Successful Scam*

Three years after his release from prison, Al Forman is a grateful man. Speaking at symposium in Las Vegas in 1994, he thanked credit managers, investigators and even the FBI agent who ultimately arrested him.

These people brought down one of the most successful bust-out artists ever and Forman credits them with helping him straighten out his life and enabling him to make strides in the art of living.

Standing at a podium facing a crowd of more than 100 credit managers and financial professionals from around the country, Forman began his foray into public speaking fumbling with index cards and telling his life story before finally getting down to what everyone was gathered to hear: how he did it.

What Al Forman did fooled creditors and investigators for a decade while setting up and deliberately bankrupting numerous companies. He was involved in more than 20 different businesses during this time and, at his peak, had four separate bust-outs operating simultaneously.

Forman, who was 54 at the time, admits he has no idea where the term bust-out originated, but he certainly understands its meaning. A bust-out is a planned bankruptcy or insolvency, often of a phony company that sells merchandise from other companies. By first placing small orders with suppliers, the bust-out artist gradually gains the trust of creditors and eventually works up to larger orders. By selling the products at discounts of 25 percent or more, the bust-out artist can pay for smaller orders until the time is right for the bust-out. Because creditors do not expect payment for 30 to 90 days, the bust-out artist can order and receive bulk shipments without paying right away. And when creditors finally do run out of patience, the bust-out artist files for bankruptcy or disappears.

From the early 1970s until his arrest in 1985, Forman mastered the bust-out. In all, his crimes cost creditors about $40 million, averaging $1 to $4 million per bust-out. At the time of his arrest, he was managing bust-outs in Pittsburgh, Rochester, Long Island and Ft. Lauderdale. By Thanksgiving of 1985, all four operations were in high gear with products coming in by the trailer load.

"All things have a beginning and an end," Forman said. "I really do believe that if I wasn't caught, those four bust-outs were going to be my last."

With creditors, FBI investigators and the U.S. Postal Service trailing him, Forman was finally arrested and convicted of mail fraud and interstate transportation of stolen property and sentenced to 17 years in prison. He served six years and was released in 1991.

How He Did It

According to Forman, there are six necessary components to a good bust-out:

1. Capital, preferably $100,000 or more;
2. A capable front man;
3. Good location from which to receive and ship merchandise;
4. Equipment;
5. Financial statement; and
6. A corporation.

Once these elements were in place, 99 percent of suppliers that Forman contacted shipped to his phony companies without a thought and were defrauded. In addition to the six elements above, Forman found that it is unwise to place too many orders at trade shows, because all orders are checked by a credit reporting agency. He made sure that a front man attending a trade show never placed more than six orders.

By adhering to a few basic rules and lining up the six elements, everything just fell into place—creditors approved orders, merchandise was shipped without payment, and the bust-out company in turn sold at discount to retailers and suppliers. Creditors readily increased credit lines and Forman was surprised at how easy it was to go from a $3,000 limit to more than $10,000.

"A good bust-out is an illusion where you paint a picture that I'm going to buy your merchandise and sell your merchandise. But I'm not going to pay the bills," he said. "There isn't a salesperson around who doesn't like large orders."

The Fall

After a long run of successful bust-outs, investigators began asking questions. Forman was questioned by the FBI in Boston about a company that had filed for bankruptcy. That deal had started with Forman's father-in-law and Forman was one of the company's clients. After that, more questions arose and Forman was followed by FBI agents. A few days before Christmas in 1985, all of the warehouses were closed and Forman and his father-in-law were arrested.

"All I could think about was that famous expression, 'I woulda, coulda, shoulda.'"

Although Forman expresses remorse for his crimes, and served time in prison, credit and financial professionals were not satisfied.

"I'm very surprised that his sentence was so light and that he's out right now and gainfully employed talking about it," said a credit manager from Procter & Gamble, Cincinnati. "He should probably still be [in jail] or at least making some restitution and that didn't come through in his speech at all."

A credit manager from Ralston Purina, St. Louis, agreed, explaining, "After many years of seeing his name, it was interesting to see him face to face. But I agree that he probably shouldn't be out."

Forman served six years in prison for his crimes. Many would say that isn't enough, but compared with many other white collar crime offenders (Michael Milken and Ivan Boesky served less time), that is a substantial amount of time.

Practices like Forman's bust-outs are not uncommon today and the problem of fraud in American business is growing.

With law enforcement concentrating on problems like drugs and violent crime, fraud is increasing. Law enforcement's resources are limited in its fight against white collar crime and private industry must institute internal and external controls to protect itself from fraud.

Forman's Future

After all that Forman learned during his decade-long bust-out spree, perhaps no lesson proved more profound than that of getting caught. He went on to work in the health food industry and began lecturing on his experiences. But Forman insists that creditors will not have to worry about any future problems from him.

"I have done harm for what at the time seemed to be good motives," Forman said. "Sometimes my supposed love of others was in reality only a desire to dominate them. Looking back, I wish I had learned to master myself, to control my impulses, and curb my cravings for power, possessions, and pleasure. What has happened to my life's progress the last three years, I've made strides in the art of living so that what I admire in people, others can admire in me. Perhaps a little, but certainly not enough."

Reprinted from NACM's Business Credit magazine, January 1995. Originally written by Kevin C. Naff, former communications associate editor.

Key Terms and Concepts

Comprehension Check

1. List four basic questions that can be asked about a credit reference to protect from business credit fraud.
2. Explain how an unusually large number of credit reference requests may indicate a possible business credit fraud.
3. Why can a sudden increase in orders or an unusual product mix be an indicator of a business credit fraud?
4. Describe why a change in ownership, unverifiable background of principals, hidden ownership and unavailable principals need further investigation and may be warning signs of fraud.
5. List some warning signs of a bad check.
6. Why is it important to keep an eye on a customer's assets and make sure they are not improperly removed?
7. Explain how **EINs** make identity theft easier.

Summary

- Business fraud costs businesses billions of dollars every year. It is critical for a credit professional to be aware of business practices that may seem out of the ordinary.
- Fraud takes a variety of forms, but is normally done through the intentional manipulation of the truth in order to do harm to another party. Common techniques used to commit fraud include:
  - **Bust-out scams**
  - **Same name scams**
  - **Unsolicited orders**
  - **Unverifiable references**

- Large number of reference requests
- Increased orders or unusual product mixes
- Undisclosed changes in ownership
- Unverifiable backgrounds of principles
- Hidden ownership
- Financial statement irregularities
- Identity theft

- There are often very reasonable explanations for irregularities in business operations. However, it is very important that, if a credit professional believes something is out of the ordinary, a credit investigation be conducted. This can be as simple as calling the customer in order to prompt an explanation. If a company applying for credit seems to be holding back information that should be readily available, or a principal is avoiding inquiries at all costs, they may be stalling in order to commit fraud.

- The best sources of information for a credit professional who suspects fraud are the sales force and industry credit groups.

- Due to a creditor's need for the free flow of information, businesses are often not afforded the same protection as individuals. Credit reports and business **EINs** may make it easy for a thief to steal a business's identity. Over 30 types of fraud have been identified with the top three complaints being identity theft, debt collections schemes and imposter scams. It is critical that a credit professional be aware of these scams and remember that, "If it seems too good to be true, it probably is."

References and Resources . . . .

Business Credit. Columbia, MD: National Association of Credit Management. (This 9 issues/year publication is a continuous source of relevant articles and information. Archived articles from *Business Credit* magazine are available through the web-based NACM Resource Library, which is a benefit of NACM membership.)

Carr, Matthew. "Attack of the Doppelgangers: A Case Study." *Business Credit.* Columbia, MD. National Association of Credit Management. June 2008.

Naff, Kevin. "Bust-out King Reveals Secrets to a Successful Scam." *Business Credit.* Columbia, MD. National Association of Credit Management. January 1995.

Office of the Attorney General of Florida, Consumer Protection. http://myfloridalegal.com/consumer.

U.S. Department of Justice, Criminal Division/Fraud Section. www.usdoj.gov/criminal/fraud.

Supplementary Material

Attack of the Doppelgangers: A Case Study*

WESCO Distribution

In 1922, Westinghouse Electric Company created WESCO to sell and distribute its growing catalog of products. The organization flourished and in 1994, the management team of WESCO, in partnership with the private investment company Clayton, Dubilier & Rice, purchased WESCO from Westinghouse. The holding company WESCO International was formed following another purchase in 1998, and the following year the company went public on the New York Stock Exchange. It is a Fortune 500 success with more than $5 billion in annual sales, 7,000 employees in 400 full-service centers and over 110,000 customers around the globe.

But in July 2006, an individual claiming to be the manager of WESCO's Cleveland, Ohio branch began placing purchase orders with several computer distributors for seemingly innocuous items such as toner, ink cartridges and computer memory sticks. The distributors took the orders and began sending invoices to the Cleveland branch, which then forwarded them on to corporate.

"That's basically how it started," said William Coe, asset protection manager, WESCO. "We initially thought, as I started the investigation, that it was an isolated incident; that somebody was impersonating this branch manager in the Cleveland area. I had no idea that it had far-reaching implications into international areas."

Shortly after, a similar situation came to light as someone posing as WESCO's chief executive officer (CEO) began submitting orders for the same items. They'd place an order for several thousand dollars and ask for a line of credit. Almost all of the transactions took place over the Internet and the salesmen for the distributors failed to place a single phone call to verify any of the information or authority. The emails from the individual claiming to be WESCO's CEO and others arrogantly provided a series of phone numbers, knowing that if any of these would have been dialed, they would have been found out to be fictitious or disconnected.

In trying to convince law enforcement to take up the case, WESCO found itself in a strange situation as it wasn't a victim in the classic sense; the company wasn't suffering a loss. It was the network of suppliers and customers that WESCO did business with that were targeted and faced the loss of tens of thousands of dollars.

"I guess the sad thing about this is, legally, we're not out any money," stated Coe. "The biggest problem we had was that because we are publicly traded, our reputation was at stake. We could ill-afford to have the Wall Street analysts or others start bad-mouthing WESCO for being mixed up in some type of scam. That's one of the reasons why we started collecting all this data and contacting the U.S. Secret Service once we found out it was a large operation that was organized and targeting hundreds of companies. They targeted everything from Dells to HPs down to the mom-and-pops running out of their garage."

Simplicity and Villainy

Between July 2006 and the end of 2007, fraudsters parading as WESCO representatives hit at least 1,500 companies. The assault didn't slow as another 200 companies contacted WESCO in the first quarter of 2008, reporting they had received fraudulent purchase orders in the company's name. The approach the scammers used is simple, yet elegant. It also clearly demonstrates that, even though there are countless warnings about email scams, there is still a broad naïve base out there for criminals to readily and successfully prey upon.

The perpetrators would pose as anything from a corporate executive at WESCO, to a purchasing agent, to one of the company's 400 branch managers. The vast majority of the contact was done via email, originating from addresses that have WESCO somewhere in the name. Coe has identified more than 40 different email addresses and at least two dozen different individuals for whom the scammers have posed. In some cases it would be a genuine person, like the CEO, CFO or a number of other executives, or it would be a common name plucked from the air that by chance would match with someone from WESCO's large employee base.

"We have an Internet site of wescodist.com. The fraudsters would use wescodistr.com or they might have wescodists.com or wescocompany.com," explained Coe. "It's just a little variation. Then it started appearing as the first part of the address, like wescosales@earthlink.net or wescoppm@gmail.com. So, they started using all sorts of free email providers like Yahoo! and EarthLink."

Even more devious was that the perpetrators also began contacting distributors using TTY/TDD telephones for the hearing impaired. The service is toll-free and uses an operator to relay responses between a hearing impaired person and another party by reading aloud what was typed by the hearing impaired individual and then by typing what was said by the other party. This allowed the perpetrators to hide their voices.

The basic scenario consists of the fraudsters asking for a quote on first contact, and once that was received, they would come back with a purchase order. The purchase order, a fairly uniform document, would be legitimate looking enough, including a WESCO logo that had been extracted from one of the company's websites and placed in the letterhead to make it look more official. When the fraudulent purchase order was sent, it was typically for between $30,000 and $60,000 and they would ask for net 30 terms. On a few occasions, multiple credit cards were used to pay for the order, but most of the time they were given a line of credit. If a credit application was sent to be filled out, the information was readily available. Since WESCO is a publicly traded company, the pertinent information could be gathered through one of the company's websites or through its prospectus.

"They tried to target salesmen versus management ... to dangle that nice commission for that guy out there," said Coe. "Once they got that initial purchase, it would quickly be followed by several other purchases of equal or greater value, but it would be the same type of items, almost identical. They would try to instill a sense of urgency by insisting that they needed the items yesterday and needed them shipped overnight to a particular address. Basically, they didn't care how much it would cost for them to ship it." Coe added, "They were counting on a degree of greed from the commissioned sales person and then they were also counting on this sense of urgency to keep those sales people from practicing due diligence."

To add to the convincing scheme, the fraudsters were armed with WESCO's Dun & Bradstreet number, which is also readily available, as well as some of WESCO's references. "The problem is some of the suppliers dealing with us on a regular basis would naturally send the products out," stated Coe. "They would not question it because we had already established lines of credit." Unfortunately, the lack of follow-through has cost some of the duped companies as much as $750,000, the result of a single salesman who hurriedly sent out product in anticipation of a big commission.

As usual, there were plenty of warning signs, but they were simply ignored. As Coe related, "The dollar tends to blind individuals to some of these obvious red flags." For example, after making an order, the fraudsters would provide a point of contact which was usually a residential address somewhere in the United States. And in every single case, the address was different than where the person making the call was supposedly located.

The sad truth is that the individuals that lived in the homes that these items were being shipped to were victims themselves. In some cases, they had met the criminals online in a chat room or some other virtual venue and had fallen in love with them. The fraudsters said that they needed a favor, and the love-struck individuals readily accepted. The perpetrators found others by trolling job search sites, and, knowing these people were in need of work, asked if they would like a position with WESCO as a "freight forwarder." The job was easy enough: the individuals could work from home accepting deliveries and all they had to do was re-label the boxes to have them shipped outside of the country. The fraudsters even got these people to pay for the overseas shipping charges out of their own pockets with the promise that any money they spent would be reimbursed. A little while back, WESCO had a series of checks sent out to suppliers stolen in transit. These were reproduced in a variety of different forms, and even sent as paychecks, just like a regular WESCO employee, to these duped "freight forwarders." Unfortunately, 10 to 12 days later, the bank would come back and inform them that the check was fictitious. But by then it was too late, the fraudsters had gotten to use these individuals and their homes for close to 40 days, with shipments arriving and being sent overnight. They had already moved on to their next victim.

"There were no arrests of these people because they were basically unaware of what they were doing," recounted Coe. The freight forwarders shipped the boxes to a legitimate importer/exporter in the United Kingdom, who then forwarded them on to Nigeria. From Nigeria, many items like toner and ink cartridges don't have serial numbers and are readily disposable. They then make their way back into the U.S. via Canada and Mexico and are reportedly sold at discount outlets. Computer supplies and peripherals aren't the only items to have been targeted.

Larger ticket items like earth-moving equipment from Caterpillar, diesel engines and diesel engine parts and LCD projectors have also been scammed.

Even WESCO itself has been a victim. A company that WESCO purchased was contacted by the fraudsters with the standard script. In an act of overzealousness, and wanting to show the new parent company that they could ship with the best of them, this newly acquired company shipped over $100,000 worth of product to the criminals. Fortunately, this worked to WESCO's advantage, to a degree. Since the company had all the tracking information, the Secret Service was able to trace the merchandise to locations in Washington State and Florida, where it had been forwarded to London. In London, the Secret Service had a detachment that went to the importer/exporter and located some of the boxes. Others had already been sent on to Nigeria. A short time after that, the Secret Service made two arrests of Nigerian nationals and confiscated tens of thousands of dollars worth of merchandise. The two men were incarcerated in Nigeria, as extradition to the United States is a tangled and complicated process.

Even more frustrating than its name being blighted said Coe is that WESCO has now become a mark. "The thing that I am more concerned about than anything else, and we've found this in the past couple weeks, is that we're seeing evidence that the fraudsters are impersonating other large companies and using their identities to target WESCO," explained Coe. "We've put out several fraud alerts to our people because I knew the other shoe was going to drop; it was just a matter of time before we would be a target."

Lessons Learned

The WESCO case, which is just one of a seemingly growing number, shows that there has to be greater due diligence on the part of everyone and, most importantly, sales staff. The Federal Trade Commission and the U.S. Secret Service do not keep statistics on how many companies are affected each year by these attacks, or how much money is ultimately lost. WESCO alone has had nearly 2,000 companies report receiving fraudulent purchase orders in its name. The company made a bold move by posting a security caution on its website informing any company that has even the slightest suspicion about an order to contact the company directly via telephone.

"I think that in putting something like that on our website shows we are concerned, not only about our business and our reputation, but also in trying to protect the public and our fellow distributors," said Coe.

The larger issue is how easily the fraudsters are able to perpetrate these scams and often how easily some individuals are fooled. "I could register www.cocacolacorp.com today, create a fake website and offer you a free case of Coke if you go to my website and give me personal information," said Tzanis. "I am sure it happens everyday via spam emails. But I doubt that spammers are specifically targeting companies that often. They will take what they can get."

Tzanis relayed information easily obtained from a public website that provided instructions on how to "spoof" emails and pose as an employee of a company. It also demonstrated how shockingly simple it was to perpetrate with even modest computer skills. "In the WESCO case, that person could have actually used the president's email address to send those 'spoofing' orders," explained Tzanis.

The onus is on all staff members to be vigilant.

"You really can't prevent this from happening. The only thing you can do is the security caution, which we did eventually," Coe said. When your company is a publicly traded Fortune 500, your company's information is out there, you can't prevent that and you can't prevent ID theft. "It's almost impossible," Coe said. "And it's not until you start getting the invoices or you start getting queries from third parties do you know that it's even occurring."

Legally, it's a difficult situation when a company's name is being used to defraud others. Enforcement oftentimes builds a case on substantiated loss. WESCO had to convince the Secret Service that the fraud posed a potential loss of reputation, which could be even more damaging in the long run. "Reputational damage is long-lasting," stated Coe. "Thousands of dollars in a loss is nothing versus the millions lost in a downtick of stock prices that can decimate a company."

Credit and sales staff have a variety of tools available to them. If an email with a suspicious originating web address is received, a simple search on registration sites like GoDaddy.com or a "Who Is" search on NetoworkSolutions.com will tell when a web address was registered, who the administrator is and where they're located. "Practice a modest amount of due diligence," recommended Tzanis. "Just run the address; just run the phone number. If you Google either and they're supposed to be from a well-known company but there's no match, then it's probably a scam."

"The first point is that if it sounds too good to be true, it probably is," added Coe. "I don't know if we'll ever be able to prevent it from happening. I think it's going to be more of an educational type of thing on the part of the potential victims. They are the ones that are going to have to look out for themselves, because it's going to happen and it continues to happen."

Reprinted from NACM's Business Credit magazine, June 2008. Originally written by Matthew Carr, former NACM staff writer.

13 Making Credit Decisions

OVERVIEW

The basic objective in making credit decisions is to find ways to approve an order with reasonable expectation that the customer will pay in accordance with established credit terms. A decision to grant or not to grant credit affects sales revenue, profit, production and procurement. If the customer is a good credit risk, the order may be approved as submitted. Otherwise, alternatives should be developed that are acceptable to the credit department and the sales department—and still meet the customer's needs.

It is desirable to establish routine procedures for making most credit decisions. Credit approval, through the use of order limits or overall credit limits, can streamline the workload in the credit department. The goal is to approve credit with minimum delay, provide customers with prompt service and control administrative costs. If routine orders can be processed quickly and efficiently, the credit professional has additional time to devote to more demanding credit matters. This chapter discusses approaches and decision factors associated with making credit decisions with speed, accuracy and efficiency.

THINK ABOUT THIS

Q. What influences when or how often a customer's credit file should be reviewed?

Q. When can it be beneficial to take on marginal business?

Q. What should be taken into consideration when approving credit for new customers?

Q. What factors influence the introduction, use and review of credit limits with customers?

Q. What constitutes marginal business, and how can marginal business be an essential component of a credit portfolio?

DISCIPLINARY CORE IDEAS

After reading this chapter, the reader should understand:

- ✓ Approval of credit for new customers.
- ✓ Establishing credit limits for customers.
- ✓ Available security devices.
- ✓ How credit scoring is used to help manage credit.
- ✓ Credit approval for marginal credit accounts.
- ✓ Making credit decisions using limited customer information.
- ✓ Conducting reviews of credit limits.

CHAPTER OUTLINE

Accounts for New Customers

Introduction

All orders should be processed as quickly as possible, particularly first orders from new customers. Prompt handling of initial orders often means continuing sales. Many credit grantors take a conservative approach with initial orders, unless the customer's reputation and history are such that credit risk is not an issue. Under certain circumstances, the Equal Credit Opportunity Act (ECOA) requires notification of an adverse action in connection with an application for credit. Depending on the applicant's gross revenue, the creditor must notify the applicant either orally or in writing within 30 days or within a reasonable amount of time. The same procedures for approving initial orders from new customers can also be used for established business customers that have not purchased for some time. When processing first orders, or sporadic orders from existing customers, there are several issues to consider:

- How much credit is required?
- What is the profit margin on the product being sold?
- Does the customer have the resources to pay? Is the use of trade credit for convenience as designed, or is the trade creditor being used as a substitute for a bank loan?
- When will the customer pay? Does the customer's history suggest that, regardless of creditworthiness, there might be a potential risk of slow-pay, dispute or litigation?
- If the customer does not currently have resources to pay timely, is it likely that the customer will have them by the time payment is due?
- How much credit do other vendors offer this customer, and is the request in line with like suppliers?

Approval of Small Initial Orders

If initial orders are small, the time and expense of a credit investigation may be unjustified. Automatic credit approval may be established for all orders that fall below a specified amount. This system might be considered *criteria-based,* meaning that one or more decisive factors are used to automate credit approval. In this case, the criteria would be the maximum amount of credit all new customers receive without investigation. Criteria-based automated credit approval should be guided by the credit grantor's credit policy and should be reviewed from time to time according to market conditions, the effect of competition, credit terms, loss experience and other elements. While individual losses will occur, the impact of extra collection expenses on overall results can be reduced by accelerating the collection procedure, writing off non-performing or under-performing accounts, or placing them with third-parties for collection. Follow-through is an important requirement of an automated approval system. Small first orders may be trial shipments that could lead to long-term, profitable relationships. The automated approval system might suggest criteria for sales personnel to include an estimate of the customer's potential credit requirements, thereby initiating a credit investigation to determine credit ability of the customer in preparation for larger orders from the customer in the future.

> **Comprehension Check**
> Some companies establish a way to automatically approve small orders. Supply a justification of this policy.

Approval Based on Credit Reporting Agency Ratings and Scores

Another method of handling initial and future orders without extensive investigation is to use credit report scores as the basis for the amount to be approved. This method of approving orders provides the following advantages:

- Documentation of actions taken.
- Little or no need for exhaustive investigation for each account when it falls within set criteria.
- Efficient use of time for other, more exacting duties.

- Exceptions to the policy or marginal cases are more easily identified and can be examined carefully by the credit department.

Many companies have developed a credit scoring system and initial order limit based on key factors such as third-party credit scores, clear bankruptcy history and clear public records.

Non-Routine First Orders

If a first order fails to meet the requirements for streamlined approval, the decision to investigate may rest on the answers to the following questions:

- Is the order large enough to warrant the cost of investigation?
- Is the potential for future sales large enough to merit a full credit analysis?
- Is the treatment of non-routine orders covered by company policy?

Terms Other than Open Account

If the circumstances do not warrant open account credit, the sale may be made on some other basis, such as cash in advance, cash on delivery, sight draft, certified check, cashier's or bank check, or standby letter of credit. Of these methods of payment, only a cashier's or bank check and standby letter of credit can guarantee payment, because in these instances the bank's credit is substituted for the customer's.

A payment on a certified check can technically be stopped for just cause by the customer, and many banks are encouraging their depositors to use bank checks instead of certified checks.

Cash on delivery can be troublesome if the cash is not available when delivery is attempted. If materials are produced especially for the buyer and are not salable through other outlets, the buyer's refusal to accept delivery could create additional costs or even cause total loss to the seller. In such cases, if the credit risk is not acceptable, the seller may want to ask for full cash payment in advance. Even on goods that are not perishable, terms other than open account, except for cashier's or bank checks and letters of credit, may expose the seller to the risk of paying for such expenses as round-trip transportation, repacking and losses in transit if the buyer refuses to accept delivery. This risk should be considered in evaluating the prospect.

Credit Availability and Limits for New/Existing/Repeat Customers

Purpose

As soon as possible after first-order approval, controls should be established to ensure prompt and appropriate disposition of further orders. The basic means of control is the credit limit or maximum amount of risk to be taken on any customer.

While credit limits should not limit sales potential, a company must ask itself two key questions: How much exposure is it willing to take with its customer base? Will it be liberal or conservative in its credit granting philosophy?

Difference between Credit Line and Credit Limit

The description "credit line" is sometimes used when "credit limit" is meant. The two terms are not the same because a **credit line** *implies that credit has been committed or will be granted up to a specific amount usually for a given period of time, as in the case of a bank line of credit.* A **credit limit** *indicates that a credit grantor retains discretion over the granting of credit.* In other words, a credit limit is the maximum amount that a seller is willing to risk in an account.

Comprehension Check
What is the difference between **credit line** and **credit limit**?

A maximum dollar amount is placed on orders that can be made or accumulated on open account credit, without promise or commitment to reserve a certain amount of purchase money in that amount at any time.

Underlying Factors

A **customer's credit limit** *is usually based on the requirements for the supplier's products and the ability of the customer to pay its debts. Other factors include the seller's credit policy, demand for the product, the size and financial condition of the buyer and seller, and the extent of competition.* In all cases, the ability of the customer to pay its debts must be evaluated by an analysis of:

- Financial information.
- Agency ratings, reports and credit scores.
- Bank checks.
- Trade clearances and other data as warranted.

A new customer's requirements can often be estimated by the sales staff at the time the initial order is placed, or the credit professional may be able to determine the customer's credit requirements through direct contact with the customer. A customer that furnishes all information requested by the credit department is usually considered less of a risk than one who is not accommodating.

Influences on Credit Decisions for the Credit Grantor

Profit Margin

For the credit grantor, net profit margins on the products or services sold are a significant factor in the decisions about how much and when to grant credit to its customer base. Company credit policies are generally closely correlated with profit margins, as described below. (*See* Figure 13-1 for additional details about profit margins.)

1. If the profit margin on a particular product is high, the seller can afford to accept a greater credit risk and make more credit available.
2. If the company's credit policy is conservative and profit margins are slim, credit limits may be more restrictive.
3. If demand for a company's product is greater than its production capacity or if there is an industry-wide supply shortage, sales may be made primarily to the most select class of customers, with credit limits to marginal customers curtailed.

Consideration must always be given to the long-term supply outlook for products the credit grantor sells. Greater credit risks may be taken when a credit grantor operates under one or more of the following:

- High overhead which demands increased production for profitability.
- A highly competitive market which affects profit margin by meeting the competition.
- Introduction of a new product line or expansion into a new territory/market means higher expenses.
- Product sales that require major capital investment such as equipment and/or fixed assets.

Figure 13-1   Lost Profits

The table below demonstrates what happens when a company with a net margin of profit of 2% does not collect $5,000 in accounts receivable. The sales force must make up that loss by selling $250,000 in products or services in order for the company to "break even" on the loss of $5,000. This means more time and expense are associated with staying even than can be exercised in getting ahead. This does not take into account the necessary efforts to collect each new sale within credit terms. In common vernacular, this scenario could be called "spinning your wheels."

If you have an actual loss of:	and your net profit is:				
	2%	3%	4%	5%	6%
	you will require this amount in additional sales to offset the loss:				
$300	$15,000	$10,000	$7,500	$6,000	$5,000
500	25,000	16,666	12,500	10,000	8,333
1,000	50,000	33,333	25,000	20,000	16,667
3,000	150,000	100,000	75,000	60,000	50,000
5,000	250,000	166,666	125,000	100,000	83,333

Terms of Sale Influence Credit Limits

Financial exposure is greater when credit terms are longer. A credit limit of $10,000 might be adequate for a company purchasing $5,000 per week on terms of net 10 days. But if the terms were net 60 days, a much larger limit would be required. The credit limit is also influenced by the collection effort that may be required. The seller must determine if sufficient personnel, time and information are available to follow a large number of high-risk accounts. If such factors are inadequate, lower limits most likely should be set. In the final analysis, profits on the good sales should exceed losses on the bad sales. A high bad-debt record is not necessarily the mark of poor credit judgment because it may be an indication that excellent credit judgment is being used to maximize net profit. On the other hand, low bad-debt losses with a high record of order refusals could be an indication that the credit policy is actually inhibiting sales efforts and restricting net profit. A certain amount of bad-debt loss has to be anticipated and should be acceptable to management.

> **Comprehension Check**
> Explain how the profit margin and terms of sale of the selling company influence credit decisions.

Establishing Credit Limits

Credit-granting companies establish their credit limits based on factors that represent their own set of unique circumstances, policies, conditions, etc. No two companies are the same and no two sets of policy are the same. Some factors to be considered are:

Competition. In this method, the amount of the credit limit is determined by matching the amount (or average amount) granted by like or similar competitors. Outside reports and other credit information sources are used to identify competitive limits. If the creditor is not the same size as comparable competitors or plays a distinctly different supply role (much larger or smaller), it will be difficult to establish reasonable credit limits using this method.

By Formula. In this method, several calculations are made and averaged to determine the credit limit to be assigned to the customer. Key financial data, such as net worth, inventory, current assets and/or net working capital are used, assuming the customer accommodates the credit grantor's request for information. These data items are divided by the number of creditors to determine the amount per creditor. Amounts are then averaged to set the credit limit. It may be difficult to obtain an accurate estimate of the number of creditors. This method is often used to calculate a preliminary estimate and is then further developed by one or more of the other methods.

Payment Record. The credit limit can fluctuate depending on the customer's ability to pay on terms. This has the advantage of making credit decisions more routine, unless the customer does not pay on time, when a more detailed credit review process would be triggered. This type of limit encourages additional sales and is popular with sales staff.

Payment Performance. This popular method adopts a conservative risk management approach and rewards new customers as they continue to do business with the company. This is often used when little payment history is available. While limiting the company's exposure, it does limit the speed at which sales can grow.

Period of Time. Purchases made over a specific period of time, such as a week or month, cannot exceed the credit limit. This is useful in cases where many shipments may be made to a customer from various company locations. Orders can be approved in a more routine manner using this method, as long as the overall credit provided does not exceed the credit limit.

Expectation of Use. Sometimes referred to as requirements, this method sets a credit limit based on the expected dollar volume of credit sales over a period of time (i.e., a year). This figure is then divided by the number of orders expected throughout the year to estimate the credit limit. This method, like the formula method, is often used to obtain a preliminary estimate that can be defined further by one or more of the other methods.

Agency Scoring and Ratings. This method may be used for new or existing customers to assess risk and determine credit limits. Figure 13-2 details NTCR and D&B rating guidelines.

Comprehension Check

Discuss three common methods used to establish a credit limit.

Figure 13-2   Agency Scoring and Ratings

NTCR Predictive Score

Predictive Score is based on the unique tradelines gathered by NACM Affiliates. The scoring model predicts late payments and severe delinquency looking forward six months. The predictive variables include current aging status, historical aging (including trends and variance in payment trends) and other business characteristics. From the data on hundreds of thousands of businesses, common characteristics are examined on the business subject and, depending on how closely or remotely that subject matches the characteristics, the score is assigned a range, from high risk to low risk. In cases where not enough data exists, no score is assigned. If the business subject is already delinquent to the degree that the score is trying to predict, no score is assigned in the low to high range because there is no need to predict something that has already occurred. Each report contains a complete credit score explanation. The Predictive Score ranges from 450 (high risk) to 850 (low risk). The Risk Class includes 1 (low risk), 2, 3, 4A, 4B and 5 (very high risk). The score leverages 12 months of historical trade data to predict future behavior.

D&B Viability Rating

Viability Score assesses the probability that a company will no longer be in business within the next 12 months compared to all U.S. businesses within the D&B database. The Viability Score is best used when ranking all businesses within a portfolio especially for identifying the most valuable prospects for sales and marketing. The score ranges from 9 (high risk) to 1 (low risk).

Portfolio Comparison compares a company to businesses assigned a similar D&B "model segment" classification which is determined by the amount and type of data available. The four model segment types include: Available Financial Data, Established Trade Payments, Limited Trade Payments and Firmographics (a set of characteristics of organizations which are most likely to spend money on your product or service) & Business Activity. This score analyzes the risk level of a business for credit risk management purposes. The score ranges from 9 (high risk) to 1 (low risk).

Data Depth Indicator represents the level of predictive data available for a company. This indicator is based on a scale from A to G where A indicates the greatest level of predictive data, such as financial statements, and G reflects a minimal level of data, such as firmographics only.

Company Profile describes a company based on a combination of five categories: Financial Data Available, Number of Trade Payments, Company Size, Years in Business and Firmographic Data. The five categories are rated based on: not available, available (3+ trades), medium and established.

Credit Scoring*

Scoring to assign credit limits is a popular tool of credit analysis. Companies identify the factors they consider most meaningful and create a scoring matrix to increase efficiency in making routine decisions and to determine the creditworthiness of a customer. A **credit score model** can be built to include internal information or a combination of internal and external information such as business and personal credit information on the principals. Such models *convert available data about a customer to a statistical number (scale) based on influencing elements including NAICS code, payment history, principal information, financial data, outside credit information, etc.* Credit scores make credit decisions data driven and less reliant upon subjectivity.

The variables are input into a computer model, which assigns them point values creating a scoring matrix. According to Charles L. Gahala in his book *Credit Management, Principles and Practices*, credit scoring can be based upon any of three different approaches to developing the scoring model:

1. **Behavioral Models.** These models require a significant pool of customers' records that are carefully analyzed to identify factors that can be used as predictive variables. With the use of statistical predictability, these models allow identifying the relevant tradeoffs or correlations among factors and assigns statistically derived weights, which constitute the base of the scoring model.

2. **Rules-Based Models.** These models are based on traditional standards of credit analysis and they require a set of simplistic rules. Factors such as the business's payment history, bank and trade references, credit agency ratings (such as D&B rating), number of years in business, and financial ratios are scored and weighted to produce an overall credit score.

   The decision of which factors to use, and how each of these factors will be scored and weighted, is generally based on the credit executive's past experience with their company, the products or services offered, and the industry that the company is in. For this reason, these models are also known as **Judgmental Models**, and are enhanced by benchmarking industry financial profiles with peer groups, and by the use of factors that reflect the company's policies and individual's characteristics .

3. **Neural Models.** Artificial Neural Networks (ANNs) or Neural Network Models are "distributed information-processing systems composed of many simple interconnected nodes inspired biologically by the neurons of the human brain." These models employ "the parallel processing of math-based historical experiences and logic-based patterns." ANNs have emerged effectively in credit scoring because of their ability to model non-linear relationship between a set of inputs and a set of outputs.

The Use of an Internal Credit Scoring Model

Banks and credit card companies were the first to use credit scoring models due to the high volume of low amount transactions involved in consumer credit. Credit scoring became a necessity for these financial institutions to approve and service their clients in a cost-effective and timely manner. Today, most retail credit decisions are taken automatically on the basis of statistically derived models that score consumer behavior.

For commercial credit underwriting, the use of scoring models as a tool can also be beneficial. However, it can have a negative impact if it is overestimated over human judgment. Businesses often use scoring models as a platform for building an overall view of the customer, which will become a basis for forming a credit decision, like establishing a payment term and amount of credit, frequency of credit monitoring, delegation of authority, and approving credit limits.

The Pros of Credit Scoring Models

1. **Increase speed and reduce response time.** The use of models allows credit professionals to evaluate borrowers faster, and consequently reduce their response time to customers. In addition, models can be easily modified to either ease or restrict credit granting depending on the company's strategies.

2. **Quantify risk and improve management control.** Credit scoring allows the credit professionals to quantify risk, and to fine tune credit risk guidelines over time. It also allows credit professionals to put a limit on the amount of risk the company is willing to take based on the company's risk appetite corresponding to each risk category.

3. **Consistency, accuracy and objectivity.** The use of a scoring model generates consistency in data gathering and decision-making, minimizing the subjective component that results from humans weighing factors according to personal experiences, and in many cases, the personal relationship developed with customers. When efficiently used, a well-structured credit rating system helps the credit monitoring functions to have consistent check on credit assessment. A company that has multiple credit functions can achieve consistency in its methodology by adopting a credit scoring.

4. **Reduce personnel and credit investigation costs.** The use of credit scoring can reduce the need for research, verification, analysis, and the elaboration of reports, resulting in fewer personnel costs.

5. **Decision support and planning tools.** Credit scoring also enables the credit professional to assess the quality of the accounts receivable portfolio, and take preventive actions and/or adjust policies accordingly. It can also be used to forecast bad debt reserves based on the past bad debt experience for customers falling within each risk category.

6. **Prioritization of collection activities and reduced bad debt loses.** Credit risk scores facilitate the development of collection strategies for low-, medium- and high-risk customers because the credit scores can quickly identify high-risk customers.

7. **Comply with audit mandates.** Scoring provides a sound basis for consistent processes which makes compliance with regulations such as the Sarbanes-Oxley Act, and the Antitrust laws easier.

8. **Knowledge transfer mechanism.** A credit scoring model can be developed to replicate a proven decision-making process which can be shared and utilized by new staff.

9. **Ease of implementation.** A credit scoring model that is rules-based can be developed in-house using the company's credit policies and decision processes without requiring the services of a costly third party to create and maintain the model.

The Cons of Credit Scoring Models

1. **Qualitative factors and situation-specific judgment.** Credit scoring models limit the use of subjective factors, such as the customer's management team, its strategy and/or competitive position, exposure to litigation, etc. There is a chance that making a sale to a favorable customer based on qualitative factors may be missed, if decision is solely based on the credit score.

2. **Dependency and lack of judgment.** In some cases, scoring models can cause credit professionals to only rely on the credit score and make poor credit decisions.

3. **Insufficient and/or heterogeneous pool of customers.** In order for statistical models to work effectively, the pool of customers must have similar characteristics to consistently predict behaviors.

4. **Obsolescence of historical information.** Due to the rapid changes that have taken place in the last 10 to 15 years, past events may be less relevant to predict the future and obsolete data may provoke statistical errors.

5. **Statistical Difficulties.** One of the challenges encountered by credit professionals is the selection of predictable variables and weighting of predictable variables that will be utilized in the model. There is also a challenge if data is not sufficient to establish behaviors.

> **Comprehension Check**
> Explain credit scoring techniques and the pros and cons for their use.

Other Factors to Consider in the Credit Decision Process

In commercial lending, the decision to grant credit based on a credit scoring system alone may not consider other factors that may significantly impact the credit risk determination of accounts. Judgment should be exercised by considering the following additional factors:

- Country risk.
- Appetite for risk.
- Willingness to pay.
- Age of credit and financial data used for credit scoring.
- Potential of customer.
- Competitor's action.
- Notes to financial statements.
- News reports, periodical articles, etc.
- Weather patterns.
- Credit insurance.

*Excerpted from the NACM Graduate School of Credit and Financial Management project, 2015.

Implementing Credit Limit Decisions

Credit limits serve a variety of purposes: as a guideline for order approval, to minimize upward spiral of orders and to call immediate attention to any change in a customer's purchasing or payment behavior. Any order that does not exceed the limit can be approved without further investigation or analysis. Orders exceeding the limit signal the need for examination of the account and may lead to holding shipments to the customer until the over-limit situation has been resolved.

Some companies would rather not establish a firm credit limit, opting instead for a flexible limit based on previous experience with the account. Flexible limits have the advantage of being easy to implement with little impact to the customer and the sales department. Unless payments are not made on time there may be little need for further involvement at the credit department level.

Those who favor a more formal system of establishing credit limits point out that the account may become overvalued quickly. Prompt payments initially are not necessarily indicative of future payment trends.

A formal analysis might set a credit limit high enough to eliminate the need for a review every time a new order is received. However, after a period of time, the credit limit may simply become a matter of course, meaning that any order the customer places is approved. This basis for credit decisions should be reserved for only very substantial and financially sound customers.

An **order limit** *specifies the dollar amount that may be released without delay on any single order.* It differs from a credit limit, which is established without regard to the size of any particular order and is generally set at an amount that can be justified by the available credit information. Some companies place an order limit on every account. This usually serves as a secondary credit check, so the customer's file is reviewed when either the credit limit or order limit is exceeded. An order limit may be particularly useful in a decentralized credit organization where it is impractical for order processing points to keep complete records of receivables.

One variation of the credit limit is based upon the amount that the creditor is willing to have outstanding at any time. This method requires complete records of unpaid invoices and of orders approved but not yet shipped. When the total outstanding balance exceeds the limit, any further orders are referred for approval.

Credit Limit Management

Companies will often create their own in-house forms with formulas which reflect their company's tolerance for risk. Some of the forms are created in Excel and are manually populated and routed for approvals. Other companies have invested in ERP solutions which provide electronic workflow documents to increase or decrease a customer's credit limit, as well as route the documents through several layers of management, depending on the requested credit limit amount and risk class of the customer. Generally, different levels of management approvals are required before credit limits are assigned to customer accounts. For example, if a credit limit is over a certain level, the credit analyst is the final approver. If the credit limit is above the first level, but below a higher level, the credit manager is the final approver, and if the limit is over the highest threshold, the treasurer, CFO or executive credit committee is the final approver. Credit limit form formulas will provide the credit analyst with a recommended credit limit sufficient for the opening order and ongoing purchases, according to the payment terms, time frame and volume of purchases, and in line with the customer's risk class, payment history, trade volume, etc.

Communicating Credit Limit Decisions

Many companies advise their sales department of the credit limits assigned to customers, often expressing the limits in terms of units (300 tons, 20 carloads) or dollars allowed during a given period of time. If, for example, a customer has a credit limit of $5,000 on terms of 1/10, net/30 and consistently discounts, this customer could be

---

Real World Perspectives

RWP 13-1

FIVE BIGGEST MISTAKES B2B CREDIT MANAGERS MAKE

Credit managers must balance the conflicting needs of revenue and business credit. But there are core best practices which are universal to all our efforts to bring the money in. Below are five mistakes credit and collection professionals make and how to fix them.

1. **Not giving reasons for your credit decisions.** Credit professionals should verbalize their well-thought-out, sound reasons to the stakeholders when presenting the bad news. Too many credit professionals impose, rather than sell their credit and collection decisions. When someone simply says "no," even if they have the authority, their credibility and reasoning can be questioned. If decisions are always supported with facts, data and experience, then stakeholders will come to understand that the decisions are based on sound judgment.

2. **Not meeting folks halfway.** Rarely are credit decisions black and white. There are situations where credit professionals need to stick to their assessment and give solid reasons for the decision. However, most day-to-day credit decisions exist in a grey area where company exposure can be controlled by limiting credit lines, modifying terms of payment, or allowing other functional groups to take a portion of the financial risk. Collaboration with other stakeholders can make all the difference between a new business partnership and no revenue.

3. **Operating in a silo.** No department or function can operate in a vacuum. A company is made up of individuals who work in groups, and they must rely on each other as if it is a living ecosystem. Hold weekly meetings with staff; have weekly meetings with direct stakeholders. Get out of the office/cube and visit with internal customers, who know who and what problems may emerge.

4. **Focusing solely on bottom-line savings, while ignoring top-line growth.** Credit and collection managers have a reputation for wanting to collect all of the receivables on every sale, at the expense of not making every sale. Credit professionals must find a balance between the two: develop a certain appetite for risk that is based on historical bad debt expense, as well as current data and information regarding the true financial health of the customer in both the short and medium range; long-term financial health is something that can be managed throughout the life of the customer relationship. It is dynamic and always changing. To keep it all in check, put strong processes and procedures in place to monitor exposure and periodically evaluate current and future risk.

5. **Not identifying the root cause of collection issues.** What's stopping the money from coming in the door? There's always a reason invoices aren't getting paid. Typically, the least common of these reasons is a customer's cash flow; the most common reason for non-payment (or late payment) is that the invoice is incorrect or not in a "format" that the customer can use. The ultimate goal of any order-to-cash process is to make the customer happy and to allow them to be a self-payer. In other words, don't provide customers any excuse not to pay the bill; this needs to be a constant driver for every organization and is one that requires a great deal of collaboration and diplomacy between the various order-to-cash stakeholders.

George Waters, Global B2B Credit Professional, Published on LinkedIn July 2016

---

sold from $10,000 to $15,000 per month. Because of discount payments, the highest credit would still be expected to remain within the credit limit of $5,000.

Informing Customers of Credit Limits

There is considerable debate about whether to inform customers of their credit limits. There is no law or regulation that requires such compliance. Of course, a credit grantor cannot discriminate when approving credit, and certain rules apply whenever an adverse action is taken either upon approval or after the account has been established. Review the ECOA rules when facing these circumstances.

In some companies, the credit limit is the maximum amount that will be shipped to the customer before initiating a review of the credit file for that customer. In other companies, it is simply the maximum amount that will be shipped to the customer before that amount is paid down or paid in full. The particular definition depends on the creditor's policy regarding credit extension. There are distinct advantages and disadvantages of advising customers of credit limits. The decision to advise or not to advise is dependent on each creditor's company policy and management philosophy. Here are some advantages and disadvantages to consider:

Advantages

- Opportunity to discuss and possibly adjust the limit in order to sell more.
- Opens discussion about payment expectations and to obtain more information.
- Reduces embarrassment of holding orders when/if customer is over limit.
- Creates a chance to help a marginal customer become more solvent.

Disadvantages

- Possibly damages goodwill.
- May restrict purchases to the credit limit imposed.
- Customer may be offended/insulted by what it perceives to be an insufficient credit limit.
- Raises questions as to how or why the credit limit was determined.

Security Instruments and Actions against Default

- **Guarantee.** An instrument containing a promise by a person, persons or company to pay or perform an obligation owed in the event the debtor does not pay or perform. It can take the form of a personal or corporate guarantee.
- **Cross-Corporate Guarantee (CCG).** This ties a parent company to a subsidiary. *Action: If the subsidiary does not pay, the parent company will pay.*
- **Irrevocable Letter of Credit.** This substitutes a bank's credit for that of the customer. It allows the supplier to initiate a draft against the letter of credit upon delivery of goods.
- **Subordination Agreement.** This agreement can improve a supplier's priority position by establishing a higher priority claim to the customer's assets, especially if a significant portion of a customer's debt is owed to officers or stockholders.
- **Security Agreements.** *Action: Request security documents, such as bond forms for construction, before creating a new account.*
- **Financing Statements.** Article 9 of the Uniform Commercial Code, titled Secured Transactions, deals with the creation of security interests in personal property. The most common forms are inventory, accounts receivable and equipment. *Action: These can be used to secure* **inventory**. *They can be filed in conjunction with a Purchase Money Security Agreement or Interest (PMSA or PMSI). A PMSI is a security interest or claim on property that enables a supplier to have a priority ranking on their products ahead of other secured creditors. It allows the suppliers to repossess the products sold to the customer should that customer default on their payments.*

- **Mechanic's Lien.** A statutory lien on a building (and usually the land it occupies) in favor of suppliers of material and contractors to secure their interest on a particular construction project. *Action: Follow the statutory requirements of each state for filing liens.*
- **Notice to Owner (NTO).** *Action: Follow state guidelines for NTO schedules as they vary by state.*
- **Payment and Performance Bonds.** *Action: Before relying on a payment bond, the supplier should send a letter to the bonding company to confirm the existence of the bond and learn its coverage with respect to the material. Since the type of project and the notification rules vary substantially, questions should be referred to the legal department through the chief credit professional.*
- **Bond Claims.** They are usually provided by the General Contractor (GC), especially if it is a public job. Occasionally, the sub-contractors under the GC will have to provide their own bonds, but other times the sub-contractors work under the umbrella of the GC. *Action: Follow the state guidelines for bond deadlines because these vary by state.*
- **Joint Check Agreements (JCA).** A joint check agreement is a device whereby the ultimate user or beneficiary of material supplied by an original seller agrees with the original seller and its supplier to make all payments to the supplier by checks payable to both the seller and the supplier. *Action: When the General Contractor (GC) pays the sub-contractor for materials, the GC writes the check to the sub and seller's company. The sub endorses the check and forwards the check to seller for deposit. This check does not include labor and is for materials only. Sometimes the GC wants to use their own form, but the seller's can use their own form as well.*
- **Real Estate Mortgages (Deeds of Trust).** Sometimes a customer will offer a first or second real estate mortgage (deed of trust) as security for open account arrangements. *Action: This can be an effective method of securing an account but a number of factors must be considered, such as determining the value of the property, the marketability of the property, liens and encumbrances on the property, the payoff on the first mortgage, and whether the first mortgage permits a second mortgage.*
- **Job Contracts.** They are terms of sales for specific job. *Action: Sales usually handles these, but they can be handled by the credit manager.*
- **Accounts Receivable (A/R) Insurance.** This is a form of credit insurance offered by commercial insurers to businesses. A/R insurance can take the form of multi-buyer insurance (a pool of receivables) or key buyer insurance. *Action: The cost-benefit must be weighed. A/R insurance can be particularly useful for new or rapidly growing businesses that cannot afford to do credit checks. For a relatively low fee, A/R insurance protects a company against loss on receivables, including default, bankruptcy or simply slow payment.*

Comprehension Check
List some available security devices.

Handling Marginal Business

General Considerations

Marginal customers *fall short of expectations and present an abnormal risk even when full information is available.* Many companies define marginal risks as having one or more typical characteristics:

- Management can be either inexperienced or lack depth and succession planning.
- Finances are inadequate. Companies are not adequately capitalized for their transaction volume or are not generating sufficient profits.
- Payments are slow. Terms of sale are not observed, requiring extra collection efforts.
- Merchandise is bought in too small quantities and/or provides low profitability.

RWP 13-2

Real World Perspectives

THE ONE THAT GOT AWAY

I had worked for a company as credit manager for less than a month when we received an order for $3.1 million from a customer with a credit limit of $500,000 and a high credit of less than $400,000. I updated the credit report and went to meet with my boss, the division CFO, and his boss, the general manager (GM). I explained that there was not enough information on file to justify releasing the order pending. I was told to make arrangements to fly out the next day—if possible—to meet with the customer to try to qualify the account for a $3.1 million credit limit.

After meeting with the customer's CFO and reviewing the customer's financial statements, which were weak and showed a significant downward trend, I was convinced that there was no way that the order pending could be released on open account terms. I shared my insights, observations and concerns with the CFO and GM as soon as I returned to the office. They thanked me for my efforts and my input, and then the GM instructed me to release the order anyway. In response, I sent him an email with a copy to my manager. In part, it said:

> "As you instructed in our meeting this morning, I have released the order pending for $3.1 million for production and shipment. I remain concerned about the possibility of default and will keep you informed of any problems involving this customer."

Approximately 50 days later, the customer filed for Chapter 11 bankruptcy protection still owing the $3.1 million—making our company the single largest unsecured creditor. On a dotted line basis, I reported to the corporate treasurer, and when he was notified of a potential $3.1 million loss, he told me to fly out and meet him ASAP to discuss this problem—and to bring the credit file.

The treasurer started the meeting by telling me that this was one of the largest bad debt losses the company had ever incurred. He added that he was disappointed and deeply concerned that the loss had occurred less than three months after I was hired. In response, I produced from the credit file my trip summary memorandum, which read in part:

> "There is no safe way to make this sale. The only reason to do so would be if our need for this $3.1 million in sales exceeds our concerns about a potential $3.1 million loss."

The second document I handed him was a copy of my email confirming the general manager's verbal instructions to release the order pending. In total, the meeting lasted about 10 minutes. The treasurer thanked me for making the trip, and instructed me to leave the credit file with him and to take the next day, a Friday, off. The following Monday, the general manager was fired and the CFO was given an opportunity to accept early retirement. I continued to work for that company for more than five years before leaving for greener pastures, but this incident was never discussed with me again.

What is the moral of the story? **Document, document, document!** Document your decision-making process, and *always* document management overrides. You never know when adequate documentation might save your job.

Michael C. Dennis, MBA, CBF

- Orders often exceed predetermined credit limits.
- The customer has a low composite credit score.

Marginal customers may be a necessary and important source of business. Those with good growth prospects offer an excellent opportunity for a supplier to make profitable sales, despite the fact that credit requests are high in relation to net worth. A well-balanced receivables portfolio should include a percentage of marginal accounts because they satisfy the need for additional business in a specific market. A supplier that has excess production capacity or needs a wider market base should be willing to take a greater credit risk. This is especially true when the better customers have absorbed fixed costs, and marginal accounts are required only to cover incremental or out-of-pocket costs.

Comprehension Check
List and discuss the characteristics of a **marginal account.**

Profit Issues

Profit on incremental sales to marginal customers may materially improve the earnings of the business, even allowing for increased credit losses. Assume a company is operating at less than capacity. If all of its fixed costs and acceptable profit are covered at present levels of production, any increase in output would only require expenditure for the direct, out-of-pocket costs of the additional sales. If these make up 40 percent of the selling price, the remaining 60 percent would be profit. Any incremental sales that sustained less than 60 percent bad-debt losses would increase the company's profit. A number of factors related to profit margins may influence the decision to sell to marginal accounts. A seller with a wider profit margin can afford to take greater credit risks. The higher the prospective customer's profit, the fewer units it must sell to pay its supplier. Disposition of the customer's profit should also be considered. As the marginal account customer reinvests its earnings during good times, its improved financial condition tends to ensure its continued existence.

Other Decision Factors

Product distribution affects the credit decision on marginal business. When new products are being promoted or when new distribution channels are being developed, marginal risks offer the seller an opportunity to maximize effectiveness. Alternative outlets must also be considered. Selling to one of a few marginal accounts may be considerably more economical than handling hundreds of direct retailer or manufacturer accounts. It may be constructive to refuse credit to a marginal risk and explore the possibility of selling to alternative outlets that present a more attractive financial picture. Obsolete or slow-moving inventory may be better sold to a marginal risk than disposed of or written off. Protective measures such as guarantees or security agreements perfected under the Uniform Commercial Code may reduce risk. Terms shorter than standard terms, COD, part cash in advance and cash before delivery may also be considered.

Comprehension Check
Why can selling to a marginal account be important to a business?

Decisions Based on Limited Information

Reasons for Limited Information

Credit information is readily available from many sources, and normal investigation usually produces adequate data for sound credit evaluation. Despite this, a credit department is sometimes obliged to act upon limited information—such as when a customer refuses to supply customary banking and trade references or financial details. Bank and trade reports can be gathered independently but with delays and greater cost. When customers refuse to supply information, their reasons should be ascertained. It is often possible to work out a basis upon which they will furnish adequate information. For example, financial data are sometimes refused because "we don't want our competition to know what we're doing." Assurances of confidential handling may satisfy this objection.

Time is of the essence and the urgency for credit action does not permit normal investigation. If the credit professional can find no way to obtain adequate information within the time available, the decision must be made on whatever information can be gathered. Unless the business is new, a payment record is almost always available. Perhaps full information is not available due to recent formation of the business or inadequate records kept by the customer. Here, the principals' past business records may be more important than financial details of the business itself. If historic information is lacking, credit grantors should proceed with caution. Sales may ask credit not to press

---

Real World Perspectives

ASK AND YE SHALL RECEIVE

I worked for 12 years at a small manufacturing business. When it was sold, I found myself looking for another position in credit. I was open to trying something new and different, and I went to work at a Big 7 accounting firm managing its receivables. I found myself in a different world!

This company had offices all over the country and internationally as well. I had a lot to learn. It became obvious that accountants are a little different in the way they think about and collect their receivables. The ones with the largest clients became partners, and these partners would do nothing that might offend their clients.

My first challenge was the New York office—the largest billing office of the firm. I had heard horror stories about how the partners there would allow no one to collect their money. So I booked my flight (Did I mention I live in a small town in North Carolina?), pulled out my best black business suit and headed to the "Big Apple."

The office on Madison Avenue was very impressive; the partners were so nice and seemed to welcome my help. Okay, not all of them, but one in particular had a major client that brought in millions. I gasped when I looked at the receivables and found that $500K was over five years old! In my old job, no money went uncollected, much less $500K.

When asked, the partner confessed that he had inherited this client, and that they were unlikely to pay because of the age of the invoices. Of course, this drove me crazy. Can you imagine my frustration? I humbly asked if I might try to collect this money. Literally, he wrung his hands, agreed, but made me promise not to upset them. UPSET *them*!

I began to prepare for my meeting with this important client, gathering time records, billing information—everything I could put my hands on. This went on for a couple of months. The information was professionally bound into a beautiful book—I was going in armed with everything I needed. Finally, the appointment was made.

The partner declined to attend the meeting. Big surprise; he had such *pressing matters* that day. For backup, I decided to take the tax administrator instead. I painstakingly briefed her on how we would handle it—who would present the information, what kind of deal we would cut and so on.

Let me set the scene as it was on that fateful day. In my best black suit again, I grabbed a taxi and headed down to the client's office. We rode the elevator and stopped on the top floor—the penthouse, no less. We were ushered into the main conference room and offered a wide selection of beverages. As we waited for the VP of Finance, I gazed out the window at the Statue of Liberty. What a view!

The VP arrived, and I told him we had $500K outstanding and that we would like to get that paid. He asked a few questions. (I had my hand on the beautiful, professionally bound book, ready to spring it on him.) Then he looked at me and said, "I will have my accounting department write you a check. You should have it by the end of the month."

My mouth must have dropped open—could it really be that easy? I thanked him for his time and for making this so easy. He just looked at me and said, "If we owe it, we will pay it. It's just that simple."

My heart was pounding as I got into the elevator. I looked at my co-worker and told her that we couldn't tell anyone how easy it was! Needless to say, I was the hero of the day, adding $500K to the bottom line—that money had been reserved as bad debt. The Partner was ecstatic but mystified. What kind of magic powers did I have??? I never did tell him!

I've since moved on, but I keep that story close to my heart. After nearly 20 years in accounts receivables, I always remind myself and those who work beside me: *"Sometimes, all you have to do is ask!"*

Amy D. McGuinn, CICP

for information because of possible adverse effects on future sales. This is an internal problem that should be resolved by discussion between the sales and credit departments. After review, departments should decide what action to take and how to proceed.

Other Factors

Decisions based on limited information involve factors that relate not only to the prospective customer but also to the supplier company. The general condition of the economy is very important. If times are prosperous, the risk of financial loss is reduced and the credit professional may be more likely to approve orders. Under depressed conditions, the risk of loss is higher and the credit professional may be more conservative in extending credit to customers.

In highly competitive situations, it may be necessary to approve orders on limited information. When there is an overabundance of products or a buyer's market exists, it is common to extend credit on a more liberal basis to maintain a reasonable market share. Conversely, when products are in short supply and a seller's market exists, credit analysis can be more strictly applied. Compiling information costs time and money, and a point is eventually reached at which more information is not worth the added cost. Properly interpreted and evaluated, limited information may be adequate for a yes-or-no decision, while a delay in reaching a decision may cause the seller to lose the order, the customer or both. The factors that apply to setting credit limits enter into decisions based on limited information. It may be helpful to review the situation with immediate superiors and top sales management. Such discussion creates common understanding of the problem, broadens the perspective of the credit professional and makes salespeople more aware of why it is desirable for them to obtain information from customers.

Review of Credit Limits

Regular Reviews

Credit limits *are based on information, assumptions, experiences, estimates, forecasts and economic conditions.* Since all of these factors can change, it is important to review credit limits and to identify the criteria that trigger such reviews. Credit procedures should provide for periodic review of all active files. For active customers, the review should be made annually, timed if possible to coincide with receipt of the year-end financial statements or before the customer's active season. For marginal risks, the review should occur at more frequent intervals: semiannually, quarterly or, in extreme cases, monthly. The periodic review can help keep credit limits flexible in order to meet the business needs of customers, and to accommodate the development of business obtained from aggressive and expanding concerns. The frequency and scope of review will vary with the type of customer, quality of risk and the amount of credit exposure involved. For top-tier accounts, it will tend to be nominal. As the quality of the account declines and the risk increases, the scope and intensity of the review will increase. A thorough and complete review should include the following steps, with particular attention to trends:

- Secure from the sales department an estimate of the customer's current and near-term needs.
- Request from the sales department an estimate of the customer's potential growth.
- Review the customer's recent payment record with the company.
- Review the latest agency reports to check for changes in ownership, operation, payment record, rating and financial information.
- Review and analyze latest financial statements, whether received directly or contained in an agency report. Obtain current figures if necessary.
- Review the most recent trade credit data and compare it with previous reports.
- Review the latest information from the customer's bank and obtain new information if necessary.
- Review notes resulting from direct contact with the customer.

- Make a personal call, if considered advisable, on the customer.
- Appraise historical information on the new principals when important changes in management take place.
- Decide whether the credit limit and payment terms are reasonable for the customer's financial strength and credit standing, in line with company credit policy, and adequate to supply the customer's needs.

Comprehension Check
When should credit limits be reviewed?

Improved Credit Situations

The most desirable reason for an off-schedule review of a customer's credit limit is a marked improvement in its credit position. Being aware of this type of improvement offers great sales possibilities. When a customer's financial condition and payment performance improve substantially, it may be possible to extend larger amounts of credit, with fewer orders referred for review. These steps can result in increased sales and profits and in better service to the customer.

Changes in Business Conditions

Changing conditions in business, in a particular industry or in a geographic area generally may warrant a review of accounts. Improving conditions in the country, market area or industry of the customer should trigger a review for the purpose of raising its credit limit. A nationwide recession, poor crops in a given section, a prolonged strike and many less dramatic changes can each have serious consequences. If prolonged or severe enough, they not only can affect the marginal business but the well-financed, well-managed company as well. Reassessment of credit availability in terms of new situations can be advantageous to both supplier and customer.

Exceeded Credit Limit

Orders that exceed the customer's credit limit require a review to determine whether the customer will pay and when it will do so. The credit professional will need financial and background material that justifies additional credit. Answers must be obtained to such questions as:

- Do current liabilities exceed current assets on the customer's balance sheet?
- Are trade payments prompt?
- What is the experience of other suppliers on the risk?
- Are other suppliers placing undisputed claims for collection?
- Is there any evidence of careless or unreliable performance by the customer?

If satisfactory answers to these questions cannot be obtained, it may be possible to work out a collateral security or other special arrangement reducing or eliminating the credit risk. However, if the available information indicates ability to pay but not within terms, the question is whether additional cost of the expected delinquency will make the receivable unprofitable.

Extraordinary Credit Needs

Requests for credit not warranted by the customer's financial condition may lead to sales and profits which otherwise would not materialize or, on the other hand, to increased credit losses or expanded slow receivables. Thorough investigation and current information should support a decision to extend unusually high credit.

Reasons for Unusual Needs

The common reasons for extraordinary credit needs are:

- Expanding sales.
- Initial or seasonal buildup of inventory.
- Special contracts.
- New or recently established business. In a highly competitive economy, buyers frequently count upon credit from suppliers as the principal source of operating capital.
- Continuing credit for normal needs when there is a moratorium on previously incurred debts.

Probability of Collection

Once the reasons for unusual needs have been established, the seller must evaluate the probability of collection. Since the amount of credit is excessive by accepted financial standards, the decision usually must be based on non-financial factors, such as the personal background and integrity of the principals, business ability, experience with other suppliers, relations with their bank, and willingness to supply financial information. Legal advice should be sought on special contracts to avoid difficulty in connection with performance, payment specifications or quality of goods. Payment specifications merit particular attention. Long-term payments carry greater hazards than short-term payments. A general guide is to negotiate for payment schedules that match the customer's cash receipts.

Seller Considerations

It is also important to determine whether the seller's accounts receivable will be adversely affected. If an unusually high accounts receivable concentrates overall portfolio credit risk in a set of customers, it may be advisable to determine the value of continuing to sell to those accounts based on the concept of return on investment.

Accounts may be classified into risk categories and incremental sales compared to incremental profits for each category. Overall company policies should also be considered on requests for unusually large amounts of credit. Such factors as profit margins, desirability of the revenue generated by the customer, distribution requirements, competition, establishment of a new product, opening a new sales territory and efficient use of production facilities must be considered.

Extended Terms

While the element of risk is common to all credit transactions, the degree of the risk varies with the credit period (i.e., the longer the credit, period, the greater the risk). When circumstances appear to justify credit terms that extend beyond the usual period, and which are not generally offered to the same classification of customer, a credit grantor must determine if there is a reason to extend terms that will satisfy antitrust regulations. Antitrust regulations are intended to avoid anti-competition, restraint of trade and pricing issues. Often, considerations such as geographic anomalies or economic conditions will meet concerns involving antitrust. Other reasons include meeting the competition, financial hardship and rehabilitation of the customer. Legal counsel may be helpful in certain circumstances and a review of antitrust regulations is recommended.

Terms of sale may be regarded as a part of the price. Credit professionals should be aware that extended payment terms may be regarded as a change in price favoring a particular customer. If extended terms are granted to one customer, they should be available to others under comparable circumstances. In addition, it should be recognized that terms concessions to some customers may be unfair to those that pay on standard terms. Accordingly, the seller should make some provision for recovery of the added costs that extended credit terms may create.

> **Comprehension Check**
> Explain the statement:
> The longer the credit period,
> the greater the risk.

Establishing the Necessity for Extended Terms

In any individual case, the need for additional time must first be confirmed. The conditions that bring about this need are similar to those that underlie requests for unusually high credit, such as expanding sales, seasonal financing of accounts receivable and inventory, and special contracts. Occasionally a customer with limited resources requests longer terms until additional capital becomes available. Current financial information is essential. In a new business, the financial data alone may justify the decision. Where the customer seems to lack operating capital to finance expanding sales, the credit professional should try to determine whether the sales forecasts are realistic. Here, the views of the sales representative handling the account can be valuable. If the need stems from a special contract, it should be examined with particular regard to the payment schedule. When additional time is needed until other capital becomes available, seek verification from the source of expected funds.

Terms Offered by Competitors

Another reason for considering extended terms, and an important one in many industries, is often simply a matter of meeting competition, and is not related to actual customer need. This issue requires the attention of both the sales and credit teams. The credit professional should analyze the risks involved, but the ultimate decision is usually that of senior management. Claims of extended terms should be verified before a decision is made to meet competition. Requests for lengthened terms to meet competition frequently stem from customer reports of special arrangements offered by competing suppliers which may be misunderstood or mistaken. If the reports are verified, a decision mutually acceptable to sales and credit management can be achieved.

Determining Whether Extended Terms Are Realistic

If the customer's need is established, the credit professional must decide whether the proposed extended payment arrangements are a realistic means of meeting this need. This means answering such questions as:

- Will temporary assistance from the supplier give adequate financing?
- Does available information, including sales forecasts and cash inflow forecasts, indicate that funds will be available to meet obligations as they mature?
- Will there be adequate funds to resume normal payments as agreed?
- Does close analysis indicate that such aid would serve no long-term purpose and that the actual need is for equity capital or long-term debt?

A manufacturer can help a customer by supplying products on extended terms, but this is not realistic if the supplier-customer relationship is relatively new and not profitable to the seller. On the other hand, if a long-time customer fails, the profit earned by the supplier over the years may more than offset any one-time loss. In deciding whether to offer extended terms, the determining factor is often the bigger picture of the entire relationship between buyer and seller. If a customer's need is established and extended terms are considered, the credit professional should give close attention to the amount of credit to be granted under these terms, keeping in mind the increased risk and the legal implications.

Overdue Accounts

Slow payment is one of the factors that most frequently lead to account review. If slow-paying customers are approached as a partner to the sale, it may be possible to convert them to prompt and profitable accounts. As a starting point, credit information should be reviewed and brought up to date. The sales department's appraisal of the risk and potential may also help decide how a past-due account should be handled. If the review indicates that additional credit is too risky, friendly but firm efforts should be initiated to collect the past-due amount. Internal controls can be set up to prevent shipment of new orders until the past-due amount has been paid. If a new order is received, the credit department may tell the customer that additional credit will be extended after past-due bills are paid.

Some problems associated with past-due accounts may be solved by amortizing payment of all or a portion of matured balances over a period of time, with a provision for prompt payment of any new credit. Amortization plans may also provide for conversion of extended open account balances to interest-bearing notes. The objective is to return the accounts to a current basis by liquidating the frozen balances. However, unless such plans are based realistically on the customer's ability to meet the schedule of payments out of profits or otherwise, they may serve only to complicate the situation. The assessment of late-payment service charges can provide inducement to pay promptly and is used for that purpose in a number of industries.

Other Reasons for Reviews

A credit file should also be reviewed upon receipt of information that is deemed unusual or significant, such as:

- Receipt of a new financial statement.
- A change in the accounting method for reporting sales and income.
- New auditors.
- The death of one of the principals.
- The admission of a new partner or other change in management.
- A change of banks.
- A change in the legal structure of the entity (e.g., from a proprietorship to a corporation or LLC).
- A merger or an acquisition.

Figure 13-3

	NEW CUSTOMER RISK REVIEW CHECKLIST	Comments	Completed?
1	Completed and signed credit application (or written approval from management if requirement is waived)		
2	Sales-initiated customer form is completed and approved		
3	Financial statements (Full set if purchases are expected to exceed a certain level. If lesser volume, obtain written or verbal information to calculate key ratios.)		
4	Resale tax certificate (if a U.S. entity) is sent to tax department (dated copy retained by credit deptartment)		
5	Legal name verification via Secretary of State websites		
6	Third-party credit reports, including key scores		
7	Bank references		
8	Trade references (3)		
9	Review customer's website and online presence		
10	Generate internal credit score		
11	Credit limit determination		
12	Security instruments		
13	Evaluation and approval		

Information from other sources may also spark a review. Local newspapers often publish changes in ownership and management while public record sources document suits filed, legal actions and information on customers. Industry and trade publications are useful sources of information about individual customers and conditions in the industry. General business conditions are discussed in financial newspapers and financial sections of leading newspapers, and periodic analyses are issued by prominent banks and a number of government publications. *These sources are reliable methods of learning about customers and can be proactively researched using various online search engines and news alerts.*

Credit professionals should be alert for any indications of a customer's financial difficulty, including reduced agency ratings, increasingly irregular or delayed trade payments, reports of contentiousness, protested checks, filing of tax claims, perfected security agreements or failure to maintain scheduled payments on debentures, mortgages or other fixed obligations. There is a great danger in presumptions based on incomplete surface indications. These should always be explored. Thorough investigation is often required to assess their significance. Any decision to curtail credit or to question a customer's creditworthiness should be delayed until complete information can be ascertained. A selling firm's own experience with bad debts, slow collections, financial requirements or marketing strategy can cause credit policy changes that would call for review of all customer credit files.

Figure 13-4

	EXISTING CUSTOMER RISK REVIEW CHECKLIST	Comments	Completed?
1	Completed and signed credit application (or written approval from management if requirement is waived)		
2	Sales-initiated customer form is completed and approved (if requesting additional credit limit)		
3	Financial statements (Full set if purchases are expected to exceed a certain level. If lesser volume, obtain written or verbal information to calculate key ratios.)		
4	Resale tax certificate sent to tax department (if a U.S. entity and if the previous certificate has expired)		
5	Legal name verification via Secretary of State websites		
6	Third-party credit reports, including key scores		
7	Bank reference to update availability and relationship		
9	Review customer's website and online presence		
10	Generate internal credit score		
11	Credit limit determination		
12	Security instruments		
13	Evaluation and approval		

Key Terms and Concepts

Comprehension Check

1. Some companies establish a way to automatically approve small orders. Supply a justification of this policy.
2. What is the difference between **credit line** and **credit limit?**
3. Explain how the profit margin and terms of sale of the selling company influence credit decisions.
4. Discuss three common methods used to establish a credit limit.
5. Explain credit scoring techniques and the pros and cons for their use.
6. List some available security devices.
7. List and discuss the characteristics of a **marginal account.**
8. Why can selling to a marginal account be important to a business?
9. When should credit limits be reviewed?
10. Explain the statement: The longer the credit period, the greater the risk.

Summary

- The basic objective in making credit decisions is to find ways to approve an order with reasonable expectation that the customer will pay in accordance with established credit terms.
- New orders should be processed as quickly as possible in order to ensure continued sales. When processing new orders, consider:
  - How much credit is required?
  - What are the profit margins on the products being sold?
  - When will the customer pay?
- Credit investigations may not be necessary for all sales. Credit policies that establish terms for automatic credit approvals and approvals based on a creditor reporting agency's rating or score can save time and money for a credit department. Some, but not all, benefits include:
  - Documentation of actions taken
  - No need for exhaustive investigation
  - Efficient use of time
- When first orders cannot be streamlined by using an automatic credit approval system or credit ratings, an organization may sell on other terms such as cash in advance or certified check.
- **Credit limits** may be assessed based on:
  - **Financial information**
  - **Agency ratings, reports and credit scores**
  - **Bank checks**
  - **Trade clearances and other data**
- Profit margin of a product can have serious implications for a credit decision. For example, high profit margin can allow a seller to accept a greater credit risk.
- Financial exposure is greater when credit terms are longer.
- Factors to consider when **establishing credit limits** are:
  - **Competition**
  - **By formula**
  - **Payment record**
  - **Payment performance**
  - **Period of time**
  - **Expectations of use**
  - **Agency scoring and rating**
- **Credit scoring** is a popular tool of credit analysis. A credit matrix can be used to assign certain credit bands to specific terms. Credit scoring models are also popular tools when making credit decisions. They can take into account various factors like the NAICS code, payment history and financial data to make an appropriate, unbiased credit decision.
- Many companies advise their sales department of credit limits. It also may be appropriate to inform the customer of credit limits. However, there are advantages and disadvantages to this practice including an opportunity to discuss and possibly adjust the limit in order to sell more, or the potential to damage goodwill between a customer and the seller.

- There are various security devices that may be used during a credit decision. Some include: guarantees, irrevocable letters of credit and subordinate agreements.
- Marginal risks may be essential to a business' receivables portfolio allowing for increased profit if the risk is justified.
- Credit managers may need to make credit decisions with limited information because of limited time or increased cost. There are many factors to consider when making decisions with little information, one being the overall economic environment at the time of the decision.
- **Credit decisions** should always be done on a specific timeline based on when certain information becomes available for that particular business. However, the frequency of review may be subject to change based on the business as well as other factors that include:
  - **Improved credit situations**
  - **Changing business conditions**
  - **Exceeded credit limits**
  - **Extraordinary credit needs**
  - **Extended terms**
  - **Overdue accounts**
- Other reasons for **review** include, but are not limited to, the following:
  - **New financial statements**
  - **New auditors**
  - **Merger or acquisition**
  - **Death**

References and Resources

Altman, Robert. *Corporate Financial Distress and Bankruptcy,* 2nd ed. John Wiley and Sons, Inc., 1993.

Business Credit. Columbia, MD: National Association of Credit Management. (This 9 issues/year publication is a continuous source of relevant articles and information. Archived articles from *Business Credit* magazine are available through the web-based NACM Resource Library, which is a benefit of NACM membership.)

Cole, Robert H. and Lon L. Mishler. *Consumer and Business Credit Management,* 11th ed. Boston: Irwin/McGraw Hill, 1998.

Credit Professional's Handbook: The Technical Reference Manual for Credit and Customer Financial Management. The Credit Research Foundation, 1999.

"Credit Risk Review." NACM Graduate School of Credit and Financial Management project, 2016. Kathie Knudson, CCE; Lisa Ball, CCE; Stacy Parker, CCE; and Dawn Dickert, CCE.

Dean, Jerry. *The Art and Science of Financial Risk Analysis.* Columbia, MD: National Association of Credit Management, 2001.

Dennis, Michael C. *Credit & Collection Handbook,* 1st ed. Paramus, NJ: Prentice Hall, 2000.

"Developing an Internal Credit Score for Businesses." NACM Graduate School of Credit and Financial Management project, 2015. Estela Frias, CCE; Roseanne Genise, CCE; Sandi Langdon, CCE; and Gerry Moran, CCE.

Gahala, Charles, L. *Credit Management Principles and Practices*, 4th ed. rev. Columbia, MD: National Association of Credit Management, 2013.

Gallinger, George and Jerry Poe. *Essentials of Finance.* Englewood Cliffs, NJ: Prentice Hall, 1995.

PART V

FINANCING AND PAYMENT

14 International Trade

OVERVIEW

Companies selling internationally have a number of unique decisions to make before shipping an order. The first of these will be based on an analysis regarding the country in which a seller is planning to do business. Once the country risk is understood, a credit decision can then be made on the customer placing the order. Consideration should be given to how the shipment will be billed and financed.

The simplest way of extending credit is on open account, however, with this method comes the greatest risk. Other methods of payment include selling by means of various drafts, letters of credit and cash prior to delivery. All of these methods are used extensively in international trade and will be discussed later in this chapter.

THINK ABOUT THIS

Q. What factors must be considered while conducting business internationally versus domestically?

Q. What payment methods are used for international transactions and why?

Q. When does risk completely pass from seller to buyer, and what tools can be used to mitigate the risk of selling internationally?

DISCIPLINARY CORE IDEAS

After reading this chapter, the reader should understand:

- ☑ Country risk analysis versus international customer credit decisions.
- ☑ Common problems for the exporter.
- ☑ Different methods of international payment.
- ☑ Letters of credit.
- ☑ Commercial invoice.
- ☑ Sight drafts.
- ☑ Dated drafts.
- ☑ Incoterms®.
- ☑ The role of the freight forwarder.
- ☑ Credit insurance.
- ☑ Factoring and forfaiting.
- ☑ Bankers acceptances.
- ☑ Foreign exchange.

CHAPTER OUTLINE

International Credit Decisions

Country Risk*

Background

When selling outside country boundaries, an exporter should take into account **country credit risk factors** such as the *political, economic, legal, cultural, geographical and financial risks of the countries where they are doing business.* The economy and business climate of any country is impacted by its policies and laws. Export sales credit decisions are impacted by the way trade is promoted or regulated, the politics of the government and the nationalism or political unrest of nations.

In many countries outside of the United States, the government may take a much larger role in economic development. For example, a large amount of construction may be driven by projects funded by the government either alone or blended with private investment. If a company stands to benefit from this situation, the credit professional should understand the philosophy of the current government and the likelihood of a change. In the case of a democratic country with periodic elections, a regime change in government can trigger a slowdown in payments during the transition as well as a change in investment priority. Anticipating and adjusting to this change may minimize exposure and risk.

Any number of events can impair a customer's ability to pay its overseas vendors. On the economic side, events can include currency devaluations, weak local demand, high inflation and the availability of foreign currency. On the political front, local instability will negatively impact the economy by harming investor and consumer confidence. Poor policy decisions can hurt local business conditions. Even more serious are threats of terrorism, revolutions or hostilities with other countries.

Foreign Exchange

When selling internationally, a critical consideration is the selling and receiving of currency. There are significant sales, treasury and tax implications. Each of these issues is reliant on the other and while credit is not generally considered in the actual transaction, it is important to realize potential problems which may become a credit issue. Often competitive reasons dictate the currency that will be used for the sale.

Both parties must be in agreement when selling/buying currency. A U.S. company, selling and expecting to be paid in U.S. dollars, must be aware that the purchaser may have to acquire U.S. dollars to pay in U.S. dollars. This may come at a gain or loss to the purchaser because of currency valuation differences. Global credit managers may find international customers extending payment terms while waiting for currency valuations to change. In some countries, it is not a simple matter of purchasing U.S. dollars with which to pay: for example, Venezuela has a Central Bank system which regulates the country's monetary policies. Buyers must apply to the Central Bank to receive funds to send outside the country which can take several months.

If sellers elect to be paid in the buyer's local currency, the same valuation issues between the local and foreign currency would occur. It is important to have treasury resources either in-house or with a bank to assist in determining the effects of these transactions because a currency exchange loss may have an impact on the seller's product margins.

Culture

Culture plays an important role in what an export customer expects from the relationship with the exporter. How credit information will be presented or in what form it is made available, and how negotiations are influenced by face-saving actions are all included in the cultural package that is part of the risk analysis process. The exporter has the extended role of not only analyzing the creditworthiness of the customer but also the need to evaluate the country itself as part of the business decision process.

Dimensions of Country Risk

The concept of country risk becomes a combination of factors that are critical in the risk assessment process for the international credit manager. Illustrated in Figure 14-1 is a tool that can be used by export credit managers in classifying the major risk issues and attributes of each risk by country. For example, in the "Current Economic Momentum" category, the credit professional may apply knowledge obtained through various direct and indirect sources of information. This information could be valuable if meeting with business management to determine if the current customer opportunity in a particular country has long-term implications for the seller. Political and Social Risks are an area that can severely impact the credit manager's ability to collect. While a company in another country may be well financed, with an excellent payment reputation, changes in the political make-up of the government may result in payments being frozen to creditors outside the country. Sources of valuable country risk material include FCIB, the Political Risk Letter written by the PRS Group (available through FCIB) and information published by global credit insurers or banks. This information includes topics specific to a country that need to be researched and evaluated including debt burden: the economic diversification of the country, reliability of available data and the stability of balance of payments.

It should be noted that country risk is mitigated in certain situations. For example, there are overseas customers who sell back to U.S. customers and collect receivables in dollars rather than local currency. Overseas apparel manufacturers buy cloth from U.S. suppliers, manufacture the garments in their country and then ship back to U.S. retailers. In these situations, exchange risk issues are minimized, and the customer may be able to borrow from local banks at rates comparable to U.S. interest rates, as opposed to the usually much higher rates offered in their own country.

Country Risk section and figure 14-1 provided by Paul Beretz, CICE, Pacific Business Solutions, Clayton, CA.

Figure 14-1   **Dimensions of Country Risk**

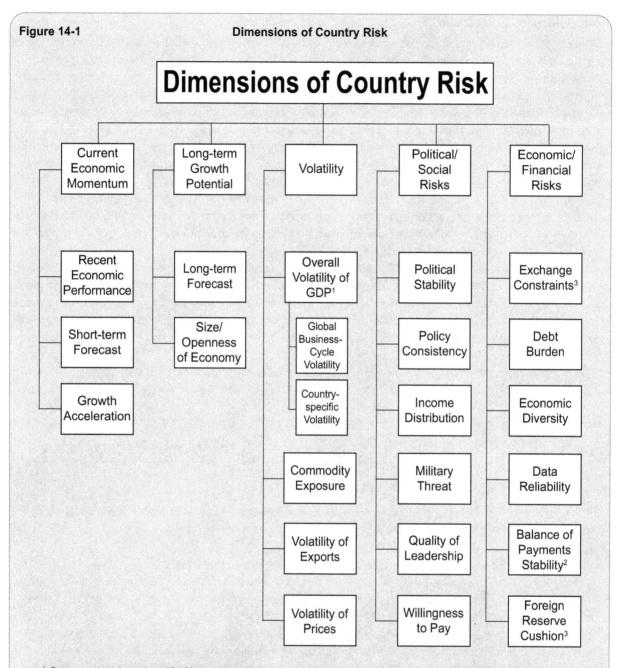

Dimensions of Country Risk

[1] **Gross national product (GNP)** *is the total of ALL economic activity in a given country, regardless of who owns the productive assets and, therefore, includes everything produced in the country by both domestic and foreign ownership.*

[2] The **balance of payments (BOP)** *is a simple accounting record of international flows.* Financial inflows, such as receipts for exports or foreign investments in a domestic stock market, are recorded as credits or positive entries. Financial outflows, such as payments for imports or purchase of shares in a foreign stock market, are debits or negative entries. The current account covers trade in goods and services, **RIPDs** *(rents, interest, profits and dividends)* and transfers.

By definition, debits must equal credits so the net BOP must equal zero. Any references to deficits or surpluses reflect imbalances in individual accounts.

[3] *See* currency convertibility under Foreign Exchange section in this chapter.

Customer Risk

Once a decision to sell has been made on a country, investigating the customer in accordance with company policies can proceed. Credit information, using domestic references, can be exchanged as in any other credit transaction. However, exchanging credit information with foreign references can be time consuming and may produce little result. Because many foreign suppliers use credit insurance, references may not be as candid. International credit reports are often used to provide business and financial information not readily available through direct sources.

Financial information may be the most difficult to receive. Many foreign customers may refuse to disclose their financial statements. Unless they are a large or publicly owned company, those that do provide financial information may have more than one set of figures, depending on the needs of the time. It may be challenging for the credit professional to understand foreign financial information and accounting standards.

Export and Customs Compliance

Export and customs compliance are critical areas for the international credit professional. For example, the United States currently has a trade embargo prohibiting the movement of goods to the Crimea Region of Ukraine, Cuba, Iran, North Korea, Sudan and Syria (as of March 2016). Shipping into these countries from the U.S. comes with severe sanctions and penalties. Beyond specific countries, there are also denied persons lists, which include individuals, concerned parties and entities. These databases are provided by the Bureau of Industry and Security through the U.S. Department of Commerce and can be found at https://www.bis.doc.gov/index.php/policy-guidance/lists-of-parties-of-concern/denied-persons-list.

Equally important are specific sanctions or penalties imposed by the U.S. Department of Treasury. These sanctions vary in their restrictions and again, come with significant penalties for violation and may include financial fines and even jail time. There are approximately 28 sanction programs which may be found at https://www.treasury.gov/resource-center/sanctions/Programs/Pages/Programs.aspx.

Depending on the size of the company, or the magnitude of the international shipments, export and customs compliance may be handled internally or by an outside third party. In both cases, it should be assured that the persons or agencies responsible are fully aware of requirements and restrictions of shipping from one point to another, especially when crossing country borders. The main purpose of customs compliance is to protect the border, safeguard duty payments, control the flow of goods and enforce legal regulations.

It is also important to realize the regulatory compliance rules when exporting. For example, U.S. companies are always subject to U.S. law, regardless of where they are shipping from. There are always two sides to international transactions which require credit professionals to check the export laws of the country from which the shipment originates and the import laws of the country of the product's destination.

 Comprehension Check
Define **country credit risk** and list resources that can be used to analyze the risk.

International Methods of Payment

Once the country and customer credit investigations have been completed, selling terms to the customer can be established. It is important to remember that the terms of sale being offered to the customer should not be more liberal than the threshold of terms established for the country. Part of this decision will be determined on the profitability of the product or service being sold. If the product or service has a large bottom line contribution, the seller should be willing to accept more risk; for products and services with a smaller profit margin, more restrictive terms should be considered.

The following methods of payment most likely to be used in international sales are:

Cash-in-Advance

With cash-in-advance payment terms, an exporter can avoid credit risk because payment is received before ownership of goods is transferred. For international sales, wire transfers and credit cards are the most commonly used cash-in-advance options available to exporters. Escrow services are another cash-in-advance option for small export transactions. However, requiring payment in advance is the least attractive option for the buyer because it creates unfavorable cash flow. Foreign buyers are also concerned that the goods may not be sent if payment is made in advance. Exporters who insist on this payment method as their sole manner of doing business may lose to competitors who offer more attractive payment terms. Cash-in-Advance terms include:

- **Cash With Order (CWO)** *is the most conservative term offered and most commonly used if the product or service is unique to the customer.*
- **Cash Before Delivery (CBD)** *is much the same as Cash with Order; however, it is normal to wait until the product or service is ready to ship before collecting the balance.*

Consignment

Consignment in international trade *is a variation of open account in which payment is sent to the exporter only after the goods have been sold by the foreign distributor to the end customer.* An **international consignment** transaction is based on *a contractual arrangement in which the foreign distributor receives, manages, and sells the goods for the exporter who retains title to the goods until they are sold.* Exporting on consignment is very risky as the exporter is not guaranteed any payment and its goods are in a foreign country in the hands of an independent distributor or agent. Consignment helps exporters become more competitive on the basis of better availability and faster delivery of goods. Selling on consignment can also help exporters reduce the direct costs of storing and managing inventory. The key to success in exporting on consignment is to partner with a reputable and trustworthy foreign distributor or a third-party logistics provider. Appropriate insurance should be in place to cover consigned goods in transit or in possession of a foreign distributor as well as to mitigate the risk of non-payment.

Open Account

An **open account transaction** *is a sale where the goods are shipped and delivered before payment is due, which in international sales is typically in 30, 60 or 90 days.* This is one of the most advantageous options to the importer in terms of cash flow and cost, but it is consequently one of the highest risk options for an exporter. Because of intense competition in export markets, foreign buyers often press exporters for open account terms since the extension of credit by the seller to the buyer is more common abroad. Exporters who are reluctant to extend credit may lose a sale to their competitors. Exporters can offer competitive open account terms while substantially mitigating the risk of non-payment by using one or more of the appropriate trade finance options.

Letters of Credit

Definition

A **letter of credit (L/C)** *is a written understanding by a bank (issuing bank), acting at the request and on the instructions of its customer (applicant for the credit)* to:

- Make payments to, or to the order of, a third party (beneficiary).
- Accept and pay bills of exchange (drafts) drawn by the beneficiary.
- Authorize another bank to effect such payment or to pay, accept, or negotiate such bills of exchange (drafts).

Letters of credit are one of the most secure instruments available to international traders. An L/C is useful when reliable credit information about a foreign buyer is difficult to obtain, but the exporter is satisfied with the credit-worthiness of the buyer's foreign bank. An L/C also protects the buyer since no payment obligation arises until the goods have been shipped as promised. The terms and conditions of the credit must be complied with before payment, negotiation or acceptance can be made.

A variety of documents, including documentary requirements, may have to be presented for a drawing under a letter of credit, such as:

- A draft.
- A bill of lading or other transport document, which may be a document of title in negotiable form.
- A commercial invoice.
- A certificate of origin.
- An insurance policies or certificates.

International letters of credit are generally governed by the current International Chamber of Commerce (ICC) publication, the *Uniform Customs and Practices for Documentary Credits,* commonly referred to as UCP 600. An example of basic L/C requirements is shown in Figure 14-2. Standby letters of credit may be governed by UCP 600, International Standby Practices ISP98 or Article 5 of the Uniform Commercial Code.

Contents of the Letter of Credit

Banks normally issue letters of credit in computerized formats that clearly indicate the bank's name and the extent of the bank's obligation under the credit. In general, commercial letters of credit contain the following information:

- **Expiry date,** *which specifies the latest date for presentation of documents.* In this manner, and by including a latest shipping date, the buyer may exercise control over the date of shipment.
- **Name of the seller,** *who is also known as the beneficiary.*
- **Name of the buyer,** *who is also known as the applicant or account party.*
- **Amount of the credit,** *which should be the value of the merchandise plus any other charges the seller intends to collect under the credit.*
- **Tenor of the draft,** *such as at sight,* 90 days after date of shipment, *which is normally dictated by the terms of the sale contract or purchase order.*
- **General description of the merchandise,** *which briefly and in only a general manner describes the merchandise covered by the letter of credit.*
- **Shipping terms,** *such as FOB, FCA, CIP, indicating whether the price includes freight and insurance, where responsibility for damage to the goods changes, who is to arrange transportation.*
- **Documents required,** *which, under a commercial L/C, will normally include commercial invoices, original transport documents, and, if the insurance is to be effected by the seller, insurance policies or certificates.*

Participants under a Letter of Credit

The **buyer** or **importer** *is referred to as the* **applicant** *or account party.* The **beneficiary** *is the seller/exporter.* Upon the instructions of the **applicant** *(importer),* the issuing bank opens or issues the letter of credit. The **advising bank,** *usually a branch or correspondent of the issuing bank located in the beneficiary's local area, advises or checks the apparent authenticity of the letter of credit it transmits to the beneficiary.*

Figure 14-2   Letter of Credit Instructions

LETTER OF CREDIT INSTRUCTIONS

This format is for use in designing a Letter of Credit Instructions Form appropriate for your company.

Date:_____

To:_____

From:_____
Address:_____
City/State:_____
Country:_____ Zip Code:_____
Attn:_____
Telephone:_____
Fax:_____

RE: ☐ Our Pro-Forma Invoice # _____   Dated:_____
      ☐ Your Purchase Order # _____   Dated:_____
      ☐ Commercial Contract # _____   Dated:_____

Gentlemen:

In connection with your above-referenced purchase, the following terms and conditions are for inclusion in your irrevocable letter of credit. We are providing you with these details as a confirmation of our understanding of the terms of sale covering this transaction. If these details do not agree with your understanding or if you are unable to comply with these terms and conditions, please notify us prior to the issuance of your letter of credit to avoid unnecessary delays and costs. Thank you for your patronage and cooperation.

1. The letter of credit must be issued no later than _____ by a bank acceptable to us.

2. The letter of credit must be irrevocable and be subject to the 2007 Revision of the Uniform Customs and Practice for Documentary Credits published by the International Chamber of Commerce (UCP 600).

3. The letter of credit must state that it is available with any bank by negotiation.

4. The letter of credit must be opened with full details by SWIFT or tested telex

   In favor of:_____   [indicate the company name and address you will use in
              _____   your invoices; if this is ***not*** the address you want your
   Attn: _____   L/Cs mailed to, give separate instructions for where
   Telephone: _____   this L/C is to be sent]

   While we will not initiate shipment until the actual letter of credit is received, it may expedite processing if you scan and email a copy of the letter of credit to [name] at [email address]. This must be a copy of your bank's actual SWIFT message sent to the advising bank. A copy of your letter of credit application is not sufficient.

5. The letter of credit must be payable in U.S. dollars for

   ☐ up to an amount of   _____
   ☐ an approximate amount of   _____

6. The letter of credit must be advised through an acceptable "prime" U.S. bank such as:

   [*list your preferred letter of credit advising banks*]

7. The letter of credit must authorize the advising bank to add its confirmation only if requested by beneficiary.

8. The letter of credit must authorize the negotiating bank to debit the issuing bank's account with a U.S. reimbursing bank with no deductions. It will expedite processing, and possibly reduce the reimbursing bank's charges, if your bank indicates their account number with the reimbursing bank in the L/C.

9. The letter of credit must be payable against drafts drawn, at the beneficiary's option, on the issuing bank, on the advising bank, or on the reimbursing bank. Drafts must be

   ☐ at sight
   ☐ at _____ days from the date of the transport document/forwarder's receipt.
   ☐ at _____ days from the date of the invoice.

Figure 14-2   Letter of Credit Instructions continued

10. The letter of credit must indicate:

☐ All banking charges outside the applicant's country, including any amendment charges, are for the account of the ☐ applicant ☐ beneficiary.

☐ Discount and acceptance charges for time drafts shall be for the account of the ☐ applicant ☐ beneficiary.

☐ Reimbursement related charges must be for the account of the issuing bank. Please instruct your bank to reflect this in their reimbursement authorization as well as in the letter of credit.

11. ☐ The letter of credit must be transferable by any bank.

12. ☐ The letter of credit must allow partial shipments.

13. The latest shipping date in the letter of credit must be at least _____ days after the issuance date of the L/C.

14. The letter of credit must allow a minimum of _____ days after the date of transport document/forwarder's receipt for presentation of documents. Add 14 days if any documents required must be consularized or legalized or if they include an inspection certificate issued by S.G.S. or similar inspection service. Expiration should be this same number of days after the latest shipment date at the counters of the negotiating bank.

15. The letter of credit must require the commercial invoice to describe the merchandise, in accordance with our pro-forma invoice, as (use only generic terms, avoiding details as to grade, quality, etc.):

_____
_____
_____
_____

☐ EXW (Ex Works, Ex Factory)	☐ cleared for export ☐ loaded on departing vehicle
☐ FCA (Free Carrier At)	☐ Seller's premises ☐ Consolidator's terminal in Seller's country ☐ Carrier's terminal ☐ Airport of departure
☐ CPT (Carriage Paid To)	☐ Customs terminal in Buyer's country ☐ Consolidator's terminal in Buyer's country ☐ Buyer's premises ☐ Airport of destination
☐ CIP (Carriage & Insurance Paid To)	☐ Customs terminal in Buyer's country ☐ Consolidator's terminal in Buyer's country ☐ Buyer's premises ☐ Airport of destination

16. If you have selected a freight forwarder who will be receiving the goods for consolidation and/or shipment, payment must be available against a Forwarder's Cargo Receipt showing merchandise consigned to/at disposal of yourselves. Otherwise the L/C must require either a multimodal transport document consigned to order of the issuing bank showing place of receipt as _____ and place of delivery or final destination as _____ or an air waybill consigned to yourselves showing airport of departure as _____ and airport of destination as _____ L/C must require the multimodal transport document or air waybill be marked "Freight Prepaid" if terms are CIP or CPT or "Freight Collect" if terms are EXW or FCA.

17. If terms are CIP, you may require a marine cargo insurance certificate covering

☐ All risks
☐ All risks including SRCC and War Risks

If terms are EXW, FCA or CPT and we are arranging the shipment, you may require a copy of a cable or fax message to yourselves giving date and means of shipment and description and value of the goods shipped, certified by the beneficiary (ourselves) to be true and accurate and to have been sent no later than two days after shipment.

We anticipate receipt of your letter of credit conforming to these requirements.

Other banks may become involved in a letter of credit transaction. The **paying/accepting bank** *is the bank on which the draft is drawn. The* **negotiating bank** *is the bank that gives value for drafts and/or documents under the credit.* The **confirming bank** *is the bank that may, at the request of the issuing bank, confirm or obligate itself to the beneficiary to ensure payment and acceptance of a draft under the letter of credit, upon presentation of documents that are in compliance with the letter of credit.*

Types of Letters of Credit

Standby Letter of Credit. This is a letter of credit where *the issuing bank agrees to make payment upon the presentation of a document, preferably only a statement in writing by the beneficiary, that the customer did not pay according to terms.* In a trade transaction, for instance, a bank may issue a standby letter of credit on behalf of a buyer to provide assurances of their ability to perform under the terms of a contract with the seller. The parties involved with the transaction do not expect that the letter of credit will ever be drawn upon. The seller knows they can draw on the letter of credit if necessary. The seller is usually able to draw under the credit simply by presenting a draft and a statement that the buyer has not performed its payment obligation. The bank is obligated to make payment if the documents presented comply with the terms of the letter of credit. A standby L/C is issued by the bank and held by the seller. The buyer is provided open account terms. The seller pursues the customer for payment directly. If payments are made in accordance with the sellers' terms, the L/C would not be drawn on and would be allowed to expire. If the buyer is unable to pay, the seller presents a draft and required documents to the bank for payment.

Commercial Letter of Credit. This L/C is *a contractual agreement between the issuing banks, on behalf of one of its customers, authorizing another bank known as the advising or confirming bank, to make payment to the beneficiary.* Both commercial and standby letters of credit can be confirmed. The primary purpose of confirmation is to cover political and economic events that may impede the ability of an issuing bank in another country to honor the L/C. By getting the letter of credit confirmed, a seller will receive a guarantee from the confirming bank to disburse to it the amount of the letter of credit if that seller presents the documents required by the letter of credit to the confirming bank. Generally a seller will request that a trusted bank in that seller's country be tapped by the issuing bank to act as the confirming bank. Also called **Export/Import Letter of Credit** depending on who uses it.

Revocable Letter of Credit. This creates leverage for the issuer. It is contractually legal for one party to either amend or cancel the exchange at any time, normally without the consent of the beneficiary. These types of letters are not seen very frequently, since most beneficiaries do not agree to them, and the UCP has no provision for them.

Irrevocable Letter of Credit This is more common than revocable letters of credit. It stipulates that *no amendments or cancellations can occur without the consent of all parties involved.* Irrevocable Letters of Credit can either be confirmed or unconfirmed. Confirmed letters require that another financial institution guarantees the payment, which is usually the case when the beneficiary does not trust the other party's bank.

Confirmed Irrevocable Documentary Letter of Credit. This type of letter of credit transaction *transfers the payment responsibility from the customer to a bank, usually located in the same country as the seller, that did not open the letter of credit but agrees, at the request of the issuing bank, to be bound by the terms of the letter of credit.* The confirming bank agrees to make payment upon presentation of documents conforming to the contract of sale. It is important to understand that this is a documentary transaction. The bank will make payment upon presentation of documents that are in compliance with the letter of credit. No consideration is given to the quality of the product.

Irrevocable Documentary Letter of Credit. This type of letter of credit is similar to a confirmed irrevocable letter of credit except that *the payment responsibility lies with the bank that issued or opened the letter of credit.* This would normally be the buyer's or customer's bank. With this type of transaction, it is important to determine the financial responsibility of the foreign bank since it will be making payment.

Every letter of credit, regardless of type, is written in an official document agreed to by both parties before it is submitted to the guaranteeing financial institution for review.

> **Comprehension Check**
> Discuss the purpose of **letters of credit** and list the types available.

Figure 14-3   **Letter of Credit Cycle**

Although the letter of credit cycle appears quite complex at first, it is not difficult to understand. This cycle merely involves the exchange of documents for money through intermediaries.

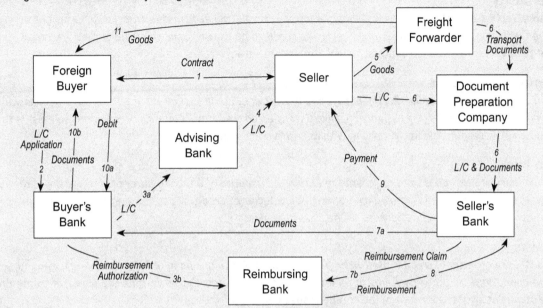

Step 1: The buyer agrees to purchase goods from the seller using a letter of credit as the mechanism of payment.

Step 2: The buyer applies to his bank for a letter of credit, signing the bank's letter of credit application/agreement form.

Step 3a: After approving the application, the issuing bank issues the actual letter of credit instrument and forwards it to their chosen advising bank.

Step 3b: At the time the L/C is sent, the issuing bank also sends a reimbursement authorization to their chosen reimbursing bank. This bank is the clearing bank the issuing bank uses when making payments in the currency of the L/C and will play a role when the time comes to pay the L/C.

Step 4: The advising bank authenticates the letter of credit and delivers it to the beneficiary (the seller). If the issuing bank has requested them to do so, the advising bank may add its confirmation to the L/C (and thereby become the confirming bank).

Step 5: Having received the issuing bank's assurance of payment (and that of the confirming bank if the L/C has been confirmed), the seller entrusts the goods to a freight forwarder, who arranges to ship the merchandise to the buyer.

Step 6: The seller, the freight forwarder, and/or a document preparation company prepares the documents called for in the letter of credit and presents them to the "nominated bank." The L/C may nominate a specific bank where documents are to be presented or it may say it is "available with any bank," giving the seller the freedom to choose where to present documents. If the L/C has been confirmed, documents must be presented to the confirming bank.

Steps 7a and b: The nominated bank examines the documents and, if they comply, obtains funds for payment to the beneficiary in accordance with the terms of the letter of credit, generally by sending the documents to the issuing bank and a reimbursement claim to the reimbursing bank named in the credit.

Step 8: The reimbursing bank matches the nominated bank's claim against the reimbursement authorizations they are holding, charges the issuing bank's account and transfers funds to the nominated bank.

Step 9: The nominated bank transfers payment to the beneficiary (seller).

Steps 10a and b: The issuing bank examines the documents. If it agrees with the nominated bank that the documents comply with the letter of credit, the issuing bank obtains payment from the applicant (buyer) in accordance with the terms of the applicant's letter of credit agreement and forwards the documents to the applicant.

Step 11: The applicant (buyer) uses the documents to pick up the merchandise from the carrier, completing the letter of credit cycle.

Special L/C Arrangements

Letters of credit may include special arrangements, such as:

Transferability

A **transferable credit** *allows the beneficiary of a letter of credit (the exporter) to transfer all or part of the rights under the credit to a third party (the transferee).* For a credit to be transferable, the exporter must arrange for the importer to have a credit opened expressly stipulating that it is transferable.

Assignment of Proceeds

Under an **assignment of proceeds,** *the beneficiary of a letter of credit assigns all or part of the proceeds under a letter of credit to a third party (the assignee).* Unlike a transferred credit, the beneficiary maintains sole rights to the credit and is solely responsible for complying with its terms and conditions.

Back-to-Back

When one letter of credit is used as security to obtain the issuance of a second letter of credit to cover the same transaction, that arrangement is known as a **back-to-back letter of credit.** Most banks are reluctant to enter into back-to-back credit arrangements because of the associated risks.

Red Clause

A **red clause** *in a letter of credit is used when a beneficiary needs financing in order to complete the manufacturing of merchandise or to purchase items to fill a particular order.* A red clause permits the exporter to obtain an advance of part or all of the amount of the credit, as specified in the credit.

Installment Credit

The applicant for an L/C may need to be assured of receiving the merchandise over a period of time in specific installments. *When a bank issues an* **installment credit** *or a credit stipulating shipments by installment within given periods, that credit should clearly state, "Shipment must be effected in the following installments."*

Revolving

A **revolving letter of credit** *contains instructions that allow the beneficiary to draw up to a specific limit for a specified period.* Revolving credit uses the same letter of credit to cover numerous scheduled shipments over a long period without the necessity of issuing new credits for each shipment or amending the existing credit. However, revolving L/Cs usually restrict the amount of money available for each shipment and control the frequency of shipments and amounts available. Revolving credits are either cumulative or noncumulative. A cumulative revolving credit allows an unused portion of a credit to be added to a subsequent period. In a noncumulative letter of credit, any portion not used in one period cannot be added to the next.

Deferred Payment

Under a deferred payment L/C, the exporter presents complying documents to the negotiating/paying bank after shipment.

Discrepancies

All documents under a letter of credit must comply with the L/C's terms and conditions before payment/acceptance can be made. Surveys of banks in major money centers reveal that approximately half of all drawings presented contain one or more discrepancies.

When the documents presented do not conform to the terms of the L/C, the exporter has the following options:

- To ask the negotiating/paying bank to return the documents for corrections and then resubmit the documents.
- To request that the negotiating/paying bank contact the issuing bank for permission to negotiate/pay or accept despite discrepancies.

- To instruct the negotiating/paying bank to forward the documents to the issuing bank on approval, that is, for honor under the L/C.
- To request that the negotiating/paying bank honor the drawing under reserve or against a guarantee.

It is important to examine all the documents for compliance with terms and conditions of the credit, such as:

- Spelling, such as company name, bank or address does not agree with spelling of required letter. All names and addresses, applicant, beneficiary and bank details must match. Shipment documents are not the place to correct misspelled names and addresses.
- The bill of lading indicates damage or states goods or packaging are defective in some manner.
- Bills of lading dated after the latest shipment date; credit will have either an explicit or an implicit latest shipment date.
- Failure on the part of the shipper to show the correct consignment; the manner in which the bill of lading is consigned is one of the terms and conditions of the credit.
- Bill of lading does not indicate goods have been shipped "on board"; somewhere on the face of the bill of lading must indicate goods have been loaded on board the named vessel.
- Unless the credit expressly permits on deck shipments, banks will not accept such notation on a transport document.
- No evidence on bill of lading of payment of freight; bill of lading must indicate whether freight is either "Collect" or "Prepaid."
- Unauthorized charter party bill of lading; the use of a charter party bill of lading must be expressly permitted within the credit to be accepted by the banks.
- Failure to comply with the named ports; the credit will stipulate a port of loading and destination.
- Unauthorized transshipment; credit will explicitly state whether goods may or may not be transshipped.
- Draft and documents presented after expiration date of credit.
- Description of goods on invoice differs from that in the credit.
- Marks and numbers on packages not identical on all documents.
- Weights not identical on all documents.
- Amount on invoice differs from that on draft.
- Draft, shipping documents or insurance documents not properly signed or endorsed: draft must be signed on the face and correctly endorsed on the reverse side. Shipping document originals must be properly signed by the correctly identified freight party and originals endorsed on the reverse side as required. Insurance certificates must be signed on the face and properly endorsed on the reverse side as required.
- Insurance documents not consistent with what the credit requires; wrong currency, incorrect coverage value, document dated after date of the departure of the freight, wrong coverage, etc.
- Insurance coverage in currency other than that of credit; coverage must be stated in the currency of the credit unless expressly stated otherwise.
- Effective date of insurance not as specified in the credit or shown on shipping documents; banks will not accept an insurance document which bears a date later than the on board or dispatch or taking in charge as indicated on the transport document.

- Cargo underinsured; goods must be insured for a minimum of 110 percent of the invoice value or the amount for which payment, acceptance or negotiation is requested, whichever is greater.

There are also other key items to consider in international trade, such as:

- A **green clause** *is very similar to a red clause in that it also allows the drawing of a clean draft, but it requires that the merchandise be stored by the paying bank until all documents are received.*
- A **telegraphic transfer clause** *speeds payments when the receiver of funds is not located in a financial center.*
- An **evergreen clause** *provides a periodic expiry date with an automatic extension and usually states one final date.*
- A **bill of lading (transport document)** *is issued by a carrier and serves as a receipt for the goods and as a contract to deliver the goods to a designated party or to its order.*
- *The person shipping the goods is the* **shipper** *or* **consigner.** *The company or agent transporting the goods is the* **carrier,** *and the party to whom the goods are destined is the* **consignee.**

Documentary Collections

A **documentary collection (D/C)** *is a transaction whereby the exporter entrusts the collection of the payment for a sale to the* **remitting bank** *(its bank), which sends the documents that its buyer needs to the* **importer's bank** *(collecting bank), with instructions to release the documents to the buyer for payment.* Funds are received from the importer and remitted to the exporter through the banks involved in the collection in exchange for those documents. D/Cs involve using a draft that requires the importer to *pay the face amount either at sight* **(document against payment)** *or on a specified date* **(document against acceptance).** The collection letter gives instructions that specify the documents required for the transfer of title to the goods. Although banks do act as facilitators for their clients, D/Cs offer no verification process and limited recourse in the event of non-payment. D/Cs are generally less expensive than L/Cs.

Commercial Invoice

The **commercial invoice** *is the document that lists the value of the shipment.* This invoice is one of several documents often required for an exporter/seller to obtain payment from the buyer for the value of goods or services supplied to an international customer. In addition to the commercial invoice, documents commonly required include a draft, a certificate of origin, a certificate of insurance, a bill of lading or air waybill. All such properly completed documents must be presented along with the original letter of credit when claiming payment. Copies of these documents must also accompany the shipment of product.

All documentary letters of credit are governed by the Uniform Customs and Practices for Documentary Credits, commonly referred to as the UCP 600. Commercial invoices are covered under Article 18 and should contain the following information:

1. Complete name and physical address of the seller.
2. Date of issue.
3. Invoice number.
4. Complete name and physical address of the buyer.
5. Order or contract number.
6. Quantity and description of the goods, unit price, details of any other agreed upon charges not included in the unit price and the total invoice amount.
7. Shipping marks and numbers as required.

8. Terms of delivery and payment.

9. Any other information required by the letter of credit (documentary credit).

10. The regulations of the buyer's country may require a consular invoice. A **consular invoice** *describes the shipment of goods and shows information such as the consignor, consignee, and value of the shipment and is notarized by the local consulate.* If required, copies are available from the destination country's embassy or consulate in the U.S.

Many credit professionals make the mistake of attempting to use an invoice that has been generated by their billing or ERP system as a commercial invoice. This can be a mistake on international shipments because Ship to and Bill to information, product descriptions or payment and FOB terms stated on system-generated invoices may not exactly match the letter of credit instructions.

Drafts

Sight Draft/Bill of Lading

The seller issues an **order bill of lading** made out to the order of the shipper (*see* Figure 14-4). The seller endorses this bill of lading and forwards it, attached to a sight draft to a bank agreed upon by the buyer and seller. A **sight draft** *requires that the buyer pay the amount of the draft immediately, before it can obtain the bill of lading or original shipping documents that enable the buyer to take possession of the goods from the carrier/warehouse.* Once paid, the bank transmits the funds to the seller. The bill of lading, if not endorsed, will *not* enable buyer possession. This procedure is designed to ensure that the buyer renders payment before taking possession. A bill of lading simply made out to order of the buyer/consignee would not provide such safeguards. Under these terms, the bill of lading will not be released by the bank until the customer pays the draft, or agrees to pay in accordance with any loan provisions provided to him by the bank. In the latter event, the supplier still receives payment from the bank, and the loan agreements exist between the bank and the buyer. As with COD shipments, the seller faces the risk of paying for transportation and packaging costs if the buyer does not honor the draft. Consequently, the seller may wish to obtain a deposit from the buyer as protection against such events. These arrangements are employed fairly frequently in sales of container quantities of meats, grains and flour.

Cash against Documents

Cash against documents shipment are consigned to the customer's bank. The product is shipped to the customer's port of entry and once payment has been made by the customer to their bank, documents will be released so the customer can now clear the shipment through customs and take possession.

Dated Draft/Documents against Acceptance

Dated drafts allow the customer to sign a **time draft,** *similar to a postdated check* with their bank for payment at some time in the future. Normally the time period is between 30 and 90 days from the date of acceptance.

Comprehension Check

What are the types of international methods of payment?

International Shipping Terms

Incoterms® Establish Passage of Risk

First introduced in 1936, the terms are endorsed by the United Nations Commission on International Trade Law and are updated periodically. Short for International Commercial Terms, **Incoterms®** are a set of internationally recognized trading rules created by the International Chamber of Commerce (ICC) which are used define and guide the purchase and shipping of goods in the international marketplace. *Incoterms® establish where the passage of risk passes between the buyer and the seller.*

Incoterms® are part of language of international trade; they are three letter codes that describe the responsibility of an international seller to an international buyer. They outline the liabilities and responsibilities of the exporter and

Figure 14-4 Sample Bill of Lading

	DATE	BOL/INVOICE	3516677

SERVICE CHARGES

NOTE: IF A SERVICE BOX IS NOT CHECKED, STANDARD SERVICE WILL APPLY.

☐ EXPRESS SERVICE ☐ STANDARD SERVICE ☐ 3 DAY SERVICE ☐ DEFERRED SERVICE
☐ PREPAID ☐ COLLECT ☐ 3RD PARTY

NOTE: IF "3RD PARTY" IS CHECKED, "BILL TO" AREAS BELOW MUST BE COMPLETED.

FROM SHIPPER	SHIPPER'S ACCT. #	TO CONSIGNEE	CONSIGNEE ACCT. #

SHIPPERS MUST INITIAL ONE OF THE BOXES BELOW

☐ CONTAINS DANGEROUS GOODS DESCRIBED BELOW ☐ CONTAINS NO DANGEROUS GOODS

PHONE

BY SIGNING, I HEREBY ACKNKOWLEDGE AND ACCEPT THE TERMS AND CONDITIONS OF WAYBILL (INCLUDING THE BACK SIDE AND TARIFF) AND AGREE TO BE BOUND THEREBY.

SHIPPER'S SIGNATURE:

X

DECLARED VALUE: OUR LIABILITY IS LIMITED TO $100.00 UNLESS A HIGHER VALUE IS DECLARED. SEE BACK FOR DETAILS

DECLARED VALUE $ _____
INSURANCE $ _____
CUSTOMS VALUE $ _____

ANY CUSTOMS VALUE GREATER THAN $2,500.00 MUST HAVE A SHIPPERS EXPORT DECLARATION.

NO. OF PCS / PKGS	DESCRIPTION OF PIECES NATURE OF CONTENTS, MARKS, AND NUMBERS	GROSS WEIGHT (LBS)	CHARGEABLE WEIGHT	SCALE/TARIFF	RATE

REFERENCE NUMBERS

SPECIAL INSTRUCTIONS

BILL TO

ACCT. #

☐ COLLECT SHIPPER'S C.O.D. ON DELIVERY. CERTIFIED CHECK PAYABLE TO SHIPPER.

C.O.D. AMOUNT	

RECEIVED IN GOOD ORDER AND CONDITION EXCEPT AS NOTED HEREON

X _____   X _____

Consignee or Consignee's Agent Signature   PLEASE PRINT CONSIGNEE NAME

RECEIVED FOR CARIBBEAN BY: X _____

DATE / /	TIME	AM	PM	DATE / /	TIME	AM	PM

NAME AND PRO NUMBER FOR ADVANCED CHARGES	ADVANCED CHARGE	OTHER CHARGES	OTHER DESC.	C.O.D.

FREIGHT	PICK-UP	DELIVERY	DECLARED CHARGE	C.O.D. FEES	BEYOND CHARGES	TOTAL CHARGES

WEIGHTS SUBJECT TO DIMENSIONAL CORRECTIONS

#	L	W	H	#	L	W	H	#	L	W	H	#	L	W	H
#	L	W	H	#	L	W	H	#	L	W	H	#	L	W	H
#	L	W	H	#	L	W	H	#	L	W	H	#	L	W	N

IMPORTANT NOTICE: Cargo items tendered or directed to be tendered by your firm for air transportation are subject to Aviation Security controls by air carriers and when appropriate, other Government Regulations. Copies of all relevant shipping documents showing the cargo's consignee, consignor, description, and other relevant data will be retained on file until the cargo completes its transportation. Carrier's liability is limited under Terms & Conditions on reverse side unless shipper requests additional declared value (subject to additional charge). WARNING: These commodities, technology or software were exported from the United States in accordance with the export administration regulations. Diversion contrary to U.S. law prohibited.

ORIGINAL SHIPPER RECEIPT

buyer. **Incoterms®** *establish the passage of risk between the seller and the buyer and govern the delivery of goods between the parties engaging in international trade.* Sellers must look to the country of the buyer when using Incoterms®; some countries stipulate which Incoterms® must be used and other countries specify which are preferred.

Incoterms® define the seller's obligation within an international sales contract to complete delivery. Incoterms®:

- Identify the physical point in the supply chain where the risk of loss or damage shifts from the seller to the buyer.
- Define the physical point the responsibility for all transportation, customs clearance, duties and related charges shift from the seller to the buyer; and.
- The responsibility between the seller and the buyer to complete delivery obligations; under Incoterms®, delivery means transfer of risk.

Incoterms® Updates

Given the explosive growth of importing and exporting, Incoterms® have been updated every ten years since 1980. In 2010, the ICC revised and simplified its Incoterm® rules by decreasing the number of individual terms from 13 to 11 and moving from four groups to two. The reduction in individual terms was accomplished by replacing four of the five D-terms with DAT (Delivered at Terminal) and DAP (Delivered at Place). Under DAT and DAP, the mode of transport is no longer the defining factor. Broadly speaking, DAT replaces DEQ (Delivered Ex Quay [Named Port of Destination])—delivery occurs at the buyer's disposal unloaded from the arriving vehicle. DAP replaces DAF (Delivered At Frontier [Named Place]), DES (Delivered Ex Ship [Named Port of Destination]) and DDU (Delivered Duty Unpaid [Named Place of Destination])—delivery occurs at the buyer's disposal, but ready for unloading.

There are two, rather than four, Incoterm® groups. The bigger group, which comprises seven terms (EXW, FCA, CPT, CIP, DAT, DAP and DDP), is applicable regardless of transport type. The smaller group of four terms (FAS, FOB, CFR and CIF) is applicable only for those transactions involving sea and inland waterway transport.

According to the ICC, all contracts made under Incoterms® 2000 remain valid even after 2011. In addition, although the ICC recommends using Incoterms® 2010 from January 2011 onward, parties to a sales contract can agree to use any version of Incoterms® after 2011. It is important, however, to clearly specify the chosen version of Incoterms® being used (i.e. Incoterms® 2010, Incoterms® 2000, or any earlier version).

Incoterms® 2010 with Definitions

Rules for any mode/modes of transport:

EXW: Ex Works (Named Place): This places the minimum obligation on the seller, as the seller makes the goods available to the buyer at the seller's premises or any other named place, such as a different warehouse or factory. Delivery is deemed to occur at this named place. The buyer bears all costs and risks after taking the goods from the seller's premises. The goods must also be cleared for export by the buyer.

FCA: Free Carrier (Named Place): The seller has fulfilled its obligation (for delivery, freight costs and risk of loss) when the goods are delivered, cleared for export, to the carrier that has been appointed by the buyer at the named place. The buyer then has to bear all costs and risks of loss for damage to the goods (insurance) from that point forward. This term may be used regardless of the mode of transport, including multimodal transport (transport by more than one carrier—truck, rail, ship, etc.).

CPT: Carriage Paid To (Named Place of Destination): This term means that the seller has fulfilled its delivery obligation when the goods are delivered to the carrier that has been nominated by the buyer. However, in addition to paying the freight costs to that point, the seller must also pay the costs of carriage necessary to bring the goods to the named destination. The buyer bears the risks of loss or damage occurring after delivery. The CPT term requires the seller to clear the goods for export. This term may be used regardless of the mode of transport including multimodal transport.

CIP: Carriage and Insurance Paid To (Named Place of Destination): Identical to CTP except with CIP the seller also has to obtain insurance against the buyer's risk of loss or damage to the goods during the carriage. The seller contracts and pays the insurance premium. As with CIF, the seller is only required to obtain the minimum cover and anything in

Figure 14-5   Incoterms® 2010

Incoterms® 2010

① First National Bank Omaha

Responsibility Matrix - Obligations of Importer (Buyer) and Exporter (Seller)

Terms of Sale	"E"	"F"			"C"				"D"		
	EXW	FAS	FOB	FCA	CFR	CIF	CPT	CIP	DAT	DAP	DDP
	Ex-Works (named place)	Free Alongside Ship (named port) of shipment)	Free on Board (named port) of shipment)	Free Carrier (named place of shipment)	Cost and freight (named port of destination)	Cost, Ins., & Freight (named port of destination)	Carriage Paid To (named place of destination)	Carriage & Ins. Paid to (named place of destination)	Delivered at Terminal (named terminal at port or place of destination)	Delivered at Place (named place of destination)	Delivered Duty Paid (named place of destination)
OBLIGATIONS AND CHARGES											
Warehouse Services (Seller's Country)	Seller	Seller	Seller	Seller	Seller	Seller	Seller	Seller	Seller	Seller	Seller
Export Packing	Seller	Seller	Seller	Seller	Seller	Seller	Seller	Seller	Seller	Seller	Seller
Documentation/Handling fees	Seller	Seller	Seller	Seller	Seller	Seller	Seller	Seller	Seller	Seller	Seller
Forwarder Fees	Buyer	Buyer	Buyer	Buyer	Seller	Seller	Seller	Seller	Seller	Seller	Seller
Loading	Buyer	Buyer	Seller	Seller/Buyer	Seller	Seller	Seller	Seller	Seller	Seller	Seller
Pre-Carriage	Buyer	Seller	Seller	Seller/Buyer	Seller	Seller	Seller	Seller	Seller	Seller	Seller
Export Clearance	Buyer	Seller	Seller	Seller	Seller	Seller	Seller	Seller	Seller	Seller	Seller
Main Carriage	Buyer	Buyer	Buyer	Buyer	Seller	Seller	Seller	Seller	Seller	Seller	Seller
Insurance Charges	No Responsibility	No Responsibility	No Responsibility	No Responsibility	No Responsibility	Seller	No Responsibility	Seller	No Responsibility	No Responsibility	No Responsibility
Charges in Foreign Port	Buyer	Buyer	Buyer	Buyer	Buyer	Buyer	Seller/Buyer	Seller/Buyer	Seller/Buyer	Seller/Buyer	Seller
Unloading in Foreign Port	Buyer	Buyer	Buyer	Buyer	Buyer	Buyer	Buyer	Buyer	Seller	Buyer	Buyer
Custom Clearance	Buyer	Buyer	Buyer	Buyer	Buyer	Buyer	Buyer	Buyer	Buyer	Buyer	Seller
Customs Duties and Taxes	Buyer	Buyer	Buyer	Buyer	Buyer	Buyer	Buyer	Buyer	Buyer	Buyer	Seller
Delivery Charges (On-Carriage)	Buyer	Buyer	Buyer	Buyer	Buyer	Buyer	Seller/Buyer	Seller/Buyer	Seller/Buyer	Seller/Buyer	Seller
"RISK OF LOSS" TRANSFERS FROM SELLER TO BUYER WHEN THE SELLER DELIVERS GOODS UNDER THESE RULES:											
	At the seller's premises, factory, or warehouse	Alongside the vessel (designated by the buyer) at the port (in seller's country) of shipment (designated by the buyer)	Loaded on board the vessel (designated by the buyer) at the port (in seller's country) of shipment (designated by the buyer) (or procured goods already so delivered)	At the named place (in the seller's country) into the custody of the carrier named by the buyer	Loaded on board the vessel (designated by the seller) at the port of shipment (or procedured goods already so delivered)	Loaded on board the vessel (designated by the seller) at the port of shipment (or procured goods already so delivered)	Into the custody of the first carrier (assumed to be at the **seller's place** unless noted differently) in the seller's country	Into the custody of first carrier (assumed to be at the **seller's place** unless noted differently) in the seller's country	At the Terminal (quay, warehouse, container yard, road, rail, or air cargo terminal a the port or place of destination) in the buyer's country	On arriving means of transport, not unloaded, at named place of destination in buyer's country	On arriving means of transport, not unloaded, at named place of destination in the buyer's country
MODE OF TRANSPORTATION											
	Any	Ocean	Ocean	Any	Ocean	Ocean	Any	Any	Any	Any	Any

Remember Title does not pass under Incoterms - make sure you address the issue of where title passes in your Contract, Purchase Order, or Proforma Invoice
Remember with the four "C" Rules, risks and costs are transferred at two different points (risks pass in the seller's country, costs pass in the buyer's country at the place of destination)

excess should be expressed to the seller or arranged for by the buyer. The CIP term requires the seller to clear the goods for export. This term may be used regardless of the mode of transport, to include multimodal transport.

DAT: Delivered At Terminal (Named Place of Destination): The delivery occurs at the buyer's disposal unloaded from the arriving vehicle (as under the former DEQ rule). This new rule, like its predecessor, is delivered, with the seller bearing all the costs (other than those related to import clearance, where applicable) and risks involved in bringing the goods to the named place of destination.

DAP: Delivered At Place (Named Place of Destination): The delivery occurs at the buyer's disposal unloaded from the arriving vehicle, but ready for unloading (as under the former DAF, DES and DDU rules). This new rule, like its predecessor, is delivered, with the seller bearing all the costs (other than those related to import clearance, where applicable) and risks involved in bringing the goods to the named place of destination.

DDP: Delivered Duty Paid (Named Place of Destination): The seller has fulfilled its obligation when the goods have been delivered to the buyer, cleared for import, but not unloaded from the means of transport at the named place of destination. The seller must pay all the costs and risks involved in bringing the goods to that named place of destination including any applicable duties, taxes, customs formalities and carrying out of the customs formalities for the import of the goods into the country of destination. If the parties wish to leave out certain import costs that would be the obligation of the seller, then this should be made very clear in the contract of sale by adding that specific wording. This term should not be used if the seller cannot obtain the import license directly or indirectly, if applicable. This term can be used regardless of the mode of transport.

Rules for sea and inland water transport:

FAS: Free Alongside Ship (Named Port of Shipment): The seller has fulfilled its obligation (for delivery, freight costs and risk of loss) when the goods are placed alongside the vessel at the named port of shipment. The buyer then has to bear all costs and risks of loss or damage to the goods from that point. This term requires the seller to

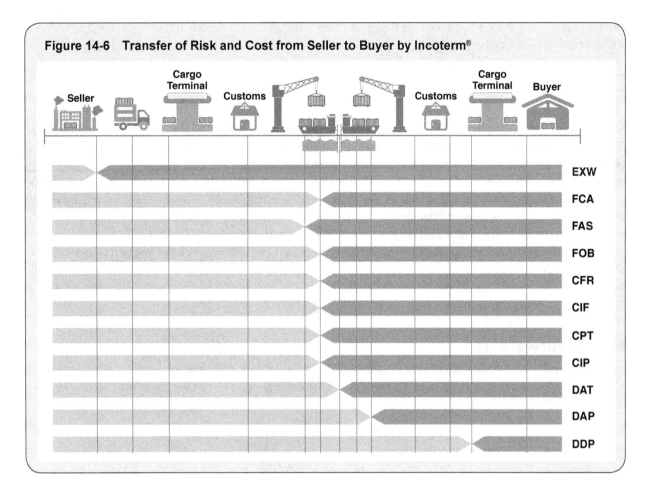

Figure 14-6   Transfer of Risk and Cost from Seller to Buyer by Incoterm®

clear the goods for export; however, if both parties wish that the buyer perform clearance that intent should be made clear in the contract of sale. This term can only be used for sea or inland waterway transport.

An example of FAS is a seller of iron who may load its ore onto a river barge in order to move its ore to the outbound commercial vessel at a shipping terminal or port. The ore is available for loading onto the cargo ship from the river barge, which is parked alongside the cargo ship for loading. The ore is free alongside the cargo ship on a river barge. FAS is commonly used when shipping to grain by river barge to the outbound shipping port.

FOB: Free On Board (Named Port or Shipment): The seller has fulfilled its obligation (for delivery, freight costs and risk of loss) when the goods have passed over the ship's rail at the named port of shipment. The buyer then bears all costs and risks of loss or damage to the goods from that point forward. This term requires the seller to clear the goods for export. This term can be used for sea or inland waterway transport only.

U.S.-based sellers are cautioned not to confuse the term, FOB Factory, with the Incoterm®, FOB. Under the Uniform Commercial Code, the terms FOB shipping point and FOB destination point are used to describe delivery terms. FOB Factory is not an Incoterm®; this GAAP term is equivalent to the Incoterm®, EXW or ExWorks.

CFR: Cost and Freight (Named Port of Destination): The seller must pay the costs and freight necessary to bring the goods to the named port of destination. However, delivery occurs when the goods pass over the ship's rail in the port of shipment. The risk of loss or damage to the goods, as well as any other additional costs incurred after delivery, are transferred from the seller to the buyer at that point. This term requires the seller to clear the goods for export. This term can be used for sea and inland water transport only.

CIF: Cost, Insurance and Freight (Named Port of Destination): Identical to CFR except with CIF the seller must obtain marine insurance against the buyer's risk of loss of or damage to the goods during the main carriage. The seller contracts for insurance and pays the insurance premium, and is only required to obtain minimum cover. If the buyer requires more protection, then that should be expressed to the seller in the contract or it may make its own extra arrangements. The CIF term requires the seller to clear the goods for export, and only can be used with sea and inland waterway transport.

Other Considerations

It is important to recognize that international sales encompass an entirely different set of rules. The typical sale is not governed by the Uniform Commercial Code (UCC), which is the foundation of commercial transaction in the United States. Many international sales are governed by the Convention for the International Sale of Goods (CISG), which may have a completely different interpretation of the UCC. Unless the contract of sale specifically rejects the CISG or the customer resides in a country that has not adopted the CISG, the seller will be bound by the conditions of the agreement. A copy of the Convention can be obtained from the International Chamber of Commerce (ICC) and should be reviewed by counsel to determine the differences between the UCC and CISG.

Documentation is another important consideration in any export transaction. Since the freight forwarder may be preparing much of the export documentation, it is important that they become involved in the transaction as early as possible. The improper preparation of an Ocean Bill of Lading, for example, can be a very expensive mistake, in the event of a claim, if the forwarder does not know or understand the seller's business.

Freight Forwarders

Freight forwarders can be excellent third-party resources to assist with international trade. Forwarders can supply an array of services to assist in export business. The following services are examples of some of the services forwarders provide:

- Letter of credit documentation preparation.
- Air freight or ocean freight service.
- Consolidation service.
- Inland transportation service.
- Customs clearance handling.
- Warehousing and distribution service.
- Packing and crating service.

Since the forwarder can provide such valuable assistance to the exporter, it is important to carefully evaluate and choose which forwarder will be contracted to provide the services. Although foreign customers may specify the use of a freight forwarder they would prefer to handle the services, exporters should use their chosen freight forwarder, in order to have more control over the quality of services to be provided.

Mitigating Risk with Trade Financing Options

There are a number of programs available that will help to mitigate the risk of an export transaction.

Credit Insurance

Export credit insurance provides protection against commercial losses, (such as default, insolvency and bankruptcy) and political losses (such as war, nationalization and currency inconvertibility). It allows exporters to increase sales by offering more liberal open account terms to new and existing customers. Insurance also provides security for banks that are providing working capital and are financing exports. Credit insurance policies include:

- **Multi-Buyer Comprehensive Insurance** is normally used for transactions having a maturity of 180 days or less. The principal amount covered will be an agreed percentage of the transaction and a maximum annual deductible will apply. This insurance can be considered much like the typical automobile insurance policy. There is a fixed annual premium based on risk, a maximum amount of coverage in each category and a deductible for each occurrence. Typically the insurance company will require that the credit file contain current information, including bank references, trade references and a current credit report.

- **Country Limit (Multi-Buyer) Insurance** includes the same conditions as multi-buyer comprehensive; however, it adds the limitation of a country maximum limit.
- **Political Risk (Multi-Buyer) Insurance** is used in the most extreme circumstances. Usually it is limited to sales into politically unstable countries where the risk of doing business because of political, economic or other reasons suggests a high degree of risk and possibility of default. This type of policy only covers the insured in the event of war, currency inconvertibility, political unrest, the overthrow of a government or some other specified event. This is the most expensive of the credit insurance options.

Export credit insurance policies are offered by many private commercial risk insurance companies and specialty insurance brokers as well as the Export-Import Bank of the United States (Ex-Im Bank), the government agency that assists in financing the export of U.S. goods and services to international markets.

Comprehension Check
Explain how credit insurance can be used to mitigate credit risk in international transactions.

Factoring

Factoring *is the process by which a business sells its receivables to a financial institution known as a factor.* Export factoring is offered under an agreement between the factor and exporter, in which the factor purchases the export-er's short-term foreign accounts receivable for cash at a discount from the face value, normally without recourse. The factor also assumes the risk on the ability of the foreign buyer to pay, and handles collections on the receivables. By practically eliminating the risk of non-payment by foreign buyers, factoring allows the exporter to offer open account terms, improves liquidity position, and boosts competitiveness in the global marketplace.

Comprehension Check
What is a **factor** and how can it be used in transacting international sales?

Forfaiting

The name forfaiting is derived from the French term for the technique *a forfait*. **Forfaiting** *refers to the concept that the seller forfeits the right to a future payment on a receivable in return for immediate cash.* Forfaiting allows exporters to obtain cash by selling their medium- and long-term foreign accounts receivable at a discount without recourse. A forfaiter is a specialized finance firm or a department in a bank that performs non-recourse export financing through the purchase of medium- and long-term trade receivables. **Without recourse** or **non-recourse** *means that the forfaiter assumes and accepts the risk of non-payment.* Similar to factoring, forfaiting virtually eliminates the risk of non-payment, once the goods have been delivered to the foreign buyer in accordance with the terms of sale. However, unlike factors, forfaiters typically work with exporters who sell capital goods and commodities, or engage in large projects and therefore need to offer extended credit periods from 180 days to seven years or more. In forfaiting, receivables are normally guaranteed by the importer's bank, which allows the exporter to take the transaction off the balance sheet to enhance key financial ratios. The current minimum transaction size for forfaiting is $100,000. In the United States, most users of forfaiting are large, established corporations, but small- and medium-size companies are slowly embracing forfaiting as they become more aggressive in seeking financing solutions for exports to countries considered high risk.

The cost of forfaiting to the exporter is determined by the rate of discount based on the aggregate of the London Inter Bank Offered Rates (LIBOR) for the tenor of the receivables and a margin reflecting the risk being sold. In addition, there are certain costs that are borne by the importer that the exporter should also take into consideration. The degree of risk varies based on the importing country, the length of the loan, the currency of the transaction, and the repayment structure. The higher the risk is, the higher the margin is and therefore the discount rate. However, forfaiting can be more cost-effective than traditional trade finance tools because of the many attractive benefits it offers to the exporter.

The major advantages to forfaiting are:

- **Volume.** Forfaiting can work on a one-off transaction basis, without requiring an ongoing volume of business.
- **Speed.** Commitments can be issued within hours or days depending on details and country.
- **Simplicity.** Documentation is usually simple, concise and straightforward.

Comprehension Check
What is the difference between **factoring** and **forfaiting?**

Ex-Im Bank

The **Export-Import Bank of the United States (Ex-Im Bank)** assists U.S. exporters by: (a) *providing direct loans;* or (b) *guaranteeing repayment of commercial loans* to creditworthy foreign buyers for purchases of U.S. goods and services. These loans are generally used to finance the purchase of high-value capital equipment or services or exports to large-scale projects that require medium- or long-term financing. Ex-Im Bank's foreign buyer financing is also used to finance the purchase of refurbished equipment, software, and certain banking and legal fees, as well as some local costs and expenses. There is no minimum or maximum limit to the size of the export sale that may be supported by the Bank's foreign buyer financing.

Other organizations and agencies such as Overseas Private Investment Corporation (OPIC) and Commodity Credit Corporation (CCC) are available to assist the exporter in insuring, financing or otherwise supporting the export transaction.

Key Features of Ex-Im Bank Loan Guarantees

- Loans are made by commercial banks and repayment of these loans is guaranteed by the Ex-Im Bank.
- Guaranteed loans cover 100 percent of the principal and interest for 85 percent of the U.S. contract price.
- Interest rates are negotiable, are usually floating and lower than fixed rates.
- Guaranteed loans are fully transferable, can be securitized and are available in certain foreign currencies.
- Guaranteed loans have a faster documentation process with the assistance of commercial banks.
- There are no U.S. vessel shipping requirements for amounts less than $20 million.

Key Features of Ex-Im Bank Direct Loans

- Fixed-rate loans are provided directly to creditworthy foreign buyers.
- Direct loans support 85 percent of the U.S. contract price.
- Exporters will be paid in full upon disbursement of a loan to the foreign buyers.
- Generally, goods shipped by sea must be carried exclusively on U.S. vessels.
- Direct loans are best used when the buyer insists on a fixed rate.

Collection Techniques

Role of the Banking System

The banking system plays an important role for any exporter. It acts as the collection agent in documentary collections such as drafts and letters of credit, a source of foreign exchange and the vehicle to transfer funds from the foreign customer to the seller.

To facilitate payments in an export transaction, it is recommended that payment be made electronically through SWIFT (Society for Worldwide Interbank Telecommunications). This method will allow immediate access to the funds as soon as the seller's bank receives confirmation of funds transmittal. Allowing the foreign customer to pay by check drawn on a foreign bank will result in extensive collection delays while the check works its way through the international banking system. Foreign checks not only delay receipt of collected funds, but also potentially increase the credit exposure if there is a problem with payment and any potential loss due to foreign exchange fluctuations.

Banker's Acceptances

A **banker's acceptance** *is a time draft drawn on and accepted by a bank and payable at a fixed or determinable future date.* It can be created either from a letter of credit transaction or from time drafts drawn independently of a letter of credit.

The following is a simplified example of how a banker's acceptance is used in the United States:

1. A time draft is drawn on a U.S. bank by an exporter or importer.
2. The drawer endorses the draft and presents it to the bank for acceptance.
3. The bank accepts the draft, discounts it and pays the net proceeds to the drawer.
4. The bank has the option to hold the draft in its own portfolio as a loan or to rediscount it in the open market.
5. At the maturity of the draft, the bank pays the face amount to the holder/presenter (if it has not been rediscounted) and looks to its customer for reimbursement.

Discount Eligibility

Acceptances are generally classified as eligible for discount or ineligible for discount at the Federal Reserve. Currently, the basic criteria for eligibility are as follows:

- The term of the draft cannot exceed 180 days.
- The shipment must be current, that is, the acceptance must be created within a reasonable period of time after the shipping date of the goods (usually within 30 days).

The underlying transaction must fall into one of the following categories:

- The import or export of goods, either to or from the United States or between foreign countries.
- The domestic shipment of goods within the United States that cross state borders or travel a minimum of 25 miles from the point of origin.
- The storage of readily marketable staples in the United States or a foreign country, provided the bank possesses a warehouse receipt or other such document conveying the security title to the goods at the time of acceptance until maturity.

Acceptances that are not eligible for discount by the Federal Reserve are defined as **ineligible acceptances.** The Federal Reserve requires that, unlike eligible acceptances, ineligible acceptances are not exempted from the definition of deposit and as such, an ineligible acceptance is subject to reserve requirements.

Comprehension Check
What is a **banker's acceptance?**

Foreign Exchange

Foreign exchange *is the conversion of a freely usable or freely convertible currency of one country into the currency of another.* Foreign exchange transactions differ depending upon when they are scheduled to occur. A **spot transaction** *is for the immediate sale and delivery of a foreign currency,* normally two business days from the transaction date for Europe and Asia and one business day for Canada and Mexico. A **forward transaction** *is a contract between two parties that have agreed to exchange currencies at a fixed rate on an agreed future date.* Forward transactions can be done for any currency, for any trade date and for any amount, although there are standards for each of the variables. For instance, regular trades are in 30-day increments, with maturities that fall on weekends or holidays, for either currency's country, rescheduled to the nearest business day.

Forward transactions are important because they allow a creditor who sells in a foreign currency to hedge its risk of exchange loss. To understand this, visualize a creditor in the United States who sells on open credit terms to an overseas customer, with invoices valued in the customer's currency. If the exchange rate at time of sale is, for example, 1.8 units of the customer's currency in exchange for one dollar, but at time of payment becomes two units per dollar, the creditor will experience an exchange loss. Conversely, overseas customers who pay creditors in dollars may avoid exchange loss by using forward contracts to fix the conversion rate at date of payment.

Real World Perspectives

RWP 14-2

SHOW ME THE MONEY?

Several years ago, I worked in the credit department of an outdoor power equipment manufacturer. Our customer base ranged from Mom and Pop fix it shops to international distributors. There was one distributor I will never forget.

The gentleman, who we will call Rafael, was having difficulty paying his bills on time. It didn't take long before his credit limit was removed and prepayment was required for all orders. In order to get his first prepaid order, Rafael had to bring his account current. It was obvious that the distributorship was struggling when he had to give me two different credit cards (his and his brother's) to cover the low four figure balance. But payment was received so the parts shipped as promised.

Then one day, I received an email from Rafael stating that he would be in town to pick up his parts order in person. He wanted to be sure I would be there to take his prepayment. Did I mention that Rafael was the owner of an outdoor power equipment distributorship in Brazil? I emailed him back to verify that I would be in the office. In my email, I questioned the fact that he was really coming to pick up the parts himself since the order consisted of several thousand dollars worth of parts and accessories. In his reply, he explained that it was less expensive for him to fly to the United States and coordinate purchases from several suppliers into one container load for shipping purposes than it was to order from each individual supplier and have the orders shipped separately. He also admitted that it was like a vacation for him.

So, the day arrived that I would meet my Brazilian friend. We proceeded to the office of the VP of International Sales. That is when I learned my first lesson about taking prepayment in person.

Rafael had a schedule to keep, so it wasn't long before the conversation turned to the amount due for the parts and accessories order. When I showed him the total, he politely asked where the men's room was. It seemed strange to me that he needed to use the men's room so urgently that he interrupted our conversation about the order. But I quickly showed him where it was and returned to the office. When I returned, the VP of International Sales was laughing and asked if I wanted to know why. I was afraid to ask, but did. He finally explained that in Brazil, many people keep their money on their bodies rather than using a wallet. That way, the money is safer from the pick-pockets. Rafael promptly returned from the men's room with a fist full of cash.

Has your mother ever told you not to put money in your mouth because you never know where it has been? Well, believe her.

Jill Westrich , CCE, CICP

Other risks of foreign exchange include **currency convertibility,** *which involves the availability or unavailability of dollars in the banking system of the overseas customer.* In other words, despite the customer's creditworthiness, IT may not be able to pay an invoice rendered in dollars due to unavailability of dollars in his local banking system for the purpose of foreign exchange. In publications on country risk issues this is called FX/Bank Delays, with the delay stated in the amount of time a creditor might expect to wait for dollars to become available. Possible solutions to this include: (a) billing in the customer's currency with a forward contract; (b) having the customer establish an account with a U.S. bank, in dollars, with which to pay the invoice; and (c) in extreme cases, barter. Other political factors, such as embargos, might result in the outright freezing of payments by overseas customers.

Rules Governing Collections

International collections are usually governed by the International Chamber of Commerce (ICC), Uniform Rules for Collections (URC 522). The general provisions of this ICC publication are binding on all parties to a collection unless otherwise expressly agreed or unless contrary to the provisions of a national, state or local law and/or regulation from which no departure may be made.

Collecting Overdue Accounts

Like domestic collections, it is important to have uniform collection procedures and systems to ensure timely recognition of potential problems of international accounts. Collection efforts should begin when the account becomes due for payment plus a reasonable processing time.

Depending on the country, routine collection efforts may become the responsibility of the agent representing the company. It is not uncommon for the local agent to pick up payment for the previous shipment while writing a new order. Caution needs to be exercised in accepting checks drawn on a foreign bank.

As a last resort, legal remedies may become necessary to collect the debt. If the receivable has been insured or factored, it becomes the responsibility of the insurance or factoring company. If the seller is carrying the receivable on its own, it will be necessary to locate a collection agency proficient in international collections or a foreign attorney to represent its interests. Many of the better known collection agencies advertise their international expertise and can represent a seller quite well, however, at a fee which is usually higher than domestic collections. Foreign attorneys should come recommended by a reliable source, because in most situations, up-front fees will be required to represent a seller's position. FCIB may be able to assist with an attorney referral.

Local consulates, Chambers of Commerce, Departments of Commerce and other governmental organizations may be helpful resources.

Comprehension Check

There are several special challenges associated with collecting international accounts. Discuss these.

Real World Perspectives

CHILEAN ADVENTURES

One of my first international credit problems involved a distributor in Chile. This particular distributor purchased product from the company I was working for in the amount of $250,000. The terms offered were D/P (documents against payment) through his bank in Chile.

We shipped the cargo and presented documents through our bank in the U.S. Our bank in turn communicated with the customer's bank in Chile as to status of the paperwork. After a period of time, we were advised by our bank that the customer had not sighted the documents for the cargo we shipped. However, after investigation by our logistics department, we discovered that the customer did have control of the cargo. Not a good thing.

I placed a phone call to the distributor and inquired if he really had the cargo as we had not received the draft. He indicated that he did and there must be some mistake at the bank; he would find out what it was. While this was going on, we were performing our inquiries in the U.S. to determine what actually happened. We were able to determine, after much effort, that our customer bribed the port official and obtained the cargo without the documents. The customer finally admitted to me that he had done just that and also stated that if we pressed the issue, he could end up in jail as it was a serious problem in Chile.

At the time this order was a major portion of our export A/R and we wanted to do whatever it took to get our money as soon as possible. The receivable was deemed a risk and we needed to do something.

The customer had no money to pay for the product, and he also was pleading for time. We finally settled on a time payment but with security. The security was his mother's house. I inquired as to what the house was worth and was told it was worth more than $250,000 and was lien free. I was also told his mother would not object to the transaction. We agreed to at least look at this potential solution as an answer to our problem. I of course spoke to the mother and she reiterated her agreement with the scheme and also indicated that her son had problems but was honorable.

In my previous employment, I had made several mortgage loans and my first call was always to my local title company. Well, guess what? Chile does not have title companies (at least not at the time), but it requires attorneys to do lien searches that go back 50 years on a property. I could tell this scheme was getting complicated (hire attorney, appraise property, inspect property, generate loan papers, record lien, etc.). I booked my flight to Santiago, Chile.

The customer picked me up at the airport in Conception and offered to drive me to Los Angeles (the location of the property). I took him up on the offer as it was 200 kilometers. Los Angeles is up in the Andes; part of the road was gravel and quite desolate. It was beautiful country though.

Upon arrival I was able to hire a local English-speaking attorney who agreed to handle the transaction at a reasonable rate. I was also able to inspect the property and arrange for a representative from a local bank to provide me a value. That value met my needs, and we agreed to go forward with the transaction. It does take time to do a lien search on the property as it is all done by hand by an attorney at the local recorder's office. Therefore, the closing of the loan could not occur while I was in country and would need to be done after I had left.

I did, however, want to meet my customer's mother. She did not live in the house we agreed to mortgage but lived on a farm higher up in the mountains. I traveled to see her and over lunch we discussed the issues that brought me to Chile. She reiterated her belief that her son would repay the loan and agreed, again, to pledge her property so we could complete the deal. I thanked her for the lunch (it was at her home) and advised that our attorney would draw up the paperwork and get it to her for her signature. I also indicated that I would keep in contact so she would know the status of the loan.

I did communicate with our customer's mother a couple of times since I was in her home (once by Christmas card), and the dialogue occurred both ways. The loan was made and repaid with interest, and all of our attorney's fees were paid by our customer as well.

Success stories are not unusual in international business. This one though was very early on in my company's sales dealings in the global arena. If the outcome had been different, we might have changed sales strategy, but as it worked out, we all learned from our experiences and moved forward in a more educated manner. Knowing your customer is very important for credit managers; prior to this situation, I had not traveled. Afterwards though, I made regular trips into the marketplace, met customers, understood their business, joined FCIB and have not had any problems since.

Jay Miller, Trident Seafoods Inc.

Key Terms and Concepts

Comprehension Check

1. Define **country credit risk** and list resources that can be used to analyze the risk.
2. Discuss the purpose of **letters of credit** and list the types available.
3. What are the types of international methods of payment?
4. Explain how credit insurance can be used to mitigate credit risk in international transactions.
5. What is a **factor** and how can it be used in transacting international sales?
6. What is the difference between **factoring** and **forfaiting**?
7. What is a **banker's acceptance?**
8. There are several special challenges associated with collecting international accounts. Discuss these.

Summary

- When selling internationally, businesses and credit managers must take into account the international and domestic economic environment, legal, political, cultural, financial and geographic factors that may influence a sale, because they all can amount to increased risk in a sale.

- One major risk is foreign exchange rates during a sale because the revaluation of currency can impose serious costs of business internationally.

- It is important to understand that the UCC does not govern international sales as the Convention for the International Sale of Goods (CISG) does. It is also of critical importance to adhere to export and customs compliance. Currently, there are several U.S. embargoes placed on countries like North Korea and Cuba that restrict trade. Therefore, if a seller is found shipping to those countries from the U.S., they can face penalties including sanctions and heavy fines.

- When selling internationally, the terms of sale should never be more liberal then the terms of sale in domestic transactions. The following **payment methods** are most likely used in international sales:
  - **Cash-in-advance**
  - **Consignment**
  - **Open account**
  - **Letters of credit**
  - **Documentary collections**

- Each type of payment in an international setting holds its benefits and costs to sellers and buyers due to the varying distribution of risk between the buyer and the seller.

- The three types of **letters of credit** include:
  - **Confirmed irrevocable documentary letter of credit**
  - **Irrevocable documentary letters of credit**
  - **Standby letter of credit**

- Within letters of credit there are also several **special arrangements** to consider including:
  - **Transferability**
  - **Assignment of proceeds**
  - **Back-to-back**

- Red clause
- Installment credit
- Revolving letter of credit
- Deferred payment

- When documents presented do not conform to the terms of the letters of credit there are several actions that may be taken. Such as asking the paying bank to return the documents for corrections and then resubmit the documents.

- Documents should always be examined for compliance with the terms and conditions. One aspect to ensure compliance is the correct spelling of all contents including company name, addresses and applicant names.

- Other **key terms** to consider in international trade includes:
  - **A green clause**
  - **A telegraphic transfer clause**
  - **Evergreen clause**
  - **Bill of lading**

- **Incoterms®** establish international trade rules when shipping, and establish when risk passes from the seller to the buyer. Given the globalization of today's economy, Incoterms® have been updated every ten years since 1980. Common rules for any mode of transportation include:
  - **EXW: Ex Works (Named Place)**
  - **FCA: Free ca Carrier (Named Place)**
  - **CPT: Carriage Paid To (Named Place of Destination)**
  - **CIP: Carriage and Insurance Paid To (Named Place of Destination)**
  - **DAT: Delivered At Terminal (Name Place of Destination)**
  - **DAP: Delivered At Place (Named Place of Destination)**
  - **DDP: Delivered Duty Paid (Named Place of Destination)**

- Rules for sea and land water transport include:
  - **FAS: Free Alongside Ship (Named Port of Shipment)**
  - **FOB: Free on Board (Named Port of Shipment)**
  - **CFR: Cost and Freight (Named Port of Shipment)**
  - **CIF: Cost, Insurance and Freight (Named Port of Destination)**

- Freight Forwarders can be an excellent third-party resource to assist in international trade as they have a host of services that include, but are not limited to, air or ocean freight service and warehousing and distribution service.

- Three ways to **mitigate the risk** of selling internationally include:
  - **Credit Insurance**
  - **Factoring**
  - **Forfaiting**
  - **Ex-Im Bank**

- Forfaiting normally deals with capital goods and commodities that typically have extended credit periods. The minimum U.S. transaction size is $100,000. The major advantages of forfaiting include:
  - Volume
  - Speed
  - Simplicity

- The main role of the Ex-Im Bank is to assist U.S. exporters by providing direct loans, or by guaranteeing repayment of commercial loans to creditworthy foreign buyers for purchases of U.S. goods and services. There is no maximum or minimum limit to the size of the export sale that may be supported by the Bank's foreign buyer financing.
- A bank plays the role of a collections agent for an exporter in documentary collections like drafts and letters of credit. They also serve as a vehicle to transfer funds and as a source of foreign exchange.
- International rules of collection are governed by the International Chamber of Commerce, Uniform Rules for Collections (URC 522). It is essential to have uniform collection procedures and systems to ensure timely recognition of potential problems of international accounts. As a last resort, legal remedies may become necessary to collect debts.

References and Resources

Beretz, Paul. Pacific Business Solutions. Clayton, CA. pacbiz.blogspot.com.

Business Credit. Columbia, MD: National Association of Credit Management. (This 9 issues/year publication is a continuous source of relevant articles and information. Archived articles from *Business Credit* magazine are available through the web-based NACM Resource Library, which is a benefit of NACM membership.)

Cole, Robert H., and Lon L. Mishler. *Consumer and Business Credit Management,* 11th ed. Boston: Irwin/McGraw Hill, 1998.

"The Five Most Common Misconceptions about Credit Insurance." *Trade Credit & Political Risk Practice.* Arthur J. Gallagher & Co. April, 2016. www.ajg.com

Manual of Credit and Commercial Laws. Columbia, MD: National Association of Credit Management, current edition.

Parsonage, Christine. Transport International. Charleston, SC.

Trade Finance Guide: A Quick Reference for U.S. Exporters. U.S. Department of Commerce, International Trade Administration, 2012.

15 Financing and Business Insurance

OVERVIEW

Customers often borrow money as a means of financing their operations. These sources of financing such as banks, finance companies, factors and other institutional lenders, usually have first claim on a significant portion, if not all, of the customer's assets by becoming a secured creditor through a filing under the Uniform Commercial Code. The customer's reliance on the lender, and the lender's superior collateral position, make it important for a grantor of unsecured trade credit to fully understand the relationships between the two parties. This chapter explores the various choices available to borrowers, as well as alternative methods of financing.

? **THINK ABOUT THIS**

: **Q.** What financial tools may be used to reduce the credit risk of marginal customers?

: **Q.** How can a creditor reduce its risk exposure without denying a marginal account?

DISCIPLINARY CORE IDEAS

After reading this chapter, the reader should understand:

- ✓ The basic reasons for borrowing.
- ✓ Types of loans and lines of credit from banks.
- ✓ Different forms of leasing and leasing arrangements.
- ✓ Aspects of leveraged buyouts and what a creditor should know about them.
- ✓ How finance companies work and what a creditor should know about them.
- ✓ Accounts receivable factoring.
- ✓ Types and features of trade credit insurance.
- ✓ How a trade receivable put options can protect a single account.

CHAPTER OUTLINE

Financing Needs

Reasons for Borrowing

A **balance sheet** *is a financial statement that shows a company's assets, liabilities and owners or stakeholders' equity at a specific date.* The balance sheet discloses sources of capital, such as equity contributions by proprietors, partners or shareholders, as well as liabilities, such as debts owed to trade credit, accrued payroll expenses, taxes, capitalized lease debt and borrowed funds.

The reasons most businesses borrow money are to:

- Purchase property, plant and equipment, which often cannot be funded from working capital and require mortgages or other types of long-term debt.
- Borrow under short-term credit facilities to build and finance inventory volumes in advance of heavy selling seasons.
- Take advantage of tax incentives:
  - Interest is tax deductible, whereas profits and dividends are taxable. Therefore, businesses can balance debt and equity for the maximum cash flow or return on shareholder investment. This receives a high level of management attention.
  - Owners often make investments in the form of notes payable to shareholders (payable to themselves) rather than equity.
- Take advantage of payment discounts offered to the company by vendors at rates higher than the lender's interest rates.
- Protect existing ownership positions. Using debt financing, as opposed to allowing equity investments by others, enables existing owners to prevent dilution of their control of a company or corporation and share of profits.

Because lenders provide financing for critical business needs, they are usually able to demand a senior secured position in the debt priorities of a business. Trade debt is often unsecured, making it possible for secured creditors or lenders to strengthen their position by virtue of liens against major portions of a borrower's assets including the inventory supplied by trade creditors. Securitization gives lenders an advantage over trade credit grantors.

Choice of Lender

Trade creditors should be aware of a customer's reasons for using outside financing and for choosing a particular lender. The lending community includes not only traditional institutional sources such as banks and finance companies, but also insurance companies, pension funds, venture capital groups, bondholders, government entities and other sources.

Credit and risk management professionals are encouraged to think like a fixed-income portfolio manager or an investor in the debt of companies: when a risk manager is responsible for $1 of product shipped to a customer on credit terms, the risk manager should consider the transaction as a $1 loan to the customer/borrower.

A formal lender, such as a bank or bondholder, considers each loan to borrowers in terms of risk-adjusted return. Not all borrowers are created equal and a diligent lender is always re-evaluating the risk profile of the borrower and adjusting the rate/price on the loan accordingly, if possible. As a risk manager, it's not always possible to alter the price of product or, even the profit margin to reflect the customer's risk.

Finance companies provide a form of long-term financing through capitalized lease arrangements. Factoring companies provide a form of financing through the outright purchase of receivables.

Lending Relationships

Creditors should also be aware of other important aspects of a lending relationship, which include the:

- Amounts outstanding.
- Terms of repayment.
- Costs involved.
- Collateral pledged.
- Existence of loan covenants or promises, that certain conditions or activities will or will not be met or done, and the possibility of defaults.

It is important for businesses to use the appropriate borrowing mechanism for the intended application of loan proceeds. Short-term borrowing should be used to fund seasonal inventory acquisitions and other short-term assets, while long-term borrowing should be used to fund the acquisition of long-term assets such as major purchases of property, plant and equipment. Any other uses can be a warning signal for the credit professional. A thorough analysis should be conducted on a customer who is unable or fails to use borrowed funds to keep its trade accounts payable current.

Close attention should also be paid to a customer who builds its base of fixed assets by paying its trade creditors slowly, as opposed to seeking long-term financing or borrowing short term in order to meet its current obligations.

Banks

Background

Banks provide a wide array of credit products that satisfy the financing needs of their customers. From small, unsecured lines of credit which may have a credit card feature to very large and complex multi-bank credit agreements that are extended to international businesses, banks are an important commercial funding resource. Many banks have developed a standard credit product set which includes several different offerings with various terms, pricing and loan servicing characteristics. Business borrowers take advantage of direct debit loan payments from deposit accounts, floating to fixed interest rate options and customized loan statement rendering. Special features for lines of credit, such as overnight investments and overdraft protection for primary demand accounts, are readily available. Customized documentation, servicing and pricing features are also available.

Types of Bank Lending

Loans Based on Borrowing Base Certificates

In bank lending, the borrowing firm makes its own sales, conducts its own credit investigations, makes its own credit decisions, approves its own orders, initiates its own collections and absorbs its own bad-debt losses. When a bank extends a business credit line, a loan agreement will be prepared. The agreement will define the maximum amount to be borrowed. Collateral for the credit, such as inventory, contracts and other assets, will be perfected with a security agreement and a UCC filing. The bank loan agreement with the borrower will identify the intervals for required submission by the customer to the bank of the **borrowing base certificate,** *a customer-certified document which details accounts receivable, ineligible accounts based on predetermined aging along with other criteria and amounts available to the collateral pool.* Inventory valuation may also be included in the borrowing base certificate. Also defined in the loan agreement will be *the percentage amounts a bank is willing to lend against qualified receivables, inventory or other collateral,* called the **advance rate.** These will determine the actual amount that can be loaned at any given time. When completed, the borrowing base certificate will assist the banker in determining the amount of available credit per the terms of the loan agreement.

Unsecured Loans

Unsecured loans cover the client's temporary working capital needs, are short term in nature (under one year) and are made based on the client's superior financial condition.

Mortgage Loans

Mortgage loans are usually made on the client's plant and equipment. They are considered long-term debt and are repaid with regularly scheduled interest and principal payments. Often these loans are fixed-rate loans or have an option for the borrower to fix the interest rate at a predetermined interval in the future, generally for a fee. Banks will usually allow a loan amount as a percentage of the property's market value of 75-80 percent. In the event of default, this allows the bank a margin of error on value and expenses.

Lines/Loans Secured by Miscellaneous Assets

Lines or loans are negotiated to meet the particular needs of each client. They may be secured by life insurance policies, deposit accounts, stocks and bonds or any other valuable assets owned by the borrower company, its endorsers or its guarantors. Often these loans are extended for short periods of time, generally for less than one year.

Equipment Loans

Equipment financing enables a company to acquire fixed assets, such as industrial equipment and machinery, and pay for them on an installment basis. Terms are arranged based on the creditworthiness of the borrower and include such considerations as financial strength and cash flow, credit repayment history, the seasonal characteristics of the borrower's line of business and the useful life of the equipment to be purchased. The borrower makes a down payment at the time the equipment is purchased and then pays the balance, including installation, delivery and carrying charges, in a series of installment payments including principal and interest. These may be paid monthly, quarterly, semi-annually or annually. Sometimes payment schedules and amounts are geared to the depreciation charges to be taken on the purchased equipment. The length of the contract should not exceed the useful life of the equipment. Sometimes the company acquiring the equipment can finance it directly with the manufacturer, who takes a secured position in the equipment.

Revolving Lines of Credit

Bank customers often require lines of credit that provide a **revolving credit** feature *whereby amounts may be borrowed, repaid and borrowed again.* The credit underwriting methodology for this credit type is similar to most other bank loan offerings. Loan documentation to evidence the transaction will sometimes include a loan agreement. This agreement will list any special requirements such as cleanup periods when the borrower is expected to rest the line at a zero balance or include loan covenant restrictions. These credit arrangements may have the personal guarantors of company owners and officers and are most commonly fully secured.

Short-Term Loans

Short-term loans or **lines of credit** *are extended to customers to temporarily support working capital.* These credit accommodations can be secured or unsecured and often are evidenced by signing a promissory note. Maturities for short-term loans range from 30 days up to one year. Loans of this nature made to small firms may be secured by the personal guarantee of company principals.

Long-Term Loans

Many firms cannot fulfill their financial needs solely through additional investment and retained profits. Consequently, they may find it necessary to look for long-term financing which often is used for long-term asset acquisition.

Although long-term borrowing cannot be considered part of the owner's investment in a business, the company does have the opportunity to use those funds over a relatively long period of time. These funds are used to purchase machinery, fixtures, equipment, real estate and other assets of a durable nature. This borrowing choice frees the firm's invested capital to carry accounts receivable, pay for inventories and meet the daily cash requirements of the business.

Long-term financing *usually has a maturity date of between three and five years, though can extend to 20 or 25 years for certain types of financing arrangements.* Monthly installment payments are common. Payment arrangements may also be structured for other intervals such as quarterly or semi-annually, depending on the capital needs of the business. Prepayment of the loan is usually allowed; however, prepayment penalties sometimes apply to early payoff of debt and should be considered in the overall cost of any transaction. The prepayment penalty fee is designed to assist the bank in defraying any loss of income due to early retirement of the debt and their loss of income stream. There may be a provision in the loan agreement for the interest rate to change over the period of the loan, and such loans may be tied to a floating prime rate index. Loans may also have fixed-rate pricing throughout their term.

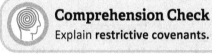

Comprehension Check
List types of loans provided by banks and explain the key points of each.

Restrictive Covenants

In any type of bank lending, it is common for the bank to include **restrictive covenants** in the loan agreement. *Covenants set performance measures that the company is required to meet or the bank is allowed to call or renegotiate the loan.* The more risk taken by the bank, the more restrictive and abundant the covenants are likely to be. Examples of loan covenants are shown in Figure 15-1.

Comprehension Check
Explain **restrictive covenants.**

Figure 15-1   Typical Covenants in a Borrowing or Loan Agreement

The borrower may not pay excessive dividends, borrow from other sources, sell business assets, guarantee the debts of other companies, merge or consolidate with other companies, or buy back any outstanding shares of stock.

The borrower generally is required to maintain an acceptable relationship between current assets and current liabilities (often as a minimum financial ratio, such as the current ratio), maintain the physical and real assets of the company in good condition, employ the proceeds of the loan in the way prescribed, provide adequate insurance coverage on the business, maintain accounting records and have them available for review and submit periodic financial statements to the lender.

Property acquired by the borrower after the agreement is signed may become subject to the terms of the loan agreement by the **after-acquired clause**. *This means that the property is automatically pledged, although the borrower did not own it at the time the loan was made.*

The interest rate may change during the life of the agreement through the use of an escalator clause.

The entire loan may become due immediately if the borrower fails to live up to the agreement. This is called an **acceleration clause.** Where the borrower cannot meet the terms of the note, the lender may institute foreclosure proceedings. The court renders a judgment and orders the property sold to satisfy the claim. If the proceeds of the sale satisfy the amount owed to the creditor, any excess is returned to the debtor. Should the proceeds be insufficient to pay the claim, the creditor may seek a deficiency judgment against the personal assets of the debtor for the difference.

There will also be a **cross-default clause,** *which states that if the borrower defaults on any long-term borrowing agreement, all such agreements will be in default (including the one being negotiated).*

U.S. Small Business Administration

Designed to assist small businesses in financing capital needs for growth and expansion, the **U.S. Small Business Administration (SBA)** *participates in loans made by private lenders.* For business loan purposes, the SBA defines a small business as one that is independently owned and operated, not dominant in its field and meets sales standards developed by the agency. Its clients are businesses that may be undercapitalized, lack sufficient collateral and have not established an operating history. The SBA establishes loan ceilings and provides its clients with free management assistance.

Types of Loans

Of the loans offered by the SBA, the general small business loan, called 7(a), is the most common. Under the **7(a) loan program,** *all funds come from the commercial lender.* The SBA guarantees a portion of the loan with loan amount ceilings that can vary depending on the loan's term and purpose. If the borrower defaults on the loan, the SBA reimburses the bank for its share of the defaulted loan. The SBA doesn't lend money directly to small businesses but rather sets the guidelines for the loans made by the partners who are lenders, community development organizations and micro-lending institutions.

> **Comprehension Check**
> Explain the purpose of the U.S. Small Business Administration and what it offers.

Leasing

Background

Leasing is a long-established practice. In the period following World War II, rapid industrial expansion and inadequate depreciation allowances enabled leasing to become widely accepted as a method of acquiring the use of assets. **Lease contracts** *allow use of equipment, buildings and other assets by lessees in return for periodic rental payments to lessors over a specified time period.* They stipulate the number, size and time sequence of lease payments; and include clauses covering cancellation rights, conditions for renewal or, if applicable, a purchase option, the treatment of tax benefits and obligations, and maintenance, insurance and servicing responsibilities of lessor and lessee. Often the lessee is responsible for upkeep, insurance and repairs.

Lessors include manufacturing companies, independent leasing companies, lease brokers, commercial finance companies and many of the large commercial banks. Many equipment manufacturers use leasing as a marketing tool, offering equipment either for sale or on operating leases.

Types of Leases

The **Financial Accounting Standards Board (FASB)**, which provides the Generally Accepted Accounting Principles (GAAP), *sets forth comprehensive guidelines for classifying leases into two broad categories: operating leases and capital leases.*

Operating Leases

Operating leases *are short-term rentals of property, plant or equipment* where non-financial services such as insurance, delivery, maintenance and repair are usually provided by the lessor. Operating leases do not transfer the risks of ownership from the lessor to the lessee. The lessee often rents the asset for only a fraction of its useful life and deducts the lease payments as an expense. The most significant difference between an operating lease and a capital lease is that operating leases are shorter and the lessee does not record the equipment as an asset or the lease payment stream as a liability.

The FASB updated its accounting standards to recognize lease assets and liabilities on the balance sheet. The core principle of the update is that a lessee should recognize the assets and liabilities that arise from leases with a term of more than 12 months. However, lessor (the owner of the asset to be leased) accounting did not fundamentally change in the update.

Accounting standards have been criticized by financial accountants for failing to meet the needs of users of financial statements because they did not always provide a faithful representation of leasing transactions. In particular, they did not require lessees to recognize assets and liabilities arising from operating leases on the balance sheet. Moving lease obligations onto the balance sheet could impact debt-to-equity ratios. Under operating leases, usually debt and lack of cash flow to service that debt cause companies to fail.

The new standards will take effect for public companies for fiscal years beginning after Dec. 15, 2018, while the update will affect other organizations for fiscal years beginning after Dec. 15, 2019, and for interim periods within fiscal years beginning after Dec. 15, 2020.

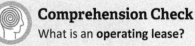

Comprehension Check
What is an **operating lease?**

Capital Leases

The economic substance of a lease contract transfers the asset from the lessor to the lessee. *When substantially all the benefits and risks of ownership are transferred by the lease,* accountants refer to the agreement as a **capital lease.** Terms of capital leases include: (1) the lease term makes up the majority of the asset's life; (2) ownership of the asset transfers to the lessee at the end of the lease term; (3) the asset can be purchased by the lessee for a bargain price; or (4) the lessee's rental payments exceed a significant portion of the asset's value. For accounting purposes, the liability and the asset are recorded for the same amount at lease inception. Theoretically, they are recorded at the lesser of the present value of the total minimum lease payments versus the fair value of the leased asset under the agreement. The leased asset is considered a fixed asset and is depreciated over its useful life. The liability accrues interest at the lessee's borrowing rate over the lease term.

This accounting treatment was designed by the Financial Accounting Standards Board (in their pronouncement SFAS No. 13) to address incomplete disclosure by lessees. Without the recording of the asset and the liability, significant debts would become off-balance-sheet items and would not be revealed to the credit analyst.

With either form of lease, additional charges may be added for services that the lessor is providing. These might include administration, insurance, maintenance and property taxes. In both types of lease contracts, legal title is retained by the lessor. Where no purchase option is provided in a lease contract, residual value reverts to the lessor, which may recoup costs by selling or releasing the asset. Entering into a capital lease has many characteristics of an investment decision in that once the contract is signed, the stream of payments to be made cannot be changed by management's subsequent decisions.

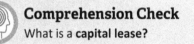

Comprehension Check
What is a **capital lease?**

Sale-Leaseback Arrangement

Sometimes a firm will be in a weak cash position and will enter into a **sale-leaseback arrangement,** *where a company sells property, plant or equipment to an investor and arranges for a long-term lease.* The stream of lease payments represents the amortized value of the asset plus a return on investment for the investor. The liquidity shown on the balance sheet can suddenly improve, but the analyst should recognize that payment obligations increase and profits may decrease. The lessee generally pays all costs an owner would pay, e.g., insurance, property taxes, etc.

Leveraged Buyouts

General Considerations

A **leveraged buyout (LBO)** *is a special acquisition process that uses borrowed money (leverage) to acquire a company.* Specifically, a management or venture capital group borrows substantial capital by pledging the assets of the company to be acquired as collateral. Simultaneously, the group uses that capital to purchase the equity necessary to acquire and control the company. This is accomplished with only a token amount of capital coming from the buyers. The technique can be used to take a public company private, to purchase a division or subsidiary spun off by the parent company or to fulfill the financial goals of a company owner who may be seeking to retire.

LBOs take advantage of the taxation principles listed in the Reasons for Borrowing section of this chapter. One example of an LBO involves a large profitable public company with thousands of shareholders. Such an entity would pay enormous taxes. When an LBO is performed on such an organization, interest costs dilute the profits, but there are now only a few shareholders among whom to distribute those profits. Also, those shareholders benefit from the tax deductibility of the interest costs. In a successful LBO, the structure allows for a higher percentage return on investment than was achieved under the original structure.

LBOs were popular acquisition techniques in the mid- to late-1980s during which time a tremendous amount of liquidity and equity capital was wrung out of corporate America. During those years, public stock prices were low and other opportunities for lending institutions were limited, providing the fuel for the technique to flourish. While the process is still in use, it has faded in popularity because many LBOs failed due to their inability to service their resultant debt loads. Figure 15-2 presents an overview of the most important considerations for credit grantors where LBOs are concerned.

Figure 15-2   Evaluating Leveraged Buyouts

1. The company must have proven products and markets. Unlike venture capital financing, leveraged buyouts aim for reliability and staying power.

2. Key management personnel must have a proven track record. They must be experienced in production, sales, finance and operating the company or a similar one.

3. Management should have enough of their own cash invested in risk equity to ensure their total commitment.

4. The company must have a steady and reliable cash flow to support the purchase price, carrying charges and related debt.

5. The physical plant should be reasonably modern so that heavy capital expenditures can be avoided during the payback period.

6. The company's industry should not be vulnerable to sudden technological shifts that can cause obsolescence.

7. Preexisting debt should be minor because the leveraged buyout will add a major layer of new debt.

8. The company should be willing to supply sufficient detailed financial information to creditors, to reassure them that the company can handle the heavy debt load.

9. Suppliers should be consulted so that previous trade terms will continue after the buyout. Harsher terms can cause liquidity problems.

An LBO, like any other heavily indebted company, requires in-depth analytical attention by the credit professional. Balance sheets and operating statements should be compared to pre-buyout statements in order to evaluate cash flow and debt effectively. It is best to review at least three years of pre-buyout balance sheets and operating statements and to perform the analysis shown in Figure 15-3. Other factors to be considered include assessments of the abilities of new management. For example, will there be closer and tighter attention to operations helping to offset the higher interest expenses and debt loads? It is important that the credit professional obtain enough information to ensure a thorough analysis.

Comprehension Check

Define the term **leveraged buyout.**

....

List nine factors to consider when evaluating an LBO.

....

List nine important items to analyze when reviewing the financial statement of an LBO.

Investinganswers.com reports that "the world's most famous LBO is the approximately $25 billion takeover of RJR Nabisco by private equity firm Kohlberg Kravis Roberts in 1989. The deal was so famous (and so brazen) that it was immortalized by the book and movie *Barbarians at the Gate*. In those days, *many companies used LBOs to purchase undervalued companies only to turn around and sell off the assets* (these acquirers were called **corporate raiders**). Today, however, LBOs are increasingly used as a way to make an average company become a great company.

Figure 15-3   Analyzing Financial Statements for a Leveraged Buyout

1.   Examine cash to uncover any seasonal peaks and valleys.

2.   Check trade receivables for the average age of past-due receivables and their rate of change. Significant customers that provide 10 percent of sales should be listed. The probability of collecting long overdue accounts needs to be evaluated.

3.   Check notes receivable from customers as to nature of loan, terms and history of collection.

4.   Examine inventories to determine the current market value, pricing sensitivity and obsolescence factor.

5.   Evaluate plant and equipment to assess their remaining useful life by comparing the appraised value with the remaining book value.

6.   Check short-term borrowing requirements for peaks and valleys beyond the debt service associated with the buyout.

7.   Analyze accounts payable to determine whether there are any payment problems arising from a reduced inventory turnover or slowdown in accounts receivables turnover.

8.   Review operating income by product lines, industry segments, geographic locations, trend of major customers, pricing strategies, sales agreements and customer base.

9.   Review operating expenses to establish the stability of cost structure by looking into each major element of expense. Lease rates, labor and fringe costs should be checked. Leases need to be examined to see if they are assignable and if they are economically advantageous to the buyer.

Finance Companies

Functions

Finance companies *make loans against pledged or assigned collateral, such as accounts receivable, inventory or fixed assets.* They do not actually purchase receivables or other assets; rather, they make loans based on the value of the asset and expect repayment of the loans by their clients.

Accounts receivable financing was pioneered in the early 20th century as a method to advance operating cash to business, but did not become a significant source of funds until 1941. Now many banks in America have financing operations and many finance companies are subsidiaries of bank holding companies. Many commercial finance companies specialize in accounts receivable financing.

One important result of this evolution is that accounts receivable financing has become increasingly important in the world of finance. The necessity for the use of receivables as collateral arises because the borrower is trading actively on invested capital and needs funds to finance current operations. With the variety of institutional sources available, small businesses as well as mid-sized and large companies are able to obtain funds through receivables financing when they might not be able to obtain unsecured financing.

Accounts Receivable Financing Procedures

A company entering into an **accounts receivable financing agreement** *which is a loan secured by accounts receivable assigned to the finance company,* continues to operate its own credit department as before. It makes credit decisions, maintains customary detailed accounts receivable records and handles its own collections, dealing directly with its debtors. Meanwhile, *the company signs a formal covering agreement with the finance company*. This is known as an **underlying agreement** or **working plan** and is a continuing arrangement for funds to be advanced by the finance company. The lender takes security in the assets by filing a lien using the normal procedures described under the Uniform Commercial Code.

The agreement outlines the overall terms and conditions of the borrowing relationship, such as maximum limit, interest rate, service fee, if any, and the rights and obligations of each party. The procedure for obtaining funds varies according to the agreement. In some instances, the borrower signs a note and submits it with a schedule of specific accounts to be assigned, duplicate invoices and evidence of shipment or delivery. In other cases, invoices and shipping documents are not required, and the borrower continuously assigns its total accounts receivable, which are normally certified by an outside accountant. For the most part, finance companies use the non-notification method, which means that the borrower's customer is not aware that the account has been pledged. Payment is made by the customer to the borrower in the normal manner and, in turn, by the borrower to the lender.

Loans against Inventory by Finance Companies

A finance company may also make inventory loans that are processed in much the same way as a factor or bank. Occasional inventory inspections may be performed by external auditors at the direction of the finance company. This audit would be discussed in the financing agreement.

Evidence of a Financing Arrangement

A company borrowing against receivables should show evidence of this either on the balance sheet or in the accompanying footnotes. Receivables and corresponding short-term loans are often linked together by an explanatory note. If that is not done, the credit professional should look for signs that a financing arrangement does exist. NACM Business credit reports and other sources can also reveal the presence of secured loans. Questions to ask are shown in Figure 15-4.

Comprehension Check
What purpose do **finance companies** serve?

Figure 15-4   Questions to Ask about Arrangements with a Finance Company

An understanding of a customer's arrangement with its finance company may be reached by obtaining answers to the following questions:

1. Is the arrangement normal? With a normal financing arrangement, there is no notification to the client's customer that receivables are being pledged to secure a loan. If the agreement differs from the normal arrangement in that it provides for notification, this should act as a warning that the finance company considers the client a higher than ordinary risk.

2. What is the contract percentage advanced by the finance company against pledged receivables?

3. What is the customer's overall line with the finance company? A finance company will advance a contract percentage against pledged assets, although there is an overall dollar limit to the loan.

4. Does the customer draw the full amount available? Are there any arrangements for advances above the contractual percentage? If the customer does not draw the full loan amount available, this is probably a favorable sign. If it is doing so, it either signals full dependency on the finance company or possibly indicates that finances are in a strained position. On the other hand, overadvances may indicate a great deal of confidence by the finance company. A conclusion as to which way the scale is balanced can only be drawn after all the facts and circumstances are weighed.

5. What is the customer's gross receivables amount and its current loan balance with the finance company? The difference between these two items is the customer's equity. Equity can be diluted by discounts and reserves, contras and concentrations, or delinquent accounts receivable. Discounts and reserves are direct reductions of the face amount. Contras are potential reductions, in that the client's customer may offset an amount owed by the client to the customer. Concentration of receivables from a few large companies poses a danger to those receivables and the market position of the seller. Finally, delinquent accounts are potential bad debts.

6. What is the usual delinquency percentage? The quality of the accounts receivable gains in importance because the company is contingently liable for them.

7. What is the accounts receivable turnover experience?

8. Is there any pledge of the accounts receivable equity to the finance company, the finance company's affiliates or subsidiaries, or to any other third party?

Factors/Factoring

Background

Factoring has its roots in Colonial America, when factors acted as commission merchants, handling goods on consignment. During the late 19th and early 20th centuries, factors generally de-emphasized their roles as sales agents and focused on the buying of receivables.

Factoring *is a transaction whereby a business (seller) sells its accounts receivable to a third party, usually a financial institution (called a* **factor**)*, at a discount in exchange for immediate payment with which to finance continued business operations.* Factoring services may be provided on a **recourse basis** or on a **non-recourse basis,** *meaning the factor must absorb any loss due to the subsequent insolvency or inability to pay by the customer.* In other words, factoring without recourse means that the factor accepts the risk that the accounts receivable may be uncollectable. Non-recourse factoring costs more than factoring with recourse. Even if the general agreement is non-recourse, any individual sale of receivables could be negotiated between the parties to include **recourse** *(seller risk).* Where recourse is involved, the factor usually handles collections until the account is 60 days past due. If still unpaid after that point, the account is charged back to the seller.

Features of Factoring

Typically, sellers are required to factor their entire accounts receivable portfolio, meaning a factor will not purchase the most risky accounts receivable without including in the purchase higher quality accounts receivable. The factor usually will place caps and limits on the maximum factorable balance from each customer. Under most factoring arrangements, factors do not have a continuing obligation to purchase accounts receivable. For particularly risky customers, the factor may cease purchase-related accounts receivable. Historically, factors have been most active in the retail and consumer goods business sectors. Factoring services are not normally available for a customer operating in bankruptcy. In the case of high-risk customers, factors often levy a surcharge or a deductible on the particular accounts receivable.

> **Comprehension Check**
> Briefly describe what a **factor** is.

Business Case for Factoring

Businesses choose this financing tool for various reasons; risk mitigation and administrative expense control are among the relevant considerations:

- Factoring can provide the same benefits as borrowing against receivables. A factor can close the gap between a business's operating cycle and the time allowed for payment by suppliers. For example, factoring is popular in industries where terms granted by suppliers are shorter than terms granted to customers (carpet manufacturing).

- Receivables are sometimes purchased on a non-recourse basis. This insulates the seller from bad debt losses on factored receivables.

- Because factoring involves the outright sale of receivables, it allows a business to avoid some of the costs associated with the collection process. Therefore, businesses that seek to minimize middle management costs sometimes use factoring (smaller apparel manufacturers).

- A factor does not assume responsibility for deductions taken by the seller's customers. Sellers must post to their own records any payments received from the factor against factored accounts receivable. For these reasons, a seller must usually maintain some level of credit and accounts receivable staffing to reconcile records, research and collect deductions and manage any sales made at seller risk. Seller risk includes receivables sold to factors on a recourse basis and credit extensions made by the seller without approval from the factor.

Factoring Procedure

A factor has two primary missions: to recruit new, profitable clients and to successfully collect purchased accounts receivable. The latter calls for the establishment of a credit and collection function quite similar to that of the trade supplier. The factor obtains bank references, credit references and financial information from the client's customers, obtains reports from credit agencies, establishes credit lines for these customers and collects money owed on accounts. Because factoring fees are generally much lower than the profit margins of their clients, factors will often take a more conservative approach to establishing credit limits.

Factoring arrangements are available in a variety of forms and are negotiated based on several variables. The fees paid to the factor are determined by the following:

- The volume of business factored.
- The degree of risk assumed by the factor, determined by the recourse/non-recourse agreements as well as the creditworthiness of the seller's customers.
- The seller's terms of sale.
- The terms for advances made by the factor to the seller, if any.
- Whether payment is made upon collection, based on the obligation's maturity.
- Other factors such as average invoice amount, billing and other services provided by the factor, if any.

The agreement may require a minimum commission to the factor based on anticipated volume. Should that volume not be achieved, the actual rate paid by the seller, as a percentage of factored receivables, will be higher than the contract rate.

Timing of Payment to Seller

There are two timing options; each may also include advance privileges:

1. **Payment upon Collection.** The factor remits payment to the seller upon collection from the seller's customer. In non-recourse factoring agreements, if customer default still exists after a defined period of time, the factor must then make payment to the seller.
2. **Payment at Maturity.** The factor issues payment to the seller upon maturity of the factored receivables according to the terms granted by the seller. Remittance is made monthly on the average due date of the invoices maturing in any given month.

Advance Arrangements

Under either of the timing arrangements, the seller must still wait some period of time to receive payment from the factor, with Payment upon Collection usually being the longest delay. To fully use all the cash flow enhancements of factoring, agreements are often structured to allow the seller to take advances against the balance due for purchased receivables. The factor and seller negotiate an interest rate for these advances. On occasion, the factor may also allow overdraft privileges, but require security in the seller's assets, other than receivables, to do so.

Normally, the seller forwards the invoices and usually receives 85 to 90 percent of the face amount purchased before maturity; *the factor holds back the balance for such contingencies as returns and discounts, disputed receivables and seller's risk receivables.* This reduction is called **dilution.**

The term, **old line factoring arrangement,** still used in many industries, simply means that *the agreement contains borrowing privileges.*

Notification

The seller's customers may or may not be aware that a factoring arrangement exists. Under a notification arrangement, the invoices contain advice to pay directly to the factor, naming the factor as payee.

Under non-notification arrangements, there are two options. The seller's invoice may direct the customer to make payment to a blind lockbox, with such receipts actually being under the factor's control. Or the seller may collect directly from customers and report transactions to the factor monthly, paying fees simultaneously. Under such arrangements, the factor does not actually buy receivables or advance funds but merely agrees to be liable for default of any approved receivables. Under this arrangement, the seller is mainly concerned with risk mitigation. These arrangements bear more resemblance to credit insurance than to traditional factoring.

Order to Order or Credit Line

With order-to-order agreements, the seller obtains factor approval for each transaction prior to shipment. Since factors have their own internal credit limits for acquired receivables, any seller may be squeezed out of its position by other sellers who have obtained previously approved sales to a particular customer. Clients may have agreements with more than one factor to ensure that every invoice can be factored.

Under direct collection arrangements, the factor may authorize the seller to establish its own credit line for each account. In the event of a default, any balances owed in excess of the line become the seller's risk.

Loans against Inventory by Factors

In addition to purchasing sellers' accounts receivable, some factors offer a number of other services, including loans against inventory. This method of secured borrowing is often used by clients to finance temporary needs for working funds. When the seller sells inventory, it turns over the resulting receivable to the factor to repay the loan. Other institutions, such as finance companies and banks, also offer loans against inventory.

Ledger Lines

A business may find itself as a client of a factor and a customer of trade creditors selling their receivables to the same factor. Under such circumstances, the factor may establish a **ledger line.** That is, *the agreement with this business includes a provision that a credit line of some amount, on the part of the factor, will be made available to the other creditors.* If this business also has advance arrangements with the factor, the amount available for advance may be reduced by the total amount of the ledger lines granted.

Factor Guarantees

Occasionally, a factor will assist its sellers in obtaining trade credit by guaranteeing payment of the seller's obligation to the creditor. The amount guaranteed is subtracted from the advance amount made available to the client seller. Any supplier asked to extend credit on the basis of a factor guarantee should ascertain the financial strength of the factor, mitigating the risk that might be associated with such a guarantee.

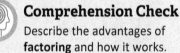

Comprehension Check
Describe the advantages of **factoring** and how it works.

Considerations for the Credit Analyst

When analyzing a customer's creditworthiness, a trade creditor should be aware of the existence of a factoring agreement and its impact on cash flow. The balance sheet entry, Due From Factor, under current assets, reveals the existence of a factoring arrangement. If all customer receivables have been sold as of the statement date, there will be no entry for accounts receivable. If accounts receivable do exist, they have either not yet been sold or may be client risk. If client risk, the collectability of these may be questionable.

The balance of the asset, Due From Factor, is usually the net amount of (a) receivables sold but not yet remitted to the client and (b) advances taken by the client. Dramatic changes in this balance, from one year to the next, may be warning signs for the analyst. A sharp reduction in this amount may mean the customer is strapped for cash and is borrowing more heavily than before.

Some highlights of a factoring agreement will normally be spelled out in the footnotes to the customer's financial statement. However, details such as

Comprehension Check
List the important questions to ask about a factoring arrangement.

How do factors differ from finance companies?

advance rates, dilution rates, etc., often require further research. Other considerations and questions to ask about factoring agreements appear in Figure 15-5.

Figure 15-5   Questions to Ask about a Factoring Arrangement on an Advance Basis

It is important to determine whether the factoring arrangement is on an advance basis. If so, the balance sheet of the customer may hide more meaningful data than it reveals, and any figure shown as Due from Factor should not be taken at face value. If the arrangement calls for advances on accounts receivable, the credit department should ask the factor the following:

1.   What is the contractual advance percentage? Is it fully used?

2.   Are there any arrangements for unsecured overdrafts? If so, what are they? An **overdraft** *is a verbal agreement by the factor to provide funds in excess of the contractual advance percentage on receivables, usually to a stated limit for a specific period of time.*

3.   Are there any overdrafts outstanding? If so, how much?

     When an arrangement calls for overdrafts in addition to advances, the reason should be determined. It could indicate that the customer is financially strained, because inordinately high sales would necessitate increased purchases of merchandise. Therefore, it is essential to obtain profit and loss figures to ascertain whether this increased activity yields commensurate profits and does not weaken the firm. In addition, interim trial balance figures are an aid in determining the current profitability of operations.

4.   Are the overdrafts stated as an amount over 100 percent of the purchased receivables or over the contractual advance percentage?

5.   Have overdrafts been requested but refused or restricted?

6.   If the maturity arrangement calls for payment on the average due date, it is essential to determine the following:

     • Is the item Due From Factor pledged to a third party, such as a bank, to secure a loan?
     • Is there an intercompany offset situation?
     • Does the factor have other affiliates or subsidiaries that are suppliers of credit to the customer?

Insurance

The position of the going concern may change radically if something unforeseen happens to its earning power and financial strength. Fire, death of a principal, embezzlement, robbery, business interruption or extraordinary bad-debt losses can change the financial condition of a business overnight. Given that these circumstances can also affect a creditors' position, it is important for creditors to know the types and amounts of insurance carried by their customers.

There is no way to foretell misfortunes that can hit a business. Adequate insurance coverage is available against these contingencies, thereby protecting company assets and earning power as well as creditors' interest. The creditor should be satisfied that major risks are covered.

Although types of insurance differ in detail, they all have points in common: people join together to protect the value of their lives and property, and each participant contributes a relatively small amount in exchange for protection against a disastrous personal loss. The ultimate purpose of insurance is self-protection, but each participant cooperates with all others to carry common risk.

Trade Credit Insurance*

The practice of insuring commercial accounts receivable against default has existed in the United States for more than 120 years. In fact, like many technological and financial innovations implemented by companies globally, credit insurance was invented in the United States. As a risk mitigation strategy undertaken in the normal course of business, the use of credit insurance by U.S. companies pales in comparison to corporations in Western Europe. Easily one-third of European corporations of all sizes have credit insurance; in the United States, it is fewer than 1 in 10 but has grown from 1 in 50 companies since the early 1990s.

From the early 1980s until the mid-1990s, the U.S. marketplace had at most five or six insurance underwriters. In the last 20 years, that number has swelled to at least 13 insurers, excluding the United States Export-Import Bank. During the U.S. market's first century as an oligopoly, companies were usually obliged to cover their entire customer base in order to obtain coverage. Underwriting guidelines have become much more flexible, particularly with the entry of several new underwriters. With a far more competitive marketplace, underwriting standards have now evolved to the point where companies can elect to insure only specific customers or even just one customer. Insureds can now request coverage on their customers based upon a much wider range of selection criteria, such as those buyers within a certain subsidiary, division, size range, distribution channel and even credit quality.

Credit insurance is a risk transfer mechanism. **Trade credit insurance** or **trade insurance** *protects a seller's commercial accounts receivable from loss, whether caused by commercial or political risk events; it protects businesses from non-payment of commercial debt.* Trade credit insurance ensures that invoices will be paid and allows companies to reliably manage the commercial and political risks of trade that are beyond their control. Capital is protected, cash flows are maintained, loan servicing and repayments are enhanced, and earnings are secure from these events of default. The insurer agrees to compensate the seller in the event that its customer becomes insolvent or bankrupt or, in some cases, there is a protracted default of payment on accounts receivable or non-payment after an agreed number of months after the due date.

A credit insurance policy protects against excessive bad-debt losses, promotes safe sales expansion, provides effective collection assistance, strengthens borrowing and purchasing power, improves planning and budgeting accuracy and provides loss prevention guidance on key risks. For a contract of credit insurance to apply, there must be a sale, shipment and delivery; or a service must be provided for which there is a legally sustainable claim against the debtor or the debtor's estate. Generally, coverage is limited to sales on regular terms of not more than one year.

Credit insurance is not a substitute for prudent, careful credit management. Sound credit management practices must be at the foundation of any credit insurance policy and partnership. Credit insurance goes beyond indemnification and does not replace a company's credit practices, but rather supplements and enhances the job of a credit professional.

Excerpted from "The Five Most Common Misconceptions about Credit Insurance," Trade Credit & Political Risk Practice, Arthur J. Gallagher & Co.

Limits

Trade credit insurance policies are often cancelable by the insurer upon notice to the seller. Credit insurance policies have total policy limits and also have customer-specific limits. Like other forms of insurance, there are often deductibles and loss-sharing rates, that is, not full-coverage. The **trade credit limit** *is the amount of loss that the insurer will reimburse to the policy holder, prior to any coinsurance or deductible, for a specific customer.*

Terms

The term of a credit insurance policy normally covers 12 months, with annual review and renewal; the arbitrary expiration and renewal date may preclude a seller from taking advantage of low rates when they are prevalent if it doesn't coincide with a renewal period. If there is a particularly risky customer at a renewal date, the insurer can choose to refuse renewal with respect to that particular customer.

Cost

Generally, the cost to insure export receivables is higher than domestic receivables. The risk associated with export receivables insurance is usually greater because of distance and unfamiliarity with the laws and customs of the country or countries. Insuring export receivables not only protects against the commercial risk of slow pay customers or bankruptcy, but also protects against a political event that may impede or completely stop payment. On the other hand, domestic receivables may have challenges within specific industries; other factors are loss experience, existing credit management procedures and personnel. Premiums are generally charged either as a percentage of sales or as a per annum rate on limits.

Premium rates are influenced by various factors including country risk, obligor risk, length of payment terms and loss experience. Premium rates can range typically from .05% to .75% as a percentage of the insured sales. Insurance policies don't usually cover accounts receivable for sales to customers in bankruptcy or operating in Chapter 11.

Policy Purchasers

The ideal purchaser of credit insurance is either:

1. A seller seeking to protect itself from unforeseeable catastrophic risk (for example the bankruptcy of a key customer without any warning or tell-tale signs, which would normally alert the insurer to the risk and cause the insurer to cancel the insurance as it relates to such customer); or
2. A seller that cannot afford the resources to perform in-house credit analysis and prefers to outsource the credit risk management to an insurer (for example, the monitoring of 50,000 small customers).

Policy Coverage

Credit insurance is available only to firms engaged in manufacturing, wholesaling and certain service businesses. It is written with deductible and primary loss provisions, and may provide for coinsurance. In every policy, the insured and the insurer agree on a maximum amount of coverage, which is the policy amount. It is the maximum amount the insured can recover for all covered losses sustained during the one-year term of the policy.

With a **coinsurance type policy,** *the insured company participates in a percentage of the bad-debt loss sustained on a debtor.* This coinsurance feature causes the insured to participate in each loss. A higher premium is charged if the insured wants a policy without coinsurance.

With a primary loss policy and because credit insurance is not intended to eliminate all credit risk, a **primary loss policy** *covers losses over and above an agreed-upon annual deductible.* This deductible is based on the normal expected loss for the business and the overall risk to be insured. *This initial deductible loss is termed the* **primary loss** *and is not reimbursed to the insured.* It is set as a percentage of sales, but in no case is less than a stated dollar amount.

A number of endorsements can be made to the credit insurance policy to cover particular situations, including the following:

*   **Bank Endorsement.** This endorsement is used when an account uses its receivables as collateral for bank borrowing. It gives the lending bank the right to file accounts in the same way as the insured does. Not all insurers give the beneficiary the right to file, but all have the right to proceeds.
*   **Construed Coverage.** In case a customer's credit agency rating is changed downward between the time an order is accepted and the merchandise is shipped, this endorsement provides coverage at the higher rating for up to 120 days after the order is accepted. This is generally being replaced by Delayed Effect of Cancellation which has less conditionality to it and offers more protection to the insured.
*   **Interim Claim Settlement.** This endorsement allows the insured to request three interim settlements within 60 days after filing a claim rather than waiting until the end of the policy term. Most insurers have automatic claim settlement.
*   **Claim Settlement.** Within one month after the expiration of the insolvency period of the policy, the insured submits a Final Statement of Claims listing all claims to be included in the loss settlement. A settlement date is made with the insured within two months after receipt by the insurer of the Final Statement of Claims, at which time the amount ascertained to be due the insured will be paid.

Cancelable Versus Non-Cancelable Limits

A number of trade insurance companies offer both cancelable and non-cancelable limit type trade credit products. Both products have been sold successfully in the United States for many years, and in a sense, each tends to service a different constituency. Some insurers went through a credit limit withdrawal exercise for some of their cancelable limits during the financial crisis. The magnitude and frequency of the withdrawals, if any, were driven by each insurer's risk assessment and underwriting models, business decisions and the characteristics of its policyholder's base.

Under a **cancelable limit,** *the insurance company may, at its discretion, amend or withdraw coverage attaching to future transactions between the policyholder and its specific customers.* Each insurer typically has conditions about how much notice may be given prior to withdrawal and whether there are any exemptions or appeals that may apply to the withdrawal. While the policy language allows the insurer to amend coverage at its discretion, limit reductions or withdrawals will typically be the result of a serious deterioration in the risk being insured, such as the credit quality of the policyholder's customer. Such heightened risk may arise from factors specific to that customer, such as a serious breach of loan covenants or material cash flow deficits, or by virtue of an industry-wide or country-wide problem that suggests a loss event is likely within the policy period.

Policyholders who opt to purchase a credit insurance program with cancelable limits often use credit insurance more holistically than for reimbursement of a loss. Some companies perceive value in having the insurer serve as an adjunct to their own internal credit management function and an early warning beacon about problems associated with their customers, in addition to helping manage and avoid potential losses.

In simple terms, under a non-cancelable limit, the insurer may not amend or withdraw a limit, once issued, for the duration of the validity period of that limit. Most policies typically have conditions that can cause coverage not to attach to future transactions between the policyholder and its customer if a dangerous adverse circumstance occurs. Such situations are that the customer is becoming bankrupt, is in grave financial difficulty, is more than a certain number of days overdue on existing, undisputed obligations, or other known facts that reasonably may be expected to cause a loss under a policy.

Purchasers of non-cancelable limits value the fixed certainty of the limit, but understand that these limits are not intended as a carte blanche or free pass coverage, irrespective of circumstances. As managers of the risk, the policyholder accepts the responsibility, in the event of a claim, to have demonstrated proper effort, due diligence and expertise. Similar to policyholders with cancelable limits, the non-cancelable limit policyholder must be aware of their duty to behave prudently and to handle their customers as if they were uninsured. Certainly, there are many reasons why companies buy a non-cancelable limit policy and often it can relate to the overall insurance program being offered.

Comprehension Check
What are the advantages of **trade credit insurance?**

Trade Receivable Put Options

Trade receivable put options, or puts, protect a seller's accounts receivable on a single-account, non-cancelable basis in the event that the seller's customer files for bankruptcy during the period of the put. **Receivable puts** *amount to a promise by one party to buy a seller's trade receivables claim in the instance of a buyer's default or bankruptcy.* In a put, a seller delivers a product to their customer and undertakes that receivable, then purchases the right to put those outstanding receivables to, for example, a financial institution in the instance of a credit event, meaning either a bankruptcy filing or a liquidation. When that credit event occurs, the put is triggered, and pays the seller a predetermined level of protection on the claim.

When a credit event takes place, the seller is able to deliver its accounts receivable that it had with its now defaulting customer to the financial institution, which has to confirm the validity of the trade claim before making any payout to the seller. It's important to note that a put doesn't require the seller to deliver its outstanding receivables to the financial institution; it gives them the right to do so, meaning that a seller could pay a put fee and never cash anything in because their customer succeeds, or because they would rather not, for whatever reason, in the instance of the customer's liquidation or bankruptcy.

A put can be a more effective hedge than other potential trade financing options, such as factoring or credit insurance, mainly due to the fact that puts offer a bit more flexibility in terms of tenor, meaning how long the instrument provides coverage. Whereas factoring and trade insurance typically have minimums of six months or a year, puts can be structured for short-term coverage, up to three years.

Comprehension Check

What is a trade **receivable put?**

Distinguishing Factors

Puts are offered on a single customer, in contrast to factoring and credit insurance, which are normally available only on a portfolio basis. Moreover, puts are routinely offered on financially-distressed customers and, therefore, tend to be more expensive than factoring or credit insurance on a per-customer basis. Puts are non-cancelable and not modifiable by the seller of the put. Puts are available on varying tenors; normally, they are offered on periods of time spanning three months to 12 months. Puts are effective immediately on all the outstanding accounts receivable from the subject customer. Also, puts are offered on customers operating in bankruptcy and under Chapter 11. Finally, puts don't have a deductible, although, in certain cases, the purchase rate may be less than 100%.

The ideal purchaser of accounts receivable put options is either:

1. An experienced in-house credit team that doesn't use credit insurance or factoring and doesn't want to lose profit from sales to a risky customer, which would otherwise be avoided or limited due to credit risk (e.g., distressed, concentration, in bankruptcy); or

2. A seller desiring to supplement its factoring arrangement or credit insurance (e.g., credits not covered/dropped by factoring/insurance, seasonal spikes).

Figure 15-6 Comparison of the Features of Factoring, Trade Insurance and Put Options

	Factoring	Trade Insurance	Put Option
Flexibility	• Normally, requires entire portfolio of accounts receivable • Retail and consumer goods focused • Minimum receivables thresholds for primary factors • Caps and limits for maximum exposure to particular companies • Only protects prospective (new) accounts receivable incurred after the coverage becomes effective	• Normally, requires entire portfolio of accounts receivable • Caps and limits for maximum exposure to particular companies • Only protects prospective (new) accounts receivable incurred after the coverage becomes effective • Usually limited to annual policies with limits decided by the insurer (annual cycle renewal constraints open clients to undesirable pricing to market risks upon renewal)	• Available on a single customer basis, rather than a portfolio of accounts receivable • Focus on high-risk and distressed accounts receivable • Effective immediately on all outstanding accounts receivable to the customer (not just new receivables incurred after put option is purchased) • Range of variables for put options (e.g., expiration date, amount, etc.)
Modification and Termination	• Generally, factor may modify or terminate coverage	• Normally, cancelable on notice at the will of the insurer • Triggered on a default (bankruptcy) or failure to pay	• Non-cancelable • Triggered on a bankruptcy filing
Product Availability	• Not normally available in bankruptcy	• Not normally available in bankruptcy	• Available before bankruptcy and during (in) bankruptcy
Pricing/Cost	• Only available to fully cover outstanding receivables (cannot protect cost only) • Surcharge or deductible added to high-risk accounts	• Only available to fully cover outstanding receivables (cannot protect cost only) • Deductible costs must be considered. Surcharge added to high-risk accounts	• Can be structured to protect sale-price (with your profit), or to cover only cost of goods sold • No deductibles or surcharges or other additional costs

Key Terms and Concepts.........................

Comprehension Check

1. List types of loans provided by banks and explain the key points of each.
2. Explain **restrictive covenants.**
3. Explain the purpose of the U.S. Small Business Administration and what it offers.
4. What is an **operating lease?**
5. What is a **capital lease?**
6. Define the term **leveraged buyout.**
7. List nine factors to consider when evaluating an LBO.
8. List nine important items to analyze when reviewing the financial statement of an LBO.
9. What purpose do **finance companies** serve?
10. Briefly describe what a **factor** is.
11. Describe the advantages of **factoring** and how it works.
12. List the important questions to ask about a factoring arrangement.
13. How do factors differ from finance companies?
14. What are the advantages of **trade credit insurance?**
15. What is a trade **receivable put?**

Summary

- Customers often borrow money as a means of financing their operations. These sources of financing such as banks, finance companies, factors and other institutional lenders, usually have first claim on a significant portion, if not all, of the customer's assets by becoming a secured creditor through filing under the UCC.
- There are a variety of reasons way a business may **borrow money**. Here are a few:
  - **Purchase of property or equipment**
  - **Build inventory before a heavy selling season**
  - **Tax advantages**
- The securitization of loans gives lenders an advantage over trade creditors.
- Important aspects of the lender relationship that a creditor should be aware of include:
  - Amount outstanding
  - Terms of repayment
  - Costs involved
  - Collateral pledged
  - Existence of loan covenants or promises
- Loan types differ greatly, and if a bank feels as though they are taking on more risk, it may include restrictive covenants in the agreement. Types of **bank lending** include:
  - **Loans based on borrowing base certificates**
  - **Unsecured loans**
  - **Mortgage loans**
  - **Loans secured by miscellaneous assets**
  - **Equipment loans**
  - **Revolving lines of credit**
  - **Short-term loans**
  - **Long-term loans**

- The **U.S. Small Business Administration (SBA)** assists the growth and expansion of small businesses in the United States. The SBA helps small businesses to obtain loans from financial institutions and in many cases insuring the banks from any defaults on those loans.

- **Leases** come in several forms. The major difference between a capital lease and a operating lease is that operating leases are shorter and the lessee does not record the equipment as an asset or payment stream as a liability. However, the FASB is in the process of updating the accounting standards associated with leases. A sale-leaseback arrangement is another type of lease that a creditor should be aware of because of its effect on the balance sheet, which may look favorable, but may ultimately spell out a greater risk to the creditor.

- **Leveraged buyouts (LBOs)** were very popular tools used by financial institutions in the late 1980s. A leveraged buyout is when a company borrows money in order to acquire another company. Leveraged buyouts should be evaluated in depth using financial statements of at least three years prior to the buyout.

- **Finance companies** make loans against pledged or assigned collateral, such as accounts receivable, inventory or fixed assets. There are several questions a creditor may want to ask such as, is this a normal arrangement?, or what is the contract percentage advanced by the finance company against pledged receivables?, but ultimately signs of borrowing against receivables should show up in the balance sheet or in its accompanying footnotes.

- **Factoring** can occur on a recourse or non-recourse basis. Typically sellers are required to factor their entire accounts receivable portfolio. Some benefits of factoring may include:
  - Insulating the seller from bad debt losses on factored receivables
  - Avoiding some costs with the collection process

- Fees that are paid to the factor are determined by many considerations including the volume of the business factored, the degree of risk and the seller's terms of sale. Timing of payment may either be upon collection or at maturity. Advanced arrangements can be made with the factor in accordance with the various payment methods.

- Because the financial condition of a business can change overnight, it is important for the credit manager to know the types and amounts of insurance carried by the customer. **Credit insurance** is a risk transfer mechanism. Policies have evolved to where companies can insure individual customers. The ideal purchaser is:
  - Protecting itself from catastrophic events
  - Unable to afford in-house credit management

- Several **endorsements** can be made to the credit insurance policy to cover specific circumstances, including:
  - **Bank endorsement**
  - **Construed coverage**
  - **Interim claim settlement**
  - **Claim settlement**

- Trade insurance may also have cancelable or non-cancelable limits.

- Another option to protect the account receivables for a single-account is **put options.** These are non-cancelable and tend to be more expensive than factoring or credit insurance. Ideal users include:
  - Experienced credit staff that do not use credit insurance or factoring
  - Those using it as a supplement to factoring or credit insurance

References and Resources

Battersby, Mark. *Factoring On-Line and Off.* Textile Industries. May, 2001.

Business Credit. Columbia, MD: National Association of Credit Management. (This 9 issues/year publication is a continuous source of relevant articles and information. Archived articles from *Business Credit* magazine are available through the web-based NACM Resource Library, which is a benefit of NACM membership.)

"The Five Most Common Misconceptions about Credit Insurance." *Trade Credit & Political Risk Practice.* Arthur J. Gallagher & Co. April, 2016.

Investinganswers.com. http://www.investinganswers.com/financial-dictionary/businesses-corporations/leveraged-buyout-lbo-961.

Woodruff, Cosby. "Globalization Makes Textiles, Factoring a Good Match." *Textile World.* November, 2001.

Negotiable Instruments

OVERVIEW

As commerce and trade developed, people moved beyond the reliance on barter to the use of money. Gradually, there was a need to use substitutes for money, such as commercial paper. **Commercial paper** *is a contract for the payment of money.* It can serve as a substitute for money payable immediately, such as a check, or it can be used as a means of extending credit. Commercial paper, consisting of notes and drafts, reflects the needs of merchants, traders and importers. These groups were responsible for the development of the negotiable instrument and the eventual creation of a set of rules for settling disputes in the courts they established for that purpose. These instrument's rules became known as the law of negotiable instruments.

Gradually, the rules were codified and a uniform negotiable instruments act was passed by every state legislature. When the Uniform Commercial Code was drafted, Article 3 contained the statutory law that governs commercial paper. This Article (as enacted in different states) was in part superseded in 1987 when the U.S. Congress passed the Expedited Funds Availability Act, implemented by Availability Act Regulation CC of the Federal Reserve Board, which effectively superseded prior state laws. Article 3 of the UCC was then rewritten to comply with applicable federal laws and regulations and is now the principal source of law governing negotiable instruments.

? THINK ABOUT THIS

Q. In your company's line of business, what are the most frequently used negotiable instruments and why?

Q. How can endorsements or notes change the negotiability of an instrument?

DISCIPLINARY CORE IDEAS

After reading this chapter, the reader should understand:

- ☑ The concept of negotiability.
- ☑ Various kinds of negotiable instruments.
- ☑ The difference between special types of checks.
- ☑ Certificates of deposit.
- ☑ What negotiation of commercial paper means.
- ☑ Various types of endorsements.
- ☑ What checks marked "Paid in Full" mean.

CHAPTER OUTLINE

The Concept of Negotiability

The concept of negotiability is one of the most important features of commercial paper. A negotiable instrument is basically a piece of paper that can be transferred multiple times from one person/entity to another without the use of actual cash. It signifies or replaces money. A common example of a negotiable instrument is a check that can be endorsed multiple times by different parties. Each time it is endorsed and given to another, it represents payment to that party. Because of this feature, negotiable instruments are highly trusted and are used daily by millions of people. A **negotiable instrument** *is a written document, signed by the maker or drawer, containing an unconditional promise to pay, or order to pay, a certain sum of money on delivery or at a definite time to the bearer, or to the order of. It can be transferred from party to party and accepted as a substitute for money.* It is important to know whether an instrument is negotiable; if it is, any dispute concerning the instrument is resolved under Article 3 of UCC. (Figure 16-1)

Figure 16-1	Negotiable Instrument

$ __1,500.00__   ___Anytown, USA, March 10, 20--___

___Sixty Days___ after date ____I____ promise to pay to

the order of _____Robert Jones_____

___One thousand five hundred and 00/100___ Dollars

Payable at ___Third National Trust___

Value received with interest at 7%

No. __746__   Due __June 18, 20 --__   *John Doe*

UCC 3-104(a) specifies that in order for an instrument to be negotiable, it must:

1. Be in writing.
2. Be signed by the maker or the drawer.
3. Be an unconditional promise or order to pay.
4. State a specific sum of money.
5. Be payable on demand or at a definite time.
6. Be payable to order or to bearer.

Comprehension Check
Define the term **negotiable instrument.**

Written Document

Negotiable instruments must possess the quality of certainty that only formal written expression can give, but the requirement is somewhat flexible in how it can be satisfied. The writing may be done in pen, printing, typewriting or pencil as long as it is legible. .

The surface on which the writing is executed must be capable of being circulated. The fact that an instrument is in writing means that the parol evidence rule governs the admissibility of oral evidence to contradict the terms of the instrument. **Parol evidence** *is a substantive rule of contracts under which a court will not receive into evidence prior oral statements that contradict a written agreement if the court finds that the written agreement was intended by the parties to be a final, complete and unambiguous expression of their agreement.*

Therefore, evidence of fraud, incompleteness, inconsistency, etc., is required before testimony on the terms of the instrument is allowed in court. There are also rules for interpreting problems that tend to occur frequently in the making out of such an instrument. Where there is a conflict of terms, the written terms take precedence over the typewritten terms or over any printed form term. In other words, if there is a conflict between the written amount and the amount expressed in numbers, the written amount wins out, due to the deliberation required to state it.

Signed by the Maker or Drawer

This second requirement is relatively straightforward: *The actual or authorized signature of the issuer is required for the instrument to be negotiable.* The **maker** *is the person or company who makes or executes a note.* A **note** *is an instrument containing an express and absolute promise of signer or maker to pay to a specified person, order or bearer a definite sum of money at a specified time.* The **drawer** *is the person or company who makes or executes a draft.* A **draft** *is a written order by the first party,* called the drawer, *instructing a second party,* called the **drawee** (*such as a bank*), *to pay money to a third party,* called a **payee.** Oral evidence is admissible to identify the signer of an instrument. For example, there are typically several people bearing a common name—such as John Smith. The appropriate person is allowed to testify as to which John Smith was the actual maker of the note.

If another person signs for the issuer (corporations may employ this method to utilize commercial paper), the person signing must be authorized to do so or be bound personally to pay the instrument. A failure to indicate that a person is signing in such a capacity, even if so authorized, obligates the signer personally. However, if the instrument is accepted and the signature is recognized as that of an authorized signer for the corporation, case law has shown that the person may not be individually liable.

Any form of signature is permissible as long as it indicates an intent to issue the instrument. Therefore, an instrument signed with an "X" is sufficient; witnesses to such a signing are a good idea but are not required technically. Also, the signature may appear anywhere on the face of the instrument although the usual place is the lower right-hand corner.

Unconditional Promise to Pay

The **unconditional promise to pay** requirement *maintains that the promise or order to pay contained in the commercial paper must not be conditional on the occurrence or nonoccurrence of some other event or agreement.* Requiring that something be done, or that a specific event occur before an instrument can be collected on, reduces the instrument to the status of a simple contract whose rights, at best, can merely be assigned.

A Sum Certain in Money

One requirement of a **sum certain** *is that the amount must be clearly ascertainable from the face of the instrument.* To qualify the instrument as negotiable, the sum certain must be calculable at two distinct times: at purchase and at maturity. When the holder considers buying the instrument, the exact minimum amount payable on it must be calculable from the information on its face. At maturity, the holder must be able to calculate from the face the exact amount due. For instance, a demand note payable with 10% interest meets the requirement of a sum certain because its amount can be determined at the time it is payable.

A second requirement is that *the instrument be payable in money.* **Money** *is defined as the medium of exchange that any domestic or foreign government has officially adopted as part of the currency.* If the instrument's value were stated in terms of services or merchandise, it would be too difficult to determine the market value at the time the instrument was to be paid. A promissory note that provides for payment in tin or hours of service is not payable in money. An instrument payable in shares of stock or government bonds is not negotiable, because neither stocks nor bonds are a medium of exchange recognized by the U.S. government.

On Demand or at a Definite Time

To satisfy this requirement, the time the instrument is payable must be determined in one of two ways. **On demand** *is synonymous with "at presentment" or "at sight" meaning that the holder has the option of choosing the time to receive payment.* Equally acceptable is specifying the time when the instrument matures. Such expressions as "due and payable 60 days from March 3, 20__," "due and payable 60 days from sight," or "due and payable on or before March 3, 20__" are all acceptable. The holder must be able to determine from the face of the instrument the latest possible time it can be paid without default.

Even if the instrument is subject to an acceleration clause, as long as a specific date is otherwise named, the instrument is still negotiable. An acceleration clause allows the obligee to declare the full amount due and payable upon the occurrence of a particular event, such as the failure to make a payment. An acceleration clause hastens the maturity date. An example is, "In case of default in payments of interest, or of an installment of the principal, the entire note shall become due and payable." Example: John lends Robert $1,500. Robert makes a negotiable note promising to pay $150 per month for 10 months. If the note contains a provision that if Robert fails to make a payment, the balance of the note is due at that time. If Robert fails to make the fourth payment, the balance of $1,050 is due to John immediately.

Payable to Order or Bearer

The last requirement is the most straightforward: An order or bearer instrument must be "payable to the order of the named payee(s)," "payable to the named payee's order" or some equivalent wording. A bearer instrument must be written "pay to bearer," "pay to cash," "pay to the order of the bearer," "pay to the order of the named payee(s) or bearer" or the like. Finally, if an instrument is made out to an obviously fictitious person, such as Superman, it is treated as a bearer instrument.

CONCEPT SUMMARY:
Eight Requirements for Negotiable Instruments

1. Must be in writing.	• A writing can be on anything that is readily transferable.
2. Must be signed by the instrument.	• The signature can be any place on the instrument. • It can be in any form (such as word, mark or stamp) that purports to be a signature and authenticates the writing. • It can be signed in a representative capacity.
3. Must be a definite order or promise to pay.	• A promise must be more than a mere acknowledgement of a debt. • The words "I/We Promise" or "Pay" meet this criterion.
4. Must be unconditional.	• Payment cannot be expressly conditional upon the occurrence of an event. • Payment cannot be made subject to or governed by another agreement. • Payment cannot be paid out of a particular fund (except for a government issued instrument).
5. Must be an order or promise to pay a sum certain.	• An instrument may state a sum certain even if payable in installments, with interest, at a stated discount or at an exchange rate. • Inclusion of cost of collection and attorney's fees does not disqualify the statement of a sum certain.
6. Must be payable in money.	• Any medium of exchange recognized as the currency of a government is money. • The maker or drawer cannot retain the option to pay the instrument in money or something else.

7. Must be payable on demand or at a definite time.	• Any instrument payable on sight, presentation or issue is a demand instrument.
	• An instrument is payable at a definite time even though it is payable on a stated date, or within a fixed period after sight, or the drawer or maker has an option to extend time for a definite period.
	• Acceleration clauses, even if unenforceable, do not affect the negotiability of the instrument.
8. Must be payable to order or bearer.	• An order instrument must name the payee with reasonable certainty.
	• An instrument whose terms intend payment to no particular person is payable to bearer.

Comprehension Check
Give a brief explanation of the elements of a **negotiable instrument**.

Kinds of Negotiable Instruments

To some extent, commercial law is a reflection of customs and usages of trade in the business world. The development of the law concerning commercial paper—checks, promissory notes and the like—grew from commercial necessity. In 1896, the National Conference of Commissioners on Uniform Laws drafted the Uniform Negotiable Instruments Law. This law was reviewed by the states, and by 1920 all had adopted it. The Uniform Negotiable Instruments Law was the forerunner of Article 3 of the Uniform Commercial Code (UCC).

There are four types of instruments specified in UCC 3-104, which serve as a substitute for money and as a credit device:

1. Drafts.
2. Checks.
3. Notes.
4. Certificates of deposit.

Comprehension Check
List the basic types of negotiable instruments.

Drafts

A **draft**, also known as **a bill of exchange**, *is an instrument that orders someone else to pay.* The order is given by the drawer, who issues the draft usually by signing it in the lower right-hand corner. The one who is ordered to pay the money is called the drawee. The one who is to receive the money is known as the payee.

Drafts may be presented to the drawee for payment or for acceptance. When a draft is presented for acceptance, the drawee is asked to become liable on the instrument. To accept a draft, the drawee writes "accepted" across the face of the instrument, and dates and signs it. By doing this, the drawee agrees to pay the instrument at a later date when it becomes due. (*See* Figure 16-2.)

Figure 16-2   **Sight Draft**

$ __576.00__	__Anytown, USA, May 3, 20--__
__At sight__	Pay to
the order of _____	
__Five hundred seventy-six and 00/100__	Dollars
__Bill of lading attached__	

Value received and charge the same to account of
To __World Shipping__   }   Davis Company
No. __361__   __Anytown, USA__   }   *John Doe*

Checks

A **check** *is a draft on which the drawee is a bank that is ordered to pay on demand;* it is the most common form of a draft. It is drawn on a bank by a drawer, who has an account with the bank, to the order of a specified person or business named on the check, or to the bearer. Ownership of a check may be transferred to another person by the endorsement of the payee. In this manner, a check may circulate among several parties, taking the place of money. Banks provide regular and special printed check forms. These check forms display a series of numbers printed in magnetic ink, known as the MICR line, which makes it possible to process checks electronically and accurately. Among the information found on a MICR line is the check number (usually located to the far left). If the magnetic numbers do not match the printed numbers at the upper right, the check is likely fraudulent and should not be accepted.

The use of printed forms is not required. Any writing, no matter how crude, may be used as a check if it is a draft drawn on a bank and payable on demand.

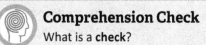

Comprehension Check
What is a **check**?

Special Types of Checks

Bank Drafts

A **bank draft,** sometimes called a **teller's check or a treasurer's check**, *is a check drawn by one bank on another bank in which it has funds on deposit in favor of a third person, the payee.*

Cashier's Checks

A **cashier's check** *is a check drawn by a bank upon itself.* The financial institution is both the drawer and the drawee. The bank, in effect, lends its credit to the purchaser of the check. Courts have held that payment cannot be stopped on a cashier's check because the bank, by issuing it, accepts the check in advance.

Certified Checks

A **certified check** *is a check that is guaranteed by the bank.* At the request of either the depositor or the holder, the bank acknowledges that sufficient funds will be withheld from the drawer's account to pay the amount stated on the check. The UCC provides that "certification of a check is acceptance." This means that a drawee bank that certifies a check becomes primarily liable on the instrument just the same as the acceptor of a draft. The bank has absolute liability to pay.

Whether anyone is secondarily liable depends upon who had the check certified. If the drawer had the check certified, the drawer and all endorsers remain secondarily liable on the instrument. If, on the other hand, the holder had the check certified, the drawer and all prior endorsers are discharged. The UCC places no obligation on a bank to certify a check if it does not want to do so.

Money Orders

A **money order** is usually presumed to have the significance of cash, but one must be aware of the issuer's identity and validity. In some areas of the country, money orders are sold by companies other than financial institutions or the U.S. Postal Service. They are privately-owned companies and may or may not have sufficient cash to cover the money order when it is presented for payment. Caution is advised when accepting a money order as payment if the issuer is not known. Investigate the issuer before negotiating the instrument.

Traveler's Checks

A **traveler's check** *is similar to a cashier's check in that the issuing financial institution is both the drawer and the drawee.* The purchaser signs the checks in the presence of the issuer when they are purchased. Technically, most traveler's checks are not checks but drafts, because the drawee—for example, American Express—is not ordinarily a bank.

Postdated Checks

A check may be **postdated** *when the drawer has insufficient funds in the bank but expects to have sufficient funds to cover the amount of the check at a future date.* A postdated check is not usually covered in the bad check laws of the states. Third-party collectors subject to the Fair Debt Collection Practices Act are restricted in their reliance on postdated checks.

Sight Drafts, Time Drafts and Trade Acceptances

A **sight draft** *is payable as soon as it is presented to the drawee for payment.* A **time draft** *is not payable until the lapse of a particular time period stated on the draft.* A **trade acceptance** *is a draft used by a seller of goods to receive payment and also to extend credit.* It is often used in combination with a bill of lading, which is a receipt given by a freight company to someone who ships goods. For example, a seller ships goods to a buyer and sends a bill of lading, with a trade acceptance attached, to a bank in the buyer's city. The trade acceptance is drawn by the seller ordering the buyer to pay either the seller or someone else. If it is a sight draft, the buyer must pay the draft immediately to receive the bill of lading from the bank. If it is a time draft, the buyer must accept the draft to receive the bill of lading from the bank. The freight company will not release the goods to the buyer unless the buyer has the bill of lading. (*See* Figures 16-2 and 16-3.)

Figure 16-3   **Time Draft**

$ __250.00__   Anytown, USA, July 12, 20--

__In or within 30 days__   Pay to

the order of _____Robert Jones_____   *Accepted*

__Two hundred fifty and 00/100__   *Jim Wilkes*   Dollars
                                                               July 16, 20--

Value received and charge the same to account of

To __Jim Wilkes__

No. __1025__   __Anytown, USA__   }   *John Doe*

Domestic Bill of Exchange

A **domestic bill of exchange** *is a draft that is drawn and payable in the United States.* A draft that is drawn in one country but is payable in another is called an **international bill of exchange** or **foreign draft**.

Notes

A **note,** or **promissory note,** *is a written promise by one party, called the maker, to pay money to the order of another party, called the payee.* In contrast with drafts, notes are promise instruments rather than order instruments, and they involve only two parties instead of three. They are used by people who loan money or extend credit as evidence of debt. *When two or more parties sign a note, they are called* **co-makers.**

Demand Notes

A **demand note,** *as its name implies, is payable whenever the payee demands payment.* A **time note** *is payable at some future time, on a definite date named in the instrument.* Unless a note is payable in installments, the principal (face value) of the note plus interest must be paid on the date that it is due. In an **installment note,** *the principal, together with interest on the unpaid balance, is payable in installments at specified times.* (*See* Figure 16-4.)

Figure 16-4   **Demand Note**

Anytown, USA, February 27, 20--

On demand, the undersigned, for value received, promise(s) to pay to the order of

anytown trust company

Five thousand two hundred and 00/100   **Dollars**

at its offices in Anytown, USA, together with interest thereon from the date thereof until paid at the rate of __10__ percent per annum.

500 Anyroad Street

Anytown, USA   *John Doe*

Promissory Notes

Promissory notes come in the following forms:

- **Single-name paper** *is a note signed by only one maker.* No one else is liable on it.
- **Double-name paper** *is a promissory note signed by two or more makers or signed by the maker and endorsed by others.* With additional people standing behind the note, the likelihood of payment is increased.

A **straight note** *is the more common instrument, used merely as evidence of indebtedness.* To make certain that the note is negotiable, the word "order" must be used.

In a **serial note,** *the amount to be paid is covered by a series of notes usually of equal amounts and with maturity dates equally spaced.* A provision is usually added, stating that in the event of a default in payment, all subsequent notes become due and payable. Thus, notes with stated maturities are converted into demand instruments under this provision.

Promissory notes are commonly used for bank loans. They are not frequently used for merchandise transactions. However, some credit executives will ask their customers to sign a note for past-due accounts, believing that it will stimulate payment and make collection of the account easier. This practice provides written acknowledgment of the past-due debt, while also postponing the due date of the account until the date stated on the note.

Collateral Notes

A **collateral note** *is a note that is secured by certain collateral, such as stocks, bonds, personal property or mortgages.* Its outstanding feature is that the collateral is held by the creditor while the note is outstanding. Such a note may be negotiated in the same manner as any negotiable note, whether the collateral is assigned or not.

Judgment Notes

Judgment notes *are controlled by state law and have many technical requirements associated with them.* These promissory notes are generally given in connection with a separate agreement by the maker who consents to have a judgment entered should payment not be made on the note when due. *The separate agreement consenting to the judgment is known as a* **confession of judgment.** Clauses that sanction confession of judgment prior to maturity are not authorized by the UCC because they do not contain an unconditional promise to pay at a definite time.

The note may be endorsed and negotiated by the payee in the same manner as any other negotiable instrument. The confession of judgment is not negotiable but may be assigned by the payee to an endorsee along with the note. *In essence, the confession of judgment enables a creditor to enter a judgment without going to trial. Because it usually can be entered without advising the debtor, it has been criticized as violating the constitutional rights of due process.*

Comprehension Check
What are some of the types of payment?

Certificates of Deposit

A **certificate of deposit (CD)** *is an acknowledgment by a bank of the receipt of money and its promise to pay the money back on the due date, usually with interest.* Certificates of deposit generally pay more interest than regular savings accounts because the depositor cannot withdraw the money before the due date without penalty. Their negotiability allows them to be sold, to be used to pay debts or to serve as security or collateral for a loan or credit agreement.

Negotiation of Commercial Paper

Assignment

Commercial paper that does not meet all of the requirements of negotiability may only be transferred by assignment, which is governed by the ordinary principles of contract law. An **assignment** *is the transfer of contract rights from one person to another.* Commercial paper is assigned either when a person whose endorsement is required on an instrument transfers it without endorsing it or when it is transferred to another person and does not meet the requirements of negotiability. In all such transfers, the transferee has only the rights of an assignee and is subject to all defenses existing against the assignor.

An assignment of commercial paper also occurs by operation of law when the holder of an instrument dies or becomes bankrupt. In such cases, title to the instrument vests in the personal representative of the estate or the trustee in bankruptcy.

Negotiation

Negotiation *is the transfer of an instrument in such a form that the transferee becomes a holder.* A **holder** *is a person who is in possession of an instrument issued or endorsed to that person, to that person's order, to bearer or in blank.* For example, XYZ Supply issues a payroll check "to the order of Mary Jones." Jones takes the check to the supermarket, signs her name on the back (an endorsement), gives it to the cashier (at delivery) and receives cash. Smith has negotiated the check to the supermarket.

If an instrument is payable to order, such as "pay to the order of," it is known as **order paper.** To be negotiated, order paper must be endorsed by the payee and delivered to the party to whom it is transferred. *If an instrument is payable to bearer or cash, it is called* **bearer paper** *and may be negotiated by delivery alone, without an endorsement.* When order paper is endorsed with a blank endorsement, it is turned into bearer paper and may be further negotiated by delivery alone. The use of bearer paper involves more risk through loss or theft than the use of order paper.

Assume Susan Smith writes a check "payable to cash" and hands it to John Doe (at delivery). Smith has negotiated the check (a bearer instrument) to Doe. Doe places the check in his wallet, which is subsequently stolen. The thief has possession of the check. At this point, negotiation has not occurred, because delivery must be voluntary on the part of the transferor. If the thief "delivers" the check to an innocent third person, however, negotiation will be complete. All rights to the check will be passed absolutely to that third person, and Doe will lose all right to recover the proceeds of the check from the third person. Of course, Smith can recover her money from the thief if the thief can be found!

Comprehension Check
Define the concept of **negotiation**.

Endorsements

An instrument is **endorsed** *when the holder signs it, thereby indicating the intent to transfer ownership to another.* Endorsements may be written in ink, typewritten or stamped. They may be written on a separate piece of paper that becomes part of it. Although the UCC does not require endorsements to be on the back of the instrument, they are usually placed on the back of the instrument for convenience purposes. Each endorsement of a negotiable instrument is a separate contract, standing apart from that of the maker or any other endorser.

Once an instrument qualifies as a negotiable instrument, the form of endorsement will have no effect on the character of the underlying instrument. Endorsement relates to the right of the holder to negotiate the paper and the manner in which negotiation must be done.

Common Types of Endorsements

Blank Endorsement

A **blank or general endorsement** *consists merely of the signature of the payee and converts the instrument into a bearer instrument and may be transferred by delivery alone.* No particular **endorsee,** *person to whom an instrument is endorsed,* is named. If the instrument is lost or stolen and gets into the hands of another holder, the new holder can recover its face value by delivery alone. (*See* Figure 16-5.)

Figure 16-5   **Blank Endorsement**

ENDORSE HERE

Robert Jones

BELOW THIS LINE

September 15, 20--

Robert Jones $ 132.00

ty-two and 00/100   Dollars

The Oakwood Grill

By   *John Oakwood*

When an instrument is made payable to a person under a misspelled name or a name other than that person's own, the payee may endorse in the incorrect name, in the correct name or in both. Signatures in both names may be required by a person paying or giving value to the instrument.

Special Endorsement

A **special endorsement,** *also called an endorsement in full, is made by writing the words "pay to the order of" or "pay to" followed by the name of the person to whom it is to be transferred (the endorsee) and the signature of the endorser. A special endorsement is one that specifies to whose order an instrument is payable.* (*See* Figure 16-6.)

Figure 16-6   Special Endorsement

ENDORSE HERE

Pay to the order of
Anytown Service Station
John Doe

DO NOT WRITE, STAMP OR SIGN BELOW THIS LINE
RESERVED FOR FINANCIAL INSTITUTION USE*

Restrictive Endorsement

A **restrictive endorsement** *limits the rights of the endorsee in some manner in order to protect the rights of the endorser.* An endorsement is restrictive if it is conditional; attempts to prohibit further transfer of the instrument; includes the words "for collection," "for deposit," "pay any bank" or like terms signifying a purpose of deposit or collection; or otherwise states that it is for the benefit or use of the endorser or of another person. (*See* Figure 16-7.)

Figure 16-7   Restrictive Endorsement

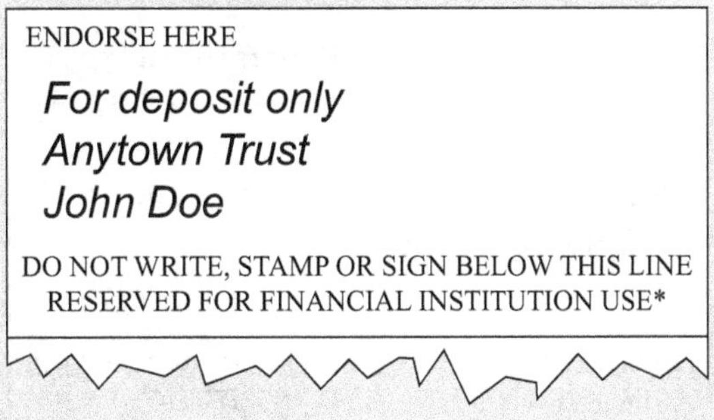

ENDORSE HERE

For deposit only
Anytown Trust
John Doe

DO NOT WRITE, STAMP OR SIGN BELOW THIS LINE
RESERVED FOR FINANCIAL INSTITUTION USE*

Conditional Endorsement

A **conditional endorsement,** *a type of restrictive endorsement, makes the rights of the endorsee subject to the occurrence of a certain event or condition.* (*See* Figure 16-8.)

Figure 16-8   Conditional Endorsement

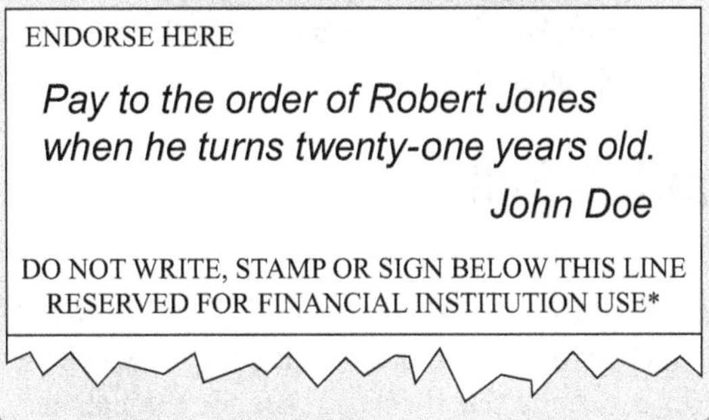

ENDORSE HERE

Pay to the order of Robert Jones
when he turns twenty-one years old.
                    John Doe

DO NOT WRITE, STAMP OR SIGN BELOW THIS LINE
RESERVED FOR FINANCIAL INSTITUTION USE*

Endorsements for Deposit or Collection

Endorsements for deposit or collection are designed to get an instrument into the banking system for the purpose of deposit or collection. *When a check is endorsed "for deposit only," the amount of the instrument is credited* *to the endorser's account before it is negotiated further.* Retail stores often stamp each check "for deposit only" when it is received. This wording provides protection in the event the check is stolen. Checks mailed to a bank for deposit should always be endorsed in this way.

Qualified Endorsement

A **qualified endorsement** *is one in which words have been added to the signature that limit the liability of the endorser.* By adding the words "without recourse" to the endorsement, the endorser disclaims liability on the instrument and cuts off their obligation to future endorsers and holders to pay on the instrument. The mere use of the words "without recourse" does not wholly relieve the endorser from liability. Under UCC 3-417, it is provided that every person who signs their name as a qualified endorser of a negotiable instrument warrants, by their signature, that:

1. they have good title to the instrument or are authorized to obtain payment or acceptance on behalf of one who has good title and the transfer is otherwise rightful;

2. all signatures are genuine or authorized;

3. the instrument has not been materially altered;

4. they have no knowledge of any defense of any party that is good against them;

5. they have has no knowledge of any insolvency proceeding instituted with respect to the maker, acceptor or drawer of an unaccepted instrument. (*See* Figure 16-9.)

Figure 16-9   Qualified Endorsement

ENDORSE HERE

Pay to the order of Robert Jones without recourse.

John Doe

DO NOT WRITE, STAMP OR SIGN BELOW THIS LINE
RESERVED FOR FINANCIAL INSTITUTION USE*

General Endorsements

A **general endorsement** *is without reservation or qualification.* A general endorser warrants everything mentioned in 1, 2, 3 and 5 above and that they have good title. There is no defense of any party that is good against them and that they have no knowledge that the drawer's or maker's signature is unauthorized and that the endorsement has not been materially altered.

Comprehension Check
List and describe the types of **endorsements**.

Checks Marked "Paid in Full"

The general rule when receiving a check marked "Paid in Full" is as follows: If the claim is paid and there is no dispute as to the amount due, a check for a lesser amount than the claim, even though marked "Paid in Full" does not settle the account. The creditor may keep the check and sue for the balance. If, however, there is a *bona fide* dispute as to the amount of the claim, and the same claim is not liquidated, a check sent and marked "Paid in Full," or "In full payment of account" is payment in full. Consequently, the creditor must either return the check and sue for the amount claimed or accept the check in complete payment. Whether a *bona fide* dispute exists can be a matter of dispute in itself, and obviously a debtor wishing to pay a lesser sum can very easily make such a claim. A good practice before accepting a check marked "Paid in Full" is to be very certain there is no dispute. It is all too common for someone outside the credit department to be aware that the customer has disputed the amount due because of pricing, time of delivery, damage, merchandise not meeting specifications, etc.

The retention and deposit of the check by the creditor may constitute an accord and satisfaction even though the creditor notifies the debtor that it has only received a partial payment on account. The creditor is therefore placed in a difficult position: either they must reject such a check and demand payment of the full amount, or accept the check and possibly be deemed to have made an accord and satisfaction. One possible solution to this problem is to stamp all collection checks with a legend that states:

> "This check is accepted without prejudice and with full preservation of all rights pursuant to Section 1-204 of the UCC."

Under this UCC section, a party who explicitly so reserves their rights does not prejudice the rights reserved. Some courts have held that this section of the UCC applies only to UCC-covered transactions such as the sale of goods, and does not apply to service contracts; other courts have entirely rejected the application of the UCC to checks marked "Paid in Full." In some instances, however, the courts have held that where a creditor gave a release under seal, the acceptance of a smaller amount than the amount due, even in a liquidated claim, releases the debt.

Comprehension Check
What is the general rule for handling a check marked "Paid in Full"?

Check Writing Alternatives*

During the past several years, the financial services industry has made significant progress in migrating consumers from paper checks to electronic payments such as credit and debit cards at the point of sale, online bill payment through Internet banking and biller websites, and traditional ACH applications of direct payment and direct deposit. However, the same level of progress has not occurred in moving businesses from checks to electronic payments.

The research confirms that businesses continue to write checks because they perceive this to be the most convenient method of payment to trading partners and sellers. A primary reason cited for using checks is the availability of remittance information that flows with the payment.

While most companies use both checks and wire transfers, more than 80 percent of the volume of all corporate payments is sent using checks.

This broad finding is consistent with recent studies from The Clearing House Payments Company, Association of Financial Professionals and the Federal Reserve Banks. Corporations remain slow to adopt electronic payments for the following reasons:

- Checks are easier to initiate and have perceived float advantages.
- Cash management and accounting systems do not provide the features desired to send and receive payments electronically.
- For wire transfer payments, no standard exists for sending remittance information that allows efficient reconciliation and posting of electronic payments once they are received.

Excerpted from Business-to-Business Wire Transfer Payments: Customer Preferences and Opportunities for Financial Institutions *prepared by the The Clearing House and the Federal Reserve Financial Services.*

EFT/ACH BECOMING THE NEW BAD CHECKS?

As the ratio of business-to-business transactions increasingly moves away from paper checks and surface mail toward technology-fueled options like electronic funds transfer (EFT) and automated clearing house (ACH), problems generated by bad actors are becoming more frequent. Creditors familiar with bad check writers in the past are now finding more rejections of EFT and ACH transactions because of insufficient funds, especially in high-turn/frequent-delivery industries related to food products and other perishables.

The vast majority of NACM members polled in an NACM survey (78%) indicated that customers have increased their EFT and ACH payments over the last few years. Those working for companies slow to adopt, noted expanded plans to accept electronic payment with greater efficiency, usually at the company's request.

"We do more and more with EFT and ACH every day; and for the most part, we have great success with it. But, as with checks, there are returned items, and there are more issues simply because this is where the industry is going," said Michael Castania, controller and former credit manager at McAneny Brothers, Inc.

Though far from widespread, bad EFT/ACH payment incidents have become more frequent. Statutory language from state to state typically addresses "bad check" situations, but it rarely specifies or defines EFT or ACH protocol and can be wildly inconsistent. In addition, enforcement at the local level can be even more unpredictable.

"With EFT, the laws are kind of nebulous," said Sam Rousseau, of Liberty USA, Inc. "With bad checks, in states including Pennsylvania, you'd traditionally go to your magistrate, which is the lowest level of the judiciary, and present your case to an assistant district attorney. They're not quite sure of the position they can take [on electronic payment] and the law on this. It leaves us hanging out there."

In addition, ill intent is difficult to prove, significantly more so than with bad checks. According to NACM business partner United Tranzactions (UTA), a check is a legal binding contract with a signature, and there is definite intent to pay somebody; with ACH, most often you don't have a signature. Because of this, all you can do in a lengthy dispute is go to court and make your case and explain your agreement with the debtor. But you won't have much case law behind you and intent is harder to prove. For that reason, UTA has always been careful to remind that you don't necessarily have that legal binding contract with ACH and EFT.

Rousseau noted that laws in many states don't even cover bad checks well, let alone iterations like EFT. "It would be nice on a state or federal level to get it defined because EFT is the future of payment," he noted.

In the absence of widespread statutory language changes or demands from state or federal officials for greater enforcement, consider the following:

- Look at your forms/documents. "With the right documents and forms, you can more easily get legal professionals involved," said PACM President Harold Booth, CGA.
- Document relationships with customers thoroughly and early. "The better-worded and more clear-cut your documentation is, the better your chances are," said Castania.
- Try to reach out/work with the customer first. "If they're willing to work with us, it doesn't need to go further," said Castania.
- Change access to certain payment methods. "Require checks or wire transfers or some other form of payment for a habitual offender," said Rudet Fountain, NACM-National.
- If not resolved quickly, try using bad check precedent with the customer and "send a Notice of Dishonor saying they need to make good," said Nick Krawec, Esq., partner at law firm Bernstein-Burkley, PC. Payment will often follow, despite legal statute vagaries.
- If all else fails, go to court. "The only way to find out if bad check law applies to EFT is to take it to court ... Maybe it takes a court decision or two to show what the appetite for this issue is," said Krawec.
- Contact state or federal elected representatives. Tell lawmakers, "I couldn't get a judgment because of the way the statute is written. What are you going to do about that?" Remind them that you vote, said Krawec.

Business Credit *magazine, October/September, 2015*

Key Terms and Concepts

Comprehension Check

1. Define the term **negotiable instrument.**
2. Give a brief explanation of the elements of a **negotiable instrument.**
3. List the basic types of negotiable instruments.
4. What is a **check?**
5. Define the following terms:
   a. **bank draft**
   b. **cashier's check**
   c. **certified check**
   d. **money order**
   e. **traveler's check**
   f. **postdated check**
   g. **sight and time drafts**
   h. **domestic bill of exchange**
   i. **demand note**

j.   **promissory note**

k.   **collateral note**

l.   **judgment note**

6.   Define the concept of **negotiation.**

7.   List and describe the types of **endorsements.**

8.   What is the general rule for handling a check marked "Paid in Full"?

Summary..

- A negotiable instrument is basically a piece of paper that can be transferred multiple times from one person/entity to another without the use of actual cash.

- Each time it is endorsed and given to another, it represents payment to that party, which makes it a highly trusted instrument used by millions of people.

- The elements of a negotiable instrument include:

    - Be in writing

    - Be signed by the maker or drawer

    - Be an unconditional promise or order to pay

    - State a specific sum of money

    - Be payable on demand or at a definite time

    - Be payable to order or to bearer

- A drawer is the person or company who makes or executes a draft

- A draft is a written order by the first party, instructing the second party to pay money to a third party.

- **Negotiable instruments** include

    - **Drafts**

    - **Checks**

    - **Notes**

    - **Certificates of deposit**

- Checks are the most **common form of draft.** Special types of checks include:

    - **Bank drafts**

    - **Cashier's checks**

    - **Certified checks**

    - **Money orders**

    - **Traveler's checks**

    - **Postdated checks**

    - **Sight drafts, time drafts or trade acceptances**

    - **Domestic bill of exchange**

- **Notes** are a written promise by one party to pay money to the order of another party. Types include:

    - **Demand notes**

    - **Promissory notes**

    - **Collateral note**

    - **Judgment notes**

- A certificate of deposit is an acknowledgement by a bank of the receipt of money and its promise to pay money back at a future date, normally with interest. It normally pays more interest because the money cannot be withdrawn by the depositor before the due date without a penalty.
- Commercial paper does not meet all of the requirements of negotiability and may only be transferred by assignment.
- Negotiation is the transfer of an instrument in such a form that the transferee becomes a holder.
- An instrument becomes endorsed when it is signed by the holder, thereby transferring the ownership to another. **Common endorsements** include:
  - **Blank endorsement**
  - **Special endorsement**
  - **Restrictive endorsement**
  - **Conditional endorsement**
  - **Endorsement for deposit or collection**
  - **Qualified endorsement**
  - **General endorsement**
- The general rule for receiving a check labeled "Paid in Full" is as follows: an account is not considered settled even if labeled as "Paid in Full" and the check is for a lesser amount than the claim. The creditor may keep the check and sue for the balance. However, there are benefits and costs associated with the steps taken by the creditor depending on whether they decide to liquidate the payment or send the payment back to be paid in full.

References and Resources

Business Credit. Columbia, MD: National Association of Credit Management. (This 9 issues/year publication is a continuous source of relevant articles and information. Archived articles from *Business Credit* magazine are available through the web-based NACM Resource Library, which is a benefit of NACM membership.)

"Business-to-Business Wire Transfer Payments: Customer Preferences and Opportunities for Financial Institutions." The Clearing House and the Federal Reserve Financial Services.

Cole, Robert H. and Lon L. Mishler. *Consumer and Business Credit Management,* 11th ed. Boston: Irwin/McGraw Hill, 1998.

Credit Professional's Handbook: The Technical Reference Manual for Credit and Customer Financial Management. The Credit Research Foundation, 1999.

Manual of Credit and Commercial Laws. Columbia, MD: National Association of Credit Management, current edition.

PART VI

BANKRUPTCY

17 Bankruptcy Code Proceedings

OVERVIEW

The term **bankruptcy** comes from Latin and means *"broken bench."* Originally, when a merchant failed to repay suppliers in a timely manner, the suppliers would break the benches that displayed the goods of the merchant. With a broken bench, that merchant was unable to conduct business. Today, bankruptcy is far more complex and is governed by federal law. This chapter presents the general basics of bankruptcy. As with all legal issues, credit professionals are urged to seek legal counsel.

THINK ABOUT THIS

Q. What are the most important factors to ensure the business receives payment when a customer files for bankruptcy?

Q. What steps can a creditor take to mitigate risk exposure if the possibility of a bankruptcy exists?

Q. After learning a customer has filed for bankruptcy, what steps should a creditor take?

DISCIPLINARY CORE IDEAS

After reading this chapter, the reader should understand:

- ☑ The automatic stay provisions of the Bankruptcy Code.
- ☑ Chapters 7, 11, 12 and 13 of the Bankruptcy Code.
- ☑ How to establish a response to bankruptcy filings.
- ☑ How to pursue claims.
- ☑ How the Office of the U.S. Trustee works.
- ☑ The basic recovery procedure.

CHAPTER OUTLINE

Bankruptcy Code History and Summary

The **Bankruptcy Code,** found in Title 11 of the United States Code, *is the federal law that provides an organized procedure under the supervision of a federal court for dealing with insolvent debtors.* The Bankruptcy Code was adopted in 1978 and became effective on October 1, 1979. The 1978 Code was the first substantial revision of the bankruptcy laws in effect in the United States. Prior to 1979, the **Bankruptcy Act of 1898** (or the **Bankruptcy Act**) was in force. *Although the 1898 Act allowed for individual bankruptcy filings, it was primarily a business law for the winding down of failed businesses.* The **Bankruptcy Abuse Prevention and Consumer Protection Act of 2005 (BAPCPA)**, enacted on April 20, 2005, became generally effective on October 17, 2005. While many of the provisions of the BAPCPA address consumer and individual bankruptcies, the BAPCPA also affects corporations, small businesses and farmers, and deals with multinational debtors.

The Code consists of nine chapters. The first three chapters, **Chapters 1, 3** and **5,** *contain administrative provisions that apply in all cases under the Bankruptcy Code.* The remaining six chapters, **Chapters 7, 9, 11, 12, 13** and **15** *are the operative chapters for filing different types of bankruptcies.* The threshold amounts in the chapters are periodically adjusted for inflation.

Chapter 7 *is a liquidation bankruptcy,* sometimes called a straight bankruptcy, in which a trustee is appointed by the United States Trustee in every case to liquidate nonexempt assets.

Chapter 9 *pertains to municipalities and governmental units.* A Chapter 9 bankruptcy can only be filed on a voluntary basis.

Chapter 11 *is the business reorganization chapter.* Most Chapter 11s involve a debtor in possession of assets who is attempting to rehabilitate a business. A small business may reorganize under an expedited Chapter 11 proceeding. A small business is defined as a business with total debts of less than $2,566,050.

Chapter 12 *is commenced only by a voluntary petition by family farmers who have debt up to $4,153,150 and family fishermen who have debts up to $1,924,550.* There are also set percentages of the debt which must have arisen from the operation of the family farm or fishing operations (50 percent for farmers and 80 percent for fishermen) while in each instance, 50 percent of the annual gross income must have been derived from the farm or fishing operation. The purpose of Chapter 12 is to provide family farmers and family fishermen with a chance to reorganize debt and retain their assets.

Chapter 13 *is sometimes called the wage earner's plan. Any individual with regular wages or income is eligible to file under Chapter 13, including certain professionals or business owners.* The threshold limits for a debtor to be eligible to file are $394,725 for unsecured debts and $1,184,200 for secured debts.

Chapter 15 *provides mechanisms to deal with multi-national insolvencies.* It is intended to establish cooperation among U.S. courts, trustees and debtors and their foreign counterparts.

One of the most important things to know about the Bankruptcy Code is that adherence to deadlines is critical; noncompliance can affect a creditor's rights under the law.

> **Comprehension Check**
> Provide a brief definition of the following chapters of the Bankruptcy Code: **7, 9, 11, 12, 13** and **15.**

Federal Rules of Bankruptcy Procedure

Congress has empowered the Supreme Court to adopt rules of procedure for bankruptcy cases, called the **Federal Rules of Bankruptcy Procedure.** There are nine chapters of rules containing deadlines and other regulations that govern pleadings, motions, practice and procedures in the bankruptcy court. They also provide for the Bankruptcy Courts and the United States District Courts to adopt local rules. If there is a conflict between the provisions of the Bankruptcy Code itself and the various applicable rules, the Bankruptcy Code prevails.

The Automatic Stay

The filing of a bankruptcy petition imposes an **automatic stay** *which is an injunction that halts actions by creditors, with certain exceptions, to collect debts from a debtor who has declared bankruptcy.* These actions include:

- Beginning or continuing judicial proceedings against the debtor.
- Obtaining possession of the debtor's property.
- Creating, perfecting or enforcing a lien against the debtor's property.
- Setting off indebtedness owed to the debtor that arose prior to the bankruptcy proceeding.

The purpose of an automatic stay is to ensure a fair distribution of the debtor's nonexempt, unencumbered assets among creditors. It prohibits any action to collect the debt from the debtor or the debtor's property. Governmental agencies, such as the IRS, cannot seize or file liens against the assets of the debtor without permission of the Bankruptcy Court. Generally, creditors cannot offset credits or returns against the debtor's debt. Any violation of the stay is in contempt of court and may be punishable by fines and fees.

A creditor may seek permission of the court to lift, terminate or modify the automatic stay if that creditor can show cause. One reason to lift the automatic stay is a lack of adequate protection of an interest in property. The creditor must show that the debtor does not have any equity in such property and such property is not necessary for a successful reorganization. In order to lift the automatic stay, the creditor must file a motion for relief from the automatic stay. Usually a filing fee is required. In routine Chapter 7 consumer cases, motions rarely have hearings; complex Chapter 11 cases almost always do. An unsecured creditor seeking to lift the automatic stay should consult with counsel upon receipt of the bankruptcy filing.

 Comprehension Check
What is the purpose of an **automatic stay** in bankruptcy?

What Happens When the Owner Goes Bankrupt?*

A mechanic's lien serves as a powerful tool for contractors, subcontractors and materials suppliers to secure payment for their work, labor or supplies. The lien, placed on real property, is based on the value added to the property during the construction process. It gives claimants the ability to force a sale of the property to obtain funds necessary to pay the delinquent debt, said William Porter, Esq., a principal in the Porter Law Group, Inc., based in Sacramento, CA.

Mechanic's liens holders file against property owners of a project as protection against not getting paid by a general contractor or subcontractor. But what happens if the property owner files for bankruptcy?

The owner/developer's bankruptcy does not automatically negate a mechanic's lien, said Wanda Borges, Esq., principal of Borges & Associates, LLC, in Syosset, NY. "A mechanic's lien gives a creditor a good position because it has an interest in the debtor's property. It's secured debt and has a greater chance of being paid in a bankruptcy proceeding. That lien will stay intact." A mechanic's lien also is not subject to preference payment rules because the creditor has that legal right to file, Borges added. Mechanic's liens are statutory liens and as such are unavoidable in a bankruptcy proceeding and will survive the bankruptcy unaffected.

Secured creditors hold significant advantages over unsecured creditors in nearly all bankruptcy cases, Borges said. A holder of a valid mechanic's lien is treated as a secured creditor and entitled to full payment, provided that the property securing the lien has value in excess of prior liens and encumbrances.

Perfecting the Lien

Being able to perfect and enforce mechanic's liens is important in bankruptcy. "Ideally, a contractor, subcontractor, or supplier does so before the owner files bankruptcy," said law firm Fabyanske Westra Hart & Thomson, out of Minneapolis, MN, in a briefing paper on its website. "If a party properly perfects its mechanic's lien pre-bankruptcy, the lien will typically 'pass through' the bankruptcy unaffected." Despite the bankruptcy, the mechanic's lien holder must still perfect its lien within the time provided under state law.

"Even if a creditor hasn't filed at the time of the bankruptcy filing, it can still file that lien," Borges said. "The circumstances vary state by state." The mechanic's lien is treated as any other secured claim.

"In a Chapter 7 case, this means that the full value of the lien claim remains in place if the property has sufficient unencumbered value to satisfy the entire claim," FWH&T said. "In a Chapter 11 case, the rights of a mechanic's lien claimant may be modified by the terms of the reorganization plan. If a lien is not perfected before the bankruptcy is filed, a claimant may be relegated to the status of an unsecured creditor, which are last in line, and only recover their claims if there is money left over after the secured creditors are paid."

If it's a Chapter 11, that means there's enough money in the company for it to operate, said Chris Ring, of STS. Then it's a reorganization of the business. The lien would likely stay intact as a secured creditor. However, if it's a Chapter 7, it could be stripped away because that involves liquidating assets.

The timing of lien filings matter, Ring said. "In some states, it's 'first in time, first in right.' It's all based on a state's statute." If a state follows the "first spade rule," all liens have an equal position based on when the project started and then it sometimes becomes a battle of who gets paid.

The Automatic Stay

A debtor's bankruptcy filing triggers the automatic stay, which halts collection or enforcement activities against the owner, via Bankruptcy Code Section 362(a). "Collection or enforcement activities include beginning or continuing litigation, any efforts to collect money, or unilaterally terminating or enforcing a contract," said Christine Barker, Esq., senior counsel with Gordon & Rees LLP, in Irvine, CA.

The stay prohibits a creditor from creating, perfecting or enforcing a lien against the debtor and/or property of the debtor's estate, said Bruce Nathan, Esq., partner with Lowenstein Sandler LLP. The code, however, prescribes certain exceptions. Under the law, mechanic's lien creditors whose lien arose prior to bankruptcy may perfect, maintain or continue the perfection of an interest in the property if, under state law and in the absence of bankruptcy, the creditor could have perfected or maintained its mechanic's lien, Nathan said.

State laws vary. For instance, in some, the lien arises at the start of the project. Typically, however, it's when materials are delivered or the work is performed—before a lien is perfected. For that reason, the Bankruptcy Code allows a mechanic's lien creditor who performed work and/or supplied materials prior to the filing of the bankruptcy petition to perfect or maintain the lien.

Enforcement

Exceptions pertaining to mechanic's liens, however, do not pertain to enforcement. Section 546(b)(1) does not deal with a creditor's post-petition enforcement of its mechanic's lien rights, Nathan said. That means the bankruptcy stay applies to a creditor's post-petition action to enforce its lien rights, and the creditor cannot take any post-petition action to enforce its lien unless it obtains a Bankruptcy Court order granting relief from the stay.

"The automatic stay does prohibit filing a lawsuit to foreclose on the mechanic's lien without first obtaining Bankruptcy Court approval," Porter said. "In addition, any state court lawsuit already on file against the bankrupt party is automatically stayed (or suspended) until the Bankruptcy Court grants relief to allow the plaintiff to proceed with the action. ... State court lawsuits filed against a bankrupt debtor after the bankruptcy filing are void and of no effect."

If you have already filed a lawsuit to foreclose on your lien, this action is also paused by the automatic stay and all proceedings cease until the automatic stay is lifted, the bankruptcy is dismissed, or the property securing the mechanic's lien is abandoned, Barker said. If you have not yet filed a lawsuit to foreclose, the automatic stay prohibits you from filing suit at this time.

A mechanic's lien creditor may file a notice of continued perfection with the bankruptcy court to preserve its rights to enforce its lien against the property. Creditors can't do anything with a mechanic's lien unless they make a motion to lift the automatic stay and the court approves the motion, Borges said. If there's plenty of equity, the court could remove the stay. In that case, however, the debtor will likely try to work something out, she said.

The creditor could also petition the court for relief from the automatic stay. After the holder of the lien perfects it, enforcement of the lien may be tolled during the stay period until enforcement is possible. The holder can also petition the court to lift the stay.

Claimants must enforce mechanic's liens within a certain time period. Once the mechanic's lien claimant learns that the automatic stay is lifted, it should then proceed in state court with an action to foreclose its mechanic's lien, keeping in mind that it could lose its rights if it fails to act promptly, Porter said.

Reprinted from Business Credit *magazine. July/August, 2016. Written by Diana Mota, NACM associate editor.*

Chapter 7 Liquidation

Chapter 7, the most common type of bankruptcy filing in the U.S, *is a straight bankruptcy or liquidation.* Most *Chapter 7 filings are consumer cases.* In all Chapter 7 cases, a trustee is appointed to take possession of nonexempt assets and sell them for the benefit of creditors. There are usually few, if any, nonexempt assets to sell.

In order to be eligible to seek Chapter 7 bankruptcy relief, an individual debtor must seek credit counseling within 180 days before filing a petition and pay a filing fee. Otherwise, the Chapter 7 will be dismissed. An individual Chapter 7 debtor must also satisfy a **means test** *where net income exceeds certain amounts* in order to proceed. If the individual Chapter 7 debtor cannot satisfy the means test, the case will be dismissed or converted to a Chapter 11 or 13. Once the case is filed, the U.S. Trustee appoints an **interim trustee,** *who is usually an attorney or an accountant assigned at random from a panel of qualified individuals.* The interim trustee has two main duties: to review the file and take possession of any unencumbered assets and to preside at the **Section 341 (§341) meeting** *which is the first meeting of creditors and equity holders.* Creditors may elect a different trustee at this meeting. There are legal qualifications and steps that must be followed. If no trustee is elected at the §341 meeting, the interim trustee's position becomes permanent. After the §341 meeting, the creditors cannot elect a new trustee, although the court may replace the trustee.

The trustee has several legal responsibilities:

- Sell any assets of the estate that are not encumbered or exempt for the benefit of the creditors.
- Investigate the financial affairs of the debtor.
- Investigate and examine proofs of claims of the creditors.
- In the rare instances when there are unencumbered assets, the trustee takes possession and prepares to liquidate them.
- Liquidate the assets and notify all of the creditors of the details in advance.

If a creditor has an interest in the property to be sold, such as a lease, consignment or secured position, that creditor must file an objection before the sale date. Objections are usually filed to ensure that the creditor's security interest in the sold asset will be recognized and, if the security interest is valid, that the creditor will receive the proceeds of sale. Without the filing of an objection, assets sold by the trustee are normally sold with clear title to the property and free of any liens.

Trustee's Compensation

Chapter 7 trustees are paid a small fee per case handled plus a percentage of the assets distributed to creditors. Compensation is so low that courts usually award the maximum compensation possible. Except for office overhead, trustees may be reimbursed by the estate for their expenses. Creditors are notified of intended payments to trustees and others and may file objections within the stated deadline in the notice.

Comprehension Check
What are the basic duties of a **trustee?**

Filing a Proof of Claim

In a Chapter 7 bankruptcy, a creditor must file **proof of claim form 410**, *which is used by creditors to indicate the amount of debt owed by the debtor on the date of the bankruptcy filing,* to participate in the distribution of estate assets. By filing a proof of claim, a creditor may be waiving its right to a jury trial on certain preference and fraudulent transfer actions and submitting to the jurisdiction of the bankruptcy court for other purposes. It is prudent to discuss the filing of a claim with counsel unless it is certain that the debtor does not have a potential claim for fraudulent or preferential transfer or otherwise against the creditor.

Distribution of Assets

To close a case, the trustee files a final report with the court and with the approval of the U.S. Trustee when all the issues of a case have been settled and the trustee is prepared to distribute the funds. It is common practice for the trustee to notify the creditors of the recommended distribution of funds and their fees. If there are no objections, the final hearing is waived and the distribution is approved as stated in the notice. If a hearing is scheduled, the trustee is usually required to appear before the court. Written objections to the recommended distribution or to the tentative fees must be filed before the deadline given in the notice. The bankruptcy court then makes the final determination.

The trustees are required to satisfy claims in a particular order. The priorities are clearly established. Proceeds from assets are distributed in a sequence of priorities:

1. **Secured Creditors.** A secured creditor is entitled to have a first claim on proceeds from the sale of collateral assets. Any excess amount received from security is available to other creditors. Any deficiency in funds resulting from the sale of collateral makes the secured creditor an unsecured creditor for the amount of the deficiency. An additional first level priority claim is an allowed unsecured claim for domestic support obligations which are claims due to a spouse, former spouse, or child of the debtor, or such child's parent, legal guardian, or responsible relative.

2. **Administrative Expenses.** These are expenses related to the bankruptcy proceeding, such as professionals retained during the bankruptcy and the actual costs and expenses of preserving the estate. They also include claims for post-petition sales to a debtor in possession. This encourages creditors to extend new credit to a bankrupt business during a Chapter 11 proceeding. In addition, there is an administrative priority claim for the value of any goods received by the debtor, in the ordinary course of such debtor's business within 20 days before the date of commencement of a bankruptcy case that remain unpaid on the bankruptcy filing date.

3. **Involuntary Case Claims.** In an involuntary case, this is a claim arising in the ordinary course of debtor's business or financial affairs after the commencement of the case but before the earlier of the appointment of a trustee and the order for relief.

4. **Wages and Compensation Claims.** Wages earned within 180 days prior to a bankruptcy filing receive a priority claim limited to $10,950 per wage earner (subject to increase for inflation).

5. **Employee Benefit Plans.** These are unsecured claims for contributions to an employee benefit plan arising from services rendered within 180 days prior to a bankruptcy filing to the extent of $10,950 (subject to increase for inflation) multiplied by the number of employees covered by the pension plan less any amounts paid to the wage and compensation claims and less any amounts paid on behalf of the estate to any other benefit plan.

6. **Grain Producers or Fisherman Claims.** These are allowed unsecured claims of persons engaged in the production or growing of grain where the debtor owns or operates a grain storage facility, or a fisherman who has sold to a debtor who is engaged in operating a fish produce storage or processing facility.

7. **Customer Deposits.** A maximum of $2,425 per claimant (subject to increase for inflation) is available to individuals who place a deposit on property or services for personal, family or household use.

8. **Taxes.** Federal, state, country or any other type of government agency receives a priority.
9. **Unsecured Claims of a Federal Depository Institutions Regulatory Agency.** These are claims based upon any commitment by the debtor to a Federal depository institutions regulatory agency (or its predecessor) to maintain the capital of an insured depository institution.
10. **Claims Arising from the Unlawful Operation of a Motor Vehicle or Vessel.** These are allowed claims for death or personal injury resulting from the operation of a motor vehicle or vessel if such operation was unlawful because the debtor was intoxicated from using alcohol, a drug, or another substance.
11. **Unsecured Creditors.** These claims are often referred to as general creditors' claims. They include trade creditors, deficiency claims of secured creditors and debenture holders. A subordinated debenture also holds this type of claim but generally must turn over proceeds to the party to whom they have subordinated until the party is paid in full.
12. **Preferred Stockholders.** Preferred stockholders are paid after all creditors are paid in full.
13. **Common Stockholders.** Last in line are the common shareholders who bear the residual risk. Any remaining funds are paid to common stockholders after all other claimants are paid in full.

Trustees may not give creditors legal advice about the case. They are fiduciaries and hold the estate in trust for all the creditors. A creditor that has concerns about how a case is being handled has two options:

1. Retain counsel to object to the trustee's final report.
2. Contact the U.S. Trustee for the district in which the case is pending.

Monitoring the notices of sale and the notice of distribution is usually sufficient. A creditor with information about the estate or the conduct of the debtor's business may be helpful to the trustee.

The Bankruptcy Code permits individual debtors to claim either state or federal exemptions in an effort to give the debtor a fresh start after bankruptcy. Creditors who wish to file an objection to such exemptions must do so within 30 days of the §341 meeting. This requires familiarity with the exemption laws of the state where the debtor resides and some knowledge of the debtor's assets. Creditors must review notices as early as possible in order to meet the deadline.

Comprehension Check
In a Chapter 7, **trustees** must satisfy claims in a particular order. List the priority of claims in order.

Discharge Litigation

A **discharge** *releases individual debtors from personal liability for most debts and prevents the creditors owed those debts from taking any collection actions against the debtor.* Only debtors who meet all of the criteria and adhere to all of the rules of the Bankruptcy Code are granted a discharge through the Bankruptcy Code. Creditors may file an objection to a discharge within 60 to 90 days of the §341 meeting.

Chapter 11 Reorganization

Chapter 11, one of the most important provisions of the Bankruptcy Code, was designed to be a *single, unified way of dealing with a reorganization of most businesses.* One objective of Chapter 11 is to reorganize a troubled debtor while maximizing the return to creditors. Another objective is to retain employment and other economic benefits that the community derives from the business.

Comprehension Check
What is the purpose of **Chapter 11?**

Key Players

The key players in a Chapter 11 case include the judge, who decides the relevant legal issues; the U.S. Trustee, who appoints the creditors' committee and has general oversight responsibility; secured creditors; equity security holders; the debtor; and the creditors' committee. Where appropriate, the court may order the appointment of a trustee to operate the debtor's business or an examiner to investigate its affairs.

Comprehension Check

Who are the key players in a Chapter 11 proceeding?

Types of Petition and Jurisdiction

A case starts with the filing of a voluntary or involuntary bankruptcy petition. The petition may be filed by either a debtor or by its creditors. A petition is required to be filed in the location where the principal place of business or principal assets of a debtor have been located for 180 days or the longer portion of 180 days immediately preceding the filing of the petition than in any other location. Often, a Chapter 11 debtor may advocate for a jurisdiction that is more convenient to it and attempt to choose friendly courts. Improper filings are not permitted and are transferred to the proper venue. Jurisdiction and venue can be important to the case. Creditors can file a motion with the court to move the venue of the case.

Most bankruptcy petitions are initiated by the debtor. The filing of a petition by a debtor automatically creates an automatic stay, which generally prevents creditors from enforcing prepetition claims or from seeking recourse against the debtor's assets without permission from the court.

An **involuntary petition** may be filed by creditors under either Chapter 7 or Chapter 11. As a general rule, *if a debtor has 12 or more creditors, at least three creditors—with unsecured, noncontingent, undisputed claims—are needed to be petitioning creditors.* The three creditors' claims must aggregate $15,775 (subject to increase for inflation) in order to force an involuntary bankruptcy. The involuntary petition is served upon the debtor together with a summons in the same manner in which an adversary proceeding would be commenced. Normally, a debtor has 20 days to contest an involuntary petition.

Role of the Trustee

Under Chapter 11, the U.S. Trustee is required to attempt to appoint a creditors' committee, except in small business cases, in which a committee is not appointed. The Code specifically authorizes the U.S. Trustee to approve and appoint a prepetition committee if it is appropriately representative.

In most instances, the U.S. Trustee may contact the seven largest unsecured creditors from the list filed with the petition for relief by the debtor and solicit their willingness to serve on the committee. Committees generally have odd numbers of members to avoid the issue of tied votes. Unless and until a liquidating or operating trustee is appointed, *a debtor remains in possession of its assets and will manage its own affairs, protected by the automatic stay.* The **debtor in possession,** or **DIP,** *has a fiduciary obligation to the creditors, much the same as a court-appointed trustee.* The U.S. Trustee will normally file a formal pleading with the court stating the names and addresses of the particular creditors appointed to serve on the committee.

Debtor in Possession

The debtor in possession is required to file periodic, standardized financial reports with the U.S. Trustee and the bankruptcy court. The reports are usually provided to the creditors' committee and are available to all creditors. Creditors can review the reports to monitor the financial affairs and performance of the debtor. Failure to file these financial reports could be grounds for the case to be dismissed or converted to a Chapter 7 (liquidation). The debtor in possession has the broad authority to conduct the business under the general supervision of the U.S. Trustee and the creditors' committee, if there is one. The debtor usually has the exclusive right to file a reorganization plan for the first 120 days of the bankruptcy case, subject to extensions up to a maximum of 18 months following the filing of the bankruptcy petition. This deadline cannot be further extended by the court.

Proof of Claim

As in a Chapter 7, creditors in a Chapter 11, should always file a **proof of claim** *which is a written statement that notifies the bankruptcy court, the debtor, the trustee and their parties that a creditor wants to assert its rights to receive a distribution or payment from the bankruptcy estate.* Creditors who have filed a claim but are not listed as a potential distributee must file an objection to determine why their claim is not included for distribution. It may have been a simple oversight by the trustee. A creditor that does not object may lose its claim for good when the court approves the distribution.

A superpriority claim can be authorized by a court during a Chapter 11 proceeding. The **superpriority claim** *has priority over other administrative claims.* The court generally authorizes a superpriority claim to a post-petition lender when a debtor in a Chapter 11 case is unable to obtain new credit during the Chapter 11. If the Chapter 11 is converted into a Chapter 7 liquidation, the superpriority claimant has the first claim on all unencumbered assets. Technically, a bank that lends to a debtor in possession during a Chapter 11 is an administrative creditor equal with all other administrative creditors; yet, if granted superpriority status, the bank is in a relatively safe position.

Notifications

The Bankruptcy Code gives all creditors the right to be notified about many actions that affect the operation of the business and the assets of the bankruptcy estate. The debtor is limited in its ability to use cash collateral, such as cash from the sale of inventory or the collection of receivables that is subject to a prepetition lien. If the cash collateral is subject to valid prepetition security interests, the debtor will attempt to obtain the express permission of the creditor holding the security interest. With the creditor's permission or upon a motion by the debtor, a court order allowing the use of cash collateral will be sought. Before the debtor and the bank can arrange for the use of cash collateral, the debtor must notify all parties in interest of the proposed agreement and its terms.

Any post-petition unsecured credit obtained by the debtor outside the ordinary course of business needs court approval before it can become effective. Some types of unsecured post-petition credit, such as post-petition trade credit, which the debtor requires in its ordinary course of business operations, do not require notice or court approval. Unsecured creditors should examine, and may wish to object to, notices of post-petition credit requests that may affect their claim on remaining unencumbered assets.

The Creditors' Committee

The Bankruptcy Code requires the U.S. Trustee to attempt to form a creditors' committee of creditors willing to serve. The **creditors' committee** *has the responsibility to protect all unsecured creditors' interests, and it oversees the debtor's operations until, and sometimes after, confirmation of the plan.* It will investigate the debtor's affairs, monitor its business and negotiate a Plan of Reorganization for the benefit of unsecured creditors. It has the right to investigate questionable transactions in which the debtor or its principals might have engaged.

Congress intended that the committee be a key player in a Chapter 11 case. The committee consists of unsecured creditors selected by the U.S. Trustee, often the holders of large claims who have the most at stake. The Code provides that a small creditor whose claim is disproportionately large is also entitled to serve on a committee. The goal is for the committee to be truly representative of its constituents. The U.S. Trustee can approve a prepetition committee as the official committee if it fairly represents the creditors. The committee has a fiduciary duty to represent all creditors rather than the specific interest of an individual creditor appointed to the committee.

The financial stake of committee members, along with their expertise in the industry, gives them tremendous influence in a case. The committee may participate in all aspects of a case. Courts often rely on the committee and its positions in deciding how to act on various issues. The committee's recommendation is often the decisive factor on the question of whether a plan will be confirmed.

The law does not stipulate how committees must operate. Most committees meet at the members' convenience and operate according to committee-approved bylaws, which address issues such as meeting frequency and location, quorum and voting protocol. Official creditors' committees are allowed to retain counsel, accountants, and other professionals at the expense of the estate, with these professional fees paid before any distribution is made to creditors. Creditors serving on the official creditors' committee are allowed to submit their necessary and reasonable expenses for approval by the bankruptcy court for reimbursement. All fees by professionals are subject to review and approval by the court.

The committee cannot tell the debtor or the debtor's officers how to run the business, but if its suggestions are not considered, it may bring the issue before the court for ruling. The committee may have to deal with fraudulent or preferential transfer actions, sometimes against committee members. The committee may also ask the court for the authority to pursue an avoidance action against a secured creditor with an improperly perfected claim. A particular strength of the committee is its ability to recommend or oppose confirmation of a proposed plan of reorganization.

The committee must provide all creditors it represents with access to information concerning an ongoing Chapter 11 proceeding. Further, the committee is directed to seek comment from its constituent creditors. Many committees establish websites for the use of the committee in fulfilling this responsibility. These websites will generally provide the following:

1. General case information including dockets.
2. Monthly committee reports summarizing ongoing events in the case.
3. Highlights of significant events in the case.
4. Access to the claims docket.
5. Press releases (if any).
6. A non-public forum for creditors to submit questions, comments and requests for information.
7. Responses to creditor inquiries, if appropriate. The committee may also send private responses to a specific creditor.
8. Answers to frequently asked questions.
9. Links to other relevant websites.

Comprehension Check
What is the role of a **creditors' committee** in a Chapter 11 proceeding?

Assumption or Rejection of Executory Contracts

Section 365 of the Bankruptcy Code governs the debtor's and creditor's rights under an executory contract. Neither §365, nor any other section of the Bankruptcy Code, defines an executory contract. Congress has left it to the courts to develop a definition. Most courts define an **executory contract** *as an agreement under which both parties remain obligated to perform their obligations under the contract, and any party's failure to perform excuses the other party from continuing to perform its remaining duties under the contract.* Examples of executory contracts include long-term supply agreements where there is an ongoing requirement for the supply and purchase of goods, and where the buyer is required to purchase a certain minimum quantity of goods. Other executory contracts include purchase orders, consignment agreements and service agreements, such as advertising and subscription fulfillment contracts.

Section 365(a) of the Bankruptcy Code permits a Chapter 11 debtor to assume or reject an unexpired executory contract or lease, subject to court approval. This provision enables a debtor to retain valuable contracts and reject burdensome, unprofitable contracts. A debtor that decides to assume an executory contract or lease must satisfy Bankruptcy Code §365(b)'s requirements. They include curing all payment and other defaults under the contract, including fully paying the creditor's prepetition and post-petition claims, and providing adequate assurance of the debtor's ability to fully perform all of its future obligations under the contract.

Comprehension Check
How long does a debtor have to assume or reject **executory contracts,** with court approval, under a Chapter 11 proceeding?

With court approval, the debtor has up to the earlier of confirmation of a Chapter 11 Plan or 120 days after the bankruptcy filing to assume or reject unexpired leases of nonresidential real property. The court may extend this period for up to one additional 90-day period, provided it is granted before the expiration of the initial 120-day period. The criteria used by the debtor are whether it will be financially more advantageous to reject the leases, assume them and sublease, or sell them. The committee will monitor executory contracts very closely. Creditors will not want an executory contract assumed with the risk of subsequent rejection because that would give the contractor an administrative claim for all or most of the post-petition balance of the contract.

Plan of Reorganization

A minority of all Chapter 11 cases result in a reorganization plan. Most filings are either converted to Chapter 7 or dismissed. The classification and treatment of claims is the heart of any reorganization plan. Under the Bankruptcy Code, a **claim** is a *right to payment or a right to some equitable remedy such as injunctive relief in the event of a breach of contract.* A claim may be contingent or disputed and may not have matured at the time of filing. **Secured creditors** *are creditors holding liens or security interests in assets of the estate.* **Undersecured claims** *are those where the value of the collateral is less than the amount of the claim held by the creditor; they are partially secured and partially unsecured.* All other claims are unsecured. An **unsecured creditor** *is one who extended credit to a debtor without a collateral security.* Secured claims and priority claims (including wage claims and taxes) are entitled to be satisfied from unencumbered assets of the estate ahead of general unsecured claims.

Underlying any plan of reorganization is the method for classifying claims and the proposed treatment for each class. The Bankruptcy Code requires that at least one class must accept the plan before the court will consider it.

In most Chapter 11 cases, the debtor in possession has the exclusive right to file a plan of reorganization for 120 days up to 18 months, if extended following the petition for relief. This is reduced to 180 days, or if extended, to a 300-day deadline for filing a plan for small businesses. Depending on the complexity of the case, some of the requirements regarding the filing of the reorganization plan and disclosure statement are simplified for small business cases to allow them to exit bankruptcy sooner. When a trustee is appointed, the exclusive right is automatically terminated. When the debtor's exclusive period has ended, any interested party, including the debtor, can file a reorganization plan. If the debtor is a corporation, the corporate officers or the board of directors may propose a plan. Shareholders also can propose a plan, but not on behalf of the debtor. Partners may propose a plan for a partnership. The creditors' committee or even a single creditor can propose a plan. Outsiders may attempt to acquire the debtor's assets or even the debtor as a form of corporate takeover.

The Code also provides a fast track for small businesses. A **small business** *is defined as a person engaged in commercial or business activities, excluding real estate, whose aggregate noncontingent liquidated and unsecured debts as of the date of the petition do not exceed $2,566,050* (subject to increase for inflation). In addition, a debtor who owns only a single real estate asset is also provided with a means to a fast resolution. A **single asset real estate debtor** *is defined as real property constituting a single property or project with less than four residential units, which generates substantially all of the gross income of a debtor and on which no substantial business is being conducted by a debtor other than the business of operating the real property and activities incidental thereto.* Plans and other deadlines in these cases are far shorter than in the normal Chapter 11 case.

Comprehension Check

Define the term **claim,** under the Bankruptcy Code.

··

How is a **small business** defined under Chapter 11 of the Bankruptcy Code?

Secured Creditors

Usually the courts require each secured creditor to be placed in a separate class. If two or more secured creditors have equal claims against the same collateral, they all may be placed in one class. The potential treatments of secured creditors often depend on the value of their collateral. If the value is the same as or more than the amount of the claim, the proponent of the plan may surrender the collateral in full satisfaction of the claim. In other cases, the debtor may propose retaining the collateral and reamortizing the debt, selling the collateral and giving the secured creditor an equivalent lien on other assets, or selling the collateral and using the proceeds to pay administrative expenses and the secured creditor. The creditors' committee or an individual creditor should review the validity of secured creditors' security interests to see if they have cause to object if one or more of them adversely affect the payment to unsecured creditors.

Unsecured Creditors

The Bankruptcy Code requires that all claims of a similar nature in a single class be treated the same. Courts will generally approve a plan that puts all unsecured creditors in a single class, but this may cause problems when the unsecured creditors have to vote on a plan if there is great disparity among the claims. Plans must be approved by a minimum of one-half the number and two-thirds the amount of the claims that vote in any one class. In such cases, one large claim or many small claims could prevent acceptance of the plan. Courts may also approve a plan where unsecured creditors are divided into several classes based on their relationship to the creditor or another factual basis relating to the case. This allows for more homogeneous classes. Creditors should examine plans to see how the classification process affects their interests. Specific things to watch for are:

- Multiple classes of unsecured creditors where one or more classes receive more favorable treatment than other classes.
- A single class of unsecured creditors that logically should be split into more than one class.
- An administrative convenience class where the minimum size of the claim is set at a relatively high figure to include all trade creditors (and win acceptance by this class) and exclude creditors with unsecured deficiency claims.

Creditors may file objections to the classifications of claims in a plan before the confirmation hearing, or earlier. Plans vary from **extension plans** *which provide unsecured creditors full payment over time* to **compromise plans** *(partial payment)* to no payment at all. The creditors' main concern in the reorganization plan is the kind of payment the plan proposes for the creditors' class. The only reason an unsecured creditor might consider a plan that provides no payment at all for its class is if there are no assets to be salvaged by liquidation, operation, or by sale. **Partial payments** *are usually for a percentage of unsecured claims either when the plan is confirmed or over time.* The timing of payments will affect the willingness of creditors to approve the plan. Unsecured creditors evaluating a proposed reorganization plan should compare the payment being offered against the liquidation value of the debtor's assets. **Pot plans** *set aside some of the debtor's assets for liquidation and distribution to the unsecured creditors.* This is usually done to gain the approval of the unsecured creditors although the value of the assets in the pot to be divided is usually difficult to estimate. Extension plans are uncommon, but sometimes the debtor will offer a **debt for equity swap** *which is a transaction in which the obligations (debts) of a company or individual are exchanged for something of value (equity).*

Comprehension Check

How are claims classified under the Bankruptcy Code?

In the case of a publicly-traded company, this would generally entail an exchange of bonds for stock. A plan can include a variety of payment plans and can offer payment choices to the classes of creditors. The danger in liquidation for unsecured creditors is that secured, administrative and other priority claims may absorb all of the liquidation proceeds, leaving nothing for general unsecured claims.

Interest Classification and Treatment

Whether the business is a sole proprietorship, partnership or corporation, the plan must classify the ownership interest and propose treatment. Equity holders are normally the last to receive any payment, and a plan must be accepted by creditors or pay them in full before equity holders may receive any payment.

Provision for Execution of Plan

A reorganization plan should spell out how the assets, claims and interests will be treated, as well as give specifics and a time schedule for any sale, liquidation or restructuring of the business, including deadlines for the distribution of any payments. A plan may also contain additional optional provisions. A plan may not discharge the guarantee claim of a creditor against a principal of the business if the guarantee holder objects.

The Bankruptcy Code requires that a proponent of a plan disclose certain information in conjunction with the solicitation of the votes on the plan and that the court must approve the disclosure statement. In general, protracted litigation over the amount of the information disclosed by the proponent of the plan is counterproductive. Such litigation wastes estate assets and can delay a plan whose success depends on speedy action and distribution to the creditors. The disclosure statement is sent pro forma to the creditors' committee and the major secured creditors only, and a hearing date is set. Other creditors must request a copy in writing from the debtor's lawyer. Objections must be received before a deadline set by the court and can be argued at the hearing. Under §1111(b), certain undersecured creditors may elect to have their claim treated as though it were fully secured for confirmation purposes. Creditors with this option should consult counsel. No one may solicit rejections or acceptances of a plan until the court has approved the disclosure statement.

Comprehension Check
What information is contained in a **plan of reorganization?**

Voting Process

For a plan to be accepted, a majority in each class must vote to accept it. A **majority** *is defined as those holding at least two-thirds in amount and one-half in number of the allowed claims voting on the plan.* The bankruptcy court may disallow votes procured in bad faith, such as in return for a payment, or not in accordance with the Bankruptcy Code. The law requires that a formal ballot either accepting or rejecting the proposed plan be returned to the court or to counsel in order to be counted.

Ballots are sent to the creditors with the proposed plan. Ballots must be returned before the deadline in order to be counted. After the deadline, counsel for the plan's proponent files a certificate of voting that lists all ballots, including those that are disputed or were returned late, and gives the result of the voting. The plan proponent or the debtor will sometimes object to a particular claim and request the court to disallow it for voting purposes. This is usually done to affect the results of the vote on the plan. Creditors that receive such an objection to their claim must respond by a given deadline and request a hearing or risk having the claim disallowed. Sometimes competing plans are sent to creditors simultaneously. It is permissible to have only one ballot that allows creditors to express their preference for one plan over the other.

The Confirmation Process

Confirmation *refers to court approval of the plan.* The first step is to file the reorganization plan and the disclosure statement. After the disclosure statement is approved as presenting the necessary information, all creditors entitled to vote receive a notice of the confirmation hearing, a copy of the reorganization plan and the disclosure statement. The court may choose to combine the hearings on the plan and the disclosure statement to save time and expense. A combined hearing also occurs in small business Chapter 11 cases. The notice also includes the identity of the proponent of the reorganization plan, a ballot for voting on the plan, deadlines for filing objections and for returning ballots, and provides directions on where to send completed ballots. Objections should be explained as specifically as possible and filed promptly—usually a week or so before the date set for the confirmation hearing. The ballots are tallied and reported to the court. Plan proponents are allowed to submit modifications to the reorganization plan up until the confirmation hearing. If the modification does not affect all classes or improves the treatment for one class, it does not have to be resubmitted to the creditors for another general vote. There is no set procedure for a confirmation hearing. The procedure is determined, to a large extent, by the objections filed and the complexity of the case. The court is likely to confirm the plan if all classes of creditors and interest holders have accepted it by the necessary majorities, and the unsecured creditors will get a distribution that equals or exceeds what they would receive in liquidation. *The bankruptcy court is allowed to confirm a plan that has been rejected by one or more classes. This is known as a* **cramdown,** *and is more often a threat than a reality.* Cramdown procedures differ depending on the creditor class involved.

Comprehension Check
In order for a **plan of reorganization** to be accepted, what is necessary?

The Absolute Priority Rule

An **absolute priority rule** *stipulates the order of payment in the event of liquidation. Debts to creditors will be paid first and shareholders (partial owners) divide what remains.* The absolute priority rule prevents confirmation of a reorganization plan without the consent of the necessary classes of creditors if the plan provides that the shareholders in the corporation or the individual debtor in an individual case will retain an interest in assets after confirmation. The rule comes into play if the debtor proposes to pay less than 100 percent of all allowed claims and the holders of those claims do not accept the plan by the necessary majority. The absolute priority rule bars confirmation of the reorganization plan unless the creditors accept it by the necessary majority, or it provides for full payment to the creditors or wipes out all junior classes.

Comprehension Check
What is the **absolute priority rule?**

Postconfirmation Problems

The Bankruptcy Code permits the proponent of the plan to make postconfirmation modifications only if a substantial transfer of assets as outlined in the plan has not already taken place. Only the plan proponents can request such a modification. Postconfirmation modifications tend to be for the purpose of correcting technical errors and are not significant changes in the plan. If the modification changes the rights of the creditors in the original confirmed plan, then the creditors must vote on the modifications. The court may consider dismissing a case after a plan has been confirmed if the plan has not been substantially consummated. This is rare because of the difficulties in reversing the effects of the confirmation. Postconfirmation conversion of a case to Chapter 7 is possible if the debtor fails to substantially consummate the confirmed plan or materially defaults on the plan. If this happens, the creditors are notified in advance about the court motion required for the conversion. If the confirmation was obtained by fraud, the court may revoke it, but only within the first 180 days after the confirmation order was entered. The authority for enforcing the plan is split between the bankruptcy court and the state court. The bankruptcy court usually has jurisdiction until the plan is substantially consummated. Generally, creditors may use the state courts to sue a debtor who has defaulted on an extension payment under a confirmed plan.

Prepackaged Chapter 11

A **prepackaged bankruptcy,** referred to as a **prepack,** is a Chapter 11 case *where the debtor reaches an agreement with its creditors and other relevant constituencies prior to the filing of the Chapter 11 case.* The agreement is documented in a plan of reorganization and voted on by the relevant constituencies before a bankruptcy petition is filed. Trade creditors are usually paid in full in a prepackaged plan.

There are various reasons prepackaged bankruptcies are favored. First, they allow a debtor to shorten and simplify the bankruptcy process. The process to obtain approval of a prepackaged Chapter 11 plan could be as short as 30-60 days after the Chapter 11 filing date. Second, the debtor is able to minimize its legal and other professional fees and other costs generally associated with operating in Chapter 11. Third, a prepackaged bankruptcy limits the uncertainty associated with the Chapter 11 process because the votes needed to confirm a plan are already solicited prior to the filing. Finally, this avenue allows a debtor to maximize going concern value and, in turn, minimize the bankruptcy's impact on trade creditors, customers, employees and day-to-day operations.

Prearranged Chapter 11

A **prearranged Chapter 11 case,** unlike a prepackaged case, *occurs when the debtor reaches an agreement with one or more, but not all, of the debtor's creditor constituencies (most often the debtor's secured lender owed significant sums) on the terms of a Chapter 11 plan prior to the filing of the Chapter 11 case.* In a prearranged case, the debtor negotiates with the lender for debtor-in-possession financing, prepares first-day pleadings, and prepares a disclosure statement and plan of reorganization for an immediate post-filing solicitation of creditors. The goal is to file for Chapter 11 and oftentimes obtain expedited approval of the disclosure statement and plan of reorganization, and then to exit bankruptcy within several months of the bankruptcy filing date. Trade creditors are not assured full or any payment in a prearranged Chapter 11 case.

Chapter 12 Adjustments of Debts of a Family Farmer or Fisherman with Regular Annual Income

Congress adopted **Chapter 12** of the Bankruptcy Code in 1986 *providing special provisions relating to the reorganization of family farmers and family fishermen.* It has some of the provisions found in Chapters 11 and 13 of the Bankruptcy Code.

Family farmers include individuals and spouses, corporations and partnerships whose aggregate debts do not exceed $4,153,150, of which 50 percent must be from farming operations. Total liabilities for a family fisherman cannot exceed $1,924,550, of which 80 percent must be from a commercial fishing operation. The thresholds are periodically adjusted for inflation. The *debtor initiates Chapter 12 by filing a document called* a **petition for relief** with the bankruptcy court. A **standing trustee** is appointed in each Chapter 12 case *to serve as the disbursing agent for payments under the plan of repayment.* However, due to the relative infrequency of filing of petitions for Chapter 12 (family farmer debt adjustment) relief, trustees for these cases are typically appointed on an *ad hoc* basis.

A Chapter 12 plan of repayment must be filed only by the debtor within 90 days after the filing of the petition for relief. As in Chapter 11, plans must classify creditors and propose treatment for each class.

Confirmation

Chapter 12 eliminates the absolute priority rule, which means the farmer may retain the family farm and make minimal payments to unsecured creditors. Creditors do not vote on the plan, and the debtor is not required to make a disclosure statement. Plans must satisfy two conditions:

1. Creditors are to receive what they would receive under liquidation (the liquidation test).
2. All the debtor's disposable income for three to five years must be paid to creditors (the best efforts test).

Chapter 12 allows a debtor keep the farm, revalue secured creditors over time on the current market value of the land, treat the balance of the debt as an unsecured claim and discharge all unsecured claims with nominal payments.

Trade Creditors' Primary Concerns

Creditors' concerns in a Chapter 12 case are to protect their secured position. Unsecured creditors may assert their right to the debtor's disposable income and any liquidation dividend. The trustee usually checks the debtor's income and expenses and claims the difference for distribution to creditors.

> **Comprehension Check**
> What two conditions must a plan satisfy under **Chapter 12**?

Chapter 13 Adjustments of Debts of an Individual with Regular Income

Chapter 13 *affords an individual with regular income an opportunity to reorganize their debts.* Prior to the 1978 code, only wage earners were eligible. Now the source of income is not relevant, but it must be regular as opposed to sporadic income received.

There are three criteria for filing under Chapter 13:

1. The debtor must be an individual.
2. The individual must have regular income.
3. The debt's limit is $394,725 in unsecured debt and $1,184,200 in secured debt. The thresholds are periodically adjusted for inflation.

Summary of a Typical Case

The debtor files a petition and a plan for handling the debts with the bankruptcy court in the district where the debtor resides. A plan must be filed within 15 days of filing the petition.

The case is then referred to the standing trustee who handles all Chapter 13 cases in a designated locality. The standing trustee will move to dismiss the case if the debtor fails to file a plan. The **standing trustee** *handles the administration of the case and presides at the §341 meeting, making recommendations to the court regarding confirmation of the plan.* The standing trustee is also responsible for collecting money from the debtor and distributing it to the creditors, as outlined in the confirmed plan. The standing trustee should be able to answer questions pertaining to the status of the case or about distributed payments.

The plan must classify creditors and propose treatment for their claims. Total payments to unsecured creditors must meet the liquidation test under Chapter 7. Like most Chapter 7 cases, which make no payments to unsecured creditors, Chapter 13 cases often make no payments to unsecured creditors as well. The plan may provide for payments to make up a monetary default for a homestead mortgage or other secured debt to prevent these assets being foreclosed and sold by the creditors.

Creditors must file claims in order to receive any distributions under the plan. Plans tend to be either extension plans or composition plans. **Extension plans** *pay all creditors in full over the duration of the plan.* There are two types of composition plans. *Both types of* **composition plans** *make only partial repayments of the total debt to creditors, and both must continue for not more than five years.* In one type, the debtor pays a fixed dollar amount monthly that is the surplus of net income after deducting expenses and payments to secured creditors. This amount is distributed *pro rata* among the unsecured creditors. In the second kind of composition plan, the plan pays a fixed percentage of the allowed claims to each unsecured creditor in monthly payments that continue until the percentage of each allowed claim has been paid. The court may stipulate that payments be for more than five years, even if it means that creditors receive more than the plan calls for.

The confirmation hearing may be brief unless the trustee or a creditor objects. The standing trustee's main concern is meeting the confirmation tests. One test is the **liquidation test:** *Will the total amount of plan payments equal the amount distributed to unsecured creditors through a Chapter 7 liquidation?* The second test is the **best efforts test:** *Will the debtor be paying creditors all of their disposable income for at least five years?* The court usually will not confirm the plan unless objections of the standing trustee are amended. Under Chapter 13, the discharge comes only after the debtor has made all payments required under the plan. The discharge is only for the claims dealt with under the plan.

Comprehension Check

List the three criteria for filings under **Chapter 13.**

The Chapter 20 and Chapter 22 Maneuver

This refers to serial bankruptcy filings where, because of the size of the debt, a debtor files a Chapter 7 petition to discharge the unsecured claims and, as soon as the discharge is granted, files a Chapter 13 petition to deal with the secured claims. The name Chapter 20 refers to the combination of 7 plus 13. This is expected to occur less frequently as Congress raised the debt limits and imposed a means test for Chapter 7 debtors. Chapter 22 refers to a company that has filed Chapter 11 twice.

Establishing a Systematic Response to Bankruptcy Filings

Creditors must establish an efficient internal system of routing bankruptcy notices so that information gets to the proper individuals. The Bankruptcy Code requires a debtor to send notices to an address specified by the creditor in communications sent to the debtor within 90 days of the bankruptcy filing.

The credit professional, or whoever is in charge of bankruptcy cases, needs to be aware of deadlines for meetings of creditors, filing of proofs of claim, objections to the sale of assets, etc. The sales department should be provided with instructions concerning the effect of the bankruptcy filing on existing credit limits and any need for consultation on post-petition sales. Many of the deadlines are relatively short, so a creditor may need to send a notice with a change of address to the bankruptcy court if the debtor or the trustee is mailing notices to a lockbox or another office where rerouting may involve unnecessary delay. It is imperative to establish procedures for staff that deal with receipts at the lockbox address for handling bankruptcy notices.

A separate system should be established to deal with adversary proceedings in which the company is sued by the debtor or some other party in the bankruptcy case. A company's bankruptcy system should include a periodic review with the sales and other staff members who have direct contact with a customer. The staff should be educated about the importance of being alert to bankruptcy danger signs and what actions to take upon learning of a bankruptcy filing.

Comprehension Check

Why is it important to establish a systematic response system for bankruptcy cases?

Filing a Proof of Claim

In cases under Chapters 7, 12 and 13, the filing of a proof of claim is generally required to participate in any distribution of the bankruptcy estate assets to unsecured creditors. In a Chapter 11 case, a claim is deemed to be filed for any claim or interest that the debtor correctly lists in the schedules without indicating that the claim is disputed, contingent, or unliquidated. The creditor should review its claim as listed by the debtor in the schedules. The creditor must file a proof of claim if the claim listed is incorrect or listed as disputed, contingent or unliquidated. Technically any document filed with the bankruptcy court in order to set forth your rights to payment of a debt may be considered a proof of claim.

In a Chapter 7, all proofs of claim must be filed within 90 days after the first date set for the §341 meeting of creditors unless the creditor receives notice of a no asset case and of the non-necessity to file a claim. When dealing with a Chapter 11, the Federal Rule of Bankruptcy Procedure Rule 3003(c) allows the bankruptcy court to establish a deadline. Chapter 12 follows Rule 3002(c) that provides that all claims must be filed within 90 days of the first date set for the §341 meeting. In a Chapter 13, all proofs of claim must be filed within 90 days after the first date set for the §341 meeting. If the §341 meeting is rescheduled, the filing date does not change. If the 90th day falls on a holiday or a weekend day, the next workday is the deadline.

The Official Proof of Claim Form

The official **Proof of Claim Form 410** should be used to file proofs of claim in all cases and can be downloaded from the United States Court website at uscourts.gov. Claims should be prepared in duplicate and may be signed by any person within the creditor company authorized to do so. This includes an officer or an attorney for the company. Most bankruptcy courts have electronic filing systems for court documents and proofs of claims. The creditor should check with the court as to whether electronic filing of the claim is required.

Comprehension Check

Under what chapters of the Bankruptcy Code must a proof of claim be filed?

Figure 17-1   Proof of Claim Form

Fill in this information to identify the case:

Debtor 1 _____

Debtor 2 _____
(Spouse, if filing)

United States Bankruptcy Court for the: _____ District of _____

Case number _____

Official Form 410

Proof of Claim

04/16

Read the instructions before filling out this form. This form is for making a claim for payment in a bankruptcy case. Do not use this form to make a request for payment of an administrative expense. Make such a request according to 11 U.S.C. § 503.

Filers must leave out or redact information that is entitled to privacy on this form or on any attached documents. Attach redacted copies of any documents that support the claim, such as promissory notes, purchase orders, invoices, itemized statements of running accounts, contracts, judgments, mortgages, and security agreements. **Do not send original documents;** they may be destroyed after scanning. If the documents are not available, explain in an attachment.

A person who files a fraudulent claim could be fined up to $500,000, imprisoned for up to 5 years, or both. 18 U.S.C. §§ 152, 157, and 3571.

Fill in all the information about the claim as of the date the case was filed. That date is on the notice of bankruptcy (Form 309) that you received.

Part 1:   Identify the Claim

1. **Who is the current creditor?**	Name of the current creditor (the person or entity to be paid for this claim) _____	
	Other names the creditor used with the debtor _____	
2. **Has this claim been acquired from someone else?**	☐ No ☐ Yes. From whom? _____	
3. **Where should notices and payments to the creditor be sent?** Federal Rule of Bankruptcy Procedure (FRBP) 2002(g)	**Where should notices to the creditor be sent?** Name _____ Number Street City State ZIP Code Contact phone _____ Contact email _____	**Where should payments to the creditor be sent?** (if different) Name _____ Number Street City State ZIP Code Contact phone _____ Contact email _____
	Uniform claim identifier for electronic payments in chapter 13 (if you use one): _	
4. **Does this claim amend one already filed?**	☐ No ☐ Yes. Claim number on court claims registry (if known) _____	Filed on _____ MM / DD / YYYY
5. **Do you know if anyone else has filed a proof of claim for this claim?**	☐ No ☐ Yes. Who made the earlier filing? _____	

Official Form 410

Proof of Claim

page 1

Figure 17-1 Proof of Claim Form continued

| **Part 2:** | **Give Information About the Claim as of the Date the Case Was Filed** |

6. Do you have any number you use to identify the debtor?

❑ No
❑ Yes. Last 4 digits of the debtor's account or any number you use to identify the debtor: ___ ___ ___ ___

7. How much is the claim?

$_____. **Does this amount include interest or other charges?**

❑ No
❑ Yes. Attach statement itemizing interest, fees, expenses, or other charges required by Bankruptcy Rule 3001(c)(2)(A).

8. What is the basis of the claim?

Examples: Goods sold, money loaned, lease, services performed, personal injury or wrongful death, or credit card.

Attach redacted copies of any documents supporting the claim required by Bankruptcy Rule 3001(c).

Limit disclosing information that is entitled to privacy, such as health care information.

_____

9. Is all or part of the claim secured?

❑ No
❑ Yes. The claim is secured by a lien on property.

Nature of property:

❑ Real estate. If the claim is secured by the debtor's principal residence, file a *Mortgage Proof of Claim Attachment* (Official Form 410-A) with this *Proof of Claim*.
❑ Motor vehicle
❑ Other. Describe: _____

Basis for perfection: _____

Attach redacted copies of documents, if any, that show evidence of perfection of a security interest (for example, a mortgage, lien, certificate of title, financing statement, or other document that shows the lien has been filed or recorded.)

Value of property:	$_____
Amount of the claim that is secured:	$_____
Amount of the claim that is unsecured:	$_____ (The sum of the secured and unsecured amounts should match the amount in line 7.)

Amount necessary to cure any default as of the date of the petition: $_____

Annual Interest Rate (when case was filed)_____%
❑ Fixed
❑ Variable

10. Is this claim based on a lease?

❑ No
❑ Yes. **Amount necessary to cure any default as of the date of the petition.** $_____

11. Is this claim subject to a right of setoff?

❑ No
❑ Yes. Identify the property: _____

| Official Form 410 | Proof of Claim | page 2 |

Figure 17-1 Proof of Claim Form continued

12. Is all or part of the claim entitled to priority under 11 U.S.C. § 507(a)?

A claim may be partly priority and partly nonpriority. For example, in some categories, the law limits the amount entitled to priority.

❑ No

❑ Yes. *Check one:*

Amount entitled to priority

❑ Domestic support obligations (including alimony and child support) under 11 U.S.C. § 507(a)(1)(A) or (a)(1)(B).

$_____

❑ Up to $2,850* of deposits toward purchase, lease, or rental of property or services for personal, family, or household use. 11 U.S.C. § 507(a)(7).

$_____

❑ Wages, salaries, or commissions (up to $12,850*) earned within 180 days before the bankruptcy petition is filed or the debtor's business ends, whichever is earlier. 11 U.S.C. § 507(a)(4).

$_____

❑ Taxes or penalties owed to governmental units. 11 U.S.C. § 507(a)(8).

$_____

❑ Contributions to an employee benefit plan. 11 U.S.C. § 507(a)(5).

$_____

❑ Other. Specify subsection of 11 U.S.C. § 507(a)(__) that applies.

$_____

* Amounts are subject to adjustment on 4/01/19 and every 3 years after that for cases begun on or after the date of adjustment.

Part 3: Sign Below

The person completing this proof of claim must sign and date it. FRBP 9011(b).

If you file this claim electronically, FRBP 5005(a)(2) authorizes courts to establish local rules specifying what a signature is.

A person who files a fraudulent claim could be fined up to $500,000, imprisoned for up to 5 years, or both. 18 U.S.C. §§ 152, 157, and 3571.

Check the appropriate box:

❑ I am the creditor.

❑ I am the creditor's attorney or authorized agent.

❑ I am the trustee, or the debtor, or their authorized agent. Bankruptcy Rule 3004.

❑ I am a guarantor, surety, endorser, or other codebtor. Bankruptcy Rule 3005.

I understand that an authorized signature on this *Proof of Claim* serves as an acknowledgment that when calculating the amount of the claim, the creditor gave the debtor credit for any payments received toward the debt.

I have examined the information in this *Proof of Claim* and have a reasonable belief that the information is true and correct.

I declare under penalty of perjury that the foregoing is true and correct.

Executed on date _____
MM / DD / YYYY

_____
Signature

Print the name of the person who is completing and signing this claim:

Name _____
First name   Middle name   Last name

Title _____

Company _____
Identify the corporate servicer as the company if the authorized agent is a servicer.

Address _____
Number   Street

_____
City   State   ZIP Code

Contact phone _____ Email _____

Official Form 410   Proof of Claim   page 3

Objections to Proofs of Claims

The trustee in Chapter 7, 11 and 13 cases and the debtor in possession under Chapter 11 are statutorily responsible for reviewing claims filed, or listed in a Chapter 11 schedule, to determine whether the claims are proper claims against the estate. Objections to claims can range from inadequate documentation to lender liability lawsuits to the inclusion of precomputed interest. Routine objections often result from communication problems and can usually be resolved without much difficulty. The trustee will charge the estate for all legal expenses relating to claim objections. As this reduces the amount available for distribution to the unsecured creditors, creditors have an incentive to present claims that are as objection-free as possible. Procedures for objecting to claims and resolving those objections vary from court to court. Legal counsel should be sought when dealing with objections. It is imperative that a creditor responds timely to an objection to claim. Failure to respond timely may result in the loss of a claim. While the court may reconsider a claim if a creditor fails to respond, the burden will be on the creditor to prove its reason for not responding. The criteria are **excusable neglect** (refers to a legitimate excuse for the failure to take some proper step at the proper time which is an extremely high burden.

Reclamation

The concept of **reclamation** *is to protect a creditor who delivers goods to a debtor while the debtor is insolvent.* The law provides for return of the goods: The eligible pool of goods subject to reclamation is all goods the debtor had received up to 45 days prior to the filing of bankruptcy, if certain conditions are met. The creditor must send a written reclamation demand for return of the goods. The creditor may send the reclamation demand to the debtor prior to bankruptcy and also has up to 20 days from the filing date to send the demand, but the demand can only cover goods received by the debtor no more than 45 days prior to the receipt of the reclamation demand. This written notice, with a proof of delivery, should include a clear description of the goods, the date of delivery and their value. Because the goods must be in the possession of the debtor in their original unused condition at the time the notice of reclamation is received, it is in the creditor's best interest to send the demand as soon as possible. Sending the debtor the demand via email and then sending the originals via overnight delivery provides a good tracking of when the notice was delivered. The creditor should also maintain proof of the debtor's receipt of the demand. There are no other rights provided to a successful reclaiming creditor other than return of the goods.

One of the flaws in reclamation is that the rights of a reclaiming creditor still remain subject to the rights of a prior secured creditor with a lien in the same collateral sought to be reclaimed.

Reclamation Catch-22: Darned If You Do, Darned If You Don't*

The Bankruptcy Abuse Prevention and Consumer Protection Act of 2005 ("BAPCPA") amended Bankruptcy Code Section 546(c)(1) and expanded the reclamation reachback period to 45 days in bankruptcy cases filed under BAPCPA. Although BAPCPA's change to Section 546(c) suggests that trade creditors would have substantially expanded reclamation rights, it most certainly has not played out that way in practice.

Reclamation rights have already been besieged in cases, such as Advanced Marketing Services in the Bankruptcy Court for the District of Delaware, where the court denied a reclaiming creditor's motion for injunctive relief to bar the debtor from selling that creditor's goods, and Dana Corporation in the Bankruptcy Court for the Southern District of New York, where the court ruled that reclamation rights were rendered valueless by virtue of the debtor's pre-petition and Chapter 11 secured lenders' alleged floating security interest in all of the debtor's inventory. More recently, in the Circuit City Stores Chapter 11 case, reclamation creditors were dealt a blow for failing to seek emergency injunctive relief at the beginning of the case, exactly the relief that the bankruptcy court in Advanced Marketing Services had rejected because reclamation rights were viewed to be valueless by virtue of the debtor's pre-petition secured lender's floating inventory security interest. The United States District Court for the Eastern

District of Virginia held that a creditor's failure to diligently pursue its reclamation rights resulted in a forfeiture of those rights.

This leaves reclamation creditors in the lurch with the impossible choice of deciding whether to seek emergency injunctive relief at the beginning of the case, a battle they will likely lose at great expense, or forfeit the ability to assert their reclamation rights at a later date (perhaps when secured creditors with floating liens on the reclamation creditors' goods have been paid in full).

State Law Reclamation Rights

Reclamation rights arise under state law and are governed by Section 2-702 of the Uniform Commercial Code (UCC), the uniform state law enacted in all 50 states. Under state law, a trade creditor could reclaim goods delivered to a buyer if the creditor satisfies all of the following conditions: The goods were sold to the debtor on credit terms; the debtor was insolvent at the time it received the goods; and the creditor demanded return of the goods within ten days of the debtor's receipt of the goods.

The UCC defines insolvency based on either a balance sheet test, of liabilities exceeding assets, or an "equity" test, where the debtor has ceased paying its debts in the ordinary course of business or is unable to pay its debts as they become due. A trade creditor that can prove all of the elements of a state law reclamation claim is entitled to recovery of all goods in the debtor's possession that are the subject of its claim.

However, a creditor's state law reclamation rights are subject to the rights of a "good faith purchaser." The UCC defines a "good faith purchaser" to include a secured creditor with a security interest in the debtor's inventory. That means a secured creditor with a floating inventory lien has priority over the rights of a reclaiming creditor.

Reclamation Rights under Bankruptcy Code Section 546(c)

Bankruptcy Code Section 546(c)(1) addresses reclamation rights as follows:

(1) ...[S]ubject to the prior rights of a holder of a security interest in such goods or the proceeds thereof, the rights and powers of the trustee under Sections 544(a), 545, 547 and 549 are subject to the right of a seller of goods that has sold goods to the debtor, in the ordinary course of such seller's business, to reclaim such goods if the debtor has received such goods while insolvent, within 45 days of the commencement of a case under this title, but such a seller may not reclaim such goods unless such seller demands in writing reclamation of such goods—(A) not later than 45 days after the date of receipt of such goods by the debtor; or (B) not later than 20 days after the date of the commencement of the case, if the 45-day period expires after the commencement of the case.

Section 546(c)(1), as enacted by BAPCPA, has brought about three significant changes to trade creditors' reclamation rights in bankruptcy cases, compared to their reclamation rights under the pre-BAPCPA version of Section 546(c). First, the reclamation reachback time period has been extended to 45 days. A creditor can reclaim goods that it had sold in the ordinary course of its business on credit to the debtor that the debtor had received within 45 days of bankruptcy. A creditor's reclamation rights are contingent upon the creditor sending a written reclamation demand, identifying the goods, to the debtor not later than 45 days after the debtor's receipt of the goods. If the 45-day period expires after the bankruptcy filing, the creditor has up to 20 days after the bankruptcy filing to send a reclamation demand. This sounds like a substantial expansion of reclamation rights, compared to the shorter time periods provided to reclaiming creditors under state law and the reclamation rights provided in the pre-BAPCPA version of Section 546(c). But don't pop open the champagne bottles quite yet!

Section 546(c)(1) now states that the rights of a reclaiming creditor are subject to the prior rights of a creditor with a security interest in the debtor's inventory, including the goods subject to reclamation. This raises the specter of the pre-BAPCPA case law holdings that a pre-existing pre-petition floating inventory secured claim renders reclamation rights valueless, even when the value of the secured creditor's collateral substantially exceeds the amount of the secured creditors' claim.

Section 546(c)(1) has also eliminated the alternative remedies of an allowed administrative priority claim or replacement lien in lieu of return of the goods that existed in the pre-BAPCPA version of Section 546(c). Current Section 546(c)(1) provides that reclamation of the goods is the sole remedy for a creditor that has satisfied the requirements for reclamation. BAPCPA's deletion of the alternative remedies for reclamation has raised many questions. Is reclamation a "wasting" right that diminishes as the debtor continues to sell the goods subject to reclamation, because relief is limited to only the goods on hand when the court grants relief? Must reclaiming creditors immediately commence suit in the bankruptcy court to seek injunctive relief at the beginning of the bankruptcy case to block the debtor's sale of, or grant of a security interest in, the goods subject to reclamation? If so, at what cost will reclamation creditors pursue such rights where the probability of success, at least at the beginning of the case, appears bleak? If reclamation creditors choose not to seek injunctive relief at the beginning of the case, will they have forfeited their reclamation rights?

All these issues were addressed in the Circuit City Stores Chapter 11 case.

Circuit City Stores

Background

On November 10, 2008 (the petition date), Circuit City Stores, Inc. and its affiliates filed Chapter 11 in the United States Bankruptcy Court for the Eastern District of Virginia. Prior to its liquidation, Circuit City was a national retailer of consumer electronics. Paramount Home Entertainment Inc. sold and delivered millions of dollars of home entertainment products to Circuit City each year.

Debtors' Financing Arrangement

On the petition date, Circuit City requested approval from the Bankruptcy Court to obtain debtor-in-possession (DIP) financing secured by a first priority lien in substantially all of Circuit City's existing and after-acquired assets, including "inventory" and the proceeds thereof. This inventory included the goods that Paramount had sold to Circuit City. Paramount did not object to the proposed DIP financing. Upon approval of the DIP loan, Circuit City used the DIP loan proceeds to repay all of its outstanding indebtedness under its pre-bankruptcy credit facility, and to finance its ongoing post-petition operations.

Reclamation Procedures

Shortly after the petition date, the Circuit City court approved an order for proposed reclamation procedures, which, among other things, required reclamation claimants to file reclamation demands consistent with Bankruptcy Code Section 546(c) no later than 20 days after the petition date, and required Circuit City to send notice by March 10, 2009 containing what Circuit City considered the allowed amount of reclamation creditors' claims. To the extent Circuit City did not believe a reclamation claimant had an allowed claim, Circuit City was not required to send notice and the claimant's reclamation demand was deemed rejected by Circuit City after March 10, 2009. The reclamation procedures order expressly provided that:

> Nothing in this Order or the above procedures is intended to prohibit, hinder, or delay any Reclamation Claimant from asserting or prosecuting any of its rights to seek to reclaim goods provided to the Debtors, or affect, alter, diminish, extinguish, or expand the rights or interest, if any, to recover goods (or proceeds thereof) sought to be reclaimed.

Paramount's Reclamation Demand

Shortly before the entry of the reclamation procedures order, Paramount sent a reclamation demand—requesting the return of goods totaling approximately $11.6 million—that was compliant with the reclamation procedures order. Circuit City, however, did not send a notice to Paramount by March 10, 2009, pursuant to the order, indicating that Paramount had an allowed reclamation claim, and accordingly, Paramount's demand was deemed rejected by Circuit City. Unrelated to Paramount's reclamation demand, Paramount also filed a proof of claim seeking priority status on account of its reclamation claim.

Circuit City Liquidates

Barely two months into its bankruptcy case, Circuit City decided to liquidate its assets by way of going out of business sales, which, of course, included the sale of Paramount's goods in Circuit City's possession. At no time after sending its reclamation demand did Paramount object to the sale of its goods, nor did Paramount take any steps to exercise its reclamation rights, such as by commencing an adversary proceeding to stop Circuit City from selling the goods subject to Paramount's reclamation demand.

Circuit City Objects to Paramount's Claim

In June 2009, Circuit City objected to Paramount's priority proof of claim based on Paramount's reclamation claim. Circuit City sought to have the claim reclassified from a priority claim to a non-priority pre-petition general unsecured claim. Paramount objected to Circuit City's proposed reclassification of the priority status of Paramount's reclamation claim. Thereafter, Circuit City filed a summary judgment motion, asserting that there were no disputed issues of fact and that as a matter of law, Paramount's claim should be reclassified from a priority claim to a general unsecured claim.

The Bankruptcy Court granted Circuit City's summary judgment motion, sustained Circuit City's objection to Paramount's reclamation claim as a priority claim and reclassified the claim as a non-priority general unsecured claim. The Bankruptcy Court stated that reclamation rights are not self-executing and that Paramount had sat on its rights by failing to take the following actions to enforce its reclamation rights: (1) failing to seek relief from the bankruptcy automatic stay to enforce Paramount's rights in the goods that were subject to its reclamation demand; (2) failing to object to the proposed DIP financing that granted the secured party a floating lien on inventory, including Paramount's goods; and (3) failing to object to Circuit City's motion seeking approval of going out of business sales, which clearly included the liquidation of the goods subject to Paramount's reclamation claim. The court declared that simply following the reclamation procedures order and serving a reclamation demand was not sufficient to preserve Paramount's reclamation rights.

The Bankruptcy Court also ruled that Paramount would not have been granted relief on its reclamation claim, even if Paramount had timely taken action to enforce its reclamation rights. Paramount's reclamation rights were rendered valueless because the goods subject to Paramount's reclamation demand were encumbered by Circuit City's pre-petition lenders' floating lien on inventory on the petition date. Accordingly, Circuit City's secured lender was a "good faith purchaser" under the UCC with priority over Paramount's rights in the goods it sought to reclaim.

Furthermore, the Bankruptcy Court held that reclamation is an "in rem" remedy that under the UCC and the Bankruptcy Code would solely allow Paramount to seek the return of its goods and not take an interest in the proceeds of the goods once they were sold. The Bankruptcy Court also held that Paramount was not entitled to an administrative priority claim because Section 546 of the Bankruptcy Code, as amended by BAPCPA, does not require the Bankruptcy Court to grant an allowed administrative claim in favor of reclamation creditors.

Paramount Appeals

Paramount appealed the Bankruptcy Court's decision to the United States District Court. Paramount argued that it was entitled to relief on its reclamation claim because it had complied with both the statutory requirements for reclamation, as well as the reclamation procedures order. Paramount had timely served a written reclamation demand, which is all that it was required to do. Paramount also argued that requiring reclamation creditors to commence suit at the beginning of the bankruptcy case would create a race to the courthouse, which bankruptcy is supposed to prevent, and would unduly burden and create expense for both trade creditors and the debtor. Interestingly, one of the rationales asserted by Circuit City in support of the reclamation procedures order was that without the order, Circuit City would need to expend substantial time and limited resources contesting and litigating reclamation demands. Paramount also argued that once a reclamation demand was served, Circuit City was prohibited from disposing of the goods subject to reclamation, without obtaining an order from the Bankruptcy Court.

Circuit City asserted that reclamation is a state law remedy and that Section 546 of the Bankruptcy Code simply allows creditors to enforce such state law rights to the extent they exist. It argued that state law and courts across the nation have ruled that serving a reclamation demand is not sufficient without, in fact, pursuing such demand on a timely basis with sufficient diligence. Paramount forfeited its reclamation rights by not taking any further action, such as (1) seeking relief from the bankruptcy automatic stay to enforce its rights in the goods that were subject to its reclamation demand, (2) objecting to the proposed DIP financing, to the extent the DIP secured lender was granted a security interest in the goods subject to Paramount's reclamation claim, or (3) objecting to Circuit City's motion seeking the approval of going out of business sales that included Paramount's goods subject to reclamation.

The District Court's Decision

The District Court sided with Circuit City and held that Paramount should have diligently asserted its reclamation rights, especially in the context of such a large bankruptcy case like the Circuit City case, and it forfeited such rights by failing to do so. In fact, the District Court stated that Paramount's failure to take action in the manner enumerated above likely created more litigation and pressure on the Bankruptcy Court. Although Paramount served a reclamation demand, it failed to seek court intervention to "perfect" that right. In addition, Paramount's failure to take further action was fatal because, in the words of the Bankruptcy Court, the Bankruptcy Code is not "self executing." Once Paramount became aware that its goods were being pledged as collateral in connection with Circuit City's DIP financing facility, Paramount should have taken action. "To make matters worse," Paramount should have objected once it became aware that Circuit City was seeking permission to conduct going out of business sales, which undoubtedly included the sale of Paramount's goods.

The District Court did not consider whether Paramount's reclamation claim was deemed "valueless" because on the petition date, the goods that were subject to the reclamation demand were encumbered by Circuit City's pre-petition lenders' floating lien on inventory; and whether Paramount's reclamation rights extended to the proceeds of its goods. The District Court, however, made clear that Section 546, as amended by BAPCPA, does not require granting an administrative expense if the Bankruptcy Court denies a reclamation claim, and even assuming the Bankruptcy Court has the discretion to award an administrative claim, the District Court did not believe the Bankruptcy Court erred in denying any relief to Paramount where Paramount had failed to diligently pursue its reclamation rights.

Conclusion

The United States District Court's decision in Circuit City is ample proof that reclamation has become a hollow remedy in bankruptcy cases. Even worse, as a result of the court's holding, a creditor who is not willing to incur the expense to enforce its reclamation rights at the beginning of the bankruptcy case, in what will likely be a losing effort, will lose those rights altogether. Where there are no reclamation procedures in place in a bankruptcy case, reclamation creditors should decide whether to act fast or risk losing their reclamation rights. If a debtor is proposing reclamation procedures, reclamation creditors should object to the procedures unless the procedures, like the procedures in the Advanced Marketing Services case, make clear that reclamation creditors will not be prejudiced by their failure to commence a reclamation lawsuit or seek injunctive relief to prevent the debtor from selling their goods, thus allowing reclamation creditors in such case the opportunity to fight another day.

Reprinted from Business Credit *magazine. May, 2011. Written by Bruce S. Nathan, Esq. and David Banker, Esq. of Lowenstein Sandler PC.*

20-Day Administrative Claim

A right granted by the Bankruptcy Code is referred to as a 20-day administrative claim or §503(b)(9) claim. *For goods sold to a debtor in the ordinary course of business, and delivered within 20 days prior to the bankruptcy filing, that creditor is granted protection, separate and apart from its reclamation rights as a **20-day administrative claim.*** The creditor can assert an administrative expense claim for the value of the goods. The creditor is not required to send written notice, prove that the goods are still in the debtor's possession, or satisfy any of the other requirements mandated for a successful reclamation claim. The creditor must, however, prove that the goods were received by the debtor within 20 days before the onset of the case. The claim is not automatic and will be granted only upon notice and a hearing. The creditor generally will have to make an application in the bankruptcy court for allowance and payment of an administrative expense claim for the value of the goods. Administrative expenses are paid before most of the other creditors' claims, and are frequently, but not always, paid in full.

Alternatively, a debtor may request court approval of procedures for handling reclamation and administrative claims. If a court order is entered providing such procedures, it is the creditor's responsibility to follow the procedures to obtain more favorable treatment of its claim. In some jurisdictions, local rules of the court set deadlines for when the 20-day administrative claim must be asserted.

Discharge and Dischargeability

The goal of any bankruptcy proceeding is the discharge of some or all of the debtor's debts and obligations. A **discharge** *is a permanent order that releases the debtor from personal liability for certain specified types of debts, thereby releasing the debtor from any legal obligation to pay any discharged debts.* The Bankruptcy Code allows for a debtor to be denied a discharge completely in Chapter 7 for reasons including fraud, perjury, concealment of assets, or destruction of relevant records.

Reasons for Denial of Discharge in Chapter 7 Cases

- Corporations are not normally discharged, although they may be under Chapter 11.
- Concealing assets.
- Failure to keep records.
- Perjury in connection with the bankruptcy case.
- Failure to explain disposition of assets.
- Failure to obey court orders to testify.
- Prior discharge in bankruptcy within eight-year limit.
- Waiver of discharge by the individual debtor.

Certain debts are excepted from the discharge, but only upon action by the bankruptcy court. The following is a checklist of excepted debts:

- Taxes due less than three months before filing bankruptcy.
- Credit obtained by false financial statement or fraud.
- Unlisted creditors (not in every case).
- Breach of fiduciary duty claims.
- Intentional torts/conversion of collateral.
- Fines and penalties/taxes.
- Student loans.
- Driving Under the Influence (DUI) liabilities.
- Debts excepted from discharge in prior bankruptcy proceedings.
- FDIC claims.
- Securities law violations.

In order to have a debt excepted from a discharge under Bankruptcy Code §523 or to deny the discharge generally under Bankruptcy Code §727, a creditor, the trustee or the U.S. Trustee must file a timely complaint under one of those sections. A complaint to deny discharge under 11 U.S.C. §727 may be filed up to the conclusion of the hearing on confirmation of the Chapter 11 plan.

Pursuing Claims for False Financial Statements and Fraud

Trade credit professionals should be familiar with the provisions of Bankruptcy Code §§523(a)(2)(A) and 523(a)(2)(B) relating to fraudulent misconduct and the use of false financial statements.

Debts arising from the extension, renewal or refinancing of credit obtained through false pretenses, false representation or actual fraud are excepted from the discharge under Bankruptcy Code §523(a)(2)(A). Creditors must show that the debtor made a false representation or committed fraud, that the debtor was aware of the false representation or fraud at the time it occurred, that the debtor intended to deceive the creditor, and that the creditor relied upon the misrepresentation with the resultant loss.

Under Bankruptcy Code §523(a)(2)(B), the Bankruptcy Code excepts from discharge claims arising out of the use of a materially false financial statement in writing. The creditor must show that the debt arises from the use of a false written financial statement that is materially false regarding the debtor's financial condition that the debtor caused to be published with intent to deceive. Conversions of collateral require showing a willful conversion of the proceeds, which is not easy to prove.

The Trustee's Strong Arm and Avoiding Powers

To further the equitable distribution of assets to creditors, bankruptcy trustees have the power to recover certain fraudulent transfers, recover preferential payments to creditors, and avoid certain improperly perfected security interests and mortgages. Collectively, these rights or powers are referred to as the trustee's strong arm and avoiding powers. Trade creditors want to make sure that any payments they receive are not subject to recovery as a preference, fraudulent transfer, or otherwise. It is the fiduciary duty of the creditors' committee to make sure that the debtor presses all possible claims for recovery, including preferences or fraudulent transfers that benefit insiders.

Basic Recovery Procedure

For both Chapter 7 and Chapter 11 filings, the procedure for recovering preferential and fraudulent transfers and setting aside improperly perfected security interests requires the filing of an adversary proceeding under Rule 7001 of the Federal Rules of Bankruptcy Procedure. Once the adversary proceeding is filed, the trustee or debtor in possession can obtain nationwide service of the summons and complaint pursuant to the Federal Rules of Bankruptcy Procedure. If the defendant does not answer the complaint within the time specified by the bankruptcy court, a default judgment will be entered. Once the defendant files an answer, an adversary proceeding is handled as any other lawsuit. If no jury has been demanded, the bankruptcy court tries the proceeding.

Settlement Considerations

As in any litigation, credit professionals should watch the bottom line: What will the action by the debtor or the creditors' committee bring into the bankruptcy estate for distribution to unsecured creditors?

The Trustee's Strong Arm Powers

Bankruptcy Code §544, the **strong arm clause,** *empowers a trustee or a debtor in possession to avoid any lien or security interest in personal property or any lien or mortgage on real estate which is not properly perfected as of the date of the bankruptcy petition.* Bankruptcy Code §544 grants to the trustee the rights of three different hypothetical types of creditors or purchasers:

Hypothetical Judicial Lien Holder

This allows the trustee or debtor in possession to set aside any security interest or mortgage of creditors for the benefit of all creditors. Trade creditors that advance credit through the sale of goods should understand the purchase money security interests and their special protection under both the UCC and the Bankruptcy Code. Any security interest or lien not properly perfected as of the date of the bankruptcy filing is subject to attack under Bankruptcy Code §544(a)(1).

Unsecured Creditor

The trustee has the rights of any actual creditor with an allowed unsecured claim as of the date of the petition permitting the trustee to set aside an improper bulk transfer of the debtor's property, located in states with a bulk sale statute, or a fraudulent conveyance under state law. This allows the trustee to take advantage of the longer state law statute of limitations for fraudulent conveyance actions, rather than the shorter period provided in §548.

Bona Fide Purchaser for Value of Any Property Owned by the Debtor as of the Date of the Petition

This gives the trustee priority over the holder of an inaccurate or unrecorded deed or mortgage. When a debtor has a large business involvement in real estate and files for bankruptcy before all business is recorded, there may be a substantial recovery of assets for general unsecured creditors. In most states, a judgment lien or a *bona fide* purchaser for value takes priority over any improperly recorded deed, mortgage, deed of trust or other real estate encumbrance.

Legal Audit

Persons dealing with security interests and mortgages in personal and real property will want to be sufficiently familiar with the law governing the creation and perfection of security interests and mortgages to perform a legal audit or review of either their own documentation or documentation of lending creditors in a case. A **legal audit** *is a review of all documentation to determine whether all security interests were properly perfected and all mortgages were correct and properly recorded, paying special attention to legal descriptions of the covered real estate.*

Preferences

A **preferential payment,** *which refers to a creditor who gets paid before dividing the assets equally among all those to whom it owes money, often by making a payment to a favored creditor just before filing a petition to be declared bankrupt,* to an unsecured creditor can be recovered by the trustee under Bankruptcy Code §547. To prove a preference, the trustee or the debtor in possession must prove that a transfer of the debtor's assets was made:

- To or for the benefit of a creditor.
- For or on account of an antecedent debt.
- While the debtor was insolvent.
- Within 90 days of the petition for relief, or within one year if the transfer was to an insider.
- The effect of the transfer was to give the creditor more than the creditor would otherwise receive in a Chapter 7 liquidation.

Exceptions to the Preference Rules

- A transfer to a creditor that is intended to be and is contemporaneous with the extension of credit or the delivery of goods by the creditor.
- Subsequent new value is given to the debtor after receipt of payment.
- Payment in the ordinary course of business or financial affairs of the debtor and the creditor; or made according to ordinary business terms.
- Preference actions for recovery of less than $6,425 cannot be pursued.
- Preference actions to recover less than $12,475 can be commenced only in the district court for the district where the trade creditor is located.

> **Comprehension Check**
>
> Before a **preferential payment** to an **unsecured creditor** can be recovered, what must the **trustee** prove?
>
> What are the exceptions to the preference rules?

Fraudulent Transfers

Two types of **fraudulent transfers** made within two years of bankruptcy may be set aside under Bankruptcy Code §548 (a) and (b). *The transfer of the debtor's property made with the actual intent to hinder, delay, or defraud creditors* is one type. The debtor's intent is usually inferred from the circumstances of the transfer. If the court concludes the debtor had the necessary fraudulent intent, it will usually set aside the transfer unless the debtor can prove it received an equivalent value in money or money's worth for the asset transferred. The second type is *the transfer of property for less than market value at a time when the debtor was insolvent or under capitalized.* However, under the Bankruptcy Code, a transferee that takes for value and in good faith is entitled to a lien on the property transferred or may retain any interest transferred to the extent that such transferee gave value.

Comprehension Check
What is a **fraudulent transfer?**

Involuntary Bankruptcy

The filing of an involuntary bankruptcy is used by creditors for several reasons. Often, an involuntary bankruptcy is the only way to force the debtor to provide full financial disclosure. Creditors may also want to force recovery of fraudulent and preferential transfers. As the common law does not prevent a debtor from preferring one creditor over others and gives creditors only a limited ability to recover fraudulent transfers, the filing of an involuntary bankruptcy may be the only way of stopping and recovering these types of transfers.

An **involuntary petition** may be filed by creditors only under Chapter 7 or 11. To do so, *three creditors must have noncontingent, undisputed claims.* The Code has emphasized that a petitioning creditor's claim must not be subject to a *bona fide* dispute in either liability or amount. Three creditors are generally necessary to file an involuntary petition. For debtors with 12 or more unsecured creditors, the three creditors' unsecured claims must aggregate at least $15,775 (subject to increase for inflation) in order to force an involuntary bankruptcy. The involuntary petition is served upon the debtor together with a summons in the same manner in which an adversary proceeding would be commenced. Normally, a debtor has 20 days to contest an involuntary petition. Typically, the petitioning creditors must demonstrate that the debtor is generally not paying its undisputed debts as such debts become due.

Strategy

Creditors should accept all payments offered by a debtor in financial difficulty. The worst that can happen is the creditor may have to return the money if it is later deemed to be preferential. The trustee or creditors' committee should carefully review all the debtor's security agreements and transfers for the year prior to the bankruptcy filing to rule out possible fraudulent transfers that might be set aside. It is important to evaluate the bankruptcy case at the beginning so as not to use up the assets of the estate in legal and other fees to the detriment of the unsecured creditors.

Beginner's Guide to Bankruptcy*

First Things First

How Do I Confirm It?

What do I do? Find out if the information is true and accurate or simply a rumor.

> **Tip:** Verification is extremely important as there are strict legal consequences for attempting to collect a debt if a bankruptcy has been filed.

PACER (Public Access to Court Electronic Records). PACER is an electronic access service that allows you to get case information directly from bankruptcy courts. Requires login and password. https://www.pacer.gov/.

Google search. Why not? Google knows all!

> **Tip:** Pay close attention to the filing date! This will dictate other rights such as potential preference issues (having to send money back) and reclamation (trying to get your stuff back).

Get Your Ducks in a Row!

Do we have orders pending or in transit?

Yes? If you were paid up front, good for you! If not, you should consider cancelling or rerouting those shipments back to your warehouse. If already delivered, you may have a chance to reclaim your material.

No? Mark the account for non-shipment.

> **Tip:** If you have a contract in place, you need to explore what your options are before you cancel, but you may want to seek legal counsel first.

What does the account look like? People are going to ask a lot of questions so you need to be ready. Gather the proper documentation, to include two years of account records on:

- ✓ Delivery tickets (bills of lading, proof of delivery), credit application, guarantee and current statement. This is the start of it, but you will need all the info below retained for later consideration.
- ✓ Payment information such as check remittance copies, ACH/wire receipts, etc.
- ✓ Invoices (paid and unpaid) and a statement of account.
- ✓ Purchase orders which could be emails, voicemail, fax, etc.
- ✓ How much do they owe you?

Who Do We Need to Tell?

The Big Dogs. This will include notification to salespeople, managers, CFOs and others in your credit department (including other branches).

Your Peers. Luckily, NACM can help with this process. Visit NACM's portal, they will verify and then send out notification to others in your industry group.

Watch Out for the Automatic Stay!

What is it? The automatic stay or "stay" bars you from all collection efforts. The automatic stay is put in place immediately after filing and there is no notification sent to anyone. The automatic stay protects the debtor and its

How to get selected as a critical vendor? To be considered a critical vendor, the debtor must file a motion with the bankruptcy court and prove to the judge that a creditor's products are necessary to the survival of the business and difficult or impossible to get from other vendors. If the debtor is able to carry this burden, then it will be authorized to pay its critical vendors in full.

In order to grant a supplier critical vendor status, courts look at several factors:

✓ Debtor needs particular products for the company to survive.

✓ Vendor likely would stop selling the debtor absent payment of its prepetition claim.

✓ Whether payment to critical vendors (and therefore continued supply from those vendors) would increase the likelihood of a successful reorganization.

> **Tip:** Tread lightly when discussing critical vendor status because if you approach the debtor, it can be deemed a violation of the automatic stay.

Creditors' Committee

What is it? Are you one of the largest unsecured creditors? If so, you might consider becoming a member of the creditors committee. The unsecured creditors' committee is appointed by the U.S. Trustee, in a Chapter 11 case, and is made up of the largest unsecured creditors (usually seven, but sometimes fewer) of the debtors who are willing to serve. Committee members have a more active role than other creditors and have greater access to information and to the debtor's representatives. The committee represents the interests of all unsecured creditors in a fiduciary capacity.

What do I do? A creditors' committee must first be formed. The U.S. Trustee owns the process of forming the committee.

- The U.S. Trustee may appoint a committee as soon as possible after the bankruptcy case is filed if there is significant interest among unsecured creditors.

- The process begins with the U.S. Trustee sending a questionnaire to the largest unsecured creditors. Creditors interested in becoming a member of the committee complete and return the questionnaire to the U.S. Trustee. From that point, the U.S. Trustee convenes an in-person meeting of those creditors that are interested in serving. The trustee will select members of the committee from among those who submitted questionnaires and are present at the meeting (although sometimes this is done based on the questionnaires alone without an in-person meeting).

What does it mean to me? The committee has official duties and responsibilities. There is a time commitment involved with being a committee member.

✓ Review the progress and status of the case and discuss the same with the debtor. Also, the debtor is required to file periodic financial reports with the Court and the Office of the United States Trustee. These reports should provide valuable information for the committee.

✓ Investigate the financial condition of the debtor, the operation of the debtor's business and the desirability of the continuance of the business.

✓ Participate in the formulation of a plan.

✓ Ask the Court to appoint an examiner in the case. An examiner is a professional (often a CPA) with the expertise to investigate the business and file a report drawing conclusions regarding the viability of the same, the competence of past or current management, possible fraud, etc.

✓ Request the appointment of a trustee. A trustee is an independent third party charged with the responsibility of controlling estate assets.

✓ Ask the Court to either dismiss the case or to convert it to one under Chapter 7 (liquidation).

One cause for dismissal or conversion is unreasonable delay which is prejudicial to creditors.

What must the debtor do? The Bankruptcy Code provides further that the debtor must meet with the creditor's committee to transact such business as may be necessary and proper, and that the debtor shall furnish to the committee, upon request, information concerning the debtor's business and its administration. If in the performance of its duties, the committee would be aided by the services of an attorney, accountant or other professional, the Bankruptcy Code provides a means for the appointment of such individuals as may be selected by the committee. The compensation of such individuals will be paid from assets of the debtor's estate, and will not be chargeable directly to individual committee members.

Considerations Throughout the Entire Case

Post-Petition Sales

What is it? Some creditors may decide to sell to a debtor after they've filed Chapter 11 bankruptcy. The debtor in bankruptcy, known as a **Debtor in Possession (DIP)**, is now essentially creating new debt that is not part of the bankruptcy case.

What do I do? Vendors need to manage their post-petition credit risk very closely. Due to the possibility that a debtor may have limited cash flow through the bankruptcy process, vendors may want to consider whether to continue doing business, and if so, under what terms. Steps in determining a debtor's post-petition liquidity include searching PACER to determine whether the debtor has authority to use its lenders cash collateral or has obtained DIP financing. This information might help you as the creditor feel more comfortable with the debtors' ability to pay you for post-petition shipments. In addition, if the debtor fails to pay you for any post-petition shipment you are entitled to a higher priority administrative claim for those shipments (although there is no guarantee administrative claims are paid in full). If you are not comfortable extending credit post-petition, you can impose COD or cash in advance terms or elect not to ship at all.

Preference Claims and Fraudulent Transfers

What is it? Preference and fraudulent transfer actions are some of the most common bankruptcy-related claims that creditors face. It may not seem fair, but it's a reality of bankruptcy. The U.S. Trustee will review all payments made to creditors going back 90 days from the date of filing. Any transfer (payment) made by the debtor to the creditor will be analyzed by the trustee. The intent of preference and fraudulent transfers analysis is to prevent a debtor from "preferentially" paying one creditor over another or "fraudulently" transferring assets to another party. The concept is rooted in fairness.

What does it mean to me? No creditor wants to receive a preference action. Nonetheless, you have to deal with it. You may receive a "demand letter" from the U.S. Trustee. The demand letter lists the payments that the trustee or debtor in possession identifies as having been made to you within the 90-day period. The demand is for immediate payment, usually less some small discount. When a creditor receives a preference demand letter, the creditor should always have experienced bankruptcy counsel review the case to determine whether the creditor has valid defenses.

> **Tip:** Creditors often are concerned about taking payments from their customers when the customer is known to be headed into bankruptcy. The reason is that the payment might be subject to clawback as a preference. Consider, however, that it often is better to have the money in-hand for several reasons: (1) you have use of the money, (2) the burden is then on the trustee to come after you to try to recover it as a preference, and (3) you might have defenses to a later preference claim. As it is often said, "possession is 9/10ths of the battle!" So, take the payment.

What do I do? You have to defend the preference action. The trustee or debtor in possession has the initial burden of proving that the elements of a preference exist. For starters, a prepayment is not a preference (even if the prepayment was received within the 90 days before bankruptcy). The Bankruptcy Code provides defenses to preference actions. The three most common are all "affirmative defenses," meaning that the creditor has the ultimate burden of proof on these issues. The most common defenses used by creditors are:

- **Ordinary course of business defense.** This defense is highly subjective, but the most common methodology is to look at the debtor's payment history to evaluate its average time to pay your invoices for some period of time prior to the 90-day preference period. Did the timing stay consistent before and during the 90-day preference period? You may also use the average time for payment in the relevant industry to prove the ordinary course of business defense. What is the typical payment timing for other companies in the same industry? Depending upon the court, the relevant industry might be the creditor's or the debtor's industry, if they are different.

- **Contemporaneous exchange for new goods or services defense.** The creditor proves the "contemporaneous exchange" defense by showing that the creditor provided new goods or services contemporaneously (i.e., at or near the same time) with a payment that was of equal value to the goods or services provided and that the parties intended the transaction to be a "contemporaneous exchange." For example, if the creditor delivers goods worth $100 on June 1 and is paid $100 for those goods on June 2, so long as the parties intended the $100 payment to be for the $100 in new goods and intended that the payment would occur "substantially contemporaneously" with delivery of the goods, then the contemporaneous exchange defense applies.

- **New value defense.** This defense gives you credit for goods that you ship during the 90-day period after you have received an otherwise preferential payment. The value of any "new" goods or services shipped during the 90-day period after an otherwise preferential payment can be offset dollar-for-dollar against any prior preferential payments made by the debtor. In order to use this defense, most courts require that the later shipment remain unpaid, although some courts will count the later shipment as new value even if you have been paid for that shipment. Using a simple example, this defense works as follows: you receive a $10,000 payment on day 80 prior to the bankruptcy filing and ship $7,500 of new goods (for which you were not paid) on day 70 prior to the bankruptcy filing. Under this scenario, assuming that the $10,000 payment meets all of the elements of a preference and would otherwise be avoidable by the trustee, you are entitled to offset the $7,500 shipment such that your net exposure is $2,500. This defense is much more objective than the ordinary course of business defense.

> **Tip:** They have two years from the date of filing to file a preference lawsuit.

Existing or Executory Contracts

What is it? An executory contract is a contract that has not yet been fully performed, that is to say, fully executed. Put another way, it's a contract under which both sides still have important performance remaining, even if your customer is in bankruptcy.

What does it mean to me? If you are a party to a prepetition contract (executory contract), debtors and bankruptcy trustees are authorized to "assume or reject" these contracts in bankruptcy.

Are you serious? Yes, property interests of the debtor filing for bankruptcy become property of the estate. An executory contract is property of the bankruptcy estate.

Why? The Bankruptcy Code allows debtors to shed (i.e., reject) burdensome contracts (e.g., those where the debtor is paying more than current fair market value) and to retain (i.e., assume) beneficial contracts.

How? Only with bankruptcy court approval can the debtor "assume or reject" an executory contract. As a party to an executory contract, the debtor is required to send you notice of a motion seeking authority to assume or reject your contract and you are given an opportunity to object, if appropriate. Bankruptcy courts defer to the debtor's business judgment when deciding whether to permit assumption or rejection of an executory contract.

What does assumption mean for me? A debtor may assume an executory contract by: Obtaining an order from the bankruptcy court permitting assumption of such contract after notice and an opportunity for the non-debtor counterparty to be heard in the bankruptcy court, or confirming a plan of reorganization, which provides for assumption of the contract. If your contract is assumed, you are entitled to a cure of all defaults (with limited exceptions). This means that if you are owed money under a contract for prepetition sales, if your contract is assumed, you will receive payment in full of your prepetition claim (as opposed to payment of some cents on the dollar).

What does rejection mean for me? Rejection of an executory contract is essentially the debtor's declaration that it will not perform its remaining obligations. Upon rejection, the debtor no longer can be compelled to perform.

What do I do? If you receive a notice that the debtor is seeking to assume your contract, it should include what the debtor believes is the amount needed to cure any defaults. You should review this carefully to be sure that you agree with the amount. If you do not, you will want to retain bankruptcy counsel who can file an objection for you to assert the correct cure amount.

What if the debtor rejects the contract? If you receive a notice that the debtor is seeking to reject your contract, first consider whether it is a leverage play by the debtor to try to get you to renegotiate the terms of your contract in exchange for continued business. If the contract is one you would prefer not to lose, you might wish to contact the debtor to see whether negotiations are possible. But know that it is ultimately the debtor's right to reject your contract. If your contract is rejected, you are entitled to file a "rejection claim." The order authorizing the rejection or a subsequent notice should tell you the deadline to file your rejection claim. A rejection claim is a claim based upon the debtor's breach of your contract, which is what is deemed to have happened upon rejection. It is as though you are filing a lawsuit in state court against the debtor seeking damages for the debtor's breach, but instead are asserting those damages in the form of a rejection claim in the debtor's bankruptcy case. The rejection claim is treated as a general unsecured claim.

Monitor, Monitor, Monitor!!

What do I do? Be cautious and monitor all filings and due dates. Late or misfiled paperwork can cost you the **entire** amount of your claim.

> **Tip:** Most proceedings take months and sometimes years to unwind. Use this time to read up on bankruptcy proceedings so next time, you will be ready.

Excerpted from NACM's Graduate School of Credit and Financial Management project, 2016. Adam Easton, CCE; Alejandro Ojeda-Nonzioli, CCE; Eve Sahnow, CCE; Jessica Pierre, CCE; Kevin Quinn, CCE; Tawnya Marsh, CCE; Jason M. Torf, Esq.; Ryan L. Haaland, Esq.; Holly C. Hamm, Esq.; and The Meridian Group.

Key Terms and Concepts..

Comprehension Check..

1. Provide a brief definition of the following chapters of the Bankruptcy Code:
   a. Chapter 7
   b. Chapter 9
   c. Chapter 11
   d. Chapter 12
   e. Chapter 13
   f. Chapter 15
2. What is the purpose of an **automatic stay** in bankruptcy?
3. What are the basic duties of a **trustee?**
4. In a Chapter 7, **trustees** must satisfy claims in a particular order. List the priority of claims in order.
5. What is the purpose of Chapter 11?
6. Who are the key players in a Chapter 11 proceeding?
7. What is the role of a **creditors' committee** in a Chapter 11 proceeding?
8. How long does a debtor have to assume or reject **executory contracts,** with court approval, under a Chapter 11 proceeding?
9. Define the term **claim,** under the Bankruptcy Code.
10. How is a **small business** defined under Chapter 11 of the Bankruptcy Code?
11. How are claims classified under the Bankruptcy Code?
12. What information is contained in a **plan of reorganization?**
13. In order for a **plan of reorganization** to be accepted, what is necessary?
14. What is the **absolute priority rule?**
15. What two conditions must a plan satisfy under Chapter 12?
16. List the three criteria for filings under Chapter 13.
17. Why is it important to establish a systematic response system for bankruptcy cases?
18. Under what chapters of the Bankruptcy Code must a proof of claim be filed?
19. Before a **preferential payment** to an **unsecured creditor** can be recovered, what must the **trustee** prove?
20. What are the exceptions to the preference rules?
21. What is a **fraudulent transfer?**

Summary

- The Bankruptcy Code is federal law that provides an organized procedure under the supervision of a federal court for dealing with insolvent debtors. This became law in 1979. The Bankruptcy Abuse Prevention and Consumer Protection Act of 2005 (BAPCPA) is the most recent update of bankruptcy law that establishes rules governing bankruptcies for individuals, corporations, small businesses and farms, as well as multination debtors.

- Chapters 7, 9, 11, 12, 13 and 15 are chapters of the Bankruptcy Code that outline the filing of different types of bankruptcies. One of the most important things to know about Bankruptcy Code is the adherence to different filing deadlines because noncompliance can affect a creditor's rights under the law. If there are is any conflict between the provisions of Bankruptcy Code itself and the various applicable rues, the Bankruptcy Code always takes precedence.

- An **automatic stay** is immediately instituted when a bankruptcy petition is filed. Its purpose is to ensure the fair distribution of nonexempt, unencumbered assets among creditors. This resulting actions that are halted include:
  - Beginning or continuing judicial proceedings against the debtor
  - Obtaining possession of the debtor's property
  - Creating, perfecting or enforcing a lien against a debtor's property
  - Setting off indebtedness owed to the debtor that arose prior to the bankruptcy proceeding

- **Chapter 7** bankruptcy is the most common and involves liquidation. The debtor must satisfy a means test. During a Chapter 7 bankruptcy a trustee is appointed. The trustee has several legal obligations that include, but are not limited to, the following:
  - Sell any assets of the estate at the benefit of the creditor
  - Investigate the financial affairs of the debtor

- If a creditor wishes to participate in the distribution of the estates assets, the creditor must file a proof of claim. It indicates the amount of debt owed by the debtor.

- **Trustees** must satisfy all claims in a particular order. The order of priority includes:
  - Secured creditors
  - Administrative expenses
  - Involuntary expenses
  - Wages and compensation claims
  - Employee benefits plans
  - Grain producers or fisherman claims
  - Customer deposits
  - Taxes
  - Unsecured claims of a federal depository institutions regulator agency
  - Claims arising from the unlawful operation of a motor vehicle or vessel
  - Unsecured creditors
  - Preferred stockholders
  - Common stockholders

- A creditor that has any concern about how the case is being handled by the trustee has two options: retain counsel to object to the trustee's final report, or contact the U.S. Trustee for the district in which the case is pending.

- A petition for bankruptcy must be filed in the location where the principle business exists, or where the principle place that assets of the debtor have been held for 180 days or longer. Most petitions are initiated by the debtor, but may be filed by creditors under Chapter 7 or Chapter 11.

- The Bankruptcy Code gives all creditors the right to be notified about any actions that affect the operation of the business and the assets of the bankruptcy estate. Any post-petition unsecured credit obtained by the debtor outside the ordinary business operations must get approval from the courts.

- The U.S. Trustee forms a creditors committee. The financial stake of the committee members, as well as expertise in the industry, give them tremendous influence in the case. They are often the deciding factor for the plan to be confirmed. The committee must also provide access to information by all creditors. Many create websites to fulfill this rule, and the sites provide information like monthly committee reports, or access to the claims docket.

- **Chapter 11** allows a debtor to assume or reject an unexpired executory contract or lease if the court approves. The debtor has 120 days after the bankruptcy to assume or reject unexpired leases of nonresidential real property.

- Many Chapter 11 bankruptcies fail to reorganize and end up being converted to Chapter 7 bankruptcies or dismissed.

- A **plan of reorganization** incorporates a method of classifying claims, secured and unsecured creditors being put into separate classes. Creditors should examine the plans in order to see how classification affects their interests. Creditors may file objections to the classifications before the confirmation hearing, or earlier. **Plans** may include:
  - **Extension plans**
  - **Compromise plans**
  - **Partial payments**
  - **Debt for equity swap**

- In order for reorganization plans to be accepted, a majority from each class must accept the plan. The court is likely to confirm a plan if all classes of creditors and interest holders have accepted the plan with necessary majorities. The court, through a **cramdown**, also has the right to accept the plan even if one or more classes doesn't accept the plan.

- Chapter 11 bankruptcies may also come **prepackaged** (prepack) or **prearranged**. Prepacks make an agreement with all creditors, while a prearranged bankruptcy only makes an agreement with some creditors. There are several advantages to a prepack or prearranged Chapter 11 bankruptcy, such as shortening the timeframe of the bankruptcy process, lowering cost and fees, and limiting uncertainty. However, a prearranged Chapter 11 bankruptcy doesn't ensure that trade creditors receive full or any payment.

- **Chapter 12** eliminates the absolute priority rule, and the plans must satisfy two conditions:
  - Creditors are to receive what they would receive under liquidation (**liquidation test**)
  - All the debtor's disposable income for three to five years must be paid to creditors (**best efforts test**)

- The three criteria for filing a **Chapter 13** Bankruptcy include:
  - The debtor must be an individual
  - The debtor must have a regular income
  - The debt's limit is $494,725 in unsecured debt and $1,184,200 in secured debt. Thresholds are subject to periodic adjustment for inflation

- An efficient internal system for handling bankruptcy should be created. This includes the routing of bank notices so the information goes to the correct individual. Generally a proof of claim is required for Chapters 7, 12 and 13. In all cases, official proof of claim **Form 410** should be used. Objections to claims can be filed, but should be limited due to the administration costs associated with an objective, which inevitably is removed from the total amount available to unsecured debtors.

- The law provides for the protection of creditors who deliver goods to an insolvent debtor through the concept of reclamation. Goods subject to reclamation include those received up to 45 days prior to the bankruptcy filing. Creditors have up to 20 days after the filing to send a demand for reclamation.

- The goal of any bankruptcy proceeding is the discharge of some or all debtor's debts and obligations. Some reasons for denial of discharge under Chapter 7 cases include:
  - Corporations are not normally discharged
  - Concealing assets
  - Failure to keep records

- Certain debts are allowed to be discharged. Some of these debts include:
  - Student loans
  - Credit receive using false financial statements
  - DUI liabilities

- Before a **preferential payment** can be recovered the trustee or debtor must prove that a transfer of the debtor's assets was made:
  - To or for the benefit of the creditor
  - For or on account of an antecedent debt
  - While the debtor was insolvent
  - Within 90 days of the petition of relief, or within a year if it was to an insider
  - The creditor received more than it would have under Chapter 7 liquidation

- Often, involuntary bankruptcy is the only way to force the debtor to provide full financial disclosure.

- Creditors should accept all payments offered by the debtor in financial difficulty.

References and Resources

Bankruptcy Abuse Prevention and Consumer Protection Act: An Overhaul of U.S. Bankruptcy Law. Columbia, MD: National Association of Credit Management, 2005.

"Beginner's Guide to Bankruptcy." NACM's Graduate School of Credit and Financial Management project, 2016.

Business Credit. Maryland: National Association of Credit Management. (This 9 issues/year publication is a continuous source of relevant articles and information. Archived articles from *Business Credit* magazine are available through the web-based NACM Resource Library, which is a benefit of NACM membership.)

Commencing an Involuntary Bankruptcy Petition: The Credit Executive's Perspective. Credit Research Foundation, 2001.

Credit Professional's Guide to Bankruptcy. Credit Research Foundation, 2001.

Credit Professional's Guide to Creditors' Committees in Chapter 11. Credit Research Foundation, 2001.

Creditors' Committee Manual. American Bankruptcy Institute, 1994.

Dunham, Mark Lieutenant Colonel (Retired). U.S. Navy & Air National Guard.

Haaland, Esq., Ryan L. Law Offices of Ryan L. Haaland, Nevada, IA.

Hamm, Esq., Holly C. Snow Spence Green LLP, Houston, TX.

Manual of Credit and Commercial Laws. Columbia, MD: National Association of Credit Management, current edition.

Mota, Diana. "What Happens When the Owner Goes Bankrupt?" *Business Credit* magazine. Columbia, MD: National Association of Credit Management, July/August, 2016.

Nathan, Bruce S., Esq. and David Banker, Esq. "Reclamation Catch-22: Darned If You Do, Darned If You Don't." *Business Credit* magazine. Columbia, MD: National Association of Credit Management, May, 2011.

Schnieder Downs Meridian LP. Pittsburgh, PA.

Torf, Esq., Jason M. Horwood Marcus & Berk Chartered, Chicago, IL.

The United States Department of Justice. "Information For Prospective Creditor Committee Members On Chapter 11 Cases." 2011.

Online Articles/Resources

http://www.hmblaw.com/presentations/bankruptcy-back-to-basics,-cfdd-credit-retreat,-troutdale,-ore-(february-2014).aspx

http://www.coveringcredit.com/business_credit_articles/Bankruptcy/art938.shtml

http://www.lexisnexis.com/legalnewsroom/bankruptcy/b/bankruptcy-law-blog/archive/2010/12/09/critical-vendor-status-in-a-business-reorganization.aspx

http://www.klgates.com/files/Publication/6eb5ac92-1b27-474f-8bf6-9a4ef5ea1ead/Presentation/PublicationAttachment/bd899918-1c17-4c99-af5a-9ce01e73728b/ba0906.pdf

https://www.justice.gov/sites/default/files/ust/legacy/2011/07/13/credcom.pdf

18 Bankruptcy Alternatives

OVERVIEW

There are many ways of handling the affairs of insolvent or financially distressed business debtors. One is to keep the debtor in business and restore the business to profitability. Another is to put the debtor out of business, sell the assets and distribute the proceeds among creditors.

Creditors usually prefer to rehabilitate a distressed debtor by voluntary out-of-court settlement. When rehabilitation is not possible they may liquidate assets outside of bankruptcy proceedings through a general assignment for the benefit of creditors. The credit professional who is familiar with both of these methods, and their advantages and disadvantages, will be able to participate effectively in whatever action is taken when a customer becomes insolvent.

THINK ABOUT THIS

Q. How can alternatives to bankruptcy be advantageous to both the debtor and its creditors?

Q. How can the time of the settlement payment affect the amount the creditor receives?

DISCIPLINARY CORE IDEAS

After reading this chapter, the reader should understand:

- ✓ How to identify a financially distressed debtor.
- ✓ What is involved in a voluntary settlement of claims.
- ✓ The different kinds of settlement plans.
- ✓ The different methods of resolution.
- ✓ The two types of assignments for the benefit of creditors.
- ✓ How to evaluate settlement offers.

CHAPTER OUTLINE

Identifying the Distressed Debtor

Prompt action must be taken if a distressed debtor is to be restored to solvency and maintained as a customer. Credit professionals learn to recognize symptoms of approaching business difficulties through experience, investigation and analysis.

Warning Signs

The credit professional should watch for changes in a customer's business behavior that may signal financial distress. There are several warning signs:

- The debtor has stopped taking advantage of available discounts.
- There is a general slowdown in payments to vendors.
- Lawsuits are being filed against the debtor.
- Tax or vendor liens are being filed against the debtor.
- The debtor is constantly shifting from one supplier to another.
- The debtor is in default with its lending institutions.
- The financial condition of the company is deteriorating.

Comprehension Check
List the warning signs of financial distress.

Public Information and Records

Newspapers are a primary medium to publish statutorily required legal notices because they are readily accessible by the public. By definition, **public records** *are information recorded in a public office and available for public inspection.* Although the types of statutorily required notices are too many to list, examples include judgments, state or federal tax liens, mechanic's liens and release of liens.

Insolvency and Non-Liquidity

In business, **insolvency** *is the situation where the liabilities of a person or firm exceed its assets. In practice, however, insolvency is the situation where an entity cannot raise enough cash to meet its obligations, or to pay debts as they become due for payment* (i.e., even if it could sell all its assets, it would still be unable to replay its debts). **Non-liquidity** occurs when a firm has a temporary cash flow problem. It *is a measure of the extent that a person or organization has cash to meet immediate and short-term obligations, or assets that can be quickly converted to do this. Its assets are greater than its debts, but some assets are illiquid* (e.g. it takes a long time to sell a house. A bank can't suddenly demand a mortgage loan back). Therefore, although in theory assets are greater than debts, it can't meet its current payment requirements.

Credit professionals should be able to distinguish between a business that can be financially rehabilitated and one that should be liquidated for the benefit of its creditors, in or out of a bankruptcy proceeding. Credit professionals should also be able to recognize the dishonest debtor that could be rehabilitated, but should instead be liquidated and prosecuted. Careful consideration should be given to whether a company can be rehabilitated with the current management in place or whether the rehabilitation should be under the guidance of a trustee. There may be situations where a better recovery in a workout plan with a trustee in place is more effective than a bankruptcy plan which may involve a large number of administrative claims. Management's ability to adapt to a different business perspective and plan of action may be an influential factor in this determination. Prosecution of a dishonest debtor is frequently desirable, but not always in the creditors' best interest. It takes money, usually from the estate and reduces the amount available for creditors' claims.

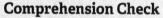

Comprehension Check
Explain the difference between **insolvency** and **non-liquidity.**

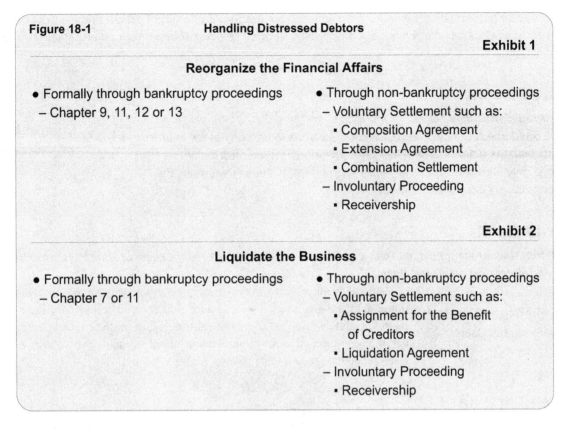

Figure 18-1   **Handling Distressed Debtors**

Exhibit 1

Reorganize the Financial Affairs

- Formally through bankruptcy proceedings
  - Chapter 9, 11, 12 or 13

- Through non-bankruptcy proceedings
  - Voluntary Settlement such as:
    - Composition Agreement
    - Extension Agreement
    - Combination Settlement
  - Involuntary Proceeding
    - Receivership

Exhibit 2

Liquidate the Business

- Formally through bankruptcy proceedings
  - Chapter 7 or 11

- Through non-bankruptcy proceedings
  - Voluntary Settlement such as:
    - Assignment for the Benefit of Creditors
    - Liquidation Agreement
  - Involuntary Proceeding
    - Receivership

Voluntary Settlements

A **voluntary settlement** *is a contract between the debtor and its creditors that settles their claims for the most the debtor can pay and the most the creditors can realize.* It keeps the debtor in business and avoids substantial bankruptcy costs that few debtors can afford under the circumstances. The creditors may take a temporary loss, but expect the debtor to emerge stable and solvent as a continuing customer. Voluntary settlements between debtors and creditors are preferred to a bankruptcy filing.

Advantages and Complications

The principal advantage of a voluntary settlement is its simplicity. There are no cumbersome court proceedings. They are essentially informal but legally binding on the debtor with specific penalties for nonperformance.

Because they are relatively uncomplicated, voluntary settlements are more economical than bankruptcy proceedings. There are no court costs and trustee fees, and the general costs of administration are lower. This means there are likely to be more assets left to satisfy the amounts due to creditors.

In some cases, the use of non-bankruptcy alternatives may not be the best option. They may be difficult to arrange when there are priority secured claims such as bank loans or tax liens on the debtor.

Initiating the Voluntary Settlement

Voluntary settlements may be initiated by either the debtor or the creditors. Most frequently, a debtor in financial difficulty goes to an attorney for advice. The attorney may consult with a few of the largest creditors and arrange a meeting to be attended by the debtor and its largest creditors. A meeting may also be initiated by a few of the most interested or largest creditors that are suspicious of the debtor's financial condition. Adjustments of debts are an alternative for creditors, as well as debtors, to attempt to gain greater recoveries on unsecured claims than might be otherwise be possible. Where a debtor has expressed the desire to try to solve financial problems out of court, adjustment specialists can effectively assist organizing unsecured creditors to ensure fair and equitable recoveries for all creditors.

Secured Claims

Secured claims *may consist of mortgages on the debtor's real property, other secured assets or any perfected security interests in property made in accordance with the Uniform Commercial Code provisions.* In general, a bankruptcy discharge only eliminates personal liability for a debt. It doesn't wipe out the creditor's security interest in the property.

Comprehension Check
What may a **secured claim** consist of?

Priority Claims

Priority claims *may consist of taxes, wages and unpaid rent which under federal or state laws are entitled to priority payment over unsecured claims.*

Comprehension Check
What may a **priority claim** consist of?

General creditors should not accept voluntary settlements or extensions unless they are given absolute assurance that secured and priority claims have been adequately disposed of by the debtor. Failure to do so could result in any voluntary settlement arrangement being unenforceable. The validity of such claims should be reviewed by counsel for the creditors.

Settlement Plan

Working out a settlement plan is largely a matter of bargaining. Armed with the information acquired, the creditors are in a position to bargain for a settlement that will ensure maximum return to creditors, but will still enable the debtor to emerge solvent.

Voluntary settlements usually take one of three forms: extensions, *pro rata* cash settlements, or combinations settlements. Which plan evolves depends in large part upon the negotiating ability of the creditors' committee. Occasionally, a committee of creditors may arrive at a plan in which an extension is accepted by some of the creditors while a *pro rata* cash settlement payment is made to other creditors.

Importance of Unity in Voluntary Settlements

The success of a voluntary settlement depends upon the full cooperation of all creditors and the debtor. For example, a secret or previously undisclosed preferential arrangement between the debtor and even one creditor, giving this creditor a larger settlement than the others, is a valid basis for any creditor to rescind the settlement on the basis of fraud.

During the negotiation period, objecting creditors are free to sue or levy against or attach the debtor's assets in satisfaction of their claim, and taxing authorities are free to levy. One creditor or taxing authority may prevent the settlement from being consummated.

Comprehension Check
Why is unity important in voluntary settlements?

The debtor can prevent this by executing a statutory assignment for the benefit of creditors or by filing a petition under the bankruptcy laws.

Creditors' Committee

At the first meeting of creditors, a committee should be selected. This committee generally consists of five or seven of the largest unsecured creditors and perhaps one or two representatives of the larger body of smaller creditors. Although the proceedings are out of court, the committee should be limited in number, with other creditors serving as alternates or ex-officio members. Sometimes only the larger companies can spare the expense of sending a representative to the creditors' meetings; having some of the creditor company names may lend credence to the proceedings.

The people serving on the committee must be knowledgeable in this type of work and have the time to serve and work in the best interest of all creditors. There must be complete disclosure by all members of the committee of their interests.

The committee should select a chairman, secretary and counsel. While the chairman is often from the largest creditor, it is of the utmost importance that the chairman be knowledgeable and willing to serve and work. Counsel is usually a lawyer experienced in this work, representing one or more of the larger creditors, or independent of all creditors. The counsel sometimes acts as the secretary.

The creditors should also ask that an accountant be retained to make an independent examination of the debtor's books and records at the expense of the debtor or its estate. It is most helpful to the creditors if the debtor will come to the first meeting well-prepared, accompanied by both counsel and accountant. The debtor should have current financial statements, be prepared to give the entire financial history of the business as well as the reasons for its distressed condition, and be able to answer most questions.

It is possible, but unlikely, that a satisfactory plan of settlement will be agreed upon at the initial creditors' meeting. In order to assess any settlement plan the debtor proposes, the creditors need their own evaluation of the debtor's business and financial situation.

Comprehension Check
Explain the important requirements of a creditors' committee.

••

What items should be examined by the creditors' committee?

Objects of the Investigation

The creditors should obtain an up-to-date inventory count and valuation if appropriate. One or more members of the creditors' committee who are experts in the type of business may evaluate the inventory, or an appraiser may be retained, at the expense of the debtor or its estate. It is important to ascertain what the assets would realize at a forced sale; this is an indication of what the dividend might be in bankruptcy proceedings and sets the floor for a voluntary settlement. Creditors should request copies of tax returns for the last several years to determine the changes that have occurred and whether they were completed and filed properly.

Causes of Financial Distress

Creditors should try to ascertain the reasons for the current financial distress: excessive rent and overhead, high general and administrative expenses which include salaries, unusually large withdrawals from the business, declining sales volume, or inadequate markup on goods. Questioning the debtor about these matters can help determine whether a workout with a 100 percent payment or reduced settlement amount is the better goal. The answers should help decide the size of a proposed settlement and whether the offer is the best possible. During its investigation, the creditors' committee may uncover indications of dishonesty or lack of management skills. If the committee determines that the business is viable, but management is lacking, a turnaround consultant or management evaluation firm may be considered. The debtor that remains outside of a formal bankruptcy statistically has a better chance of survival, improving the chances that creditors can be repaid and the relationship with the debtor as a paying customer can be reestablished.

Comprehension Check
List the causes of financial distress.

Questionable Actions by Debtor

These include:

- Sudden increases in purchases without corresponding increases in sales.
- Materially false financial statements.
- Unaccountable or unexplained reduction in inventory or cash.
- Recent repayment of loans.
- Pledging of assets.

- Missing financial records.
- Evasiveness by the debtor in answering questions or supplying information.
- Big salaries or expense accounts.

Reaction of Creditors' Committee

In such instances, the reaction of the creditors' committee to the debtor may be unfavorable. The committee may decide that court proceedings are preferable, with opportunities for investigating fully, denying the debtor a discharge from its obligations, or even imposing criminal sanctions. The committee may decide to retain a forensic accountant to piece together how the decline happened.

Positive Findings by the Creditors' Committee

If the committee finds that the debtor has been honest and a worthwhile customer in the past and that the business can be saved, it should ask the debtor to present a plan. A review of the debtor's buying and payment history may enable the creditors to assist the debtor with a plan that would work for everyone's benefit. The goal is to rehabilitate and retain a previously valuable customer.

Methods of Resolution

Alternative Dispute Resolution

The increasingly complex nature of commercial agreements and the substantial delays and expense associated with litigation have given rise to alternatives for accommodating the needs of creditors when disputes occur. There are two types of **alternative dispute resolution (ADR)**, or ways to resolve conflicts between parties without litigation; *mediation and arbitration*. While not totally inconsistent with one another, arbitration and mediation are different and have their own uses.

Normally, both parties must agree to use ADR, making it appropriate for voluntary settlements. Mediators and arbitrators are neutral, they represent neither side. Each of the parties in a voluntary settlement should have its own legal counsel for the ADR process.

Mediation

Mediation *is the non-binding attempt by parties to solve a dispute using an independent mediator or facilitator in order to allow the parties to reach common ground.* Unlike arbitration, mediation can be chosen after the dispute has arisen. The parties usually select and agree upon a qualified, skilled and experienced mediator.

The mediator's role is to separately review each party's position as to their respective claim or defense, and then bring the parties together on sufficient common grounds so that a settlement can be effected. The mediator does not make a decision as to who is right or who is wrong, nor is there any final order or award entered as a result of mediation, unless the parties reach a voluntary settlement. The mediator manages the process, helps the two sides prioritize their demands, and keeps negotiations on a realistic basis. The mediator may suggest compromises or terms but cannot impose them. Mediators are usually lawyers but can be business people or other professionals.

 Comprehension Check
Define **mediation**.

Arbitration

In **arbitration,** *the parties use an independent arbitrator to act in lieu of a judge or jury in resolving a dispute.* Arbitration is usually provided for in a contract. In arbitration, both parties present their case to an impartial arbitrator. As with mediation, it is critically important that the arbitrator not only have the training necessary, but also be well schooled in the law and industry practices.

In most arbitrations, the normal courtroom evidence rules do not apply (Figure 18-2). This permits the parties to present their case and the arbitrator to hear the entire case. After the presentation of all of the evidence, the arbitrator announces a ruling and an award, which is binding on the parties. Arbitrators are often lawyers, retired judges, or may even be business people who have additional training in dispute resolution. They may be located through national and state professional associations.

Comprehension Check
Define **arbitration**.

> **Figure 18-2   Advantages of Arbitration**
>
> ■ May be faster and less expensive than litigation.
> ■ The business relationship may continue while arbitration is occurring.
> ■ An arbiter with special knowledge of the industry may be selected.
> ■ Subject matter may remain confidential.

Extension Agreement

Under an **extension plan,** *the debtor proposes to pay creditors in full over a period of time.* An extension is, in effect, a deferral of payment of debts. The debtor remains in possession, continues to operate the business and temporarily buys on a cash basis. The creditors' committee acts in an advisory capacity only and does not assume active control of the business. An extension requires an optimistic prospect of future operations.

Establishing Controls

Creditors should make sure that adequate controls are instituted for the operation of the business and, in the event rehabilitation is not possible, over the liquidation of assets and disposition of the proceeds. This is done to provide reasonable assurance that assets are protected from improper use and to produce records from which reliable reports can be prepared.

 Comprehension Check
What is an **extension agreement?**

Transfer of Stock

This is effective when the debtor is a corporation. The creditors' committee may have the stockholders transfer their stock certificates to the committee or to be held in escrow. If the extension plan is fully performed, the shares are returned. If not, the transfer becomes effective and the entire corporation becomes the property of the committee, to be liquidated for the benefit of creditors.

The committee may also receive and hold in escrow the written resignation of all officers and directors of the debtor corporation. The committee will thus be in a position to assume complete ownership and control if the debtor defaults under the plan.

Financial Controls

During the extension period, the committee may designate its accountant to monitor or, if necessary, supervise operations or have a representative countersign all checks and control expenditures.

Security

Under the extension plan, the debtor presumably will execute extension notes to the creditors, payable in installments. In addition, the creditors' committee may request or demand some form of security for payment such as a:

- Mortgage on the debtor's real estate, which is frequently owned by the debtor and spouse.
- Security interest in accounts, inventory and other assets of the debtor.
- Assignment of accounts receivable.
- Guarantee of the extension notes by a responsible third party acceptable to the committee.

A security interest in accounts, inventory and other personal property must be perfected under the Uniform Commercial Code (UCC).

New Trade Creditors

In order to obtain the cooperation of new trade creditors, a security interest under the UCC could be given to creditors with the old debt, and they in turn could subordinate that debt to the new trade creditors to give them a priority and encourage shipments to the debtor.

This type of arrangement has to be fully documented, and comply with the UCC with respect to the lien and the subordination. It is widely used in rehabilitation cases and gives a good measure of flexibility in working out problems.

Composition Agreement

A **composition agreement** *is a pro rata settlement in which the debtor proposes to settle with creditors for less than the full amount owed.* It is the quickest of all voluntary settlements.

How it works:

1. The debtor pays a uniform percentage of its obligations in cash to all its creditors, who accept the partial payment in full settlement of their claims.
2. The percentage depends upon what the debtor's assets are, what the debtor is able to pay and the amount that the creditors are able to procure in the negotiating process.
3. The debtor may obtain third-party loans or equity capital to make a settlement with creditors.

The Settlement Percentage

The most important criterion in determining the rate of settlement is what the dividend would be in bankruptcy proceedings. A *pro rata* voluntary settlement should be at least as high as the proceeds would be from bankruptcy proceedings. The costs of administration are low and the debtor avoids the stigma of bankruptcy. However, negotiating for a *pro rata* cash settlement is sometimes difficult. Some creditors will, as a matter of policy, accept extensions of time but not *pro rata* cash settlements.

If all creditors cannot agree to accept the *pro rata* cash settlement, it may be necessary to proceed to liquidate under Chapter 7 or 11 of the federal Bankruptcy Code, and creditors may realize a smaller percentage of their claims.

Creditors with Small Claims

Creditors with small claims frequently hold out for payment in full. It is often advisable to provide that payment to reduce the number of creditors and eliminate all small claims. Also, some creditors agreeing to reduce their claims to a specified amount may receive 100 percent of their claims, while a payment of 25 percent is paid to larger creditors.

Combination Settlement

A **combination settlement** is voluntary and *contains both a pro rata cash payment and an extension of time.* For example, the settlement may provide a cash payment of 20 percent immediately and three future installments of 5 percent each, or a total of 35 percent in full settlement. The installment payments, usually evidenced by notes, may be payable at three, six, nine or 12-month intervals. The disbursements are usually made by an adjustment bureau rather than by the debtor company. Because this method involves payments over time, control over the debtor's business and security for creditors during the extension period should be carefully provided.

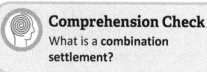

Comprehension Check
What is a **combination settlement**?

Real World Perspectives

VARIATION ON A THEME: SMALL CLAIMS IS A BREEZE

My first position as a credit manager was at a local seafood company in St. Louis. It was decided in the interest of saving money, that I would do all of my own small claims cases. After a few days of training, I began haunting the courthouses in St. Louis City and St. Louis County and observed several cases over the next few weeks. I watched and took a lot of notes. I tried to figure out what the judges did and didn't like. I began to get a feel of how the whole process worked.

There was a limousine company being sued by its customers because the driver had spun the tires on their lawn and damaged the landscape. The driver claimed that the passengers were rude and abusive, did damage to the limousine and told him to drive on their lawn in the first place since there was no place to turn around. The judge ended up splitting the fee between them, so no one really prevailed.

There was another case of payment due on the sale of a cockatoo. The judge asked if any payment had been received on the $1,500 balance due.

"Yes your honor," was the plaintiff's answer. "Five hundred dollars and an iguana."

"Excuse me, what's an 'iguana'?"

"It's a big green lizard, your honor"

My first suit was against a restaurant on South Broadway. They owed us almost the limit of what you were allowed to sue for in that particular court. I filed all my papers and got a court date. I prepared spreadsheets and copies of delivery receipts, invoices and call records. I was a wreck. I paced. I practiced in the mirror. I fretted and had a slight melt down. "You can do this," was my mantra.

The court date finally arrived. I took great care in getting ready that morning. I took out my brand new navy blue suit, navy blue pumps and crisp white blouse. I even left my skirt hanging on the hook on the back of the bedroom door until the last minute so I wouldn't muss or wrinkle it. I did my hair and makeup and made a quick final inspection in the bureau mirror. I looked professional. I was ready.

I arrived at the court house just over two hours early. I had a briefcase full of every document ever created for any transaction having to do with that account. I had spent hours preparing. As I walked the three or so blocks from my car to the courthouse, I was thinking that it was pretty brisk out for a St. Louis spring morning and wished I had worn a coat. Wow, it was downright breezy. As I climbed the steps of the old courthouse, I glanced down to check my skirt for wrinkles and, to my horror, discovered that I had forgotten to put it on. There I was on the courthouse steps, briefcase in hand, in my brand new blue blazer, blue pumps, crisp white blouse—and my slip.

I raced back to my car and broke every speed record in the state of Missouri driving back to my house. I grabbed my skirt off the back of the door, threw it on, raced back to the courthouse and, though breathless, still arrived in time to have my case heard. The defendant arrived late, with little scraps of crumpled paper he called records, which he pulled in fistfuls from his pockets and placed on the table. We were awarded the judgment.

A few months later, after numerous attempts to collect the debt, I paid a visit to the restaurant during a very busy lunch hour, fully clothed I might add. I was accompanied by an extremely large and extremely patient deputy sheriff, who assisted me in enforcing my court order allowing me to seize the contents of the cash drawer. When the proprietor protested loudly, my companion gently took my arm and led me around behind him as if to shield me. He reached to his side, patted his gun and said, "Son, don't cause me to draw my weapon."

We collected what we were owed in full and went on our way. I still believe to this day that it will never be safe for me or anyone in my family to dine there or at any of the proprietor's other restaurants.

I discovered then that I loved working in credit. I loved everything about it. These days, though, when I walk out of my house and have the feeling that I'm forgetting something, I check for keys, purse and wallet. Most importantly, I check my attire in a full-length mirror instead of the one on my waist-high bureau.

Patti Guard-Younce

Administration Costs

Over and above the settlement amount to creditors, the plan must provide for payment of all administration costs. Administration costs include any expenses incurred by the creditors' committee, such as cost of counsel and accountant, court costs and out-of-pocket expenses of committee members. The costs of administration for voluntary settlements are usually lower than for formal proceedings.

Execution of the Settlement

When the creditors' committee has approved a plan it should, with the aid of counsel, prepare a notice to all creditors with details of the settlement plan recommending that creditors accept it. A form of acceptance should accompany the notice for signature by creditors and return to the committee. If the transaction is complicated, the notice should include a form of agreement drafted by the committee's counsel. Funds necessary for immediate payment to creditors are usually deposited by the debtor with the secretary of the creditors' committee. The secretary may also hold the outstanding notes on behalf of creditors.

Assignment for the Benefit of Creditors

While creditors' efforts are ordinarily directed toward rehabilitating the distressed debtor, some are too indebted and lacking in prospects to be turned around. In those cases, the debtor may be asked to execute a general assignment for the benefit of creditors, a liquidation technique by which the debtor goes out of business. There are two types of assignments: statutory assignment and common law assignment.

Statutory Assignment for the Benefit of Creditors

One of the vehicles to liquidate a failed or no longer viable business is an assignment for the benefit of creditors (ABC or Assignment). ABCs are a state law, rather than a federal law. This method of liquidating or transferring assets has the advantage of avoiding the unpredictability and expense of a Chapter 7 or a liquidating Chapter 11 of the Bankruptcy Code. It has long been popular in states such as Illinois and California and is regaining popularity in many other states such as Florida, Michigan, New Jersey, New York, Ohio, Pennsylvania and Texas.

An **assignment** *is a transfer of the debtor's legal and equitable title to property to a trustee, with authority to liquidate the debtor's affairs and distribute proceeds equitably to creditors.* In reality, an assignment is very similar to Chapter 7 liquidation under the Bankruptcy Code. The difference is that the bankruptcy court is not involved and the trustee does not report to the bankruptcy court. The trustee or assignee receives the debtor's assets which are to be liquidated for the benefit of all of the creditors of the debtor.

An assignment is subject to the state law of the state in which it is made. Many states do not have state statutes which regulate assignments, but depend on common law (case law) which has developed over the years. Other states, such as Florida and Indiana, have assignment statutes which proscribe how an ABC is conducted and may require court approval for the actions of the assignee. In spite of these differences, the concept remains the same; an assignment is a liquidation tool which places the assets with an independent fiduciary for benefit of all the creditors. Although there is not an automatic stay as under the Bankruptcy Code, the practical effect is that actions to reach the assets are stopped while the assignee acts to liquidate the assets. The creditor pursuing a judgment against the debtor may find that the assignee is willing to allow the judgment so long as the judgment creditor submits its claim as described below. The assignee may also defend against a claim if the plaintiff is seeking a judgment which is unjustified and not fair to other creditors.

Assignor and Assignee

The debtor company is the **assignor** *who transfers its assets to the* **assignee** *who acts as a fiduciary to all of the creditors of the debtor company.* The assignee and assignor enter into a contract by which the assignor agrees to liquidate the assets assigned for the benefit of the creditors of the assignor company. The assignee is generally an unrelated individual who agrees to act in this fiduciary capacity and is experienced with liquidating assets. Upon acceptance of the assignment, all of the assets previously belonging to the assignor become the property of the assignee for the purpose of liquidation.

The assignee is generally chosen by the debtor and perhaps with the approval of the secured lender. They should familiar with liquidations, sales of businesses and knowledgeable about the debtor's industry. A board of a debtor corporation may want to consider an assignment to a professional assignee to ensure that the board acting while in the zone of insolvency is using a professional and experienced individual who is able to be a true fiduciary to the creditors. Unlike a Chapter 7 Trustee who is randomly assigned from a panel of trustees, the assignee can be selected as knowledgeable with liquidations and the particular industry of the debtor.

Because the assignor is able to pick the professional assignee, the assignor and the prospective assignee are able to discuss what is likely to happen in the assignment, to negotiate the cost and payment of the assignee's expenses and determine whether the making of an assignment is worth pursuing. For example, if the assignor is to sell the debtor's business as a going-concern, the prospective assignee may want to make arrangements to retain certain valuable employees to run the business under the direction or administration of the prospective assignee. If the prospective assignee determines initially that there is not enough revenue expected during the assignment to support the ongoing business, the assignment may take another form such as liquidation. The advantage of an ABC over a Chapter 7 filing is that the parties can largely determine, prior to executing the assignment documents, what is going to happen during the assignment.

For the creditors of the assignor corporation, the assignment of assets to the professional assignee may be relief that the prior management is no longer in control.

Effect of the Assignment

The assignee accepts the assignment of the assignor property with all existing liens remaining in place. The assignee is likely to seek consent of the debtor's secured lenders prior to accepting the assigned assets. This ensures the assignment from being disrupted by a UCC or mortgage foreclosure. Many banks are happy to see an assignment and may in fact suggest an ABC as a reasonable way of liquidating a bad loan. The assignee will examine Uniform Commercial Code filings and other documents to determine who has valid and perfected liens on the assets.

The acceptance of the assignment by the assignee creates an estate which remains subject to all of the claims of creditors, both unsecured and secured. In states where the state court supervises assignments, the assignment contract will be filed with the court and supervision of the liquidation by the court begins. In common law states, the assignee may proceed to liquidate the property in a commercially reasonable fashion. In most cases, the assignee will advertise the sale or auction of the property in a manner which is economically realistic for the sale of that type of property. The assignee will also notify creditors of the debtor company as it is possible the creditors may know likely buyers or may be buyers themselves.

An ABC does not provide a discharge for the assignor debtor company, just as a Chapter 7 liquidation for a corporation does not either.

Cost of an ABC

The biggest advantages of an assignment over a Chapter 7 petition are the cost savings to the estate and the predictability of the outcome. Although less expensive than a Chapter 7 case, there are still significant costs such as the following for which payment must be provided:

- **Administrative rent.** This cost involves the cost of the assignee staying in the premises previously occupied by the assignor debtor. The assignee may be able to negotiate a reduction in rent or possibly a waiver if the premises are leased by the debtor's principal or related party.
- **Fees of assignee and other professionals.** The assignee is generally paid through a fee which is negotiated initially and is part of the assignment contract. The cash necessary to cover the costs of the assignment need to be there at the initiation of the ABC or there must be an agreement with the secured lender to advance monies to administer the estate

and preserve the assets. Fees may be determined as a percentage of the amount realized from the liquidation of the assets. The fees may also be fixed or capped by the assignment contract. In a state requiring that a court monitor the process, the court will approve the fees. In addition to the fees of the assignee, the assignee may require the assistance of attorneys, accountants or real estate brokers. Each of these professionals will need to receive payment for their services and this must come out of the estate assets, as well. The assignee, as a fiduciary to the creditors, has a duty to act efficiently and not incur fees needlessly.

Each assignment is different and the professionals required may differ depending on the type of business being liquidated and whether the business will continue to operate during the assignment. Because fees can be negotiated as part of the assignment contract, they can be predicted prior to being incurred. For example, if the debtor is aware of an interested buyer for the assets at the time of the assignment, the assignee may be able to negotiate the terms of a sale with the interested buyer and then use this buyer as the stalking horse to advertise a sale which may bring in other competitive bidders at an auction. If, however, no interested buyers have been identified, the assignee may have to spend time and expense attempting to locate buyers and drumming up interest for the assets. If the primary asset is liquidated, the assignee will be required to pay legal fees to continue the prosecution of the action. In many states, the costs of administration are considered a lien on the assets of the estate. In most circumstances the assignee will negotiate with the secured creditor the right to be paid, prior to even taking on the obligations of the assignment.

Steps of an Assignment

At the beginning of an assignment, the assignor is required to give the assignee a complete list of creditors and a list of all assets being assigned. Based upon this list, the assignee will send a letter to all creditors notifying them of the fact that the assignment has been made, providing information on the probable distribution that will be made to creditors and providing a claim form for each creditor to submit a claim to the assignee. After claim forms are returned, the assignee will determine the proper amount of each claim and inform the creditors if there are problems with the amount of a claim. After all the assets have been liquidated, the assignee will determine the distribution amounts based upon the priorities of claim type.

The assignee will generally inform the Internal Revenue Service that the assignment has been made and will file a notice with the local county and state recording offices. The assignee will also immediately determine whether there are any additional liens that have previously not been disclosed. The assignee will conduct Uniform Commercial Code searches and real estate lien searches, if real estate is involved, and to make sure that all creditors and interest holders receive notice of the ABC.

The assignee will take control of the assets, changing locks, taking over bank accounts, the debtor's books and records and generally securing all assets. The assignee may on limited occasions continue to operate the business to maintain going-concern value. This step is taken very cautiously and only where the business has sufficient funds to operate on a cash basis without incurring any additional debt. Most assignees will not operate a business because the cash is simply not sufficient.

Priority of Claims

Although state law may determine the priority of claims, where this is not determined, the assignees follow the priorities set forth in the Bankruptcy Code. Properly perfected secured claims will be paid prior to those of taxing authorities, wage claims and general unsecured claims. Certain states may alter this scheme if there are requirements under state laws that create a trust for certain categories of creditors such as employees, customer deposits or employee benefits. The assignee must also be aware of state reclamation laws which may provide rights to creditors delivering goods during the period of the assignor's insolvency.

Avoidance Actions

In a Chapter 7 case, the trustee will attempt to recover preference payments and fraudulent transfers. In an assignment, the assignee may pursue fraudulent transfers and preferences only as allowed under state law. State statutes in most states give the assignee the right to recover payments or transfers where the payments or transfers were made with the intent to defraud other creditors. Not all states offer the same right to recover payments which may simply be preferential. Even in states such as California, where a state statute does provide the right to recover preferential payments, a court decision has called this right into question outside a bankruptcy proceeding. If there are significant preferences to be recovered, the assignee may want to avoid taking on the assignment as a Chapter 7 case may be more appropriate.

Actions to Take When Notified of an ABC

There are many considerations to make upon receipt of a notice of an assignment for the benefit of creditors; some will depend on the industry or on the specifics of an individual situation.

Here are some questions to ask and considerations to consider:

1. Is the assignee qualified?

- Does the assignee have the type of experience that makes them qualified to act as a fiduciary for the creditors?
- Is the assignee disinterested?
- Is the assignee bonded?
- What is the relationship of the assignee to the assigning company, its principals and its secured lender?

2. Preferences

- If the debtor has been paying other creditors to the disadvantage of a creditor or other creditors, will the assignee be able to effectively pursue them for the distribution to other creditors?

3. Fraudulent Transfers

- Has the assignee examined the payments to insiders during the several years prior to the assignment?

4. Reclamation

- Were goods delivered during the last 10 days? State law reclamation rights remain in place.

5. Is a sale to insiders being proposed?

- If so, will the sale be tested in a commercially reasonable way so that the highest and best price for the assets can be obtained?
- If the sale appears not to be conducted in a public manner, why not?
- Is the sale being conducted to merely "cleanse the assets" so that the previous management can continue conducting business without debt?

6. Executory leases or contracts?

- If there are leases or contracts that should be rejected, it is possible that an assignment is not in the best interest of the estate and that the Bankruptcy Code may be the better vehicle?

If the checklist questions cannot be adequately answered and the assignee or their attorney will not provide satisfactory answers, the creditors should consider other remedies such as filing an involuntary petition to place the debtor in a Chapter 7 case. The filing of an involuntary bankruptcy petition is a serious issue which should not be done without consulting an attorney, but it may be the best alternative. This is especially true where preferences will be left without recovery or where the sale of the assets does not appear to be commercially reasonable. If the assignee or the debtor is unwilling to provide information concerning the assignment, then there may be information that is being withheld and a bankruptcy proceeding may be a better method for liquidation with the full disclosure which would be provided to creditors.

On the other hand, if there are no significant preferences and the sale or liquidation of the assets appears to be commercially reasonable, an ABC may be the most efficient and cost-effective means of liquidating the assets for creditors. Even if there are preferences that may not be otherwise recovered without a bankruptcy, certain bankruptcy judges recognizing the professional assignee's expertise in the sale and liquidation of assets may abstain from administering the estate until after the sale. After that time, the bankruptcy court may adjudicate the case as well as the proceeds of the sale. If there are no preferences or other assets which can be better administered by the bankruptcy court, then the bankruptcy court will likely abstain from administering the estate. The assignment avoids the cost of filing motions with the bankruptcy court and seeking approval throughout the process. The assignee can object to claims informally and negotiate with individual creditors if necessary. The sale of assets can, if a known buyer has been identified, occur within three weeks or perhaps less if necessary. Thus, the value of the assets may be more readily available.

Assignments have become a more attractive vehicle for selling or liquidating companies. The increased cost of liquidating Chapter 11 cases and the Chapter 7 cases makes the use of professional and experienced assignees a good avenue for liquidating assets and creating a better return for creditors.

Comprehension Check
Describe the process of **assignment for the benefit of creditors.**

Common Law Assignment

The **common law assignment** *is a device whereby a debtor transfers title to all assets to a third party, designated as assignee or trustee, with instructions to liquidate the assets and distribute the proceeds among creditors on a pro rata basis.* The assignment may be made by a debtor without prior consultation with creditors, or it may be executed after meetings with creditors or a creditors' committee, when it becomes obvious that a voluntary settlement cannot be made. In the latter instance, an adjustment bureau is frequently appointed assignee.

Sale of Assets

The assignee proceeds to liquidate the assets, most frequently by public sale through a recognized auctioneer with adequate advertising to ensure competitive bidding. In rare instances, the assignee may sell at a private sale when a better price can be achieved. The assignee also takes steps to collect or sell accounts receivable.

Distribution

After deducting administration costs, the assignee distributes the proceeds from the sale of assets *pro rata* among all unsecured creditors. Because a common law assignment is not under the supervision or control of a court, administration costs are low and dividends to creditors may be correspondingly higher.

Acceptance

No creditor is obliged to accept a *pro rata* settlement. The creditor may refuse the settlement and file a claim in full. As a practical matter creditors usually accept it because the dividends are generally larger than those obtainable in bankruptcy, and their old claim may have little or no value unless the debtor subsequently acquires new assets.

Discharge from Obligations

In a common law assignment, the debtor does not receive a discharge from obligations. The debtor merely has its assets sold and the proceeds distributed among creditors. If, for example, the *pro rata* distribution is 35 percent, creditors retain their claims against the debtor for the balance of 65 percent. The principal users of this device are corporations that are going out of business; a claim for the balance is immaterial since the corporation will be dissolved. Individual debtors seeking discharge from their obligations will couple the assignment with a proposal for settlement in full.

The credit professional should keep in mind that if dividend checks issued under a common law assignment are not accompanied by an agreement for discharge, no discharge is granted. The creditors may therefore cash the checks and receive their dividends without agreeing to discharge the debtor. Claims for the balance are retained.

The creditor must read the wording on the check to determine whether it can be cashed only by creditors accepting it in full settlement.

Receivership Proceedings (A Non-Bankruptcy, Court Proceeding)

Unlike compositions and assignments for the benefit of creditors, receivership proceedings are rarely voluntary. In most states, receivership proceedings can only be instituted by the commencement of any adversary-type proceeding. The receivership is instituted only after the court has made the determination that it is necessary and proper.

States may have different rules governing receivership administration, therefore careful attention should be paid by creditors to all communications received in the case so that they can maximize their return. If creditors feel that the receiver is not looking out for their best interests, it is possible to consider filing an involuntary bankruptcy case against the debtor to control the situation in either a Chapter 7 or 11.

Evaluating Settlement Offers

Traditionally, these offers are made and considered with little attention given to the time value of funds involved. A 100 percent settlement over two years or longer is usually deemed full recovery of a claim. Furthermore, in tax accounting, write-offs and recoveries are always depicted at face value, regardless of when they are made. In order to choose effectively, the credit executive should be familiar with the cost of capital and time value of funds concepts.

To establish the analysis, it is assumed that a creditor has been approached by a debtor in financial difficulty that wants to make an out-of-court settlement on a claim of $100,000 that is now owing and past due. The regular series of collection efforts has been exhausted, and it does not appear likely that the debtor can pay all of the outstanding debt at this time. However, the creditor is satisfied that the customer proposing the settlement is an honest debtor. The analysis shows the best choice to yield the greatest financial recovery to the creditor.

One-Time Partial Payment

The simplest offer would be for the debtor to pay a percentage of the outstanding debt and have the creditor agree to forgive the rest. This would benefit the creditor as the longer a debt is outstanding, the less is realized over time because of the cost of carrying an accounts receivable. For example, the agreement may be for 20 percent payment and the balance to be written off. The creditor would receive 20 percent of the total receivable, or $20,000. At the same time, the creditor writes off $80,000 as a bad debt expense, assuming that the creditor keeps financial records on an accrual basis and originally recorded $100,000 in sales and accounts receivable.

Present Value of Serial Payments

In the previous example, all of the actions take place in the present. Consequently, there is no need to consider the time value or the present value (PV) of funds when deciding whether to accept or decline the debtor's offer. However, when a schedule of serial payments is offered, a new set of variables must be considered. Because a dollar collected today is worth more than a dollar collected sometime in the future, the creditor should consider more than the face amount of any extended offer. Instead, the offer should be regarded as a stream of future payments to be discounted back to the present. The full offer is equal to the sum of the present values of all the payments.

They do not take into account nonfinancial factors, such as the desire to rehabilitate a particular customer or the need to make a vital penetration into a desirable market area. The consideration of nonfinancial factors may outweigh the potential financial recovery in any given instance.

Settlements That Benefit Debtors

Stretched out repayment schedules cause large losses in the present value of total recovery for the creditor, even if the debtor adheres to the schedule. Schedules that provide for small early payments and large payments made later in the plan also erode the creditor's present value of total funds recovered. The worst possible plan from the creditor's point of view is one that provides for a long period of repayment and also proposes installments that are small in the beginning and increase as time goes on.

Impact of the Cost of Capital

Potential losses in the present value of total funds recovered are directly related to the cost of capital of the creditor firm: they are lowest when cost of capital is low, and increase directly as the cost of capital increases. Furthermore, if the cost of capital tends to rise while a plan is in effect, the creditor will realize a lower maximum present value recovery than was projected by the earlier calculations.

Comprehension Check
What are the different ways to evaluate settlement offers?

Key Terms and Concepts

Alternative dispute resolution (ADR)

Arbitration, 18-7

Assignee, 18-11

Assignment, 18-11

Assignment for the benefit of creditors (ABC),

Assignor, 18-11

Combination settlement, 18-9–18-10

Common law assignment, 18-10

Composition agreement, 18-8

Extension plan, 18-6

Insolvent, 18-2

Mediation, 18-7

Not liquid, 18-2

Priority claim, 18-4

Public records, 18-2

Secured claim, 18-4

Voluntary settlement, 18-3

Comprehension Check

1. List the warning signs of financial distress.
2. Explain the difference between **insolvency** and **non-liquidity.**
3. What may a **secured claim** consist of?
4. What may a **priority claim** consist of?
5. Why is unity important in voluntary settlements?
6. Explain the important requirements of a creditors' committee.
7. What items should be examined by the creditors' committee?
8. List the causes of financial distress.
9. Define **mediation.**
10. Define **arbitration.**
11. What is an **extension agreement?**
12. What is a **combination settlement?**
13. Describe the process of **assignment for the benefit of creditors.**
14. What are the different ways to evaluate settlement offers?

Summary

- There are many ways of handling insolvency or financially stressed debtors. Generally, one way is to keep the debtor in business and restore it to profitability, and the other is to put the debtor out of business, sell the assets and distribute the proceeds among creditors.

- There are many warnings signs that a business is financially distressed. A few include:
  - The debtor has stop taking advantage of available discounts
  - Tax or vendors liens are being filed against the debtor
  - Lawsuits are being filed against the debtor

- When a debtors liabilities exceed its debts it is deemed insolvent, and may not be liquid if the business cannot pay debts when they come due. It is imperative that credit professionals distinguish between a business that can be rehabilitated and one that should be liquidated.

- Voluntary settlements are simple and may be the best choice if the creditor is willing to take the temporary loss and if the debtor may emerge stable and continue as a customer.
- Voluntary claims are generally not advised unless secured claims and priority claims have already been taken care of by the debtor.
- **Voluntary claims** usually take one of the three forms:
  - **Extensions**
  - **Pro rata cash settlements**
  - **Combination settlements**
- The success of any credit dispute will be the full cooperation of all creditors and the debtor. If there is any preferential treatment, any creditor can rescind the settlement under the basis of fraud.
- During the first meeting of the creditors, a committee should be formed. It should select a chairman, secretary and counsel. The creditors should also ask an accountant be retained to make an independent examination of the debtor's books and records at the cost of the debtor. In these meetings, the creditor should obtain up-to-date objects of investigation, such as inventory and several years of tax returns. With this information, the cause of financial distress may be assessed.
- The debtor that remains outside of the formal bankruptcy statistically has a better chance of survival, which ultimately improves the chances that creditors get repaid. Questionable actions can include, but are not limited to, the following:
  - Sudden increases in purchases without corresponding increase in sales
  - Missing financial records
  - Excessively large salaries or expense accounts
- **Extension agreements** can be made, but are only advised if there is a good probability that operations will continue in the future. Creditors can institute controls to ensure the repayment of loans. Controls may include:
  - Transfer of stock
  - Financial controls: security and new trade creditors
- Each method of resolution includes payments of administration costs incurred by the creditors. **Methods of resolution** include:
  - **Alternative Dispute Resolution (ADR)**
  - **Composition agreement**
  - **Combination settlement**
- **Mediation** and **arbitration** are both methods of resolution. Mediation is non-binding, while an arbitrator acts in lieu of a judge. There are advantages to arbitration. One being, the arbiter may have special knowledge of the industry.
- The difference between a **composition agreement** and a **combination settlement** is that a combination settlement contains, not only a pro rata cash payment, but an extension of time.
- The two types of **assignments** are:
  - **Statutory assignment for the benefit of creditors (ABC)**
  - **Common law assignment**
- **ABCs** are state law, rather than federal law, and ABCs may be advantageous when liquidating assets by avoiding the unpredictability of a Chapter 7 or Chapter 11 bankruptcy proceeding. The biggest advantage may be the cost savings to the estate. Payment must be provided for the following:

- Administrative rent
- Fees of assignee and other professionals

- In a common law assignment, the assignee distributes the proceeds of the sale on a pro rata basis among the creditors. However, in a common law assignment, the debtor does not receive a discharge from obligations. Therefore, if the sale of assets is 35 percent of the claim, the debtor still owes the other 65 percent.

- When evaluating settlement offers, a creditor should pay attention to the time value of funds involved. A 100 percent settlement over two years or longer is usually deemed full recovery of a claim. Stretched out repayment schedules cause large losses in the present value for the creditor, even if the payments are made on time. These losses are directly related to the cost of capital at the time.

References and Resources

American Arbitrators Association. www.adr.org/index.asp.

American Bankruptcy Institute. www.abiworld.org.

Business Credit. Columbia, MD: National Association of Credit Management. (This 9 issues/year publication is a continuous source of relevant articles and information. Archived articles from *Business Credit* magazine are available through the web-based NACM Resource Library, which is a benefit of NACM membership.)

Credit Professional's Guide to Bankruptcy. Credit Research Foundation, 2001.

Credit Professional's Guide to Creditors' Committees in Chapter 11. Credit Research Foundation, 2001.

Creditors' Committee Manual. American Bankruptcy Institute, 1994.

Manual of Credit and Commercial Laws. Columbia, MD: National Association of Credit Management, current edition.

Miller, Roger, and Gaylord Jentz. *Business Law Today.* 5th ed. London: Thomson Learning, 2000. *See* Unit 7.

Glossary

absolute priority rule: Stipulates the order of payment in the event of liquidation. Debts to creditors will be paid first and shareholders (partial owners) divide what remains. (17-14)

acceleration clause: An acceleration clause is ordinarily used in connection with bank loans. It gives a bank the option to a call a loan ahead of time if the financial conditions of the borrower change so much that it increases the bank's risk. (15-5)

accounts: As one of the categories of collateral covered under UCC Article 9, accounts include the right to payment arising from the sale, lease, license and other disposition of all types of tangible and intangible property. Accounts include fees and royalties, credit card receivables and health care insurance receivables. (7-11)

accounts receivable (A/R) insurance: Sometimes a customer will offer a first or second real estate mortgage (deed of trust) as security for open account arrangements. (13-12)

administrative priority claim: One of the highest priority claims when settlements are paid in a bankruptcy. (17-25)

advance rate: In the loan agreement it will be the percentage amounts a bank is willing to lend against qualified receivables, inventory or other collateral. These will determine the actual amount that can be loaned at any given time. When completed, the **borrowing base certificate** will assist the banker in determining the amount of available credit per the terms of the loan agreement. (15-3)

Advanced Shipment Notice (ASN): A document that provides detailed information about a pending delivery. (8-14)

adverse action as defined by the ECOA: Under the Equal Credit Opportunity Act, a creditor must provide a written explanation for four kinds of actions. They are as follows: (6-11)
   1. **Refusal to grant credit.** A refusal to grant credit occurs when credit is denied in substantially the amount or terms requested by the credit applicant. However, if the business credit grantor makes a counter offer that is accepted by the applicant, it is not considered as adverse action taken. For example, if the applicant has applied for $100,000 in credit availability and the business credit grantor offers to extend $10,000 rather than $100,000, and if the applicant accepts this offer, the action is not considered to be adverse.
   2. **Refusal to increase credit on an existing account.** This situation occurs when an existing customer requests additional credit and that request is denied. This action is considered as adverse action.
   3. **Reduction of credit availability on an existing account.** This situation occurs when a business credit grantor reduces credit in any way. For example, if a credit limit is reduced from $100,000 to $10,000, it is considered an adverse action.
   4. **Termination of credit on an existing account.** This situation occurs when credit is terminated. For example, if a customer is placed on COD, credit has been effectively terminated. *Placing a customer on credit hold or COD because of its credit history (e.g., slow paying or delinquent) is not considered an adverse action.*

advertising: This occurs when a company agrees to pay another company for promoting their product in various mediums including print or electronic. Typically, specific dates, products and reduced pricing are involved in the contract. Proof of performance (copy of the ad) is normally required before claims will be validated or paid. (8-14, 11-12–11-13)

advising bank: Usually a branch or correspondent of the issuing bank located in the beneficiary's local area, advises or checks the apparent authenticity of the letter of credit it transmits to the beneficiary. (14-7)

affiliated interests: A person is said to have affiliated interests when he/she is a principal in more than one company. (5-17)

after-acquired clause: Based on such a clause, property acquired by the borrower after the agreement is signed may become subject to the terms of the loan agreement. This means that the property is automatically pledged, although the borrower did not own it at the time the loan was made. (15-5)

aggregating credit reporting agencies: Typically resellers of the general or specialized agencies and use either individual data elements or entire credit reports from these agencies, and may also include news feeds and external econometric or publicly available data, to create a consolidated report. (11-20)

agricultural credit: Credit related to the farming industry and the family farmer. It often presents more risk to the creditor and is sometimes separated into its own unique category. The farming industry is highly seasonal and is subject to natural hazards such as drought, flood, frost, wind and insect damage. Consequently, many laws and regulations that govern credit regulations treat this type of credit separately. (1-13, 1-14)

alternative dispute resolution (ADR): An out-of-court settlement using binding arbitration or mediation. Arbitration is binding and eliminates litigation or trial by jury whereas mediation is not binding and does not circumvent litigation if either party is not satisfied with the mediator's decision. (9-22, 18-6–18-7)

anticipation: A type of early payment allowance wherein a discount is allowed based on the number of days an invoice is paid early, using a pre-established annual rate converted to a daily rate. (10-8–10-9)

anti-defamation: Libelous statements among creditors must be carefully avoided; they may subject all creditors to major damage suits by persons who consider themselves to have been defamed. Creditors must also avoid giving opinions or making statements which imply that any individuals are dishonest, fraudulent or immoral since no specific damages need to be proven in court to recover for these kinds of statements. Statements which might be considered **libelous** or hearsay should not be used unless it can be proved from clear evidence that the statement is true. (11-2, 11-4)

antitrust: In an industry credit group meeting, the collection and exchange of credit experience information relevant to the credit of accounts must be based upon actual experience or present knowledge as it relates to past and completed transactions only. It does not imply in any manner that the creditors, party to such exchange, recommend that any credit relationship be conducted or modified in any way. There should be no agreement or understanding, express or implied, to fix or determine to whom sales should be made or credit extended, establish joint or uniform prices, terms or conditions under which sales are made or credit extended; and creditors may not boycott or blacklist any customers or suppliers. Creditors may not plan with another, or report, any future actions or policies. Creditors may not give advice or otherwise attempt to influence the independent judgment of other creditors in the extension of credit. (11-2–11-4)

Antitrust Procedures and Penalties Act: Passed in 1974, this Act increased the penalties for offenses under the Sherman Act, changed consent decree procedures and revised the provisions for appellate review of antitrust cases. (6-6)

applicant: In a letter of credit, the account party or the buyer or importer. (14-7)

approval subject to confirmation: A situation that usually means that the customer is being asked to do something before goods are released, such as pay an overdue balance, reduce an outstanding balance to an acceptable level, or submit an interim or annual financial statement. Conditional approval usually allows the goods to be manufactured for delivery on time to the buyer. (2-9)

arbitration: A type of alternative dispute resolution where the parties use an independent arbitrator to act in lieu of a judge and/or jury in resolving a dispute. Arbitration is usually provided for in a contract. (18-7)

arbitration clauses: Language that binds parties to the use of arbitration in lieu of a judge and/or jury in resolving a dispute. (10-20)

articles or certificate of incorporation: A description of the purposes and powers that the corporation expects to comply with and exercise respectively. These are called the **express purposes** or **powers of the corporation. Implied powers** include the right to buy and sell real estate when used as a plant or office location, the right to borrow, the right to have a bank account and the right to have a corporate seal as part of the corporate signature. (5-7)

asset-backed bonds: Created in the mid-1980s, this type of bond is secured or backed up by specific holdings of the issuing corporation such as equipment or real estate. (1-12)

assignee: The company that acts as a fiduciary to all of the creditors of the debtor company. (18-10–18-11)

assignment: The transfer of contract rights from one person to another. (16-9, 18-10–18-15)

assignment of proceeds: The beneficiary of a letter of credit assigns all or part of the proceeds under a letter of credit to a third party (the assignee). Unlike a transferred credit, the beneficiary maintains sole rights to the credit and is solely responsible for complying with its terms and conditions. (14-12)

assignor: The debtor company that transfers its assets to the **assignee.** (18-10–18-11)

Automated Clearing House (ACH): An electronic funds transfer system developed jointly by the private sector and the Federal Reserve in the early 1970s as a more efficient alternative to checks. ACH payments are pre-authorized and large-volume, and are transmitted in batches to a Federal Reserve processing center by a depository institution. ACH credit transfers are used to make direct deposit payroll payments and corporate payments to contractors and vendors. ACH debit transfers are used by consumers to make payments on insurance premiums, mortgages, loans and other bills and by businesses to make payments to other businesses. Although the Fed is the primary operator, regional ACHs are owned by member financial institutions. The National Automated Clearing House Association (NACHA) is the member-run organization that sets policies for the ACHs and performs other functions such as research training and marketing. (1-22)

automatic stay: An injunction that halts actions by creditors, with certain exceptions, to collect debts from a debtor who has declared bankruptcy. (17-3, 17-4)

availability float: The delay between the time a check is deposited at the bank and the time the depositor's account is credited with collected funds by the bank. (1-21)

"back-to-back" letter of credit: An arrangement where one letter of credit is used as security to obtain the issuance of a second letter of credit to cover the same transaction. Most banks are reluctant to enter into a back-to-back arrangement because of associated risks. (14-12)

bad debt: An accounting method of deleting from a company's books and from regular accounts receivable records by writing off the outstanding receivable. Some companies establish Allowance for Bad Debt Accounts, contra asset accounts, in order to recognize that write-offs are inevitable and to provide management with estimates of potential write-offs. (8-13)

balance of payment (BPO): A simple accounting record of international flows. Financial inflows, such as receipts for exports or foreign investments in a domestic stock market, are recorded as credits or positive entries. Financial outflows, such as payments for imports or purchase of shares in a foreign stock market, are debits or negative entries. (14-4)

balance sheet: A financial statement that shows a company's assets, liabilities and owners or stakeholders' equity at a specific date. (15-2)

bank credit: This differs from business credit in a number of ways, but primarily in terms of the type of resource which changes hands in a transaction. A bank furnishes money, while a business (supplier, wholesaler, manufacturer or other service provider) furnishes goods or services. After the transaction is completed, both the banker and the business supplier are creditors: the customer owes money to each entity. (1-14, 1-15)

bank draft: A check drawn by one bank on another bank in which it has funds on deposit in favor of a third party, the payee. Also known as a **teller's check** or a **treasurer's check.** (16-6)

bank endorsement: This endorsement is used when an account uses its receivables as collateral for bank borrowing. It gives the lending bank the right to file accounts in the same way as the insured does. Not all insurers give the beneficiary the right to file, but all have the right to proceeds. (15-16)

banker's acceptance: A time draft drawn on and accepted by a bank and payable at a fixed or determinable future date. (14-23)

bankruptcy: From the Latin meaning "broken bench." (17-1)

Bankruptcy Abuse Prevention and Consumer Protection Act of 2005 (BAPCPA): Enacted on April 20, 2005, became generally effective on October 17, 2005, a revision of the **Bankruptcy Act of 1898.** While many of the provisions of the BAPCPA address consumer and individual bankruptcies, the BAPCPA also affects corporations, small businesses and farmers, and deals with multinational debtors. (17-2)

Bankruptcy Act of 1898: This Act was enforced until the adoption of the Bankruptcy Code in 1978. Although the 1898 Act allowed for individual bankruptcy fillings, it was primarily a business law for the winding down of failed enterprises. (17-2)

Bankruptcy Code: The federal law that provides an organized procedure under the supervision of a federal court for dealing with insolvent debtors. It is found in Title 11 of the United States Code, was adopted in 1978 and became effective on October 1, 1979. The Bankruptcy Code comprises nine chapters. (17-2)

barter arrangements: A form of payment which allows a buyer to pay with merchandise instead of currency, often using a third-party clearinghouse as an intermediary. The intermediary facilitates the transaction and collects a fee for its services. The intermediary can also function as a broker, working with buyers and sellers that wish to take part in barter arrangements. (10-20)

bearer paper: An instrument that is payable to bearer or to cash, which may be negotiated by delivery alone, without an endorsement. (16-9)

Beige Book: A report published eight times a year. Each Federal Reserve Bank gathers anecdotal information on current economic conditions in its district through reports from bank and branch directors and interviews with key business contacts, economists, market experts and other sources. (1-20)

beneficiary: In a letter of credit, the seller/exporter. (14-7)

best efforts test: In a Chapter 7 liquidations, will the debtor be paying creditors all of their disposable income for at least five years? (17-16)

Bill and Hold (B&H) terms: Terms that are utilized in some industries, such as textiles, to permit sellers to invoice buyers under normal payment terms on the agreed-upon completion date, whether or not shipment has actually occurred (10-17)

billback allowances: These are special deals offered to incent the customer to move a product. Rather than being given off-invoice, these items are "billed back"' to the manufacturer. Depending on the contract/deal, there may be requirements to earn the additional sums. (8-14)

bill of lading: A transport document issued by a carrier, which serves as a receipt for the goods and as a contract to deliver the goods to a designated party or to its order. (14-14)

bill-to-bill terms: Some terms for bill-to-bill shipment include "drop ship," "drop delivery" or "load-to-load" terms and require payment for the previous shipment when a new delivery is made. (10-5)

blank endorsement: An endorsement that consists of a signature alone written on the instrument. (16-10–16-11)

blanket financing statement: An instrument used by a manufacturer in UCC security agreements to protect its interests. Normally found in floor-plan financing. (10-18)

Board of Governors: The part of the Federal Reserve responsible for the regulations, writing the rules that will keep the banking system stable and competitive. The 12 regional banks, along with the Board, are responsible for supervision, enforcing those rules. (1-15, 1-19)

bonds: Loans that investors make to corporations and governments through which borrowers obtain the cash they need while lenders earn interest. Bonds are also known as **fixed-income securities.** Generally long-term (more than 10 years) securities that pay a specified sum (called the **principal**) either at a future date or periodically over the length of a loan, during which a fixed rate of interest may be paid on a regular basis. Every bond has a fixed maturity date when the bond expires and the loan must be paid back in full. The interest a bond pays is also set when the bond is issued. The rate is competitive, which means the bond pays interest comparable to what investors can earn elsewhere. As a result, the rate on a new bond is usually similar to other current interest rates, including mortgage rates. Unlike stockholders who have equity in a company, bond holders are creditors. The word "bond" once referred to the piece of paper; it now is used more generally to describe a vast and varied market in debt securities. (1-12, 1-13)

borrowing base certificate: A customer-certified document which details accounts receivable, ineligible accounts based on predetermined aging along with other criteria and amounts available to the collateral pool. Inventory valuation may also be included in the borrowing base certificate. In the bank loan agreement with the borrower, it will identify the intervals for required submission by the customer to the bank. (15-3)

bulk transfer/bulk sales: Any transfer of a major part of the materials, supplies, merchandise or other inventory of an enterprise that is not made in the ordinary course of business; under revised UCC Article 6, the transferor must be going out of business as well. (7-8–7-9)

business: The word "business" first appeared around the 14th century and was originally defined to mean "purposeful activity." Now a more inclusive term, the term designates the activities of those engaged in the purchase or sale of commodities or in related financial transactions. (2-2)

business credit: This refers to extensions of credit primarily for business or commercial purposes. Important characteristics include:

- Selling terms are relatively short
- Transactions are usually on open account or unsecured, but may be partially secured or secured in full
- Cash discounts may be offered for payment before the net due date
- The terms include transactions to manufacturers, wholesalers and retailers, but specifically exclude the consumer.
- The timeliness in reaching a decision whether or not to extend credit is often much more critical in the business setting. Delays in the manufacturing process can increase costs and reduce the quality of perishable goods

The fact that business credit finances the intermediate and final stages of production and distribution distinguishes it from consumer credit. Business credit sales also yield a profit on goods sold rather than interest or investment income, which distinguishes it from bank and investment credit. (1-14)

business organization: A combination of functions, people and materials aimed at producing goods or services, and selling them to customers at a profit. (2-2)

bust-out fraud (sleeper fraud): Primarily a first-party fraud scheme. The fraudster makes on-time payments to maintain a good account standing with the intent of bouncing a final payment and abandoning the account. (12-2)

buyer: A company or individual consumer that decides to purchase a product or service from a seller, which either makes or provides a product or service. (1-10)

buyer/importer: In a letter of credit, the applicant or account party. (14-7)

– C –

cancelable limit: The insurance company may, at its discretion, amend or withdraw coverage attaching to future transactions between the policyholder and its specific customers. (15-17)

Canons of Business Credit Ethics: A cornerstone of the global business economy for the extension of commercial credit. They establish standards relating to the proper exchange of credit information among creditors which contains historical and current factual information to support the process of independent credit decision-making. (1-9, 9-11)

Capacity: One of the 5 Cs of Credit. The inclination or propensity of a business to operate profitably and its ability to pay trade creditors, banks, employees and others as those debts become due. (1-7, 8-9)

Capital: One of the 5 Cs of Credit. The value of a customer's business in excess of all liabilities and claims is referred to as its equity or net worth, and represents its financial strength. (1-7, 8-9)

capital lease: An agreement where substantially all the benefits and risks of ownership are transferred by the lease. (15-7)

carrier: The company or agent transporting the goods. (14-14)

cash: Different types of cash-like instruments include a buyer's company check, a certified check or a cashier's check. (10-6)

cash before delivery (CBD): Similar to **cash with order;** however, it is normal to wait until the product or service is ready to ship before collecting the balance. (14-6)

cash discount elements: These include (a) the amount of the discount, usually expressed as a percentage of the invoice face amount excluding freight and other third-party charges and (b) the length of time allowed for the buyer to pay on a discounted basis. (10-7)

cash in advance (CIA): These terms require the buyer to make payment via one of the cash methods (e.g., electronic transfers, company check, certified check, cashier's check, etc.) before an order will be shipped. CIA terms are most often used for very weak credit or when unsatisfactory, limited or no credit information is available. (10-5)

cash inflows: These are the funds collected from customers or obtained from financial sources. (2-4)

cash management: As a key component of a company's financial activities, cash management is the efficient management and use of cash in a manner that is consistent with the strategic objectives of the business. A major goal of cash management is to manage cash flows in order to increase the long-term value of the business while balancing the inflow and outflow of cash so that the business can meet its demands for cash by creditors. (2-4)

cash on delivery COD): These terms require payment to the transportation company for the full invoice amount at the time of the delivery. (10-5)

cash outflows: These are the funds disbursed from cash reserves to pay for purchases of inventories, to pay for operating expenses such as salaries, rent and insurance; to pay for the purchase of long-lived assets such as buildings or land; or for the repayment of debt principal or payment of dividends. (2-4)

cash terms: Payment received prior to the transaction or at the time of the transaction. Also referred to as prepayment or closed terms. Cash terms include Cash in Advance (CIA), Cash Before Delivery (CBD), Cash With Order (CWO) and Cash on Delivery (COD). (10-5)

cash with order (CWO): The most conservative term offered and most commonly used if the product or service is unique to the customer. (10-5, 14-6)

cashier's check: This instrument is drawn by a bank on its own funds. (The financial institution is both the drawer and the drawee—that is, the bank, in effect, lends its credit to the purchaser of the check. Courts have held that payment cannot be stopped on a cashier's check because the bank, by issuing it, accepts the check in advance.) (10-6, 16-6)

CBA: The Credit Business Associate℠ is an academic-based designation which signals mastery of three business-credit related disciplines: Basic Financial Accounting, Financial Statement Analysis I and Business Credit Principles. (3-13)

CBF: The Credit Business Fellow℠ is an academic and participation-based designation which illustrates that achievers are knowledgeable about and have contributed to the field of business credit by first having earned the CBA designation as well as having completed additional course work. The CBF signals competence in business and credit law. (3-13)

CCE: The Certified Credit Executive® is NACM's executive level designation which endorses its achievers as capable of managing the credit function at an executive level. Candidates must pass a rigorous, four-hour exam which tests application skills in the areas of accounting, finance, domestic and international credit concepts, management and law. (3-13)

CCRA: The Certified Credit and Risk Analyst℠ is an academic-based designation which signals mastery in the analysis and interpretation of financial statements and the ability to make informed credit risk assessments. (3-13)

centralized management: A requirement of a corporation, but one of three elements that an LLC can possess or avoid in order to retain its LLC status. (5-11, 5-12)

centralized structure: The credit function is controlled and administered from a principal or central location. Smaller businesses or companies operating in only one geographic area often have centralized credit functions. (3-2–3-3, 3-5)

certificate of deposit (CD): An acknowledgment by a bank of the receipt of money and its promise to pay back the money on an established due date, usually with interest. (16-9)

certified check: With this instrument, a bank guarantees that funds are on deposit when the check is certified. The UCC provides that "certification of a check is acceptance." This means that a drawee bank that certifies a check becomes primarily liable on the instrument just the same as the acceptor of a draft. The bank has absolute liability to pay. (10-6, 16-6)

CFR (Cost and Freight) (Named Port of Destination): The seller must pay the costs and freight necessary to bring the goods to the named port of destination. However, delivery occurs when the goods pass over the ship's rail in the port of shipment. The risk of loss or damage to the goods, as well as any other additional costs incurred after delivery, are transferred from the seller to the buyer at that point. This term requires the seller to clear the goods for export. This term can be used for sea and inland water transport only. (7-4, 14-19)

chain discount: An allowance that represents a manner in which a trade discount and a payment discount can be combined in a single set of terms. (10-9)

Chapter 1, 3 and 5: The first three chapters contain administrative provisions that apply in all cases under the Bankruptcy Code. (17-2)

Chapter 7: A liquidation bankruptcy, sometimes known as a straight bankruptcy, in which a trustee is appointed by the United States Trustee in every case to liquidate nonexempt assets. (17-2, 17-5–17-7)

Chapter 7, 9, 11, 12, 13 and 15: The operative chapters for filing different types of bankruptcies. (17-2)

Chapter 9: Pertains to municipalities and governmental units. Chapter 9 bankruptcies are only filed on a voluntary basis. (17-2)

Chapter 11: Known as the business reorganization chapter. (17-2, 17-7–17-15)

Chapter 12: Commenced only by a voluntary petition by family farmers who have debts up to $3,792,650 and family fishermen who have debts up to $1,757,475. (17-2, 17-15)

Chapter 13: Known as the wage earner's plan. Any individual with regular wages or income is eligible to file under Chapter 13, including certain professionals or business owners. Eligible debtors must meet the following threshold limits: $360,475 in unsecured debts and $1,081,400 for secured debts. (17-2, 17-15–17-16)

Chapter 15: Provides mechanisms to deal with multi-national insolvencies. Chapter 15 is intended to establish cooperation among U.S. courts, trustees and debtors and their foreign counterparts. (17-2)

Chapter 20 and Chapter 22: This refers to serial bankruptcy filings where, because of the size of the debt, a debtor files a Chapter 7 petition to discharge the unsecured claims and, as soon as the discharge is granted, files a Chapter 13 petition to deal with the secured claims. The name Chapter 20 refers to the combination of 7 plus 13. Chapter 22 refers to a company that has filed Chapter 11 twice. (17-16)

Character: One of the 5 Cs of Credit. The willingness of a debtor to pay its obligations and imputes a level of ethics, integrity, trustworthiness and quality of management that is provided or available to the business customer (proprietorship, corporation, etc.). (1-7, 8-8)

chattel paper: Any writing evidencing both a monetary obligation and a security interest in specific goods, including electronic as well as tangible chattel paper. Also includes promissory notes as a subcategory of instruments. (7-12)

check: A draft on which the drawee is a bank that is ordered to pay on demand. (16-6)

check truncation: The process of taking the physical paper check out of circulation, capturing the check information electronically, and moving the electronic copy through the clearing system. The paper check is destroyed or put into storage.

   Check truncation is a result of the Check Clearing for the 21st Century Act (**Check 21**), which became effective October 28, 2004. Check 21 creates a more efficient system of moving checks through the banking and clearing system. (1-22)

Check 21 (Check Clearing for the 21st Century Act): The purpose of this Act is to remove barriers to the electronic collection of checks allowing banks to truncate checks. (1-22)

CIF (Cost, Insurance and Freight) (Named Port of Destination): Identical to CFR except with CIF the seller must obtain marine insurance against the buyer's risk of loss of or damage to the goods during the main carriage. The seller contracts for insurance and pays the insurance premium, and is only required to obtain minimum cover. If the buyer requires more protection, then that should be expressed to the seller in the contract or he may make his own extra arrangements. The CIF term requires the seller to clear the goods for export, and only can be used with sea and inland waterway transport. (7-4, 14-19–14-20)

CIP (Carriage and Insurance Paid To) (Named Place of Destination): Identical to CTP except with CIP the seller also has to obtain insurance against the buyer's risk of loss or damage to the goods during the carriage. The seller contracts and pays the insurance premium. As with CIF, the seller is only required to obtain the minimum cover and anything in excess should be expressed to the seller or arranged for by the buyer. The CIP term requires the seller to clear the goods for export. This term may be used regardless of the mode of transport, to include multimodal transport. (14-17)

claim: A right to payment or a right to some equitable remedy such as injunctive relief in the event of a breach of contract. (17-11)

The Clayton Act of 1914: The Clayton Act was designed to amend the Sherman Act and fix its broad language. It adds certain offenses when the effect is to substantially lessen competition or to tend to create a monopoly. These offenses include exclusive dealing arrangements, tying leases and agreements to one another, and the acquisition of another corporation's stock. (6-3–6-4)

Clearing House Interbank Payments System (CHIPS): An independent message-switching system established in 1970 and operated by the New York Clearing House Association, CHIPS substitutes electronic payments for paper checks arising from international dollar transactions, such as Eurocurrency or foreign exchange, between foreign and U.S. banks. It is also used for payments under letters of credit and documentary collections and for third-party transfers. (1-22)

closed-end credit: All consumer credit that does not fit the definition of open-end credit. It consists of both credit sales and loans. Closed-end credit means credit which is to be repaid in full (along with any interest and finance charges) by a specified future date. Most real estate and auto loans are closed-end. (1-13)

closed terms: These terms call for payment before the transaction or at the time of the transaction. (10-5)

coinsurance type policy: The insured company participates in a percentage of the bad-debt loss sustained on a debtor. (15-16)

collaboration: One of the Three Cs of Credit. In order to meet the goals of the credit and sales department, collaboration is essential to allow for each department to find ways to meet customer demands, while mitigating risk. (4-3–4-4)

Collateral: One of the 5 Cs of Credit. Property may be pledged as security for the satisfaction of a debt. (1-7-1-8, 7-9, 7-11–7-12, 8-9)

collateral note: A note that is secured by certain collateral, such as stocks, bonds, personal property or mortgages. (16-8)

collateral trust bond: Such bonds are similar to mortgage bonds except they are backed by securities of a company through its pledge of stocks and bonds. (1-12)

collections: The credit policy should identify what methods credit personnel will use to collect receivables, particularly past due accounts. The best collection process is one which is proactive and consistent, and which reflects the mission and goals of the credit department. The collection procedure should be prioritized according to both the customer's risk and exposure level. (8-11)

collection stage or cycle: The process point where the customer pays for the goods that were initially purchased on credit. (1-10, 2-5)

co-makers: When two or more parties sign a note. (16-8)

combination settlement: A voluntary settlement that contains both a pro rata cash payment and an extension of time. For example, the settlement may provide a cash payment of 20 percent immediately and three future installments of 5 percent each, or a total of 35 percent in full settlement. (18-8)

commercial invoice: A document that lists the value of a shipment. A commercial invoice should provide: complete name and address of the seller; date of issue; invoice number; complete name and physical address of the buyer; order or contract number; quality and description of the goods, including unit price and total invoice amount; shipping marks and numbers as required; terms of delivery and payment; any other information required by the (documentary) **letter of credit**; and, possibly, a **consular invoice** (a commercial invoice notarized by the local consulate). (14-14)

commercial letter of credit: This L/C is a contractual agreement between the issuing banks, on behalf of one of its customers, authorizing another bank known as the advising or confirming bank, to make payment to the beneficiary. (14-10)

commercial paper: A contract for the payment of money. It can serve as a substitute for money payable immediately, such as a check, or it can be used as a means of extending credit. Commercial paper, consisting of notes and drafts, has played an important role in business and commerce since the 12th century. (16-1)

commercial tort claim: A tort claim in favor of an organization or in favor of an individual that arises in the course of the individual's business or profession. (7-12)

commercial unit: Any unit of goods that is treated by commercial usage as a single whole (such as a machine or a dozen, bale or carload of something). (7-3)

common law assignment: A device whereby a debtor transfers title to all assets to a third party, designated as an assignee or trustee, with instructions to liquidate the assets and distribute the proceeds among creditors on a pro rata basis. (18-14)

common law trust: This form of organization generally derives its power from a trust agreement as opposed to statutory law, as in the case of corporations. Common law trusts are formed by an agreement between owners of property (or a business) and a trustee or group of trustees. Also known as a Massachusetts trust or business trust. (5-14–5-15)

common stock: From a balance sheet perspective, common stock represents all or a portion of the money that was received when the company issued its shares. (5-8)

communication: One of the Three Cs of Credit. Communication is essential to fostering a healthy and efficient working relationship between the credit and sales department. A couple ways to enhance this relationship is to share information, use technology and have the sales team join the credit department on occasion. (4-3)

competition: An important factor that influences terms of sale. (10-3)

compiled reports: Those pulled together from automated sources of data and matched, merged de-duplicated and updated without any or much human intervention. (11-20)

composition agreement: A pro rata settlement in which the debtor proposes to settle with creditors for less than the full amount owed. It is the quickest of all voluntary settlements. (18-8)

composition plans: Two types of composition plans are available. Both make only partial repayments of the total debt to creditors, and both must continue for not more than five years. (17-16)

compromise plans (partial payment): Where a debtor negotiates to pay only a part of the debt. (17-12)

conditional endorsement: A type of restrictive endorsement that makes the rights of the endorsee subject to the happenings of a certain event or condition. (16-11)

Conditions: One of the 5 Cs of Credit. The external events, occurrences, phenomena and factors that may interrupt or otherwise disturb the normal flow of business that the credit professional considers when examining a new or existing customer's credit. (1-8, 8-9)

confession of judgment: A separate agreement that establishes consent for the judgment note. In essence, a confession of judgment enables a creditor to enter a judgment without going to trial. (16-9)

confidentiality: All information obtained by credit grantors must be considered strictly confidential and not to be divulged or discussed with any person outside of the creditors own credit department under any circumstances. (11-2, 11-6–11-7)

confirmation: Refers to court approval of the plan of reorganization is a bankruptcy. (17-13)

confirmed irrevocable letter of credit: This type of letter of credit transaction transfers the payment responsibility from the customer to a bank (usually located in the same country as the seller) that did not open the letter of credit but agrees, at the request of the issuing bank, to be bound by the terms of the letter of credit. The confirming bank agrees to make payment upon presentation of documents conforming to the contract of sale. (14-10)

confirming bank: The bank that may, at the request of the issuing bank, "confirm" or obligate itself to the beneficiary to ensure payment and acceptance of a draft under the letter of credit, upon presentation of documents that are in compliance with the letter of credit. (14-10)

consignee: The party to whom the goods are destined. (10-17, 14-14)

consignment: A consignment is a delivery of goods having a value of at least $1,000 to a merchant for sale provided that: (7-25–7-26, 14-6)
- the transaction does not create a security interest;
- the goods are not consumer goods immediately before delivery;
- the merchant deals in goods of that kind under a name other than that of the consignor, is not an auctioneer and is not generally known by its creditors to be engaged substantially in selling the goods of others.

consignment terms: A special (other) term that offers an alternative to an open account sale. Consignment is not truly a sale until the buyer, known as the **consignee,** actually sells the goods to a third party or moves them from consigned inventory into the buyer's own inventory. Until the goods are thus sold or moved, title remains with the supplier, usually the manufacturer, who is known as the **consignor.** (10-17–10-18)

consignor: Until the goods are thus sold or moved, title remains with the supplier, usually the manufacturer. (10-17)

consolidation: A process whereby a completely new corporation is formed. Shares from the corporations involved are exchanged for shares in the newly formed entity. The credit professional must determine what factors have been brought into the credit situation by the consolidation or merger of the two or more companies. (5-18)

construed coverage: In case a customer's credit agency rating is changed downward between the time an order is accepted and the merchandise is shipped, this endorsement provides coverage at the higher rating for up to 120 days after the order is accepted. (15-16)

consular invoice: A commercial invoice notarized by the local consulate. (14-15)

consumer credit: Credit extended to a natural person primarily for personal, family or household purposes and may be closed-end, open-end or incidental. It excludes business and agricultural credit, and loans exceeding $25,000 that are not secured by real property or a dwelling. It must also be extended by a creditor, although it can be advertised by someone else, such as a builder, real estate broker or advertising agency. (1-13)

Consumer Financial Protection Bureau (CFPB): Created by the Dodd-Frank Act, the CFPB's primary mission is related to consumer lending. (6-13–6-14)

contemporaneous exchange: Where the parties agree to contemporaneously exchange goods and/or services for payment in a bankruptcy case. (10-7)

continuity of life: The idea that an organization does not end solely based on death, bankruptcy or change of the principles. (5-2, 5-4–5-5, 5-7, 5-10, 5-13, 5-14, 5-15)

contra account: This offsets the balance in another, related account with which it is paired. If the related account is an asset account, then a contra asset account is used to offset it with a credit balance. If the related account is a liability account, then a contra liability account is used to offset it with a debit balance. (10-18)

contract terms: These are the terms outlined and agreed to by the customer and the organization. They typically outline beginning and end dates, proof of performance requirements, products involved, etc. The more detailed the contracts are, the less room there is for third-party auditors to "re-interpret" the deal a year or more in the future. (8-14)

contractual clearing balances: An amount that a depository institution agrees to hold at its Federal Reserve Bank in addition to any required reserve balance. (1-19)

control: In terms of perfection, situations where a secured party may not be in physical possession of the collateral but can still exercise a sufficient amount of power over the collateral to control it. (7-16)

cooperation: One of the Three Cs of Credit. This element is essential to the credit-sales relationship in order to prevent a silo environment between the two groups. To prevent this from occurring, the credit and sales department can engage in customer visits together as well as presenting options other than declining a sales agreement. (4-5–4-6)

cooperative: A private, independent entity owned and controlled by the members of the cooperative who use its services. (9-8)

cooperative society: Organizations of mutual help and betterment that are formed when individuals or corporate businesses combine their financial, capital and other resources to advance their particular trade or industry. By combining resources, a cooperative society seeks to obtain marketing and/or purchasing advantage. (5-16)

corporate bonds: These are usually applied to longer-term debt instruments, with maturity of at least one year, and are higher risk than government bonds and thus higher yielding. (1-12)

corporate guarantee: This is used when a corporation agrees to be held responsible for completing the duties and obligations of a debtor to a lender, in the event that the debtor fails to fulfill the terms of the debtor-lender contract. (9-26–9-27)

corporate raiders: Companies that use LBOs to purchase undervalued companies only to turn around and sell off the assets. More common in the past, LBOs are increasingly used as a way to make an average company become a great company. (15-8)

corporation: A voluntary association of persons, natural or legal (i.e., other corporations); organized under state or federal law and recognized by the law as being a person, fictitious in character, having a corporate name, and being entirely separate and distinct from the people who own it; having continuous life; and set up for some specified purpose or purposes. The classic definition, as described by U.S. Supreme Court Justice John Marshall (1755-1835): "...an artificial being, invisible, intangible, and existing only in contemplation of the law." (5-6–5-7, 9-7)

cost of capital: This refers to the opportunity cost of making a specific investment. It is the rate of return that could have been earned by putting the same money into a different investment with equal risk. Thus, the cost of capital is the rate of return required to persuade the investor to make a given investment. (10-11)

cost to buyer formula: A way to help convince the buyer that a bank loan may be cheaper than trade credit when discount terms are available. (10-15)

country credit risk factors: The political, economic, legal, cultural, geographical and financial risks of the countries where they are doing business. (14-2)

country risk: An element of the Five Cs of Credit that must be accounted for when dealing in international credit transactions. (1-14)

cover: As defined by the UCC, cover gives the buyer an alternative right to purchase substitute goods and to recover from the seller the difference between the contract price and the purchase of the replacement goods as an absolute measure of damages, provided the buyer purchases in a reasonable manner. (7-3)

CPT (Carriage Paid To) (Named Place of Destination): This term means that the seller has fulfilled his delivery obligation when he delivers the goods to the carrier that has been nominated by the buyer. However, in addition to paying the freight costs to that point, the seller must also pay the costs of carriage necessary to bring the goods to the named destination. The buyer bears the risks of loss or damage occurring after delivery. The CPT term requires the seller to clear the goods for export. This term may be used regardless of the mode of transport including multimodal transport. (14-17)

cramdown: The actions of a bankruptcy court when it confirms a plan that has been rejected by one or more classes of creditors and interest holders. Cramdown procedures are usually more of a threat than a reality and differ depending on the creditor class involved. (17-13)

credere: Latin for "to believe or trust." (1-5)

credit: A concept describing the transfer of economic value now, on faith, in return for an expected economic value in the future. Important elements of credit include risk of nonpayment, timing, security, extra costs, legal aspects and economic influences. (1-5, 1-6)

credit card payment: It indicates that the seller obtains the promise of payment from a financial institution on behalf of the buyer rather than extending credit. That financial institution extends credit to the buyer and renders payment to the seller. The duration of payment timing is determined by the contractual agreement with the institution involved. The institution must issue, to the buyer, advance approval of the transaction. The payment received by the seller will involve a discount from the sales price taken by the financial institution as a fee for its handling of the transaction. (10-6)

credit evaluation: A credit decision based on the credit applicant's willingness to pay, as evidenced by its payment history, and on its ability to pay, as evidenced by its financial situation. Other factors relating to the applicant, such as its legal form and the industry in which it operates, plus years in existence, should also be considered. (8-8–8-9)

credit function, boundaries: A specific assignment of responsibility and delegation of authority. Credit policy establishes the broad limits for decisions over a long period of time. (8-7–8-8)

credit limit: By establishing credit limits for customers, a creditor retains discretion over credit granting. In other words, a ceiling has been placed on the amount of orders that can be placed, but no promise is made to extend credit at any given time.

Companies use different criteria and experience patterns when establishing credit limits. Some determine credit limits based on payment records while others consider the amount of credit granted by competing firms. Still other companies set terms for a defined period of time. Credit terms can also be set by basing them on credit agency ratings and/or by formula. Additional limit options include determining how much credit a customer is expected to use during a specific period of time and initially setting a limit low and progressively increasing as the customer displays acceptable payment performance. (8-10, 13-3–13-6, 13-9–13-11, 13-16–13-21)

credit line: A term that implies that credit will be or has been granted up to a specific amount usually for a given period of time, as in the case of a bank line of credit. (13-3)

credit policy: A credit policy is a general statement that provides a framework for making effective credit decisions. Credit policies should identify who has the authority to do the job, establish consistent credit guidelines, and incorporate credit and sales cooperation. Other factors identified in a credit policy include: terms of sales; monitoring credit risk; relationship to the sales department; training and development of credit personnel; amount of capital committed to accounts receivables; and measurement of the status of the accounts receivable investment. An effective credit policy permits and encourages the fullest development of the opportunities in administering credit. A credit policy can be either implied or stated. (3-7, 8-1–8-20)

credit procedure: The actual working steps that should be followed in the appropriate order in order to accomplish the desired credit result or decision. (3-7, 5-3, 8-3, 8-20–8-22)

credit scoring model: Such models convert available data about a customer to a statistical number based on influencing elements including NAICS code, payment history, principal information, financial data, outside credit information, etc. Credit scores make credit decisions data driven and less reliant upon subjectivity. (13-7)

creditors' committee: It has the responsibility to protect all unsecured creditors' interests, and it oversees the debtor's operations until, and sometimes after, confirmation of the plan. (17-9–17-10, 18-6)

creditworthiness: The purchaser's ability to obtain a product or service based on its promise to pay at a later date. (1-10)

Cross-Corporate Guarantee (CCG): This ties a parent company to a subsidiary. Action: If the subsidiary does not pay, the parent company will pay. (13-11)

cross-default clause: Under this clause, if the borrower defaults on any long-term borrowing agreement, then all such agreements will be in default (including the one being negotiated). (15-5)

culture: An additional component of the Five Cs of Credit that must be taken into account when assessing risk in a international credit transaction. (1-14)

currency convertibility: The availability or unavailability of dollars in the banking system of an overseas customer. This situation is known as "FX/Bank Delays" in publications on country risk issues. (14-25)

currency issues: An additional component of the Five Cs of Credit. Currency issues involve the strength and stability issues of a country's currency when dealing in international trade. A less stable currency may lead to increased risk when dealing in international credit transactions. (1-14)

customer's credit limit: A customer's credit limit is usually based on the requirements for the supplier's products and the ability of the customer to pay its debts. Other factors include the seller's policy, demand for the product, the size and financial condition of the buyer and seller, and the extent of competition. (13-4)

– D –

DAP (Delivered at Place) (Named Place of Destination): The delivery occurs at the buyer's disposal unloaded from the arriving vehicle, but ready for unloading (as under the former DAF, DES and DDU rules). This new rule, like its predecessor, is "delivered", with the seller bearing all the costs (other than those related to import clearance, where applicable) and risks involved in bringing the goods to the named place of destination. (14-18)

DAT (Delivered at Terminal) (Named Place of Destination): The delivery occurs at the buyer's disposal unloaded from the arriving vehicle (as under the former DEQ rule). This new rule, like its predecessor, is "delivered", with the seller bearing all the costs (other than those related to import clearance, where applicable) and risks involved in bringing the goods to the named place of destination. (14-18)

date of receipt payment: It is considered to be the date a check for good funds was received by the seller. (10-7)

DDP (Delivered Duty Paid) (Named Place of Destination): The seller has fulfilled his obligation when the goods have been delivered to the buyer, cleared for import, but not unloaded from the means of transport at the named place of destination. The seller must pay all the costs and risks involved in bringing the goods to that named place of destination including any applicable duties, taxes, customs formalities and carrying out of the customs formalities for the import of the goods into the country of destination. If the parties wish to leave out certain import costs that would be the obligation of the seller, then this should be made very clear in the contract of sale by adding that specific wording. This term should not be used if the seller cannot obtain the import license directly or indirectly if applicable. This term can be used regardless of the mode of transport. (14-18)

debentures: The most common corporate bonds. They are backed only by the financial strength or standing of the organization issuing it, rather than by any specific assets. A debenture buyer relies on the issuer's faith and credit as the only assurance of being paid the principal and interest. (1-12)

debt: Obligation of a company to pay creditors. (17-12)

debt for equity swap: It is a transaction in which the obligations (debts) of a company or individual are exchange for something of value (equity). (17-12)

debtor: The party who owes payment or other performance of a secured obligation. (7-9)

debtor in possession (DIP): A debtor that remains in possession of its assets and manages its own affairs, protected by the automatic stay, during a bankruptcy. (17-8)

decentralized structure: The credit function may report to a principal location (headquarters) with credit personnel located at remote offices. (3-2, 3-3–3-5)

defamation: A false statement made to others that injures the name or reputation of a third party. (11-4–11-6)

defining responsibility: The credit department's structure should be flexible and clearly delineate responsibility for each function to be performed and for each customer account. (2-10)

demand note: A note that is payable whenever the payee demands payment. (16-8)

deposit account: A bank account (including demand, time, savings, passbook or savings) maintained with a bank. (7-12)

developed reports: Those freshly investigated, potentially using compiled reports as a source, but often including interviews with the subject itself and **direct verification of references.** (11-20)

direct investigations: Investigations where credit information is collected by the creditor either through direct contact with the customer or through direct contact with noncommercial sources of information such as individuals, banks or other trade references that may have relevant details to share. (11-8)

discharge: A release of individual debtors from personal liability for most debts, preventing the creditors owed those debts from taking any collection actions against the debtor during a bankruptcy. (17-7, 17-26)

discount period: A specific period of time in which a cash discount is calculated if the customer pays. (10-8)

discount rate: The interest rate banks must pay when they borrow money from the Federal Reserve. (1-15, 1-17–1-18)

division: The internal arrangement of a corporation made for the convenience of its management. (5-18)

document against acceptance: A draft that requires the importer to pay the face amount on a specified date. (14-14)

document against payment: A draft that requires the importer to pay the face amount at sight. (14-14)

documentary collection (D/C): A transaction whereby the exporter entrusts the collection of the payment for a sale to the **remitting bank** (its bank),which sends the documents that its buyer needs to the **importer's bank** (collecting bank), with instructions to release the documents to the buyer for payment. (14-14)

Dodd-Frank Wall Street Reform and Consumer Protection Act of 2010 (Dodd-Frank Act): This Act established the Consumer Financial Protection Bureau (CFPB). (6-13–6-14)

domestic bill of exchange: A draft that is drawn and payable in the United States. (16-7)

domestic corporation: A corporation is known as such when located in the state in which it is incorporated. (5-6)

double debtor issue: This situation occurs when collateral is either transferred to a successor debtor or the original debtor merges with a third party. (7-26)

draft: A written order by the first party, called the **drawer,** instructing a second party, called the **drawee** (such as a bank), to pay money to a third party, called a payee. (16-3, 16-5)

drawer: The person (or company) who makes or executes a draft. (16-3)

dynamic discounting: This allows buyers more flexibility to choose how and when to pay their suppliers in exchange for a lower price or discount for the goods and services purchased. The "dynamic" component refers to the option to provide discounts based on the dates of payment to suppliers. (10-9)

– E –

economies of scale: The economic concept that describes the fact that as production increases, the cost of operations decrease. (3-5)

EDI/ASN – Electronic Data Interchange (EDI): The transfer of data from one computer system to another by standardized message formatting, without the need for human intervention. It is most commonly used for invoices. Advance Shipment Notice (ASN) is a document that provides detailed information about a pending delivery. The purpose is to notify the customer when shipping occurs and provide physical characteristics about the shipment so the customer can be prepared to accept delivery. (2-9, 8-14)

effects test: This is the means of which price discrimination is measured under the ECOA. (6-12)

8% 10 EOM: An 8% percent discount is earned if payment is made by the 10th of the month following shipment. (10-8)

8% 10th Prox: Similar to 8% 10 EOM. "Prox" terms are similar to EOM terms—except that under prox terms individual invoices are usually billed at the time of shipment. (10-8)

EIN (Employer Identification Number): A business form of a Social Security number used to identify a business. (12-11)

Electronic Data Interchange (EDI): EDI is the movement of data electronically from one computer to another in a structured, processable format. EDI converts documents such as quotes, purchase orders and invoices to electronic messages, which are routed directly between the parties, either in a standard, widely accepted format or in a proprietary, mutually agreed upon format. (2-9)

electronic funds transfer (EFT): The electronic transfer of money is from one bank account to another, either within a single financial institution or across multiple institutions, through computer-based systems and without the direct intervention of bank staff. (1-22, 9-16, 10-6)

electronic signature (e-signature): An electronic or digital signature created through fingerprint readers, stylus pads or encrypted "smart cards." (6-18–6-19)

Electronic Signatures in Global and National Commerce Act ("E-Sign Act"): Effective October 1, 2000, the Act permits a party to accept an e-signature in order to form a binding contract. Regulated by the Federal Trade Commission, the Act creates a uniform, nationwide system previously lacking among the states, legally recognizing that a vendor may engage in e-credit transactions throughout the country. The Act uses UCC provisions that allow any symbol to constitute a signature if it is executed or adopted by a party with a present intention to authenticate a writing. (6-17–6-18)

elements of contract common law: Elements include offer and acceptance, mutual assent, capacity to contract, legality of subject matter, and consideration. (7-2–7-3)

end-of-month (EOM) terms: Shipments made during a given month are billed as of the last day of that month and assigned a single due date in the following month (usually the tenth of the following month). (10-7)

endorsed: The point when a holder signs an instrument, thereby indicating the intent to transfer ownership to another. (16-10)

endorsee: The person to whom an instrument is endorsed. (16-10)

endorsement for deposit or collection: A type of endorsement designed to move an instrument into the banking system for the purpose of deposit or collection. When a check is endorsed "for deposit only," the amount of the instrument is credited to the endorser's account before it is negotiated further. (16-11–16-12)

The Equal Credit Opportunity Act and Regulation B: The purpose of this regulation is to promote the availability of credit to all creditworthy applicants without regard to race, color, religion, national origin, sex, marital status or age (provided the applicant has the capacity to contract); to the fact that all or part of the applicant's income derives from a public assistance program; or to the fact that the applicant has, in good faith, exercised any right under the Consumer Credit Protection Act. The regulation also requires creditors to notify applicants of action taken on their applications and to retain records of credit applications. (6-8–6-13, 9-28, 11-30)

equipment trust certificates (ETC): These bonds are issued to pay for new equipment, secured by a lien on the purchased equipment. ETCs are frequently issued by airlines, railroads and shipping companies to finance the purchase of railroad freight cars, airplanes and oil tankers. (1-12)

equity: Value of assets of a company. (17-12)

escheatment: A reversion of property to the state upon the death of an owner who has neither a will nor any legal heirs. Today companies with funds that cannot be traced to the owner must be remitted to the state. This unclaimed property can include the following type of checks: payroll, vendor, expense, rebate and commission. (6-19–6-22, 9-20)

e-signature: An electronic or digital signature created through fingerprint readers, stylus pads or encrypted "smart cards." (6-17–6-18)

evergreen clause: Such a clause provides a periodic expiry date with an automatic extension and usually states one final date. (14-14)

excusable neglect: In a bankruptcy, refers to a legitimate excuse for the failure to take some proper step at the proper time. For example, this is claimed to set aside a default judgment for failure to answer or neglecting to answer a lawsuit within the period set by law. (17-21)

executory contracts: An agreement where each party still has material obligations to perform. (17-10)

Expedited Funds Availability Act (EFAA): Limits the time that banks can hold funds from checks deposited into customer accounts before the funds are available for withdrawal. (1-21)

Export-Import Bank of the United States (Ex-Im Bank): This bank assists U.S. exporters by: (a) providing direct loans; or (b) guaranteeing repayment of commercial loans to creditworthy foreign buyers for purchases of U.S. goods and services. (14-22–14-23)

express warranty: An oral or written statement, promise or other representation about the quality of a product. (7-6)

Ex-Ship: Seller is responsible for the expense and risk until the goods are unloaded from whatever ship is used. A commonly used shipping term that creates a destination contract. (7-5)

extension plan: Under such an agreement, the debtor proposes to pay creditors in full over a period of time. An extension is, in effect, a deferral of payment of debts. (17-12, 17-16, 18-7)

extra dating terms: Terms that can be used to extend the net period and/or the discount period. For example, terms of "2% 10, 60 extra" extend both the discount period and the next credit period to 70 days from the date of the invoice. (10-18–10-19)

EXW (Ex Works) (Named Place): This places the minimum obligation on the seller, as the seller makes the goods available to the buyer at the seller's premises or any other named place, such as a different warehouse or factory. Delivery is deemed to occur at this named place. The buyer bears all costs and risks after taking the goods from the seller's premises. The goods must also be cleared for export by the buyer. (14-17)

face amount (non-discounted amount): The amount of the invoice (cost). (10-7)

factoring: As defined by the Federal Reserve Board, factoring is a purchase of accounts receivable. Factoring usually involves small continuous streams of receivables with maturities of one to six months. It does not fall under the purview of the ECOA or Regulation Z. Factoring services may be provided on a **recourse basis** (seller risk) or on a **non-recourse basis,** meaning the **factor** (financial institution) must absorb any loss due to the subsequent insolvency or inability to pay by the customer. Factoring without recourse means that the factor accepts the risk that the accounts receivable may be uncollectable. After an invoice is 60 days past due, the account is charged back to the seller. The seller forwards the invoices and usually receives 85 to 90 percent of the face amount purchased before maturity; the factor holds back the balance for such contingencies as returns and discounts, disputed receivables and seller's risk receivables **(dilution). Old line factoring arrangement** means that the agreement contains borrowing privileges. A business may find itself as a client of a factor and a customer of trade creditors selling their receivables to the same factor. The factor may then establish a **ledger line** where the agreement with this business includes a provision that a credit line of some amount, on the part of the factor, will be made available to the other creditors. (6-9, 14-21, 15-11–15-14)

Fair Credit Billing Act: Requires creditors to correct errors promptly while at the same time preventing the errors from showing up on consumer credit reports. (6-16–6-17))

Fair Credit Reporting Act (FCRA): As Title VI of the Consumer Credit Protection Act, the FCRA became effective on April 25, 1971. The purpose of the Act is to require consumer reporting agencies to adopt reasonable procedures for meeting the needs of consumer credit, personnel (employment), insurance and other information that is fair and equitable to consumers. It guarantees consumers the right to know all credit information that is maintained by credit bureaus and consumer reporting agencies and to be given a specific reason or reasons why they as consumers were denied credit. The Act was intended to apply only to consumer credit transactions and not to commercial credit transactions. (6-6–6-8, 9-25–9-26)

Fair Debt Collection Practices Act (FDCPA): FDCPA was passed in 1977 and became effective on March 20, 1978. Prior to its enactment, there was no federal law on debt collection. This Act identifies the ways in which a debt collector, defined as any person who regularly collects debts owed to others, may go about pursuing payments from a debtor. In July 1986, the FDCPA was amended to include attorneys who collect debts as well. It is the most important act within the credit and collection profession. The FDCPA attempts to eliminate all unethical practices of collecting a debt that were clearly present prior to its installation. Consequently, it prohibits creditors from attempting collection by employing tactics such as extortion; physical threats; threats of defamation among family, friends and colleagues; and annoying inconveniences. (6-14–6-15)

FAS (Free Alongside Ship) (Named Port of Shipment): The seller has fulfilled his obligation (for delivery, freight costs and risk of loss) when the goods are placed alongside the vessel at the named port of shipment. The buyer then has to bear all costs and risks of loss or damage to the goods from that point. This term requires the seller to clear the goods for export; however, if both parties wish that the buyer perform clearance that intent should be made clear in the contract of sale. This term can only be used for sea or inland waterway transport. (7-4, 14-18–14-19)

FCA (Free Carrier) (Named Place): The seller has fulfilled his obligation (for delivery, freight costs and risk of loss) when he delivers the goods, cleared for export, to the carrier that has been appointed by the buyer at the named place. The buyer then has to bear all costs and risks of loss for damage to the goods (insurance) from that point forward. This term may be used regardless of the mode of transport, including multimodal transport (transport by more than one carrier—truck, rail, ship). (14-17)

Federal Deposit Insurance Corporation (FDIC): The FDIC was created in 1913 by the Federal Deposit Insurance Corporation Improvement Act to provide insurance protection for depositors if their bank fails. Since 1933, the FDIC has responded to thousands of bank failures, and its insurance protection has been expanded to include accounts in savings and loans associations. The FDIC insures deposits up to $250,000 per personal or corporate depositor per institution in all federally chartered and most state banks.

One of its most important roles is in determining the course of action in the event of a bank failure. The FDIC usually makes the decision that a bank is insolvent and is charged with liquidating a failed bank's remaining assets and paying insured depositors. The FDIC also is the federal bank regulator responsible for supervising certain savings banks and state-chartered banks that are not members of the Federal Reserve System. (1-23)

federal funds rate: The level of balances that depository institutions hold at the Federal Reserve Banks and the rate at which banks lend each other money from their Federal Reserve Bank balances. (1-18)

Federal Open Market Committee (FOMC): The part of the Federal Reserve which is charged with buying and selling securities on the open market in order to change the supply of money held in deposit at the Federal Reserve Banks. The FOMC is made up of all seven governors from the Board of Governors, the President of the Federal Reserve Bank of New York and four presidents of other regional banks. The four positions for regional Bank presidents rotate each year. The notes from their discussions are called **Fed Minutes.** (1-17)

Federal Reserve System (the Fed): The Federal Reserve System is the central bank of the United States. It was created as an independent agency to provide the nation with a safer, more flexible and more stable monetary and financial system. Given its key roles in supervising, regulating and providing services to the banking community, the Fed has a substantial effect on credit management.

The Federal Reserve was organized under the Federal Reserve Act of 1913. It currently comprises 12 districts and 25 regional branches. Approximately half of all banks in the U.S., and all of the largest banks, are members of the Federal Reserve System. National banks must be members.

All banks must maintain Federal Reserve accounts to be able to move or receive funds through the Federal Reserve System. The initial link between monetary policy and the economy occurs in the market for reserves. Federal Reserve policies influence the demand for, or supply of, reserves at banks and other depository institutions and, through this market, the effects of monetary policy are transmitted to the rest of the economy. The Federal Reserve is structured to be independent within the federal government and is made up of the **Board of Governors,** the **Federal Open Market Committee** and 12 **regional banks.** (1-15–1-20)

Federal Rules of Bankruptcy Procedure: The rules of procedure for bankruptcy cases as adopted by the U.S. Supreme Court, which has been empowered to do so by the U.S. Congress. (17-2–17-5)

Federal Tax Identification Number (FEIN): The federal Social Security number sed to identify a business and required to file a tax return. (9-4)

The Federal Trade Commission Act of 1914: As the broadest of antitrust acts to be passed, this Act states that all unlawful methods of competition and unfair or deceptive acts or practices in commerce to be unlawful. Its prohibitions include the false advertising of foods, drugs, devices and cosmetics, and any other practice that is designed to deceive the public. (6-4)

Fed Minutes: The notes from the **Federal Open Market Committee** discussions. (1-20)

Fedwire: Fedwire is a national clearing house for check clearance and real-time electronic funds transfer system provided by the Federal Reserve. It works by transferring cash value from one bank to another, in real time, and using Federal Reserve account balances. (1-22)

finance companies: These organizations make loans against pledged or assigned collateral, such as accounts receivable, inventory or fixed assets. They do not actually purchase receivables or other assets; rather, they make loans based on the value of the asset and expect repayment of the loans by their clients. A company entering into an **accounts receivable financing agreement** which is a loan secured by accounts receivable assigned to the finance company, continues to operate its own credit department as before. The company then signs a formal covering agreement with the finance company (an **underlying agreement** or **working plan**) which is a continuing arrangement for funds to be advanced by the finance company. The lender takes security in the assets by filing a lien using the normal procedures described under the Uniform Commercial Code. (15-9–15-10)

Finance, Credit and International Business Association (FCIB): A wholly-owned subsidiary of NACM, which serves professionals involved in worldwide export financing, credit, treasury and international subsidiary management. FCIB provides **International Credit Reports** and **Country Reports.** FCIB has two certifications that it awards—**CICP** and **ICCE.** (11-28)

finance lease: A lease in which the lessor does not manufacture or produce the goods and only acquires the goods in connection with the lease and is governed by Article 2A. (7-7)

Financial Accounting Standards Board (FASB): An organization that provides the Generally Accepted Accounting Principles (GAAP), which set forth comprehensive guidelines for classifying leases into two broad categories: operating leases and capital leases. (15-6)

financial services: They are provided to member banks and to the federal government by the **Federal Reserve** and include payment systems policies and solutions as well as currency distribution operations. (1-17, 1-20)

financing statement: Known as the UCC-1 form, this document is usually filed in order to give public notice to third parties of a secured party's security interest. (2-9, 7-9)

Five Cs of Credit: The Five Cs—**character, capacity, capital, collateral** and **conditions**—represent the most significant features of a credit applicant. The ability to analyze each of the Five Cs provides an important foundation in the credit process. For those working in the international arena, **country risk, currency issues** and **culture** add three more dimensions to the Five Cs of Credit. (1-6–1-8, 1-14, 8-8–8-9, 12-6, 12-7, 12-10)

fixed-income securities: Generally long-term (more than 10 years) securities that pay a specified sum (called the principal) either at a future date or periodically over the length of a loan, during which a fixed rate of interest may be paid on a regular basis. (1-12)

floating lien: A lien where the parties have the right to create a security interest in property the debtor does not yet own or possess at the time that the security interest is created. A floating lien attaches to all of the debtor's property of a particular kind, described in the security agreement, even though the property is acquired long after the execution of the agreement.

Property that is acquired thereafter is automatically covered and is likewise automatically released from the lien as items are sold by the debtor in the ordinary course of business. (7-11)

floor-plan financing: A special (other) term involving an inventory financing company, called the floor-plan creditor, that has contractual arrangements with both the supplier/seller and the buyer. (10-18)

FOB (Free on Board) (Named Port or Shipment): The seller has fulfilled his obligation (for delivery, freight costs and risk of loss) when the goods have passed over the ship's rail at the named port of shipment. The buyer then bears all costs and risks of loss or damage to the goods from that point forward. This term requires the seller to clear the goods for export. This term can be used for sea or inland waterway transport only. (7-4, 14-19)

FOB Destination: An FOB term that has a named place of destination of the goods and that puts the expense and risk of delivering the goods to that destination on the seller. (7-5, 14-19)

force majeure: These events can include "acts of God," such as floods, earthquakes and hurricanes, as well as other events, such as war, terrorist activities, labor disputes and electrical failures. (9-25, 10-20))

foreign corporation: A corporation is known as such when not located in the state in which it is incorporated. (5-6)

foreign exchange: The conversion of a freely usable or freely convertible currency of one country into the currency of another. (14-24)

forfaiting: The concept that the seller forfeits the right to a future payment on a receivable in return for immediate cash. While this idea may sound similar to factoring, forfaiting usually covers very large single transactions for terms of one to five years. Derived from the French term for the technique *a forfait.* (14-21–14-22)

Form B10: The official proof of claim form to be used in a bankruptcy. (17-16–17-17)

forward transaction: A contract between two parties that have agreed to exchange currencies at a fixed rate on an agreed future date. Forward transactions can be done for any currency, for any trade date and for any amount, although there are standards for each of these variables. (14-24)

fraud: An intent to deceive and an intentional perversion of the truth for the purpose of inducing another to rely on it to part with some valuable thing. It is a false representation of a matter of fact, whether by words or conduct, by false or misleading statements or by concealment of that which should have been disclosed, which deceives and is intended to deceive another so that a person shall act upon it to their legal injury. Unless creditors were at some point intentionally deceived on a material fact, the principal cannot properly be charged with fraud. (12-2)

fraudulent transfer: In a bankruptcy case, a transfer of assets for less than reasonably equivalent value, to a third party, at the time when the debtor is insolvent or which transfer renders the debtor insolvent. (17-29)

free transferability of assets: The ability to transfer equity in a company without permission from all the other members. This is one of the three characteristics that LLCs can avoid to remain an LLC. (5-11, 5-12)

funds transfer: A series of transactions, beginning with the originator's payment order, made for the purpose of making a payment to the beneficiary of the order. (1-22)

future value: To recover the profit erosion caused by the time value of funds, a seller would determine the present price at the required profit, then project the resulting value forward to the maturity date by applying the cost of capital factor. (10-12)

general credit reporting agencies: Those that gather credit information on any business regardless of industry or upon receipt of an inquiry from a subscriber or member, delivering the information to the inquirer and then storing that information on file for future delivery and updating of the subject file. (11-20)

general endorsement: An endorsement without reservation or qualification. (16-10, 16-12)

general ledger: Typically sales departments have budgets or "wallets" with promotion funds allocated to their customers on an annual basis. Sales usually monitors these accounts to prevent overspends. When a customer takes a deduction for a promotional-related reason, often times those deductions are banked against the appropriate funds. (8-14)

general partnership: An association where all partners are entitled to take an active part in the affairs of management, unless this is amended by the partnership agreement. Each partner is considered an agent for the firm. (5-4, 9-7)

goods: All things, other than money, stocks and bonds, that are movable. Goods also include the unborn young of animals and growing crops. Goods that are not yet in existence or not yet under the control of people are called future goods. (7-2–7-3)

Gramm-Leach-Bliley Act: Requires financial institutions—companies that offer consumers financial products or services like loans, financial or investment advice, or insurance—to explain their information-sharing practices to their customers and to safeguard sensitive data. (9-26)

green clause: While similar to a red clause in that it allows the drawing of a clean draft, a green clause requires that the merchandise be stored by the paying bank until all documents are received. (14-14)

gross national product (GNP): The total of ALL economic activity in a given country, regardless of who owns the productive assets and, therefore, includes everything produced in the country by both domestic and foreign ownership. (14-4)

guarantee: An instrument containing a promise by a person, persons or company to pay or perform an obligation owed in the event the debtor does not pay or perform. It can take the form of a **personal** (obtained from a principal of an entity such as a president or other officer or shareholder; a member or multiple members of an LLC; or from any third-party source unrelated to the business but who can be offered as a signatory) or **corporate** (obtained from a principal of an entity such as a president or other officer or shareholder; a member or multiple members of an LLC; or from any third-party source unrelated to the business but who can be offered as a signatory) guarantee. Consider including exhibits of both types in a company credit manual. (8-17, 8-19, 13-11)

— H —

holder: A person who is in possession of an instrument issued or endorsed to that person, to that person's order, to bearer or in blank. (16-9)

horizontal rotation: A popular on-the-job training method involving lateral transfers that enable employees to work at different jobs. Also known as job rotation. (3-11)

— I —

implied credit policy: Exists, but it is not officially stated (or written). (8-2)

implied powers of the corporation: A corporation's implied powers include the right to buy and sell real estate when used as a plant or office location, the right to borrow, the right to have a bank account and the right to have a corporate seal as part of the corporate signature. (5-7)

implied warranty: A warranty that is imposed by law rather than by statements, descriptions or samples given by the seller.
It relates to all sales transactions, whether they are business-to-consumer transactions or business-to-business transactions. Implied warranties are designed to promote high standards in business and to discourage harsh dealings. There are four basic types of implied warranties: (7-7)

1. An implied warranty of merchantability.
2. An implied warranty of fitness for a particular purpose.
3. An implied warranty that is derived from a course of dealing or usage of trade.
4. An implied warranty of title (owner has title to the item).

importer's bank: The collecting bank. (14-14)

incidental credit: Credit extended by service providers, such as a hospital, doctor, lawyer or retailer, that allows the client or customer to defer the payment of a bill. There is no credit card involved. There is no finance charge and no agreement for payment in installments. (1-13)

Incoterms®: A set of internationally recognized shipping terms, defined by the International Chamber of Commerce (ICC), which are used for the purchase and shipping of goods in the international marketplace. Short for International Commercial Terms. *(See also* EXW, CFR, CIF, CIP, CPT, DAP, DAT, DDP, FAS, FCA and FOB.) (9-16, 10-20, 14-15–14-20)

indirect investigations: Investigations where credit information is acquired from third-party sources, which are in the business of preparing information on companies (e.g., a credit report purchased from a commercial credit reporting agency). (11-18–11-26)

industry credit group: A third-party reporting resource that can yield information for credit grantors who make open account credit decisions. Also known as a trade credit group. (11-19, 15-9)

ineligible acceptances: Acceptances that are not eligible for discount by the Federal Reserve. (14-23)

insolvent: Characterization of a debtor whose liabilities exceed assets. (18-2)

installment credit: A credit stipulating shipments by installment within given periods, that credit should clearly state, "Shipment must be effected in the following installments." (14-12)

installment note: A note where the principal, as well as interest on the unpaid balance, is payable in installments at specified times. (16-8)

insurance: Trade credit insurance or **trade insurance** protects a seller's commercial accounts receivable from loss, whether caused by commercial or political risk events; it protects businesses from non-payment of commercial debt. The **trade credit limit** is the amount of loss that the insurer will reimburse to the policy holder, prior to any coinsurance or deductible, for a specific customer. With a **coinsurance type policy,** the insured company participates in a percentage of the bad-debt loss sustained on a debtor. A **primary loss policy** covers losses over and above an agreed-upon annual deductible. This deductible is based on the normal expected loss for the business and the overall risk to be insured. This initial deductible loss is termed the **primary loss** and is not reimbursed to the insured. It is set as a percentage of sales, but in no case is less than a stated dollar amount. Under a **cancelable limit,** the insurance company may amend or withdraw coverage attaching to future transactions between the policyholder and its specific customers. (15-14–15-17)

interest payment: Charges made by financial institutions for loans. (10-16)

interim claim settlement: This endorsement allows the insured to request three interim settlements within 60 days after filing a claim rather than waiting until the end of the policy term. Most insurers have automatic claim settlement. (15-16)

interim trustee: Usually an attorney or an accountant assigned at random from a panel of qualified individuals to handle a bankruptcy. (17-5)

international bill of exchange: A draft that is drawn in one country but is payable in another. It is also known as a **foreign draft.** (16-8)

international consignment: A variation of open account in which payment is sent to the exporter only after the goods have been sold by the foreign distributor to the end customer. (14-6)

investment credit: The long-term borrowing of large amounts of money to finance productive assets. It consists primarily of loans made to governments or businesses to raise capital to pay for expansion, modernization or public projects such as highways or schools. (1-12–1-13) involuntary bankruptcy: A legal proceeding in which a person or business is requested to go into **bankruptcy** by creditors, rather than on the person or business' own accord. Creditors seeking **involuntary bankruptcy** must petition the court to initiate the proceedings, and the indebted party can file an objection to force a case (17-29).

involuntary petition: Filed by creditors under Chapter 7 or 11. To do so, three creditors must have noncontingent, undisputed claims. (17-8, 17-29)

irrevocable documentary letter of credit: This type of letter of credit is similar to a confirmed irrevocable letter of credit except that payment responsibility lies with the bank that issued or opened the letter of credit. This would normally be the buyer's, or customer's, bank. (14-10)

irrevocable letter of credit: An irrevocable letter of credit substitutes a bank's credit for that of the customer. It allows the supplier to initiate a draft against the letter of credit upon delivery of goods. Copies of all types of letters of credit should be included as exhibits in a company credit manual. (13-11)

— J —

job description: A statement of the duties, responsibilities and authorities of a position in the credit department. (3-8–3-9)

job specification: A statement of qualifications—such as educational and experiential—that an individual should possess in order to fill a particular job. (3-8)

joint check agreement (JCA): A joint check agreement is a device whereby the ultimate user or beneficiary of material supplied by an original seller agrees with the original seller and its supplier to make all payments to the supplier by checks payable to both the seller and the supplier. A copy of the agreement should be shown as an exhibit in a company credit manual. (13-12)

joint venture: Also known as a syndicate, a joint venture is a combination of two or more persons (including corporations) formed to undertake a specific, and usually large, contract or project. For credit analysis purposes, a joint venture is similar to a partnership. (5-15–5-16, 9-8)

judgment note: A note controlled by state law that often has many technical requirements. (16-9)

— L —

late charges: The means by which a seller recovers or attempts to recover the cost of carrying an unpaid account after its maturity date. (10-16)

lease contract: Such contracts allow for the use of equipment, buildings and other assets by lessees in return for periodic rental payments to lessors over a specific period of time. They stipulate the number, size and time sequence of lease payments and include clauses covering cancellation rights, conditions for renewal or (if applicable) a purchase option, the treatment of tax benefits and obligations, and maintenance, insurance and servicing responsibilities of lessor and lessee. (15-6)

leases: The transfer of the right to possession and use of goods for a term in return for consideration. Leasing allows the lessee to use valuable assets without making an initial large capital investment and allows firms with limited capital budgets an alternative way to obtain resources. Leases are frequently tailored to meet the cash budget requirements of the lessee. (7-7)

ledger line: The agreement with this business includes a provision that a credit line of some amount, on the part of the factor, will be made available to the other creditors. (15-13)

legal audit: A review of all documentation to determine whether all security interests were properly perfected and all mortgages were correct and properly recorded, paying special attention to legal descriptions of the covered real estate. (17-28)

letter of credit (L/C): A written understanding by a bank (issuing bank), acting at the request and on the instructions of its customer (applicant for the credit) to:
- make payments to, or to the order of, a third party (beneficiary)
- accept and pay bills of exchange (drafts) drawn by the beneficiary
- authorize another bank to effect such payment or to pay, accept or negotiate such bills of exchange (drafts)

A letter of credit contains the following: amount of the credit, contents, documents required, expiry date, general description of the merchandise, name of the buyer, name of the seller, shipping terms and tenor of the draft. (14-6–14-14)

letter of credit right: A right to payment or performance of a letter of credit. (7-12)

leverage: The relationship of debt to equity. (5-10)

leveraged buyout: A special acquisition process that uses borrowed money (leverage) to acquire a company. (15-7–15-9)

libel: Defamation in some permanent form, such as printed media or writing in form. (11-4–11-6)

limited liability company (LLC): An LLC is based on the concept that an unincorporated business association, which desires to do business under the corporate structure, may do so by combining the benefits of a traditional C corporation and a partnership. (5-11–5-13, 9-7)

limited liability partnership (LLP): While an LLP is very similar to a limited liability corporation (LLC), it is specifically designed for professionals who do business as partners in a partnership. LLPs are formed and operated in compliance with state statutes. (5-5–5-6)

limited partnership: An association comprising one or more general partners and one or more limited partners. (5-4–5-5, 9-8)

lines of credit: Terms extended to customers to temporarily support working capital. (15-4)

liquidated damages: Damages that the parties agree will compensate an injured party upon a specified breach. (9-24)

liquidation test: Will the total amount of plan payments equal the amount distributed to unsecured creditors through a Chapter 7 liquidation? (17-16)

lockbox: A check collection system operated by a bank. Two major types of lockboxes are usually offered: wholesale (ideal for a moderate number of large-dollar remittances, usually from business payors) and retail (ideal for a large number of relatively small-dollar remittances). (2-12, 8-22)

— M —

magnetic ink character recognition (MICR) system: In the 1950s, the Federal Reserve developed and implemented the magnetic ink character recognition (MICR) system for encoding pertinent data on checks so that the data could be read electronically. The characters are printed at the bottom of a check in what is called the **MICR line.** (1-21)

The first section, or the first eight digits, of the MICR line is called the **transit routing number,** which provides information about the financial institution on which the check is drawn. Additional sections of the MICR line identify the:
- payor's account number: Within a depository institution, each account is assigned a unique number. This enables the bank to debit or credit the appropriate account after the check is processed.
- sequence number: This optional field enables the bank to sort checks to a particular account in numerical order. Usually, this sequence of numbers contains the check number.
- encoded amount: At the bank, the amount for which the check is drawn is read by people and then printed or encoded on the right-hand side of the MICR line. Unless an error has been made, this number (in cents) will agree with the amount written or typed in the body of the check. Once a check is encoded, it is completely readable from that time on.

majority: Defined as those holding at least two-thirds in amount and one-half in number of the allowed claims voting on the plan. (17-13)

majority vote: Where those holding at least two-thirds in amount and one-half in number of the allowed claims vote on the reorganization plan in bankruptcy. (17-13)

maker: The person (or company) who makes or executes a note. (16-3)

marginal accounts: Accounts with poor payment history, inadequate working capital or a deteriorating financial condition. Marginal accounts are taken on for strategic reasons and should be identified as such when receivables investment is being analyzed. (2-8)

marginal customer: A customer who falls short of expectations in one or more ways; consequently, potential sales to such a customer may present an abnormal risk even when full information is available. (13-13–13-14)

market and product characteristics: Important factors that will likely influence a company's terms of sale. (10-3–10-4)

master limited partnership: A type of limited partnership that is publicly traded over-the-counter or on a stock exchange. (9-8)

matter libelous per se: Any communication that falsely suggests a criminal act or immorality, or which tends to deprive a person in business of public confidence and esteem. (11-5)

means test: Where net income exceeds certain amounts in order to proceed in a Chapter 7 bankruptcy. (17-5)

mechanic's lien: A statutory lien on a building (and usually the land it occupies) in favor of suppliers of material and contractors to secure their interest on a particular construction project. (7-10, 13-12)

mediation: A non-binding attempt by parties to solve a dispute using an independent mediator or facilitator in order to allow the parties to reach common ground. Mediation can be chosen after a dispute has arisen, unlike arbitration. (18-6)

merchant: The UCC defines a merchant as "a person who deals in goods of the kind...involved in the transaction or a person who regularly deals in the kind of goods being sold." The Code recognizes that more reliance can be placed on professional sellers—in effect, holding them to a higher standard. (7-3, 9-16)

merchantability: Merchantability is the concept that goods are reasonably fit for the general purpose for which they are sold. (7-7)

merger: The complete integration of corporate entities, as defined by state statutory procedures. The survivor corporation basically absorbs all components of the other corporation, including stock, files and liabilities. The credit professional must determine what factors have been brought into the credit situation by the consolidation or merger of the two or more companies. (5-18, 17-26–17-27)

middle of the month (MOM) terms: Shipments made from the 1st through the 15th of a given month are invoiced as of the 15th of that month; shipments made from the 16th through the end of a given month are invoiced as of the end of that month. (10-8)

mission statement: This expresses the long-range focus of company policy and defines the purpose of the credit department. It summarizes how the credit function will contribute to sales growth and profitability though risk management and customer relationships. (8-6)

money: The medium of exchange that any domestic or foreign government has officially adopted as part of the currency. Negotiable instruments must be payable in money. (16-3)

money order: While money orders are usually presumed to have the significance of cash, payees must be aware of the issuer's identity and validity. Caution is advised when accepting a money order as payment if the issuer is not known. Investigate the issuer before negotiating the instrument. (16-7)

monitoring accounts: The process of re-evaluating credit for existing customers with the sources of information commonly used. Establishing regular credit evaluation will allow the company to monitor any changes in the risk level of the receivable portfolio. The company can then adjust credit and collection policy accordingly. If the portfolio is becoming a little more precarious than tolerance for risk permits, the credit policy and collection plan should be tightened. (8-10–8-11)

mortgage bonds: A mortgage bond is secured or collateralized with specific corporate assets such as buildings. Mortgage bonds are backed by a pool of mortgage loans. (1-12)

municipal utility: A not-for-profit public entity owned and operated by the state or a political subdivision of the state (for example, cities, public utility districts or a locally elected utility board). (9-8)

NAICS: The North American Industry Classification System (NAICS) is the standard used by Federal statistical agencies in classifying business establishments for the purpose of collecting, analyzing and publishing statistical data related to the U.S. business economy. The **NAICS code** identifies companies by their product or service and industry. (9-6)

National Association of Credit Management (NACM): Founded in 1896, the National Association of Credit Management promotes good laws for sound credit; protects businesses against fraudulent debtors; improves the interchange of credit information; develops better credit practices and methods; and has established a code of ethics. NACM currently represents the interests of more than 19,000 credit professionals worldwide and is a well-regarded advocate for the business credit and finance sector. Its purposes and objectives are as follows: (1-3–1-4, 3-13–3-14)
- To promote honest and fair dealings in credit transactions
- To ensure good laws for sound credit
- To foster and facilitate the exchange of credit information
- To encourage efficient service in the collection of accounts
- To promote and expedite sound credit administration in international trade
- To encourage training for credit work through colleges, universities, self-study courses and other means
- To foster and encourage research in the field of credit
- To disseminate useful and instructive articles and ideas with respect to credit management techniques
- To promote economy and efficiency in the handling of estates of insolvent, embarrassed or bankrupt debtors
- To provide facilities for investigation and prevention of fraud
- To perform other functions as the advancement and protection of business credit may require

negotiable instrument: A written document, signed by the maker or drawer, containing an unconditional promise to pay, or order to pay, a certain sum of money on delivery or at a definite time to the bearer, or to the order of. It can be transferred from party to party and accepted as a substitute for money. An accepted substitute for money that can be transferred from party to party. (16-2)

negotiating bank: In a letter of credit, the bank that gives value for drafts and/or documents under the credit. (14-10)

negotiation: The transfer of an instrument in such a form that the transferee becomes a holder. (16-9–16-10)

net credit period: The length of time allowed for payment of the face amount (non-discounted amount) of the invoice. (10-7)

net present value: The value of any receivable to be paid in the future must be discounted backwards in time to determine its present value. (10-11)

net working capital: The difference between current assets and current liabilities. If positive, net working capital represents the amount of working capital the company expects to generate in the short term and have available to pay operating expenses. As such, it is an excellent predictor of future cash flows. Also known as working capital. (2-3)

nexus: A legal term that refers to the requirement for companies doing business in a state to collect and pay tax on sales in that state. (9-5)

The 1976 Antitrust Act: This Act grants the federal government new disclosure powers in antitrust litigation. It also requires companies of a certain size to file pre-merger notices, and it permits a state attorney general to sue for damages on behalf of the state's citizens. (6-6)

No Arrival, No Sale: Seller is responsible for the expense and risk during shipment. If the goods fail to arrive through no fault of the seller, the seller has no further liability to the buyer. A commonly used shipping term that creates a destination contract. (7-5, 9-16)

non-liquidity: This occurs when a firm has a temporary cash flow problem. It is a measure of the extent that a person or organization has cash to meet immediate and short-term obligations, or assets that can be quickly converted to do this. Its assets are greater than its debts, but some assets are illiquid (e.g. it takes a long time to sell a house. A bank can't suddenly demand a mortgage loan back). Therefore, although in theory assets are greater than debts, it can't meet its current payment requirements. (18-2)

non-recourse (without recourse): The forfaiter assumes and accepts the risk of non-payment. (14-21, 15-11)

note: An instrument representing a written promise by one party, called the **maker,** to pay money to the order of another party, called the **payee.** In contrast to drafts, notes are promise instruments rather than order instruments, and they involve only two parties instead of three. (16-3, 16-8)

not-for-profit organization: The Internal Revenue Service recognizes the designation "not-for-profit" for certain organizations, which may be either corporations or associations. They are often formed to carry out work or business as a service to the community rather than for profit. (5-16)

notice to owner (NTO): A notice sent to the owner to inform them that services or materials will be sent to their property. Follow state guidelines for NTO schedules as they vary by state. (13-12)

not liquid: Characterization of a debtor that is unable to pay debts as they become due. (18-2)

old line factoring arrangement: The agreement contains borrowing privileges. (15-2)

onboarding: A method of in-house training, which is especially important when dealing with credit professionals because of the wide range of functions members of this staff perform and the reality that most new credit professionals have not studied trade credit. (3-11, 3-18–3-23)

on demand: Terms that mean the holder has the option of choosing the time to receive payment. "On demand" is synonymous with "at presentment" or "at sight." (16-3)

1% 10 net 30: A 1% discount is earned from the face amount if an invoice is paid within 10 days. If a buyer does not take the discount, the full amount of the invoice is due within 30 days. (10-8)

online business banking: A simplified money management method which makes it easier to monitor accounts, financials, account history and statements; transfer funds between accounts and banks; pay bills and more. (1-23)

open account credit: Where creditor reasonably expects the customer to make repeated transactions and generally makes more credit available to the buyer as the outstanding balance is paid. It is also called ordinary terms or standard terms. (1-14)

open account terms: Such terms includes as many as three elements: a net credit period and, if terms provide a discount option, a cash discount and cash discount period. (10-7–10-8)

open account transaction: A sale where the goods are shipped and delivered before payment is due, which in international sales is typically in 30, 60 or 90 days. (14-6)

open credit terms: Arrangements of goods or services that may be delivered on an unsecured basis; a period of time is allowed for the buyer to render payment. Such terms are offered when the seller believes that the customer is a good credit risk. (10-2)

open-end credit: is an agreement by a bank to lend a specific amount to a borrower and to allow that amount to be borrowed again once it has been repaid. Also called revolving credit or revolving line of credit. It can also be defined as: credit extended under a plan where a creditor may permit an applicant to make purchases or obtain loans from time to time directly from the creditor or indirectly by the use of a credit card, check or other device. Examples include bank and retail gasoline credit cards, department stores' revolving charge accounts and cash-advance checking accounts. (1-13)

open market operations: The purchase or sale of securities, primarily U.S. Treasury securities, in the open market to influence the level of balances that depository institutions hold at the Federal Reserve Banks and the rate at which banks lend each other money from their Federal Reserve Bank balances (the **federal funds rate**). Open market operations are conducted at the Federal Reserve Bank of New York. (1-18)

operating cycle: The period of time between the acquisition of material, labor and overhead inputs for production and the collection of sales receipts. A business must first purchase the resources it needs to make its product. It then sells that product and collects the funds from the sale. Cash flows into and out of the business during the operating cycle: cash flows out of the business, during the production stage, when it purchases the resources needed, and cash flows into the business, during the collection cycle, when it finally sells the product to a customer. Rarely do these events occur at the same time; the challenge of business is to maintain sufficient levels of cash throughout the operating cycle to ensure smooth and ongoing operations. (1-10, 2-5, 10-3–10-4)

operating leases: Short-term rentals of property, plant or equipment. (15-6–15-7)

opportunity cost: Represents the return that the seller can obtain by investing funds elsewhere at comparable risk or by investing funds in corporate growth through acquisitions or other means. (10-10)

order bill of lading: A bill of lading made out to the "order of the shipper." The seller endorses this bill of lading and forwards it, attached to a sight draft to a bank agreed upon by the buyer and seller. (14-15)

order limit: An order limit specifies the dollar amount that may be released without delay on any single order. (13-9)

order paper: An instrument that is payable to order (e.g., "pay to the order of"). (16-9)

Organization for Economic Cooperation and Development (OECD): An organization of 34 member countries that enables its members to consult and cooperate with each other in order to achieve the highest sustainable economic growth in their countries and to improve the economic and social wellbeing of their populations. (11-28)

parent of its subsidiary: When a corporation owns more than 50 percent of the stock of another company, it is said to be the parent of its subsidiary. (5-18)

parol evidence: A substantive rule of contracts under which a court will not receive into evidence prior oral statements that contradict a written agreement if the court finds that the written agreement was intended by the parties to be a final, complete and unambiguous expression of their agreement. (16-2–16-3)

partial payment: Usually for a percentage of unsecured claims either when the plan is confirmed or over time. (17-12)

partnership: An association of two or more persons to carry on as co-owners of a business in order to share profits and losses. (5-3–5-4)

par value: A specific dollar amount that is shown on the face of the stock certificate. (5-7)

paying/accepting bank: In a letter of credit, the bank on which the draft is drawn. (14-10)

payment and performance bonds: Security instrument as an action against default (13-12)

payment intangibles: A subcategory of general intangibles as defined by UCC Article 9 where the obligor's principal obligation is the payment of money. Examples include loan agreements and commercial debt instruments. (7-12)

payment terms: Arrangements that specify whether or not open credit is part of the sales transaction, the length of time for which credit is to be granted and other features such as discounts. (10-1)

penalties for non-compliance: Any time a manufacturer does not meet all requirements from their customers, they could be subject to a penalty fee. This could be a set amount per incident or a percentage of the total invoice/order involved in the violation. While they originally were designed to bring attention to quality or other viable issues, they can be punitive so it is important to pay close attention to these issues and involve all appropriate parties for resolution. (8-14)

perfection: The process of taking the legal steps necessary to ensure that a secured party's interests in collateral will withstand attack by competing secured creditors, judgment lien creditors and a bankruptcy trustee. (7-14–7-16)

Perishable Agricultural Commodities Act (PACA): An Act that regulates and protects businesses dealing in fresh and frozen fruits and vegetables by establishing and enforcing a code of fair business practices and by helping companies resolve business disputes. Perishable items have a short shelf life, rapid turnover rate and short selling terms. Less perishable foods have a longer turnover period, since they can be stocked in larger quantities by the retailer and are sold on longer terms. (10-4)

personal guarantee: Obtained from a principal of an entity such as a president or other officer or shareholder; a member or multiple members of an LLC; or from any third-party source unrelated to the business but who can be offered as a signatory. (9-26–9-28) petition for relief: A document filed by the debtor to initiate a Chapter 12 filing. (17-15)

plan: In a bankruptcy, there are many types of plans. They include: **compromise plans** (partial payment), **debt for equity swaps** (obligations of a company or individual in exchange for something of value), **partial payment** (usually for a percentage of unsecured claims either when the plan is confirmed or over time) and **pot plans** (some of the debtor's assets are set aside for liquidation and distribution to the unsecured creditors) (17-12)

postdated check: A check is postdated when the drawer has insufficient funds in the bank but expects to have sufficient funds to cover the amount of the check at a future date. (16-7)

prearranged Chapter 11: Occurs when the debtor reaches an agreement with one or more, but not all, of the debtor's creditor constituencies (most often the debtor's secured lender owed significant sums) on the terms of a Chapter 11 plan prior to the filing of the Chapter 11 case. (17-14)

preemptive rights: Based on state laws, the corporate charter or both, preemptive right prevents dilution of stockholders' equity without their consent. (5-8)

preference: In a bankruptcy case, if it can be shown that the buyer made a payment that is deemed preferential to a seller within 90 days of the bankruptcy, then the payment can be questioned. (17-28)

preferential payment: Refers to a creditor who gets paid before dividing the assets equally among all those to whom it owes money, often by making a payment to a favored creditor just before filing a petition to be declared bankrupt, to an unsecured creditor can be recovered by the trustee under Bankruptcy Code §547. (17-28)

preferred stock: The claims on assets of preferred shareholders generally have a higher priority than do the claims of common shareholders. In the event of a liquidation of the business, preferred stockholders are entitled to be paid before a distribution is made to common stockholders. (5-8–5-9)

prepackaged bankruptcy (prepack): A Chapter 11 case where the debtor reaches an agreement with its creditors and other relevant constituencies prior to the filing of the Chapter 11 case. (17-14)

prepayment: A call for payment before the transaction or at the time of the transaction. (10-5)

presumption rule: Where the secured party fails to comply with UCC Article 9, there is a presumption that the value of its collateral equaled the amount of the secured claim, which eliminates its deficiency claim. (7-30)

price discrimination: Consumers are protected against price discrimination by the Robinson-Patman act. Price discrimination can take the form of giving different price to different purchasers, differences in terms and conditions of sale and preferential credit terms. (6-4–6-5)

price-fixing: The extending of interest-free credit for a period of time or the equivalent to giving a discount equal to the value of the use of the purchase price for that period of time. (6-5)

primary loss: The initial deductible loss. It is not reimbursed to the insured. (15-16)

primary loss policy: Covers losses over and above an agreed-upon annual deductible. This deductible is based on the normal expected loss for the business and the overall risk to be insured. (15-16)

priority: Article 9's long-standing rule is that the first secured party to file a UCC financing statement or otherwise perfect its security interest has priority over competing secured parties. However, there is an exception to this rule for certain categories of collateral: A later perfection by possession or control of the collateral has priority over an earlier perfection by UCC filing. (7-22)

priority claim: Includes taxes, wages and unpaid rent that are entitled to priority payment over unsecured claims under federal or state laws. (18-4)

private credit: Credit extended to or used by individuals or businesses to carry on the exchange of goods and services in the private sector. Private credit is divided into five broad categories: investment credit, consumer credit, agricultural credit, business credit and bank credit. (1-11–1-15)

privileged communications: Statements made by one person in pursuance of a duty to another person having a corresponding duty or interest. (11-5–11-6)

proceeds: Whatever is realized from the sale, exchange, collection or other disposition of collateral. (7-12)

process mapping: A technique that breaks down key processes into primary activities, including actions, decision points and information/transportation flows. (2-9)

production stage: The process point where material is converted into goods. A manufacturer usually must pay its supplier for the materials. (1-10)

pro forma invoice: An abbreviated invoice sent in advance of a shipment. (10-20)

promissory note, double-name paper: A note signed by two or more makers, or signed by the maker and endorsed by others. (16-8)

promissory note, serial note: A series of notes usually of equal amounts and with maturity dates equally spaced that covers the amount to be paid. (16-8)

promissory note, single-name paper: A note signed by only one maker. Liability is limited to that one maker. (16-8)

promissory note, straight note: The more commonly used instrument, which serves as evidence of indebtedness. (16-8)

promotion account (promo account): Typically sales departments have budgets or "wallets" with promotion funds allocated to their customers on an annual basis. Sales usually monitors these accounts to prevent overspends. When a customer takes a deduction for a promotional-related reason, often times those deductions are banked against the appropriate funds. (8-14)

proof of claim: A form used by creditors to indicate the amount of debt owed by the debtor on the date of the bankruptcy filing. (17-5–17-6, 17-9, 17-17–17-20, 17-21)

Proof of Claim Form 410: This is used by creditors to indicate the amount of debt owed by the debtor on the date of the bankruptcy filing. (17-5)

proprietorship: A business owned and operated by one person. (5-2–5-3)

proximo terms: Individual invoices are usually billed at time of shipment rather than on a monthly basis. Also, prox terms may offer a net period that is different from the discount period. (10-8)

publication: As an element essential to an action in libel, publication refers to communication of the libel to some third person. (11-5)

public credit: Credit extended to or used by governments or governmental divisions, agencies or municipalities. Also known as government credit. (1-11)

public records: Information recorded in a public office and available for public inspection. (18-2)

purchase money security interest: A security interest granted to a trade creditor in goods sold on credit terms to the debtor for the purchase price of the trade creditor's goods. It may also be a security interest granted to a third party lender in goods purchased by the debtor and paid for by loans or advances made by that lender. (7-23, 10-18)

purchasing debit card (P-cards): Used extensively in industries characterized by high volume, spontaneous purchasing. This type of purchase is funded directly by the buyer's bank account; the transfer of funds occurs from the buyer's bank account to the seller's bank account. (10-6)

– Q –

qualified endorsement: A type of endorsement in which words have been added to the signature that limit the liability of the endorser. (16-12)

quantitative data: Reports that include number of invoices, checks, credits, discount or other terms violations, short payments and overpayments. (2-11)

– R –

Receipt of Goods (ROG) terms: A special (other) term that permits the buyer to compute the cash discount period or net credit period from the date the merchandise is received rather than from the invoice date. ROG terms are common in the importing of raw sugar and other situations where long transit times exist. (10-17)

receipt of invoice terms: This requires the customer to render payment immediately upon receipt of seller invoice or on some predefined short dating. Typically payment must be received before the next order is to be shipped, therefore making it similar to Bill-to-Bill in its intent. (10-5)

receivable puts: A promise by one party to buy a seller's trade receivables claim in the instance of a buyer's default or bankruptcy. (15-17–15-18)

reclamation: In a bankruptcy case, the seller's right to require an insolvent buyer to return goods purchased on credit. (17-21)

reclamation claim: In a bankruptcy, a written demand for the return of the goods. (17-24)

record: Information that is inscribed on a tangible medium, such as on paper as a written security agreement, or is stored in an electronic or other medium and is retrievable in perceptible form. (7-13)

red clause: When placed in a letter of credit, a red clause is used when a beneficiary needs financing in order to complete the manufacturing of merchandise or to purchase items to fill a particular order. (14-12)

red flags: Laws which require most creditors and financial institutions to adopt a written program to detect, prevent and mitigate identity theft in connection with the new opening of a covered account or any existing covered account. Every creditor and financial institution covered by the rule must adopt a risk-based program that identifies red flags relevant to its own operation and, more importantly, how it will respond to them. (6-25–6-34)

regional banks: There are 12 regional banks within the Federal Reserve System. Each bank is run by a bank president and nine directors, chosen from outside the bank. Three of those directors represent member banks and the rest are from the public, designed to represent a diverse selection of the region's population. (1-15–1-16)

registered organization: A business such as a corporation, limited liability company and limited partnership, located in the state where it is organized and registered. This term refers to an entity organized solely under the law of a single state or the United States by the filing of a public organic record with the issuance of a public organic record by, or the enactment of legislation by the state or the United States. (7-16)

remitting bank: The exporter entrusts the collection of the payment for a sale to the **remitting bank** (its bank), which sends the documents that its buyer needs to the importer's bank (collecting bank), with instructions to release the documents to the buyer for payment. (14-14)

rents, interest profits and dividends (RIPDs): When assessing country risk, trade in goods and services. (14-4)

reorganization plan: Filed with a bankruptcy court judge by a company in bankruptcy proceedings in which the disbursement of assets is stipulated. The plan must be approved by the firm's creditors and by the court. A reorganization plan results in new securities being given to creditors in trade for old securities. (17-9–17-10, 17-11–17-12)

reporting to management: Reporting is delivered to senior management, executive management or the management team, which is generally a team of individuals at the highest level of organization management who have the day-to-day responsibilities of managing a company or corporation; holding specific executive powers conferred onto them with and by authority of the board of directors and/or the shareholders. (8-15–8-16)

reserve requirement: All depository institutions—commercial banks, saving banks, savings and loan associations and credit unions—must retain a percentage of certain types of deposits to be held as reserves. The reserve requirements are set by the Federal Reserve under the Depository Institutions Deregulation and Monetary Control Act of 1980. (1-18–1-19)

restrictive covenants: In the loan agreement, covenants set performance measures that the company is required to meet or the bank is allowed to call or renegotiate the loan. The more risk taken by the bank, the more restrictive and abundant the covenants are likely to be. (15-5)

restrictive endorsement: Such an endorsement limits the rights of the endorsee in some manner in order to protect the rights of the endorser. (16-11)

revocable letter of credit: This creates leverage for the issuer. It is contractually legal for one party to either amend or cancel the exchange at any time, normally without the consent of the beneficiary. (14-10)

revolving credit: A type of credit whereby amounts may be borrowed, repaid and borrowed again. (15-4)

revolving letter of credit: This type of letter of credit contains instructions that allow the beneficiary to draw up a specific limit for a specified period. (14-12)

right of setoff: A depository bank's security interest. With respect to a debtor's deposit account, it has priority over all other security interests in the account, whether such competing security interests are taken as original collateral or are proceeds of other collateral. A security interest in favor of the debtor's securities intermediary perfected by control of the debtor's brokerage account always has priority over a competing security interest in the account perfected by control. (7-22)

risk premium: The risk of possible nonpayment. (10-11)

Robinson-Patman Act of 1936: This Act forbids price discrimination where the effect of such discrimination is to substantially reduce competition or to create a monopoly. Among the business practices covered: a different price charged to different purchases; differences in terms and conditions; and preferential credit terms. (6-4–6-5)

routing guides: Documents which contain routing instructions and the rules of engagement for shipping products from suppliers and to customers. They include modes and carriers to use in specific lanes. They can also contain rates and service requirements. (8-14)

— S —

sale-leaseback arrangement: In this situation, a company sells property, plant or equipment to an investor and arranges for a long-term lease. (15-7)

The Sarbanes-Oxley Act of 2002: SOX, as it is commonly known, was created and enacted to protect investors by improving the accuracy and reliability of corporate disclosures made pursuant to the securities laws and for other purposes. The Act comprises the following 11 titles: (6-23–6-24)

> Title I: Public Company Accounting Oversight Board
> Title II: Auditor Independence
> Title III: Corporate Responsibility
> Title IV: Enhanced Financial Disclosures
> Title V: Analyst Conflicts of Interest
> Title VI: Commission Resources and Authority
> Title VII: Studies and Reports
> Title VIII: Corporate and Criminal Fraud Accountability
> Title IX: White-Collar Crime Penalty Enhancements
> Title X: Corporate Tax Returns
> Title XI: Corporate Fraud Accountability

S corporation: A corporation in all respects, except that stockholders rather than the corporation pay federal income taxes. Formerly known as a Subchapter S Corporation. (5-9–5-11)

seasonal dating terms: Used when there is a high seasonal demand for a product and sellers wish to encourage off-season purchases. Seasonal terms postpone payments to coincide with the buyers' heavy selling seasons. These terms are common in the toy (December dating) and agricultural (crop terms) industries, among others. (10-19)

Section 341 meeting: The first meeting of creditors and equity holders in a bankruptcy. (17-5, 17-16)

secured bonds: Such bonds have specific titles attached to them, such as mortgage bonds, equipment and trust certificates and collateral trust bonds. (1-12)

secured claim: Secured assets (e.g., mortgages on the debtor's real property) or any perfected security interests in property subject to the UCC. (18-4)

secured credit arrangement: An arrangement in which collateral is provided to the creditor. By obtaining some form of security, the creditor can reduce repayment risk. Examples where secured credit may be useful are a start-up business or an undercapitalized business or an opportunity to sell an account that cannot justify a high credit exposure. Security is obtained not only when the buyer's financial condition is weak, but in order to guarantee payment if the buyer's financial condition changes. While it cannot strengthen a buyer's financial weakness, a secured credit arrangement does reduce the likelihood of loss. Secured credit is defined in UCC Article 9. (1-14)

secured creditor: A creditor who holds liens on assets of the estate. (17-6, 17-11)

secured party: A creditor who has a security interest in a debtor's collateral. According to the UCC, a creditor can be a seller, lender, cosigner and ever a buyer of accounts or chattel paper. (7-9)

secured transaction: A very basic modern business practice where payment of a debt is guaranteed, or secured, by personal property owned by the debtor or by property in which the debtor has a legal interest. (7-9)

securitization: An important aspect of credit which includes but is not limited to letters of credit, Uniform Commercial Code (UCC) filings, liens and guarantees. (2-3)

security agreement: Generally speaking, an agreement that creates or provides for a security interest. Article 9 of the Uniform Commercial Code details the creation of security interests in personal property. The most common types are inventory, accounts receivable and equipment. (7-9, 13-11)

security instruments: Various methods to secure open account credit, such as guarantees, letters of credit, mechanic's liens, **payment and performance bonds, real estate mortgages,** etc. (13-12)

security interest: The interest in the collateral (personal property, accounts and so forth) that secures payment or performance of an obligation. (7-9, 7-12)

seller: A person who sells or contracts to sell goods. (9-16)

Sherman Act of 1890: As the first antitrust act passed in the United States, the Sherman Act was designed to prevent monopolies, contracts and combinations that would unduly interfere with those engaged, or who wish to engage, in trade and commerce; in short, the Act sought to preserve, in general terms, the right of freedom of trade. (6-2)

shipment contract: Under such contracts, both title and risk of loss pass to the buyer when the goods are given to the carrier. The seller has no responsibility for seeing that the goods reach their destination. (9-16)

shipper/consigner: The person shipping the goods. (14-14)

short-term loans or lines of credit: Terms extended to customers to temporarily support working capital. (15-4)

short terms: As befits its name, such terms are of truncated duration and are usually offered as a matter of industry practice (i.e., highly perishable goods); in situations where credit limits are very tight; or in situations where the seller wishes to provide some token amount of credit support. Bill-to-Bill and Receipt of Invoice are two types of short terms. (10-5–10-7)

sight draft: A draft that is payable as soon as it is presented to the drawee for payment. Otherwise, the buyer/drawee cannot obtain the bill of lading or original shipping documents that will enable the buyer/drawee to take possession of the goods from the carrier/warehouse. (14-15, 16-7)

single asset real estate debtor: Real property constituting a single property or project with less than four residential units, which generates substantially all of the gross income of a debtor and on which no substantial business is being conducted by a debtor other than the business of operating the real property and activities incidental thereto. (17-11)

single payment terms: Purchases made over a period of time, usually a month, are assigned a single due date, usually in the following month. Examples include End-of-Month (EOM) terms, Middle of the Month (MOM) terms and Proximo terms. (10-7)

"sinking fund" preferred stock: The issuing company promises to buy back or redeem the preferred stock at some fixed time in the future. (5-9)

SKU – Stock Keeping Unit: Normally each item in a warehouse is assigned a unique SKU. It is often referenced on deals and invoices. (8-15)

slander: Defamation in a temporary form, such as speech. (11-4–11-5)

slotting fees: A slotting fee or slotting allowance is a fee charged to companies by retailers in order to have their product placed on their shelves. The fee varies greatly depending on the product, manufacturer and market conditions. (8-14)

small business: Under the Bankruptcy Code, a small business is defined as a person engaged in commercial or business activities, excluding real estate, whose aggregate non-contingent liquidated and unsecured debts do not exceed $2,343,000 as of the date of the petition. (17-11)

special endorsement: Such an endorsement is made by writing the words "pay to the order of" or "pay to" followed by the name of the person to whom it is to be transferred (the endorsee) and the signature of the endorser. Also known as an endorsement in full. (16-10–16-11)

specialized credit reporting agencies: Those that are more restrictive in the scope of the industry(ies) on which credit information is gathered and of the type of information reported. (11-20)

spot transaction: A foreign exchange draft for the immediate sale and delivery of a foreign currency (normally two business days from the transaction date for Europe and Asia, and one business day for Canada and Mexico). (14-24)

standard terms: The basic terms offered uniformly to all accounts, which must be set independently from other sellers and without collusion or conspiracy with other sellers in order to avoid violation of antitrust laws. (10-2)

standby letter of credit: A letter of credit where the issuing bank agrees to make payment upon the presentment of a document, preferably only a statement in writing by the beneficiary, that the customer did not pay according to terms. (14-10)

standing trustee: A trustee appointed in a bankruptcy case to serve as the disbursing agent for payments under the plan of repayment. (17-15, 17-16)

stated credit policy: It is set forth in writing and usually has the support and approval of senior management. (8-2)

statutory period of time: A period of time usually spanning six months to one year in most states. (5-14)

stock certificates: When issued by a company, stock certificates are evidence of corporate ownership in a proportion of the number of shares held to the total number of shares outstanding. (5-7–5-8)

strategic planning: The coordination of long-range plans with a particular focus on strategies, controls and desired results. (2-2)

strategy: The art of devising or using plans to achieve a goal. (2-2)

strong arm clause: Bankruptcy Code §544 empowers a trustee or a debtor in possession to avoid any lien or security interest in personal property or any lien or mortgage on real estate, which is not properly perfected as of the date of the bankruptcy petition. (17-27)

structure, Federal Reserve: The United States' central bank, more commonly known as the Federal Reserve or simply the Fed, charged with ensuring the stability and flexibility of the nation's monetary and financial systems. The Federal Reserve is structured to be independent within the federal government. The Federal Reserve System is made up of the **Board of Governors,** the **Federal Open Market Committee** and 12 **regional banks.** (1-15–1-17)

subordination agreement: This agreement can improve a supplier's priority position by establishing a higher priority claim to the customer's assets, especially if a significant portion of a customer's debt is owed to officers or stockholders. A copy should be shown as an exhibit in a company credit manual. (5-11, 13-11)

sum certain: A requirement of commercial paper whereby the amount must be clearly ascertainable from the face of the instrument. (16-3)

superpriority claim: A claim that has priority over other administrative claims in a bankruptcy. (17-9)

SWIFT (Society for Worldwide Interbank Financial Telecommunication): A dedicated computer network to support funds transfer messages internationally between member banks worldwide. (1-22)

TARGET2: The real-time gross settlement (RTGS) system owned and operated by the Eurosystem. TARGET stands for Trans-European Automated Real-Time Gross Settlement Express Transfer System. TARGET2 is the second generation of TARGET. (1-22)

telegraphic transfer clause: This clause speeds payments when the receiver of funds is not located in a financial center. (14-14)

tender delivery: Where a seller must make the goods available to the buyer. The basic obligation of the buyer is to accept the goods and to pay in accordance with the contract. Additionally, the buyer has the right, before payment or acceptance, to inspect the goods, to reject the goods if they fail to conform to the contract or to accept the goods in spite of non-conformity. The seller has the right to correct or cure improper delivery. Acceptance of goods occurs when the buyer, having had a reasonable opportunity to inspect the goods, either accepts or rejects them. (7-3-7-4)

terms and conditions of sale: Arrangements that specify the contractual conditions of transactions between sellers and buyers for the sale of goods or services. (8-9, 8-21, 10-1)

terms based on invoice date: The most common open terms category. Here, the net credit period is a certain number of days from the date the invoice was billed (e.g., "net 30" where payment is due within 30 days of the date of the invoice). In a few industries, the period is computed from the date the goods are received by the customer. (10-7)

third-party sources: Organizations in the business of preparing information on businesses/companies as opposed to individuals (principals of businesses/companies). These third-party sources are referred to as commercial credit agencies, bureaus or "repositories." (11-18)

Three Cs of credit and sales partnership: They are Communication, Collaboration and Cooperation. (4-3–4-4)

time draft: A draft that is payable only after the lapse of a particular time period stated on the draft. (14-14, 16-7)

time note: A note that is payable at some future time—on a definite date named in the instrument. (16-8)

TIPANET (Transferts Interbancaires de Paiement Automatisés): The international payment system set up by the European cooperative banks. (1-22)

trade acceptance: A draft presented by a seller of goods to receive payment and also to extend credit. Often used in conjunction with a bill of lading. (16-7)

trade credit: The Federal Reserve Board defines trade credit as limited to a financing arrangement that involves a buyer and a seller—such as a supplier who finances the sale of equipment, supplies or inventory; it does not apply to an extension of credit by a bank or other financial institution for the financing of such items. (1-4, 6-9)

trade credit insurance or trade insurance: Protects a seller's commercial accounts receivable from loss, whether caused by commercial or political risk events; it protects businesses from non-payment of commercial debt. (15-14–15-17)

trade credit limit: The amount of loss that the insurer will reimburse to the policy holder, prior to any coinsurance or deductible, for a specific customer. (15-15)

trade discount: An allowance offered to buyers based on industry custom or the volume of purchases. (10-9)

trade reference: The payment experience information provided by a supplier on its customer. (11-15)

trade-related deductions: These deductions are claims taken to claim monies specifically offered in exchange for promotion of a particular product. They can come in several forms, but are typically contractually based for a period of time and have specific requirements that must be met in order to claim the funds, either via deduction, check, or credit memo. (8-14)

transferable credit: Allows the beneficiary of a letter of credit (the exporter) to transfer all or part of the rights under the credit to a third party (the transferee). For a credit to be transferable, the exporter must arrange for the importer to have a credit opened expressly stipulating that it is transferable. (14-12)

transit routing number: This proves information about the financial institution on which a check is drawn. (1-21)

traveler's check: Similar to a cashier's check in that the issuing financial institution is both the drawer and the drawee. Technically, most traveler's checks are not checks but drafts, because the drawee—for example, American Express—is not ordinarily a bank. (16-7)

trustee: A person who is appointed by the United States Department of Justice or by the creditors involved in a bankruptcy case. (17-5, 17-6–17-7)

Truth in Lending Act and Regulation Z: The Truth in Lending Act was first signed into law in 1968 by President Lyndon Johnson. The Act and Regulation Z, which comprises its rules and regulations, attempt to give consumers the opportunity and right to shop for credit.

In an effort to protect and educate consumers, sellers of credit are mandated by law to disclose certain information when offering credit. Such information allows the consumer to know exactly what interest rates, finance charges and fees will apply before accepting such credit. Using this information, consumers can choose rates, terms and conditions that are the best for their needs. This Act only applies to consumer credit. (6-15–6-16)

20-day administrative priority claim: Under section 503(b)(9) of the Bankruptcy Code, the seller is granted a priority clam for the value of all goods sold to the buyer in the ordinary course of the buyer's business and received by the buyer within 20 days of bankruptcy. (17-25)

2% 10 MOM: Shipments made from the first through the 15th of a given month are due on the 25th of the month; those made from the 16th through the end of the month are due on the 10th of the following month, with the credit period being the same as the discount period. (10-8)

2% 10th Prox, Net 30th: A 2% discount is earned if payment is made by the 10th of the month following shipment. Otherwise, the full, undiscounted amount is due by the 30th of the month following shipment. (10-8)

UCC financing statement: Filing a UCC financing statement is the most common means of perfecting a security interest under the UCC. A UCC financing statement qualifies as such as long as it meets all statutory requirements and is filed with the proper authorities. It must provide the following: name of debtor; name of secured party or its representative; and a description of collateral. (7-9, 7-16, 7-17–7-20, 7-25, 13-11)

UCC gap fillers: Provisions of the UCC that cover specific issues when courts review contract disputes (i.e., terms and conditions that conflict with one another). (10-22)

ultra vires **acts:** Those acts outside the powers of the corporation. (5-7)

unclaimed property: Tangible or intangible property owed to a person or entity (i.e., "owner"), which is held by another (i.e., "holder"). All states, the District of Columbia, the U.S. Virgin Islands, Puerto Rico and Guam have enacted unclaimed property laws based, in whole or part, on the 1954 Uniform Unclaimed Property Act. (6-19)

unconditional promise to pay: A requirement that maintains the promise or order to pay contained in commercial paper must not be conditional on the occurrence or nonoccurrence of some other event or agreement. (16-3)

underlying agreement: The formal covering agreement signed by the finance company. It is a continuing arrangement for funds to be advanced by the finance company. (15-9)

undersecured claims: Claims where the value of the collateral is less than the amount of the claim held by the creditor; they are partially secured and partially unsecured. (17-11)

unearned cash discounts (UCDs): If a company offers terms, they list the percentage of the discount (normally 1-2%) and by when the customer must pay their invoice in order to earn the discount. For example, 2% 10, net 30 would mean a 2% discount is offered if the invoice is paid by the 10th day (normally, payment must be sent by the 10th date in order to receive the discount) If no discount is taken, the customer would have up to 30 days to pay. Other associated terms are **DOI** (date of invoice), **ROI** (receipt of invoice) and **ROG** (receipt of goods) (8-14)

unearned discount: A customer payment that reflects a discount even though the discount period or terms have expired. (10-9–10-10)

Uniform Commercial Code (UCC): This Code is based on the premise that the personal property commercial transaction is a single subject of law. It contains nine articles that make uniform the laws for the sale of and payment for goods in a simple, clear and modern fashion. (7-1–7-35)

Uniform Disposition of Unclaimed Property Act (the Uniform Act) of 1954: Introduced to unify the state statutory scheme of escheatment. It attempts to prevent multiple state claims for property by designating the last known address of the owner as the basic test of jurisdiction. (6-19–6-20)

Uniform Partnership Act (UPA): A uniform act established by the National Conference of Commissioners on Uniform State Laws that covers the rights and duties of partners. Several states have enacted versions of this model statute or its revised counterpart, the Revised Uniform Partnership Act (RUPA). (5-4)

unsecured creditor: One who extended credit to a debtor without a collateral security. (17-5, 17-10–17-11, 17-20)

unsecured, open account credit: The most widely used form of domestic business credit. In open account credit, the creditor reasonably expects the customer to make repeated transactions and generally makes more credit available to the buyer as the outstanding balance is paid. A typical business creditor who sells on open account terms is relying specifically on the full faith and credit of a purchaser. The seller establishes the terms of sale. Open account terms are also called ordinary terms or standard terms. (1-14)

U.S. Small Business Administration (SBA): A federal organization that participates in loans made by private lenders. One loan, called 7(a), is the most common. Under the **7(a) loan program,** all funds come from the commercial lender. The SBA guarantees a portion of the loan with loan amount ceilings that can vary depending on the loan's term and purpose. If the borrower defaults on the loan, the SBA reimburses the bank for its share of the defaulted loan. The SBA doesn't lend money directly to small businesses, but rather sets the guidelines for the loans made by the partners who are lenders, community development organizations and micro-lending institutions. (15-5–15-6)

usury, laws of: The laws of usury pertain to the ceilings of interest rates. Most usury limitations are defined at the state level, although some important exceptions are found at the federal level. Credit managers must be aware of the various limitations of state laws as well as the complex relationship between federal and state usury laws. (6-16)

valid security agreement: In order to be valid, a security agreement must contain a sufficient description of the collateral and be authenticated by the debtor. (7-13)

venture capital: Capital invested in a project in which there is a substantial element of risk, typically a new or expanding business (6-9)

venue: The customer's location. (9-14)

vertical rotation: A popular on-the-job training method where a new employee serves under an executive as an observer or assistant to become familiar with the functions and area of responsibility. Also known as job shadowing. (3-11)

voluntary settlement: A contract between the debtor and its creditors that settles their claims for the most the debtor can pay and the most the creditors can receive. Such a settlement keeps the debtor in business and avoids the substantial bankruptcy costs that few debtors can afford. (18-3)

warranty: A contractual promise by the seller regarding the quality, character or suitability of the goods sold. An **express warranty** is an oral or written statement, promise or other representation about the quality of a product. An **implied warranty** is a warranty that is imposed by law rather than by statements, descriptions or samples given by the seller; it relates to all sales transactions, whether they are business-to-consumer transactions or business-to-business transactions. (7-6, 7-7)

wire transfer: When setting up a wire transfer, a buyer arranges to move funds electronically from its bank account to the seller's bank account electronically. (10-6)

work in process (WIP): Inventory in the process of being manufactured from raw materials to finished goods. That is, a lender may make a secured loan to a buyer based on raw and finished goods values, but not WIP. This is because WIP has little or no intrinsic value while in that state. This can create problems for buyers as they seek to finance their operating cycles. (10-4)

working capital: The capital of a business that is used in its day-to-day trading operations, calculated as the current assets minus the current liabilities. (6-9)

working plan: The formal covering agreement signed by the finance company. It is a continuing arrangement for funds to be advanced by the finance company. (15-9)

Index

Alphabetization is letter-by-letter (e.g., "Creditor" precedes "Credit scoring").